THE ENGLISH CABALAH

VOLUME I

The Mysteries of Pi

By
WILLIAM EISEN

DeVORSS & COMPANY
P.O. Box 550, Marina Del Rey, CA 90291

The English Cabalah: An Agashan Book by William Eisen
Copyright © 1980 by William Eisen

First Edition

ISBN 0-87516-390-4
Library of Congress Catalog Card Number: 79-57053

Manufactured in the United States of America
by DeVorss & Company, Publishers

Dedicated to all of the Teachers of the Great White Way who have assisted in the dissemination of the material contained herein, and especially to that Illumined One known to the writer as Rhebaumaus Tate.

The Scribe

TABLE OF CONTENTS

PART II

THE SEARCH

PART III

THE APPLICATION

INTRODUCTION

In the first volume of this series, *Agasha: Master of Wisdom*, the reader was introduced to the Great White Brotherhood of the Ascended Masters, great Arisen Adepts who have watched over the affairs of mankind since the dawn of time. In that work we pointed out how these Masters have gradually revealed from time to time, through various inspired and enlightened individuals down through history, different aspects of that which is known as the Ancient Wisdom.

In the 19th century their instrument was Helena Petrovna Blavatsky. Of course, there always are many instruments that they work through, but during this period without any doubt whatsoever we can say that she was the principal one. In two great works, *Isis Unveiled*[1] which was first published in 1877, and then again in 1888 when *The Secret Doctrine*[2] made its appearance, these Masters once again brought mankind to the threshold of pure, spiritual awareness. In particular, we speak of the Master Morya—one of the world's great souls and an Arisen Adept from the heights of the Himalayas in Tibet—and the Master Koot Hoomi Lal Singh, a co-worker in the same Brotherhood and one who distinguished himself in a previous lifetime as the Greek philosopher Pythagoras.

12

In the 20th century, although there are many, many great souls who are bringing forth New Age teachings, the name of Richard Zenor Slocum will undoubtedly stand out among them and eventually be placed in its rightful category. For almost 67 years (August 25, 1911 to March 17, 1978), this great soul lived a life completely dedicated to serving others and allowing the Masters of Light to speak through him. Just the 2,200 classes alone that have been tape recorded for posterity—where the Master Teachers from the Consciousness of Immensity have talked upon practically every subject imaginable—are no small achievement. But did the work of these Arisen Adepts end with the passing of their principal channel into the spirit side of life? No indeed, it did not.

It was barely four months later (August 1, 1978), when they were once more conducting classes on a weekly basis at the Agasha Temple of Wisdom in Los Angeles. Only this time, of course, they were using a different instrument. Yet the classes were basically the same, in essence, the only real difference being that in Dr. Lane's class the principal speaker is the Master Teacher Araskas, the brother of Agasha whose discourses and philosophy were the subject of our two previous works. Some of the other Teachers have also gone on; yet many of the same ones remain including Dr. Navajo, Earshin, Kraio, and a host of others. The changeover is much the same as when a new pope moves into the Vatican or a new president into the White House. Yet this is not a true analogy since the Hermetic Wisdom as taught by Araskas is identically the same, even to the use of the same terminologies, as that given by his brother Agasha before him.

It is especially interesting to hear Richard Zenor himself, the former instrument who used to go into trance on this very same platform, return and speak to the class through a completely different set of vocal cords, and in his own inimitable style and manner, in much the same way that one would after returning from a short journey into a foreign country. His remanifestation is perhaps one of the best pieces of evidence proving the continuity of life beyond the earthly grave that the writer has had the privilege of witnessing—and he has seen many return, through different mediums, in the course of his lifetime.

Yet all in all, it still seems rather amazing that the program originally begun by Agasha, and now being carried on by his brother Araskas, should be able to continue with hardly even a break in the normal flow of the teachings. Dr. Barry Lane, the instrument for the present manifestations, is a much younger man than Richard Zenor and should be able to carry on with his work for many years to come. His channelship is equally as versatile as his brother's (yes, even Barry Lane and Richard Zenor were brothers 7,000 years ago in Egypt at the time of Agasha's manifestation), and the lectures by the various ones who manifest are dramatic, inspirational, and quite educational. Such is the way of Destiny.

However, as the months went by, the obligations and responsibilities of Dr. Lane's own church of which he is the founder (The Sanctuary of Revelations in Woodland Hills, California) forced him to transfer his classes back to the San Fernando Valley again, and that is where they are now being conducted. But the tapes of the original Agashan classes are still being played at 8:00 P.M. every Monday and Thursday evening at the Agasha Temple of Wisdom, 460 North Western Avenue, in Los Angeles, and they are open to the public for any who wish to drop in from time to time.

Perhaps we should now say something about the format and subject matter of the present volume. The dream of bringing forth a Cabalah based upon the English language had been with the writer for some time. He had discussed the subject at great length with the teacher Rhebaumaus Tate during many private contacts through the Zenor instrument, which date back to when he first began attending the Agashan classes in October, 1952. Of course, at that time it was only a very nebulous idea—something that I sort of knew was possible, and yet had absolutely no conception of how it was to come about. The teacher did, however, inform the writer that I had had a close relationship with Pythagoras many lifetimes ago in Greece, having attended his academy at Croton. He further went on to say that my mission in the present life was along those lines.

But the years went by, and it was not until my return to the Agasha Temple in 1969 after an absence of several years, that the project was begun in earnest. Thus the material for all three of the Agashan books that we have published to date—*Agasha: Master of Wisdom, The Agashan Discourses*, and *The English Cabalah* (of which this present volume is only the first part)— began to be gathered together at one and the same time. The only reason that the first two were published before the present one was on the insistence of the teacher Rhebaumaus Tate (the real author of this present work) that such should be the case. "Otherwise you would be putting the cart before the horse," he said on numerous occasions. Yet all three volumes are but different aspects of the same Hermetic philosophy that the Teachers of Light wish to have clarified in this present generation.

The Cabalah, for those of you who don't know the meaning of the term, means a system of theosophy, mysticism, and thaumaturgy marked by belief in creation through emanation and a cipher method of interpreting Scripture. Agasha has many times referred to it as the numerology of the ancient Hebrews, and of the Atlanteans before that. It is a universal system that has no real beginning in time, since it has always existed and it always shall exist. It only needs to be rediscovered when each civilization reaches a critical point in its evolution.

Its basic aspects are amazingly simple; but we, in our present civilization, have lost sight of them because we have divorced letters from number. Even the ancient Hebrews had no separate system for identifying numbers from words. Every letter in the Hebrew language stood for a number; therefore, the only way for them to record a number was by means of its appropriate word. This, then, accounts for the tremendous importance given in the Old Testament, especially in the Book of Genesis, to number, to names, to the number of years that each generation lived after Adam, and even to the numerical number of each chapter and verse.

All of these things were important to the Hebrew priests, to those who were learned in the esoteric wisdom, because through the real meaning of number they could interpret the past. Yet this was not for the public at large; it was only for those who were admitted into the Mysteries.

"All well and good," you say, "but how does this affect us today in our present civilization, when the ancient Hebrew terminologies are no longer used and, in fact, even our language is completely different?" Aha! Here is where the absolutely incredible, almost unbelievable, aspect of the English language unfolds before our very eyes. The English alphabet, believe it or not, was actually *designed* by the God Consciousness so that mankind in the 20th century would be able to understand the nature of his very BEING. Whatever the magical qualities of the ancient Hebrew alphabet were, the English alphabet of today goes it one better! And with the aid of the cipher code that it contains, all of the hidden meanings of Scripture can once more be easily understood by the lay mind. This is what this book is all about.

The late Eric Temple Bell, Professor of Mathematics at the California Institute of Technology, subconsciously knew that we had not yet discovered the real secret of number. In his book on *Numerology: The Magic of Numbers,*[3] he discusses at considerable length the *geometrical* aspects that the Pythagoreans attributed to number. Yet, he did not feel that they went far enough. On page 105 of his immensely informative volume, he states:

"But, as a student of the theory of numbers, I have often wondered whether that great theory might not have followed an entirely different course, and perhaps one closer to reason and nature, if Pythagoras had never lived. Being unable to suggest any more rational thing to do than what is now being done, I merely throw out the suggestion to any curious mind which may, possibly, penetrate to a deeper stratum of the relations between numbers than any we have yet struck. My own feeling is that the theory of forms is a beautiful bypath, and that it is such because arithmetic has not yet had its Descartes, let alone its Newton or Einstein. So much for my own numerological confession of unfaith."

The French philosopher Descartes, of course, is looked upon today as the first modern mathematician. But his great contribution was in the field of analytical geometry. He was the first one to apply the principles of algebra to form. But as yet, no one has seen fit in our modern-day world to remove number from its imprisonment in form and quantity, and instead apply it in a *qualitative* way to words, to language, to the very *sounds* attributed to each letter of the alphabet. In this way then a whole new dimension opens up in the understanding of what number really is—a far cry from the limited understanding that we have had of it previously. "Every Word Is a Number and Every Number Is a Word" is the title of the first chapter in this work, and we hope it will prove interesting to the average reader.

One more thought before we close this Introduction to the present volume. Even Madame Blavatsky herself knew the ways of the Masters, and that their teachings were given to the world in cyclic intervals. Manly Palmer Hall, in his commentary on *The Secret Doctrine*, and Madame Blavatsky in particular, tells us on page 95 of his classical treatise, *The Phoenix:*[4]

"*The Secret Doctrine* contains practically all that is known on the subject of occultism that is permissible to print, and every page is a veritable treasure-house of esoteric lore. . . . H.P. Blavatsky herself realized that her writings were out of sympathy with the age and that the full significance of *The Secret Doctrine* could not be fully recognized until the advent of a more auspicious time. It was to be the occult textbook of the twentieth century, to stand without addition or subtraction until the coming of the next emissary of the Masters, which, according to H.P.B., was to be about 1975. Mohammed well said that each age has its book, and *The Secret Doctrine* is unquestionably the *magnum opus* of the literature of the modern world."

Let us hope, then, that the teachings of Agasha, Araskas, Rhebaumaus Tate, and all of the other Teachers of the Great White Brotherhood fulfill this prophecy, and that they eventually become the *magnum opus* of the present day.

The Scribe
William Eisen
Los Angeles, Calif.
August 26, 1979

NOTES

1. H.P. Blavatsky, *Isis Unveiled* (Pasadena, Calif., Theosophical University Press, 1877, 1950)

2. H. P. Blavatsky, *The Secret Doctrine* (Wheaton, Ill., The Theosophical Press, 1888, 1938)

3. Eric Temple Bell, Ph.D., *Numerology: The Magic of Numbers* (New York, United Book Guild, 1945) p. 105

4. Manly Palmer Hall, *The Phoenix* (Los Angeles, Calif., Philosophical Research Society, 1931) p. 95

PART I

THE BEGINNING
AND
THE END

Chapter 1

EVERY WORD IS A NUMBER AND
EVERY NUMBER IS A WORD

In the english Cabalah, letters are shown to be a manifestation of number. Therefore every word, being built up
entirely from letters, must also represent a number. And the
converse is also true. This, then, explains the seemingly contradictory statement of Agasha when he tells us on page 296 of
The Agashan Discourses that "every word is the equivalent of a
number, and every number can be said to be a word."

Now since the English alphabet is composed of 26 different
letters from A to Z, we can also number the letters accordingly.
Thus A is one, B is two, C is three, etc., all the way up to Z
which represents a manifestation of the number 26. Let us
study the following table:

C O L U M N S

	1	2	3	4	5	6	7	8	9	
DIGITS	1	2	3	4	5	6	7	8	9	R
LETTERS 1st Row	1 A	2 B	3 C	4 D	5 E	6 F	7 G	8 H	9 I	O
2nd Row	10 J	11 K	12 L	13 M	14 N	15 O	16 P	17 Q	18 R	W
3rd Row	19 S	20 T	21 U	22 V	23 W	24 X	25 Y	26 Z	27 O	A C E / S

Figure 1
A Table of the Letters and Digits

21

It can readily be seen that all of the digits from 1 to 9, the letters from A to Z, and the zero (which represents a vacant space or the absence of a letter) occupy their appropriate positions on the table. We thus have three separate and distinct manifestations of the numbers—three orders, degrees, or octaves of vibration—in this table of 36 squares. The top row, which represents the digits themselves in their unmanifested state, could be said to represent the zero row from which the numbers spring forth into manifestation into the various letters or degrees of consciousness.

Some very interesting relationships also become apparent. The *ones* manifest as the A, J, and S. These three letters phonetically sound out as the AGES—the various periods in the history of human progress. The *twos* are the B, K, and T. These could be said to represent a BUCKET—a vessel for carrying or containing something. The *threes* become the C, L, and U and being a trinity, offer us a CLUE or a piece of evidence that can lead us towards the solution to any problem.

Agasha states the *fours* represent a blockage, an obstruction, or an obstacle in our path (*The Agashan Discourses*, page 294) and indeed they do. They come into manifestation in the letters D, M, and V. The two letters, D and M, literally build a DAM over the letter V, thus preventing any flow of liquid from escaping from the V when it is turned upside down and becomes a Δ (the letter *Delta*, the fourth letter of the Greek alphabet). Therefore, the *fours* DAM the V.

The *fives* become the bearer of the *unexpected* (*The Agashan Discourses*, page 294) and bring forth something NEW with the letters N, E, and W. This new "something" turns out to be the FOX who is brought into manifestation with the F, O, and X. This "fox" is very sly and clever since he represents the famous Beast of the Book of *Revelation* whose number is "Six hundred threescore and six." Yet he functions very much on the *material* plane since, according to the Agashan philosophy, the *sixes* have to do with the material, and it is on the material plane where all the action is, at least as far as the mortal is concerned.

Therefore, much can be gained from a proper understanding of the FOX whose number is 666.

We come now to the *sevens* as they manifest in the letters G, Y, and P. Those who are on the spiritual path often complain of the required sacrifices that one must make as he struggles along the path of the number seven, and, accordingly, the *sevens* can sometimes manifest as a GYP—but this is only illusionary. If you feel that you are being gypped or cheated out of something because you are on the spiritual path, always remember that these sacrifices will eventually be returned to you a thousandfold. Even the Gypsies, who have been forced to wander about in their migratory way of life without the security of a home, will eventually come into their own.

The *eights* come into manifestation with the letters H, Q, and Z. The Q and Z represent a QUIZ—a short oral or written test. And the letter H in the English Cabalah always means EACH. The letter H also represents the Teacher, as we will discover a little later in this book. Therefore the *eights* can quite materially benefit a person as he passes EACH QUIZ that is given by the Teacher along the pathway of life.

And now we come to the most profound number of them all —the number *nine*. The *nines* manifest in the letters I and R, but why does Agasha state that the nine is so profound? He also tells us that it can be a disturbing factor if it is not utilized properly (*The Agashan Discourses*, page 295), and why is this so? The answer lies in the letters themselves. The disturbing factor comes about when we experience the IRE or wrath of the great I AM. And what is the "I AM"? The I AM is simply the I ARE. The letter R in the English Cabalah is spelled ARE, and it means the present indicative, plural, of the verb BE. But when we consider all of the many "I"s individually, and as a whole, we must out of necessity consider them in the plural and not the singular form. Therefore, in this context it is grammatically correct to say "I ARE" when we are in reference to all of the many individuals who are a part of the great I AM.

The letters I and R can also be said to represent AIR. It is the vehicle through which sound is brought into manifestation when the "Word" is uttered either by God or by Man. But I AM or I ARE what? It is the *zero* or the vacant square following the letter Z. Thus, what ever letter eventually fills this space, God Is. It is represented by the return of the letter A in the form of the ACE. The ACE of the Tarot deck represents the letter A; yet its numerical value is 1 + 3 + 5 or the number 9. Thus the ACE can very aptly fill the space under the great I ARE. In the English Cabalah, the A-C-E means the All-Seeing-Eye that goes before us to prepare a place in a new or forthcoming incarnation or world of consciousness. Therefore, it can be said that the I R represents I ARE 0 (zero) OR (reading up the column) I ARE ACE. But I (also) RACE. And whom do "I" race? I race the AGES, the *ones*, time itself, as I hurriedly race ahead to prepare a place for a new manifestation of MY existence. And who am I? I am the entire human race; in other words, you might call it the "I" race—a race of "I"s.

Now laying this little excursion as to the meanings of the letters aside for the moment, let us take a look at the actual method used whereby we can change any word or group of words into a number, and any number into a word. Of course, all numbers cannot be converted into a correctly spelled word of the English language. Of course not. But at least we can single out the correct letters, or combination of letters, that make up that number and then analyze the letters themselves to see if they can shed any light as to the true meaning of the number.

For instance: What is the meaning of the number 13,114? We can segregate the digits a little differently into 13-1-14, and we have the word MAN. Likewise, the number 381,891,920 can be more clearly identified when we break it up into the correct letters that make up the number. It can be changed into 3-8-18-9-19-20 which yields the word CHRIST. In this way then, we find that any word in the English language can very easily be changed into its corresponding number.

However, the inverse process is not always so easy. Because

many of the letters convert into two-digit numbers, it is a little more difficult to convert some of the larger numbers, especially when they contain a considerable number of ones and twos, into their appropriate words. The number for CONSCIOUS-NESS is a good example of this point. The number is 3,151,419, 391,521,191,451,919. At a cursory glance, it is not readily apparent whether to make use of the two-digit letters or the one-digit letters in making our analysis. A little practice, how-ever, will soon make the student quite proficient at this as he learns to mentally see letters instead of numbers. A good rule to follow is wherever possible start out with the two-digit letter first, and then if this doesn't work you may substitute the A D for the N in the case of the 1-4 sequence, etc.

About the only other difficulty the student will run into is in differentiating the letter O (oh) from the digit 0 (zero). Since they both have the same symbol, the situation can be quite confusing at times. For instance: Let us take the two numbers 7,154 and 704. Both of these numbers spell out the word GOD. Both are correct in this respect. The only difference between them is that in the latter case the central 0 is empty and not in manifestation, and in the former case it is in full manifestation as the letter O. However, both O's, the empty one as well as the full one, can be used to represent the symbol known as O.

The empty space, or the digit 0, is sometimes used as the connecting link between the words in a sentence. The zero in between the words will not change the numerical value of the sentence because it has no numerical value. It is simply zero. Let us take a look at the number 9,012,152,250,251,521. All of the 0 digits in this particular number simply show a vacant space between the words in the sentence. The number spells out I LOVE YOU.

Thus we find that every word or phrase in the English lan-guage can be converted into a number. This number, which represents the natural sequence of the letters, is called the "Natural number" of that particular word or phrase.

The Various Ways to Read a Number

However, the method outlined above is not the only way to "read" a number. A number may have many different meanings in much the same way that words, even though they may sound alike and sometimes even be spelled the same, also can have various meanings.

For example: Let us take the number 3 which converts to the letter C. Very well. We have converted the digit 3 to the letter C. But now we also find, in our analysis, that the letter C can be pronounced soft with an "s" sound as in ACE or CENT, or it may be pronounced hard with a "k" sound as in CAT. But this is not all. The letter C may also be pronounced in the same way that it sounds when we recite the alphabet. Thus C may be pronounced CEE as well.

There are also other words which sound the same as CEE, but they are spelled differently and consequently have different meanings. Yet the symbol is the same—C. First, we have the word SEA, which means the ocean. Then we have the word SEE, but this word has many different meanings. It means to perceive with the eyes, it means to understand something mentally, and it also means the seat or the center of authority of a bishop, as in the Holy See—just to mention a few. Therefore, when we come across the digit 3, and then convert it to the letter C, there are many ways to "read" it.

The same thing can be said for the digits themselves. We do not "have" to convert a digit to a letter when we come across it in a number. We may simply leave it alone and call it by its numerical name. For instance, the digit 4 may be read as the number FOUR or as the preposition FOR. Or then again, it may be read as the letter D. The same rule applies to the digits 2 and 8, or any other number that can be converted to a letter, for that matter. The symbol 2 may be read as the number TWO, the preposition TO, the adverb TOO, or the letter B. The symbol 8 may be read as the number EIGHT, the verb ATE, or the letter H. There are many ways to read a number.

This idea of reading a number as a word, but with a different meaning, is not new. Many advertisements have appeared in periodicals, on billboards, etc. in recent times that take advantage of this principle. Children will sometimes entertain themselves while riding in an automobile by interpreting the license numbers on the cars as they go by. For instance: The letters ICU can be interpreted to mean I SEE YOU; the symbols 24T can be read TWO FOR TEA; and the license plate UR4-ME2 makes the statement, YOU ARE FOR ME, TOO. And when they eventually learn that the digits or numbers may likewise be transformed into letters, the game should prove even more popular.

Another way to "read" a number is to read it in reverse direction. We must remember that the Hebrew language is read from right to left, and there is certainly no hard and fast rule that we cannot also read a number in the same way. For example: The number 2,013 may be expressed as 20-1-3, which spells TAC. This is not a word in the English language, but if we read it from right to left, it becomes CAT. In this way then, many numbers which normally would have no apparent meaning can be read intelligently, and sometimes the thought expressed is quite profound!

And we don't even have to stop here. We can continue on in our analysis. For once we have transformed a number into a word, even the word itself may give rise to several additional meanings when we rearrange the letters in a slightly different manner. A common method that may be used to provide supplementary meanings to a word is to write it out in the form of a circle, and then read it in either clockwise or counterclockwise directions, and from alternate starting points.

For example: Let us take the word EARTH. What is the true meaning of this word? We all know that it is the name of the planet on which we live, and that it is the third planet out from the sun in our respective solar system, but what is the word really telling us? Is there some hidden information that is not readily apparent on the surface? Well, let us find out. Let us simply write the letters out in the form of a circle. The various interpretations are then shown in the following diagram. Each figure should be read from the *.

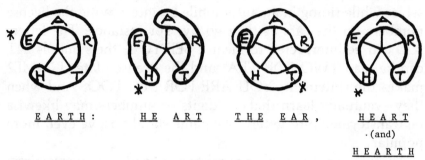

EARTH :   HE ART   THE EAR ,   HEART
                                                  · (and)

                                               HEARTH

Figure 2
An Analysis of the Word EARTH

We find then that there are several other additional meanings that the word EARTH tells us. These are all joined together in the sentence: EARTH: HE ART THE EAR, HEART, (and) HEARTH. But He is the ear, heart, and hearth of what? And why does the word refer to the Earth as He? The word *heart* refers to the breast or bosom, or the center of emotion; and the word *hearth* refers to the fireside or home. Do the words imply, then, that the Earth is functioning as the "heart" of our solar system? Or is it perhaps the home of the Solar Logos, and also one of its "ears" as it tunes itself to the Cosmos? The answers to these questions, and more, may be obtained when we differentiate the word even further by some of the more complicated methods of analysis explained in later chapters. The method that we have just described is only one of the simpler methods of analysis available to the modern-day student of the Cabalah.

At this point, we should mention that there is also no hard and fast rule that all of the words making up a sentence in the English Cabalah should always be separated. It would be wonderful if this were so, but it is not always the case. Since sometimes entire sentences are made up of only a few letters, as in the above example, the impossibility of such a rule is obvious. The student will find that sometimes the words are separated by the digit 0, sometimes there is no separation, and sometimes the last letter of one word is also the first letter of the next word. In any event though, once the code is broken, the meaning usually becomes quite clear.

The one thing that one should always remember, as he attempts to "read" a number or find the hidden meaning contained therein, is that that number or word is trying to tell you a story. The consciousness within the word is trying to speak to you. And it is doing so by means of the only language it knows —the language of number, symbology, and analogy. These three terms are what constitute the true study of semantics. Semantics, as it is practiced today, simply does not go far enough; for before we can understand the true meaning of a word, we must embrace the Cabalah and interpret it cabalistically. And when we do this, the word will stand out in all of its pristine purity, stripped of the outer garments, and in its nakedness unashamedly reveal to the onlooker its true identity.

Therefore, the only restrictions that are imposed upon the seeker as he attempts to interpret the true meaning of a word cabalistically, are the restrictions that the seeker imposes upon himself. Your only limitations are the limits of your own ingenuity, as you attempt to solve any given problem. But always remember that you must also use logic in your interpretations. The laws of any cabalistic method must always be logical and orderly. It has been said that figures do not lie, but that liars figure; and this applies equally as well to the study of the Cabalah. But always feel free to use your imagination and ingenuity to the utmost as you attempt a cabalistic interpretation of a word. Allow the word to speak to you in the language in which it is trying to express itself, and let it dictate its own rules and reasons for being.

The Alpha Number

Perhaps the most important number used in the English Cabalah is that which is called the "Alpha number." For practical purposes, this number is used far more extensively than the *Natural* number, the number from which it is derived. The Natural number, which represents the natural sequence of the letters, is ofttimes very large and quite cumbersome to handle. But the Alpha number, being a much smaller number, is quite easy to handle; and it is essentially the same as the Natural number in that it is simply the sum total of its parts. The Alpha number of any word or phrase, therefore, is the total sum of the numerical value of each letter contained therein. It has been so named because it represents the value of the letters in the English alphabet.

For example: The Alpha number for the word GOD is $7 + 15 + 4 = (26)$. The Alpha number for the word CHRIST is $3 + 8 + 18 + 9 + 19 + 20 = (77)$; and the Alpha number for the word MAN is $13 + 1 + 14 = (28)$. One can very readily see that the numbers 26, 77, and 28 are far less cumbersome to handle than their counterparts of (7,154), (381,891,920), and (13,114), respectively. Yet essentially the Alpha number and the Natural number are the same, as the whole is always equal to the sum of its parts.

Now let us not confuse the Alpha number, usually a number of several digits, with the single-digit number most students of numerology are acquainted with. All of us know that any natural whole number, no matter how large it be, can be reduced to a single digit by successive addition. This digit then strikes the keynote for the entire number (*The Agashan Discourses*, page 294). But there are still several intermediate steps that we first have to go through in order to arrive at this single-digit number, the Ultimate, the One.

The Alpha number is then the first sum that we arrive at in adding up the total value of all the letters in the word or phrase. The second sum, the sum of the digits in the Alpha number, would then be called the Beta number; the third sum, the Gamma number, etc. This would continue until we eventually arrived at the Ultimate, the One, the single-digit number, whatever it be.

The Alpha number could then be said to represent an intermediate point in that vast spectrum of vibration from the One

to the Many. At one end of the spectrum we have an immensely large number, called the Natural number. It could be any
natural whole number, and the number of its digits could range
into the thousands. Then at the other end of the spectrum we
have the One, the single digit. But the important thing to
remember is that these single-digit numbers, along with each of
the intermediate sums, are individually equivalent to the
immensely large number they were at the beginning.

One other point. The Alpha number for the word CON-
SCIOUSNESS is $3 + 15 + 14 + 19 + 3 + 9 + 15 + 21 + 19 +$
$14 + 5 + 19 + 19 = (175)$. And it is interesting to note that this
Alpha number for CONSCIOUSNESS in turn transliterates
itself into the word AGE (175). Thus the English Cabalah tells
us that Consciousness can be said to represent an AGE. But it
also says that God can be represented by the letter Z (God =
26), and that Man's number is 28 or B + H. In other words,
Man BE EACH. Man, then, is a part of *each* thing that we can
refer to—God, Age, Consciousness, or whatever.

Chapter 2

THE BOOK OF THE TAROT

Perhaps the most essential aspect of the English Cabalah is the Tarot. For without the Tarot, we would have no means of unlocking the mysteries contained within the English language. The word *tarot* is derived from the Hebrew word for *law* which is "tora" and the Latin word for *wheel* which is "rota." Therefore, by placing these four letters on a wheel in the north, east, south, and west positions respectively, we have literally the wheel (rota) of the law (tora). But the wheel must be rotated in both a clockwise and an anti-clockwise direction to bring these words into manifestation. It should be noted that the "T" is both the alpha and the omega, the beginning and the ending, of the word TAROT.

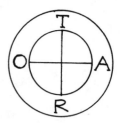

Figure 3

There are an incredible number of books that have been published on the Tarot, and it is not the purpose of this volume to reiterate and repeat the same information that has been so aptly given by many other authors. What we *are* trying to do, however, is to supplement and enhance this vast treasure-trove

32

of information that has already been published with some new material which should shed even more light on this most fascinating subject.

But first, a brief review is in order. The Book of the Tarot is a textbook of occult philosophy that was originally given in Atlantis. This is not generally known in the outer world today, inasmuch as the earliest physical evidence we have of the Tarot dates back only to the 14th century. But the Agashan teachers have stated that the philosophy contained therein goes way back into the sands of time.

One of its most prominent proponents in our modern era was Alphonse Louis Constant, otherwise known as Eliphas Levi. This 19th-century occultist has manifested on a number of occasions in the Agashan classes, incidentally, and he left us much information on the Tarot in his many published works.[1]

"The Tarot is a book which epitomizes all sciences," he writes, "while its infinite combinations can solve all problems; a book which speaks by evoking thought; the inspirer and controller of all possible conceptions; the masterpiece, perhaps, of the human mind, and undoubtedly one of the finest things which antiquity has bequeathed us."

Elsewhere he says, "The Tarot is a veritable oracle, and replies to all possible questions with precision and infallibility. A prisoner, with no other book than the Tarot, if he knew how to use it, could in a few years acquire a universal science, and would be able to speak on all subjects with unequalled learning and inexhaustible eloquence. The oracles of the Tarot give answers as exact as mathematics, and as measured as the harmonies of Nature. By the aid of these signs and their infinite combinations, it is possible to arrive at the natural and mathematical revelation of all secrets of Nature. The practical value of the Tarot is truly and above all marvelous."

Levi emphasizes this thought once more when he states, "The Tarot is a truly philosophical machine which prevents the mind from going astray, even while leaving it its own initiative and freedom; it is mathematics in their application to the absolute, the alliance of the real and the ideal, a lottery of thoughts, all of which are rigorously exact, like numbers; in fine, it is perhaps at once the simplest and grandest thing ever conceived by human genius."

Now Eliphas Levi, or Constant as he is known to members of the Agashan classes, is only one of many scholars, mystics, and writers who have come to realize and respect the universal wisdom contained within this fantastic book of 78 unbound pages. Yes, the Book of the Tarot has never been bound and it never shall be bound, for if it were, the universal symbols contained therein would not be free to move about, intermingle, and thus express the many and varied permutations and combinations that are possible with 78 freely moving and unrestricted symbols or cards.

The Book of the Tarot, then, is a deck of cards, a deck of universal symbols, which if understood in its entirety is able to express all of the laws of Man, God, and the Universe. It is therefore, in symbolical form, a microcosm of the macrocosm. It is YOU! It represents everything that you ever have been and everything that you ever shall be. Remember, there are an almost infinite number of combinations available to 78 freely moving symbols. Although each card is an entity unto itself, it is also influenced greatly by the other forces or cards within its immediate atmosphere. And is this so different from life itself? It is not.

Let us now take a brief look at the cards themselves. You will see that they very closely resemble a modern deck of playing cards. The four suits—Swords, Wands, Pentacles, and Cups— may be compared with the Spades, Clubs, Diamonds, and Hearts of the modern deck. The only difference in this respect is that the Tarot suits have one additional card—the Knight. But there is one other major difference, and this difference, as far as the occultist is concerned, is of paramount importance. Beyond the four 14-card suits which make up what is known as the Minor Arcana is the trump suit which is called the Major Arcana. This trump suit is comprised of 21 numbered cards, which represent a series of universal and absolute ideas, and also an unnumbered card or a zero card. This unnumbered card corresponds to the Joker of the modern deck. All of these cards, then, go on to make up that which has come to be known as the Book of the Tarot.

It would be wise at this time if the reader would avail himself of an actual deck of Tarot cards. But first, which deck should he buy? There have been literally hundreds of decks published throughout the years, and it is not within the jurisdiction of this writer to pass judgment on any one of them. Basically, they are all the same. By that I mean that each deck has the four suits of the Minor Arcana with each suit containing a King, Queen, Knight, and Page and ten numbered cards from the Ace to the Ten. Each deck has also a 22 card trump suit; but here the similarity ends. Some of the trump cards in some of the decks have been so changed so as to be almost unrecognizable from the original. But who am I to say that these "improvements" are necessarily wrong? You will have to be your own judge in that matter.

However, there is one particular deck of Tarot cards that is used throughout this book on the English Cabalah. It was designed by the learned occultist Arthur Edward Waite and his associate Pamela Colman Smith during the first decade of our century while they were carrying out their investigations in magic, theosophy, freemasonry, and all forms of symbology. During this time, they were also members of the magical Order of the Golden Dawn, that occult fraternity that paved the way for modern-day occultism. Waite reversed the positions of the Tarot cards denoting Strength and Justice (now cards number 8 and 11), and refined the symbolism on all of the other trump cards so as to better express their correct symbology. But this is not all. He also gave the correct interpretation to the actual meanings of all of the numbered cards from the Ace to the Ten in each suit of the Minor Arcana as well. All of the decks prior to this time simply showed pips on these numbered cards in much the same fashion as the modern playing card deck. One can see, then, that A. E. Waite most certainly added a good deal of "weight" to the entire subject of the Tarot. It is for these reasons, then, that this particular deck has now become standard for most of the English-speaking world. Since it was first published by William Rider & Son, Ltd., it is called the Rider deck.

Now that you have your cards in front of you, look at them, fondle them, and meditate on them. Cherish them as you would your dearest friend, for indeed they are just that. Treat them with the respect that they so justly deserve and they will never let you down, for these are the symbols of the soul. And the soul is your best teacher. Remember, these symbols are as old as time itself. They were never really created, for they have always existed; they have merely been forgotten at times. So don't let these strange symbols disturb you. After all, if you are to communicate with your soul, the language of symbology most certainly must contain the bad along with the good or there could be no communication. If this were not so, then how could you be informed of the negative results of a wrong action?

The reader is referred at this point to the discourse titled "Symbology: The Language of the Soul" on pages 195-200 of *The Agashan Discourses.* It is here where Dr. Navajo endeavors to explain what Agasha had been saying for many years pertaining to the various methods of soul communication. "And the truly amazing thing in all of this," Dr. Navajo goes on to say, "is that the soul, being infinitely intelligent, can work through a deck of picture symbols and cause the mortal self to so shuffle the cards, or toss the coins as in the I Ching, so that the correct symbols will appear and show the probable solution to any stated problem." But it was also stated in this particular discourse that we have to go back many generations before we can arrive at the true symbology relative to the Tarot cards of today. And this book will attempt to do just that. It is hoped that the study of the English Cabalah will enable the student to remove the final veil from these ancient symbols of the past and bring them once more out into the sunlight of understanding.

Its Basic Divisions

Now that you have your "soul" spread out before you, what is the first thing that comes to your mind? The average person will answer by saying he is confused, that there are simply too many symbols, all mingled together, to form any sort of an opinion. And this is true. Since the soul is a consciousness, a world, a kingdom, the first thing to do is to put it in order. By that, I mean the next step is to segregate its various components into their rightful categories, separate the wheat from the chaff, so to speak, and by so doing, put your house in order. So then let us begin by taking the various cards, sorting them out, and studying their relationships with one another.

Let us start with the Major Arcana. You will find that this trump suit contains 21 numbered cards plus a zero card. Since 21 is the sum of $1 + 2 + 3 + 4 + 5 + 6$, the numbered cards will very easily fall into place in the form of a triangle with the first card, the Magician, occupying the apex position. The 0 card, or the Fool, you may place outside of the triangle for the moment. Now the first thing for the student to realize is that that Fool is YOU. And being outside of the triangle or pyramid, he is doing the same thing that you are doing right now. He is looking at the pyramid, in complete wonderment, wondering what on earth that pyramid is all about. He is looking at his own BEING, and he doesn't even know it. Yes, it could be said that the pyramid that you have just built represents all of the basic, fundamental forces or ideas that permit you, as an individual, to exist. Each force or card may be considered to be one element or letter of a magical alphabet, the totality of which comprises this pyramid. The pyramid may then be said to represent the pyramid of your own Being.

Now if this Fool, which is You, wishes to know more about the mysteries contained within his consciousness, he must go on a journey. This journey is called the Fool's pilgrimage. But before he can do this, he must have some place to go. Therefore, the outer worlds are brought into manifestation. These outer worlds that our Fool is about to explore are represented by the four suits of the Tarot—Swords, Wands, Pentacles, and Cups. These four kingdoms are analogous to the four basic divisions of Nature—Air, Fire, Earth, and Water, and they go on to make up what is known as Man's outer consciousness. This is in direct opposition to, but still a reflection of, the pyramid which represents his inner consciousness.

Now these four worlds may be arranged in any number of geometric patterns. Since there are 14 cards in each suit or kingdom, they may be set up into rectangles of two rows each, with seven cards in each row. Or they may be arranged in a circle, or whatever. The important thing to remember is that we should arrange the cards of each kingdom in some orderly manner. An interesting situation arises when we try to place these 14 cards into a triangle similar to the trump suit. It cannot be done unless we leave the apex off or some other space in the triangle vacant. But this is the whole point! By doing so, you have permitted yourself to become part of the picture, to gain entry into this world or kingdom. Each suit will then have four rows of 2, 3, 4, and 5 cards respectively. This makes 14 in all. This leaves the apex position open to receive the Fool as he embarks upon his journey through life after tumbling from the lofty position he had held at the beginning.

The four court cards of each suit, the King, Queen, Knight, and Page, represent the royal family and consequently the rulers of each kingdom. The numbered cards from the Ace to the Ten represent the major experiences, or the lessons to be learned, that the Fool must encounter as he travels through that particular kingdom. The Ace always represents the beginning of the journey and the Ten its completion.

Let us now reflect upon another very interesting point. Take a look at the 10's of each suit, and what do you find? You find that two of the suits have happy endings and two have unhappy endings. And this is just the way it should be to have any balance in life. You will find that the Tarot is so structured that everything balances out to zero in the final analysis. It leaves room for every possible type of experience—the good as well as the bad. The direful ending of the 10 of Swords reemphasizes the old adage which states, "As you live by the sword, so shall you die by the sword." The 10 of Wands or Clubs is not much better. It represents *oppression.* But if you are fortunate enough to be traveling through the suits of Cups and Pentacles, and if you passed every test while in the pursuit of love and wisdom, then a glorious ending lies in store for the aspirant as he completes his final step into the heaven that awaits him. These suits may be compared to the red cards of the modern playing card deck as opposed to the black cards of the Spades and Clubs.

Now that you have put your consciousness into some sort of order, you are better able to see where you are and what life is all about. Of course, at this point we have not even scratched the surface, but at least the reader should have some glimmer of understanding relative to the various aspects of his own consciousness or soul. There you are, the Fool, the Ego, the Self, looking slightly perplexed as you contemplate the vastness of your own Being. Over there, right in front of your eyes, lie the four worlds that give expression to your outer consciousness, your Outer Self. And over here, as close to you as breathing, is the Great Pyramid of your Inner Consciousness, the ONE state of your Higher Self.

The Position of the Fool

Let us now give some attention to the true position of the Fool. Since on many decks he has no number at all, and on other decks he is simply assigned the number 0, where then should we place him in relationship with all of the other cards? Where is his own individual sanctuary in this Temple of 78 different rooms? You might ask the same thing about the Page, the King, the Queen, the Knight. If you examine these cards also, you will never see a number appearing upon them. Where then should we place them?

One will find a little later in this work that the Court cards of the four suits *do* have a particular number, and there is a very definite position that they normally occupy. But with the Fool, we have a slightly different situation. It would seem that he very aptly fits the description of the Wandering Jew, that legendary character who is condemned to roam without rest because he struck Christ on the day of the Crucifixion. And the Fool, strangely enough, *does* have a very interesting relationship with that Force that we call *Christ.*

The alpha number for the word "Christ" is $3 + 8 + 18 + 9 + 19 + 20 = (77)$. And the Tarot deck consists of 77 numbered cards *plus* the Fool or the 0 card. It would seem, then, that the body of Christ, or the Christ Consciousness, is made up of these 77 numbered cards: and that the Self, the incarnating Ego, is represented by the 0 card, or the Fool. This is borne out by the fact that *any* number to the 0 power *is* 1 ($x^0 = 1$). Therefore, the Fool becomes the individualized entity, the One, who incarnates within his own consciousness. Thus he can actually *be* any card in the deck he desires to be, or has earned the right to be, because he *is* the deck and all that is in it.

However, we must out of necessity find a place to put him because he is still an individualized entity. But where? It must be somewhere within the Major Arcana because he is a part of the Major Arcana. He is one of the 22 universal and absolute ideas which made up the original cabalistic alphabet of the ancient Hebrews. But does he stand before all of the others? Or does he come last in 22nd place? Perhaps he might even fit somewhere in between.

We should also remember that we have a perfect analogy between the 22 Tarot Keys of the Major Arcana and the 22 letters of the original Hebrew alphabet. This in itself is quite unusual, and it doesn't seem to be the result of coincidence. Therefore, many early scholars of the occult assigned a Hebrew letter to each Major Arcana card. But where did they place the Fool? The answer is quite surprising on the surface. The majority of them, including Eliphas Levi, Papus, Oswald Wirth, Arthur Edward Waite—just to name a few—chose to assign the 0 Tarot Key, the Fool, *between* Tarot Keys Number 20 and 21. Now why did they do this? Normally you and I would place the 0 before the 1, as this is quite logical. And a great many of the modern scholars have done just that. They have placed the

Fool in the Aleph or the Number 1 position. However, this course of action throws all of the Tarot Keys off by one digit from the normal sequence of the alphabet.

This situation is quite confusing to the beginner who is just taking up the study of the Tarot; for if the Book of the Tarot represents successive stages of initiation, then getting the trump sequence in correct order is of primary importance. Again, if each trump corresponds to a number and a letter of the Hebrew alphabet, then establishing the correct order is obviously a matter of primary concern. A false step in this essential process can throw one's entire system awry.

But we believe we have found a simple solution to the entire problem. Actually, it turns out that *both* of these systems are essentially correct. The correct placement only depends upon one's viewpoint in the scheme of things. You see, we must remember that all things in life are circular and cyclic. After we come to the final letter of the alphabet, there is simply no place else to go except begin all over again as we spiral out from the center or the hub. But it took the English alphabet, along with the simple evolution of the Hebrew alphabet, to give us the key.

NOTES

1. English translations of some of Eliphas Levi's works have been published by Rider & Co. in London and Samuel Weiser in New York. Titles include *The History of Magic, Transcendental Magic,* and *The Key of the Mysteries.*

Chapter 3

THE EVOLUTION OF THE ALPHABETS

PERHAPS WE SHOULD say something about alphabets in general at this time. Alphabets, like everything else, go through a state of evolution. The English alphabet of today is essentially the Latin alphabet of yesterday. Somewhere around the 11th century A.D., the letter W was added to distinguish two U's from a U and a V; and in the same fashion, the letter J came into manifestation as a variant form of the Latin letter I. Therefore, the English alphabet is nothing more than the Latin alphabet but with two additional letters—the J and the W. It is also important to realize that these two new letters came into manifestation *within* the alphabet itself; they were not just added on at the end. Growth always comes from within.

We can say the same thing about the Hebrew alphabet. It is interesting to note that the original Hebrew alphabet was evidently quite pure and without sin. I am saying this facetiously only to point out that "sin" actually was added to the Hebrew alphabet in recent times. The letter *Sin* was brought into manifestation as a variant of the 21st letter *Shin*. This new letter was also created from within the alphabet, with Sin replacing Shin as the 21st letter. The original 21st and 22nd letters, Shin and

Taw, then went on to become the 22nd and the 23rd letters respectively. Thus the original 22-letter alphabet of the ancient Hebrews has now evolved into a 23-letter alphabet.

Now all alphabets are interrelated in the final analysis. This is especially true when we consider the Hebrew, Greek, Latin, and English alphabets; for here, within these four alphabets, we can observe the primitive 22-letter magical alphabet of the Cabalah—the 22 Keys of the Major Arcana of the Tarot—go through a state of evolution and gradually become, once more, the 26-letter WORD it was in the beginning. This, it would appear, is the English alphabet of today.

Why do we say this? How can we make the statement that the English alphabet is equivalent to the Sacred Word? For a proper understanding, let us take a look at the word itself. But this Divine Word, this Sacred Tetragram of the Ancients, was never pronounced but only spelt—YOD HE VAV HE. These four Hebrew letters transliterate into the word *Jehova*, which means God. They are also sometimes referred to by the letters IHVH. Now the important thing to understand is that their numerical value in the Hebrew alphabet is $10 + 5 + 6 + 5 =$ (26). Therefore, the number 26 was considered by the Ancients to be the number for God. But the Alpha number for this same word, GOD, is also $7 + 15 + 4 = (26)$. Therefore, inasmuch as the English alphabet is likewise composed of 26 letters, we have a basis for stating that it is equivalent to the WORD that was uttered in the beginning.

But the real point that we wish to make is that the English Cabalah of 26 letters or keys is actually no different, in essence, from the Hebrew Cabalah of only 22 letters or keys. They are both a part of one and the same Cabalah. There is only one Cabalah and there always will be only one Cabalah. The only difference between the two is that in the Hebrew Cabalah of 22 letters, four of the main keys of the English Cabalah are missing. These are the Page, King, Queen, and Knight. In the English Cabalah, these four very important keys—the rulers of the Outer Kingdoms in the Book of the Tarot—are once more reunited in the Inner Kingdom of the Father.

A Table of Correspondences

Let us refer to the accompanying chart. We have matched up, for comparison purposes, the English alphabet in the right hand column with the modern Hebrew alphabet in the left hand column. We have also set up the Tarot Keys in the manner prescribed by Waite, Levi, Papus, and others; that is, we have equated Tarot Key 1, the Magician, with the first letter of the Hebrew alphabet, Aleph. We have also shortened the God Names, the full names of the Tarot Keys, to their principal words. We call this one word the *God Word* for a particular Tarot Key in contrast to the *God Name* for the full title of the Key. For instance: the God Word for Tarot Key 10 is *Wheel*; its God Name is *The Wheel of Fortune.*

The spelling of the Hebrew letters is taken from the latest (1974) edition of *Webster's New Collegiate Dictionary*. It is to be noted that the English spelling for the Hebrew letters has varied considerably down through the years. Spelling, like everything else, also goes through the process of change.

Likewise, all of the God Names used as a basis for forming the English Cabalah are those identical names used by Waite in his classic work, *The Pictorial Key to the Tarot* and also on the actual cards themselves. Although the basic symbols for the cards have been rather consistent for the past several hundred years, the actual names of the Keys have varied considerably. For instance: the Juggler has sometimes been substituted for the Magician, the Female Pope or Pope Joan for the High Priestess, the Pope for the Hierophant, Vice and Virtue for the Lovers, Judgment for Judgement, and the Universe for the World. Although there is nothing particularly wrong with these other names, it has been found that the "magical key" for unlocking the secrets of the English Cabalah is to use those particular names selected by Waite for inclusion in his deck of the Tarot. Why this is so, I have absolutely no idea. I only know that it works.

The chart also has columns which give the numerical value, the equivalent sound, and the symbolical meaning of each of the original letters in the Hebrew alphabet as determined by the

THE MAJOR ARCANA--HEBREW LETTERS							
Tarot Key	God Word	Hebrew Letter	Letter Value	Letter Sound	Letter Meaning	God Word	English Letter
1.	MAGICIAN	ALEPH	1	a	Ox	MAGICIAN	A
2.	PRIESTESS	BETH	2	b, bh	House	PRIESTESS	B
3.	EMPRESS	GIMEL	3	g, gh	Camel	EMPRESS	C
4.	EMPEROR	DALETH	4	d, dh	Door	EMPEROR	D
5.	HIEROPHANT	HE	5	h	Window	HIEROPHANT	E
6.	LOVERS	VAV	6	w, v	Pin, Hook	LOVERS	F
7.	CHARIOT	ZAYIN	7	z	Sword, Armor	CHARIOT	G
8.	STRENGTH	HETH	8	h, ch	Fence	STRENGTH	H
9.	HERMIT	TETH	9	t	Snake	HERMIT	I
10.	WHEEL	YOD	10	y, i	Hand	WHEEL	J
11.	JUSTICE	KAPH	20	k, kh	Fist	JUSTICE	K
12.	MAN	LAMED	30	l	Ox Goad	MAN	L
13.	DEATH	MEM	40	m	Water	DEATH	M
14.	TEMPERANCE	NUN	50	n	Fish	TEMPERANCE	N
15.	DEVIL	SAMEKH	60	s	Prop	DEVIL	O
16.	TOWER	AYIN	70	o	Eye, anger	TOWER	P
17.	STAR	PE	80	p, ph	Mouth	STAR	Q
18.	MOON	SADHE	90	s, tz	Fish-hook	MOON	R
19.	SUN	QOPH	100	q	Ear Back of Head	SUN	S
20.	JUDGEMENT	RESH	200	r	Head	JUDGEMENT	T
0.	FOOL	SIN	- -	s		FOOL	U
21.	WORLD	SHIN	300	sh	Tooth	WORLD	V
0.	FOOL	TAW	400	t, th	Cross	PAGE *	W
1.	MAGICIAN	ALEPH	1,495	Total		KING *	X
2.	PRIESTESS	BETH	A DIE			QUEEN *	Y
3.	EMPRESS	GIMEL			* Court Cards	KNIGHT *	Z

Figure 4: A Table of Correspondences

ancient Hebrews. Since there were no corresponding numerical symbols in use at the time, they attributed a numerical value to each letter in the alphabet. Thus the first nine letters represented the digits 1 to 9, the next nine letters the two-digit numbers from 10 to 90, and the remaining four letters the three-digit numbers from 100 to 400.

Very well. Now let us study the chart. The first thing that comes to our attention is that Tarot Key 0, the Fool, now corresponds with the new letter *Sin* that has been added to the Hebrew alphabet in recent times. In other words, it is the Fool who is doing the sinning, and that Fool is YOU. And since the Tarot Key number of the Fool is zero, no letter value is attributed to this new letter *Sin.* Therefore the total value of all of the letters in the modern alphabet of 23 letters will remain the same as it was with the original 22.

And what is this sum? Add them up for yourself. The total is 1,495, and the truly amazing thing about all of this is that the number 1,495 reads "A DIE." And who is A? Our Table of Correspondences shows us that the first letter of the English alphabet, A, corresponds with the letter Aleph, Tarot Key 1, the Magician. In other words, it is the Magician who dies. But this "death" is not permanent. He is born again in the next cycle of the letters when the letter Aleph, which represents the Magician, reappears once more.

To search for a further meaning of this life/death cycle of the Magician, let us go once more to our Table of Correspondences. We find that the second birth of the Magician is opposite the letter X of the English alphabet. Therefore we must endeavor to find the true meaning of this letter X. But this is really not too difficult, as all one has to do is to go to the dictionary. One of its meanings is that it represents the symbol for Christ. (The word *Xmas* is derived from the Greek letter chi (X), meaning Christ, + mass, which gives us the word *Christmas.*) We find that it means the birth and the resurrection of Christ. Therefore, the life/death cycle of the Magician is just that—the birth, death, and resurrection of the Christ.

From the above, one can see that the key for understanding the why and wherefore of the Hebrew sequence of letters lies in the English alphabet. For instance: Opposite Tarot Key 0, the Fool, is the English letter U. This makes sense, since we pointed out earlier that the Fool does indeed represent *You.* And opposite the second appearance of the Fool, as he begins the second cycle of the Major Arcana, is the English letter W. Therefore, this "double you" infers that we should repeat once again the U, the Fool, Tarot Key 0, so that he may be ready to embark upon the second phase of his journey into consciousness.

If we were to attribute a number other than 0 to the first position of the Fool in between Tarot Keys 20 and 21, what would it be? If the letter value for Resh (Tarot Key 20) is 200, and the letter value for Shin (Tarot Key 21) is 300, it would be reasonable to assume that the letter value for Sin (Tarot Key 0) would be 250. But let us "read" this number and see what it tells us. The number 250 reads "BE O." In other words, it reaffirms that this particular space, location, or whatever is simply *Zero*.

Another verification comes when we realize that the word *Sin* is also the abbreviation for the trigonometric function word "sine." We state that the sine of a 30 degree angle is 1/2, or that the sine of a 90 degree angle is 1, in the following manner: Sin 30° = 1/2, and Sin 90° = 1. And this becomes doubly interesting when we realize that the sine of zero degrees actually *is* zero. (Sin 0° = 0). Therefore, the mathematics of trigonometry also verifies that the correct numerical value for this position of the Fool is 0.

The use of the double 0 at and around the World (Tarot Key 21) has many connotations. First, it allows the Fool (Tarot Key 0) an opportunity to travel in both directions, clockwise as well as counterclockwise, inwards as well as outwards, as he begins his journey around the great wheel of life. Secondly, it assumes that Tarot Key 21, the last card of the Major Arcana, is in fact the entire Universe, the Infinite State, the Godhood, the Core of Life from which you sprang. It is the microcosm within the macrocosm, the true "zero" point, the dot within the circle. The circle in this context would then be represented by the two positions of the Fool (the two 0's), the distance from one 0 to the other 0 being the diameter of the circle of which Tarot Key 21, the World, is its center.

Thirdly, the use of the double 0 provides us with an empty space. And this empty space, being an alternative position of the Fool, will then enable you, the reader, to place *yourself* within the Cabalah and actively participate in the Mysteries. You, therefore, are not just "looking" at the picture we are painting, but you actually *are* a part of the picture itself.

One can also see from the Table of Correspondences that both systems currently in use for the placement of the Fool, Tarot Key 0, are basically correct; for he can either be between Judgement (Tarot Key 20) and the World (Tarot Key 21), or occupy the 0 position between the World (Tarot Key 21) and the Magician (Tarot Key 1). And you, the reader, being a counterpart of the Fool (Tarot Key 0), must out of necessity be in the alternate location where he is not.

Then fourthly, the use of these two 0's provides us with a breaking point between the inner world of the God Consciousness (the Major Arcana) and the four outer worlds of the senses (the Minor Arcana). If we assume the Fool is beginning his journey into the Major Arcana of the inner world, he is in the correct position at the letter *Sin* to face Judgement (Tarot Key 20), and then be judged accordingly. Or, if he is to be sent back again into the physical world, he may take over the body of the Page and be born into one of the outer kingdoms as the son or daughter of its King and Queen. The reader will note that the Page, the first of the Court Keys, occupies the same position in the Table of Correspondences as the Fool when he is in the Taw position of the Hebrew letter column. And since the symbol for this letter is the cross, it enables the Fool to crucify himself upon the "cross" of matter and thus be born once more upon the physical plane as the Page.

Therefore, never underestimate yourself. Even though you may occupy only a very humble position in life, you are still a member of the royal family. You must be either the son or daughter of the King and Queen of your respective consciousness; for it if were not so, you could not be living in the flesh.

This leaves us then with the fifth and final reason for the use of the double 0's. This is probably the most important one of them all, for these two 0's, placed as they are upon the Wheel of Life, will allow the Sacred Name, YOD HE VAV HE, to once more bring life into manifestation as its vibrations resound over and over again upon the still waters of the deep.

Chapter 4

IN THE BEGINNING WAS THE WORD

"İN THE BEGINNING was the Word, and the Word was with God, and the Word was God." This phrase (John 1:1), above all others, is perhaps the most significant verse in the entire Bible, insofar as the English Cabalah is concerned. It refers to a sound, a vibration, a word, which, when uttered, starts the entire Cosmos vibrating and initiates the beginning of all that is. Before the Word was uttered there was only silence, and all was null and void. But after the Word was uttered there is life, action, vibration, motion. But St. John tells us that this sound or initial vibration is dual; for the Word was not only *with* God, but it also *was* God.

Therefore, we have a dichotomy. On the one hand we have the Word, and on the other hand we have God. They must be two equal and opposite expressions of the same thing, because how could the Word be both God and also *with* God, if it were not so? The ancient Hebrews evidently understood this principle of duality quite well when they called this "Word" by its Sacred Name, YOD HE VAV HE. For even within the Word itself, the second letter is repeated twice. *He* is both the second letter and the fourth letter of this Divine Word, the Sacred Tetragram, YOD HE VAV HE.

For a further understanding, let us return once more to the words of St. John. In Verses 2-5, he continues on, saying: "The same was in the beginning with God. All things were made by him; and without him was not any thing made that was made. In him was life; and the life was the light of men. And the light shineth in darkness; and the darkness comprehended it not."

Now what is St. John telling us? If the reader would only meditate upon the words just uttered, he would realize that St. John has just revealed the true meaning of the Sacred Name, YOD HE VAV HE. In the first place, the name contains two He's. Now who or what are these two He's? One *He* is obviously God and the other *He* must be the Word that was with God in the beginning. Here is the duality in manifestation; or is it only seemingly so? In any event, the "He" force is the creator of all. He is positive and masculine, and it represents the Fatherhood of God.

The second point we would like to make, and one that is of primary importance, is that St. John has just told us that within *him* (the two He's) is life, and that this "life" is the light of men. Therefore the letter Vav, inasmuch as it is placed between He and He, must represent the life that is within him (God). And what is this "life" that is within him? St. John says that it is the "light" of men, but that it shineth in darkness, and the darkness comprehended it not.

This symbology is in perfect accord with that expressed in the Agashan classes for many years. Agasha has stated on numerous occasions that the Core of Life is like a great sun (*The Agashan Discourses*, pages 323-326). And doesn't the sun also give "light" unto men? And isn't it true that men, in a true occult understanding, comprehended it not? Therefore, this great Core of Life from which we sprang in the beginning, this great Virgin Mother of the World, is perfectly expressed by the Hebrew letter Vav, the third letter of the Sacred Tetragram. Vav is negative and feminine, and it represents the Motherhood of God.

But the symbology is not yet complete. An important fact is yet to be revealed. St. John expounds the thought further in Verses 6-9, when he states: "There was a man sent from God, whose name was John. The same came for a witness, to bear witness of the Light, that all *men* through him might believe.

He was not that Light, but *was sent* to bear witness of that Light. *That* was the true Light, which lighteth every man that cometh into the world."

We now have two other forces that enter the picture. One is Christ and the other is Man. Let us take up the Christ force first. Christ, then, is the true Light, the Light that lighteth every man that cometh into the world. The reader will note that this new *Light* is capitalized. The *light* that was described as emanating from the sun was not capitalized. But the true *Light* is the great Christ Light, the Christ Force, the Christ Power. It is the great force of Yod, the first letter of the Sacred Name, YOD HE VAV HE. Yod could be compared to the consciousness of the great Pillars of Light. It is a neutral force, and it is both masculine and feminine in its gender.

The other force, of course, is Man. It is Man who is sent into the outer world to redeem himself. It is Man who is sent to bear witness of the great Christ Light. And it is Man himself that becomes the *Word* that was made flesh (John 1:14). Therefore, the Word that was with God in the beginning was none other than Man himself. Man, then, is a co-partner with God. Man is a co-creator with God. And it is Man who is the true second He in the Sacred Name, YOD HE VAV HE.

To illustrate this point a little further, let us refer now to Figure 5.

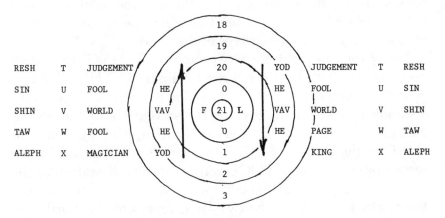

Figure 5
In the Beginning Was the Word

Let us assume that we are looking at the surface of a pond from above. The waters are very still. The air is also very still, and there is no wind to disturb the smooth surface of the pond. But suddenly, let us drop a pebble into the pond. Let us assume the pebble hits the surface at the very center of the diagram, and what do we observe? We see ripples radiating outwards from the point of contact in concentric circles, until they finally dissipate themselves and disappear into the distance.

In essence, this action is exactly the same as when the Word was first sounded in the beginning. Its sound waves are analogous to the ripples as they move outwards across the surface of the pond. From the diagram, we see that the point of impact is Tarot Key 21, the World, the Universe. It is the very Core of Life itself. It is the passive, negative, feminine principle of God. It is the Virgin Mother of the World. It is the Hebrew letter Vav, the third letter of the Sacred Name, YOD HE VAV HE.

Insofar as the Core of Life is analogous to the physical sun, each ripple may then be compared to the orbits of the various planets, which are also brought into manifestation as the vibrations from the eternal Word bring them into being.

The orbit of the first ripple is the active, positive, masculine principle of God. Agasha tells us that in the beginning, this great positive principle then makes the connecting link and brings forth the counterpart of itself within the etheric consciousness, the same as it was there in the original source (*The Agashan Discourses*, page 326). The etheric consciousness may be compared to the surface of the pond.

Therefore, this great positive principle, God the Father, then becomes the first He of the Sacred Name, YOD HE VAV HE. And the counterpart of itself, God the Son, comes into manifestation as the fourth letter or the second He of the Sacred Name, YOD HE VAV HE. We can see then, from the diagram, that God the Father and God the Son are each a part of the same ripple. The word FOOL comes into manifestation as the four cardinal points of the compass—North, East, South, and West. The two O's, or the two He's, represent the North and South points, respectively.

For purposes of simplification, the diagram shows these

ripples as moving basically in two directions only—either up or down. Of course, we know that in reality they are moving in all directions simultaneously. But even though this is true, it is still a fact that every possible point on a circle, no matter where it be, has also its counterpart that is diametrically opposite it. In other words, there are an infinite number of "Father-Son" combinations, each at a slightly different degree of rotation, that can be shown even on this simple diagram. And each pair of opposites has the God force (the creative force) at one end of the spectrum and that which was created (the Word force) at the opposite end. One force is then radiating upwards, and the other force radiating downwards, respectively.

If the force is radiating upwards into the Major Arcana, into the finer worlds of the Spirit, the Yod force begins with the Magician, Tarot Key 1, the Hebrew letter Aleph. If the force is radiating downwards into the Minor Arcana, into the dense worlds of physical expression, the Yod force then begins with Judgement, Tarot Key 20, the Hebrew letter Resh. In the latter case, the Page replaces the Fool as the fourth letter or second He of the Sacred Name, YOD HE VAV HE. And the King, Queen, and Knight, along with the other numbered forces from the Ace to the Ten, will likewise replace their spiritual counterparts in the Major Arcana as the downwards force clothes itself with the coarse vibrations of the physical plane.

The reader will note that the Yod force, or the Christ force, seems to be the one who initiates the action as the force either moves upwards into the worlds of spirit, or downwards into the physical planes of matter. The Yod, then, could be said to represent the archer, as he bends his bow, ready to send forth the arrow on a journey that is eternity. Perhaps he is comparable to Chiron, a wise and beneficent centaur, half man and half horse, who rules the ninth sign of the Zodiac as the archer, Sagittarius. In any event, the writer is reminded of a poem, learned early in childhood, that seems to express the whole saga of life—from its beginning to its end. It was written by Henry Wadsworth Longfellow, and it is entitled *The Arrow and the Song*. Here it is, in its entirety:

I shot an arrow into the air,
It fell to earth, I know not where;
For, so swiftly it flew, the sight
Could not follow it in its flight.

I breathed a song into the air,
It fell to earth, I know not where;
For who has sight so keen and strong,
That it can follow the flight of song?

Long, long afterward, in an oak
I found the arrow, still unbroke;
And the song, from beginning to end,
I found again in the heart of a friend.

Thank you, Mr. Longfellow, for leaving us with sheer, uncomparable elegance. But let us give a little thought now, if we may, to the real meaning of the poem itself. First, who is the one who shoots the arrow into the air? Who is the one who breathes a song into the air? And who is the one who finds the arrow and the song once again? Longfellow tells us that it is simply I. But who is "I"? Agasha answers this question by stating that it is the "I" within you and the "I" within me. They are one and the same. The "I" is, then, the One who states simply that "I AM." It is the Light within the soul itself. It is GOD.

But it is also Yod, the initial letter or force of the Sacred Name, YOD HE VAV HE. The English equivalent of this Sacred Name, the Divine Tetragram, are the letters I H V H. Therefore, even the English language tells us that the Hebrew Yod equates to the English I. And so does the Zodiac. The ninth house of the Zodiac is occupied by the *archer*, Sagittarius; and the ninth letter of the English alphabet is likewise the same letter, I.

Now let us analyze the "instrument" that sends the arrow into its flight. This, of course, is the bow. The bow, then, is analogous to the second and third letters or forces of the Sacred Name, YOD HE VAV HE. It therefore plays the role of the Father-Mother aspect of God, the first differentiation of the

Oneness. For in the bow, the Yod transforms himself from the One into the Two. It thus becomes male and female, positive and negative. He, the masculine force, becomes the string that bends the bow; and Vav, the feminine force, becomes the bow itself, that flexible strip of wood.

This, then, leaves only the final He to be taken into consideration. And this, of course, is the arrow. But let us take a closer look at this arrow that is shot into the air, to fall to earth, I know not where. This is YOU. This is the fourth letter of the Sacred Name, YOD HE VAV HE. You are also the song that was breathed into the air; you are the Word that was sounded in the beginning by the eternal One. Therefore, you are the arrow, the song, and the Word made flesh. This is YOU.

If you will look at the diagram, you will notice that the final He of the Sacred Name is the Fool (Tarot Key 0) only if the arrow is to be sent in its upward flight into the consciousness of the inner worlds of the Spirit. If the arrow is to be sent in a downward flight into the dense, outer worlds of physical matter, the final He will then become the Page, one of the Court Keys of the Minor Arcana. Therefore, the Page plays a role of primary importance.

The Page is the vehicle that permits a Teacher in the Higher Orders of Immensity to contact those in the outer worlds. Many times in the Agashan classes, Agasha or Araskas will say that they are sending out their "call" for others to come into the movement. But when we "call" someone, aren't we really paging him also? Therefore the Page, being in service to the Knight or the King, is also the messenger of the Gods. He delivers the message from the higher consciousness of Spirit to the lower consciousness of the physical worlds.

The analogy becomes even more convincing when we consider the structure of our solar system. Let us start with the Sun. This is our star, the star we call "Sun," the star that gave birth to all of the planets within our system. Looking at it in this respect, she becomes feminine, the Virgin Mother of the Worlds. She is Vav, and she represents the "Sun" Core of Life from which we sprang.

The first "ripple" that radiates out from the Core of Life is equivalent to the first planet within the solar system. Inasmuch as we are moving outwards into the physical worlds, the first planet on the outer side of Vav would represent the final He of the Sacred Name, YOD HE VAV HE. But He, in this case, would be the Page and not the Fool. And isn't it strange that the first planet in our solar system is called Mercury? He most certainly plays the role of the Page, because in Roman mythology he actually *was* the "Messenger of the Gods."

But this is not all. We can study our solar system from still another vantage point. Let us assume that we are starting from somewhere within the solar system itself, and that we wish to travel now in an *inward* direction. Therefore, we have to look for some other planet to play the role of the Core of Life, Vav, the Virgin Mother. This is not too hard to do because the only other planet that is considered feminine is Venus. And Venus plays the role magnificently! Why do we say this? Well, let us analyze her name. If we write her name in the form of a circle, and then read it backwards, we read EV'S SUN. This means Eve's Sun. And who was Eve? She was the first woman and the mother of the human race. She is a perfect symbol for Vav. And the Cabalah tells us that the planet Venus is her Sun, her star. Therefore, we find that Venus, the Roman goddess of love, can play the role of the "Sun" Core of Life equally as well as the Sun itself.

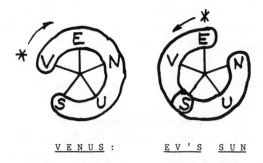

V E N U S :   E V ' S   S U N

Figure 6: An Analysis of the Word VENUS

Venus, then, becomes the bow; and the Earth becomes her string. Earth, being the next planet outwards in the system, now plays the role of the first He of the Sacred Name. Being her lover, he literally becomes the "strings of her heart." He may do this quite easily, for he merely changes his name from EARTH to HEART and becomes her "heartstrings."

Who then is Yod? Yod must be the archer himself who bends the bow and sends the arrow to its final destination on its inward journey into the Sun. But the role of Yod must out of necessity be played by the planet Mars; for Mars is the fourth planet in our planetary system, the planet next outwards from the Earth. Therefore the Yod force, in this example, is portrayed by Mars, the ancient Roman god of war.

Now Mars, surprisingly enough, also plays his role quite well. Perhaps he is not the perfect prototype of what we would expect of Yod, the initial force of the Sacred Name; but at least he has the strength of Yod and is very capable of bending the bow and sending the arrow on its homeward flight. How do we know this? The answer is quite simple. Mars, being a god, can also do the same thing his brother Earth had done. He simply changes his name from MARS to ARMS, and literally becomes Yod's "arms" as Yod bends the bow to release the arrow.

He also furnishes the missing "arms" for the goddess Venus, who was portrayed so magnificently in the famous statue, *Venus de Milo*. For without arms, our goddess presents a sorry sight, indeed. Mars then completes the picture and gives her *arms* so that she may embrace her lover, and *arms* so that she can pluck the heartstrings of her heart, the Earth.

And the arrow? Who is He? Who is the final He of the Divine Name, YOD HE VAV HE? Again the answer is very easily forthcoming. We just cannot seem to get away from the fact that Mercury wants to play the role of "Messenger of the Gods." Whether we are traveling inward toward the Sun or outward toward the outer planets, the answer is the same. It has to be the planet Mercury, because it is Mercury himself who occupies the key position midpoint between the Sun and Venus.

So then what is the final outcome? Is the Page or the "call" to be lost forever in fathomless space? Is this our fate? Is this Mercury's fate? And the answer is no, absolutely not. Longfellow tells us that you shall be found again, still unbroke; and that your song, from beginning to end, will be found again in the heart (or earth) of a friend.

The AUM and the OM

Perhaps the two greatest sounds in the Universe are those two great mantras—the AUM and the OM. In reality, they are identical; one is simply the counterpart or the inverse of the other. One represents the out-going sound and the other the in-going sound. One is the Alpha and the other the Omega—the beginning and ending of any sound ever uttered since the beginning of time. Therefore, in the AUM and the OM, we see a symbolic representation of the complete life cycle of the Divine Word that was in the beginning.

Theosophy tells us: "The primal single sound (Aum or Om) is the highest uttered word of power and knowledge. It is verily as Brahman itself. The regulation of the breath is the chiefest tapas-discipline. Higher than the Savitri is no mantra. Higher than silence is truth."[1]

And in essence, this is what the Teachers in the Agashan classes have been teaching these many years. Even Christ himself is quoted as saying (Revelation 22:13): "I am the Alpha and the Omega, the beginning and the end, the first and the last." Now what does he mean by that? Agasha explains that he is using the word "I" in relationship to the Universal Consciousness, and not to any one individual. And Araskas tells us that this Universal Consciousness is brought into manifestation with the sounding of the AUM, and that it goes out of manifestation (completes its cycle) with the sounding of the OM. The former is the Alpha and the latter is the Omega—the first and last letters of the Greek alphabet. But in reality, they are identical; as the ending of any one cycle is always the beginning of another.

The noted philosopher H. Saraydarian gives an excellent

description of this entire process in his book, *Cosmos in Man*.²
Therefore, we are taking the liberty of quoting him directly, as
there are no other words that we could use that would match
his explanation in either clarity or style.

"The Word is the vibratory expression of a meaning or a
thought," he begins. "When we think and verbally express a
thought, we create a thoughtform in space. This thoughtform
gradually condenses, attracting appropriate matter from space,
and creates a form. Thus, all of creation is a result of vibration
or Sound which slowly condenses and changes into material
form. The Word differs from Sound in that it serves as a bridge
between the Sound and manifestation or creation."

"This bridge carries sound in two directions—out-going and
in-going. The out-going Word changes to AUM. The in-going
Word is the OM. The first Word, the AUM, differentiates into
specific tones or notes and carries the purpose and the plan of
the originator into manifestation. The second Word, the OM,
is the bridge of *Return* which releases the Spirit from matter
and leads it back Home, back to its Source. When creation
reaches its lowest degree of objectivity, its involution is completed and it starts to turn back toward dematerialization as it
enters upon the path of evolution. These two Words keep the
manifestation of the Solar System in motion and form a way
for cyclic manvantara and pralaya in all kingdoms. In a sense
they are the yin and the yang within the wheel of Sound. Thus,
the AUM expresses itself as the basic principle, energy, the fire
which perpetuates existence."

He concludes with the thought, "The OM is the pilgrim
engaged in the process of leaving the not-self behind and climb-
ing the ladder of evolution. This is the time when the human
being strives to change all involutionary tendencies in himself
and to enter upon the path of evolution, discipleship and Initiation. Prior to this stage, on the arc of involution, the Spark was
on the current of out-breathing. Now on the arc of evolution,
He is on the current of in-breathing. At first He was an AUM.
Now, He is intended to be an OM. Thus the 'three' become
'two' and the 'two' become 'One'—the Sound."

Thank you Mr. Saraydarian for your excellent interpretation. But sometimes a picture can enhance a verbal description even further. So let us turn now to Figure 7 which vividly portrays that which has just been described.

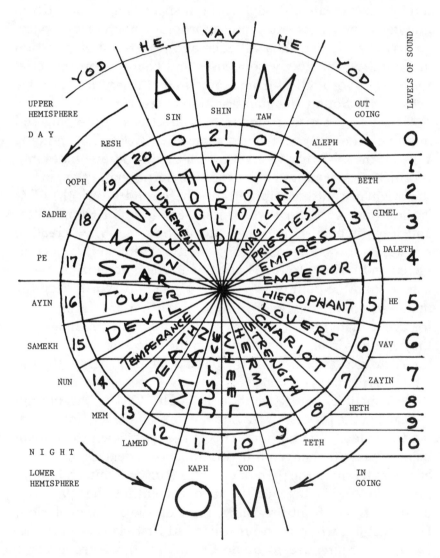

Figure 7
The Wheel of the Major Arcana as It Relates with the Hebrew Alphabet

Let us imagine that Figure 7 is a cross section through the Earth itself. We have sliced it in two, and its interior is exposed to our view. Its inner core is divided into the 22 Tarot Keys of the Major Arcana plus an empty space for the alternate position of the Fool (Tarot Key 0). Its outer shell is likewise divided; each compartment contains the numerical number of its corresponding Tarot Key. And then out in the air, out in the space surrounding the Earth, are the 23 letters of the Hebrew alphabet. The relationship of the Tarot Keys with the Hebrew alphabet is exactly the same as depicted in the Table of Correspondences, Figure 4. The letter Shin, along with Tarot Key 21 (the World), occupies the same position as the Earth's north magnetic pole.

Very well. Now let us look at Figure 8. This figure shows the magnetic field of the Earth, the planet on which we live. The magnetic currents leave the north pole, travel out into space, and then return again into the south pole. Let us assume, then, that the letters of the Hebrew alphabet in Figure 7 are likewise occupying a corresponding position in this magnetic field. In other words, for purposes of this discussion, we are dividing the Earth's magnetic field into 23 separate divisions or houses, in the same way that we divide the heavens around the Earth into the 12 signs of the Zodiac.

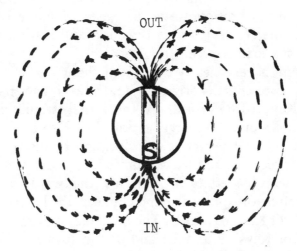

Figure 8
The Magnetic Field of the Earth

In order to clarify the point a little further, let us turn back to Figure 5. This figure, if you will remember, showed the ripples in a pond radiating outwards in concentric circles from the point of contact with a pebble. And this figure is also exactly what you would see if you were looking down upon the Earth from a point in space directly above the Earth's north magnetic pole. Of course you wouldn't "see" these concentric circles; but they would be there just the same. Each of the magnetic currents would appear as a circle, or a ripple, or a wave, gradually moving outwards from a point which would appear only as a dot. This "dot" would represent the north magnetic pole of the Earth.

By now, the reader will probably guess the point we are trying to make. That point is that sound will travel out into the air, or that ripples will move out in a pond, in much the same fashion as the magnetic currents move out into space from the Earth's north magnetic pole. But the important point to understand is that these sounds or waves will not just move out into space and be gone; but they will actually circumvent the globe and return once more to the sender. The only reason that those ripples seem to disappear a little distance out from the point of impact with the pebble, is that the "atom" vibration wave simply turns into an "anim" vibration wave. And when it turns into an anim vibration wave, it ceases to move outwards; instead, it merely reverses its direction and starts its *inward* journey back to its source.

This point is very clearly depicted in Figure 7. Let us assume the AUM represents the original sound when it was first uttered at Tarot Key 21 (the World). At this initial starting point, the sound wave would be merely a dot. The Hebrew letter Shin represents this dot. Then as the vibration builds up, the first circle or ripple of sound waves comes into manifestation. This circle connects the letters Sin and Taw (the two 0 Tarot Keys). The next circle or ripple of sound connects the letters Resh and Aleph (Tarot Keys 20 and 1). The next one connects Qoph and Beth (Tarot Keys 19 and 2); and this in turn is followed by Sadhe and Gimel (Tarot Keys 18 and 3). But one can very readily see that this out-going sound does not go on forever. At the equator of the earth, these circles or ripples of sound will gradually start getting smaller as they begin their *in-ward* journey back to the OM. And if you were watching these vibrations from a vantage point directly above the AUM, the point where the vibration was first initiated, you would see them apparently disappear at the Earth's equator. But they would not really disappear; they would just be invisible to your sight.

Figure 7 shows these various concentric circles as "levels of sound," and subdivides them on a scale of 0 to 10. This scale from 0 to 10, incidentally, is of primary importance in the English Cabalah and is the very foundation that supports the whole. "The number 10 denotes *completion*," Agasha tells us, "Therefore, it becomes silent and reverts back to 0, the point where we started. The digit 1, which stands beside the 0, is now ready to begin a new cycle of manifestations in a higher phase of the evolution of the numbers." (*The Agashan Discourses*, page 295).

Thus we find that the beginning is the AUM and the ending is the OM, but inasmuch as these are both "zero" terms, they are in reality the "voice of the silence." The actual "sound" comes into manifestation in the digits from 1 to 9. However, even the "sound" cycles are subdivided into *atom* vibration waves and *anim* vibration waves. The ripples of sound in the upper hemisphere are out-going; therefore these are atom vibration waves. The sound ripples in the lower hemisphere are in-going; these are anim vibration waves. The anim vibration waves are also sometimes referred to as "soundless sounds."

The reader should note that the total value of each level of sound is 21. (The zero level is $0 + 21 + 0 = 21$; the one level is $20 + 1 = 21$; the two level is $19 + 2 = 21$, etc.) Therefore, inasmuch as Tarot Key 21 represents the World, each of these "ripples of sound" constitutes a world in itself. Each is an individual entity. Each has its own consciousness. And each is built up of two distinct and complementary aspects of itself, such as Sin and Taw, Resh and Aleph, etc.

There is one exception. The original sound, the "AUM" that initiates the action, contains still a third aspect of itself. This is the "dot" within the circle, the spark within the fire, the 0 within the 10, the one within the all. Its letter is Shin. Its Tarot Key is the World. It is the microcosm within the macrocosm. It is God itself.

Therefore, we have the AUM which marks the beginning of a manifestation. This has three letters—AUM. And we have the OM which marks the completion of a manifestation. This has two letters—OM. But there is still one remaining part of the Sacred Name that is missing. This is the *inner* part that separates the AUM from the OM. We must remember that the AUM and the OM are vibrations that go *around* the Earth. They are the *outer* part of the Sacred Name. But there is still the *inner* part which could be said to represent the *diameter* of the Earth. This inner part is called simply the "M." It has only one letter—M. It could be symbolically represented as a pipe or a tunnel which runs directly through the Earth from the OM to the AUM. It is the "M," then, that receives the in-coming vibrations at the OM, transmits them up the diameter and through the Earth, and then sends them out again at the AUM. Thus we are back at the beginning, and the cycle is complete.

Now you might ask, "Is there any verification that what we have just pointed out is true?" And this is a very good question. After all, theorizing about something is one thing, but putting it to the test is another. But this is the beautiful thing about the Cabalah. At any point along the way—or rather, we should say, at the end of some conclusive statement—we may test a particular theory, and the Cabalah will then either verify or deny the theory as being correct or incorrect. The Cabalah gives us many methods to do this; and one of its easiest and most direct methods is to simply determine the Alpha number for the particular word or phrase in question, and then read what it says. The answer given will then either show one is on the right track and that he should proceed further, or, if the assumption was not correct, that he should discard the accumulated data and seek in a new direction.

Therefore, if we have theorized that a cycle of manifestation is complete with the "sounding" of these three words—The M, The OM, and The AUM—let us derive their Alpha numbers, both individually and collectively, and see what they say. Their Alpha numbers are as follows:

1. THE M $= 20 + 8 + 5 + 0 + 13$ $= (46)$
2. THE OM $= 20 + 8 + 5 + 0 + 15 + 13$ $= (61)$
3. THE AUM $= 20 + 8 + 5 + 0 + 1 + 21 + 13 =$ (68)

Total Alpha Number $(175) = AGE$

Well, it would appear as though our assumption was correct. The M, the OM, and the AUM are, indeed, an AGE. And what is an age? Webster says that an *age* is the length of time during which a being or thing has existed, or a particular period in history—an epoch. And a little earlier in this book, it was pointed out that the Alpha number for the word *CONSCIOUS-NESS* itself is also this same number: (175) or AGE. Therefore, we might assume that the M, the OM, and the AUM are in reality other words for the expression of CONSCIOUS-NESS. And the term *Consciousness* is related to God—the Universal Consciousness God.

Other points of verification arise when we consider the locations on the Wheel of Life that we have assigned to the AUM and the OM. Let us refer once more to Figure 7. It seemed only natural when we laid out this "wheel" that the AUM, inasmuch as it contained three letters, should occupy the 0 level of sound at the Hebrew letters Sin, Shin, and Taw. It followed then that the OM, which should in theory be diametrically opposite from the AUM, must out of necessity occupy the 10 level of sound at the Hebrew letters Kaph and Yod. And the 10 level, quite conveniently, allowed for only a two-letter word.

But enough of theory. Let us put this assumption to the same rigorous test that we applied to the total value of the names in the previous example. The Alpha number for the Hebrew letters SIN SHIN TAW is $19 + 9 + 14 + 0 + 19 + 8 + 9 + 14 + 0 + 20 + 1 + 23 = (136)$. And this number, theoretically, should be equal to the Alpha number for THE AUM. But it

is not. The Alpha number for THE AUM is (68), and there is
a discrepancy. Now what is wrong? Why shouldn't the numbers be equal? When problems of this type arise, the next step is
to find the difference between the two terms so that we may
expose that which is causing the discrepancy. In this particular
case, the answer is quite simple. Subtracting the two numbers,
(136 − 68), gives us another 68 again, and we have another
AUM. Fantastic! SIN SHIN TAW simply equates to THE AUM
+ THE AUM. And of course this is plausible; for at the beginning, the sound is dual. At the point of departure, the sound is
sent forth in two directions—clockwise as well as anticlockwise
—and we have for all intents and purposes, two AUM's.

All well and good. Now let us analyze the counterpart of the
AUM, the OM. The Alpha number for the Hebrew letters
KAPH YOD is $11 + 1 + 16 + 8 + 0 + 25 + 15 + 4 = (80)$.
And the Alpha number for THE OM is (61). Again, we have a
discrepancy. So let us once more expose that which is causing it
by subtracting the two terms, the one from the other. The difference is 19. $(80 − 61 = 19)$. So then what does the number 19
represent? Of course. Why didn't we think of it before? The
answer is self evident. 19 stands for the letter S; and the term
KAPH YOD simply equates to THE OM'S. Here again, we
have a verification that our original assumption was correct.
But the plural form at the in-going pole is THE OM'S instead of
THE AUM + THE AUM, as it is at the out-going pole. But this
way or that way, the Cabalah tells us that the OM, like its
counterpart, is also dual at the pole. The OM returns from two
directions, combines two separate OM'S into One, and the
Cabalah proves itself with flying colors.

One other point, before we close this fascinating little chapter on the OM's. It was brought out in *Agasha: Master of
Wisdom* that the various Spiritual Centers of the Earth are constantly sending out their Light and their Power unto the outer
world. They do this, in part, by chanting these OM's. One of
the Centers that was discussed quite extensively is the Earshin
Valley which, incidentally, is located in the very heart of beautiful Mount Shasta. But many have wondered from whence

came its name. The Adept Earshin has never explained the derivation of the name (to this writer's knowledge), but perhaps we may use the Cabalah, and especially this chart of the Wheel of Life that we have just constructed, to gain an insight as to its meaning.

First, let us break the name EARSHIN into its constituent parts and we have EAR + SHIN. Now what does this tell us? It tells us that the name contains an "ear" so that the AUM may be heard as it is sounded forth at the letter "Shin"—from the inner Voice of the Silence. The letter *Shin*, remember, represents God itself. It is the dot within the circle, the spark within the fire, the 0 within the 10, the one within the all. But before one can *hear* this soundless sound, one must first have an *ear*. Therefore, we have the name Ear-Shin or simply Earshin.

We may also write the name EARSHIN in the form of a circle, and we end up with SH (Silence) IN EAR. Therefore, the name hears the "silence" that is whispered into the ear. The word *Sh* is also used in a prolonged form to command one to be silent, for one must be silent before one can hear the "still-small-voice" that comes from within.

The Alpha numbers for the words EARSHIN VALLEY are also most interesting. The Alpha number for EARSHIN is (74) and the Alpha number for VALLEY is (77). "Well, there is nothing particularly unusual in this," you might say. But these names do prove quite significant when we consider that the Alpha number for JESUS is also (74); and the Alpha number for CHRIST is likewise a (77). Therefore, it can be said that the words EARSHIN VALLEY have the same numerical vibration as the words JESUS CHRIST. The writer hasn't the faintest idea for the significance of all of this; but you will have to admit, it *is* interesting.

The Spiral Aspect of All Life

Let us leave the OM's or the Sound vibration for the moment, and return once more to the Word itself—the Sacred Name that it was in the beginning, YOD HE VAV HE. Now it is certainly not our wish to belabor the point, but there are other essential aspects of the Word—by that, we mean the Name or Phrase that initiates the action—that simply must be covered before one may have even a general understanding of the workings of the Cabalah.

But first, a brief review is in order. In the previous segments we compared the initial Word, YOD HE VAV HE, to certain Tarot Keys of the Major Arcana, and we showed how each letter represents a ripple in a series of concentric circles that gradually moves outwards from its source. This was depicted in Figure 5. And then in Figure 8, we pointed out that this series of concentric circles or sound waves was in reality rising into the air from its point of origin in much the same manner as the Earth's magnetic field. But as these circles of sound waves would rise, their diameters would increase and a particle traveling in the sound wave—inasmuch as the sound was traveling in all directions—would in reality be *spiraling* out from one concentric circle to the next one. This idea of the spiral action of sound or vibration was not clearly pointed out earlier, and so therefore we must now add still another dimension to our study of the Word.

An excellent example of spiral motion is observed when we study any whirling current of air or water. These whirling eddies or currents are called whirlwinds, cyclones, or tornadoes when they are in the air; in the water they are referred to as whirlpools. And we have often watched how water in the bathtub reacts when it is being sucked into the drain. Therefore, we may theorize that a "particle" of sound—if we may use the term in this manner—will move in much the same manner as a piece of dust would move if it were in the water as the water was being sucked into a drain. This, of course, is an example of the in-going sound or the OM. The out-going sound, or the AUM, would be the reverse. But in both of these actions, the out-going as well as the in-going, our little particle of sound will be moving in a spiral. It will be spiraling upwards and outwards at the out-going sound and inwards and downwards at the in-going sound, like a particle riding in a whirlpool as it is being sucked into a drain or spun out into space in centrifugal action.

Therefore, the diagram of concentric circles as depicted in Figure 5 does not show the true motion of our little particle of sound. It shows two of the component parts of this motion (the radial and the circular), true, but it does not show the actual path followed by any one particle of sound. This would have to be depicted as one, single, continuous spiral. It starts at the inception of the sound, and then gradually spirals outwards and upwards embracing each and every one of our concentric circles or waves. Furthermore, this continuous spiral may be divided into quadrants, and we may name each quadrant by one letter of the Sacred Name as in Figure 9, below.

Figure 9
The I-H-V-H Spiral

Thus we find that each revolution yields the name YOD HE VAV HE or, if we were to express it in English, I H V H. In other words, with the utterance of the letter Yod we are in the first quadrant. The letter He will then put us in the second quadrant, the letter Vav the third, and the final He the fourth.

With the completion of this final He, we will then be ready to begin once more another revolution of the spiral.

These spiral cycles will continue outwards until they come to the equator of the sphere, and then at the equator, they will reverse their direction and turn inwards. The circles will then gradually become smaller, as this now soundless sound returns once more to its anti-source, the opposite pole, or the OM. Thus the constant repetition of the Word YOD HE VAV HE acts as a bridge between the out-going sound AUM and the in-going sound OM.

One can see then how the sounds themselves become so all important. But let us now analyze them individually, as words, in the same way that we analyzed the word EARTH in Figure 2. We may do this by arranging these two words, AUM and OM, in the form of a circle, and then simply reading what they say. In this way, then, we may understand the message that they are trying to tell us. This has been done in the following diagram, Figure 10:

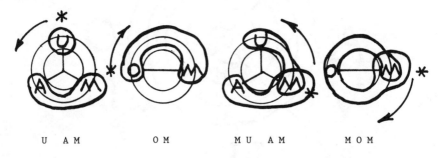

U A M   O M   M U A M   M O M

Figure 10: An Analysis of the AUM and the OM

The AUM, reading anticlockwise, reads U (You) AM. This is the mortal equivalent of the great I AM. But you are what? The answer is You are the OM. The AUM or the U AM then makes the statement, and the OM is the object of that statement. Another way of looking at it is that the Alpha is identical with the Omega; the AUM is equal to the OM. But since You *are* the OM, this entity called *You* is likewise equal to the AUM, since things equal to the same thing are also equal to each other. Therefore, you are equal to both the OM and the AUM.

We may also start with one letter and then finish the word or statement with the same letter; in other words, one letter is repeated twice. When we read words in this manner, incidentally, we are in effect bringing into manifestation the eternal symbol of the serpent swallowing its tail. For is not the head of the serpent also equal to the first letter of any word? And if this is so, then its tail must represent the last letter. Therefore, when we put the tail of the serpent into its mouth, we are for all practical purposes making the statement that the first letter of the word must occupy the same position on the circle as the last letter of the word.

Let us start with the letter M. Reading anticlockwise, the words tell us that MU AM. But who and what is MU? Mu, of course, is another word for Lemuria, the great lost continent in the Pacific. Therefore we know the subject of the statement. But again we ask, "Mu or Lemuria is what?" The answer is simple, straightforward, and to the point. MU is simply MOM, which means Mother. Thus we find that Mu, a great civilization that flourished many hundreds of thousands of years ago, is literally the *Mother* of the major civilizations of the Earth. But this is what James Churchward, the author of several works about this ancient continent (*The Lost Continent of Mu, The Sacred Symbols of Mu*, etc.), has been saying all the time. Many, many times he tells us that Mu, in reality, is the great Motherland—the mother of our present civilization. Mu, then, is the perfect symbol for Vav—the great Core of Life from which we sprang or, simply stated, the great Motherhood of God. Once again we find a verification that words contain within themselves clues pertaining to their true meaning.

Every Name Has Length, Breadth, and Thickness

There are many different ways to analyze the true meaning of a word; we have hardly even scratched the surface, as far as that is concerned. And again, if we are to proceed further, we have to get down to basics. So then let us return once more to the Word that was in the beginning. Now this Word, as we stated earlier in the chapter, could be almost any word. The "Word" simply relates to the word or phrase that initiates an action that leads to any specific result. Therefore, we must first study this "word" and break it up into its component parts.

"What then are its component parts?" you might ask. To answer this, let us consider our "word" to have length, breadth, and thickness. Let us consider it as a box. Thus it has three separate and distinct dimensions of its being. It occupies "space" (as determined by its length, breadth, and thickness), but it also exists in "time." Therefore, in reality it has three dimensions of "space" and one dimension of "time." Time, in this context, is considered to have only one dimension which is lineal, or circular.

We can see, then, that any word or phrase must out of necessity have four distinct and unrelated numbers attached to it for it to exist in four-dimensional space, or a space-time continuum. The Cabalah very expressly allows for all four of these numbers to be computed for any word, phrase, sentence, paragraph, chapter, or even book of the English language. The derivation of the number corresponding to the "time" dimension will be discussed in a later chapter, but the computation of the numbers corresponding to the "space" dimensions (length, breadth, and thickness) will be taken up forthwith.

The first number that we shall consider is called the "Word number." The computation for this number is very simple, in that it involves nothing more than counting the number of words contained within any particular phrase or sentence. For instance: The Word number for AUM is (1), since there is only one word involved. But the Word number for THE AUM is (2), since there are two words in that particular name. Therefore, the Word number is the easiest number to compute since all one has to do is count. It could be any number. The Word number for this book might be 151,200, or whatever. It is simply the total number of words in the book. The Word number is the smallest number of the three, and it corresponds to *thickness*.

The second number to be considered is called the "Alpha number." The computation of this number was discussed earlier and will not be pursued further. Needless to say, however, we will repeat that the Alpha number represents the total numerical value of the letters contained therein. The Alpha number is also the largest of the three "space" dimensions, and it corresponds to *length*.

The third number that must be derived is called the "Letter number." The computation of this number is also very simple. For like the Word number, all one has to do is count. The Letter number then is simply nothing more than the total number of letters contained within any particular word or phrase. However, it should be pointed out that the spaces in between the words of a name or a phrase are not counted as letters. Punctuation marks, empty spaces, etc. are not counted in the computation of any Letter number. The Letter number is then the middle number of the three, and it corresponds to *breadth*.

There is still a fourth number that must be considered at this time, but this fourth number that we shall take up has nothing whatsoever to do with the dimension called "time." It only relates to that which could be said to represent the "space" dimension as an entity unto itself. This number is called the "Key number," and it is nothing more than the sum total of its three individual components—the Word number, the Alpha number, and the Letter number.

It is interesting to note that Agasha also refers to the "Key number" in a somewhat similar fashion. He states that that which is called your Key number is derived from the month, the day, and the year that you were born (*The Agashan Discourses*, page 298). It relates to the "sound" that was uttered by the God Consciousness at the day of your birth. It is the "sound" or the AUM that makes you what you are today. And it is *your* number insofar as your date of birth is concerned.

But the interesting thing to be observed is that the Key number represents the Trinity; the Key number is always the three. Insofar as your date of birth is concerned, your Key number is derived from the month, the day, and the year that you were born. But if you were to take your *Name* into consideration, your Key number would then become the sum total of its Word number, its Alpha number, and its Letter number. Therefore, your Name as well as your birthday become so all-important in finding out who and what you are and the various aspects that go on to make up you as an individual in this individual life of yours.

NOTES

1. *The Theosophist*, Volume VII, p. 218
2. W. Saraydarian, *Cosmos in Man* (Agoura, Calif., The Aquarian Educational Group, 1973) p. 238

Chapter 5

YOUR JOURNEY ALONG THE SPIRAL PATH

Let us now go on a journey. Let us retrace our steps from the time we were originally spewed forth from the great Core of Life by following the Spiral Path back to the Core. It could be compared to the Yellow Brick Road that took Dorothy and her four companions (we can't forget Toto) into the City of Oz, for the City of Oz is the City of O's (zeros). This pathway that leads to the Core is depicted in Figure 11.

Upon inspection, the reader will find that Figure 11 is a magnification or a blow-up of the central core of the spiral depicted in Figure 9. From this core is where all action begins and ends. From this core is where the "Word" was originally sent forth and into which it will eventually return. And from this core—which could be said to represent the very Core of Life itself—you were originally spewed forth along one of its spiral paths when you began your journey that is eternity.

The spiral depicted in Figure 11, therefore, can be read in two directions—as an out-going force or as an in-going force. In its out-going aspects, it could be compared to a great spiritual sun bringing a new universe into manifestation, as it whirls its energies outwards and around itself, like some great spiral galaxy. And in its in-going aspects, it is like a "black hole" devouring anything and everything of a material nature that is swept into its path, as it draws its energies inwards and back into itself in the same manner as water is sucked into a drain.

75

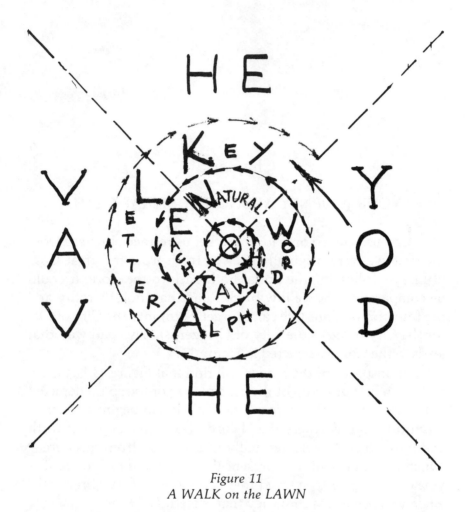

Figure 11
A WALK on the LAWN

But both of these forces are good: the "anim" force that leaves the core at the AUM, and the "atom" (at OM) force that returns to the core at the OM. You then, as you tread that spiral path on its *inward* journey, are like "atom" matter that is being called back home by its creator. For every step you take as you walk along that path, you are gradually being cleansed of the gross aspects of the material world—being freed from the confines of matter, so to speak—so that you may once again ascend into the great Light, Power, and Illumination that exists within the Core. In a nutshell, this is what Figure 11 is all about. It is the Alpha and the Omega, the beginning and the end, of anything and everything that was ever brought into manifestation of a material or spiritual nature.

So then now let us take a real look at Figure 11 and study it. Picture yourself upon that spiral path as if you were returning home to the core of your being after a lifetime of many years in the earthly plane of physical existence. You are at the Yod position at the right-hand side of the diagram, and you are now approaching your sunset years. It is a time for reflection, and a time for you to try to ascertain the reason that you had to go through the many experiences that you did. You thus look forward to the next step in your journey homeward, and your spiritual eyesight reveals that you will now be moving into the Key position of the spiral—into the upper He quadrant of the great Wheel of Life.

But first, we must determine the numerical vibration rate of the individual cells of the spiral. And since this is *your* spiral, your own individual spiral, all of the frequencies of the many cells contained within it are a function of that one number that represents you as an individual in this particular incarnation of yours. That number, of course, is your Natural number—the Natural number of the *name* that appears upon your birth certificate, or your marriage certificate, or whatever. This is your "tag" in this particular incarnation; this is the number that represents YOU.

Let us say, as a supposition that your name is JOHN JONES. Then after we know your name, we can quite easily determine the frequencies of the many cells that go on to make up the spiral of your being. The method of determining the higher and lower frequencies in the other octaves of your name, the other revolutions of your spiral, will be left for a later chapter. But at the moment, we already have the method of determining the numerical frequencies of that which could be called the Key revolution of your spiral. The frequencies for the name JOHN JONES are as follows:

Your Natural number: 10–15–8–14–0–10–15–14–5–19
            = 10,158,140,101,514,519
Your Word number: = 2 = (1+1)
Your Alpha number: = 110 = (10+15+8+14+0+10+15+14+5+19)
Your Letter number: = 9 = (4+5)
Your Key number: = 121 = (2+110+9)

These, then, are the frequencies of your serpent that swallows its tail. And since both the Key number and the Natural number lie in the same quadrant, we may say that the Key number represents the serpent's head and the Natural number its tail.

Therefore, you now find yourself in the upper Key quadrant. You have determined that its vibration rate is 121. This is a pretty good vibration since 121 transposes into AU, and AU is the symbol for the element *gold.* One must remember that the Cabalah allows for any interpretation of a number that is feasible, and this certainly does not exclude the Table of the Chemical Elements; indeed, they are most important. The Agashan teachers have long since stated that the element gold represents matter in a "pure" state; that is, it is free from contamination. Therefore, if you were to find that your Key number represents *gold,* this is an excellent sign. It means simply that the base metals which constitute its being—the Letter number, the Alpha number, and the Word number—have been literally transformed into spiritual gold. This is what all of the ancient Alchemists wished to do; and in the case of John Jones, it has been done, or rather he may look forward to its being done when he reaches the core of his life's spiral.

Why do we say that the Letter number, the Alpha number, and the Word number constitute, or rather may be changed into, the Key number? By definition; you have been told that this is so. "But why is this really so?" you ask. The answer is because it is the *Law;* the initial letters of the words Letter, Alpha, and Word are LAW. Therefore, this primary "law" of the Cabalah becomes a major "key" in its operation. All of the laws of the Cabalah are God laws, incidentally, and it is not up to us as mortals to question them. It is only up to us to try to *understand* them.

So then as you spiral home on your spiritual path, this very same "law" will bring you next into the Vav vibration, and you will find yourself walking through the Letter number of your name. This in turn will be followed by the He vibration, and then the Yod vibration, as you travel first into the southerly quadrant of the Alpha number and then up into the westerly quadrant of the Word number. And when you finally arrive in the arc of your Natural number, you will be once more back in the upper He quadrant, the point from where you began your downward descent.

The arc of your Natural number is vibrating at a tremendous frequency. In the case of John Jones, it is in the quadrillions— a number expressed by 17 digits—and with other names it is usually even larger. Therefore, when you move from the Word number to the Natural number, you are suddenly jumping from a very, very small number (usually less than 10) to an almost infinitely large one. This is so because the Natural number represents the complete differentiation of the Name itself into its raw or natural state—from the one to the many, so to speak.

But then when you move into the Vav quadrant again, you find that you have now reversed the process and integrated the Natural number back to unity. In other words, you have gone from the many back to one again. This is the reason for naming the arc just left of the Natural number as *Each*. The word "each," by definition, means every one of a group of many things considered individually or one by one. This is not as confusing as it sounds when you consider that as you move from the Word number to the Natural number to Each number, you are in reality making 90-degree turns at each step. And if you were to write the Natural number out on the face of a yardstick, and then rotate the yardstick in 90-degree turns, you would see what we mean. Looking end on end, the yardstick would appear as a simple square only one inch wide; but looking at the yardstick face on, it would appear as a long stick some 36 inches in length. Yet it is the same yardstick; we are only observing it from different viewpoints in space.

Another point to be considered is that in the same way the Key number is the sum of three successive integrations of the Natural number in an *outward* direction—Word-wise, Alphawise, and Letter-wise—so is the Core itself the sum of three successive integrations of the Natural number in an *inward* direction. In other words, the Core itself is equal to the sum of the inner Yod, He, and Vav components of the Natural number, in the same way that the Key number is the sum of its outer components. And since things equal to the same thing are also equal to each other, the Natural number must likewise also be equal to the Core number, or the "O." This will be verified a little later when we compare the Alpha number of the word NATURAL with the Alpha number for Tarot Key 19 which represents the Core. They both are 87.

Continuing on in our journey back to the Core, let us now move down into the lower He quadrant. The name for this arc of the spiral is Taw, the 23rd letter of the Hebrew alphabet. "Why is it called Taw?" you ask. The complete answer to this question will be given later on in this work and then again in Volume II, and need not be covered here. But for the moment, let us just point out that the sound of the letter Taw is the same as the English letter "T," and its symbol is the cross. It is the cross of matter on which the Fool is crucified as he begins or ends his journey from the Core. In other words, it is the doorway through which we all must pass as we leave or enter that great world of Light, Power, and Illumination that exists within the Core. The Taw or the cross then acts as a bridge between "each" number and its Core. And if the number for Each is one (or three if we were to consider it as a trinity), then the number for Taw would be two.

This concept is explained quite easily in the following diagram, Figure 12.

Figure 12
The First and Last YOD HE VAV HE

Figure 12 is titled the First and Last YOD HE VAV HE, and rightly so. This is the core of the great spiral and where all of the action really takes place. All of the other arc segments in the *outer* revolutions of the spiral were only minor acts in the great drama called Life. But Figure 12 is the Grand Finale! It embraces not only the Core of Life itself, but also the first great *inner* revolution of the spiral which, at one and the same time, is likewise its last *outer* revolution. The last of the outer is only the beginning of the inner, and vice versa.

But the outer revolutions of the spiral were in reality only maya—illusion. We can say this because the Agashan teachers have stated over and over again that life in the earthly realms of physical expression is only the *image* of reality. Therefore, when we pass from the outer part of the spiral into the inner core of the spiral, we are moving from a world of illusion to a world of reality.

The Inner Core

The inner core of the spiral is the Yod; or rather, we should say it is the first two letters of the word YOD. The final letter, the D, represents that part of the Yod that has spewed itself out from the perfect circle that represents the Core itself. One should note that this inner YO-D is even shaped like the

Hebrew letter Yod or **9**. The similarity of this symbol, which is shaped like a comma, with the inner core of a spiral is absolutely astounding! Here again, one begins to feel the devastating impact of the fantastic intelligence contained within that which we call the Cabalah. But this is only the beginning. There is more to come.

The Yod has the numerical value of the number 10 in the numerical system of the ancient Hebrews. This is so because it is the tenth letter of the Hebrew alphabet. But just look at the diagram on the right. As we return home from the 5, to the 4, to the 3, to the 2, to the Core, we find at the Core the 1 + 0 or the 10. Thus the core is 10 (ten) if read from the outside-in, and 01 (one) if read from the inside-out.

Another point of interest arises when we consider only that part of the Yod that exists within the central circle itself. This is YO, as we have just pointed out. But is not the word YO also equal to the word I? They are one and the same; their only difference lies in the language that is being spoken. In the Spanish language, the word *Yo* means the same as the English word *I*— the nominative singular pronoun used by the speaker in referring to himself. And isn't it fitting that the home of the great "I AM" is shown by the Cabalah to be in the perfect circle of the core of a spiral? The symbology just couldn't be any more perfect.

Now let us analyze the Core from the standpoint of the English word *Oh*. Webster says that the word *Oh* is used in direct address to attract the attention of the person spoken to. Thus within this same circle, we have both the speaker, the *I*, as well as the word used to attract the attention of the one spoken to, the *Oh*. There certainly seems to be a dialogue going on here, and we have the impression that a conversation is about to begin.

But as with the Yod, there is still more to come. The word *Oh* is also used to express an emotion such as astonishment, pain, or desire (Webster, again). But aren't these the feelings that one would more than likely feel after being admitted into the spiritual realms after so-called physical death? It would seem so.

But there is even one more meaning for the word *Oh* that is the greatest of all. Webster says that it also means "zero" and is often used to express a number in words such as "four oh eight" for the number 408, etc. True. But this is not the real meaning that the Cabalah intends for this word. The real meaning for the word *Oh* is that it differentiates between the letter *Oh* (O), and the number *Zero* (0). Therefore, the name of the 15th letter of the English alphabet, O, is the word *Oh*.

The reader will find a little later in this volume that the English letter attributed to Tarot Key 19, the Sun, is likewise this same letter Oh. But is this so unusual? Of course it isn't. After all, the astrological symbol for the Sun is a circle with a dot at its center, and the English letter (O) (Oh) is almost identical to the symbol. Therefore, it is not unusual that the Cabalah would place the symbol for the Sun at the Core of every spiral.

The Master teacher Agasha reinforces this thought on page 324 of *The Agashan Discourses* when he states, "It can be said that the Core of Life may be pictured as *a great sun*; and yet this would not amply describe it, for it is larger than any sun could ever possibly be. And if we were to try to measure it— and there would be no way to do this, indeed there would not —we would find that it would encircle not only one entire solar system, but many other solar systems beyond it."

The above description by Agasha of the great Core of Life, or the great "Sun Core of Life" as he has used on other occasions, tells us better than anything else that the Sun is indeed a perfect symbol for the core of every spiral. And the word *Oh* may be broken apart into the O-H in the same manner that the word *Yod* was broken into the YO-D. Thus the "O" part of *OH* is the perfect circular center of the spiral, and the "H" part is the part that spewed itself away from the Core of Life in the beginning.

A Name Becomes the Base of Every Spiral

The reader will note that in Figure 12 we have substituted the word NAME in the upper He quadrant for the word NATURAL that was used in Figure 11. In a sense, both of these words are correct. The word "Natural" implies that it is the *Natural* number of your *Name.* So Number-wise or Name-wise, it really doesn't make much difference whether you use a long number of many digits or simply the Name itself. However, the student will soon realize that it is much easier to spell out the "Name" of the words that are being analyzed, than to try to transpose this Name into an extremely long number—especially when there is really no need to do so. We only brought out the idea of the Natural number to express the principle involved, and once this is thoroughly understood by the student, there is no further need to go through this rather cumbersome process. The Name itself, written out in its English words and letters, will tell the entire story of the Natural number even clearer than the number could ever possibly do by itself. The secret, of course, is to learn to mentally transpose numbers into letters, and then reverse the process. This is not as difficult as it sounds, and with a little practice one may become quite proficient.

The Name itself then becomes the base of every spiral. And this base "Name" is then written in the upper He quadrant immediately above the Core. In the example we used a little earlier, we would write in the words JOHN JONES in the space provided on the graph. The next step would be to write in the Word number in the Yod quadrant to the right. In this example, the number would be 2, since there are two words in the Name. And in the Vav quadrant immediately to the left of the name, we would write in the number 1. Why do we do this? We write in the number 1 because the word EACH (the name of this particular arc or space) refers to the number of individual entities or groups that is implied within the Name itself. In this case, the Name refers to one individual, YOU, and therefore the number 1 is appropriate. You will find, however, that your

Word number will normally be a little larger, since your full name will usually consist of several words.

One can very readily see then how important to the spiral the Name really is. The Natural number of the Name, which means the Name itself, is actually the final HE of the Word YOD HE VAV HE that was uttered in the beginning by God. And if the spiral that we are depicting pertains to YOU, as an individual, that Name that is emblazoned in golden letters in the space provided must out of necessity be *Your* Name. And the number of that Name, whatever it is, affects each and every arc-segment of your Life Spiral.

Very well. Let us return now to Figure 11. We have just placed the name JOHN JONES in its Natural location in the He quadrant between 0 and Key. But we learned earlier that in the same way we can perform three successive integrations of this name in an *outward* direction—Word-wise, Alpha-wise, and Letter-wise—so we can also perform three successive integrations of the Name in an *inward* direction. These three inner integrations are performed in the arc-segments called EACH TAW H. Therefore, it follows that the equivalent sum of EACH TAW H is not only equal to the name JOHN JONES, but it is also equal to the Core. And the Core is symbolized by the Sun. Thus the name JOHN JONES, in its ultimate sense, becomes just as powerful as the Core of Life itself.

These concepts might be hard to grasp at first, but the Cabalah seems to bend over backwards in its endeavors to make them crystal clear. For instance: We have learned that EACH TAW H may be transformed into not only its Natural Name, but also to its Core. But what is EACH TAW H really? The answer is simple. It is EACH "WHAT." And the word "What" is a pronoun meaning "something." Therefore, the Natural Name of anything—be it man, insect, planet, or whatever—is nothing more than a symbol for each "something" or each "What." And if someone were to ask the question, "What is it?" it may be answered by just removing the question mark and stating, "What *is* it." *It* is its Natural Name. Whatever *it* is called, *it* is. Did I say the Cabalah makes things crystal clear?

The Image and the Reality

But in the same way that three successive integrations in an *inward* direction from the Symbol will bring into manifestation each "something" or the thing itself, three successive integrations in an *outward* direction from the Symbol will bring into manifestation only the reflection or the image of this inner reality. This follows from what we had said earlier when we pointed out that when we pass from the outer revolutions of a Life Spiral into its inner revolutions, we are actually moving from a world of illusion into a world of reality. Thus the outer physical worlds of *atom* matter are only the image of the inner spiritual worlds of *anim* matter.

The inner spiritual worlds are then represented by the EACH TAW H arc-segments, and the outer physical worlds are represented by the *WORD ALPHA LETTER* arc-segments. One group is positive and the other is negative; one group is real and the other is unreal. But the Symbol or the NATURAL Name is neither real nor unreal. It is neutral and represents the 0 point in the spectrum between positive and negative matter. How do we know that all of this is so? Here again, we have to refer to the Cabalah. We get our answer from the *initial* letters of the words themselves. The three inner words may be rearranged into Taw-H-Each, which gives us THE (the initial letters of "Taw-H-Each"). And the three outer words may be read in reverse order as "Letter-Alpha-Word," whose initial letters are LAW. We will just leave the middle word "Natural" as it is. Therefore, the Cabalah tells us that the relationship between the inner worlds of the anim and the outer worlds of the atom is an expression of that which is termed "THE NATURAL LAW." (See Figure 11.)

But this is only the beginning. Even the Alpha numbers of the corresponding words tell the same story. For instance: We just pointed out that the neutral or 0 point in the spectrum between positive and negative matter is represented by the word NATURAL. From this 0 position, then, we may number the arc-segments in either an inward or outward direction by 1, 2, 3, 4. And the Number 4 position is always either the KEY segment or the CORE. This is as it should be as the Alpha numbers for the word KEY and the word CORE are identical. They both are 41.

We also find that if we start at the Core (Tarot Key 19, the Sun, which is represented by the English letter O), and count outwards, H will be 1, TAW will be 2, EACH will be 3, and NATURAL will be 4. And here again, the Core letter O and the word NATURAL represent the same numerical numbers—0 or 4. And as before, the Alpha numbers for the name of the Core, THE SUN, and for the word NATURAL are also identical. In this case, the number is 87. But not only that, it should likewise be noted that $8 + 7 = 15$, which in turn also equals the English letter O. Coincidence? Hardly. (See Figure 12.)

Each of the four possible sequences of rotation are diagramed in Figure 13:

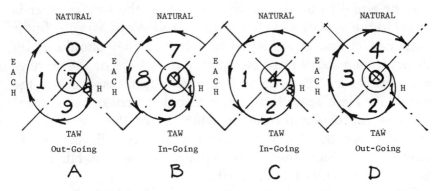

Figure 13: The Four Possible Sequences of Rotation

The reader will note that in order to end up at 10 (ten) at the Core, the NATURAL position must be at 7; and if we start with 01 (one) at the Core, the NATURAL quadrant will be at 4. These two basic assumptions, along with their inverse sequences, are what give rise to the four spirals depicted in Figure 13. The reader will also note that the 0 is in every case either in the NATURAL or the Core (THE SUN) position. Both of these names have for their Alpha value the number 87.

Very well. Let us study another very interesting relationship. The word EACH means one thing, and likewise the letter H also means "Each" or one thing. Therefore the numeral 1 is very appropriate for these two symbols. It would seem that the traveler first starts at the 0 (the Sun Core if he is being spewed forth in an outward direction, or at his Natural Name if he is to travel inwards towards the Core), and then proceeds first through the One, then through the Many (the HE quadrant), then through the One again, and finally ends up once more at the 0 at the opposite end of the spectrum, so to speak. But these final 3rd and 4th positions really represent the *Ten* position inasmuch as they are made up of the 1 and the 0. Yet, from still another aspect, the 3rd and 4th positions represent the *One* position inasmuch as the Alpha number for the word ONE is 34. Interesting, isn't it?

But this is not all. As we stated earlier, both THE SUN and the word NATURAL have for their Alpha value the number 87. Therefore, the numerical sum of EACH + TAW + H must also be equal to 87 in the same way that the Key number is equal to the sum of its Letter, Alpha, and Word aspects. But if both EACH and H are equal to 1 (which they should be by theory), then TAW must be equal to 87 − 1 − 1 or the number 85. Now let us "read" 85 and we mentally transpose it to the word HE. Here again is a perfect Cabalistic confirmation that we have not deviated from the truth during the course of our thinking, for the TAW arc-segment always falls in the HE quadrant. In fact, the TAW actually *is* the first HE of the Divine Name YOD HE VAV HE.

Before we leave the diagram, we should also point out at least two other items of interest. One is that the number 8 is also quite appropriate for the word EACH and the letter H inasmuch as the Alpha number for the former is 17 which reduces to 8, and the Alpha number for H is of course also 8. The other item is that the Alpha number for TWO is 58. 58 also relates to HE because it is the inverse of HE or EH. And more than this, it is a fact that 87 − 58 = 29. The number 29 converts to BI, and Webster says that the prefix "Bi" means twice or two. Therefore, no matter which way you look at it, HE or its inverse form EH when subtracted from 87 always leaves two 1's left over—one for EACH and the other for H. And furthermore, it should not be forgotten that TAW always falls in either a 2 or a 9 numerical segment, which, quite coincidentally, also spells out the word BI.

The Esoteric Meaning of Each Quadrant

Now are we finished with Figure 13? Or is there still another major facet of it that should be explored before we leave it? The writer had intended to conclude this discussion with the preceding paragraph but, as it happens so many times in the study of the Cabalah, when you "dig" a little further you sometimes discover real spiritual gold. And this is precisely what is about to occur in this particular instance. Yes, we can truthfully say that great spiritual wisdom lies there, under camouflage, ready to be unveiled and brought into the sunlight of understanding by the discerning reader.

Therefore, let us now look at Figure 13 objectively, as a whole. What is this diagram really telling us? Other than the fact that it gives a numerical interpretation to the sequence of events lying at the core of our Life Spiral, what else is it telling us? What have we missed in our previous discussion? Look at it. See if you can determine its overall meaning. It is actually very simple, for all you have to do is "read" it.

For instance: What is the true meaning of the arc-segment in the upper HE quadrant just above the Core? What are the four manifestations of the NATURAL number saying? The answer is simple. These four manifestations are making a flat statement which is revealed in the number 0 7 0 4. The revelation comes when it is transliterated into the phrase "O GOD." The word O, in the sense that it is used here, is an interjection which when placed before a name in direct address lends earnestness to an appeal. Therefore the true meaning of this arc-segment, which is the Natural number or the Name of something, is in effect an earnest appeal to God.

Now let us study the central Core. What do its four manifestations bring into being? This is revealed in the number 7 0 4 0. This number transliterates itself into a similar phrase, although one that has a slightly different meaning. It states that it is the "GOD O." In other words, the Cabalah tells us that the

Core of the Life Spiral is literally God itself. It is the 0 point of one's being, the God within, the one being addressed by the Natural Name in its outer state. And it is not only the God whose number is 0, but it is also the God whose letter is O (Oh). This means then that it represents the Sun, and the Sun is a symbol for the Core of Life from which we sprang.

An analysis of the meaning of the arc-segment in the lower He quadrant just below the Core is equally as astounding, although on the surface it is not so readily apparent. The name of this arc-segment is TAW, which when combined with the O in the central Core can be changed to "A TWO." And the number of its four successive manifestations tells us exactly the same thing. The number is 9 9 2 2, but it has to be placed in a circle, and then read starting with the second 9, before its meaning can be understood. If we read it in this manner, we read "I B BI," or simply, "I be Bi." And of course, *bi* means *two*.

There is still another way to read this diagram, and that way is to read it vertically starting from the upper He, then down through the Core, and finishing up at the lower He. But in order to understand this method of analysis, we have to embrace the *God Names* of the various letters of the English alphabet, and that is beyond the scope of this present chapter. Needless to say, however, it can be shown that the word NATURAL (the upper He) equates to the letter G, the words THE SUN (the central Core) equate to the letter O, and the key word TAW (the lower He) equates to the letter D. These three letters add up to the word GOD. But more than that, the Alpha numbers of the God Names of these particular letters are 87, 87, and 85. This in itself is nothing out of the ordinary, but when we add them together and obtain their sum, we are taken aback a bit in awe. The number is 259, and it restates once again that which was derived in the previous paragraphs. That statement is the simple fact that (GOD) BE I.

But that is not the only point that is intended to be made. No, indeed it is not. In fact, it is the lesser point. The greater point to be brought out is only understood when we consider the Central Core of our Life Spiral as a cross. Therefore, we must also take into consideration the arms of the cross which exist on either side of the Central Sun. These are the Vav on the left and the outer part of the Yod which protrudes on the right. One is called EACH and the other H (which is only another symbol for the same word "each"). Thus the greater meaning of the term "Be I" means that God be Each—each separate thing, no matter what it be.

Now we have even a greater meaning for the arc-segment TAW, which we determined above to be 9 2 2 9 or simply "I be Bi (two)." We could have just as easily capitalized the final "i" and stated that TAW means "I be BE I (God)." In fact, the symbol for the Hebrew letter Taw *is* the Cross. Therefore, it could be said that when one is crucified upon the cross of matter, it is in reality an *outer* manifestation of the same Universal God Consciousness that exists *within* the Central Core of each and every Life Spiral.

All of the names of these arc-segments are shown in their proper position in Figure 11. Therefore for a clearer understanding of the thoughts expressed above, we should read once again the preceding paragraphs in the light of Figure 11, and then follow the train of thought, as it were, as we spiral out or in from the Core. But are we now finished with Figure 11? Is this all that Figure 11 has to tell us? Or are there still some other aspects of this amazing spiral that must be explored before we leave it? To answer these questions, let us also look at Figure 11 in an objective manner, as a whole, and from a different vantage point.

Let us say, as an assumption, that we are traveling inwards at a pretty fast pace. We are riding our horse, our physical body as it were, and we have finally reached the upper He quadrant of our Natural Name. Then from the vantage point of our Name (the symbol that represents us), we are better able to gaze inwards towards the Core. And what do we see? We see EACH T (the T-cross upon which we have been crucified), and the realization of all of this brings us to the understanding that we have now come to the end of the trail. We have had enough of the outer world, and we pull on the reins and say to our horse, "WHOA." (The word *Whoa* is a command usually given to horses or draft animals, and it means to stop or stand still.) But we do not actually give this command until after we have passed the T-cross. The Natural Name only enables us to realize that the end of the trail is in sight.

And how do we know that we will then be at the end of our trail? We know this because the realization of the cross enables us to understand that after it lies the Core, the Central Point of our Being. We will then be AT the WHO (the One that we really are) and AT the HOW (the principle that brought us into manifestation). In other words, in the Core of our Life Spiral we not only find out *WHO* we are, or *HOW* we came into manifestation, but we also find out *WHAT* we are to become in the future. All of these things are revealed when we arrive *AT* the *O* (the Inner Core).

But this is not all. When we are *in* the Core, we are also able to look outwards again, out along the spiral path that we had just traversed. We are then able to observe in detail every step along the way and come to a clear understanding of not only "WHO A TEACH," but also "HOW A TEACH." And who is "A"? The true meaning for this word is not readily apparent at the moment, other than the fact that the dictionary defines it as the indefinite article, which means that it is *any* one thing of a particular class of things (*Each* man is *a* man). But in a later chapter we will find out that the esoteric meaning of the English letter A is that it represents the Fatherhood of God. God the Father then is the letter A, the first He of the spiral.

And who is God the Son? God the Son is the *One* whom A teaches. God the Son is the second He of the spiral, the *one* definite particular thing that is symbolized by its Natural Name. And this Natural Name or number may very well be *your* name or number. Therefore, you the reader are a manifestation of God the Son. Thus your God-Self is able to observe its outer self, You, as you manifest on each and every step along the great spiral pathway of the Wheel of Life. YOU then are WHO A TEACH. And not only that, the Cabalah tells us that the process of "HOW A TEACH" is through teaching EACH NATURAL WORD ALPHA LETTER KEY of the Sacred Name YOD HE VAV HE.

Chapter 6

THE EVOLUTION OF THE ANKH

Lᴇᴛ ᴜs ɴᴏᴡ turn our attention to one of the most ancient and sacred symbols of antiquity—the ANKH. The Ankh may be described as a Tau cross with a loop at the top, and for many thousands of years it was revered in ancient Egypt as a symbol for generation and enduring life. But the Ankh did not just appear from out of nowhere. Man may have become aware of it all of a sudden, yes, but the Ankh has always existed and it always shall exist. Yet, it too has gone through the process of evolution, the same as the Reality that it represents—LIFE. Therefore, we can state that as Life evolves, so does the Ankh.

The proof of this statement can be ascertained from a study of Figure 14. The diagram has been called the Evolution of the ANKH, and rightly so, because that is just what it is. Reading up from the bottom of the figure we read H (Each) ANKH! And not only that, but the symbol of the Ankh is likewise portrayed with the O of the Central Core sitting on top of the T.

The reader will observe that Figure 14 is really nothing more than a duplication of Figure 11, with the exception that the Names of the arc-segments have been changed from the full word to only its initial letter. Otherwise everything else remains the same. However, the outermost circle contains the English equivalent of the Hebrew word YOD HE VAV HE, which is I H V H, in lieu of the initial letters.

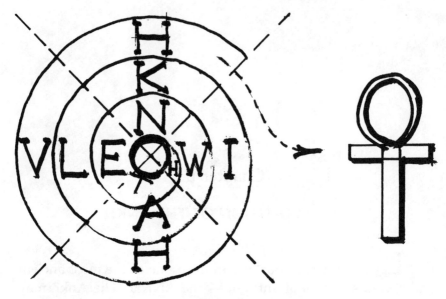

Figure 14
The Evolution of the ANKH

But what is so incredible about the whole thing is that this ancient symbol for *Life* appears at the very Core of our own *Life* Spiral! And it is even spelled correctly, with the letters appearing in their exact sequence! I am sure that even the most confirmed skeptic, at this point, must at least give the Cabalah the benefit of the doubt.

The great Master Teacher Agasha said on many occasions that eventually every word that he uttered, in its entirety, would finally be proved to our full satisfaction. And it would be the "I" within that would bring about the proof. Thus the Cabalah seems to be taking us a long ways in this direction. In any event, we are off to a good start with the knowledge that whoever invented the English alphabet, or the Hebrew alphabet, or the modern-day English spelling of the ancient words, or even the Cabalah itself, most certainly must have had a full and complete understanding of this ancient symbol for life— the ANKH.

But again this isn't all. In fact, it is safe to say that we have hardly even begun. For another "whammy" or knockout punch, let us consider only the Inner Core and one complete revolution of the spiral from Yod to Yod. In this case, we will repeat the Yod twice; the first Yod will stand for the Core, and the second Yod will complete the first outer revolution. Very well. We have the letters O H T E N W. "Well, what is so unusual about that?" you may ask. To answer this question for himself, we ask the reader to observe the Core of the spiral as if it represented the four cardinal points of the compass—North, East, South, and West. To the left of the Central Sun—the Yod, the O, or the Oh as it were—we have the EAST. Then rising above the Core, the NORTH comes into manifestation. And descending on our right, into the sunset, is the WEST. This leaves the letter T to represent the SOUTH, and it would seem, on the surface, that there is a discrepancy here. But there is no discrepancy.

For an answer to this puzzle, we have only to consider the direction SOUTH as being portrayed by the bottom portion of the symbol for the Ankh. This is the letter T. The upper part of the Ankh is then the circle, the O, the Core of Life itself which sits on top of the T. Even the letters contained within the word SOUTH tell us the same story. For here, within the Ankh, we have three of the letters of this word. They are the O, the T, and the H. Only the letters U and S are missing in order to make up the complete word SOUTH. And you know who U and S are, don't you? They can stand for no one else but US, you and I, who are quite conveniently "missing" from the Central Core of our Life Spiral. But this is as it should be because at the present time we will most certainly find ourselves spiraling around in one of the outer circles, as it were. Nevertheless, when we finally do return to the Core we will have put ourselves into the Ankh, so to speak, and then we will make up the complete word SOUTH, all spelled out so nice and properlike. Amazing, isn't it?

Now let us read the diagram horizontally, from the right to the left. Let us read inwards to the Core, and we have the letters IWHO or simply, I WHO. Thus we learn that the right arm of the Ankh cross is "I Who." But, one may ask, it is *I who* does "what?" For an answer to this question, we have to continue the sentence by reading now outwards from the Core, and we have the letters OELV. These letters, which on the surface have no particular meaning, must then be unscrambled into their true meaning which is LOVE. Therefore, the horizontal crossbar of the Ankh cross tells us that it is "I WHO LOVE." The right arm is the "I WHO," and the left arm is "LOVE."

But this is not the only statement that the horizontal crossbar of the Ankh cross makes. The letters "I WHO" can be changed into "HOW I," and "LOVE" can be read backwards in a circular fashion which yields forth the word "EVOLVE." (In this case, the first two letters of the word are repeated once again as the last two letters when we come to the end of the circle.) Therefore, the crossbar states that it is not only "I WHO LOVE," but it is also "HOW I EVOLVE." In other words, the Cabalah tells us that the "I" evolves through Love, and that crucifying itself on the cross of the Ankh, is the method by which this is accomplished.

Now have we exhausted all of the information contained within the crossarms of the Ankh? No, not by any means; in fact, by far the most important aspect is yet to be unveiled. "But how can you read these seven letters any differently?" you will ask. The answer again is to put them in the form of a circle. We did this with the left arm of the Ankh in the example above, but now let us try it with the entire crossbar. Then, reading around the circumference, we have the letters IWHOELVI. In this case, it is the "I" (the first and last letter) that is repeated twice; in the earlier example when we went inwards toward the Core, it was the "O" (the Core itself) that was repeated twice.

The next step is to read once more what the letters tell us, and we read "I WHO ELVI." But here again, the third word has no meaning until it is unscrambled. We can unscramble "ELVI" into "LIVE" and then read it backwards as "EVIL." Thus the crossarms of the Ankh also inform us that they are "HOW I LIVE." And who is the "I" they are referring to? It is the "I WHO (am) EVIL." In other words, the one who is evil suffers the consequences by living crucified upon the cross of the Ankh. And this is as it should be.

But we are not yet finished with the crossarms. There is still one final statement that will come into focus when we treat "ELVI" in *exactly* the same way that we changed "OELV" into "LOVE." If we follow through the same process, step by step, "ELVI" becomes "VEIL." Thus the Cabalah also tells us that the crossbar of the Ankh, when it is turned into a circle, is the "I WHO VEIL." And not only that, it informs us as to "WHO I VEIL" and "HOW I VEIL."

Removing the Veil from Isis

Connecting the ends of the horizontal crossbar of the Ankh should then give us a valuable clue towards understanding the true meaning of the term, "removing the veil from Isis." Or rather we should say the opposite is true, because when the veil (the left arm of the cross) is brought up over the Core and connected to the "I" at the extreme right end of the cross, Isis (the Central Core or the "Who") is truly veiled. Therefore when we cut the circle and lay the "veil" over to one side, as it is shown in Figure 14, then the Core is exposed to our view and Isis is thereby unveiled, thus revealing the true splendor of the mysteries of her Being.

But before we discuss who and what she really is, perhaps we should say a few words about what we already know of her. Occult tradition has it that she is the archetype of the Virgin Mother of the World. Her name is the Greek form of the ancient Egyptian hieroglyph meaning "throne," and the great drama of her life is the mainstay of the entire Egyptian religion. She is therefore one of the prime goddesses of ancient Egypt.

"But what is her real significance to us today, here in the modern world?" one might ask. For an answer to this question, let us ask the Cabalah. Her name, simply stated, tells us that the Goddess Isis "IS the I'S." In other words, she *is* the sum total of all the multitudinous number of individual I's contained within any one consciousness. You yourself are one entity; yet the body that you inhabit, the Temple of the Living God, so to speak, is in reality composed of billions of individual living cells. And it is the same with Isis.

We will cover her complete story in a later chapter, but for

the moment let us be content with the knowledge that the
Goddess Isis *is* the sum total of the *I's*. Therefore, she is the one
who states, "It is I WHO VEIL HOW I LIVE." She is the feminine aspect of the one-living God, the feminine aspect of the
One without a Second, the feminine aspect of *your* very own
Being. Madame Blavatsky reinforces this thought in the Preface of her monumental work, *Isis Unveiled*,[1] and I quote:

"In our studies, mysteries were shown to be no mysteries.
Names (italics ours) and places that to the Western mind have
only a significance derived from Eastern fable, were shown to
be realities. Reverently we stepped in spirit within the temple of
Isis; to lift aside the veil of "the one that is and was and shall
be" at Sais; to look through the rent curtain of the Sanctum
Sanctorum at Jerusalem; and even to interrogate within the
crypts which once existed beneath the sacred edifice, the
mysterious Bath-Kol. The *Filia Vocis*—the daughter of the
divine voice—responded from the mercy-seat within the veil,
and science, theology, every human hypothesis and conception
born of imperfect knowledge, lost forever their authoritative
character in our sight. The one-living God had spoken through
his oracle—man, and we were satisfied. Such knowledge is
priceless; and it has been hidden only from those who overlooked it, derided it, or denied its existence."

Thank you Madame Blavatsky for your exquisite interpretation of the meaning of the Temple of Isis. But wait, Isis has not
yet finished speaking. She has unveiled the meaning of the
horizontal arms and the vertical stem of the Ankh cross, but
the true purpose and message contained within its upper loop
remains still a mystery. Then how do we go about deciphering
it? The answer again is very simple. We merely ask the
Cabalah and then read what it says. But in order to ascertain
the meaning for the upper loop, we have to (1) retrace out the
letters of the cardinal points of the compass as we weave in and
out in a clockwise and then an anticlockwise direction around
its core, and (2) then proceed in a circular manner as we travel
around and around its spiral for as many revolutions as we
wish.

Therefore, let us take one more look at Figure 14 and read

the letters in this fashion. We will start at the base of the Ankh which is represented by the letters A and T. And then we will proceed in both directions around the clock, going into the core and then out again in alternate turns as if we were sewing. Now follow us carefully, step by step, as we watch each letter almost magically unfold and bring into manifestation the loop part of the Ankh cross. And note especially the magnificent symmetry and balance and order of the letters.

Are you ready? Now follow us carefully as we start at the base of the T and read—THAT. Very well. We have now brought into manifestation the T part of the Ankh upon which the circular loop rests. This also represents the direction South. Let us now proceed with the loop as it winds in and out of the core bringing into manifestation first the East, and then the North, and then the West cardinal points respectively. And doing this, we thus finish the sentence with—THAT EON NOW ONE.

Wow! Just realize what the Cabalah of the Ankh loop has now told us! It has gone through a complete cycle of manifestation, forwards and backwards, and names the time necessary to bring all of this about as an *eon*. Now an eon embraces many millions and even billions of years. And more than that, at the conclusion of this seemingly endless period of time, the Cabalah takes this tremendously large number and equates it back to unity or one. "That particular eon is now *one*," it says. And with one as a beginning, we are now ready to bring into manifestation an even greater circle which, at its completion, would also be equated back to unity. Only this new revolution of the spiral would in all probability be called *two*. And the next one *three*, and the next one *four*, and so on. But the important thing to understand is that in the eyes of the God Consciousness, a vast eon of countless years is nothing more than a moment of time.

You may look at the Natural number which represents your Name in the same way. This is a number which has many, many digits within it; and it is a very vast number, indeed. But you yourself, the entity that it represents, are One. And at the end of this particular life, a lifetime embracing a considerable number of years, you will look back upon it from your vantage point in the astral world as unity again—one life in a series of many. This same principle of equating a very large number at the end of a cycle back to unity again, or that which it was in the beginning, evidently applies throughout the Universe. Herein lies the secret for the Unity of the God Consciousness, for the many in the eyes of God are truly One.

All of the above can be lumped together and expressed by two simple words. The words are "da capo," and they are used as a musical direction to repeat once again from the beginning. In fact, the exact definition as given by Webster is "(It.): from the beginning—." The "It" is intended to mean that the words are derived from the Italian language, but I would prefer to interpret it Cabalistically and say that the occult definition of the term should literally be "It from the beginning." "It" then can apply to anything—you name it—once it has completed its cycle and is sent back to repeat once again that which it was in the beginning.

The word "It," since it is neither masculine nor feminine but completely neutral, is also an excellent expression for the God Consciousness. *It* is then the One without a Second, as the Master Teacher Araskas would say. *It* is the great Light from which we sprang. *It* is the inexhaustible, self-creating, and self-serving One—the one that was from the beginning, being without end. In each cycle *It* dies, and in each cycle *It* begins all over again. And *It* is the Word that is for ever and always One—the Alpha and the Omega, the beginning and the end.

A Walk on the Lawn

We find then that the process of retracing out the letters of the four cardinal points of the compass, in the manner prescribed above, has enabled us to bring into manifestation the upper loop of the Ankh cross. But the complete meaning for this symbol will not be forthcoming until we complete the second phase of the operation, which consists of now proceeding in a circular direction around its spiral path for at least one or two revolutions, or until the message contained therein is thoroughly understood. And we may do this in either a clockwise or an anticlockwise fashion; a clockwise movement will enable us to travel outwards towards the periphery of the spiral, and motion in an anticlockwise direction will carry us inwards towards the Core.

Very well. Let us return to Figure 14 and do just that. The previous initial cycle has left us proceeding in an inward direction along the circular arc from the "N" to the "E," and so let us continue in the same manner until we reach the Core. The complete sentence now reads, "THAT EON NOW ONETH O." "Oneth O? What does this mean?" you ask. You will not have to wait very long for an answer to your question, because if you reverse your direction and proceed outwardly you will have your answer. The Cabalah answers back as it mirrors your own thought with the words, "OH, TEN." Of course, "Oneth O" means simply "One O"; the confusion was that it was written in a Biblical format. And we all know that "One O" is 10 or *Ten*.

But if the Biblical spelling is still a bothersome point, inasmuch as *Oneth* is not a verb, you may eliminate the word entirely by proceeding directly to the Core as soon as you finish tracing out the letters ONE. The initial phrase would then read "THAT EON NOW ONE O." There is an excellent argument that can be made that this is the way we should have proceeded in the first place. Therefore, the answer could very well be that the *eon* is not only *one*, but that it is also *ten* (1 + 0 = 10).

Or perhaps it means that an eon is simply one zero or a single 0 (one 0, not two 0's). You see, there are many ways that we may read the Cabalah, and each meaning can be equally as valid as the others. For instance: if we were to consider only the Core and its first three outer arc-segments, we would then have the term THE O; and this is precisely what it is—The O.

Now let us consider the Core along with its first four outer arc-segments, and we read "O H TEN." We have now separated the "H" from the "O," and placed it somewhere along the circular arc between the "O" and the "10." The letter "H," as we pointed out earlier, is in reality only a symbol for the word "Each." Therefore the symbol "H" could also be interpreted as occupying *each* of the numbers between 0 and 10—namely, 1, 2, 3, 4, 5, 6, 7, 8, or 9. Is this true? Is "H" actually walking the pathway between 0 and 10? It would appear so, because after the word TEN, the word WALK comes into view.

Thus we find that as we proceed in a circular manner, to and fro, backwards and forwards along our spiral path, the true meaning of the upper loop of the Ankh is beginning to make itself known. We use the term "backwards and forwards" because it is necessary to proceed in both directions before we can ascertain the complete meaning.

Therefore, let us now reverse our direction again and see if we can find out what kind of terrain we have traversed in our "walk" from the 0 to the 10. Reading backwards from the final "K" of the word WALK, we find that it consists of a LAWN. We have walked on the *lawn*, so to speak, in the first two revolutions of our spiral pathway that leads outwards from the Core. And since Webster tells us that the word "lawn" means a stretch of grass-covered land usually near a house or an estate, we find that we have been traveling over a relatively level area, and that this area was more than likely the outer garden of some great Hall of Higher Learning.

This interpretation fits very closely with the way we had expected it to be, not only strictly from a mathematical point of view, but also from a philosophical viewpoint. We have learned that our spiral pathway travels outwards and upwards in much the same manner as the magnetic field of the earth. Therefore, it begins more or less on the floor of a great valley, and then it spirals upwards into the mountains that surround it. This valley floor could very well be similar to the Valley of Cocoda, a Spiritual Center that is located deep within the mountains of Tibet, and at the center of which is a fountain. The Masters in this Center have often compared their fountain symbolically with the mythical Fountain of Life—the fountainhead from which life springs forth. The fountain is then the 0, the zero point from which the spiral path begins and ends, as it slowly climbs up and away from the grass-covered *lawn* that surrounds this beautiful Spiritual Center.

But is this spiritual pathway that travels through the numbers always smooth and more or less level as if it were on the surface of a lawn? The answer is definitely not; in fact, the contrary is so in some of the outer revolutions of the spiral path that traverse through rather rugged territory in the great mountain of our Being. Thus the further we proceed outwards from the Core, the fountainhead of our Being, the path becomes steeper and steeper, and eventually our simple "walk" turns into a veritable "hike."

How do we know that this is so, other than the fact that it seems logical? Does the Cabalah say anything about it? Of course it does. We have to only proceed through the outermost revolution of our spiral glyph to find the answer. Traveling then in an outward direction from the final "K" of the word WALK, and then inwards again towards the center, we find the letters "I HV H" (reading outwardly) and "HV HIK" (reading inwardly). These letters may be translated into the sentence, "I have each 'H' have hike." Thus our "H," which in the revolutions very near to the core only had to "walk" upon the "lawn" of the valley floor, now must "hike" up the steep trail of its outer revolutions towards the summit.

Then, once he has arrived at the summit he so valiantly struggled to reach, our "H" (which means each one of us who has made it to the top) will be able to hold up his lantern to act as a guiding light so that all those on the lower levels of the spiral path may then see it and follow it. "This is the way," he beckons unto us as he seems to say, "Follow me to the promised land." He can say this with full authority, for right there on the mountaintop, exposed to his view but shielded from ours, is the most glorious Temple of Illumination ever beheld by mortal man.

This Temple then is what awaits us at the end of our spiral journey into Consciousness. This is the Temple that the "I" within would have us to hike up to. And this is the most glorious temple of them all, for it is the Temple of our own Being.

Figure 15
The Spiral Path to the Temple of Illumination[2]

The God Names

Let us return now to the Major Arcana of the Book of the Tarot and analyze the God Words and the God Names of the various forces that go on to make up the Universal Consciousness that men call God. Yes, the Major Arcana of the Tarot is just that. It is composed of the gods, forces, or principles—call them what you will—that govern this God Consciousness. In other words, it represents the rulers or the royal family of the Universal Consciousness God.

But the Major Arcana is even more than that. It also represents the rulers and the royal family of your own individual soul consciousness. Thus it is the macrocosm and the microcosm, the universal Akashic and the individual Akashic, the universe and the man.

So then let us analyze these words and names—dissect them as it were—and find out what really makes them "tick." Let us see whether we can unmask the power that lies within each word or name. Let us analyze the "numerical forces" that are contained within the words themselves, and in so doing, try to find out if these numerical forces constitute any sort of pattern, a soul pattern as it were, that can be used to identify them more clearly.

But first we must more clearly define what we mean when we speak of a God Word or a God Name. These terms were partially defined in the chapter-segment titled "A Table of Correspondences," where we defined a *God Name* as the full title of a particular Tarot Key and the *God Word* as the principal word contained within it. For example, the God Name for Tarot Key 2 is *The High Priestess;* its God Word is simply *Priestess.* But there is a far more fundamental difference between these two terms, other than the fact that they are a long form and a short form for the same Tarot Key. And this fundamental or primary difference between the God Word and the God Name is what we now want to unfold.

"In the beginning was the Word, and the Word was with God, and the Word was God." Again we want to return to this verse of St. John, for it gives us an excellent explanation for the

primary difference between the two terms. And if the Word
was in the beginning, what was in the end? The Name, of
course. The Natural number, or the Name of anything, you
will recall, is the end result of the total expansion of the Word
as it is brought into manifestation through the first, second,
and third quadrants of the spiral after being spewed forth from
the Core.

For a better explanation of what we mean, let us refer once
more to Figure 12. The God Word then is the "D" part of the
YO-D, the "H" part of the O-H, the "1" part of the 0-1. It is the
outer part of the initial word of the Divine Name, YOD HE
VAV HE, and it is located in the Yod quadrant or the first
quadrant of the spiral.

The God Name occupies the fourth quadrant of this spiral.
Being the full manifestation of the God Word, it quite naturally
falls into place in the arc-segment for the Natural Number, or
the Natural Name. It is the sum total of H TAW EACH or the
numbers 1, 2, and 3. It is the final word of the Divine Name,
YOD HE VAV HE, and it is located in the second He quadrant
or the North quadrant of the spiral.

We find then that the God Word and the God Name are
separated by two intervening quadrants. They are separated by
"Each Taw," the VAV and the HE, the Motherhood and the
Fatherhood of God, the Bow and the String. It is the archer,
remember, who occupies the initial "H" position, or the "D"
part of the YOD. This is the God Word. And by the same analogy, it is the arrow itself that occupies the second He position,
or God the Son. This is the God Name. Therefore, it can be
said that the God Word is the "force" that sends the God Name
(the arrow) out into the Cosmos, to fall to earth and come into
manifestation as the Natural number of the God Name. And
the Natural number of the God Name *is* the God Name, once
the numbers of same have been changed into letters.

The second step in the analysis of the Words and the Names
of the Major Arcana is simply to tabulate them. This we have
done in Figures 16 and 17. The first column gives the Hebrew

THE MAJOR ARCANA -- GOD WORDS								
Hebrew Letters and Number	The God Words	Numbers				Running Totals		
		Word (Yod)	Alpha (He)	Letter (Vav)	Key (He)	Key Sum	Letter Sum	Alpha Sum
1. Aleph	MAGICIAN	1	57	8	66	66	8	57
2. Beth	PRIESTESS	1	130	9	140	206	17	187
3. Gimel	EMPRESS	1	95	7	103	309	24	282
4. Daleth	EMPEROR	1	90	7	98	407	31	372
5. He	HIEROPHANT	1	114	10	125	532	41	486
6. Vav	LOVERS	1	91	6	98	630	47	577 EGG
7. Zayin	CHARIOT	1	74	7	82	712	54	651
8. Heth	STRENGTH	1	111	8	120	832	62	762
9. Teth	HERMIT	1	73	6	80	912	68	835
10. Yod	WHEEL	1	53	5	59	971	73	888
11. Kaph	JUSTICE	1	87	7	95	1,066	80	975
12. Lamed	MAN	1	28	3	32	1,098	83	1,003
13. Mem	DEATH	1	38	5	44	1,142	88	1,041
14. Nun	TEMPERANCE	1	100	10	111	1,253	98	1,141 AN A
15. Samekh	DEVIL	1	52	5	58	1,311	103	1,193
16. Ayin	TOWER	1	81	5	87	1,398	108	1,274
17. Pe	STAR	1	58	4	63	1,461	112	1,332
18. Sadhe	MOON	1	57	4	62	1,523	116	1,389
19. Qoph	SUN	1	54	3	58	1,581	119	1,443
20. Resh	JUDGEMENT	1	99	9	109	1,690	128	1,542
0. Sin	FOOL	1	48	4	53	1,743	132	1,590
21. Shin	WORLD	1	72	5	78	1,821	137	1,662
	Arcana Total	22	1,662	137	1,821			
0. Taw	FOOL	1	48	4	53	1,874	141	1,710
	Wheel Total	23	1,710	141	1,874			

Figure 16: The God Words

T H E M A J O R A R C A N A - - G O D N A M E S								
Hebrew ·Letters and Number	The God Names	Numbers				Running Totals		
		Word (Yod)	Alpha (He)	Letter (Vav)	Key (He)	Key Sum	Letter Sum	Alpha Sum
1. Aleph	THE MAGICIAN	2	90	11	103	103	11	90
2. Beth	THE HIGH PRIESTESS	3	195	16	214	317	27	285
3. Gimel	THE EMPRESS	2	128	10	140	457	37	413
4. Daleth	THE EMPEROR	2	123	10	135	592	47	536
5. He	THE HIEROPHANT	2	147	13	162	754	60	683
6. Vav	THE LOVERS	2	124	9	135	889	69	807
7. Zayin	THE CHARIOT	2	107	10	119	1,008	79	914
8. Heth	STRENGTH	1	111	8	120	1,128	87	1,025
9. Teth	THE HERMIT	2	106	9	117	1,245	96	1,131
10. Yod	THE WHEEL OF FORTUNE	4	206	17	227	1,472	113	1,337
11. Kaph	JUSTICE	1	87	7	95	1,567	120	1,424 NX
12. Lamed	THE HANGED MAN	3	100	12	115	1,682	132	1,524
13. Mem	DEATH	1	38	5	44	1,726	137	1,562
14. Nun	TEMPERANCE	1	100	10	111	1,837	147	1,662 *
15. Samekh	THE DEVIL	2	85	8	95	1,932	155	1,747
16. Ayin	THE TOWER	2	114	8	124	2,056	163	1,861
17. Pe	THE STAR	2	91	7	100	2,156	170	1,952
18. Sadhe	THE MOON	2	90	7	99	2,255	177	2,042
19. Qoph	THE SUN	2	87	6	95	2,350	183	2,129
20. Resh	JUDGEMENT	1	99	9	109	2,459	192	2,228
0. Sin	THE FOOL	2	81	7	90	2,549	199	2,309
21. Shin	THE WORLD	2	105	8	115	2,664	207	2,414 XN
	Arcana Subtotal	43	2,414	207	2,664	* Also Word Total		
0. Taw	THE FOOL	2	81	7	90	2,754	214	2,495
	Wheel Grand Total	45	2,495	214	2,754		BAD	B DIE

Figure 17: The God Names

letter that corresponds to its particular Tarot Key. These
Hebrew letters are a carry-over from Figure 4, but because they
are so all-important to any analysis we might make, they have
been repeated once again. Also in the first column is the num-

ber of the Tarot Key that appears on the card itself. It represents the *order* in which the gods make their appearance. This in turn is followed by the appropriate God Word or God Name; and the fourth, fifth, sixth, and seventh columns give its Word, Alpha, Letter, and Key numbers respectively. Thus it now becomes possible for you and me, as we study these charts, to perhaps even "walk upon the lawn" ourselves. The final three columns are simply a tabulation, or a running total as it were, of all of the values of the individual terms extending from Tarot Key 1, the Magician, to the particular Tarot Key in question. We have done this in order to see if there might be a significant meaning for the total value of a particular group of keys or forces, that would otherwise remain undiscovered if they were only analyzed on an individual basis.

Before we can proceed with an analysis of these Tables, we must also have one other very important figure or glyph in front of us. Therefore let us refer once again to Figure 7. Now Figure 7, if you recall, represents a cross section through an earth, a sphere, a globe. But it also represents the Wheel of Life; in other words, it takes all of the Tarot Keys of the Major Arcana and connects them as if they were on the rim of a wheel. But in order to show this wheel in its entirety, to be able to bring the AUM and the OM into manifestation, we must out of necessity have 23 segments or divisions. And these 23 segments are very "conveniently" represented by the modern Hebrew alphabet. This, we covered in an earlier chapter.

But in addition to all of this, Figure 7 is also a cross section through our spiral. It may be viewed as if the observer were in the Vav quadrant and looking at a cross section through the very Core of the spiral, a section that cuts through all of the "He" quadrants from top to bottom. In other words, none of the Vav or Yod quadrants would appear in Figure 7. Only the "He" arc-segments would be seen; the 2nd He or the Son arc-segments would appear to the left of the veritical axis, and the 1st He or the Father arc-segments would appear to the right of the axis. This may be quite easily visualized if the reader will observe the spiral depicted in Figure 11 with this thought in mind.

Inasmuch as the Hebrew letter Shin (Tarot Key 21, the World) depicts the Central Core of our spiral, it now should be readily apparent why the Hebrew letter Taw was chosen to designate the first He arc-segment of the spiral. It was simply the next letter of the Hebrew alphabet following Shin. And the next letter after Taw is the Hebrew letter Aleph, which is the equivalent of the Greek letter Alpha, the English letter A, the name of the He arc-segment just below Taw. And the next one is called Beth, and then Gimel, and then Daleth, etc.

In Figure 7, then, is a perfect description of how our hero, the "H," travels through all of the numbers from 0 to 10 in his hike to the top of the mountain where the Temple of Illumination exists at the in-going sound of the OM. This is at the tenth revolution around the spiral, when he finally arrives at the letters Yod and Kaph, Tarot Keys 10 and 11 respectively. It should be remembered that the completion of the first revolution was not until he reached the letter Aleph, or the Alpha number of his name. At the Taw and the Sin positions he was still whirling around the World (the letter Shin), in the 0 revolution at the center of the valley floor. He had not yet been spewed forth from this Fountain of Life.

An interesting verification that we are correct in our analysis comes about when we study the Hebrew letters that represent the two positions of our Fool in his "O" revolution around the World (Tarot Key 21). These are the Hebrew letters Taw and Sin. Therefore, let us analyze these two letters further and see if we can find out what else they are trying to tell us relative to the identity of the Fool or Tarot Key 0. We may do this by simply treating them as an anagram, rearranging their letters as it were, and then reading what they say. We find that "TAW SIN" very easily transposes into "A'S TWIN" or "TWINS' A." In other words, the Cabalah tells us that the Fool, who is you, is none other than a twin (a person closely related to or closely resembling another person) of "A." And the letter "A," in the English Cabalah, is a symbol representing the Father aspect of the Universal Consciousness God. This bears out the idea that Man was created in the image and likeness of God.

Or, if we were to arrange the letters "A'S TWIN" into a

circle, we could interpret it as saying that the two words, Taw and Sin, are "AS TWIN A'S." This is logical inasmuch as both Taw and Sin occupy the first or the "A" position as we read the letters clockwise or anticlockwise out from Shin (Tarot Key 21) which represents the O or the Core.

Thus the reader will note that Figures 16 and 17, the God Words and the God Names, have been compiled with Figure 7 in mind. But, inasmuch as they are also a tabulation of the Major Arcana as well as the Wheel of Life, two separate totals are shown at the bottom of the tables. One gives the total numerical value of the 22 elements of the Major Arcana, and the other gives the total numerical value of the 23 different segments of the Wheel of Life depicted in Figure 7.

Now let us take a look at these totals, read them as it were, and see if they contain any other interesting bits of information that the Cabalah may want to convey to us. Let us start with Figure 17, the God Names. The first thing that hits our eye is the total value of the Alpha numbers of all 23 elements of the Wheel of Life. It is 2,495 and it tells us that "B DIE." Now who and what is B? The letter B, being the second letter of the English alphabet, refers to the digit 2; and Tarot Key 2 of the Major Arcana is the High Priestess. Therefore, the Cabalah tells us that the total value of all 23 elements of the Wheel of Life brings death to the 2; and if we interpret the 2 as representing the second key of the Major Arcana, it is the High Priestess who dies. "Now why does the Wheel of Life bring death to the High Priestess?" you will ask.

Before we attempt to answer this question, let us return once more to Figure 4 titled a Table of Correspondences. And doesn't the reader observe something strange going on here? Figure 4 shows that the total numerical value of the original 22 letters of the Hebrew alphabet (when it was without "sin") was a very similar number. That number was 1,495 and it tells us that "A DIE." And we determined in this earlier chapter segment that the first letter of the English alphabet corresponds with Tarot Key 1, the Magician. Therefore it is the digit 1 or the Magician who dies when we interpret the Wheel of Life as representing the total value of the original Hebrew alphabet.

But it is still the same way with the modern Hebrew alphabet inasmuch as the letter Sin is represented by the Fool whose Tarot Key number is 0. Therefore, if we add 0 to 1,495 we still end up with 1,495, and the answer is the same. In this case it is the digit 1 or the Magician who dies.

This is absolutely incredible when you come to think about it. How is it possible that the Alpha numbers of the 23 God Names of the Major Arcana, when arranged on the Wheel of Life with the Fool appearing there twice (the second appearance of the Fool is really yourself, remember) will add up to match so incredibly the statement made by the total value of the Hebrew letters for these same Forces? In the former case it is the digit 2 or the High Priestess who dies; in the latter case it is the digit 1 or the Magician who dies.

But our wonderment grows even greater when we take ourselves (the second appearance of the Fool) off the Wheel of Life. The value of the Hebrew letters remains the same (1,495 − 0 = 1,495), and the statement is still made that the digit 1 or the Magician dies. But when we remove the Alpha number for this second "Fool," we are left with a different number and consequently a new statement. This new number is 2,495 − 81 = 2,414, and it spells out "B DAD (Be Dad)." In other words, the digit 1 or the Magician dies; and this digit 1 is none other than God the Father. "A DIE. Be DAD" is the statement that is made. And the word "Dad" is only another word for Father. Therefore, the digit 1 represents the Fatherhood of God.

But this is not all. Figure 17 also tells us *why* these entities or "Forces" had to die. We have only to read the total value of the Letter numbers for these God Names to find the answer. The number is 214 and it tells us that they were BAD. Therefore, being "bad," they must now ride the Wheel of Life once more in order to make amends for their previous transgressions, balance their karmic debts so to speak, and by so doing, thus free themselves from this process of death and resurrection. We find then that it doesn't seem to make any difference who they are—be they Gods, Forces, or just simply mortals as you or I— the law is the same. When one is "bad," he suffers the consequences for such wrong action; the Universal Spirit God never has and never shall show partiality. This, the Agashan Teachers have been teaching for many, many years; the Cabalah only seems to reinforce this thought for emphasis.

In summary, then, it could be said that riding the Wheel of Life could prove dangerous to your health, for whoever rides this wheel must DIE! It is also interesting to note that the digit 2 plus the digit 1 (the two numbers that must go through this process), when appearing alongside of each other, bring into manifestation the number 21. Tarot Key 21 is the World, and the English letter for this number is U. Therefore in the former case it is the World that dies, and in the latter case it is *You* who die.

But this "death" is not permanent because each entity is born again in the next cycle of the letters or turns of the wheel. The 1 follows the 0, the 2 follows the 1, the 3 follows the 2, etc. In each physical incarnation you are crucified upon the cross of matter and literally "die" as you are cast out of the astral realms. You then ride the Wheel of Life for a time, go through your experiences, learn your lessons, make amends, until eventually the soul releases its outer expression from the wheel and allows it to resume its spiritual life from whence it came.

Now let us study these tables strictly from the standpoint of the 22 keys of the Major Arcana, and leave out for the moment the 23rd element which turns them into a wheel. If we look at them in this way, other very interesting relationships will come to the surface. First, we find that the Alpha sum of the first half of the Major Arcana (Tarot Keys 1 through 11) is the reverse of the Alpha sum of all 22 keys taken as a whole. The total value of the first 11 God Names is 1,424 which reads NX; and the total value for all 22 God Names is 2,414 which reads XN. Now the philosophical impact of this strange relationship will not be understood until we unveil the true meaning of the letters X and N in a later chapter. But for the moment, let us be content with the knowledge that X + N = 24 + 14 = 38. And 38 is the Alpha number for Tarot Key 13 whose name is *Death*. (Fig. 17)

Secondly, we find that the first 14 keys of the Major Arcana contain within themselves a valuable clue to the hidden meaning of each of the 14-card suits of the Minor Arcana. How do we know this? We can ascertain it from the following very interesting relationships: The Alpha sum of the first 14 God *Names* of the Major Arcana is exactly equal to the Alpha sum of the entire 22 God *Words*. The number is 1,662. And for the hidden meaning of each of the 14-card suits of the Minor Arcana, we have only to "read" the Alpha sum of the first 14 God *Words* of the Major Arcana. The number is 1,141, and it says that these 14 cards represent "AN A." Thus we find that the 14-card suits of the Minor Arcana are in reality the "A" that dies. And that "A" that dies is the Father image of God.

This then leads us into a completely different thought. We have learned that the numerical sum of the 22 letters of the original Hebrew alphabet, and which in turn is equivalent to the 22 keys of the Major Arcana, yields the number 1,495, the translation of which is A DIE. And we have also learned that the sum of the Alpha numbers for these same 22 keys is the number 2,414 which transliterates into B DAD. Then, in addition to the Cabalistic statement that "A" dies and that he be Dad, we learned in the preceding paragraph that the sum of the first 14 keys of the Major Arcana (or a 14-card suit of the Minor Arcana) is in fact AN A. The letter "A" then becomes a pretty important element of the English Cabalah.

But what does "A" look like? Do we have an appropriate symbol and name for Him and for what He represents? Wouldn't you like to see a portrait of "A"? Then how about "B"? Who and what is "B"? And we could ask the same things regarding C, D, and E. Who are they and what do they represent? Do we actually have a Tarot Key that can identify these letters? Perhaps we do.

For an answer to these perplexing questions, let us return once again to Figure 4. The right-hand column lists the 26 letters of the English alphabet. Then, just to the left of the English letters, are the 22 God Words of the Major Arcana and the 4 Court Keys—the Page, King, Queen, Knight. One can see that there is a one-to-one correspondence between the letters of the English alphabet and these major keys of the Book of the Tarot. Both contain 26 separate and distinct elements. And this number is exactly the same as the number of the Divine Name that was in the beginning, YOD HE VAV HE (10 + 5 + 6 + 5 = 26 = GOD). These elements, then, apparently correspond with the 26 elements of GOD.

Here then is a thought: What if each one of the 26 letters of the English alphabet actually *can* be matched up with one of the 26 Tarot Keys? What if each Tarot picture symbol actually *is* a picture symbol of a letter in the English alphabet? What if each God Name actually *is* the real name of a particular letter? What *if* each of the English letters is a picture symbol representing some great philosophical or mathematical truth? What *if* our English letters are in reality only picture symbols in the same fashion as the Egyptian hieroglyphics?

Before we answer these questions, let us go to the dictionary and look up the definition of the word *hieroglyphic.* A hieroglyphic or hieroglyph (an alternate form) is a figure or symbol with a hidden meaning. It is also the picture script of the ancient Egyptian priesthood or any other writing, figures, or characters difficult to decipher. But more than that, hieroglyphics designate or pertain to a pictographic script in which many of the symbols are *conventionalized pictures of the thing represented by the words for which the symbols stand.*

We therefore have (1) the *image,* duplicate, or picture of a thing—anything, you name it, an elephant, a man, or a star. The next in order following its image is (2) its *name,* the word or words which describe the thing itself. But by far the simplest way of expressing the thought of this "thing" is by (3) its *symbol,* a conventionalized glyph or diagram drawn to represent it in the simplest possible manner. And then, of course, there is always (4) the original reality—the thing itself from which its image, name, and symbol gradually emerged.

Cannot these same rules apply to the God Consciousness? It would seem reasonable that they do. Therefore, we make the amazing presumption that the Book of the Tarot gives rise to the *images* and *names* of the elements of the God Consciousness and that the English alphabet letters are its *symbols.*

Look at the column of English letters in Figure 4 and study it as if each letter is in reality a hieroglyph—a conventionalized picture symbol representing some great mathematical or philosophical truth. Pretend, for the moment, that these letters are hieroglyphics. If you came from some other planet the Egyptian hieroglyphics would be no more mysterious to you than the English hieroglyphics.

Now look at the column of God Words just to the left of the column of English letters. These would be equally as mysterious to you if you had come from some other planet. The only thing that would be apparent would be that they are made up of various combinations of the hieroglyphic symbols that appear in the column to the right. But if this visitor from another planet had a Tarot deck in front of him, he could decipher the meaning of the God Words from the picture appearing on the card. Yet the meaning of each individual element of the word, the individual hieroglyphics as it were, would still remain a mystery.

But not for long. Our planetary visitor would in all probability be possessed of an intelligence at least equal to if not superior to our own. (This is not saying too much for our "planetary visitor," considering the state of our own intelligence at the moment, but we will let the statement stand.) You see, simply having a deck of Tarot cards with the English words and the graphic pictures depicted therein, would enable our planetary visitor to eventually decipher the meaning of the individual English hieroglyphics. "How is this possible?" you ask. It would be possible because the Tarot deck would act as his Rosetta stone (a stone slab, found in 1799 near Rosetta, bearing parallel inscriptions in Greek, Egyptian hieroglyphic, and demotic characters, making possible the decipherment of ancient Egyptian hieroglyphics).

For instance: He would first realize, as we have done, that there are the same number of English hieroglyphic symbols as there are picture symbols. And each picture symbol not only has an English name attached to it, but it also has a number that fits into a numerical sequence. Yet it would soon become apparent to our visitor that this numerical sequence of the Tarot Keys could in no way fit the same numerical sequence of the English hieroglyphics. (We will assume, for the purpose of this illustration, that he also has been given the order and the sequence of the English alphabet, although he has no knowledge of the meanings of the individual letters.) Therefore, with the knowledge of these two completely different numerical sequences, he would then feed this information into his computer and by so doing come up with the meaning of each of the English hieroglyphic characters. You say this is impossible? No, it definitely is not. In fact, it is even possible to do so using one's own innate intelligence and reasoning ability. We will prove this to the reader in the following section of this work.

Thus there is almost an infinite amount of information that our Rosetta stone—the Book of the Tarot including its fantastic tables of the God Words and the God Names—can tell us. Every name can be disected again and again and reveal an incredible amount of information about itself. And when we speak of names, we are not merely talking about the God Names (the individual Tarot Keys), but we are talking about every word and every name that exists in the English language. For, be it known to all of the readers of this book, the real meaning of any "Force" is hidden within its name. And this is not only applicable to the macrocosm—the Universe and the Gods—but it is equally as applicable to the microcosm as well. And please include your own name here also.

We might add as an afterthought, although we have no means of verifying this at the moment, that we might not even be limited to words in the English language. We have already seen how the English spelling of the letters of the Hebrew alphabet makes tremendous sense when interpreted Cabalistically, and perhaps words in other languages will work equally as well. Perhaps, in time, a Cabalah may be developed for every language on the face of the earth. Only experimentation and research in this direction will give us the answer.

In any event, we have now the tools at our disposal for matching up on a one-to-one basis each Tarot Key with its appropriate symbol—that particular letter of the English alphabet that it represents. Think of it! Along with all of the other knowledge the modern seeker of the occult now has at his disposal—and this includes the vast amount of information that has been published on the Tarot in recent years—perhaps the greatest key lies within the English language itself.

The Masters within the Spiritual Centers of the earth know these keys well. So do the Ascended Masters in the Consciousness of Immensity. They realize that the keys of the Cabalah, being based upon strict mathematical principles, also relate to the Universal Language of Vibration. They are eternal and they always shall be eternal. Therefore, they are never invented but only discovered. In fact, on numerous occasions the Master Teacher Rhebaumaus Tate told the writer, "There is nothing new under the sun. There is never any new knowledge that is passed on to mankind that had not been given to an earlier civilization either on this planet or elsewhere." This, of course, was through the trance mediumship of perhaps one of the greatest instruments of our time, Reverend Richard Zenor of the Agasha Temple of Wisdom.

But the search for the matching symbol, the correct English letter that corresponds to each Tarot Key, did not come easy— at least to this writer. In fact, it took a full seven years for the process to complete itself. I find from my notes that I started on this search very early in 1971, and it was not until February 21, 1978, that the final match was consummated. The story of this search, along with its many pitfalls and dead ends, will be the subject of Part II of this work.

NOTES

1. H. P. Blavatsky, *Isis Unveiled* (Wheaton, Ill. Theosophical Pub. House, 1950) p. vi

2. The original painting shown in Figure 15 was painted by Robert Zimmerman. It is shown in full color on the frontispiece of *The Agashan Discourses.*

PART II

THE
SEARCH

Chapter 7

MY QUEST BEGINS

ONCE I HAD become convinced that a one-to-one correspondence existed between the 26 letters of the English alphabet and the 26 keys of the Tarot (the 22 Major Arcana Keys plus the 4 Court Keys), I started out on my search in earnest. Actually, I had been interested in the Tarot for many years, but it was not until January or February of 1971 that I suddenly realized that this relationship existed. I remember one morning getting up from my chair, rushing to the drawer that housed my Book of the Tarot, and then rather excitedly removing these 26 pages or keys and laying them face up on the living room floor.

"Right there before your eyes are all of the letters from A to Z," an inner voice seemed to say to my mortal, conscious self. Absolutely enthralled, I gazed at them in wonderment with this new thought in mind. Why hadn't I thought of this before? It is all so simple. Of course, this is the answer. Just think of all the interesting stories that these magical symbols may now be able to tell! And with these thoughts, the pictures themselves seemed to awaken from their slumber as they returned my gaze with an inner, knowing smile.

121

First, I matched them up with obvious yin/yang relationships. Death and Judgement were an obvious pair, with death
on the physical plane corresponding with resurrection, birth,
and judgement on the spiritual planes. The Emperor and the
Empress were also equally as obvious as they became the
male and female, the positive and the negative, the God and
the Goddess. But in addition to these obvious pairs, the pictures also revealed other pairs of opposites not quite so obvious on the surface.

For instance: The Wheel of Fortune now very easily paired
up with Tarot Key 21, the World. Both symbols contained a
circle or an oval surrounded by the four living creatures of
Ezekiel—the man, the lion, the ox, and the eagle. Only in one,
the Wheel of Fortune, the figures are ascended; and in the
other, the World, they are as they appear on earth. Another
very interesting pair is Tarot Key 6, the Lovers, and Tarot Key
15, the Devil. Both picture symbols are almost identical, their
only difference being that they represent Man at completely
opposite ends of the spectrum. In the 15th Tarot Key Adam
and Eve, who represent you and me, are enslaved by the Devil,
their mortal mind. But in Tarot Key 6 Adam and Eve are now
free, and they are being blessed by the Angel Raphael who
symbolically represents their God mind.

In time, as one continues in his studies of the Cabalah, all of
the remaining seven other pairs of opposites will likewise be
revealed to the conscientious student, but the yin/yang relationships of some are very cleverly concealed. On that Sunday
morning the writer discovered a few more pairs, but on the
whole, the rest remained a mystery. And pairing them up was
only the beginning of my quest, the ultimate end being the
unveiling of the actual symbols themselves.

I tried to receive inspiration. I pleaded with them; I implored
them to reveal their secrets. Which letter do they belong to?
Which English letter is their symbol? I asked and I asked, I
meditated and I meditated, apparently all in vain. Today, the
letters are all so obvious to me, but then they were very mysterious. You see, at that time I did not know the true symbol-

ogy of the English alphabet—that it was in reality only picture symbols of great philosophical and mathematical truths.

Finally I had the great idea! I would simply ask the cards themselves to reveal the answer. I had used the Tarot on many other occasions for divination purposes to find the answer to a particular question, so then why not simply ask them for their symbol? But, unfortunately, most of the answers I received at the time were meaningless to me. There is a law of which I should have been aware, but in my eagerness to discern the truth I had completely forgotten it. That law, simply stated, is that nothing ever comes to a person that is not earned. Only when you have earned the right to know a particular truth, through your prior actions, do you receive the answer. Therefore, inasmuch as compensation can only come *after* an effort has been put forth, I knew I had more work to do on the physical level of life before these truths could be revealed in their entirety from the inner spiritual levels of consciousness.

The Soul Consciousness

Perhaps we can better explain this statement by defining once again the meaning of the word "soul." The Teacher Rhebaumaus Tate once told the writer, "My son, you must always remember that the soul is a *consciousness*." And a consciousness is what? The dictionary says that it is (1) the awareness of one's own existence and (2) the thoughts and feelings, collectively, of an individual or of an *aggregate* of people. Therefore, a consciousness may be said to be composed of many different entities or smaller "i's," the sum total of which is one greater "I." And this greater "I" is YOU. You are a soul, a consciousness. You are the equivalent of Los Angeles, America, or the World. Even though you outwardly consider yourself as a single entity, one individual, inwardly you may be considered to be a multitude of smaller "i's." You are the sum total of every individual that you had ever been in your many countless lives of earthly incarnations. Each of these personalities is alive within you. All of these entities make up your inner kingdom. That is your soul. That is You.

Now the emperor of this kingdom is your God Self. And your God Self is that same Spark of Divinity that left the Core of Life in the beginning and is still with you now. It resides in the very core of the soul, which in turn is located in the central portion of the human anatomy, the solar plexus. Its subjects, then, are the many countless entities that it ever had been or ever shall be on any earth plane whatsoever. But *It*, being neutral, must also have an empress, the feminine half of its being, to counterbalance its masculine aspects which are symbolized as an emperor. And when we combine the two together, the father and the mother, they are equivalent to their offspring, which is always symbolized as the child. This child of the God Self (God the Father plus God the Mother) is then God the Son who in turn has become known as the Christ. These three "Forces" then, taken as a whole, are what constitute the Trinity, and they are the rulers of your own individual soul consciousness.

We must also understand that the outer expression of this vast inner consciousness is a single entity, and that single entity is YOU. But your outer consciousness, which is You, is somehow divorced or separated from this inner consciousness of the soul. Yet they are one and the same consciousness. If you could somehow turn yourself inside-out, as if you were a sock or a paper bag, you would then *be* this vast consciousness of the soul. But then when you turn yourself outside-in again, you would then revert back to the mortal that you are today. Thus you yourself are a perfect example of the Yin/Yang principle. The Yang is the mortal since it is being acted upon by the centripetal force of gravity as it pulls the body towards the earth; and the Yin is the soul since it tends to rise after being released from the physical body at death.

Now what are you doing while you are "cast out" of the inner soul consciousness, so to speak? You are endeavoring to cleanse yourself, make amends for your previous errors, fulfill that which your soul is desirous for you to fulfill, and otherwise perfect yourself while in this *outer* consciousness so that you may be readmitted once again as a full-fledged entity of the soul's *inner* consciousness. Or at least this is what you are *supposed* to be doing.

Unfortunately, however, many individuals are simply motivating on the earth plane, living their lives aimlessly, and being motivated only by the mortal, outer consciousness. With these individuals, the connecting link with the inner consciousness of the soul could be said to be asleep. This "connecting link" is the real You; it is your Higher Self. Of course your God Self, your Spark of Divinity, is always awake and it always has been awake. It is only the Higher Self that temporarily sleeps. And with this Higher Self asleep, the real You asleep, how then can the God Self communicate with its outer, mortal consciousness? The answer is, it can't.

This then is the real reason and the main purpose of the Adepts and the Ascended Masters—the Teachers of the earth plane. These great Beings are constantly endeavoring to awaken the sleeping "higher selves" that still sleep within the souls of the masses of humanity. For until these souls are awakened sufficiently for them to realize the purpose of life, the earth cannot fully experience the new Golden Age of Peace that has been prophesied by so many sources to be practically upon us now.

Perhaps it is unfair to infer that communication with the soul consciousness is impossible while the soul's "higher self" is in a state of slumber. If this is the case, there are always many guides, helpers, relatives, or other spiritual teachers who will attempt to relay the information from the soul unto the mortal and act as the intermediary, we will say, between the two states of the soul consciousness. But here again, these guides are limited; sometimes the mortal will flatly refuse any assistance from these helpers and proceed merrily on its way towards its own destruction.

But usually those individuals who find themselves living good lives, abiding by the laws of the land, and otherwise trying to do the best that they can under the circumstances, are listening to these spirit guides and are perhaps well on their way to this "soul awakening." Then, somewhere along the spiritual path, it will happen. And when it does, the teacher or teachers assigned to a particular individual will most certainly be joyous, for they will have fulfilled their purpose and literally introduced the disciple to his own Higher Self. This is called the soul awakening, and from that point on you will act as your own intermediary—mentally, physically, and spiritually. It can then be said that the soul consciousness is indeed ONE.

But do not think that when this soul awakening finally occurs, the mortal consciousness will suddenly become illumined. Nothing could be further from the truth. It will be the Higher Self, the real You, who will go through this experience —not the mortal self. But do not be dismayed, because from that point on the soul will have taken over, and your life then will no longer be strictly your own. You will be about your Father's business, and what could be greater than that?

It was for all of these reasons, then, that I suddenly realized on that Sunday morning in early 1971 the futility of trying to "force" the Tarot cards into revealing that which I had not yet earned the right to know. The Tarot is indeed the mouthpiece of the soul, and it can be used at times in a truly incredible way *if* the soul deems the information to be given out right and proper. But it can just as easily *not* reveal the answer and keep it purposely hidden if it so desires. And this was most certainly the case insofar as the greater part of the information I had desired was concerned. I knew after a few unsuccessful tries that I simply had not yet earned the right to receive it.

You see, I had already been assigned the first part of my mission by the soul a few months earlier, and I had not yet accomplished it. In fact, I had hardly even begun. That mission was to transcribe a sufficient number of the Agashan classes so that the material contained therein could be compiled and correlated into systematic classifications and presented as an indepth study of the entire Agashan philosophy. This fact was verified during a contact with Rhebaumaus Tate on November 23, 1969—my first contact through the Zenor mediumship after an absence from the Agasha Temple for several years. However, it should be pointed out that I had never really been out of touch with this Master Teacher, as I had "tuned in" to his consciousness on many occasions down through the years, and still do to this day as a matter of fact.

The point that I am trying to make is that the English Cabalah could absolutely not have been brought through, in its entirety, until the Agashan material was first published. The one had to come before the other. This was a law set up by the soul, and neither I nor the Master Teacher could change it. A point in fact being that the final matching of the English letters with their correct Tarot Keys was not accomplished until *after* the final manuscript of *The Agashan Discourses* was in the hands of the publisher. And once this was done, a chain reaction of synchronistic events fairly forced the reversal of the Tarot Keys for the letters T and N.

It was also not particularly easy for me to concentrate my attention on completing the first two books, especially when the many varied concepts of the English Cabalah kept entering my mind with considerable regularity. Even as far back as the summer of 1971, I had convinced myself that I should stop work on compiling the material for the basic Agashan philosophy, and concentrate all of my attention on the Cabalah. It is with considerable amusement that I now read back my notes of the contact I had with Rhebaumaus Tate on August 11, 1971 (the second one since my return to the classes). There I recorded that the Teacher kept telling me, "My son, you are trying to put the cart before the horse. The Cabalah is the key to the entire Agashan philosophy, true; but it is absolutely essential that you first complete that which you have already started." What words of wisdom from this great Master Teacher! If I had not followed his advice the results would have been catastrophic; for what I then knew of the English Cabalah was almost nothing, and even what little I had discovered eventually turned out to be wrong.

Some Early Discoveries

But all of my first attempts at identification were not in vain. Certainly not! A notable exception to the many confusing answers I received when I simply asked the Tarot to reveal the true identity of each key was Tarot Key 4, the Emperor. I vividly remember shuffling the cards, concentrating on the letter A, and then asking myself to turn up the correct Tarot Key that represented this first letter of the English alphabet. And time after time I would draw the Emperor. The consistency of the draws which would match the letter A with the Emperor was absolutely incredible! All of the other letters yielded several different answers to the question regarding their identity, but with the letter A the answer was always the same —the Emperor.

It would seem that this particular Tarot Key almost became alive as I worked with the Tarot cards down through the years. I could say the same thing for each of the other keys of the Major Arcana, true, but with the Emperor it was different. When the going would get rough, and there just didn't seem to be any solution to a particular problem, it was always the Emperor who would appear and point the way towards its final solution. The answer would suddenly come to me. Of course, why didn't I think of that before? And then I would cut the deck and behold his commanding presence gazing back into my eyes, as if to signify that it was He, and He alone, who had brought me to the answer. Yes indeed, the Emperor is the true ruler of the House of Tarot.

The reader will now probably ask the question that if the Tarot did not reveal the true meaning for its symbology directly, then through what other method was this finally accomplished? In other words, what was the *modus operandi* for finding the solution to the problems? The answer to this question is that the writer simply had to learn to think—to reason intelligently, to think a problem through to its answer in much the same way that you would work out a problem in mathematics. Then, after a good deal of effort in this direction, and after going through the process of elimination whereby the various other alternate solutions were explored and then dispensed with, the final single correct solution would stand there in its naked splendor—stripped of all embellishments, and revealing the pure magnificence of the great truth it represents.

I started by working out problems on the back of napkins in

a restaurant or on a scratch tablet. Then I would go home and try to transcribe all of this data onto loose-leaf pages of a 3-ring binder. In this way I thought I could keep all of my notes in order and filed into systematic classifications. All well and good. But the truth is that by June of 1971 I had completely filled three of these large 3" binders, and all of these notes and data were in absolutely no order at all. Time just had not permitted any systematic rewriting of the material.

But I knew that these original notes had to be kept in some sort of order at least, and realizing that I would never get around to transcribing them, I embarked upon a system of recording everything on a one time basis into 8" x 11" quadrille ruled spiral bound tablets of 100 pages each. These tablets became a sort of magical diary, a place where I could doodle, work out problems, write down my thoughts, or otherwise record anything and everything that might be of interest of a cabalistic nature. This little book became my constant companion and I would take it with me wherever I would go. In this way then, I would no longer have to convert my sometimes almost illegible notes onto other pages. And everything was right there, recorded in order by dates. When one tablet was filled I went on to Tablet No. 2, and then No. 3, etc. At the date of this writing (November, 1978) I find I am working on Book No. 90, and at 100 pages each, this represents a total of 9,000 pages filled on both sides with scribbling, clippings, or attempts at solutions to cabalistic problems. These therefore are workbooks, with no attempt at neatness—just paper I used to think with. But they constitute an excellent method of recording one's thoughts, just as they are received, and keeping them intact from beginning to end.

By June of 1971 I also find that I had established the correct Tarot keys for four of the letters of the English alphabet—the A, T, S, and H. (Of course, I had tentative solutions to all of the others, but these letters were the only ones that were correct.) As a matter of interest, the Cabalah tells us that at that point of our undertaking (June 22, 1971) we were then at the Silence—AT SH. But this point did not last long, because I later erroneously matched another Tarot key for the letter T, leaving the correct interpretation of the Cabalah relegated or demoted to its lowest possible state—as an "Ash." The word *ash,* you will recall, relates to the solid residue of matter that remains when combustible material is thoroughly burned or oxidized by chemical means.

But as the months and years went by, these "ashes" then began to be transformed into spiritual wisdom. By May 28, 1973 (as an example to show how fast we were progressing in our quest for the truth), I find that we now had a total of 19 letters correctly matched with their appropriate Tarot keys. This left only 7 letters yet to be transformed through the process which I like to refer to as "spiritual alchemy." These letters, taking them in their natural numerical sequence, were the D, G, J, M, N, T, and Y. But doesn't the reader note something strange here? I did the moment I started writing them down. They may be grouped together into D GJMNT Y, and the letter Y, inasmuch as its Alpha number is 25, may also be read as BE. Therefore, the Cabalah tells us that after two years in the process, we had now arrived at the point where we were to finally understand what the "D JUDGEMENT BE." And the letter D, as you will find out a little later in this work, is the symbol for the Devil.

Very well. But just what is this "Devil Judgement"? Here again, the magical properties of the Cabalah may be used to answer our question as well as to ask it. "How does one go about doing this?" you will ask. The answer in this case is very simple. All we have to do is match up on a one-to-one basis the wrong letters we had erroneously assigned to these Tarot keys. And these "wrong" letters, taking them in the same order as the correct ones, are the M, Y, G, D, T, N, and J. These letters may be grouped together into MY GD TN J, and the astute reader will read this statement as "MY GOD, TEN J." Isn't this absolutely fascinating? It most certainly is, because the letter J is the symbol for the World. In summary then, we find that the answer to the question asked by the "correct" Tarot symbols, "The Devil Judgement be . . . ?" is answered by the "wrong"

Tarot symbols who reply saying, "My God, Ten—the World!"

This may be elaborated upon still further when we take the ten Sephiroth of the Hebrew Cabalah and the Tree of Life into consideration. Here, the missing Sephirah *Daath* (the 0 Sephirah or the Devil) is banished from its central position in the Tree of Life to the lowest possible point at the very base of the tree. This is the 10th Sephirah which is called Malkuth or the Kingdom. The Kingdom is analogous to the World or the letter J, the 10th letter of the English alphabet; but the 10th Tarot key is the Wheel of Fortune or the great Wheel of Life. Therefore, Judgement has decreed that the Devil, who is You, must once again ride this wheel and go through a series of lives on the Earth, or the Kingdom, to make amends for his previous transgressions.

Now how is it possible that the writer, in endeavoring to understand the great laws of the Tarot, could have by "chance" selected the wrong symbols for these Tarot keys at that particular time so that when interpreted cabalistically, they would make such a beautiful philosophical statement? *Chance* then has to be overruled; the errors must have been purposefully initiated by the "Force," whoever and whatever it is, that is revealing the laws of the Tarot at this time. But this is not the only instance of such a thing occurring, no indeed it is not. In fact, there isn't one of my 90 consecutive workbooks that doesn't contain literally dozens of similar "coincidences."

For instance: I would mysteriously find that the license plate of the car parked in front of me would contain within itself a key towards the solution of a particular problem I was working on at the time. Or I might find the key in an advertisement for a beer ad in a magazine, or on a receipt for a clothing purchase, or my bank account balance, or even by what people might say or do on TV. It was absolutely incredible! How could such things be that these seemingly unrelated events could be so directly related, sometimes to themselves as well as my own particular problem? (The question asked by the letters of the license plate of one passing automobile might be answered by the one immediately following it.) Was it "written" that these ships that pass in the night, these automobiles driven by perfect strangers, were in fact fulfilling a greater pattern on some larger network of understanding? It would appear so.

But investigating these situations was not without its dangers. I remember on one occasion that I was so intrigued by the relationship of the license plate numbers on the entire row of cars on the Sears parking lot, that I just *had* to get out of my car and carefully record in my notebook all of the information —license numbers, model numbers, make of car, etc.—of the other automobiles in the row. The information given by each car perfectly matched the consecutive terms of a certain mathematical series. I was shocked! But I was even more shocked when I was placed under arrest by the Sears security guard. Someone had reported that I was stealing things out of the cars.

Then on another occasion I was in a Midas muffler shop getting a new muffler installed. My car was up on the rack and so was another one to its immediate right. But this time I was really astounded, as right there on the car next to mine was the complete answer to my problem. It was just too good to be true! But the next thing I knew a large burly man had his hand on my shoulder. He exposed his badge. "What is the meaning of this?" he demanded to know. He wanted to know why I was meticulously recording his license number. I really had difficulty with that one.

Sometimes I would have a very vivid dream that would symbolically relate to some aspect of the Cabalah. But I soon found out that the actual precise time I awoke was also important. For instance: the time might be 8:59 A.M., which in turn could be translated into "HE I AM," and this would enhance the meaning still further. Thus I learned very early in this undertaking the importance of time, and I never receive the answer to a problem without always recording the exact time and date. Even the wind-up decorative clock on my living room wall mysteriously stopped one day, fully wound, with both hands in conjunction with each other and pointing to the 9 or the I. To me, this symbolizes that the two "I's," the larger "I" and the smaller "i," are for the moment one. Somehow this pleases me, and I never had the clock repaired. To this day the hands are stopped in that same position where only one hand may be seen.

But these particular "coincidences" I have described are only examples. My notebooks contain dozens and dozens of other coincidental events, some of which are almost unbelievable. For this reason, then, I meticulously pasted the "proof" in the notebook at the precise date that it occurred—the actual receipt, the theater ticket stub, the newspaper clipping, or whatever. These also include a great many "JUMBLES" (an anagram puzzle published on the second page of the classified ad section of the Los Angeles Times). It would seem that the writers of this scrambled word game, Henri Arnold and Bob Lee, were unconsciously functioning on the same wave length as the "Force" who was bringing forth the answers to the Cabalah. The words they chose to use would invariably enhance and explain more fully any major breakthrough *on the exact day* that it had occurred, and sometimes quite profoundly.

This principle of unrelated events affecting other unrelated events is not new to those involved in depth psychology or in the investigation of various aspects of consciousness. In fact, the great psychologist Dr. Carl Gustav Jung gave it a name and called it the principle of *synchronicity*, which means the *meaningful* coincidence between two or more events that are not in themselves causally connected. Even many famous writers, including Aleister Crowley, Arthur Koestler, Robert Anton Wilson, and Dr. John Lilly—just to name a few—have been absolutely astounded when they became aware of this principle in operation. And Jano Watts (Mrs. Alan Watts) has even given a name to this vast web of synchronicity that seems to connect everything-in-the-universe with everything-else-in-the-universe. She has called it "The Net," and it is most appropriately named.[1] If we read the word *Net* backwards, it becomes *Ten;* and the Alpha number for "The Net" is 72, which is the same as the word "World." And, of course, the 10th letter of the English alphabet is the letter J which is also the symbol for the World. Everything in the universe, it would seem, is in a network of tens.

So let us now then go through the letters individually, and find out more or less the basic reasons why a particular letter is the symbol for its appropriate Tarot key. Sometimes the answer is amazingly simple; and at other times it is immensely complicated. Looking at it in hindsight, they are all so obvious to me now; and it is not really understandable to my mortal consciousness why the answers were so long in coming. But it takes time for sowing and time for reaping; everything in the universe seems to have its time. And the time it takes for a rose to bloom, or for the soul to unfold, seems to occupy a definite set period. Therefore, inasmuch as Agasha has stated on many occasions that seven is the number of the soul, perhaps it is not so unusual that the full unfoldment of the symbols of the Tarot would take place over a span of seven years.

NOTES

1. Robert Anton Wilson, *Cosmic Trigger: The Final Secret of the Illuminati* (New York, Pocket Books, 1977) p. 17

Chapter 8

THE GREAT PYRAMID OF THE EMPEROR

As WE STATED in the previous chapter, the first symbol that revealed its true identity was the letter A, the first letter of the English alphabet. But now, other than just through a psychic manifestation, we must prove that the letter A does indeed represent Tarot Key 4, the Emperor. Let us refer then to the following Figure 18:

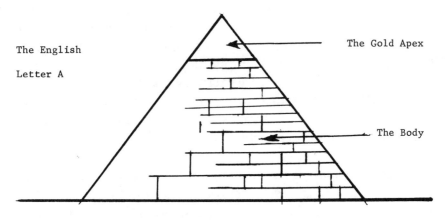

Figure 18
The Great Pyramid of the Emperor

135

One can very readily see from the above diagram that the English letter A is actually a pictograph of the Great Pyramid. But this is not so surprising when we consider the importance given the Great Pyramid in Masonic tradition, as well as the fact that it is the key symbol of the great seal of the United States of America. Look in your billfold. It even appears on the back of the one dollar bill. And this is even more significant when we realize that the English letter A, numerically speaking, is likewise equal to one.

But how do we know that the A is also the symbol for the Emperor? For an answer to this question we have to study the Alpha numbers of the words themselves. The Alpha number for "The Great Pyramid" is 170 (33 + 51 + 86). And 170 transliterates into AGO. Therefore the Great Pyramid refers to the past, to a time earlier than our present era. But this great "monument of spirituality," as the Agashan teachers so often refer to it, is the Great Pyramid of *who* or *what?* It is called the Great Pyramid of Cheops by some, and in other circles it is known as the Great Pyramid of Khufu. The writer even referred to it once as the Great Pyramid of Agasha (*Agasha: Master of Wisdom,* page 151), but that is neither here nor there. The fact remains that the Great Pyramid is the prototype or the archetype for all of the other pyramids that were later to come into manifestation; and since all of these other pyramids were tombs built for the preservation of the body of each respective king or pharaoh, it seems fitting that the prototype of all of them would simply be called the Great Pyramid of the Emperor. By using this term, we are being completely impersonal, as the word *emperor* refers to the title of the position and not necessarily to any one individual. It stands for the sovereign or supreme ruler of the land, whoever or whatever he may be.

Let us now analyze the Alpha number for this king of kings, otherwise known as "The Emperor." It is simply 123 (33 + 90), and 123 may be read as ABC. The Emperor, then, or the letter A, is very significant insofar as the simple ABC's of life are concerned. It is significant because it also represents "The God-Self

of A" (33 + 26 + 42 + 21 + 1) which is that same number—
123. And we most certainly cannot leave out the Sphinx, that
half man and half beast who stands guard by the Great Pyramid, for his number is also 123 (33 + 90). The Master Teacher
Agasha is most certainly aware of this relationship between the
Emperor (the king of men) and the Sphinx (the man/lion king
of the beasts), because he has chosen for his symbol the Sphinx
encased within the body of the Great Pyramid itself. (He is
wearing this symbol in the Keene portrait of Agasha which
appears as the frontispiece of *Agasha: Master of Wisdom*.) He
also prefaces every request for the class to sound the A-U-M
with the three words, "One . . . two . . . three. . . ."

Another proof that the true name of the Great Pyramid is
"The Great Pyramid of the Emperor" lies in the Alpha number
for the complete name itself. It is 314 (170 + 21 + 123). But
doesn't the reader notice something unusual here? The Great
Pyramid at Giza has been called in many occult circles the
"Pi" pyramid inasmuch as the ratio of its half-base with its altitude is exactly equal to Pi (the ratio of the circumference of a
circle with its diameter). Now, none of the other pyramids are
constructed in this manner. The Great Pyramid is the only one.
And the Alpha number for its name is 314—the first three digits
of the value of Pi, which is 3.14159 . . .

But this is not all. The term "of the Emperor" is likewise also
significant. The Alpha number for these three words gives us
144 (21 + 33 + 90). And 144 is twelve squared. The Alpha
number for "twelve" is 87, and it is also the Alpha number for
"the Sun," the name of the Tarot key representing the English
letter O. Therefore, the term "of the Emperor" tells us for all
practical purposes that it squares the circle (144 = "twelve"
squared = "the Sun" squared = "O" squared). And when we
come to this rather fantastic number, we know that we are at
the *end* of the cycle and that now is the time to *add* up all of its
constituent parts. How do we know this? We know this because we are able to read. (144 = ND or "end," and 144 also
= ADD). Then when we follow the instructions of the
Cabalah to add the digits of the number 144 together, we end

up with the number 9 or the "I." Thus we find out that the terms "of the Emperor," or "of the God-Self of A," or any other phrase which adds up to the number 144, relate to the inner "I" that lies within.

The Court Letters: K, Q, P, and L

Now let us leave the letter A for the moment and move on to the corresponding letters for the four Court Keys: The King, the Queen, the Page, and the Knight. Actually, these particular symbols unveiled their secrets rather easily once we came into the possession of the master key which unlocked all of the doors to the mysteries of their being. And this master key, strangely enough, has been known for centuries by all of those who have studied the game of chess. But, as in everything else in life, sometimes the most profound secrets are well concealed simply because they are so obvious. The following Figure 19 will demonstrate what we mean.

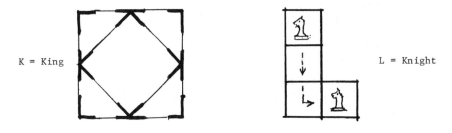

Figure 19
The King and the Knight

The master key, of course, is revealed when one studies the movements of the various chess pieces, especially the Knight. His move is always two squares vertically plus one horizontally, or one vertically and then two horizontally. It is either a 1-2 or a 2-1 and it is always "L" shaped. And the final clue that the symbol for the Knight is the letter L is the 1-2 move. 1-2 gives us 12, and the letter L is the 12th letter of the English alphabet.

The King's move is equally as instructive, although not quite as obvious. He may move only one square at a time, but this movement can be in any direction he so chooses—vertically, horizontally, or diagonally. All possible movements of both the King and the Knight are illustrated in the left-hand diagram of Figure 19. This diagram also reveals the necessity for the four suits of the Minor Arcana, for without four suits we would be unable to bring into manifestation the square within the square or the pyramid within the pyramid.

Now let us take a look at the Queen and the Page. One can see by the following diagram that these two chess pieces (the Page plays the role of the lowly pawn or foot soldier) are also very closely related. They are, in fact, complementary to each other. But this is as it should be because the Page, being the child of the Queen, may advance to the opposite end of the chessboard; and if he so succeeds in this accomplishment, he then is "knighted" and becomes as powerful a force as the Queen herself.

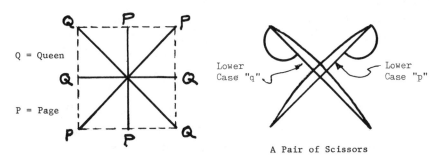

Figure 20
The Queen and the Page

The clue that we were to arrange the Page and the Queen in the order that they are shown in Figure 20 was given by the lower case forms of the leters P and Q (p, q). When connected at the center and placed back to back, these letters literally bring into manifestation a pair of scissors and may be used accordingly. In the Cabalah, two of the suits of the Minor

Arcana are the *movers* and the other two are the *moved*. The more powerful suits initiate the force, and the weaker suits react to it. In fact, the action is exactly the same as that of a pair of scissors. Therefore the symbol of the scissors is a perfect symbol for these two elements of the Cabalah. It illustrates very vividly that if we don't mind our p's and q's (be careful with our manners, behavior, or conduct), we most certainly will feel the cutting edge of the scissors as our higher "p" and "q" (our conscience) punishes us for our wrong actions.

Common sense also dictated that the Page and the Queen should be placed in the way that they are shown, rather than placing all of the Pages in the inner location and the Queens in the outer, or vice versa. For if this were the case, the Knights could never marry (be in conjunction with) a Queen, and the Kings could never have a Page or a son. Or it would be the other way around. There could be absolutely no way for any "intrigues" to develop within the kingdom, and life would become rather monotonous.

But by far the most positive proof that they are placed correctly comes about when we take their Alpha numbers into consideration. The Alpha number for "The Page" is 62 (33 + 29); and the Alpha number for "The Queen" is 95 (33 + 62). Now the circle of the outer square is composed of two Pages and two Queens; and the circle of the inner square is likewise the same. And when we compute the total Alpha number for these "circles," we find that it amazingly adds up to Pi or 314 (62 + 95 + 62 + 95). Another very interesting relationship between the Page and the Queen, and another reason for their complementary positions, is shown when we compare the God Name of the one with the God Word of the other. They both are the same. The Alpha number for "The Page" is identical with the Alpha number for "Queen." They both are 62, and this illustrates quite vividly the equality between the mother and her child.

There are still three other letters that are directly related to the base square of the pyramid, and we cannot go on to other aspects of the Cabalah until we dispense with them. They are the letters Z and N, which complement each other in a most remarkable manner, and the letter X. The latter is perhaps one of the most interesting letters of the entire alphabet, both philosophically as well as symbolically, for the very reason that it has so many meanings. But before we proceed with the identification of these letters, a little background material is in order.

A Lesson in Zen

Many years ago during one of the Agashan classes, the writer was presented with a vision from the soul. It was extremely clear and in technicolor; and it came to me in full waking consciousness while Agasha was lecturing. The vision consisted of six pyramids, laid out in two rows of three each and touching one another. They appeared to be of solid gold. And looking down on them from above was the face of a man whom I presumed to be God. I have puzzled over the meaning of this vision for many years, but perhaps Figure 21 will finally explain it.

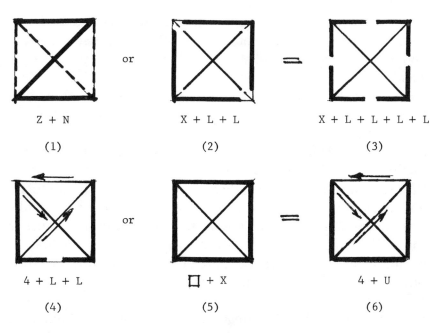

Figure 21
Zen Excels Ex-ells

This particular diagram seemed to come into manifestation through the process of evolution. It started out to be a simple explanation of the relationship of the letter Z with the letter N; but then it just grew and grew and grew, until we eventually ended up with six figures, representing pyramids, and being built up of every possible combination of symbols. It was only when I finally had it complete that I suddenly remembered this vision out of the past, and then the whole impact of it hit me like a ton of bricks. Of course, this is what I had unknowingly (to my outer mind) reconstructed! There is quite a story to tell with this little pictograph, and we hope the reader will enjoy it. Actually, all six figures are intended to be identical; the lines have been accentuated only to reveal the identity of the symbols hidden therein. We have given it the title "Zen Excels Ex-ells" because that is just what the first row says when it is read cabalistically. (The word "ex-ells" refers to former ells (L's) or Knights of the past.)

Diagram (1) constructs the pyramid with the letters Z and N and it spells "Zen." Now what is Zen? The dictionary defines the term as a form of Buddhism which attempts to bring enlightenment to the student by the most direct possible means, and which accepts formal studies only when they are a part of such means. In other words, through the practice of Zen, enlightenment comes from direct intuition by means of meditation. The writer is forced to acknowledge that this definition certainly seems to be true, and it evidently works—this book being the proof. In fact, on second thought, this seems to be the method that Agasha has been using in his classes down through the years. He has always said he comes to stimulate and awaken the soul to the point where the soul will then take over and enhance his teachings even further. And since most of the students found themselves in a deep state of meditation during at least a substantial part of his talks (some say they were asleep), this seems to be the method he was using.

Diagram (2) constructs the pyramid with the letter X plus two L's, and Diagram (3) constructs it with the letter X and four L's. The Alpha number for the former is 48 or "Fool" (Tarot Key 0); the Alpha number for the latter is 72 or "World" (Tarot

Key 21). Therefore, the first row of figures also states that Zen "fools" the World of these former Knights (ex-ells). But we may also read the statement backwards by saying that the World likewise "fools" or excels Zen. And if this be the case, these former Knights or ex-ells will in all probability accomplish this feat by means of judo. (Judo is a Japanese sport which makes use of quick movement and leverage to throw an opponent.)

Why do we use the word *judo?* We use it because that is the word that is brought into manifestation when we read the sentence backwards. The symbol for "World" is the letter J, and the symbol for "Fool" is the letter U. The Alpha number for "Z + N" is 40, and inasmuch as this number is not a specific God Name or God Word with a specific symbol attached to it, we must read it as DO. Therefore, the Cabalah tells us that these former Knights must use the martial art of JUDO if they are to "fool" or excel over Zen.

Now let us move on to the second row of Figure 21. Diagram (4) constructs the pyramid with the figure 4 plus two L's (making the L's plural), and we read it as "Four ells." Diagram (5) encloses the X in a square, and Diagram (6) builds the pyramid with the figure 4 and the letter U. Thus we read the entire statement as "Four ells square X for you"—which is true. Four L's do indeed make a square around the X. But this row, like the first row, can also be read backwards. And there is no law requiring us to keep it in the present tense. Reading it in the past tense then, and reversing the order, we find out that the "Four" you has now *squared* X for ells.

Now who and what is this "Four" you? It is simply the fourth letter of the English alphabet, the letter D, and it relates to the Devil. It is your lower self, your demon self, the challenging factor; and it is the one who puts you into all of the predicaments that you have to work out of. The Alpha number of its God Name (The Devil) is 85, and it is read as HE. The Alpha number of its God Word (Devil) is 52, and this number is exactly twice the Alpha number for God which is 26. If we were to read it backwards, we would have the verb BE.

This "Devil" then is the lower self of the mortal who is You. Your middle self, or your dense self as it is sometimes called, is the Fool (Tarot Key 0). Its symbol is the letter U. The Alpha number of its God Name (The Fool) is 81; and the Alpha number of its God Word (Fool) is 48.

This leaves only your higher self to be unveiled. This higher self is your own personal Christ—the Christ that lies within. In his highest expression he is represented by the Tarot key called *Judgement*, whose symbol is the letter X. However, this "Christ light" manifests through a series of higher selves, the most immediate one above the Fool being the Knight or the letter L. The Knight is also the reverse of the Fool because L equals 12 and U equals 21; and the unification of the Knight with the Fool can be expressed by U + L = Yule, which means Christmas or the Christ mass. U + L also means to u-nite (U-Knight). Therefore, the combination of U and L means to be united in Christ. The relationship of these various "selves" is not a haphazard one. They exist in a very definite numerical order, the general idea of which is expressed below:

		Name		Symbol	
Higher Self	Christ	77	Death	38
Delta		+ 4		– 17
Middle Self	The Fool	81	U	21
Delta		+ 4		– 17
Lower Self	The Devil	85	D	4

Thus we find that the death of Christ brings the higher self into manifestation. In the instance of the Fool, the higher self becomes one of the four Knights or the letter L. "Why is it this particular letter?" you will ask. The answer is clearly seen when all 26 letters of the English alphabet are placed on the rim of a wheel as in Figure 22.

The 0 symbol on the Tarot key for the Fool is no accident, for it is intended to denote the 0 or the starting point from which he begins his journey around the Wheel of Life—either clockwise in the direction of time or anti-clockwise backwards in time. 17 steps in one direction will take the Fool to his lower self or the Devil. 17 steps in the opposite direction will bring into manifestation his immediate higher self or the Knight. It will

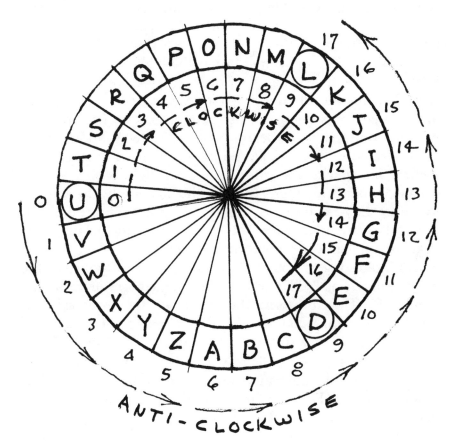

Figure 22
The Letters on the Rim of the Wheel

be seen that all three selves—the higher self, the lower self, and the middle self—divide the wheel into approximately three equal parts, and that each complete revolution of the wheel goes through all of the letters from A to Z. Therefore, it is not necessary to laboriously count the steps around the wheel to determine the letter symbol for any particular number. The remainder left after dividing by multiples of 26 will always give the correct answer. For instance: 38 − 26 = 12 = L, and if the number were a larger number such as 273, the answer would be 273/26 = 10 revolutions with 13 steps remaining into the 11th revolution. This would leave us at the number 13 or the letter M. The letter M, incidentally, is also the symbol for the Tarot key for *Death.*

Now if the death of Christ brings the higher self into manifestation, what then brings the Christ light itself into manifestation? The answer, of course, is the resurrection of Christ. We are not a complete being without both phases of these phenomena within us. Thus the death of Christ is always followed by his resurrection. His resurrection is symbolized by the Tarot key for *Judgement,* the letter X, but his *Light* is still with us even in death. It manifests through the higher self, the Knight, the letter L. And bringing them both into conjunction with each other, by adding the X to the L, we find that we once again "excel the ex-ell" (the former Knight).

It is interesting to note that all four aspects of yourself, the entity known as YOU, when added together equate to the number 61. The Christ self, the higher self, the lower self, and the middle self all equal 61. ($X + L + D + U = 24 + 12 + 4 + 21 = 61$) But 61 is also the Alpha number for "You." Therefore, we may say that YOU = XLD + U, or that You excelled U. In other words, the entity called *You* excelled the Fool; but inasmuch as the Fool is none other than your dense self, we may say that you excelled yourself.

Let us return once more to the second row of Figure 21 and analyze it in the light of what we have just learned. Superficially, from left to right it reads, "Four L's square X for you"; and then reversing the direction we read, "(4U) squared X for L's." All well and good. But what else is this series of three symbols telling us? If we dig a little deeper into the interpretation of the center symbol, Diagram (5), we may add even a further dimension to our little lesson in Zen.

First, we must remember that a *square* X is entirely different from a *squared* X. The Alpha number for "square" is 81 or the Fool; and the Alpha number for "squared" is 85 or the Devil. We can see then that by just adding a 4 to the Fool turns him into the Devil in the same way that subtracting a 4 from the Fool turns him into a Christ. Thus this Fool, who is really a "square" (one who is ignorant of or uninterested in current fads, ideas, or manners—in other words a conformer, a conventionalist) is literally "square-d" and transformed into the Devil when the D is added to his name. (4 + 81 = 85 = The Devil = D). Therefore this D, who is the Devil, is really nothing more than a 4U. But "a 4U" is the Devil in more ways than one since "a 4U" also equals 85. (1 + 4 × 21 = 85 = The Devil = D).

Secondly, a "squared X" is likewise a spell or a *hex*, since the Alpha number for "squared" is 85 or HE, and when we add X to it we have the word HEX. But a "square X" becomes a weapon or *each ax* when we treat it in the same fashion. (81 + X = HAX = H AX = Each Ax). Therefore the Knight, being the instrument of the higher self, is given a weapon to fight this "hex" from the lower self.

The whole story from beginning to end is dramatized in the following bit of epic verse:

> (4U) hex four L's
> Four L's each ax (4U)
> (4U) squared X for L's
> Four L's square X for You.

Thus Figure 21 gives us an excellent example of the principle of Zen in that it graphically illustrates the ever continuing battle between good and evil and its ultimate reward and punishment. The action is always to and fro, back and forth, first from the right and then from the left, over and over again, in much the same manner as the pendulum of a clock. The initial wrong action is followed by the punishment. Then comes the redemption in the form of right action, and this new right action brings about its ultimate reward. It is always the same story—first the one, then the two, then the three, and finally the four. The completion of these four elements brings into manifestation the decade or the ten (1 + 2 + 3 + 4 = 10), and the cycle is ready to begin all over again with the one.

For instance: it may be assumed that way back in the far reaches of time the Devil, being a 4U, put a *hex* on the four

Knights (the four L's) and cast an evil spell over them. Then, in retaliation to this wrong action by the Devil, the four Knights, each one of them, proceeded to give the "ax" to the 4U or the Devil. (To *ax* an opponent means to shape, dress, remove, kill, or curtail him.) Ultimately the Devil, having been properly chastised by the Knights, is able to make amends by being put to the labor of squaring the X for the Knights. Eventually his karma is paid, and now the four Knights square the X for You.

"But what is so important about squaring the X?" you will ask. "What is really meant by this term?" The answer is that squaring the X means to put a square around it, and the reader will see for himself in the following chapter segment why this action of enclosing the X in a square becomes so all-important. It illustrates an extremely important principle, not only insofar as it relates to you and me, but even to the Universe itself.

The Cohesive Force of the Base Letters Z, N, and X

Let us say that you wished to construct a pyramid, but the only building blocks that were available were millions of small balls or spheres. Their size would not make any difference as long as they all were the same. They might be basketballs, baseballs, billiard balls, or whatever. Let us say that they are ping-pong balls because of their small size and ability to stick to one another with the aid of an adhesive.

But you would soon find out that you would not need any other adhesive because the force of gravity would do all of this for you, keep them all packed tightly together, if—and this is a very big if—you had first secured the *outer perimeter* of the bottom layer of spheres very tightly together with a strong adhesive. The accompanying figure will illustrate what we mean.

One can very readily see from Figure 23 that three exterior forces are absolutely necessary to keep our pyramid of spheres intact—gravitation, a rack, and a base. Remove any one of them, and you no longer have a pyramid. For instance: without the aid of the bottom rack, just imagine yourself constructing a pyramid of ping-pong balls. Imagine it if you can. (Of course, we are assuming the base to be a very smooth and frictionless surface, much the same as a glass table top.) Conse-

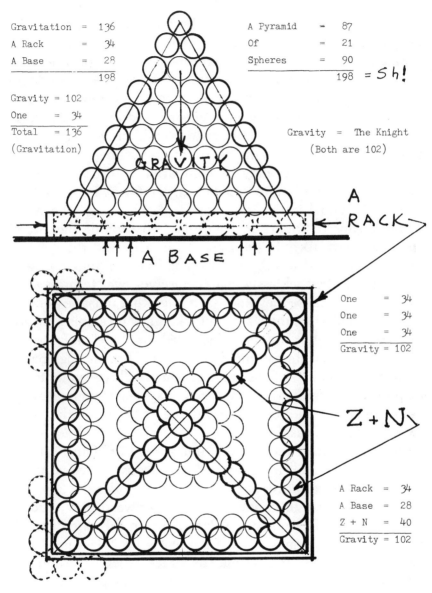

Figure 23
A Pyramid of Spheres

quently, all three of these forces are absolutely necessary in order to furnish the cohesive "glue" that holds our pyramid intact.

Now let us suddenly remove the rack or the base from our pyramid and what happens? In the twinkling of an eye the pyramid would collapse, and every solitary one of the millions of ping-pong balls that had heretofore been held together very securely, would now go bouncing off in every possible direction. Instead of the magnificent order that had previously prevailed, with each ball being snugly packed and touching its twelve companions, now utter chaos would prevail. The pyramid therefore represents the beautiful crystalline solid state of matter, and the latter may be compared to its gaseous state with atoms and molecules flying off in every way imaginable.

Now do you see the importance of "squaring" the X? It simply means to square the pyramid—to provide the lateral force necessary to hold the pyramid intact. And the Knights who normally perform this function do so out of purely unselfish motives. They selflessly give themselves over to preserving the pyramid because they know it is a job that must be done. It could be said that they are truly knights in shining *armor* because it is a labor of *love*. (The word for "love" in French is *amour* which is almost the same as the British spelling of "armor" or *armour*). Thus these knights of "love" voluntarily support *your* pyramid so that you may learn your lessons, make amends, and by so doing be in a position to be "knighted" and be as they.

But in the case of the Z and N (Diagram 1 of Figure 21), the rack is entirely built-in and no other cohesive force is necessary, with the exception of the X which provides the upwards thrust of the base to counteract the downward gravitational forces of the ZN combination. However, in the case of the X acting alone (Diagrams 2, 3, and 5 of Figure 21), it needs the four Knights (the four L's) to act as a rack as well as—and this is most important—the downward push of the pyramid itself, the letter A, to resist the upward thrust of the X. One can see then that all five of these letters, taken as a whole, are what constitute the cohesive forces of matter which react together to build form. They are the A, X, L, Z, and N (the Axle's N), and their Alpha number can be equated to Christ. $(1 + 24 + 12 + 26 + 14 = 77 = Christ)$.

Moving back to Figure 23 again, we find that it also points out the almost reciprocal relationship existing between the complex of gravitational forces and those exhibited by the Knight. For instance: the Knight moves in a "One One—One" fashion, or two steps up and one sideways. But so does the force of gravity insofar as its reaction on the ping-pong balls is concerned. (A gravitational force of $\sqrt{3}$ acting vertically is transposed into a slant edge component of 2 and a horizontal component of 1.) And the Alpha number for all three terms is the same number. "One One—One" equals "The Knight" which in turn equals the word "Gravity" or 102. But this is not all. The word "Gravitation" adds another *One* to the series making it equal to "One One One One" or the number 136.

Are you still skeptical or do you want some more proof? Since the term "The Knight" is composed of two words, one wonders what would happen to the word "Gravity" if it were broken apart accordingly—that is, breaking it into two words with the Alpha numbers of 33 and 69 respectively. We can very easily do this and we end up with "Gay Rvit." Have we lost our meaning? No. In fact, we have even enhanced it further to the point where the word "Gravity" might be revealing some of its hidden secrets. The word "Rvit" obviously should be read as *Rivit*, a word Webster defines as something that "attracts and holds completely." And isn't this just what the term *gravity* implies? But the word "Gay" staggers our imagination! *Gay* relates to a homosexual force, a male force as well as a female force, a positive force as well as a negative force. Therefore, the Cabalah infers that gravity works both ways—as a positive, masculine force of attraction, and as a negative, feminine force of repulsion. Perhaps we may eventually be able to reverse the polarity of the force of gravity—make it "Gay" as it were—and by so doing, be able to not only levitate objects into the air, but perhaps even let them "fall" away from the earth towards some distant planet or star. Harnessing these anti-gravitational energies may indeed be the secret for space travel in the future.

Let us move on now to Figure 24 where we will investigate how the Knights combat the *ills* of the World.

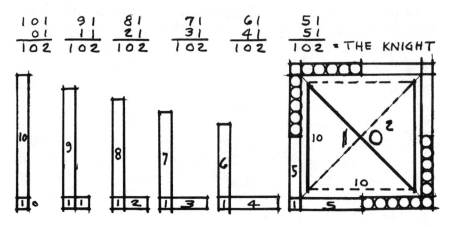

Figure 24
The Knights Combat the ILLS of the World

The reader undoubtedly noticed that our pyramid of spheres that we constructed in Figure 23 was built of ten successive layers or planes, one above the other. Actually the pyramid could have been built of any number of planes, the ten being chosen only to illustrate the principle involved. But no matter what the number, the base plane *must* contain an outer perimeter of spheres, tightly welded together, to act as a rack to resist the lateral forces imposed by the pyramid itself. The length of a side of the rack then is always two more than the length of the side of the base plane of the pyramid. In this case the rack length is 12 and the base length of the pyramid is 10.

One can see that there are several possibilities for the shape of the Knights or the L's at each corner of the rack. However, no matter what the ratio of the lengths of its legs actually is, the total length of the legs of each possible L is always a fixed constant. In the case of our example, it is a 102, which stands for the Knight. The square of the base plane of the pyramid is 100 which can be written as $(10)^2$. Here again is the number 102. And the length of the rack is 12, which is also the number for L, or the Knight. In each and every case, the power that the Knights are able to muster equates to the Alpha number for the word "Gravity." Doesn't it seem that the Cabalah is trying to tell us something?

Let us add up the total of all of the spheres in our pyramid. In this case, it is $1^2 + 2^2 + 3^2 + 4^2 + 5^2 + 6^2 + 7^2 + 8^2 + 9^2 + 10^2$, the sum of which is 385. Therefore there are 385 spheres in our pyramid. Now this is a very significant figure because through a little Cabalistic magic it can be transformed into the Emperor himself. "How do we go about doing this?" you will ask. For an answer to this question, let us move on to Figure 25 and embrace the mysteries of *Vesica Piscis*.

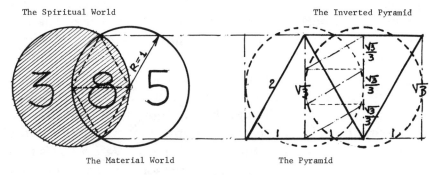

Figure 25
Vesica Piscis: The Merging of the Worlds

Vesica Piscis has been respected since the dawn of history as a symbol of the sacred marriage of the spiritual world of essences with the material world of phenomena. This "vessel of the fish," as it is often called, is brought into manifestation by the interpenetration of two circles of equal size, the center of each lying on the circumference of the other. The orifice so formed is considered to be the womb from which all of the numbers and ratios of King Solomon's Temple are generated. It has often been referred to as an emblem of Christ.

The Alpha number for "Vesica" is 59 which means "The God" (33 + 26 = 59). The Alpha number for "Piscis" is 75, a cabalistic number for "The Self" (33 + 42 = 75). And when we combine the two into one—add the God to the Self, so to speak —we end up with the term *Vesica Piscis* whose number/symbol is 134 or MD. This combination of the letter M with the letter D is perhaps one of the most significant combinations of the entire Cabalah in that it literally brings Death to the Devil. (M is the letter/symbol for "Death" and D is the letter/symbol for "The Devil.")

We learned a few pages back that our lower self is represented by the Devil, the letter D, Tarot Key 15. This is the self that gets us into all kinds of trouble—the demon self, the monster self. And he will continue to get us into trouble until we chastise him, tie him up, throw him into prison, or even put him to death. But the laws of the Cabalah state that we never can really "kill" anything, because the death of something only results in its resurrection on a different plane of life. There is not one thing in life that is really not immortal in the final analysis.

Very well. Let us say that we chastise the Devil—that is a better word—and by so doing, make him harmless. But how do we go about doing this? Rather we should ask how does the soul bring this about, because it is the soul who initiates the action. The answer is that it puts the laws of *Vesica Piscis* into operation by setting the sphere of its spiritual consciousness into a collision course with the sphere of its material consciousness. The sphere of Vesica is the God sphere, the inner sphere, the spiritual world of essences, and its symbol is the letter M. This is the force known as Death, Tarot Key 13, and whose Alpha number is 38. The sphere of Piscis relates to the Self, the outer sphere, the material world of phenomena, and its symbol is the letter D. This is the Devil, Tarot Key 15, whose Alpha number is 85.

Eventually they will meet. Figure 25 shows both spheres half way interpenetrated, thus bringing into manifestation the inner orifice or the vessel of the fish. Its number is 88, but in the diagram one of the 8's is hidden behind the other one. It is still there, nonetheless. This represents Christ the King (Christ = 77, and 11 which stands for K or King). Two equilateral triangles may also be constructed within this orifice, thus giving rise to two pyramids, one the inverse of the other. It is interesting to note that the Tarot numbers for M and D add up to 28 which is the Alpha number for Man (13 + 15 = 28 = Man).

But we are not yet complete; there is still more work to be

done. The process will continue until both spheres are merged together into one. Then at this point the Great Work will be finished, with the material and spiritual consciousnesses now joined together into the great Oneness. And what is this state? We simply add together the Alpha number for both spheres and we have the answer. It is none other than the Emperor himself, the number 123, the letter A (38 + 85 = 123). Thus our lower self, the Devil, has now met his "death" and his consciousness has been miraculously transformed into a part of the great God Consciousness of the Emperor.

But what about the 44 remaining spheres that represent the four Knights, the four L's that enclose the 10th plane of the base and act as a rack to support the whole? This number 44 is also the Alpha number for *Space*, incidentally. And in the same way that the 385 spheres that go on to make up the body of the pyramid can be transformed into the Emperor, these 44 spheres can be transformed into the Great Pyramid itself. How do we do this? We simply do the reverse of what we had done previously. The number 44 = DD, and since D is the symbol for the Devil whose Alpha number is 85, we add these two D's together and we end up with 170 (85 + 85 = 170 = AGO). And 170, you will remember, is the Alpha number for "The Great Pyramid." Therefore in our little diagram we have reconstructed the Great Pyramid of the Emperor.

One can readily see from this little exercise how important *all* of the keys of the Cabalah actually are. It is just as Agasha has said so many times, "Every solitary atom is as necessary to the Universe as the Universe is to itself." But on the other hand, it was absolutely essential that the Devil should "die" so that the Emperor may live.

The Resurrectional Powers of the Apex Letters Z, N, and X

Let us now take a brief look at the Hanged Man (Tarot Key 12). Who is this man who is hanging upside down on the Tree of Life? This card has been an enigma to students of the Tarot down through the centuries ever since the Tarot was first rediscovered in our modern era, but let us see if we can find an explanation for his predicament. "How do we do this?" you ask. The answer is to simply analyze the God Name for that particular Tarot key. It consists of three words: The Hanged Man. Its Alpha number is 33 + 39 + 28 = 100.

Our first clue as to his identity lies in the number 100. This number is ten squared (10^2), and it represents the area of a square whose side is equal to 10. This in itself is not too much to go on until we also analyze the word "hanged," and it is here where we make our first real breakthrough, for it emphasizes again the importance of the 10. The Alpha number for "hanged" is 39 which is identical with the Alpha number for "ten." Therefore, we could just as easily call Tarot Key 12 by its other name which is "The Ten Man." Even the Alpha number for "The Hanged," the first two words of its name, tells us the same story. That number is 33 + 39 or 72, which is the number for "World," the letter J, the 10th letter of the English alphabet.

But who is this man, really? The second clue to his identity is given by the first and last words of his name when combined together and read as a unit. These words are "The Man," and their Alpha number is 33 + 28 or 61. But 61 is also the Alpha number for "You"; therefore, when we speak of "The Man" independently, we are referring to *You*. But we do not find out who "you" really are until we complete our analysis and treat the second and third words of his name in the same fashion. The Alpha number for "Hanged Man" is 39 + 28 or 67; and inasmuch as this number is also the Alpha number for "Soul," we find then that the Hanged Man, the Ten Man as it were, is none other than the Soul itself.

Therefore *You* are the man who is suspended upside down on the Tree of Life; but this man is not your outer self, for that "you" is the Fool. Nor is he your lower self, otherwise known as the Devil; nor is he your immediate higher self, called the Knight. This man that is suspended therein is all of these selves and more; for he is the ten man, the complete man, the perfect man. He is all of the other selves rolled into one, for he represents the vast consciousness of the Soul.

"But why is he depicted hanging upside down on a 'T' cross?"

you will ask. The answer is that his outer self, or his body, is being tempered upon the cross of matter so that it too may become perfect "even as the Father in Heaven is perfect." One will note that there is a nimbus or a circle of radiant light drawn around the head of the Hanged Man, indicating that his inner consciousness, or his mind, is in a state of perfection. It is only his body, his outer self, that is being perfected.

"But why is he upside down?" you persist. For an answer to this question we must refer once again to the symbol of *Vesica Piscis* and the two triangles contained within it. Only to understand the symbol in its entirety, we must conceive of these triangles as representing two pyramids, each with its golden apex, and each being constructed as the inverse of the other. The following Figure 26 will present this idea a little more clearly:

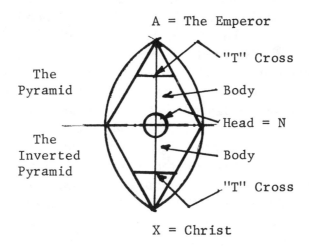

Figure 26: The Symbology of the Hanged Man

Now then: If the Hanged Man is in reality the *Ten* Man, the Man whose Alpha number is $(10)^2$, it would be logical to assume that he represents the base plane of the pyramid of spheres we constructed a little earlier in Figure 23. And this seems especially so when we take his Tarot key number into consideration. This is 12—the number of spheres necessary to form the outer edge of a base plane of 10 including the two extra spheres necessary to form a rack. (If we did not have these two extra spheres, the pyramid would collapse.)

But the thing that must be pointed out is that it is only the Hanged Man's *consciousness* that exists on the 10th plane of the pyramid. This is clearly shown to be the case because only the head has a nimbus around it. And the head symbolizes mind or consciousness. Therefore the rest of his body, inasmuch as it is not enclosed in light, must be assumed to represent other selves, or other states of consciousness.

The next step in our attempt to understand the reason for the Hanged Man's predicament is for the reader to place alongside Figure 26 the actual Tarot key itself. Right in the center of the base plane of the upper pyramid, visualize his head. The bottom line of the apex will then bring into manfestation the top of the "T" cross upon which he is hung. So there you have it: the Hanged Man depicted in the upper half of *Vesica Piscis*, the vessel of the fish. This is the Soul, with all of its various "selves" strung out upon the Tree of Life and extending downwards from the apex of the pyramid all the way to its base.

The question can now be asked that if the 10th plane represents the head of the Hanged Man, what plane is it that constitutes the crossbar of the "T" cross? Here again, we believe the Hanged Man is telling us the answer. If you will take this Tarot key, turn it upside down, and then place it in front of a mirror, what do you see? You will see that his two legs are crossed in the shape of the figure 4. But more than that, his right leg is pointing to and practically touching the crossbar of the "T." Therefore, we may assume that the crossbar of the "T," the bottom line of the apex of our pyramid, represents the 4th plane in our pyramid of spheres. And the numeral 4, indeed, is the number to labor under. The body of the Hanged Man could then be said to exist on the 5th, 6th, 7th, 8th, and 9th planes; and his head would represent the 10th. It is interesting to note that the apex of the pyramid has the same power as its base, inasmuch as it also is a 10 $(1 + 2 + 3 + 4 = 10)$.

The horizontal line through the center of *Vesica Piscis* may be said to represent the ground line that separates the earth from the sky. Therefore the lower pyramid is the dense, material world of the earth; and the upper pyramid is the ethereal, spiritual world of the heavens. The Tree of Life then towers into the sky above while its roots burrow ever so deeply within the rich soil of the earth below. And the Hanged Man, in his normal position, depicts the Soul of Mankind falling to earth from his previous high estate.

Very well. But one can very readily ascertain from a study of the diagram that if the Soul of Man continues in this downward direction, it is destined to end up deep within the bowels of the earth, separated from the light of the sun, and confined to the stygian darkness of the vast regions of the underworld known as Hades. In other words, it will end up in Hell.

So then what is to be done? The answer is that the Soul of Man must now reverse its downward flight, aspire to the higher, and by so doing ascend once more back into the worlds of Spirit from which it had fallen. But how does it do this? The answer is simple. You can do it right now and be your own Savior. Just pick up the Hanged Man card which represents your Soul, turn the poor man right-side up again, and through this symbolic gesture be on your way to becoming a great Pillar of Light.

Have you done it? Ha, ha. I caught you. You have just sold your Soul to the Devil and there is a price you must pay for your action. Look at the card again with the Hanged Man now right-side up, and visualize him occupying the lower pyramid of Figure 26, but with his head in exactly the same location as before. Now where is your Soul? The answer is that its body is now confined to Hell. The Devil has it in his grasp. Only the head remains in the light and above the surface of the earth. Before you made that fatal step your body was bathed in the sunlight of God, completely safe from being plunged into the darkness of Hades. How was it safe? Just look at the figure. You made a fatal blunder. You forgot to notice that it was safely tied to the crossbar of the "T" cross, and as long as that rope held, you would have been safe and secure from the clutches of the Devil, that monster known as your lower self.

Thus you must now pay the penalty for your action and be

as Atlas, that ancient Titan giant who for his part in the Titans' revolt against the Olympian gods was sentenced to support the Heavens upon his head and shoulders. You can see for yourself by just looking at the diagram that this is the price your Soul must pay, for the former "hanged man" is now in Hell and has a very heavy burden to bear. Even the figure itself has his shoulders outstretched as if to alleviate and remove the entire weight of the upper pyramid solely from his head and onto his shoulders. And escape is out of the question, since the rope that ties him to the base of the cross is very secure.

But you are the one who placed your Soul there, and therefore you are the one who must pay the consequences. But all is not as bad as it seems. Think of yourself as performing the complementary function to the Knight, your higher self, who counteracts the lateral thrust from the weight of the pyramid. Therefore, for a while you must counteract the vertical gravitational force of the pyramid in much the same manner that your lower self, the Devil, usually performs his function.

One can see, then, that without your lower and higher selves acting as a team, and furnishing the necessary reactions to the gravitational forces, the higher pyramid that constitutes your etheric consciousness would soon collapse and be no more. Indeed, all of the unlearned souls in the underworld are pushing up against and helping to support the entire weight of the Earth's etheric world. It is as the old saying goes: For every action, there must be an equal and opposite reaction.

But fear not. There is a way out of your predicament. All is not yet lost. If your lower self, the Devil, can get you into it through trickery, your Christ self can get you out of it through your own efforts. One must remember that in the same way the God self, the Emperor, sends power downwards from the upper apex of the pyramid to the Soul when it is on the "T" cross above the surface of the earth, so does the Christ self send power upwards from the lower apex to all of the souls motivating about and crying out for help in the underworld regions of Hades below the Earth's surface. So then help is to be had no matter where you are on the Tree of Life; but whether you receive it or not depends entirely on you.

If you find yourself in the predicament that we just mentioned, and your burden is very heavy indeed, just think of Atlas and pretend that you are he. But who was Atlas, really? All you have to do is rearrange the letters in his name, and then you will know. He was the "last A." And, of course, the last A is always the inverted A, the A that always bears the weight of the first A, the upper pyramid, upon its shoulders.

But more than that, the last A is the ten, or the return once more of the one. It is the 1 with the 0 standing next to it, which means the completion of the cycle. The upper pyramid may then be compared with the digit 1, as opposed to the lower pyramid which represents the number 10. Thus going from pyramid to pyramid means multiplying by 10, or raising the value of the previous pyramid to a higher power of 10, whatever the case may be. For this reason, then, when the Soul starts out on its journey from the apex of the upper pyramid, it is called simply by its God Word which is *Man*. (The Alpha number for "Man" is 28 which reduces to 1 or unity.) But when it falls into the lower pyramid, the figure turns right-side up and it is called "The Ten Man," meaning that it has been multiplied by 10. And finally, after the Soul redeems itself and returns once more to the upper pyramid, the figure on the cross reverses its position and turns upside down again back to the way it was in the beginning. It is then known by its God Name which is "The Hanged Man." It is interesting to note that the multiplication process is still constant, inasmuch as the Alpha number for its God Name is 10 times 10 or 100.

Now does this turning of the Hanged Man upside down affect him in any way? The answer is absolutely not, and to prove this point the designers of the Cabalah chose a most appropriate symbol for this particular Tarot key. It is the English letter N. Just try reversing this letter to an upside down position, and you will find it still completely intact and not changed a whit. It is the same with the Hanged Man or the Soul. This way, that way, upside down or inside out, he always remains the same—the letter N which is the symbol for the Soul consciousness.

Even the Alpha number for the word "Soul" relates to unity

which is forever constant. It is 67 and it is one of the most
important numbers in the Cabalah for it means "The One."
Haven't you ever heard the expression, "You're the one"? Well,
you *are* the one. You are "The One Soul," and just to prove my
point, we find that its Alpha number is 67 + 67 or 134. Here is
the MD or the death of the Devil again, or in other words—
The Emperor. And of course, we cannot forget *Vesica Piscis*.

As we reflect in our minds on the idea of turning the Hanged
Man right-side up and then upside down again, our thoughts
turn to the symbol of the hourglass. For this is exactly what we
do when "time runs out." We simply turn the hourglass upside
down again, which instantly places all of the sand in the upper
chamber, and lo—time is started anew. This idea is expressed
in the following Figure 27:

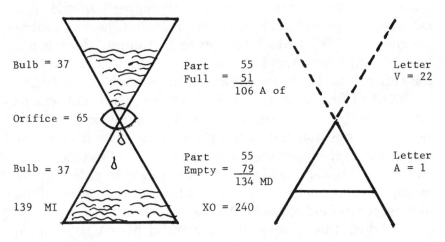

Figure 27
The Hourglass of Time (221)

The above figure illustrates one of the most basic and fundamental principles of the entire Cabalah, in that it points out the
constant interplay between the forces of birth, life, death, and
their inevitable resurrection and rebirth. These then go on to
form a continuous chain of events that governs everything in
the universe, even the very principle of time itself. For

example: Time is "born" the moment you turn the hourglass upside down, thus putting the process in operation. And when the last particles of sand have fallen from the upper chamber into the lower chamber, the process stops and death is the result. Thus we could say that Time "lived" all during the time the particles were falling and in motion, but at the moment this activity ceased, all was still and Time "died." And Time continued to remain "dead," perhaps even for several years of our time, until you brought it back to life again when you started the process in operation once more.

Who did we say brought it back to life again? It was *You.* *You* were the one who started the process operating, but it was the universal laws of *God* that kept the sand particles moving in their journey from the upper chamber into the lower chamber. Thus all that Man can do is initiate a process; it is God that doeth the work. Here again is another fundamental principle of the Cabalah. That principle is that Man is a co-partner with God. One cannot manifest without the other, in the sense that for every image there must also exist that which makes the image.

Figure 27 is really self explanatory. Here are our same two pyramids again but with their positions reversed. The lower pyramid has now become the upper pyramid, and time begins anew. And *Vesica Piscis*, which heretofore was the macrocosm, is now the microcosm—the orifice, the door through which each and every particle must pass in its journey from the one to the other. The number 221 is the Alpha number for the title of the figure, and it rather "accidentally" reads VA which is exactly what the hourglass is—a V sitting on top of an A.

We have called the upper and lower chambers a "bulb" because that is the term the dictionary uses. It is interesting to note that the Alpha number for the plural of this word (bulbs) is 56, which is the reverse of that of the orifice (65); and that the number for the sum of the three parts of the hourglass is 139, which is the Alpha number for "The Wheel of Life." Even the number for the word "part" is interesting since it is 55, the total of the numbers 1 through 10; therefore the empty part or the full part would refer to the ten planes above or below the orifice. And when we combine all of the grains of sand on all of the planes together, we end up with a "mix of O's," which is exactly what the two totals shown on Figure 27 so state.

An analysis of the words "full" and "empty" is even more interesting, in that it reveals a valuable insight as to the nature of these O's. For example, the Alpha number for "full" is 51 which means EA or Each; and the Alpha number for "empty" is 79 or GI. Therefore, the Cabalah tells us that each enlisted man in the army, each GI, or each one of *us* since we are all a member of God's army, is in reality the sum total of the full and empty parts of the hourglass. In other words, we are a combination of fullness and emptiness. And adding them together gives us 130 or MO, which is the death of the Sun since M is the symbol for Death and O is the symbol for the Sun. It follows then that you and I represent the actual death of some sun or star, and the thought is quite profound. But is it really too far fetched? After all, the Master Teacher Agasha tells us that our soul atom is as mighty as the universe, and that is *really* something.

Chapter 9

THE HIEROPHANT: THE MAN TIME HANGED

THIS CHAPTER promises to be an interesting one for it will attempt to clarify the mystery as to why the Hanged Man is hanging upside down on the cross (Tarot Key 12), as well as pinpoint his relationship with the Hierophant (Tarot Key 5). We will also attempt to shed some light on those mysterious characters we first read about in the Book of *Genesis*—Adam and Eve.

So then let us move on now to Figure 28. In the center of the glyph is the hourglass, and the Hanged Man is being poured through the orifice into the lower chamber (or vice versa). Or then again, we may interpret Figure 28 to be an enlargement of Figure 26. If we visualize it in this manner, our mind brings into focus the two pyramids of *Vesica Piscis*. But by far the most startling new concept that can be realized from a study of the figure is that Figure 28 recreates within its orifice a replica of the great Wheel of Life. And if this isn't enough, you may turn the figure 90 degrees and look into the still greater All-Seeing Eye of God!

Like so many other things in the Cabalah, we might say that the construction of Figure 28 was a happening. It started from an attempt to carry out a very simple idea and then, like some

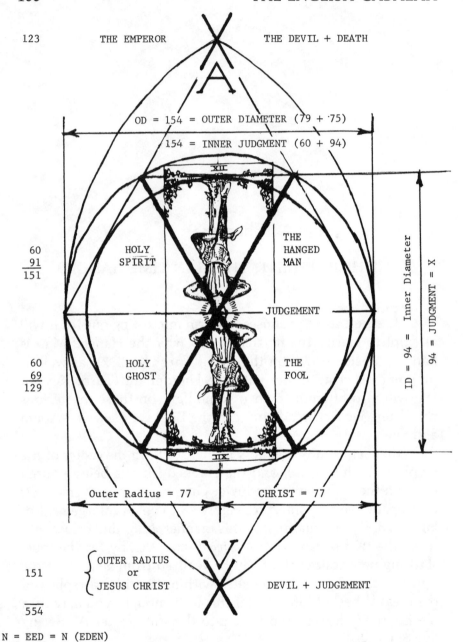

123   THE EMPEROR   THE DEVIL + DEATH

OD = 154 = OUTER DIAMETER (79 + 75)

154 = INNER JUDGMENT (60 + 94)

60
91
151

HOLY SPIRIT   THE HANGED MAN

ID = 94 = Inner Diameter

94 = JUDGMENT = X

JUDGEMENT

60
69
129

HOLY GHOST   THE FOOL

Outer Radius = 77   CHRIST = 77

151   { OUTER RADIUS or JESUS CHRIST }   DEVIL + JUDGEMENT

554

N = EED = N (EDEN)

Figure 28
The Hierophant: The Man Time Hanged

of the others, it just grew and grew and grew. I had had the idea from a very early period in my research that the nimbus around the head of the Hanged Man must indicate that the head was at the center of consciousness, the Infinite State, the Core of Life, and perhaps was even oblivious to the body which was being crucified upon the Tree of Life. But I never did realize what would really happen if I reflected a mirror image of the Hanged Man in a reversed direction below him. I had done so in my mind's eye many times, but I had never physically done it until I xeroxed several copies of the card and started to construct this diagram for the book. Then everything just seemed to happen.

The first thing that became apparent was that the crossbars of the "T" cross now formed the upper and lower parts of the capital letter "I." This was not entirely unexpected, but the visual picture of the dual nature of this "I" within us all was rather breathtaking. Furthermore, when we double the symbol for the Hanged Man we end up with the Alpha value for its God Word which is Man (N + N = 14 + 14 = 28 = Man). If the reader will meditate on Figure 28 with this thought in mind, he should have the same reaction—Wow, this is the "I"!

Now if the center of our "I," the part of us that is attuned to the Infinite State, is the Soul itself, this would account for the fact that the Soul is located at the very center of the human anatomy—the solar plexus. And seeing that the Soul Consciousness, the Infinite State, the Core of Life as it were, has been likened on many occasions in the Agashan classes to the hub of a wheel, the next step was obviously to build the wheel around the hub by adding the rim. Here then was when we hit the jackpot and discovered a part of the Cabalah that had been heretofore very cleverly concealed.

It is a fact of geometry that the hexagon is of primary importance in the construction of a circle because the radius of that circle may be marked off exactly six times around its circumference. Therefore, in the construction of our wheel we first extended the lengths of the crossbars of the top and bottom of our "I" so as to form the sides of a hexagon, and then we drew in the rim by inscribing and circumscribing circles about that hexagon. But what was completely unexpected was the fact that the circumscribed circle intersected exactly the border frame that Arthur Edward Waite and Pamela Colman Smith had placed around this particular Tarot key. This seemed to me to be absolutely incredible at the time. I checked the xerox copies I had made of this card again, and the match just could not have been any closer. If the frame had just been a little wider, or a little higher, the match could not have been made. Anyway there it is. You can check it out for yourself.

On thinking it over, I feel quite sure that Waite was not outwardly aware of this when he designed the card. But his God self was most certainly aware! Therefore it must have directed him, unbeknownst to his outer mind, to produce the border in such a way so as to define the thickness of the rim of the wheel. This incident, along with many others, shows how indispensable to a true interpretation of the Tarot the Waite deck becomes. In fact, the designs of all of the Tarot keys seem to have been divinely inspired from this Universal Consciousness or Infinite State.

Thus we find that the thickness of the rim of the great Wheel of Life is defined as the difference between the lengths of the radii of the inscribed and circumscribed circles about a hexagon. The hexagon, incidentally, also encloses the two interlaced triangles that make up another famous symbol—the Star of David or the Seal of Solomon.

All of the above now leads us up to the third discovery that is revealed from a study of Figure 28. That discovery is that the inner and outer radii of the Wheel of Life as well as its respective diameters have definite and established numerical names. For instance: the abbreviation for *Inner Diameter* is ID and the abbreviation for *Outer Diameter* is OD; but the *id* is also one of the three primary divisions of the psyche along with the *ego* and *superego*. And the *id* in Jungian psychology is completely unconscious and the source of psychic energy, but it became so only as the result of an *OD*, an overdose of a narcotic.

The *id* or inner diameter is also the individual ID number of the soul as evidenced by its "ID card" which is JUDGMENT.

The reason for this is that the Alpha number for "Judgment" (the 20th Tarot card of the Major Arcana) is this same number: 94 which means ID. And it is the awakening of this inner "I," the sleeping god within, that is the main purpose of life. The Agashan Teachers call it the *soul awakening*.

But let us not stop here. The Alpha number for "Outer Diameter" is also extremely significant inasmuch as it is 154 which is just what it is—OD. This same number 154 is likewise the Alpha number for "Inner Judgment"; therefore, the *outer* diameter represents the *inner* judgment and the *inner* diameter represents the *outer* judgment, or just plain judgment. The symbol for this Tarot Key is the English letter X, and it represents the resurrection of the dead or the awakening of the inner "I" that sleeps within. It is also significant that the letter X is likewise the Roman numeral for the number 10. Therefore, it relates to the awakening of the 10 man, the hanged man, the soul.

While we are on the subject of the God Name for the Tarot key whose symbol is X, we must emphasize that this particular word has two accepted spellings—JUDGMENT and JUDGEMENT. The eight-letter word *Judgment* relates to the resurrection of life on the rim of the wheel, and the nine-letter word *Judgement* relates to the resurrection of the inner "I," the Hierophant, the man "Time" hanged. Time hanged the man because when we invert the hourglass the man is hanged or turned upside down.

It is equally significant that the Alpha number for "The Hierophant" (the God Name whose letter/symbol is the English letter E) is identical to the Alpha number for "The Man Time Hanged." They both are 147 ($33 + 28 + 47 + 39 = 147 = 33 + 114$). But if we add "time" to the Hanged Man he is still the same number because he then becomes the Ten Man, and the Alpha number for them both is still 100. Therefore the symbol for "the Man Time Hanged" is still the letter N. And inasmuch as the symbol for the Hierophant is the letter E, the entire title of Figure 28 transliterates into EN, which is the *name* of the letter N. Have I lost you? Think it through. It isn't as complicated as it seems.

Another point that is extremely significant is that the outer radius is none other than Christ himself. How do we know this? We can figure it out mathematically; it is just as simple as that. The outer diameter of the wheel is naturally twice its outer radius. And since its outer diameter is 154, its radius must be 77 which is the Alpha number for *Christ*. But this evidence by itself is not too conclusive because there are many words with an Alpha number of 77. The real clincher comes when we compare the Alpha numbers for "Outer Radius" with the full name of Christ which is "Jesus Christ." Here again we have identical numbers. The number is 151 or OA; and this is exactly what Christ is—the Sun of the Emperor or the Son of the Father. They are one and the same.

Are you still with me? Let us continue. Figure 28 also defines the difference between the two terms used in the Bible to express the third member of the Holy Trinity called in some places the "Holy Spirit" and in others the "Holy Ghost." Yet they both refer to the same Power or Force, call it what you will. This is the Soul, the Hanged Man, the Ten Man as it were. When the Hanged Man is upside down or "hanged" he is the Holy Spirit; and when he is right-side up in the lower kingdom below the surface of the Earth, he is the Fool or the Ten Man who is You. This is the Holy Ghost. The term "Holy Spirit" relates to "Jesus Christ" since the Alpha number for them both is 151. Therefore he is the arisen "you" whereas the Fool is the "Holy Ghost" or the "you" who is still in Hades.

The Cabalah also gives us an alternate method for proving this point. The Alpha number for "Holy Ghost" is 129, and when we add this to the number for "Holy Spirit" or 151 we have the number 280 which is 28 times 10, or Man times 10, or the Ten Man. And who is this "Man" who has been multiplied by the power of 10? He is none other than You, the Fool, once he has redeemed himself and is thus resurrected by and through the inner "Judgement," the inner power of X or 10. He then is One who is Ascended, and who functions on the plane of the Holy Spirit as the Hanged Man. He is the sum total of *the Fool, Judgement,* and *the Hanged Man,* which gives us the same identical number, (81 + 99 + 100 = 280 = Man times 10). These are the letters U, X, and N, or simply NU X (new ten). The total value of their symbols is $14 + 21 + 24$ or 59 which in the Cabalah means "The God." Thus this greater "You" is the equivalent of the Soul, a spark of the Divine Consciousness, God.

The last major point that we wish to make relative to Figure 28 is the totality of the whole. And to make our inner "wheel" complete, we must extend our hexagon upwards into the golden apex of its upper pyramid and downward into the golden apex of its lower pyramid. The upper apex represents the kingdom of God the Father. Its symbol is the letter A, and its God Name is the Emperor. The lower apex represents the dual kingdom of God the Son and/or God the Sun. Its cabalistic name is Jesus Christ and/or Christ the King; and its God Name is Judgement and/or Judgment. The symbol for all of them is the English letter X.

Let us analyze them individually: The upper part of the lower apex is represented by the letter V, the God Name of which is the Lovers (Tarot Key 6). Its Alpha number is 124 which is transliterated into AX, showing that it relates both to the upper apex whose symbol is A and the lower apex whose symbol is X. The Alpha number for the Lovers is also one more than the Alpha number for the upper apex (124 versus 123); this indicates that the lower apex is dual in its nature as opposed to the oneness of the upper apex of the Father.

The Son is simply another name for the Fool who is You. The Alpha number for both of them is 81 or HA (Each A); but the Alpha number for "God the Son" is 107, which means then that it is equivalent to the Chariot (Tarot Key 7), whose symbol is the English letter W. Its counterpart is "God the Sun" whose Alpha number is 113 or AM. But to make them both equal to Jesus Christ or Christ the King (their Alpha numbers are each 151), we have to add "Death" to *God the Sun* and "of W" to *God the Son*. Therefore, the terms *Jesus Christ* or *Christ the King* are only another way of saying: "The Sun God Death" or "W: The Son of God." (The latter term means "The Chariot of W" or simply the "double you" of W.)

Figure 28 also brings the continuity of life sharply into focus.

It points out quite vividly and dramatically that it is the Emperor who puts the Devil to death, but through the powers of Jesus Christ, his Son, the Devil is resurrected and brought back to life again. (The Alpha number for *The Emperor* equates to "The Devil + Death" and the Alpha number for *Jesus Christ* equates to "Devil + Judgement.") And, of course, it is needless to say that the Devil is YOU.

There is also a remarkable continuity between the Alpha numbers for the cabalistic names of the upper apex, the inner apex within the central base, and the lower apex—the Emperor, the Hanged Man, and Christ. The numerical difference in each case is 23 or the letter W. For example: if we add W to Christ we bring the Hanged Man into manifestation (23 + 77 = 100), and if we add W to the Hanged Man we bring the Emperor into manifestation (23 + 100 = 123). The W or "double you," incidentally, is merely the letter A plus the letter V (1 + 22 = 23), and it is in these letters where we unveil the mystery of Adam and Eve.

The Adam and Eve Story

"And the Lord God caused a deep sleep to fall upon Adam, and he slept: and he took one of his ribs, and closed up the flesh instead thereof; And the rib, which the Lord God had taken from man, made he a woman, and brought her unto the man." (Genesis 2:21–22). Thus we find that Eve was created through and by the removal of a rib from Adam.

Impossible, you say? No, not at all. The Biblical creation of Eve is based upon strict, cabalistic principles. In fact, we may even repeat the process right now. But first, let us define who Adam and Eve really are. Adam and Eve are you and me—the male and the female counterparts of the one soul. They are the hero and heroine of our drama, and taken together as a whole they are the "double you," the twin souls, the letter A which stands for Adam and the letter V which stands for Eve. "But the first initial of the word *Eve* is E," you say. True, but the letter V also stands for Eve since the word *Eve* is really an anagram for *Vee;* and the word *Vee* is the name of the letter whose symbol is V. Therefore V = Vee = Eve.

Let us say that you are God and that you wish to create a counterpart for Adam. What do you do? You become the magician. You start with the symbol for Adam which is A, then you invert it to change its polarity from positive to negative, and you complete the process by removing the central "rib" from the A and lo—there stands the symbol for Eve, the letter V. The final act in our little drama, of course, (and this is a little more difficult), is for you to wave your magic wand over this symbol and in the twinkling of an eye there will be Eve herself, magnificently attired in all of her naked splendor.

The main point to this discussion is that the Cabalah tells us that the complete soul is a double pyramid, an octahedron as it were, with the positive or masculine half representing the "A" position, and the negative or feminine half representing the inverse of this, the "V" position. Then they may break apart, go their separate ways for a while, but eventually they will return to each other and become reunited once more. But the way in which they can become united, or attach themselves to each other as it were, is not always the same. In fact there are four different possibilities. They may reunite as they were in the beginning as a diamond (Figure 26), or they may unite themselves in the form of an "X," or an "M," or a "W" (Figure 34).

The Alpha number for Adam is 19 which reduces to a 1 or an A; and the Alpha number for Eve is 32 which reduces to 5 or an E. Here are their initials again—A and E. Moreover, we still do not lose these initials even if we add the Alpha numbers themselves together. The result is 19 + 32 = 51, which gives us EA. Therefore, we may conclude that the Adam-Eve combination represents each one of us since "Ea" means *Each* and "Ae" means *One*.

But let us not stop here. Since God created Adam and Eve, we may wonder what is the value of all three combined into one. The result is rather spectacular, since we find when we do so we bring Christ into manifestation (God + Adam + Eve = 26 + 19 + 32 = 77 = Christ). And even going a step further, we find that when we add Adam and Eve to Christ we bring the Empress (Tarot Key 3) into manifestation (Christ + Adam +

Eve = 77 + 19 + 32 = 128 = The Empress). This is most unusual since the Alpha number for God is 26 which is Z, and the letter/symbol for the Empress is also Z.

The Empress is the counterpart of the Emperor, and she bears the same relationship with the Emperor as Eve has with Adam. Moreover, the Empress represents the Motherhood of God in the same way that the Emperor stands for the Fatherhood of God. They are counterparts or soul mates. In the same way that you have your soul mate, so does God.

The Empress is also the Soul of Mankind (The Soul + Man = The Empress). This relationship is expressed rather dramatically just by rotating the letter Z through a 90-degree turn. It then becomes the letter N. It also is expressed numerically inasmuch as the God Name for the letter N (The Hanged Man or the Soul), when added to its God Word (Man), brings into manifestation the Empress (100 + 28 = 128).

But who is the soul of Adam and Eve? We know that the Hanged Man represents the Soul per se because the Alpha numbers for both terms are identical (100 or 10^2). But the Hanged Man is the soul of what? He is the soul of whatever name we add on to it. Therefore, to find the soul of Adam and Eve, which means the soul of you and me, we need only to add the three terms together. And when we do this, we end up with another rather startling answer because we find that it is none other than Jesus Christ himself (100 + 19 + 32 = 151 = Jesus Christ).

This, then, is the secret of the Cabalah. The word *Christ* by itself represents a tremendous *universal* consciousness—the Christ Consciousness, the Cosmic Consciousness, the Cosmic Christ. But when we add the word *Jesus* to it, we are individualizing this consciousness into a single entity—the individualized, personal consciousness that comes into manifestation when a pair of twin souls are merged together into one. Thus the souls of Adam and Eve, the souls of you and your counterpart or soul mate, when added together become the *one* soul of Jesus Christ or the Holy Spirit. You are then blended into the Oneness; yet the Agashan Teachers always state that you never lose your individuality. Are these two statements contradictory? I think not. They only appear to the limited, mortal consciousness as such.

But our story of Adam and Eve is not yet complete. True, we have found that the Adam-Eve Soul is 151 or Jesus Christ. This is symbolically represented as OA (151), and the symbol OA means literally "The Sun of the Emperor." Therefore, you and your counterpart, taken as a single entity, are also the Sun of the Emperor or the Sun of God. But a "sun" is what? A sun is a star. Therefore the Adam-Eve Soul, the individualized Jesus Christ or Holy Spirit, you and your soul mate, are in reality one of the infinite number of God's stars that exist in fathomless space. This is His Consciousness of which we all are a part.

But just knowing that the Adam-Eve Soul is Jesus Christ or a star in the sky does not solve the problem. Who and what is Christ? The word *Christ*, you will remember, is made up of Adam, Eve, and God (19 + 32 + 26 = 77 = Christ). Therefore, in order to understand the whole story of Adam and Eve, we must also embrace the consciousness of God, the Father who art in Heaven, the Creator of all. We have learned that He is symbolically represented by the letter A which stands for the Emperor, but this same symbol also stands for the Ace. This point is clarified in Figure 29, which attempts to explain the difference between the two symbols.

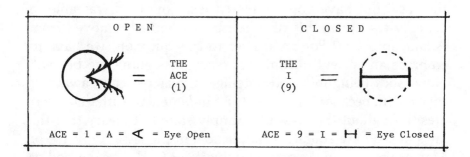

Figure 29
The Eyeball of the All-Seeing Eye (ACE)

The Ace is the All-Seeing Eye of God. The A stands for All, the C stands for Seeing, and the E stands for Eye. There you have it: the Ace, the All-Seeing Eye. It is graphically shown in its open position in the left-hand part of the diagram. The A is the open part of the eye; the C is the rest of the eyeball outside of the A, the part that sees. Therefore when the eye is open, the "All" sees. But what does this "All" see? The answer is that it sees the right part of the diagram, the eye that is closed. But this closed "eye" is a different kind of an eye; it is an "I," an individual, an entity within a circle. The circle represents the Sun; therefore the closed eye is you or I, the diameter of our respective sun or star.

The Alpha number for "Ace" and the Alpha number for "I" are the same. They are both 9. And if we were to put them together, side by side, we would have the number 99 which is the Alpha number for "Judgement." This Tarot key's symbol is X, the symbol for Christ. The open eye or the Ace represents the arisen Christ, and the closed eye is the "I" that sleeps within you and me. The Alpha number for "The Eye" is 68 which means "God-Self" (33 + 35 = 68 and 26 + 42 = 68). But the Alpha number for "The I" means just "Self" per se. Its number is 42 (33 + 9 = 42 = Self), and it can also be broken up into 21 + 21 or U + U. Thus the true *Self* is the double you—you and your counterpart and/or you and your God-Self. The symbol has a dual meaning.

All of the above pretty much explains the difference between the "I's." But have you wondered just how God was able to actually transform this rib, the rib that he had removed from Adam, into Eve? For an answer to this question, we have to embrace an ancient maxim that reads, "As above: so below." Now God, being infinitely intelligent, was perfectly aware of this maxim because it represents a fundamental truth that operates throughout the universe. Simply stated, it means that the laws of God are equally as applicable in the lesser universe of Man as they are in the greater universe of God. The method or the way of going about doing something in order to accomplish a specific result may differ in the various planes of consciousness, but the *principle* used to accomplish that result is always the same.

Therefore, if God was to produce Eve from the rib that he had removed from Adam, he knew that he must go through the same procedure with the rib as he had done with the body of Adam. That is, he must now open the rib itself, remove the necessary ingredients, and then close it up again in the same way that he had "closed up the flesh" of Adam. But how does one go about opening a rib? Figure 30 gives us the answer.

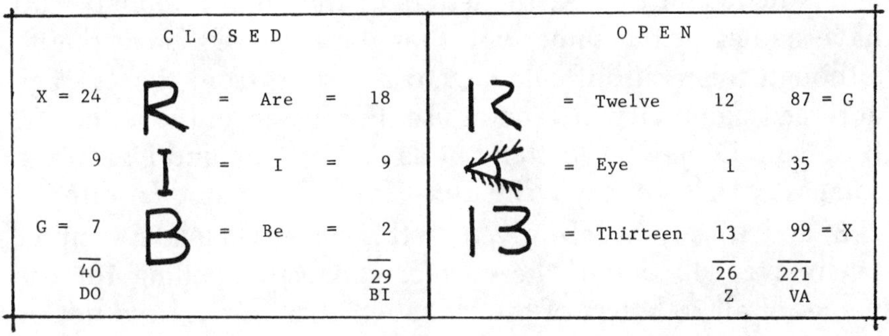

CLOSED					OPEN			
X = 24	R	=	Are	=	18	= Twelve	12	87 = G
9	I	=	I	=	9	= Eye	1	35
G = 7	B	=	Be	=	2	= Thirteen	13	99 = X
40					29		26	221
DO					BI		Z	VA

Figure 30
Adam's Magic Rib

Of course. Why didn't we think of it before? It's all so very simple once you know the answer. The letter R opens up into the number 12, the closed "I" opens up into the open "eye" or the Ace, and the letter B opens up into the number 13. Right there before your eyes is the fundamental principle of spiritual alchemy. Everything exists within everything else; therefore, in order to transform something into something else, the first thing the magician does is to simply open it up. What a fantastic way to demonstrate this principle! The writer didn't create these symbols for the English letters or numerals, nor did you. But you can see for yourself that the letter R can be opened up into the number 12 and the letter B into the number 13. And if we find that this transformation makes philosophical sense, and it most certainly does as the reader will soon find out, the inevitable conclusion must be that the symbols were designed by God.

First, let us analyze our magic "Rib" in its closed position. Its Alpha number is 29 or BI. The dictionary tells us that the word *Bi* is a prefix meaning "life" (bi-ology, bi-ogenic, etc.). It also is a prefix meaning "two" (bi-weekly, bi-axial, etc.). But the most important cabalistic interpretation of the number 29 is that it is the Alpha number for "Page," the letter P, the son of the King and the Queen.

The next step in our analysis is to analyze the *names* of the letters R, I, and B. Yes, the letters of the English alphabet do have names in the same way that the numerals have theirs, although this is a difficult fact to ascertain from the average abridged dictionary in general use. For instance: the letters A, B, C, and D may be written out as *A*, *Be*, *Cee*, and *Dee* in the same way that we may write *One*, *Two*, *Three*, and *Four* for 1, 2, 3, and 4. More will be given on this subject in a later chapter where we will derive the correct cabalistic spelling for the names of all 26 letters of the alphabet; therefore it need not be pursued any further here.

The first point of verification that our "Rib" does indeed belong to Adam comes about when we compute the total Alpha value for the *names* of its three letters. The Alpha number for *Are* is 24, the number for *I* is 9, and the number for *Be* is 7; therefore the total is 40 which transliterates into DO. This is most interesting inasmuch as it tells us that our "Rib" is made up of the Devil and the Sun (D + O), and that when we combine them together we end up with the Star (D + O = 4 + 15 = 19 = S or the Star). Our rib then most certainly does belong to Adam because Adam is that star (Adam = 19 = S = The Star = 91).

The second point of verification lies within the actual names of the three letters themselves when placed in reverse order. RIB reversed is BIR, and if we spell it out we have BE I ARE which is an anagram for BIER AE (The *bier* of Adam and Eve) or EA BIER (Each bier). Thus we find out that our "Rib" in its closed position is also a coffin, and not only that, it is the coffin of Adam and Eve.

Now let us analyze our magic "Rib" in its open position. The natural number for the sum of its parts is now 12 + 1 + 13 =

26 which is the letter Z, meaning the Empress. (In this context we are assuming the Eye or the Ace to have a value of 1.) But the amazing thing that now comes to light is when we compute the Alpha value for the *names* of its component parts in the same way that we did for the Rib in its closed position. The total is 221 which is read as VA or Eve-Adam. Thus we find we were correct in the assumption that our *Rib* was the bier or coffin of Adam and Eve, for when we open it, there they are intact.

"But you still haven't answered the question of how God was able to transform Adam's rib into Eve," you say. Ah! But I have. You have just not been alert. The answer was given in the second sentence of the above paragraph, but you were not alert enough to perceive it. It is the Divine Word—the AUM. All God had to do was sound the AUM the moment he opened the rib; and then the *life* in the rib, the "Bi" in the rib, would have immediately brought Eve into manifestation (life = 32 = Eve). And God could sound the AUM by simply transforming the numbers 12-1-13 into 1-21-13, and there it is—the AUM. The procedure is clarified in the following Figure 31:

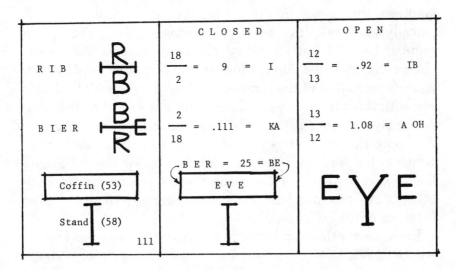

Figure 31
Eve's Magic Bier

Figure 31 is really only a duplication of Figure 30, but with one exception: The closed "I" has been rotated 90 degrees into a horizontal position, thus presenting a more correct symbolism for a closed eye (Figure 29). And since the term "closed I" has the same Alpha number as "Hanged Man" (58 + 9 = 67 = N), it implies that the figure should be inverted or turned upside down. This we have done: the result is the glyph of the word *bier* just below the glyph of the word *rib*. The bottom glyph is a visual picture of a bier as defined by Webster: a coffin together with its stand.

We can see very easily that the "I" now becomes the dividing line between the upper and lower hemispheres of the eye. In one of the hemispheres is the R—the symbol for the Lightning-struck Tower, the House of God from which two individuals are cast out (Tarot Key 16). And who are they? Adam and Eve, of course. In the other hemisphere is the B—the symbol for the Wheel of Fortune, the Wheel of Life into which they fall (Tarot Key 10).

The glyph for the dividing line that separates the two hemispheres of the inverse position of the "Rib" is most interesting. It appears to be a trident—that traditional three-pronged spear which from ancient times has been a characteristic attribute of Neptune, the Roman god of the sea. Let us check it out cabalistically and see if this assumption makes sense. The Alpha number for "Trident" is 90, which is the same as that of the "Emperor." And the Alpha number for "Neptune" is 95, which is the same as that of the "Empress." Therefore, we hit the bull's eye with this assumption, and we now can proceed further into our analysis from a rather solid foundation. It is interesting to also note that the letters A and Z add up to the number 27, which is the traditional position of the Ace or the All-Seeing Eye (Figure 1). And the I and the E when placed next to each other bring into manifestation the number 95—the number of Neptune or the Z (Empress).

Even the relationship between our Adam "I" and our Eve "I" is significant. Both terms are connected by means of a right-angle turn. For example:

ADAM I = 28 = MAN	= N)	THE ADAM I = 61 = YOU
EVE I = 41 = KING	= K) Ankle	THE EVE I = 74 = JESUS
Total = 69 = KNIGHT	= L)	Total = 135 = ACE

The Knight, of course, moves in an "L" shaped manner and his symbol is the same. Webster defines the ankle as the joint between the foot and the leg (also "L" shaped); and the Ace or All-Seeing Eye is normally at right angles to the "I" when speaking of "I" as an individual.

Now let us turn our attention to the bier itself. One can see very easily from the diagram that the "I" part of the *bier* is the stand and the "Ber" part is the coffin. Therefore, the coffin represents the letter B, the Wheel of Life. We have two points of verification that this assumption is correct because (1) the Alpha number for "Coffin" is 53 which is the same as the number for "Wheel," the God Word whose symbol is B, and (2) the Alpha number for "Ber" is 25 or BE, the *name* of the letter B.

But the amazing discovery is made when we perform a magical operation on the "Ber" part of the bier, the coffin or wheel. This is accomplished by again substituting the word "Are" for the letter R. This is perfectly permissible in the rules of the Cabalah because the name of something can always be substituted for its symbol. (A basic fundamental in the laws of mathematics is that things equal to the same thing are always equal to each other.) Therefore, we may transform "BER" to "BE + ARE" quite logically; but the magical part of the operation comes about when we change "BE-ARE" to "BEAR E." Thus we find that the Wheel of Life (the coffin as it were) bears, carries, and gives birth to "E"—one of the symbols for Eve. Now do you see what we are driving at? Now do you see how God was able to bring forth Eve from the rib of Adam through the simple procedure of opening up her "bier"?

"But how do you really know that the letter E, in this case, means Eve?" you persist. Ah, but it does! The reader can see this for himself through a study of Figure 31. The second glyph shows Eve in her coffin. Now let us pretend that we are the inner "I," the Father within that doeth the work. Through a

simple act of *will* we first open the coffin by removing it
entirely. The sounding of the AUM (the Divine Word that
gives life to all things) will then merge the "I" with Eve, with
the result that the body of Eve that slept will now become the
body of "Eye" that lives.

And it was the same with Adam. The sounding of the AUM
brings into manifestation its Alpha number which is 35. This is
the same as the Alpha number for "Eye." Therefore, when we
combine the "Eye" with the "AUM," we have a vibration rate
of 70 which is identical with the Alpha number for "Adam *and*
Eve" (19 + 19 + 32 = 70). So then we cannot exclude Adam;
and when we add "Adam" to the "Bier" we bring the "Wheel"
into manifestation (19 + 34 = 53 = Wheel = B).

In summary: If we place Eve in the bier and then open it, we
bring forth the living "Eye"; and if we place Adam in the bier
and then open it, we find only the empty *coffin* or *wheel* whose
symbol is "B." This combination of Adam and Eve in their
respective biers is of tremendous importance in the Cabalah
because it represents all of humanity. How do we know this?
We know it to be true because we are magicians who can perform magical operations with letters and symbols, and consequently prove all things mathematically. Adam in his bier is
"B," and Eve in her bier is "Eye"; and when we combine the
two together we have "B + EYE." But a "magician," one who
understands the Cabalah, will read this as "BE YE"; therefore
he knows that Adam and Eve represents humanity, either individually or collectively.

Before we close this little discourse on the true meaning of
Adam and Eve, we should bring out one other important point.
This point is expressed rather emphatically once we complete
the mathematical operation demanded by the glyphs in Figure
31. This function, of course, is division—the finding of the
quotient by dividing one term into the other. The quotient for
the closed rib is simply "I"; but the quotient for the open rib is
"IB," which means "I Be, I Am, or I Exist." In the former the "I"
is asleep; in the latter the "I" is awake.

The quotients obtained for the inverse function are equally
as interesting. The quotient for the closed bier is "KA," an

Egyptian word for *Spirit*. It is also interesting to note that the Alpha number for the words *Coffin* and *Stand*, the totality of which is the bier, is likewise this same number 111 or KA. (The Cabalah will usually verify important points so as to avoid any misunderstandings.) But the really important point is discovered when we find the quotient for the open bier. The result to the first three significant figures yields the word "A OH," which means the Emperor and his Sun or more simply—Jesus Christ. The Alpha number for Jesus Christ, you will remember, is 151 or OA, the Sun + the Emperor. The only difference between the two terms is that the order of the letters has been reversed; in the former the A comes before the O, and in the latter the O comes before the A. But the net result is the same, and the fact that the name of the letter O (Oh) is used in one case and only its symbol in the other is not material.

Thus we find that the Cabalah has again verified itself. The quotient for the closed bier is simply *Spirit* by itself (111 or KA); but the quotient for the open bier is *Holy Spirit* or Jesus Christ (the Emperor + the Sun). The Alpha number for "The Adam I" is 61 which means "You"; but the Alpha number for "The Eve I" is 74 which means "Jesus" or "The King," the total of which is 135. And, of course, we must not forget that 135 is the number for ACE, which means the All-Seeing Eye, the Oneness from which we sprang forth to become the individuals that we are today.

Banishment and Retribution

Now let us take a look at the next cycle in the lives of Adam and Eve—banishment from the Garden of Eden and its consequent retribution brought about through countless revolutions of the Wheel of Life. Even the words themselves have tremendous cabalistic meanings. The Alpha number for the word "banishment" is 105, which is the same as that for "The World" (Tarot Key 21); and the Alpha number for "and" is 19 which means "Adam." But the truly amazing thing is disclosed when we add the two words together. The result is 124 which is the Alpha number for "The Lovers" (Tarot Key 6 whose letter/ symbol is V). This Tarot key, incidentally, represents not only

Eve herself, but it also represents both of the lovers taken as a whole. Thus we find that our hero and heroine, Adam and Eve, have now been "banished" into the harsh conditions of the outer World in order to make amends and redeem themselves.

Now let us analyze the word "retribution." Its Alpha number is 151, which is the number for Jesus Christ or Holy Spirit. Therefore, the Cabalah tells us that the retribution of our lovers will be accomplished through the interaction of these two forces.

But this is not all; the Cabalah is absolutely fantastic at times! What is the total Alpha number for the title of this sub-chapter "Banishment and Retribution"? The answer is 275 which is read as BGE. But now let us total this number and we have 275 = 14 or BGE = N; and if you are a "magician" you will read this as "B GEN." And going a step further, we ask ourselves what the word "Gen." stands for. The answer is that it is the abbreviation for the word *Genesis*, the first chapter of the Bible that relates the adventures of Adam and Eve. And not only that, the word *Genesis* itself breaks apart into Gen-esis, the Alpha number of which is 26 + 52, or "God" + "Devil." Are you impressed? Maybe you are not, but I certainly am.

Let us now move on to Figure 32 which is titled "The Life Preserver, the Porthole, or Circle?" This is a strange title, but it merely asks the question as to what this figure really represents. It could be any one of the three.

The one thing that all three of these terms have in common is that they SAVE. The life preserver will save one from drowning; the porthole will act as an escape hatch from a sinking ship; and a magic circle drawn upon the floor will protect the magician from any evil spirits that he may have knowingly or unknowingly evoked. But this is not all. Besides being a visual portrayal of all three terms, even the title of Figure 32 quite remarkably brings into manifestation these four letters—S, A, V, and E. The Alpha number for "The Life Preserver" is 191 or SA (33 + 32 + 126 = 191); and the Alpha number for "The Porthole or Circle" is 225 or VE (33 + 109 + 33 + 50 = 225). Therefore, it spells out SAVE.

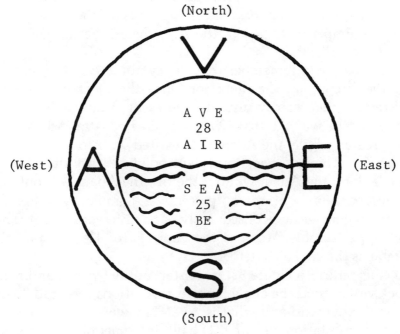

Figure 32
The Life Preserver, the Porthole, or Circle?

"But what is so unusual about these four letters?" you will ask. There is nothing particularly unusual about them except that they represent two diametric pairs of opposites, each at right angles to the other. They also signify the four points of the compass, from the north to the south to the east to the west. And last but not least, each of the four letters or symbols is directly related to either Adam or Eve or both of them. For example: At the North is the symbol V which stands for Eve, but it also stands for the Lovers, the Key that represents both; and at the South is the symbol S which stands for Adam (Adam = 19 = S), but it also stands for the Serpent/Snake that was the instrument of their banishment from the Garden of Eden. At the East is the symbol E which stands for Eve, the counterpart of Adam, but it also stands for the Hierophant, the Pope, the Christ, the instrument for their retribution; and at the West is the symbol A which stands for Adam, the Son who was created in the image of the Father, but it also stands for the Father himself, the Emperor, the God, the Ace, the All-Seeing Eye, the Creator of All.

Now we must remember that the symbols A and S, taken together, represent the plural of One—the Ones or the A's. Therefore, they can be used to represent Adam only in the sense that he was the first *One* to be created—the Adam that was created whole, the Adam who existed *prior* to the removal of his rib. This is a very important point because the incomplete Adam, the Adam without the rib, the Adam without his counterpart or soul mate, presents a completely different archetypal image and consequently has a different symbol. The archetype for this Adam is the Fool (Tarot Key 0) and his symbol is the English letter U.

Let us return to Figure 32. If we start at the letter A and read clockwise around the circle for two revolutions, we read "Ave Saves." Now who and what is Ave? The word *Ave* taken by itself is a salutation meaning (1) hail! welcome! or (2) farewell! good-by! But when we add the word *Maria* to it, it becomes "Ave Maria," the first two words of a prayer, a salutation of the angel Gabriel to the Virgin Mary. And if we were to add *the King* to it, it would mean "Hail the King" in the same way that *Ave Maria* means "Hail Mary." In any event, the word *Ave* is one of the most important words of the English Cabalah because it represents $1\sqrt{5}$ (one times the square root of five), and it truly is the mathematical instrument of "saving" whatever term is attached to it. The proof of this will be given in the second volume of this work.

Therefore, we find that Ave saves. Its Alpha number is 28 which means "Man." The Alpha number of "Saves" is 66 which means "Woman;" and when we combine the two together we end up with 94, the ID, the source of psychic energy, your "ID" card, the Alpha number for "Judgment" (Tarot Key 20), the letter X, the symbol for Christ.

Now let us read clockwise around the circle and then anticlockwise around the circle, and as we do, let us analyze each pair of letters individually. An analysis of this type usually begins by making a one-to-one correspondence with some cabalistic term of the same Alpha number. For example:

SA	=	191	The Lovers' Soul
AV	=	122	You + You
VE	=	225	Jesus Christ, the King
ES	=	519	(Judgement + the King) x 3
		1,057	

AS	=	119	All-Seeing Eye
SE	=	195	The High Priestess
EV	=	522	(Are + I + Be + Twelve + Eye + Thirteen) x 2
VA	=	221	The Universal Soul
		1,057	

But if Ave saves all of these people or forces—and they really could be most anything as far as that is concerned—the question could be asked as to who and what saves Ave. And as with almost everything else in the Cabalah, the answer is contained within the term itself. It is, "Ave's Vase Saves Ave." Just look at our glyph in Figure 32. Here is a view of the vase (looking down on it from above) and in the vase, which is solid, we find both water and air. Therefore the glyph also portrays the solid, liquid, and gaseous states of matter.

The next step in our cabalistic analysis is to add up the various terms that appear as we go around the circumference of the circle, and then read what it says. The number is 2,114; and it reads BAN or UN-BAN. Ah, ha! Reading the total once, it prohibits, forbids, or bars something from something; but reading it twice, it releases that ban or "un-bans" it. Could it be that within Ave's Vase is the secret of Adam and Eve's banishment from the Garden of Eden? Let us proceed further and find out.

The only remaining combinations of letters are those obtained by the perpendicular and horizontal diameters of the Vase. Let us first analyze the horizontal diameter—the horizon line that separates the sea from the air. This gives us the terms EA or AE. But EA is an abbreviation for "Each," and AE means

"One"; and the Alpha number for "Each One" is also 51 or EA again (17 + 34 = 51 = EA). Therefore, we must conclude that *each one* is the object or thing that is banned.

But who is doing the banning? Let us now analyze the vertical diameter and see if it will offer us any clue as to the identity of this force. The ascending term is SV and the descending term is VS. If there is a clue here, it is certainly well hidden. But wait! Let us add up the numbers in the same way that we did for the circumference of the vase, and perhaps then we may be able to "read" it better. The term SV gives us 1,922 and the VS gives us 2,219, the sum of which is the astounding number, 4,141.

"What is so astounding about that?" you ask. Absolutely everything is astounding about it! Read it forwards and backwards and then forwards and backwards once more, each time substituting different letters or symbols. And when we do this, we have the astonishing statement "DNA AND DAD: $1\sqrt{2}$" (the first four digits of the square root of two are 1.414). DNA and Dad: One times the square root of two—what a magnificent statement! The former is the famous DNA molecule, the double helix that is responsible for the transference of genetic characteristics and which is therefore the primary basis for heredity; and the latter is the counterpart of AVE, one times the square root of two, versus one times the square root of five. It is significant that if the digit 2 is inverted, rotated 180 degrees about its base, it becomes the digit 5. Try it. You will see that this is correct. And if we place them side by side they return to the 2 again, because 25 = BE = B = 2.

But this is not all. In fact, we have hardly even begun in our analysis of the meaning of Figure 32. The statement made by every possible combination of the letters SAVE is therefore, "DNA AND DAD $(1\sqrt{2})$ BAN EA. AE." Or we might say that they "un-ban" each one. But if you were DNA and Dad, how would you do this? How would you remove the ban? The answer to this question, like the other one that was asked, is contained within the primary statement. All we have to do is read it in reverse and we have, "EA AE *NAB* $\sqrt{2}$: 1 DAD AND DNA," or the contrary statement, "DNA AND DAD $(1\sqrt{2})$

NAB AE EA." In other words, the "unbanning" is accomplished by suddenly capturing, seizing, or arresting each one. But who is supposed to do it, you or Dad? Is each one supposed to capture the DNA molecule, and by so doing remove the ban himself? Or will Dad eventually forgive each Adam and Eve, nab each one, and put them all back into the Garden of Eden again? The answer is up to the reader to figure out and is a typical problem in Zen.

After you have solved this problem—but don't worry if you haven't because I haven't solved it either—the next step in the analysis is to ascertain the grand total for all of the terms in Figure 32 that we have analyzed so far. These terms are 4,141 for DNA, 2,114 for BAN, 51 for EA, and 15 for AE. This total is 6,321 and it can be interpreted as representing the smallest perfect number. (A perfect number is a number that is equal to the sum or the product of its factors.) In this case the number is six. $6 = 3 + 2 + 1$ as well as $6 = 3 \times 2 \times 1$. But this is not all. Reading the number backwards gives us another important number of the Cabalah. The number is 1.236 and it is the first 4 digits of the term $(\sqrt{5} - 1)$. But wait a minute. What have we here? If we were to add 1 to this number, we would have the square root of five pure and unadulterated—at least as far as we could represent it with only four digits. And $\sqrt{5} = 1\sqrt{5} =$ AVE, the basic number for our glyph!

Ave! Hail to Pi; Farewell to "D"

A new discovery such as this is not unique to this particular analysis, but it is typical of the average cabalistic analysis of almost anything—you name it. Usually, as one proceeds along with any cabalistic train of thought, and if his prior conclusions were correct, he will eventually reach a point where these conclusions will be verified by some startling new discovery—completely new and quite unexpected.

"But what is so startling about the fact that $1 + \sqrt{5} - 1 = \sqrt{5}$?" you will ask. There is nothing startling about that, of course. The new discovery was that our previous analysis of Figure 32 was not yet complete; there was still one element to be added to make it whole and complete within itself—to make it all there is, as it were. And this added element or factor is 1 or unity. After all, AVE is not simply $\sqrt{5}$, but AVE is "one times the square root of five" $(1\sqrt{5})$. Therefore, in addition to 4,141 for DNA, 2,114 for BAN, 51 for EA, and 15 for AE, we must also have 1 for A, the unity factor which any natural number must be multiplied by to give it *area*—to bring it into manifestation. For instance, the number 67 by itself is only an abstract idea; but when we multiply it by unity it becomes 67 ones or things, and thus it exists.

Let us look at Figure 32 again. We had previously made the statement that when we start from A and read clockwise around the circle for two revolutions, we would read "Ave Saves." But this is not true in the strict sense of the word, for we have not really *completed* two revolutions. We could say "Ave Saves, Ave Saves, Ave Saves," for ever; but we would never really bring the cycles to a conclusion until we returned to the A from whence we started. Therefore, if we were to travel for two *complete* revolutions around the circle, we would bring into manifestation the phrase, "Ave Saves A," and our sentence would be complete. It would have a subject, a predicate, and an object.

The Cabalah very subtly emphasizes this point by fairly *demanding* that the unity factor of A or 1 be added to the previous total for the sum of the terms contained within Figure 32. Otherwise, the total would only represent $(\sqrt{5} - 1)$ which is *not* AVE or $1\sqrt{5}$. The correct total is then 6,321 + 1 or 6,322. This number *is* AVE, inasmuch as when it is read in reverse it is exactly "one times the square root of five" to four significant digits (2.236).

The Alpha numbers for these particular words and combinations of words are also significant and, in fact, they will lead us towards the conclusion to this entire matter—the ultimate meaning of AVE. Let us first start with the Alpha number for "The square root of five." It is 245 and is read as XE (33 + 81 + 68 + 21 + 42 = 245). Now XE, on the surface, does not have any particular meaning, but when we reverse it and read it backwards it becomes EX, the *name* of the symbol for "Judgment," the English letter X. Therefore, the Cabalah implies that the square root of five is to be read in reverse in order to unlock its secrets. This we have done, and the sum total of every possible combination of pairs of letters in the four-letter word SAVE, along with unity, is the result. The answer is 6,322, and when this sum is read in reverse we *do* unlock its secrets for we find that it is AVE, $1\sqrt{5}$, the number 2.236.

Now let us analyze "The reverse of the square root of five." The Alpha number for this term is the fantastic number 391. This number 391 (33 + 92 + 21 + 245) is of tremendous importance in the Cabalah for it brings the CIA into manifestation; and, of course, you know what the CIA is—the Central Intelligence Agency of the United States of America. Therefore, this is what the glyph depicted in Figure 32 really is—the CIA.

But we do not yet understand AVE, that is, completely. The final clue that will lead towards the unveiling of its secrets is contained within the phrase. "One times the square root of five." It is here where we sit up and take notice of what this cabalistic ball game is really all about. Let us refer to the diagram on the following page.

Figure 33 is, of course, a pictorial representation of the famous theorem of Pythagoras which states, "The sum of the squares of the long side and the short side of any right triangle is equal to the square of the hypotenuse." This theorem, above all others, is perhaps the most basic and fundamental principle upon which the entire structure of mathematics rests. It is applicable throughout the universe, on any planet whatsoever, and the principles contained therein were never created, not even by God, but have always existed and always shall exist.

One can readily see that the area of each square circumscribed about the inner triangles of Figure 33 represents the square of its appropriate side. The lengths of the sides are designated by numerals, the areas of the squares by capital letters, and the areas of the inner triangles by lower case letters. The triangles are so chosen because each is a manifestation of AVE. (The first triangle has its hypotenuse equal to $1\sqrt{5}$, the second triangle has its long side equal to $1\sqrt{5}$, the third triangle

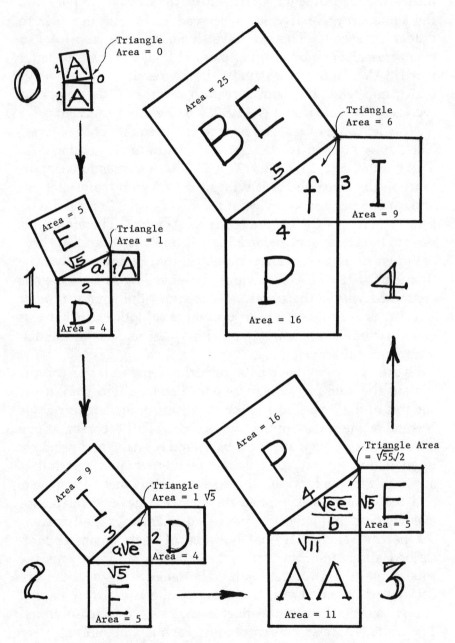

Figure 33: Ave! Each "D" Die, Ape "A," Be Pi

has its short side equal to $1\sqrt{5}$, and the last triangle is a 345 right triangle.) Otherwise, Figure 33 is self-explanatory.

"But what does a 345 right triangle have to do with AVE?" you ask. The answer is that a 345 right triangle has everything to do with AVE because it *is* the Alpha number of the phrase, "One times the square root of five." $(34 + 66 + 33 + 81 + 68 + 21 + 42 = 345.)$ And since this all-important phrase is the actual name of $1\sqrt{5}$, we may conclude that all three sides of a 345 right triangle, taken as a whole, represent AVE. This then was the clue that we spoke of earlier, and which eventually led to the construction of Figure 33.

The zero triangle is included because it represents AVE in an unmanifested state. The inner triangle has simply disappeared into the nothingness, with its hypotenuse and long side merged together into unity. Yet AVE still exists in an unmanifested condition because the diagonal of these two squares *is* $1\sqrt{5}$. The instant these two sides merge together AVE bisects them, thus bringing Triangle (1) once again into manifestation in a higher dimension.

The first thing that comes to mind, as we study Figure 33, is the similarity in the messages that seem to be given by the Cabalah once we turn the numbers for the areas into letters. For instance: Glyph (1) plainly relates to "Each Devil" since *Ea.* is an abbreviation for *each* and the letter D is the symbol for the Devil (Tarot Key 15); but then when we move on to Glyph (2) we find that he "dies." Now didn't we run across this "death of the devil" once before? In Figure 25 we found that *Vesica Piscis* represented M + D or 38 + 85 which transformed the Devil into the Emperor $(38 + 85 = 123)$. Therefore, the same message seems to be repeated again inasmuch as Glyph (3) tells us that the Devil, once he is dead, will be able to ape or copy the A or the Emperor.

This thought is certainly reinforced in Glyph (4). This glyph tells us that the entire operation results in Pi (the ratio of the circumference of a circle to its diameter), and that with the completion of these four steps we will have gone completely around the circle and the cycle will be complete. We will then be able to start all over again with the double A (Glyph 0).

Even the messages given by the squares of similar sides, taken as individual groups, make sense. For example: the squares of the short sides tell us that OA dies. Now who is OA? We have learned that OA (151) stands for the Sun of the Emperor or Jesus Christ. And didn't He also die? We can see now how all this came about because as the square of the short side becomes smaller and smaller it will eventually disappear, and this OA square will have literally "died."

The squares of the hypotenuse tell us that "EA (Each) BE PI," and isn't this statement also true? Do not all things in life go in circles, complete their cycles, and then start all over again? It would appear that this is so, and the Cabalah is simply reemphasizing this point.

The squares of the long sides tell us a little different story, one with a different twist. Starting with Glyph (2), and then moving in a clockwise direction we read, "EA (Each), A PAD," or we may start with Glyph (3) and we read, "A PAD EA (Each)." In the former case the word *pad* is used as a noun; in the latter case it is used as a verb. In any event, the Cabalah seems to be telling us that each one of these squares may be compared to a number of sheets of paper bound together into a pad or a tablet. Each square could then be said to be padded, with the binding of the pad at the edge of the inner triangle. With this as a model, one can easily visualize removing the individual sheets or layers, and yet at the same time not destroying the pad itself.

The message given by the group of inner triangles is even more interesting. If we start from Glyph (2) and then move upwards in a clockwise direction we read "AVE! A OF VEE/B." The letter A stands for the Emperor, and the symbol VEE/B means the Lovers, Adam and Eve, who are riding the Wheel of Life. Therefore the message is loud and clear as it rings out, "Ave! Hail the Emperor of the Lovers and the Wheel of Life." What an apt proclamation from this inner triangle, the source of all!

Other interesting observations can be made by breaking the inner triangles into pairs. The areas of the 1st and the 4th triangles are 1 and 6, or 6 and 1. Now 16 = P = Page, and 61 = You; therefore, someone is paging you or calling you. Who is it? Add up the numbers and find out. The answer is 77 or Christ.

The areas of the 2nd and 3rd triangles are equally as interesting. The former is $1\sqrt{5}$ (AVE) = 2.236; the latter is $.5\sqrt{55}$ (EVE E or E VEE) = 3.708 (CG of OH). And when we add them together, the answer is 5.944. "What is so interesting about that?" you say. Well, read it backwards. The result is D DIE or the Devil dies again. Interesting, isn't it?

Even the messages given by the individual glyphs are significant. For example: Glyph (2) tells us that it represents the IDEA for the $\sqrt{5}$; Glyph (4) tells us that F (the High Priestess) BE PI; and Glyph (3) makes the astute observation that even "a pea copies the life cycle of the Emperor, the Hierophant, and the Lovers." We read this information out of the symbols, "A PEA APE (copies) A (the Emperor) and E VEE (the Hierophant and the Lovers)." The reader will notice that in this case the Cabalah uses the *names* of the letters A, E, and Vee, and not just their symbols (A, E, V). We say that this is an astute observation because the word *pea* applies equally as well to the seed, the pod, or the vine itself. The writer can think of no other word that is used interchangeably to describe the three states of its being. But the Cabalah seems to take this into consideration inasmuch as the Alpha number for A + E + V is 28 which is read as B H (Be each).

One other point before we leave this subject of Ave and move on to other areas. The question has been asked innumerable times as to who *really* made the hero and heroine of our story, Adam and Eve. Some say God, some say Nature; but who was it, really? The answer is quite simple. It was Ave. How do we know it? We know it because the Cabalah says it's so. Isn't it a fact that the anagram "AVE MADE = ADAM EVE"?

Judgement: The Judgment of "E"

Speaking of Adam and Eve, let us now take a brief look at their ultimate judgment after physical death. The "Judgement" card of the Tarot deck (Tarot Key 20) depicts the scene quite beautifully as our hero and heroine, along with many other men, women, and children, arise from their coffins as the angel Gabriel blows his horn. The symbol of this card is the letter X, which means literally the *Resurrection*—the arising from a lower state of consciousness into a higher one. A double X (XX) appears at the top of the card signifying not only the Roman numeral for the number 20, but also a double judgement. It is significant that the Alpha number for "Judgement + Judgement" is identical with that of "The Resurrection." They both equal 198 (99 + 99 = 198, and 33 + 165 = 198). This number also transliterates into SH, a command to be silent.

The English language allows for two separate and distinct spellings for this Tarot key—JUDGEMENT and/or JUDGMENT. The Alpha number for the former is 99, which stands for the double I, and the number for the latter is 94 which means the ID. The *Id* is defined in the dictionary as "the undifferentiated source of the organism's energy from which both ego and libido are derived." Hence even though the words on the surface stand for the same thing, their inner meanings are somewhat different. The difference may be compared with that existing between the words EXOTERIC and ESOTERIC, two words with identical Alpha numbers (99 and 94). The word *exoteric* relates to the outer doctrine, knowledge that is imparted to the general public; the word *esoteric* relates to the inner doctrine, knowledge that is given to the higher Initiate. And it is the same with the words *judgement* and *judgment*.

The difference between the terms can be better explained in the accompanying Figure 34 titled, "The Judgment of 'E'," but before we get into a discussion of Figure 34, it is suggested that the reader reacquaint himself once more with Figure 27 titled, "The Hourglass of Time." Figure 34 shows this same

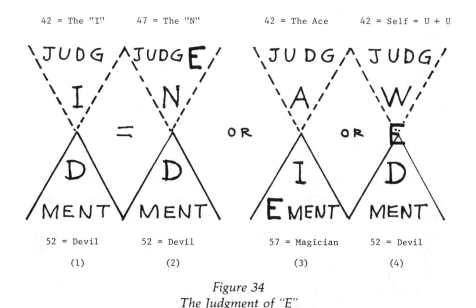

Figure 34
The Judgment of "E"

hourglass, only now each hourglass (the symbol X) is joined with another one at its side. We have symbolically joined them together in this way for two reasons: the first to show the necessity for a "double" judgement, and the second to show alternate ways in which the masculine and feminine aspects of the soul, the A and the V so to speak, may become reunited.

In the same way that there are four different types of "judge-ments," so there are four possible ways in which the soul mates can join forces. The first way is in the shape of a diamond (Figure 26) and the second way is the inverse of this, the letter X. In both of these cases the feminine half of the soul is in either a higher or a lower state of consciousness than its masculine counterpart. But this need not always be the case. They both may come together on the same *plane* of consciousness and thus be reunited in Death, the lower states of consciousness designated by the symbol M (Tarot Key 13); or they may be able to literally soar together into the higher realms of spiritual awareness through and by the powers contained within their own personal vehicle, the letter W, a veritable chariot of the gods depicted by the Chariot (Tarot Key 7). In these last two cases, of course, either the symbol A or the symbol V is inverted relative to its normal position. They then may fit quite easily into the containers that hold them, the M or the W.

But leaving this thought for the moment, let us turn our attention to the four types of "judgements" depicted by Figure 34. In the first place, *judgement* always occurs on the inside of the wheel along its diameter and never on the outside around its perimeter. It is a force of energy traveling from the outer rim into the hub and then back out again to the opposite side. But this energy also travels down as well as up. It may be the sand falling from the upper bulb of the hourglass into the orifice, and from there down into the lower bulb; or it may be the spirit rising up from the body, through the orifice, and into the higher spiritual dimensions.

First there is the Id, the undifferentiated inner source of this energy depicted by the eight-letter word JUDGMENT; and secondly, there are the double I's, the differentiated outer states of this energy at various points along its path. This outer state is depicted by the nine-letter word JUDGEMENT. But it is the letter "E" that stands for Energy that is significant here. Figure 34 then breaks out this "Energy" and shows it in its three basic positions: in the upper bulb by Glyph (2), in the lower bulb by Glyph (3), and in the orifice by Glyph (4). The hidden, *inner* source of the energy is within the symbol "X" itself; therefore, there is no *outer* "E" in Glyph (1).

We can see, then, the reason behind the spelling of the word whose symbol is X. The E part of EX stands for its outer energy state; the X part of EX stands for the inner source of this energy. If we add these two letters together we have the number 29 or BI; and this word, as we learned earlier, relates not only to "life," but also to the dual nature of this life.

The Alpha number for the first four letters of "Judgment" is 42. This is the same number as "The I"; therefore we have placed a capital "I" in the upper bulb of Glyph (1). The Alpha number for the last four letters of "Judgment" is 52 which is the same as "Devil"; this accounts for the letter "D" in the lower bulb of Glyph (1). And taken as a whole, these letters then match the Alpha number for all eight letters of "Judgment," inasmuch as it is 94 or ID.

Glyph (2) is the same as the first glyph with the exception that an E has been added to the upper bulb. This is 5 more than "The I"; therefore we have labeled it "The N" and have placed an N in the upper bulb. The upper bulbs of the third and fourth glyphs are also the same as the first. And since the Alpha number of 42 relates to each one of them, we have taken the liberty of naming each of the upper bulbs by a different letter. We have placed an A in Glyph (3) because 42 is the Alpha number for "The Ace"; and we have placed a W in Glyph (4) because 42 is the Alpha number for "U + U." Isn't a "U + U" a double you? The Cabalah quite frequently uses the two words interchangeably.

The Alpha number for the lower bulbs of the first, second, and fourth glyphs is in every case 52; and since this number is a true God Word number (the exact number of one of the 26 names of the English letters), there is no particular reason to change it. But since an E has been added to the lower bulb of Glyph (3) making its Alpha number 57 instead of 52, we have changed the D to an I because 57 is the Alpha number for "Magician," the God Word for Tarot Key 1 whose symbol is the English letter "I."

We have said earlier that there must always be a double "Judgement" in order to bring about "The Resurrection." But this does not always mean that both types of "Judgement" are the same. In fact, the contrary is usually true. For a true "resurrection" we must have the "E" (the outer energy state) combined with the "X" (the energy source); otherwise, the changeover into the higher or lower state of consciousness would not be possible.

The messages given by the various combinations of glyphs in Figure 34 are most interesting. Glyph (1) when married to Glyph (2) gives us the letters I, N, D, and D. Putting them together, we have I + N + Dee + D, or the word INDEED. The word *deed* refers to something done, a feat, an exploit; and the word *indeed* verifies that it is true, without any question whatsoever. Therefore in this particular combination, this great feat was accomplished most admirably.

Now let us marry Glyph (1) with Glyph (3). The result is the letters I, A, I, and D, which when read in a cabalistic fashion gives us, "I AID DIA (Diameter) of the I." But the really interesting message results with the marriage of Glyph (1) with Glyph (4). Here we have the words "I WED D," and we find that the "I" is married to the "Devil." Can you think of anything more unique? Well, the Cabalah has an interesting surprise in store for us when we marry all four of the glyphs together into a single entity. Glyph (1) gives us ID; Glyphs (2) and (3) give us AND I (reading counter clockwise from the A); and Glyph (4) gives us WED. Therefore, the combined statement is that the "ID AND I WED." What this really means is anybody's guess; but whatever it is, it must be good.

But wait! We are not yet through. There are even more surprises in store for us in this truly amazing glyph. The Alpha number for all three outer energy judgements, that is, the Alpha number for JUDGEMENT + JUDGEMENT + JUDGEMENT is 99 + 99 + 99 or 297 which means that it is BIG. And not only that, when combined with the Alpha number for Glyph (1), JUDGMENT, we find that it is the "BIG ID."

Therefore, let us now find out what the "Big Id" really is. How do we do it? We simply find the grand total of its Alpha number—the sum of 297 + 94. But hold on to your hats! The number is found to be 391 or the CIA—the Central Intelligence Agency again!

This is an extremely important organization inasmuch as the Alpha numbers of each of its component parts are all equal to 90. The God Name for the symbol C is "The Moon," and its number is 90; the God Name for the symbol I is "The Magician," and its number is 90; and the God Word for the symbol A is "Emperor," and its number is also 90. We could stop here, but human persistence makes us proceed further. What is the Alpha number for "Central Intelligence Agency"? We find that it is 243 (73 + 115 + 55); and this number, when it is changed into letters, is XC. This is the same number 90, but it is now expressed in Roman numerals.

Now why is the CIA so easily broken up into four equal parts? The answer is quite simple as four 90-degree angles make a complete circle of 360 degrees. We may place the C in one quadrant, the I in the second, the A in the third, and the sum total of all of them, the CIA itself, in the fourth. But what is this total? It is the number 13 (3 + 9 + 1), which equates to the letter M. Therefore, we can place the M in the fourth quadrant.

Figure 35 shows all four of these letters in their proper positions in a circle, the central circle within the symbol of *Vesica Piscis*. In this way, then, we have created one of the most powerful symbols of the entire Cabalah—the great All-Seeing Eye of God. Now as one studies this diagram, a very startling statement begins to emerge. That statement is "I AM (the) CIA." Wow! Now the Cabalah is telling us that the great "I AM" is none other than the CIA; and not only that, but it also states that the "MC," the *Master of Ceremonies* for the entire production, is the CIA. If we start with the I, and then read in a clockwise direction for two complete revolutions, we read the following statement: "I AM CIA MC."

Figure 35
I Am CIA

Yes indeed, the Cabalah seems to communicate to mankind quite fantastically at times!

Chapter 10

THE WYE OF CARA BOGA COTY

"Cara boga coty? What strange words are these?" one might ask. For those who have read *Agasha: Master of Wisdom* the words are no longer a mystery, but for those of you who are not familiar with Agasha's philosophy, the following information will be in order: The words *Cara Boga Coty* represent the totality of one's consciousness. "You are Cara Boga Coty," Agasha has said on many occasions. "The word *Cara* means the mental aspect of your being, the word *Boga* means its physical aspect, and the word *Coty* means its spiritual aspect. Each individual represents the Holy Trinity; that is, each soul has three modes of expression."

Now the words *Cara Boga Coty* are Atlantean words, dating way back to the consciousness of Atlantis. The original meaning of the word *Cara* meant "Light and Inspiration"; the meaning for the word *Boga* was "One to Obey"; and the word *Coty* meant the "Learned One." And it is the same today. The Tarot brings them back to life once more in the picture symbols on the Tarot keys for the letters W, Y, and E, the combination of which reveals the WYE (Why) of Cara Boga Coty. They are shown in Figure 36.

202

Figure 36
The WYE (Why) of Cara Boga Coty

Now let us analyze the words themselves. The word *Cara* tells us in modern English that it is "A Car"—a vehicle that moves on wheels for transportation from one place to another. Indeed, isn't a chariot a car? The symbology is perfect. Therefore the Chariot (Tarot Key 7) represents Cara, the mental aspect of your being. It is your own personal mental body which is capable of taking you anywhere in the entire Cosmos that you have earned the right to visit. It is your own personal UFO (Unidentified flying object) or "flying saucer," and it gives off a great amount of "Light and Inspiration" wherever you may send it. The Alpha number for "Cara" is 23 which brings into manifestation the letter W (Double-You), a fitting vehicle for "You and I." We use the words "You and I" because the Alpha number for "Light and Inspiration" is 219 or U + I (56 + 19 + 144 = 219).

Thus we see that Cara is dual. The "You" part is the mortal mind, the lower mind, as opposed to the "I" part which is the divine mind or the higher mind. The Alpha number for "Light" is 56 or EF, the name of the symbol for the High Priestess whose number is 6; and the Alpha number for "Inspiration" is 144 which commands us to ADD, and when we do so we find that it is "I," the Magician, the number 9. Thus Cara has its feminine aspect as well as its masculine aspect, with the two parts of its consciousness being connected by the conjunction "and," which represents the letter S or the Star.

You and I then are the number 219, Light and Inspiration, and when we add the two together we find that it represents the Moon and the Sun (21 + 9 = 30 = CO, the C being the symbol for the Moon (Tarot Key 19) and O being the symbol for the Sun (Tarot Key 19)). Thus the Sun and the Moon are the masculine and feminine chariots—the Chariots of the Gods, as it were—that we observe racing across the apparent dome of the sky in the daily cycle, and around the circle of the Zodiac in the larger cycle, as they endeavor to give forth their great light (as from the Sun) and inspiration (as from the Moon).

Boga Relates to the Past

The word *Boga* states that it relates to the past, that the "Ago Be" when we read it from the right to the left (AGO B = BOGA). Therefore, the physical aspect of Being, the Boga aspect of Being, is somehow related to the past. Perhaps it is a replay, once again, of that which existed long ago.

On page 267 of *Agasha: Master of Wisdom*, we pointed out that every star we see in the sky is only a picture, an image as it were, of the way it once did exist in the past. There is not a single star that exists in our own "now." Some of the stars even in our own galaxy are showing us the way they once appeared some 100,000 years back into the past. Therefore, the stars be in the past; when we observe the stars, we see the "ago" the way it "be," the way the past once was. Boga then would apparently represent the physical universe.

Now the Cabalah gives us astonishing proof that what we say here is true. Let us take the Zodiac. The dictionary defines the term as representing an imaginary belt in the heavens, usually 18 degrees wide, that encompasses the apparent paths of all of the principal planets except Pluto. The Zodiac has the ecliptic for its central line, and it is divided into 12 constellations or signs, each taken, for astrological purposes, to extend 30 degrees of longitude. The names of all 12 of the signs, along with their Alpha numbers, are tabulated below:

1. Aries the Ram	= 52 + 33 + 32	=	117
2. Taurus the Bull	= 100 + 33 + 47	=	180 BIG
3. Gemini the Twins	= 57 + 33 + 85	=	175 AGE
4. Cancer the Crab	= 44 + 33 + 24	=	101
5. Leo the Lion	= 32 + 33 + 50	=	115
6. Virgo the Virgin	= 71 + 33 + 79	=	183
7. Libra the Scales	= 42 + 33 + 59	=	134
8. Scorpio the Scorpion	= 95 + 33 + 109	=	237
9. Sagittarius the Archer	= 144 + 33 + 53	=	230
10. Capricorn the Goat	= 97 + 33 + 43	=	173
11. Aquarius the Water Bearer	= 107 + 33 + 67 + 49 =		256
12. Pisces the Fishes	= 71 + 33 + 66	=	170 AGO
Grand Total	912 + 1,159		= 2,071 BOGA

Think of it! The Universal Consciousness which men call God went to all that trouble to name the signs of the Zodiac in such a way so that the total value of their numerical sum, in English, would bring into manifestation the word BOGA—a most powerful word, indeed. Coincidence, you say? Not very likely when we consider that Cara and Boga are supposed to represent counterparts of each other: the one representing the chariots of the Sun, Moon, and planets, and the other representing the Zodiac, the racetrack around which they race. Indeed, the Alpha number for *Boga* which is 25, when compared with that for *Zodiac* which is 58, tells us that it BE the reason Y (Why) the *Star* exists (the Alpha number for Star is the same as that for Zodiac).

A further study of the Tarot key of Strength (Tarot Key 8) reveals why the alternate meaning for the word *Boga* is "One to Obey." It depicts a woman, garlanded with flowers and with the sign of infinity over her head, opening and closing the mouth of a ferocious lion with as much ease as if it were a lamb. She is the High Priestess, the letter F, the feminine aspect of Cara and the counterpart of the Magician, the letter I, the masculine aspect of Cara. The proof of this fact is that both she and the Magician (Tarot Key 1) have the symbol of the cosmic lemniscate above their heads, indicating an extremely close relationship. She is proving that the powers of the mind are far superior to the physical strength of the lion, and is she not indeed "One to Obey"? From the lion's point of view she most certainly is, and here again is a play on words. The lion, the king of the beasts, could also be said to be "One to Obey" in the sense that he has learned to obey the commands of his Master or Mistress.

The words "One to Obey" can also be read as "1 2 O Be Y." Now what is the significance of the number 120? Its significance is that it represents the Alpha number for "Double-You," the name of the letter W, the symbol for Cara. And since the letter Y is the symbol for Boga, the conclusion must be reached that in the final analysis, the great powers of the mind will equal, balance, and counteract the tremendous strength of the physical. Thus we have still another proof that what we have learned is true.

All Is Within the One, and the One Is Within the All

In a sense, all three of the Tarot card symbols for Cara, Boga, and Coty reflect not only the individual Force per se, but also contain within the picture both of the other two Forces as well. In the Chariot, Cara is the charioteer, the triumphant king who has conquered on all planes, and Boga and Coty are the black and white sphinxes that pull the chariot. In the Hierophant, Coty is the "Learned One," the Pope, the head of the church, and Cara and Boga are the two priestly ministers in albs who kneel before him. The Alpha number for "Learned One," incidentally, is 93 which means "I see, I understand (59 + 34 = 93 = I C). But as we study the card for Strength, there are only two individuals depicted therein: the High Priestess who represents Cara, and the lion who quite obviously represents Boga. Where then is Coty?

For the answer to this question, we have to refer back to a game we all played in childhood. Its name is Tic-Tac-Toe. All of us have played this little game at some time or another in our lives, but few today realize its cabalistic significance. So then now let us play the game once more, only this time let us play it a little differently. Instead of placing X's and O's in the squares, let us fill them in with the name of the game itself. But don't rush away for a sheet of paper; this has already been done for you in Figure 37.

Figure 37
Tic Tac Toe: Cat Eat Coti

The game is played with X's and O's, and the reader will see that we have symbolically gone through the motion of making an "X" with the two diagonal lines and an "O" with the inner circle. But what we read is almost unbelievable, because we soon discover that this action reveals the whereabouts of our missing Coty. It is very simple. The lion has eaten him. One can see that the word *Coti* is merely a different spelling for the word *Coty*. They are one and the same, and the lion is the cat that eats Coti.

The answer is also quite reasonable in a philosophical sense. Coty, the spiritual aspect of our being, is not seen in the Tarot card for Strength because it is *within* the body of the lion. And the lion, of course, is Boga, our physical body, the Temple of the Living God. "The spiritual consciousness is within you," the Agashan teachers have declared over and over again, and this particular Tarot key only reemphasizes this point once more.

Now let us see if the Cabalah gives us any verification that our Tic-Tac-Toe glyph is actually referring to the *lion*, and not just any other cat. The verification is definitely there because the Alpha number for the two diagonal words "Cat Eat" is 50 (24 + 26 = 50), which is the same as the number for "Lion"; and the Alpha number for "Coti" is 47, the same as the number for "Beast." And the lion, as we all know, is said to be the king of the beasts.

Satisfied that we are still on course, let us now continue in our attempt to remove a few more veils from the mysteries of Being. "Picture three circles, slightly separated, in a row," Agasha said one evening. "Inside the first circle is a sarcophagus. Inside the second circle is a sarcophagus. Inside the third circle is a sarcophagus. Now underneath the first circle write the word *Cara*; underneath the second circle write the word *Boga*; and underneath the third circle write the word *Coty*." With these words, he then went on to explain that these three sarcophagi, in three separate and distinct circles, are the symbol for Cara Boga Coty.

"Be aware of Being," Agasha is constantly saying. "Only by being aware of Being will you know thy true self. You are Cara Boga Coty. That is you" (*Agasha: Master of Wisdom*, page 183).

Thus we learn that if we are to truly understand Being, we must embrace all of its facets—death as well as life, darkness as well as light. Pure Being or Consciousness may be compared to white light before it is broken up into its constituent parts. Then, after it is sent through a prism, it disperses itself into three primary forces—Cara, Boga, and Coty, the mental, physical, and spiritual aspects of all life. But what is so incredible about this entire subject is that when we actually do draw the symbol for Cara Boga Coty (3 sarcophagi in a row, each within a circle), we find that the symbol itself is identical with its Alpha number. It is 111. And not only that, but it is also the Alpha number for Strength (Tarot Key 8), the letter Y, the Tarot key that stands for their *physical* embodiment.

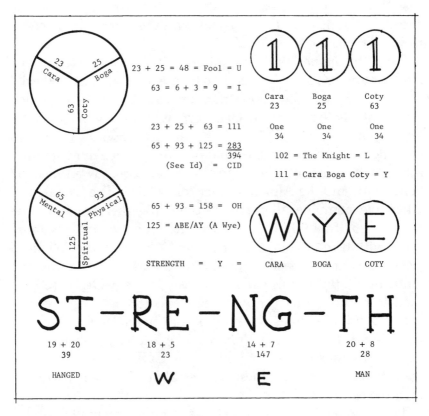

Figure 38
The Three 1's of Cara Boga Coty

One, one, one! What a truly fantastic number to express the three facets of Being because it assigns a single unit of consciousness to each of them—Cara, Boga, and Coty. If ever there were a single number that could be said to represent the Agashan philosophy in its entirety, this is it: 111. Moreover, these three units can arrange themselves in an inner way in the form of a "Y" where they all meet in the center, or in an outer way in the form of a "Δ" (the Greek letter Delta), where each force is now perpendicular to its "Y" arrangement as it revolves *around* the center. But this way or that way, we can still say that they constitute what the Agashan teachers say is the true Trinity—the mental, the physical, and the spiritual aspects of the God Consciousness.

Even the *names* of the symbols tell the same story. The Alpha number for "Wye" is 53 which is the same as "Wheel," the letter B; and the Alpha number for "Delta" is 42 which represents the Ace or the I. Therefore, we may say that "Wye + Delta" equals "Be + I." But this is exactly what GOD is because the letters of his name tell us that he "BE I." The Alpha number for G is 87 (Justice), the Alpha Number for O is another 87 (The Sun), and the Alpha number for D is 85 (The Devil); and when we combine all three of them together we have the number 259 that "BE I." Thus we find when we put the inner force within the outer force, put the "Y" within the "Δ" so to speak, this action results in GOD, the great "I AM," the one who "BE I." But in this particular case, "Wye + Delta" reflects the Motherhood of God or the Empress (53 + 42 = 95 = Empress). And, of course, the symbol for the Empress is the letter Z, the 26th letter of the alphabet, the Alpha number for the One Consciousness whose name is GOD (Z = 26 = God). Everywhere, it seems, these universal truths seem to repeat themselves.

The number 111 can be expressed either mentally, physically, or spiritually. *Mentally* it is expressed as "One One One" because the Alpha numbers of "mentally" and "One One One" are the same. They are each equal to 102, the Knight, the letter L. *Physically* it is expressed by "Strength" because its Alpha number *is* 111, the letter Y. *Spiritually*, however, it can be expressed in two separate and distinct ways, the Alpha numbers of both expressions being equal to 147, the Hierophant, the letter E. These modes of expression are (1) "Hundred + Ten + One" and (2) its alternate format of "One 00 + One 0

+ One." It seems a rather fantastic "coincidence" that the Alpha numbers of both of these terms are identical, but nevertheless they are. (74 + 39 + 34 = 147, and 64 + 49 + 34 = 147.) How do we know that these terms are *spiritually* an expression of 111, and not mentally or physically? Again the Cabalah has an answer to this question. The Alpha number for "Spiritually" is 162, which is the same as "Hundred + Ten + One + 0" (74 + 39 + 34 + 15 = 162) and, of course, we can easily see that the sum of these terms is not changed in the slightest. It is still 111 no matter which way you look at it.

Are you impressed? Well let's try another one for size. Let us take the Alpha number for "spiritual" and break it out into its component parts. The number is 125 which means that it is 5^3 (Five cubed). The Alpha number for "Five cubed" is 42 + 35 = 77, which can be translated into "The I + Eye = Christ." And isn't this a pretty fair definition of the word *Christ*? The combination of the "I" of the Ego with the "Eye" of God?

Now let us "read" the number 125 and see what it says. We find that SPIRITUAL = 125 = ABE/AY/LE. We are using the virgule (the /) to separate alternate ways of reading the number, and the combined expression "ABE/AY/LE" contains every possible way of reading 125. The Cabalist will now try to make sense out of this more complete expression of the number, and it would seem that he has now hit pay dirt indeed. We may segregate these letters into "A BE A YLE," which in turn translates itself into "A be a while" or "A be awhile." The dictionary defines the word *while* to indicate a period or an interval of time, and the word *awhile* to limit this time to only a short period. Therefore, the cabalistic interpretation of the word *spiritual* indicates that the Emperor, whose symbol is A, comes into manifestation for a period of time, and that this time period may exist for a long "while" or just for a short time (awhile).

But even more than just expressing the above rather astounding statement, the Cabalah also tells us that "A be a Y, an L, and an E"—the physical, the mental, and the spiritual expression of CARA BOGA COTY! The Alpha number for the physical, Boga expression of the Y is 111; the Alpha number for the mental, Cara expression of the L is 102; and the Alpha number of the spiritual, Coty expression of the E is 147. And when we combine all three of these numbers together to express the passage of time, we find that their total is 360 which is the exact number of degrees in a circle—one hour or a day of time, as measured by the clock.

Now let us compare the word "WHILE" with "YLE." The Alpha number of the former is 57 which means "Magician," the God Word for the letter I; and the Alpha number of the latter is 42 which means the Ace or the I. Therefore, we have two I's. The Cabalah verifies that we are correct in our assumption because the total of the two numbers is 99 or a pair of I's. The number is also the number of *Judgement*, the letter X, the Christ. This dovetails very nicely with our interpretation of the Alpha number for "Spiritual." It is 125 or "Five Cubed," the Alpha number of which is also equal to 77, the number for Christ. Yes indeed, if the Cabalah is given a chance to work, it will verify itself every time.

The Dual Aspect of Coty

Now let us analyze the word *Coty*. Its Alpha number is 63, and if we add it to the Alpha number of the Tarot Key that is its symbol, the Hierophant, we end up with the number 210, a most important number in the Cabalah (63 + 147 = 210). We will discuss this number later on in this work, but for the moment let us just say that it represents You. The number for the letter U is 21, and its God Name is the Fool whose Tarot Key number is 0. Everything always begins with the 0 or the Fool; when *you* start to count, you are at the point marked 0 before you move to the 1. All cycles begin with the Fool, the Coty Fool, the Spiritual Fool, and the number 210 brings the "U" into manifestation, Alphawise as well as Tarotwise.

We can also break the word *Coty* up into its two basic parts —COT and Y. The Alpha number for "Y" is 25, and it can be read as "BE." Therefore, we know that the word *Coty* means that a "COT BE," or that it be a cot. Now what is a cot? A cot is a light portable bed; therefore the word *Coty* means that it is a bed upon which we sleep. But what other kind of a bed is it? We may analyze the word by finding its Alpha number, and to our surprise and horror, we find that it is 38 which means Death. The Alpha number for "Cot" is indeed 38 and it equates to Death (Tarot Key 13). Therefore, an alternate meaning for Coty is that it *be* our *death bed*, the very last place on the physical plane of life that we will find ourselves before leaving the physical body and entering the spiritual consciousness.

We can see then that the Coty aspect of life, the spiritual aspect of life, is twofold. The spiritual aspect of Being represents the Death *and* the Resurrection of the spirit at one and the same time. You literally die from one plane of consciousness to be born into another. Coty therefore represents the Christ principle of eternal life.

One other point before we leave this subject and move on to some of the other letters: The Cara, Boga, and Coty aspects of life are not limited to these three particular Tarot cards. The WYE keys are only intended to show the "why" of Cara Boga Coty, the princple that brings them in and out of manifestation, and the laws that govern them. Actually, either of these Forces can manifest through any number or letter that brings it into manifestation. Any one of them can also be either masculine or feminine. They represent truly universal principles, and should be considered more like empty houses in which any of the numbers or letters can reside for a time.

Thus everything in life seems to be either circular or cyclic, and this even applies to the life and death of CARA BOGA COTY.

Chapter 11

THE LETTER B: THE FOOL'S WHEEL OF LIFE

THE NEXT Tarot key that we shall investigate and match up with its English equivalent is the Wheel of Fortune. In occult circles it is known as the Fool's Wheel of Life. Why is it so named? The answer is contained in the word *Fortune*. Its Alpha number is 99 which is the same as *Judgement* (Tarot Key 20). It is also the number for "Fool's Life." Therefore the Wheel of Fortune can either be called the Wheel of Judgement or the Fool's Wheel of Life. It is the Wheel of the Double I (99 = I + I), the male "I" and the female "I," or more simply Adam and Eve. And it is *your* Wheel of Life since you and your counterpart are that same Adam and Eve.

But you and/or your soul mate are not the only pair of "Fools" (the letter/symbol for the Fool, Tarot Key 0, is U which means You) that are riding this Wheel of Life, and by so doing suffering through your own individual "judgement" as it were, reaping the consequences either for the good or the bad, which is the inevitable result of previous action. No indeed. This planet Earth on which we live is a veritable "Ship of Fools" as it carries its many billions of inhabitants through that which in occult science is known as the Wheel of Life or the Wheel of

Fortune. Empty, it is called the *Wheel of Life;* but when occupied by the "Fools," which means when you and I are riding on
it, it is known as the *Wheel of Fortune.* In other words, it is the
Fool's Wheel of Life.

But this is not the only reason that it is so named. There is
still another reason that has to do with the numbers themselves. The Alpha number for "The Wheel of Life" is 139 or MI.
This means the Death of "I" or the Death of the Magician, and
its God-Name number is 128 or the Empress (13 + 9 = M + I =
38 + 90 = 128 = Z = God). Thus the Wheel of Life when
empty represents the Empress, the Motherood of God. But now
let us add all of these "Fools" to Mother Earth so to speak, to
the Wheel of Life, and what is the number then? The Alpha
number for "The Fools' Wheel of Life" is then 139 + 67 (the
Alpha number for "Fools") or 206. This is read as "B OF" and
it is just that, since it now *be of* "The Wheel of Fortune" whose
Alpha number is also 206.

The number 67 is an exceptionally important number in the
Cabalah because it represents "The One." But "The One" is
also dual because it is made up of two words: "The" and
"One," the masculine and the feminine, the odd and the even.
The number 67 or FG is indeed an "effigy" because it is an
image, a representation, an *effigy* of that which can only be
known to mankind as "The One." There are no other words to
describe that which cannot be described, because "The One" is
complete unto itself. It is the original archetype from which we
all sprang forth; it is the One without a second, the Oneness of
God, all that is, was, or ever will be combined into a single
entity. In other words, it is GOD.

We can glean an even greater understanding of this mysterious number 67 which represents "The One" (33 + 34 = 67)
by dissecting it in half, removing the 33 or the odd part represented by the word "The," and analyzing the remaining even
half of the term, the word "One," all by itself. The God-Name
number for ONE is 334 (87 + 100 + 147 = 334), and this is
especially significant in that it represents a *Vesica Piscis* or a
merging together of the numbers 33 and 34. The reader is asked

to refer once more to Figure 25 to reacquaint himself with how this phenomenon comes about. Thus we find that the even part of the term, the even number 34, is itself a combination of the 33 and the 34, only when we observe the 34 independently, the CD or the seed as it were, its masculine half or the definite article "The" seems to have disappeared.

It is interesting to observe the effect that adding or subtracting "The One" has on the various Tarot Forces. For instance: if we add "The One" to the Empress, we make her pregnant and change her into the High Priestess, the Virgin Mother of the World (67 + 128 = 195 = F). But if we subtract "The One" from the Empress, whom do we have left? The answer is 61 or You (128 - 67 = 61). In the same manner if we subtract "The One" from the Wheel of Life, not the Wheel of Fortune but the Wheel of Life, only the word "World" remains (139 - 67 = 72 = World). Thus You are the World, the essence of the Earth Mother, the Empress, and the Wheel of Life. Any further differentiation leaves only Energy or Death. If we subtract "The One" from "World" we have only E (72 - 67 = 5 = E = Energy); and subtracting "The One" from "The World" leaves us Death (105 - 67 = 38 = Death = M).

There are other words whose Alpha number is 67, but most of them, if traced back far enough, relate to the general idea or basic meaning of "The One." Besides the word "Fools," either in the possessive case or the plural (Fool's, Fools', or Fools), we have the words "Soul" and "Hanged Man," just to name a few. Two 67's give us "The One Soul" or the number 134. This is the Alpha number for "Vesica Piscis" and it relates to the Death of the Devil (134 = MD). And four 67's tell us that "The One Fool's Soul Hanged Man." The number four is important here because the pictorial representation of the Wheel of Fortune (Tarot Key 10) plainly depicts the four mystical beasts from the Book of Revelation at its four corners.

There is one other important point to be made before we move on to the graphical representation of the letter B. That point is that if we add "Us" to "The Wheel of Fortune," add "US" to the word "FORTUNE," it splits up into the phrase

"FOUR TUNES." Thus the Wheel, the letter B, then becomes "The Wheel of Four Tunes," and that is exactly what its true meaning is in the ultimate sense. We must all travel through the four kingdoms of Earth, Air, Fire, and Water before we are finished with this "Wheel of Life." The 1, plus the 2, plus the 3, plus the 4 gives us the decade or the 10; and the Roman numeral X, which stands for 10, is the number of this Tarot key. Thus we find that the Fool who is You, the letter U, and the Star who is the letter S, constitute the many U's or simply "Us." And the Alpha number for "Us" is 40 which means "Mind."

Why the Letter B Is Its Symbol

Now let us learn why the English letter B is the appropriate symbol for the Wheel of Fortune. The following Figure 39 shows its derivation:

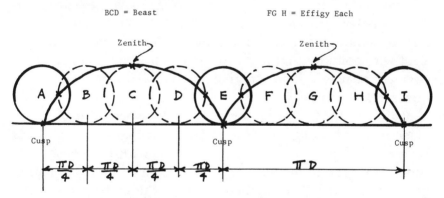

Figure 39: The Cycloid of the Wheel of Fortune

When the writer was first seeking a one-to-one correspondence between the Tarot keys and the letters of the English alphabet, the correct symbol for the Wheel of Fortune evaded him. At first glance, since a wheel is a circle, the obvious choice is the letter O. However, this particular letter had long since been appropriated by the Sun (Tarot Key 19), for as far as we can go back in history, we find the circle with a dot in its center as its symbol. Where then, among all of the other letters, was another symbol equally as expressive of the incessant motion of the wheel? I knew it was there, but in spite of my efforts, it was well over a year before I discovered it.

Then one day it happened! Of course, it was the perfect symbol. Why hadn't I thought of it earlier? These thoughts raced through my mind as I roughly sketched out the mathematical curve of the cycloid in my notebook. This is the curve that is generated by a point on the circumference of a circle (or wheel) as it rolls along a straight line. Two complete full revolutions of the wheel then trace out the English letter B, with the straight line part of the letter representing the plane upon which it rolls. But over and above the geometrical correspondence, the simple fact that it takes *two* revolutions of the wheel —not one, three, or five, but two—to make the B was overwhelming. For isn't the letter B the second letter of the alphabet, and isn't its Alpha value also a two? With this discovery, all previous misconceptions relative to the mysteries surrounding this letter vanished into the nothingness, and I had to readjust my gradually emerging cabalistic alphabet accordingly. I slept very soundly that night as I felt as if I had literally rediscovered the wheel. I am sure that its original inventor, whoever it was, felt the same way.

Figure 39 illustrates the position of the wheel at each right-angle turn of 90 degrees. It is to be noted that the position at each cusp of the "B" occurs at a vowel, with the consonants occupying the intermediate positions. But the significant fact to be pointed out is the phonetic sounds the consonants make when sounded as a group. For instance: I would like the reader to pronounce out loud the phrase "Be C D," and then immediately afterwards pronounce the word "BEAST." Can you notice any difference in the sounds? You cannot; therefore the letters BCD can be read as *Beast*.

And in the same way, we can analyze the meaning for the next group of consonants, the letters FGH. The first two letters refer to an "effigy," and the last letter, the H, means "each." Therefore, it can be construed that a "beast" (BCD) is brought into manifestation with a single turn of the wheel and "each effigy" (H FG) in the second. Or, if we read the complete letter B as one symbol, we find that it represents "each beast effigy" (H BCD FG).

This is most interesting; so now let us attempt to find out who "each beast effigy" actually is. How do we do that? We do that by integrating both halves of the cycloid and find their Alpha numbers. The Alpha number for "BCD" is 9 which stands for "I"; and the Alpha number for "HFG" (each effigy) is 21 which refers to "U" (You). Therefore, you and I represent each beast effigy. You and I are the ones who occupy the intermediate positions in this great Wheel of Life. We are the consonants, but who then are the vowels?

The answer to the latter question comes to us when we realize that the vowels represent the beginning and ending of each cycle—the cusp of the cycloid where the curve reverses its direction and starts all over again. These are evidently the Planetary Logoi, the Pillars of the Temple as it were, the great Ones who first uttered the sound in the beginning. They represent the great Universal Consciousness of God known as "The One I" since *Ae* means *One*. It follows then that "AE I" means one "I," one consciousness, but in many modes of expression. Yet this is not the entire story. There is still far more to follow.

The Jinni in the Wheel

We have all heard of the magic genie in the bottle, the one who resides therein and awaits the chance to serve his summoner. But, strangely enough, the correct spelling of the term is not in common use today. If you look up the word "genie" in the dictionary, you will be referred to the word "jinn" or "jinni." Therefore, there is no way for you to ascertain the full meaning of the term unless you spell it correctly. It is in the spelling of its name that reveals the true secrets of its power.

This fact is brought out all too clearly when we find our "jinni," not in a bottle as one might suppose, but living right within the very heart of the Wheel of Life itself! The following Figure 40 returns the phases of the cycloid back to the wheel which brought it into manifestation. It also makes it possible to view the Wheel of Life for what it really is—the symbolical iris of the great All-Seeing Eye of God.

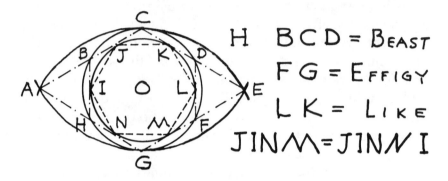

Figure 40: The Message of the Wheel of Life

Upon inspection, one will find that Figure 40 is nothing more than Figure 28 turned at a 90-degree angle. Thus the All-Seeing Eye is brought into manifestation. There is an extremely important principle hidden within these three glyphs of the Hanged Man (Figure 28), the Wheel of Life (Figure 39), and the All-Seeing Eye (Figure 40). To discover it, we must search within ourselves; we must study the *inner* circle of the iris which corresponds to the *outer* circle of the pupil. This means, then, that this particular circle represents the Wheel of Life within the Wheel of Life of "each beast effigy" (H BCD FG). Figure 39 brought it into manifestation, but Figure 40 explains it.

The dictionary defines the term *jinni* as "one of a class of spirits that according to Muslim demonology inhabit the earth, assume various forms, and exercise supernatural power." Another definition is that it is a supernatural spirit who quite often will take human form to serve his summoner. Of course this is all mythology, but there is an element of truth in all myths. Mythology was only invented in order to bring to mankind some great esoteric truth.

As an illustration: Figure 40 plainly points out that in order to bring this magic "jinni" into manifestation, to release him from his prison, you must first open the casket of Death, the letter M, and release the "N + I" contained within it. This is cabalistically valid inasmuch as "N + I = 23 = W," and "W" is only "M" turned upside down. But who are "N + I"? The letter N stands for the Hanged Man, the Soul, and the letter I is the Magician, the one "I" that exists within all of us. When you have successfully completed this operation you will have what the Agashan Teachers say is the "soul awakening," and from that point on your magic "jinni" will be free to assist you in any way that you so desire.

Mythology states that this "jinni" takes on human form, and this is quite correct. But whose form does he take? He takes on *your* form; he becomes a part of *you*, once you have allowed the soul to take over and manage your affairs. This operation is indeed a *Vesica Piscis* operation in that it brings Death to the Devil, the combination of which brings the Emperor into manifestation, and the Emperor is the God-Self.

Thus we find this inner circle or wheel within the outer wheel, the totality of which is called the Wheel of Life, to be "jinni-like" (JINNI-LK), like a jinni, and it is the source of the inner power that exists within "each beast effigy" (H BCD FG) or, in other words, you and I. But, remember, it is only available to us if we perform the above-mentioned operation, and not only that, but we must also read the inner wheel in an *anticlockwise* direction. This is most important because if we read it or turn it in the opposite direction, in a *clockwise* manner, we will miss the true *esoteric* meaning of the wheel and understand it only *exoterically*, or in its outer public sense.

For instance: the exoteric meaning of the Wheel of Fortune is illustrated quite clearly on the Tarot key itself. There you see the serpent god, Typhon, descending into the Wheel of Life and the jackal-headed god, Hermes-Anubis, ascending from it. The serpent represents the life-force in its descent into the physical world, and the jackal-man symbolizes you or me as we ascend from it into the higher spiritual realms. The one pulls you down and the other lifts you up. The spermatozan serpent

takes the male life-force through the semenal fluid to impregnate the body of the High Priestess, the Virgin Mother of the
World. Then, after you are born, you become as a god, but
with the body of a man and the head of a jackal—half man and
half beast. This is you. This is the exoteric story of the Wheel of
Life, and this is the story that is imparted to mankind as he
reads the inner wheel in a *clockwise* direction. The following
tabulation will illustrate what we mean:

	Alpha	*Number*	*Alpha*	*Number*	*Sum*
Inner	JKL	33	Jackal	38	71
Circle	MN	27	Man	28	55
	I	9	I	9	18
	Knight	69	The Self	75	144
	FI			GE	N D
Outer	H	8	Each	17	25
Circle	BCD	9	Beast	47	56
	FG	13	Effigy	58	71
	An 0	30	You You	122	152
	CO			LB	O B

One can see that we have not deviated from the normal flow of
the letters on the two wheels of Figure 40 in any way. The only
exception is when we change over from the last letter of the
inner wheel (the I) to the first letter of the outer wheel (the H).
Here, we have apparently moved downwards, but the motion
is only illusionary. The inner "I" becomes the outer "H" when
we rotate it through a right angle of 90 degrees (This is demon-
strated in Figure 29). In other words, the one "I" becomes
"each" one when it moves into its outer mode of expression.

Thus one can plainly see that there is nothing "wrong" in
reading the inner wheel in a clockwise fashion. Indeed, there is
a great story to tell. The jackal-man "I," the inner man, eyes
(looks at) each beast effigy, which is you or I, the outer man.
And if it sees that we have put forth the proper effort, put the
mortal mind or the devil self to death, then the kundalini force

within it will rise up the spinal column, awaken the psychic centers, and enable the outer man to ascend into the higher consciousness. This is clearly seen when we read the figure correctly. Even the above tabulation tells us "FIG END COL B O B." This is interpreted to mean that the figure or diagram comes to an end, and not only that, but the end column is 152 or the All-Seeing Eye. The inner circle sum is also 144 or ADD; and when we follow through with the addition we find that it is 9 or "I." The number 144 is likewise the Alpha number for "The Strength," or Tarot Key 8 with a "the" added to its name. But the letter/symbol is still the same and it is "Y." Thus when we combine the sum of the outer circle with the sum of the inner circle, we find that it is either BOY or BOND. Both terms are significant.

We can see that the inner self is indeed the Magician or the true jinni within us all. But he is the jackal I (JKL I) or the Christ I; and he was not born in the *inn* because there was no room in the "inn," as the story is told of Christ's birth. The letters M + N read INN when we break the letter M into the I + N; thus *Men* are born in the *inn*, but the Christ self, the jackal I, is born outside of it, in the manger. We could go on and on with the cabalistic interpretation of the birth of Christ, and it is most interesting, indeed, but we will leave that for another chapter.

The Hidden Meaning in the Words

Let us now look for some verification to see if the words themselves verify that what we have been saying here is true. For instance: who and what is Hermes-Anubis? The Alpha number for *Hermes* is 68, which means God-Self, Pillar, or Logos. All well and good. The Greek god Hermes, who is considered to be the herald and messenger of the other gods, would certainly fit into this category. But how about *Anubis*? What does this other half of his name mean? The Alpha number for *Anubis* is 66, and in the Cabalah, this number represents "woman." (The Alpha number for "man" is 28; and the Alpha number for "woman" is 66. The combination of them both is 94 or the Id.) Therefore, it follows that Hermes-Anubis means "Pillar Woman," meaning a female pillar or logos. And her total number is 134 or MD, the Alpha number for *Vesica Piscis*. But to say that *Vesica Piscis* or Hermes-Anubis is feminine is not entirely correct. Actually, Hermes-Anubis is neutral, since it is composed of both the male and the female force.

How about the Alpha number for "jackal-headed god," the descriptive part of its name? This number is 91, the number of the Star, the letter S (38 + 27 + 26 = 91). And according to the Ancient Wisdom, this is what you and I actually are in the final analysis—a star. But if we add "the" to the name, and find the Alpha number for "The jackal-headed god," we find that it is 124, the number for the Lovers, Tarot Key 6, the letter/symbol V. Yes indeed, as far as the numbers relating to Hermes-Anubis are concerned, our assumptions have most certainly been verified.

Let us now analyze the two symbolical creatures on the wheel: the serpent and the jackal. The Alpha number for "serpent" is 97, and the number for "jackal" is 38 which means Death; however, the combination of the two gives us 135 which is read as ACE—the All-Seeing Eye, or the initial force which brings each suit of the Tarot into manifestation. And as far as the "serpent Typhon" is concerned, her Alpha number is 195 which represents the High Priestess, the letter F. One would assume that the "serpent Typhon" is most definitely feminine inasmuch as the High Priestess is probably the most feminine force of them all. Yet, isn't a spermatozoon a male force? What is wrong? The answer is that we have not included the Alpha number for the male force of the definite article "the" in our analysis of the name. Thus the correct Alpha number for "The serpent Typhon" is 228 (33 + 97 + 98 = 228), and this number is read as BB + H or "each baby." And if we integrate the number 228 together into a single number, we end up with 12 which stands for the Knight—a most definite masculine force. However, one can see how easy it is to fall into a trap when trying to ascertain whether a particular force is masculine or feminine. And this is as it should be because that which is male now has been of the feminine sex in other lives.

Before we leave this little discourse on the merits or demerits of having to go through the Wheel of Life—I am sure we all have our individual opinions on the matter—there is one final point to be made. That is that the outer circle of the Wheel of Fortune brings you into life and the inner circle takes you out. You come in from the outside door and you leave through the inside door. Birth is from the outside and death is to the inside. "The real universe is *within* you," the Masters have said over and over again. "Now I know this seems a little paradoxical at the moment," the voice within seems to be saying, "but I assure you, before this work is complete you will have a more thorough understanding of this higher truth."

Therefore, the outer circle of "H BCD FG" (each beast effigy) must represent the serpent Typhon and the inner circle of "JKL MN I," the jackal-headed god, Hermes-Anubis. We have already proven the latter, but we have not yet established a proof for the former. Of course, there is no such thing as a real "proof" in the Cabalah, as the proof of anything is only in the eyes of the beholder; so a better word is to say "established a point of verification." This is quite easily done when we compare the Alpha number for "H BCD FG" with that of "The serpent Typhon." You will find that the former is 30 and the latter 228. But isn't 22 + 8 also 30? It would seem then that he is indeed "each beast effigy."

Chapter 12

THE LETTERS C AND D: THE LIFE IN THE SEED

THIS CHAPTER WILL cover two other very important letters in the English alphabet, the letters C and D. It did not take too much insight to allocate the letter C to the Moon (Tarot Key 18), inasmuch as the crescent, like the symbol O for the Sun, had long since been associated with that heavenly body. Therefore, it is self evident that the English letter C is the symbol for the Moon. But when we sound the name of this letter, the word *Cee*, into the atmosphere, there are two alternate ways in which we may spell the sound that is made. It may be spelled as SEA or SEE, in addition to the normal spelling which is CEE. Each of these words relates to the symbol C, but each brings into manifestation a different aspect of the esoteric meaning of the symbol.

The word *Cee* relates to the crescent, the moon, the planet: a planetary body that reflects light from the Sun. The word *Sea* refers to a body of water: the ocean, lake, pond, or whatever that is the *source* of life, that which life evolves out of to become greater than what it is. Therefore, the words *Cee* and *Sea* are counterparts of each other: the former reflects light or energy from another source, but the latter is the source itself— the source of *life* which is only *light* in a different energy state. The ability to identify *life* with *light* comes about through the word "see." This word means to perceive by the eye, but it also means to come to know, or to understand. "Oh, I see what you mean!" you exclaim, when an understanding of something suddenly bursts into your consciousness. This third meaning for the symbol C was conveyed by at least one deck of Tarot cards, where Tarot Key 18 was illustrated by a man looking through a telescope at the moon. The word *See* is also used as a noun meaning the seat of a bishop, an office of power or authority such as the Holy See, the office of the pope. And the Alpha number for all three terms, *Cee*, *Sea*, and *See*, is the number 67 which means "The One" (13 + 25 + 29 = 67 = FG or effigy). In this way we find that the symbol C has its Cara, its Boga, and its Coty aspects—the mental, the physical, and the spiritual aspects of its Being.

Now let us look at the letter D. The meaning for this letter was not quite as obvious as that of the letter C, but it is still simple to ascertain once you have the key. It is finding this key that is so all-important, and the key that we speak of is the letter B. But before we get into this more comprehensive proof, let us just look at the term itself. The letter D is the fourth letter of the alphabet; therefore it relates to the number 4. And what is the meaning of the digit 4? Agasha tells us that the 4 is a very negative number and that it spells *trouble*. "Indeed," he goes on to say, "it is a number to labor under if you have that digit in your vibration. Therefore, it can be said to be an obstacle in your path. It is something to overcome, something to be conquered so that you may become a stronger individual." These words of Agasha's are taken from Page 294 of *The Agashan Discourses*.

Now if the reader would look at all 22 of the Tarot Trumps, just which Tarot key would you select to represent the above definition as given by the Master Teacher Agasha? It is the Devil (Tarot Key 15), of course. It is the Devil, your own mortal mind, that keeps you in bondage and gets you into all sorts of trouble. Indeed, the Devil can truly be said to be an obstacle in your path and most certainly something to be over-come. Therefore, since the letter D is the fourth letter of the English alphabet, it quite obviously must represent the Devil, Tarot Key 15.

Even the meaning of the prefix "de-" points in this same direction. The dictionary tells us that when these two letters are used in front of a word, they indicate privation (*deprive*), re-moval (*depart; detach*), separation (*dehumidify*), negation (*de-merit; derange*), descent (*degrade; deduce*), reversal (*detract*), and intensity (*decompound*). Just look at all of the words in the English language that are prefaced by the two letters "de," and you will have a general idea of what role the Devil plays in life. It is a most extraordinary role, indeed, but one that is a mixed blessing inasmuch as without the number 4, or the letter D, throwing obstacles in our path, we could not grow, we could not overcome.

Now let us go back to the key that we spoke of earlier, the relationship of the letter B with the letter D. This relationship is very simply expressed as follows:

$$B = 2 = \frac{4}{2} = \frac{D}{B} = \frac{DEE}{BE} = \frac{14}{7} = \frac{2}{1} = 2 = TWO = 58 = EH$$

One can see that when we spell the Alpha number for "two" backwards, we read HE, the number of "The Devil" (HE = 85 = The Devil). Therefore, the Devil or the letter D is the reverse of "Two" or the letter B. But the D is also twice the value of B, and it takes two B's to make one D. This principle is even accentuated with the spelling of the words "Dee" and "Be"; the Alpha number for the latter is one half that of the former.

The adjoining Figure 41 brings these relationships sharply into focus. We have called it the Mysteries of the High Priestess because the area of the upper loop of our "B," when combined with the remaining area of the lower loop (after the "Be-Be" and the "Dee-Dee" have gone through the process of birth), gives us the numbers 8 and 16 or the letters H and P which stand for "High Priestess." The letters PH also combine together into the sound of "F" as in "philosophy." And "F," of course, is the symbol for the High Priestess. We will derive the proof of this in another chapter.

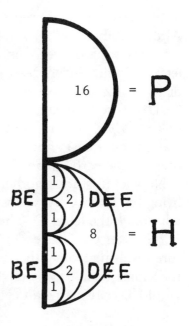

Figure 41
The Mysteries of
the High Priestess

The numerical values for the areas in Figure 41 are derived from the fact that if two circles are placed side by side within a greater circle, the area of the remaining space on either side of the two smaller circles is identical to the area of each of the smaller circles. The proof for this is quite elementary, and we need not go into it here. Instead, we must understand the meanings for the areas "Be-Be" and "Dee-Dee." Cabalistically, these areas represent the words "Baby" and "Daddy" or simply "Babe" and "Dad." It is Eve or the Lovers, the number 22, who gives birth to the "Be-Be," and the High Priestess herself who gives birth to "Dee-Dee" or Dad. Yet who is the Devil in all of this? It is "Be-Be" who is the Devil, since $1 + 1 + 1 + 1 = 4 =$ Devil. But the "Be-Be" is also Christ (Be-Be $= 7 + 7 = 77 =$ Christ), and therefore the baby can be both good and bad. The father "Dee-Dee" is then the Hermit, the Teacher (Tarot Key 9), since $D + D = 4 + 4 = 8 = H$. The fact that the father is "Dee-Dee" is also verified by simply adding the Alpha numbers of the term. (Dee-Dee $= 14 + 14 = $ A DAD.)

Another interesting situation arises when we square the Hermit "Dee-Dee" who represents the father. 8 × 8 = 64, the Alpha number for "zero." All well and good. But what happens when we square "Dee-Dee"? The answer is the numeral 2 or the letter B itself, since "Dee-Dee" = 14 + 14 = 1.414, the first four digits of $\sqrt{2}$. Thus we learn that if we square the Hermit, square "A DAD" so to speak, the answer will literally be the numeral 2 or the Wheel of Life, and we will be right back to where we started. Figure 41 shows us very clearly that the letter "Dee" is literally the verb "to be" (2 + B).

Now let us study another very interesting relationship. Let us bring the letter C very close to the letter D; in fact, let it actually *touch* the letter D. Then let us take the letter I and place it *in* the letter O. The reader will find that the geometrical structure resulting from either of these two operations is identically the same. Then if we were to place one on top of the other, we would have the left-hand glyph of Figure 42 below:

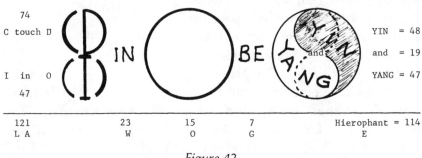

74				YIN = 48
C touch D	IN	BE		and = 19
I in O				YANG = 47
47				

| 121 | 23 | 15 | 7 | Hierophant = 114 |
| L A | W | O | G | E |

Figure 42
The Law of the Ego

The interesting thing that arises when we allow the C to touch the D in this fashion is that it brings into manifestation the CD or the SEED. Now you and I know what a seed is. A seed is the germ or propagative source of almost anything, and it makes no real difference whether a particular seed is that of a human, an animal, or a plant; but the principle of the life within the seed is the same for all. No matter what the seed may be, if we plant it in the right environment, allow it to grow and expand so to speak, we will find that it will eventually bring into manifestation a replica of that which is contained within it—no more, no less. A seed of a geranium will bring forth a geranium, and the seed of a human will bring forth another human. This is the law and it has always been so. And Figure 42 plainly points out that this entire cycle from birth to death, and then from death to rebirth again, results in the remanifestation once more of the ego, the conscious self that lives on and on and on—forever.

The God-Name for the letter C is the Moon, whose Alpha number is 90; and the God-Name for the letter D is the Devil, whose number is 85. Therefore, when we combine the two together into the CD (the seed), the resulting God-Name number is 175 or an AGE. And what is an age? An age is the complete cycle, from beginning to end. But an *age* is even more than that, for it represents *consciousness.* The Alpha number for the word "consciousness" is itself an "age" because it is just that—the number 175 or AGE. This way or that way, the Cabalah is so structured that eventually even a child may understand its basic principles; and the principle of the seed acting as the root of consciousness is of primary importance.

The God-Name number for the I and the O is equally as important. The God-Name for the letter I is the Magician, whose number is 90; and the God-Name for the letter O is the Sun, whose number is 87. Thus the combination of the two is 177, the cabalistic number for "A Christ." The term "personal Christ" may also be used because its Alpha number is the same (100 + 77 = 177). Therefore, it follows that the two circles, one above the other, represent the Christ Consciousness or "A Christ Age."

The word SEED literally says that the DEE'S SEE "D" if we were to read it first from the right, and then from the left. In other words, the seed enables the D or the Devil, which represents you and me, to virtually see or understand himself. And not only that, but it also makes the statement that the Devil is exceedingly "seedy" (SEED + D = Seedy). Thus reading it backwards and forwards through two complete cycles, we find that it is "DEE'S SEEDY SEED." This, however, can be taken two ways. Besides being extremely prolific, being full of seeds as it were, it is with some amusement that we also realize that the word "seedy" implies a seedy character, one who is in an inferior condition or state, and somewhat disreputable.

So then now that we understand ourselves a little better, let us take one final look at the Devil and remove Tarot Key 15 from the deck. Place it before you as you would a mirror, and what do you see? You see the reflection of your own mortal mind, that aspect of yourself that is this "seedy" character called the Devil. Of course, this is not the complete you, the total you. To discover all of your other aspects you would have to go through the entire Major Arcana, alternately using each Tarot key to mirror that particular aspect of yourself that you wished to see reflected.

Looking at yourself in this mirror, then, you will notice that your mortal mind has temporarily enslaved you. But the important thing to realize is that the chains around your neck are loose, and they can be removed at will. The Devil is also sitting on a half-cube, and it is this same half-cube upon which he sits that you are chained to. Therefore, you are most certainly *not* chained to the Devil—only to the half-cube. The idea of being chained to the Devil is only illusionary.

Now a half-cube implies the existence of a full-cube. Where then is the full-cube? To answer this question, let us ask ourselves which of the numbers from one to ten represents a perfect cube. Other than one, or unity, the only other number is eight ($2^3 = 8$). The volume of a cube whose side is equal to two is eight. The number four then must represent the volume of a half-cube, and either the Devil (whose number is 4) *or* the Lovers (whose number is 22 and also a 4) the remaining half. It is you, then, the "Be-Be" or the Lovers, that constitutes one half of the cube and your negative counterpart, the Devil, the other. Or, if you wish, you may free yourselves from this attachment by either kicking the Devil out entirely or loosening the chains from about your necks and flying off to another kingdom not contaminated by the mortal mind. There, in that new kingdom, you can reattach yourselves to a positive half-cube and thus become the Hermit, the Teacher, the numeral 8 that you rightfully are.

The reader will observe that when this numeral "8" is placed within the central circle of Figure 42, the result will bring the equivalent of an "eightball" into manifestation or the circle of the Yin and Yang. Now if you are behind this "eightball" you will usually find yourself in a disadvantageous or an uncomfortable situation, or so it has been said. Why is this so? The answer to the riddle lies within the real meaning of its counterpart, the *Yin and Yang.*

New Light on the Yin and the Yang

In Chinese philosophy, the Yin and Yang represent the two basic principles of life whose interaction influences the destinies of all creatures and things. The Yin is negative, dark, and feminine; the Yang is positive, bright, and masculine. We have placed these two words in their proper positions in the right-hand circle of Figure 42, and the result of their being so placed could bring about an explosion that undoubtedly will be heard throughout the metaphysical world for many years to come. Why do we make this seemingly ridiculous statement? After all, the principles of the Yin and Yang have been public knowledge for centuries. Yes, this is quite true; but the real, esoteric meaning in *English* of these *Chinese* words has not been understood by the outer world at all—at least, not to this writer's knowledge.

Before we explode our "bomb," let me preface these remarks by stating that this particular instance of the Cabalah being able to explain the real meaning of words is not so all-important. What is important, and what is particularly intriguing about it all, is that the Cabalah exists in the first place. How, when, and where did such Infinite Intelligence as seems to be at work behind the Cabalah come into being? How could it have guided the evolution of the words in the English language so that they end up being spelled the way they are today? These questions, along with many others of a similar nature, will ultimately become the real "bomb" and not the minor "firecracker" that we will now ignite.

The reader is asked to turn back once again to Figure 42. There, you will find the words Yin and Yang occupying the upper and lower "commas" respectively of the right-hand circle. But, if you will observe the diagram carefully, you will see that the central "8" figure is identified by the letters "YI-NG" and the outer spaces to the left and right by the letters "YA-N." Do you find anything unusual in this arrangement of letters? You probably have not, because the real meaning of the words is still concealed by the camouflage of the exoteric meaning of the letter Y. The Alpha number for the letter Y, remember, is 25; but this number can also be converted very easily to the word "BE." This word, "BE," is the esoteric meaning of the letter as opposed to its exoteric meaning which is "Y."

Isn't this absolutely fantastic! For now, if you will replace each of the "Y's" with its alternate symbol of "BE," you will find that the correct name of the central "8" is "BEING"; and not only that, but the name of the outer space to the left and the right of it is "BEAN"! Right here, within the Yin and the Yang, is the *Being* within the *Seed*; for the word "bean" is defined in the dictionary as the "seed" of various species of plants, or a plant producing such seeds.

The Cabalah has just revealed the source of the power contained within the seed. But this inner "Being," or the "Jinni" that lies within, cannot be found from a study of the exterior of the seed because only at the poles of the circle does this inner "8" touch its outer circumference. It is very well hidden, indeed.

One other point: Figure 42 also brings out another very interesting observation. That is that the power that brings the Yin-Yang into manifestation, or the Being along with its Seed, is none other than the AUM! "How do you come to that conclusion?" you ask. If the reader will study Figure 42 a little more carefully, he can quite easily ascertain for himself that this is actually the case. The Alpha number of "IN + O" is 38 or Death, the letter M (23 + 15 = 38 = M). Therefore, when we place the "8" *in* "O," the Alpha number sum of these three operations is "121 + 23 + 15 = 121 + 38 = AU + M = AUM." Thus the sounding of the AUM brings forth the Yin-Yang.

This is not as complicated as it first appears. The inner "BEING" resides in the two inner circles, the "BE I" part in the upper one and the "NG" part in the lower one. The higher aspect of "BEING" is then God, because the "BE I" part represents the number 259, the God-Name number for the word "God." And the lower aspect of "BEING" is the Hierophant, the letter E, because the "NG" part is the number 147, the Alpha number for the Hierophant (Tarot Key 5).

The coffin or the shell in which these two inner circles are encased is the "SEED" or the "BEAN." It is shown in Figure 42 by the letters "YA + N," the left-hand part being represented by the "YA" and the right-hand part by the "N." But if we combine this left-hand part into a single letter to correspond with its right-hand counterpart, an interesting phenomenon occurs. The "YA" is changed to "Z," which signifies that the left-hand part of a seed is merely a 90-degree rotation from its right-hand counterpart, the letter "N."

A further thought that must be mentioned here is that this entire action of the life going on within the seed is somehow connected with *Zen*. This particular philosophy, which emphasizes enlightenment by the most direct possible means, is vividly expressed in this particular instance because that is exactly what is occurring here. The higher aspect of the "BEING" encased within the seed is the "BE I," which represents God. But the seed itself, along with its lower aspect, the "NG" or the "E," is shown to be a manifestation of the principles of "ZEN," whatever those principles may be.

We mentioned a little earlier that if you found yourself *behind* the eightball of the Yin-Yang, you would undoubtedly be in a disadvantageous or an uncomfortable situation. The Cabalah seems to verify this point, because if you were *behind* the right-hand diagram of Figure 42, the Figure "S" that separates the Yin from the Yang would be reversed, and it would become the Serpent instead of the Star (Tarot Key 17). And the

Serpent, you will recall, was responsible for Adam and Eve's downfall. The Alpha number for the word "and," incidentally, is 19, the number of the letter S. Therefore, it literally does perform its function of separating these two basic aspects of life.

The Fundamental Principle

There is still another fundamental relationship between the symbols of the "C" and the "D" that we have not yet brought out, but this second relationship is more of a macrocosmic nature than a microcosmic one. It deals with the larger worlds of the planetary bodies rather than the smaller worlds of the seeds. Yet, the basic, fundamental principle that it expresses is truly universal in character in that it applies equally as well to the atom as to the cosmos. The general idea is expressed in the following Figure 43:

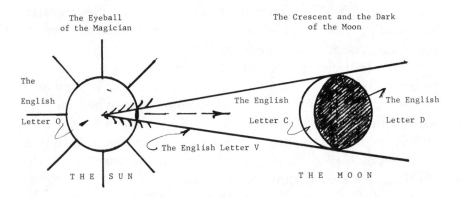

Figure 43
The Fundamental Principle

Figure 43 plainly points out the difference between a body that is the direct source of light and one that is only reflecting it. There is really no actual difference between the Moon and a planet, insofar as all planetary bodies would appear crescent-shaped at times if you were to observe them from one of their moons. Likewise if you were close to a star, it would appear as the Sun; therefore, there is no real difference between these two bodies either. The Cabalah takes all of these individual situations into account. The Star (Tarot Key 17) and the Crescent (Tarot Key 18) refer to a distant sun and its respective planets; but the Sun (Tarot Key 19) and the Moon (Tarot Key 18) refer to our own sun and our own moon as observed from the planet Earth. Therefore, their significance becomes only a question of relativity. It depends only upon one's position in space.

All planetary bodies go through their various phases of light and darkness as they revolve around their respective suns. We on the planet Earth are in a unique position to observe this phenomenon because our own moon is so located in space that it appears to us to be almost exactly the same size as the sun. Therefore, when we observe an eclipse of the sun, even the sun itself appears to go through exactly the same phases of light and darkness as any of its planets, only at a much faster pace. There is undoubtedly a lesson to be learned here; otherwise the Universal Spirit God would not have placed these celestial bodies in such a unique position relative to the planet Earth.

The various phases that a planetary body goes through are roughly set forth in Figure 44:

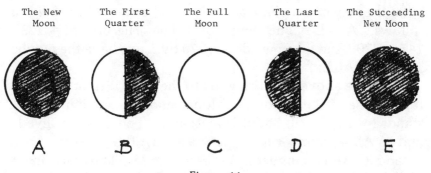

| The New Moon | The First Quarter | The Full Moon | The Last Quarter | The Succeeding New Moon |

A   B   C   D   E

Figure 44
The Phases of the Moon

The letters A, B, C and D have been used to designate each of the four quarters, with the letter E representing the end of the cycle and the consequent total eclipse of the Moon. In this position, the Earth is receiving absolutely no light at all from the Moon—only energy. Yet the true beginning of the "A" phase is identical to the letter E. They are one and the same, and it would appear as no coincidence that the word *Ae* literally means "one."

To show the interrelationship of the planetary cycle with the seed cycle, let us see just what the letters A, B, C, D tell us. First, the group as a whole states that it is "A BCD" or a beast; and secondly, it states that "A B CD" or that "A be seed." In other words, the Cabalah tells us that during the complete cycle of darkness becoming light and then light returning back to darkness again, the A, the Ace, or the Emperor is as a seed. Thus the macrocosm becomes the microcosm, only on a much larger scale of measurement.

Another interesting observation is that both the first quarter and the last quarter phases actually resemble the letters "B" and "D"; only the first quarter phase is really only half of the symbol, but in reverse order. But we cannot stop here, because the full moon is indeed designated by the letter C, the symbol for the moon itself. And going one step further, if we add the God-Name numbers for the letters A and E together and then divide by two to find their average value, the result gives us the astonishing number 135 which means ACE, and this is just exactly what the new moon phase actually is—the Ace. The proof is as follows: A + E = The Emperor + The Hierophant = 123 + 147 = 270. And when we divide 270 by 2, we have the number 135 or the ACE.

All of the above then brings us to the basic idea of the C and the D. The C stands for the Moon, and it is feminine; the D stands for the Devil, and it is masculine. The C is the "Eve I," and its Alpha number is 41 (32 + 9 = 41); the D is the "Adam I," and its Alpha number is 28 (19 + 9 = 28). Thus this "Eve I" plus the "Adam I" then become the "BEING" that dwells within the seed or the "BEAN." But who is the "BEAN"? It is the outer ego, the conscious self; or in other words, you and I. Even the Alpha number for the word "bean" tells the same story. It is 22 and it represents the Lovers (Tarot Key 6). It is also the "Be-Be" that we spoke of earlier. But if we are to consider this outer self as one entity, one person, we must represent it as the Fool (Tarot Key 0) who is You. Therefore, within the Fool, within the physical body of the conscious, outer self, lies the "Eve I" and the "Adam I," the "BEING" that dwells within.

Now let us combine all of these entities together, and let us see what we have. We have the Fool, whose Alpha number is 81; we have the "Eve I," whose Alpha number is 41; and we have the "Adam I," whose Alpha number is 28. Very well. But if we are to make the picture the way it really is, we should break up the number for the outer self or the Fool into two parts, a left-hand part and a right-hand part. Thus the number 81 becomes "8 + 1" or H (each) A. The construction of the final picture then of the inner "Eve I" and "Adam I" within the outer self called "The Fool" results in the number "8 + 41 + 28 + 1." But what is the cabalistic meaning of the number 41? It is the God-Word number for "King," the letter K. And what is the cabalistic meaning of the number 28? It is the God-Word number of "Man," the letter N. Therefore, we may now read the number "8 + 41 + 28 + 1" as 'H + K + N + A." Does this mean anything to you? Does this word look in the least bit familiar? If it doesn't ring a bell yet it is only because you have not yet mastered the art of reading words backwards, but that ability will become almost as a second nature to you in time. The answer, of course, is the word "ANKH," the tau cross with a loop at the top, the Egyptian symbol of enduring life.

Now let us move away from the planetary, indirect light of the Moon for the moment, and transfer our attention to the direct light of the Sun. This is shown as the left-hand diagram in Figure 43. The Sun has been called the eyeball of the Magician because it is just that, at least, symbolically speaking it is. This is the "I," and he is now looking at the "You." His rays of sight go out in the form of a "V" from the central dot within the Sun, the O, and he becomes conscious of each and every planet, or each and every "you" within his system. Indeed, he represents the Core of Life of the solar system itself. In our diagram we have transformed the "I" into an "eye" because it portrays the symbol all the more clearly.

In the same way that when we let the "C" touch the "D," we

end up with a figure identical to that formed by the "I" in the "O," so is the figure formed by a "C" touching the "A" identical to the one made by a "V" penetrating the "O." Figure 42 illustrated the former relationship, and the following Figure 45 illustrates the latter:

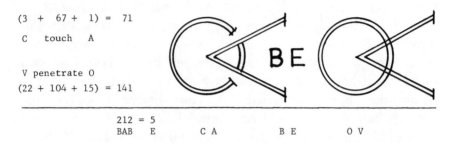

$(3 + 67 + 1) = 71$

C   touch   A

V penetrate O
$(22 + 104 + 15) = 141$

212 = 5
BAB   E   C A   B E   O V

Figure 45
The Babe Sees That Which Is Above

It is interesting to note that when we let the "C" touch the "A," we actually do bring into manifestation a "BABE" just by adding the Alpha number for "C touch A" to that of "V penetrate O." This in itself would not be too unusual, except for the fact that when we add the God-Name numbers for the letters "C + A" to the God-Name numbers for the letters "O + V," and then divide by two to find their average value, the result is the identical number 212, or BAB = E. The proof is given in the following tabulation:

Names	*Alpha Numbers*		*Names*
C = The Moon	= 90	87 = The Sun	= O
A = The Emperor	= 123	124 = The Lovers	= V
C + A	213	211	V + O
	B M	U A	
	BAC	B K	

The fantastic result of the above tabulation not only gives us the proof that the average value of the terms is 212 or BAB =

E, but it also casts more light on the great mystery of the AUM. If we read the two sums backwards from the right to the left, we read "AUM B," which means that the "AUM be," or that this action brings into manifestation that which we call the AUM. Yet if we reverse the direction of our thought, read the numbers from the left to the right in other words, we now find that it be *back*, that it returns once more, in the letters "BAC-B-K." And when this sound comes back, it is in all probability in the form of the OM, the Omega versus the Alpha.

There is still another way that we can interpret this combination of letters. Since the two terms are falling all over themselves to call our attention to the word "Babe," perhaps the two B's that exist at the beginning of each of the numbers means "Be-Be" or "Babe." If this were the case, then, it would be the *babe* that the AUM brings back, in the form of the reincarnation of the spirit for another ride on the great Wheel of Life. There are many ways in which we can interpret the meaning of these symbols, and each one is probably equally as valid as the other.

For instance: we can set up the equation "C + A = V + O." If we set it up in this manner, the A and the V (the Adam I and the Eve I) are in the middle between the C and the O. This is as it should be, because they then become the *being* within the seed. The seed is then the CO. But what is a CO? It is the abbreviation for the word "company," which means then that this "CO," this company, represents a group of people assembled together into a single organization for some united cause or purpose. Very well. But this "company" is also YOU. It is the sum total of that which you, the outer personality or ego, represent. It is composed of all of the previous characters you have played in your many lifetimes of earthly living, and this goes back for a long period of time. All of these characters or personalities, every single one of them, could be said to represent the *company* that is YOU. This company, as a whole, is then your own "personal Christ," as evidenced by the fact that if we add the God-Name numbers for CO together, the Sun and the Moon, we end up with the number 177 or "A Christ."

Now let us move on to an entirely different thought. Let us examine the fundamental principle of the eclipse, that particular phenomenon that occurs when the Moon passes briefly between the Earth and the Sun. Figure 46 illustrates its various phases, along with their possible long-range effects.

The eclipse or conjunction of two stars or planets has long been recognized in Astrology as a force which initiates or brings about a change in the lives of Man. Therefore, we have taken the opportunity in Figure 46 to compare the major phases of an eclipse with the various "isms" that mankind embraces insofar as they relate to the involution and evolution of man's philosophical thought. However, the eclipse per se only relates to Phases C through I; Phases B and J represent the Moon and the Sun as they would appear together almost anytime during the day, and Phase A is reserved only for the night. In this state, after the Sun has disappeared to the other side of the horizon, only the Moon and the stars remain to illuminate the huge vault of the sky. Thus the day is illuminated by sunlight, and the night is illuminated by moonlight and starlight. It is all illumination, but in an entirely different order and degree.

The same could be said regarding the numerous isms or doctrines of philosophical thought that are in existence today. Each is an important part of the whole; each represents a necessary step in the spiritual evolution of mankind. We have selected a few at random in order to show how they tend to exist in pairs; namely, that a particular type of thought that exists a certain number of degrees to the left of center is very similar to that type of thought that exists an equal number of degrees to the right. In the former case the ism is moving inwards towards the moment of totality of the eclipse, and in the latter case it is evolving in an outward direction and away from it. But it is the same "ism." It has only evolved into a higher state of consciousness by having gone through the experience brought about by the eclipse.

Therefore, in addition to lettering the various possible ways that the Moon can relate to the Sun in the order of their natural

The Instant Picture			Its Long-Range Effects	
Order	Action	Symbol	The "Ism" and Its Attributes	Alpha Number
NIGHT A	● Stars	C or D	ATHEISM: (The "A" Ism). Disbelief in the existence of deity. Ungodliness. Wickedness.	75
DAY B	●○ Before	W	SUPERNATURALISM: Belief in a supernatural power relating to an order of existence beyond the visible universe such as a god, demigod, spirit, ghost, or infernal being.	207
C	◕○	V	SPIRITISM: A belief that departed spirits hold intercourse with the living-- usually through a medium.	132
D	◑○	X	HUMANISM: A doctrine centered on human interests and the importance of man rather than that of the supernatural.	98
E	◑	A	AGNOSTICISM: A belief that the existence of any ultimate reality such as God is <u>unknown</u> and probably <u>unknowable</u>.	129
F	☀	M	ANNIHILATIONISM: The belief that the human soul or spirit is annihilated at physical death.	167
G	◐	A	EXISTENTIALISM: A doctrine that regards human existence as <u>not understandable</u> in scientific terms. Yet it believes in the responsibility of the individual and the isolation of subjective experiences such as anguish, guilt, etc.	179
H	◑●	X	HUMANITARIANISM: A doctrine that tries to better human conditions by promoting human welfare, social reform, and philanthropy.	170
I	○●	V	SPIRITUALISM: Essentially the doctrine of Spiritism but with the added viewpoint that spirit is a prime element of the reality of the universe.	166
DAY J	○● After	W	GODISM: A belief that God is Infinite Mind-- a Universal Consciousness that manifests throughout the universe and of which we all are a part.	67
Totals	A = 75 (AGE)		B-J = 1,315 = OM (The Death of the Sun)	1,390

(The Eclipse — running vertically between the Symbol and "Ism" columns for rows C through I)

Figure 46
A Solar Eclipse: The Death, Judgment, and Resurrectin of the Sun

occurrence (the letters A through J), we have also named the major pairs of relationships, or "isms" as it were, by an appropriate symbol to differentiate each pair of similar states from the others. These were selected from the symbols available to us (Figure 34, the Judgment of "E") which show alternate ways that the masculine and feminine aspects of the soul, the "A" force and the "V" force so to speak, may become reunited. In the "W," the *double-you* or the two of you, both the Sun and the Moon are in full manifestation as these male and female "chariots" race across the sky. Then, eventually, they must catch up with each other and merge into one, become united in Death as the "W" is inverted into the "M," and the Moon totally obscures the light of the Sun. The beginning and ending of this final confrontation phase is symbolized by the feminine force, the letter V, for it was originally Eve who was the first one to partake of the forbidden fruit that caused their downfall. Then in the final quarter, the quarter just before and after the "death" of the Sun, the masculine force of the letter A comes to the front as Adam becomes the Christ, the "Son" who is crucified upon the cross but who returns once again to prove there is no death. The midpoint of the eclipse, when the Moon has proceeded half way across the Sun, is represented by the letter X, the Judgement of the double "I's" as it were, with both the "A" and the "V" in equal manifestation.

From the above, it can be ascertained that the symbol for the Sun and the Moon, taken together as a pair or as a unit, is the W or the Chariot on any normal day. (They are also called the "CO" which stands for "company.") However, during one particular day in almost every year, they will mate and apparently merge with each other for a brief sexual encounter. At the moment of totality, the *day* will become *night* for those within the 170-mile-wide arc that usually marks the passage of the Moon's full shadow, and a "diamond ring" or a "wedding ring" will be seen to tie the bond of marriage and make the two into one. But those on earth who are privileged to witness one of these celestial marriages are few, since the frequency of a total solar eclipse from any given point on the earth's surface is only once in every 360 years.[1] Even in a country the size of America, the next total solar eclipse is not scheduled until the year 2017 —exactly 38 years from the most recent one witnessed by a few in the northwestern part of the country in the present year, 1979. The number 38 is itself significant, in that it is the Alpha number for Death, the letter M, Tarot Key 13.

It comes as rather a surprise to the writer—although nothing is really a surprise when one begins to accept the Cabalah for what it is—that the symbols we have chosen to represent this "wedding day" enhance the story even further. We see before us the letters "WV X A MAX VW." These may be read as "Wave X A (for) Maximum View." In other words, for us to have a maximum view of this celestial event, we must be in a position where the waves of light or energy coming from the Sun cross or "X" the symbol for the night, the letter A, and thus bring the Emperor into full manifestation.

The Emperor, of course, represents the *night* phase of life before the *day* phase is born. He is the Supreme Deity, that great "Master of Life" which in the Masonic Order is considered to be higher than either the Sun or the Moon, but yet manifests through both. In the nighttime He manifests through the Moon and the Stars; for when the Sun "dies" and enters the underworld of Hades as it disappears under the horizon, He is literally "born again" into the multitude of Stars in the nighttime sky. Thus the positive aspect of God which in the day is represented by only one sun or unity, is replaced in the night by a multitude of stars or infinity.

This is the Christ, for the Alpha number of "stars" is His number—77. His feminine aspect is the Moon, for the Alpha number of "The Moon" is 90 which is the same as "Emperor." Thus the Emperor becomes literally "the Man in the Moon." Even the Alpha number of "Moon" plus "Stars" tells the same story. It is 134 (57 + 77), the "MD" of *Vesica Piscis*, or the Death of the Devil. And, of course, the Death of the Devil is the Emperor or the letter A (38 + 85 = 123 = A).

Yet, strangely enough, there is a negative aspect to this same number 123 which represents the letter A. If we take the Sun

from the Moon by removing one of the O's from the word
"MOON," and if we add the Devil to the Stars by adding a "D"
to the word "STARS" (in which case the central "A" is transformed into an "E" since D + A = E), we end up with the term
"MON-STERS." And the Alpha number for these "monsters" is
the same as that of the Emperor: 123. But who are they,
really? The answer is that they are very clearly depicted on the
face of Tarot Key 18 which represents the Moon. There they
are, evolving out of the sea unto the shore. But if we want to
know who they *really* are, we have only to break the term
"monsters" into its two component parts. The Alpha number
for "mon" is 42 which represents the Ace or the I; and the
Alpha number for "sters" is 81 or the Fool whose symbol is U.
Therefore, these "monsters" are none other than you and I as
we evolve out of the sea (the "C" or the planet) and ascend that
great stairway to the stars.

Thus we find that in the same way that there is a light and a
dark side to the Moon, so is there a light and a dark side to the
letter/symbol of the A. The dark side of the A is brought into
manifestation through the term "Atheism," which denies the
existence of God. This is symbolized by the Devil or the letter
D. But the light side of the A, the letter C which means to see,
to understand, is brought into its full glory by simply changing
the letters of the word "Atheism" into "The 'A' Ism," the *one*
ism that represents the Oneness of God. The relationship of
these two letters, the positive and negative aspects of the Oneness, is made even more clear if the reader would refer once
more to Figure 44. In this way then, you will see how the Devil
is literally "aced" by the Magician (the two aspects of the ID),
as he beats the Devil by sending the Sun into the underworld,
thus revealing the Stars.

The Moon is the "I" since their Alpha numbers are identical
(The Moon = 90 = The Magician), and the Christ is the Stars.
Therefore, the combination of this "Christ I" which represents
the positive aspects of the letter A, along with its negative
aspect as symbolized by the word "Atheism," brings into manifestation an AGE. (The Alpha number for "Atheism" is 75, and
A + 75 = AGE.) And not only that, since the Alpha number

for "Consciousness" is 175 or AGE, we may safely say that the Christ Consciousness is represented by at least two or more Stars plus the Moon. The Alpha number for only one "Star" is 58; but the Alpha number for two or more "Stars" is 77 or Christ.

In the same way that the Sun is a symbol for the day, so is the Star a symbol for the night. The Alpha number for the word "day" is 30 or CO, the abbreviation for the word "company." And the Alpha number for "company" is 87, the number of the Sun. Therefore the Sun and the Moon represent the day. But the night is represented by the Star since their Alpha numbers are each 58 (Star = 58 = night). Moreover, the term "Night and Day" may also be considered to be a "double-you" since its Alpha number is 107, the number of the Chariot (58 + 19 + 30 = 107 = W).

The term "Night + Day" is likewise a manifestation of Boga Coty since ints Alpha number is 88 (58 + 30 = 88, and 25 + 63 = 88). But which one represents Boga and which one is Coty? The answer is quite simple, since the number of "The Day" is 63, the number of Coty. Therefore, Boga must represent the Night or the Star. And this only confirms our previous observation, where we learned that Boga is a symbol for the Zodiac, whose Alpha number is 58, the number of the "Star."

Now let us study the Eclipse. This phenomenon is interesting insofar as it illustrates what is happening during this "marriage" of the Sun and the Moon. We may break the letters of "The Eclipse" up as follows: "The E clips E." The Alpha number for "The E" is 38 which means Death (Tarot Key 13), the letter M. This is also the moment of totality in Figure 46, the "F" phase where it is symbolized by the letter "M." These letters "FM," taken together, represent the *feminine* aspect of the eclipse; and not only that, but they also bring about the Death of the High Priestess which results in the birth of the Star (F + M = 6 + 13 = 19 = S = The Star). And the night returns once again right in the middle of the day (Night = 58 = Star, and Day = 30 = CO).

But this is not all. We learn that "Death Clips E." And what does the word "clip" mean? The dictionary defines the term in two ways: first, it means to clutch something, or to hold it in a tight grasp; and secondly, to make it smaller, or cut out parts of it as if with a shears. But who is "E"? This is the symbol of the Hierophant (Tarot Key 5), the counterpart of the High Priestess whose symbol is F. Therefore, the entire drama seems to have all of the earmarks of a Shakespearean tragedy where not only one, but both of the Lovers are embraced by Death.

The "wedding ring," incidentally, that embraces the two of them at the moment of totality is also extremely significant. The following tabulation will prove what we mean:

Alpha	Number	God-Name	Number
T	20	Temperance	100
H	8	The Hermit	106
E	5	The Hierophant	147
W	23	The Chariot	107
E	5	The Hierophant	147
D	4	The Devil	85
D	4	The Devil	85
I	9	The Magician	90
N	14	The Hanged Man	100
G	7	Justice	87
R	18	The Tower	114
I	9	The Magician	90
N	14	The Hanged Man	100
G	7	Justice	87
Sum	147	The Hierophant	1,445
	E	(End of "E")	ND E

In other words, the Alpha numbers and the God-Name numbers for the term that seals the marriage between the Sun and the Moon, or the marriage between the Hierophant and the High Priestess, reaffirm the message given earlier pertaining to the death of the Sun and the birth of the Star. It is also significant that if the word "diamond" were substituted for the word "wedding" in the above tabulation, the resulting God-Name number would be 1,352 instead of 1,445, and it would signify that the "ACE BE" this "END." The Ace, of course, refers to the All-Seeing Eye or the initial force of each suit of the Minor Arcana of the Tarot.

This then leads us right back to our "isms" of Figure 46. The total Alpha number for all nine of the isms that we have selected to represent the phases from B to J, from Boaz to Jachin so to speak, is 1,315 or MO, the Death of the Sun. Isn't this remarkable, because the philosophies that we chose to depict were selected with an entirely different thought in mind. And then when we consider that by adding the Alpha number for "Atheism" (The A Ism) to the other nine, making ten in all, we end up with the number 1,390 (The Wheel of Life × 10), the thought becomes staggering! Imagine it! The average number for each one of our phases from A through J is 139, the number for the Wheel of Life, or the letter B. And not only that, but the Alpha number for "ism" itself is 41, the same as the number for "A C or D" (A Cord), the symbols for the night phase of our glyph. As we said earlier, the Cabalah can be absolutely fantastic at times.

All of the above then brings us to the close of our little discourse on the fundamental principle or force that operates throughout life. That principle is that for every action there must be an equal and opposite reaction, for every positive force there is a negative force to counterbalance it, and not only that, but life itself forces the constant interplay between these pairs of opposites. The struggle will go on for a time, but then eventually one of them will win; this will be the moment of the eclipse, so to speak, the point when the positive and negative are merged for a brief period into one. This is like the zero point on the swing of the pendulum, and it marks the ending of one cycle and the beginning of another. It is also the story of *your* life—the story of your death, judgment, resurrection, and ultimate rebirth upon the Wheel of Life if the lessons so given were not learned.

NOTES

1. *Life* Magazine (Time Inc., April, 1979) p. 110

Chapter 13

THE TRUE MEANING OF THE LETTER G

THE GOD-NAME for the English letter G is Justice (Tarot Key 11). But before we can understand the correct interpretation of this symbol, we must compare it with two other Tarot keys so that each may unlock the door to the others. Therefore, let us remove the following three Tarot cards from the deck and place them before us: On the left we should have the High Priestess (Tarot Key 2); in the center we should have Justice (Tarot Key 11); and on the right we should place a very important card from the Minor Arcana, the Two of Swords. The positions are illustrated in Figure 47. Very well. Now study them and see if you can determine a general theme that runs through all three of the cards.

First, you will notice that the central figure in all three of the cards is a woman. Secondly, they are all a two. The Roman numeral II appears on top of both the left-hand card and the right-hand card, indicating perfect balance between them. In a way, all three of the cards taken together as a whole resemble a pair of scales, with the fulcrum or central part of the scales being represented by Justice, whose Tarot key number is XI which reduces to a two. The High Priestess then is the object of

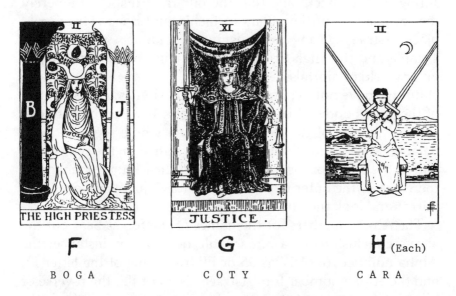

F   **G**   **H** (Each)

BOGA   COTY   CARA

Figure 47
The Balance: The Weighing of Cara by Coty

known weight in the left-hand pan, and the Two of Swords
represents the object being weighed in the right-hand pan. But
the poor girl representing the Two of Swords is blindfolded and
cannot see. This is very much of a contrast to both of the other
women who have nothing over their eyes and can see perfectly.

Thirdly, you will notice that both the High Priestess and
Justice are seated between two pillars. The pillars of the High
Priestess card are plainly marked B and J; therefore there is no
doubt but that they represent Boaz and Jachin. We are not yet
too sure of the identity of the pillars of the Justice card, but the
noted Tarot authority Arthur Edward Waite gives us a clue. He
states that "the pillars of Justice open into one world and the
pillars of the High Priestess into another."[1] He also tells us that
the female figure seated between the pillars of Justice represents
the Greek goddess Astraea and that the role of the High Priestess is played by the Egyptian goddess Isis. If this be the case, a
logical assumption would be that these two goddesses are

sitting back to back, and that the pillars of Justice are merely the reverse side of the pillars of Jachin and Boaz. This would place Astraea gazing inwards into the inner world of the Temple and the High Priestess Isis looking outwards into the outer world of mortals.

But we have not yet answered the question as to the identity of the poor hoodwinked girl on the right. If we go back to our original picture of the three figures as a whole representing a balance, she is quite obviously being weighed on the right-hand pan of the scales of Justice. She is from the Minor Arcana, and therefore of the outer world. Her identity? Just walk over to a mirror and look therein. You will find her there.

The Alpha numbers for the names of the forces bear out the above conclusions to a remarkable degree. For instance: the Alpha number for "Isis" is 56 or EF (the name of the letter F), and the Alpha number for "Astraea" is 65 or FE, the reverse of EF. And if we compute the sum of "Isis + Astraea," we find it to be 121, the same as the sum of "Two + Eleven" (58 + 63 = 121). Furthermore, the Alpha number for "The High Priestess" is 195, the identical number for "Priestess Astraea" (130 + 65 = 195).

Now Isis is quite well-known in the world today, but for those of you who are not familiar with Astraea, let me quote from *Bell's New Pantheon of the Gods, Demi-Gods, and Heroes:* [2] "ASTRAEA: goddess of justice, daughter of Astraeus, one of the Titans, or (according to Ovid) of Zeus/Jupiter and Themis. She descended from heaven in the Golden Age and inspired mankind with principles of justice and equity, but with the world growing corrupt, she reascended thither where she became the constellation in the Zodiac called Virgo. This goddess is represented with a serene countenance, her eyes bound or blinded, having a sword in one hand and a pair of equally poised balances in the other." The reader will see that this description fits almost perfectly the illustration on the face of Tarot Key 11, the only exception being that her blindfold has now been removed.

It is interesting to note that Greek mythology bears witness to the precession of the equinoxes, which enables the rulers of each sign of the Zodiac to move backwards into the preceding sign every 2,200 years. Thus in the same way that we are now moving from the age of Pisces (the 12th sign) to the new age of Aquarius (the 11th sign), Astraea, the goddess of Justice, was able to move from the 7th sign of Libra, which is designated by the Scales, to the 6th sign of Virgo which is called the Virgin.

Now the English Cabalah has taken all of this into account, and the English alphabet with its 26 letters seems to have been especially designed, among other things, to encompass two complete revolutions of the Zodiac with two letters left over to represent that which is within and had gone before, and that which is without and is yet to come. The letter A or the Emperor then represents the first sign of the Zodiac, which is Aries the Ram. He is depicted in Tarot Key 4 as seated on a throne, the arms of which are fronted by *ram's* heads, and there is much other evidence to prove this point. And we can go through all 12 signs from Aries to Pisces by simply taking the letters from A to L in alphabetical order to represent each consecutive sign. There is nothing mysterious about the Cabalah; it doesn't jump all over the place. Every action follows a simple, ordered, logical progression of the numbers or letters into whatever dimension of life we are attempting to study, and the constellations around the circle of the Zodiac—or the circle of holy animals, as it has sometimes been called—is most certainly no exception to this rule.

What, then, is the letter/symbol for Virgo, the 6th sign of the Zodiac, which is depicted as the Virgin? It is the letter F, of course, since F is the 6th letter of the English alphabet. The Cabalah verifies this by naming the High Priestess herself as *Isis*, the Alpha number of which is 56 or EF, the name of the letter F. She is the goddess Isis, the Virgin Mother of the World, and we will cover her a little more completely later on in the book.

And if the symbol for the Virgin is F, the symbol for the Scales most certainly must be G, since G is the 7th letter of the English alphabet and Libra is the 7th sign of the Zodiac. This,

too, has been verified by the Cabalah by introducing the name
of *Astraea* as the goddess of Justice, whose symbol is the scales,
and who quite logically represents Libra. Therefore, G is the
symbol for Justice (Tarot Key 11); but when she is seated in the
CG (center of gravity) position at the fulcrum of the scales, she
is no longer blindfolded, for the very word JUSTICE itself
states that the "Just I (eye) see."

It is only her image that cannot see. Therefore, when her
image is being weighed on the right-hand pan of the scales, she
is shown as being blindfolded. The Two of Swords then is the
image of Astraea as she *balances* two *swords* upon her
shoulders while being *blindfolded*. Or, more correctly, we
should state that the Two of Swords is the image of the High
Priestess plus Justice, an "effigy" of the F plus the G, if you will.
On page 250 of his book, Arthur Edward Waite describes the
Two of Swords as "A hoodwinked female figure." Is it a coincidence that the Alpha number for this term is 217 or a BAG? (1
+ 108 + 42 + 66 = 217 = BAG). And is it coincidence that the
Alpha value for "Priestess + Justice" is also this same number—
217? (130 + 87 = 217). And is it coincidence that the Alpha
number of "The Two of Swords" brings the pillars B and J once
more into manifestation? It represents their image because the
Alpha number of the term is 210 or BJ (33 + 58 + 21 + 98 = 210
= BJ). Come, come, come, simple intelligence fairly demands
that we credit at least a part of this "coincidence" to the
Cabalah.

The Alpha number for *Libra* is 42 which means "The Ace";
the Alpha number for "The Scales" is 92 which states "I Be."
Therefore, the total term states that "I be the Ace or the I." This
is verified again in the number 134 (92 + 42) which brings
Vesica Piscis or the Death of the Devil into manifestation (134
= M + D = A). Moreover, the Alpha number for "balance" is
38, the number of *Death*; and the number for "sword" is 79
which means "GI," an ordinary foot soldier or enlisted man in
the army. Therefore, the two symbols taken together mean
our death, since you and I are that GI. Making the term into
the plural form by adding an "S" doesn't change the meaning in

the slightest because the number for "swords" is 98 or IH (I each).

Let us return to Figure 47 once again. It is interesting to note that the Alpha numbers for "The High Priestess + Justice" yield a total value of 282 or BHB (195 + 87 = 282). This means that it *be each "B"* (two), or that it be the letter "H." And lest there be any confusion relative to the total value of the sum of the terms, the Cabalah has alleviated this by making the Alpha sum of the letters F and G identical to the sum of their Tarot key numbers (F + G = 6 + 7 = 13 = M or Death, and 2 + 11 also equals 13 or Death). Moreover, the number 67 means "The One," the Alpha number of "Soul" or "Hanged Man." And I suppose that it is "justice" that up until now you and I have been oblivious to this fact, because the Alpha numbers for "justice" and "blindfolded" are identical. They both are equal to 87, which means that they represent HG or "each G."

You will note that we have inserted the names *Boga, Coty,* and *Cara* under the letters F, G, and H, respectively. Now why have we done that? We have done so because the symbol of the fulcrum of the scales along with its two pans is still another manifestation of this important trinity. Boga, as we said earlier, represents the sum total of all of your previous actions in the "ago" or in the past. These past deeds are now being weighed against all that you represent yourself to be in the present. If you are in harmony with the past, the two pans will be equally poised indicating perfect balance between these two states of your BEING. These are the *Boga* state and the *Cara* state, whose Alpha numbers are 25 and 23, respectively. The total of the two is 48, the number of the "Fool" who is U (You).

Now watch the scales in Figure 47. Cara is being weighed against the known weight of Boga who occupies the left-hand pan. Which way are the scales going to tip? They will tip in the favor of Boga since her Alpha number is 25, 2 more than the weight of Cara. Now why is this? The symbol for Justice is a pair of equally poised balances, with the weights of the two pans being identical; therefore there must be something wrong. And that is precisely the case inasmuch as the term Cara, per se, means only "a car"; and in this case it is an *empty* car. It tips in the favor of Boga simply because you are not in it! Therefore, in order to bring harmony and balance into the picture, each pair of the male and the female of the species, you and your counterpart or soul mate as it were, must get into your "Cara" car before it is weighed. The two of you represent the Lovers (Tarot Key 6), whose symbol is V. And the blindfolded girl being weighed is making the symbol of the "V" in the two swords which are balanced on her shoulders. She, inasmuch as she represents the pair of you or the Lovers, will then bring the two pans into equilibrium once she gets into her car and is weighed ($2 + 23 = 25 = BE = Boga$).

The Alpha number for the word "pair" is also interesting. It is 44 or DD. Its total Alpha value is 8 which means "H" or each; and its God-Name number is 170 or AGO ($D + D = 85 + 85 = 170 = AGO$). Our "pair" then simply means Cara's 2 or Cara's B; in other words, since B represents "wheel" and Cara is 23 which is a W (The Chariot), the term "Cara's B" means the Chariot's wheel. Isn't a chariot "a car"? Of course it is. Thus Cara's "wheel" becomes an all-important part of the overall term. But "Cara's B" may be transformed into the word "Scarab"; and the Alpha number for both terms is 44, the same as the number for "pair." These are the two D's, the two mortals, the two "devils" which represent you and me while we are going through our experiences on the earth plane. And this is precisely the reason, in all probability, why the *scarab* was regarded as being so sacred by the ancient Egyptians. Moreover, these two D's, when placed one above the other, bring into manifestation the letter "B," the true wheel of the chariot called Cara.

Now let us analyze the word *Coty*. This, you will note, represents the fulcrum of the scales of Justice, and as it was with its two counterparts, it also has another meaning. Its basic meaning is that it represents the spiritual aspect of our BEING, and the spiritual aspect is, of course, the complete harmony and balance between the positive and negative, the mental and the physical, the odd and the even. In other words, Coty represents the God-Self within, or the zero point of the very term *Being* itself. "Be aware of Being," the Agashan Teachers are always saying, but that "Being" that we should become aware of is none other than the CG of our consciousness (Being = 37 = CG), and the CG of our consciousness is Coty.

Earlier we learned that an alternate meaning for Coty is that it represents our death bed, the very last place on the physical plane of life that we will find ourselves before ascending into the higher spiritual consciousness. But is this really so unusual? After all, it seems perfectly logical that when traveling through a number from the integer part to its decimal fraction, or when moving down the scale of numbers from the positive ones to the negative ones, we must first pass through the decimal point or the zero itself which is completely neutral. Coty then acts as the doorway between the two worlds of the inner and the outer, the spiritual and the material, and through its portals all must pass on this journey that is Life.

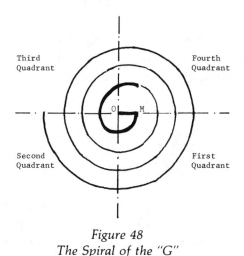

Figure 48
The Spiral of the "G"

Let us say that we are spiraling inwards on this journey. Let us say that each revolution of the spiral shown in the above Figure 48 represents one year of earthly living. There they are: the four quadrants divide the year up into its four seasons of Spring, Summer, Autumn, and Winter. You are moving along quite nicely, blissfully unaware that the road will suddenly end at some point marked M. This is the dwelling place of Coty. Here, your spiritual path will suddenly turn inwards as it makes a 90-degree, right-angle turn. You will then be traveling towards the real center of your Being, the very Core of Life itself at the point marked O. This is the final leg of your spiritual journey home, a journey that began many years ago when you fell asleep in the astral regions, only to reawaken a short time later as a small child in this present life of yours. The end and the beginning of this final phase are symbolized by the OM, the space on the diagram between the letters O and M, and the in-going portion of the Divine Sound of Creation—the AUM and the OM.

One can see that the "G" symbol very aptly portrays the beginning and ending of every coil or spiral. Yet, it in itself is a combination of two other symbols: the "C" and the "L." The "C" represents the circular path around the core, and the "L" its abrupt right-angle turn inwards at the point of physical death. Together, they add up to 15 which balances the out-going force of the Sun, the letter "O," the force that spewed you forth in the beginning. And, of course, the total for all three is 30, which represents the CO or the *Company* of which you are a part. Here, within these symbols, are perfect justice and balance, for the number 87, it must be remembered, is not only the Alpha number of "Company," but it is also the number for *Justice* and *the Sun* as well. It is indeed the number that makes the company formed by the Moon and the Sun literally and truly "go."

One other point: Death is not the only force that exists at the fulcrum of the scales, the "O" point where Coty resides. Indeed not, for its counterpart is ever present. What is its counterpart? It is Judgment, the Resurrection, Christ, the letter "X." How do we know that it is there? We know it to be true because the Alpha number for "fulcrum" is 94, the number of the ID and the number of "Judgment." The combination of Boga and Coty or "Each H" (the number 88) will see that it is so.

Where Two or Three Are Gathered Together

The Holy Bible is a veritable treasure-trove of philosophical and spiritual information once its many chapters and verses in the 39 books of the Old Testament and the 27 books of the New Testament are interpreted cabalistically. And by that interpretation, we mean applying the laws of the English Cabalah to decipher the hidden meaning of any chapter and verse. Even the very name itself implies that this is so. The Alpha number for "The Holy Bible" is 123, which means that it stands for the Emperor, the Fatherhood of God (33 + 60 + 30 = 123 = A). And the number of books contained therein substantiate this even further; for when we read 39 + 27, we read it as "C I B G" or "See, I be G (Justice)." And the Universal Consciousness God is most certainly just that.

As an illustration, let us analyze the word "Matthew," the name of the first book in the New Testament. We may break it apart as follows: M at the W, or "Death at the Chariot." The letter "M" is also the inverse of the letter "W," geometrically as well as philosophically, for when we upset the chariot (turn the "W" upside down) we literally bring death (the letter "M") to its occupants. And if we compute the Alpha number for the complete word, "Matthew," we find the reason why. For the number is 90; the number of the A, the C, or the I (Emperor = The Moon = The Magician = 90). And doesn't the term "ACI" refer to the "All-Seeing Eye"? Isn't this another manifestation of *Cara Boga Coty* or the three I's, three different aspects of God with each being equal to the other? Therefore, the term "Matthew" itself implies that it represents the CG or the central point within the God Consciousness.

There is still another way to arrive at this conclusion. The symbols "ACI" may be read as the number 139; but isn't this number the Alpha number for "The Wheel of Life," the letter B? If our assumption is correct, then, the Book of Matthew must be so placed within the overall books of the Bible that it represents the letter B. And this is precisely where it is located.

There are 39 books ahead of it, and this represents a group of 3 times 13 or three M's. There are 26 books following it, and this latter set represents a group of 2 times 13 or two M's. Where, then, is the single M? It must be at the Book of Matthew; yet Matthew represents only one book and not 13. The problem is solved by simply opening up the letter "B" into the number "13" as in Figure 30. Moreover, the letter M is also the initial letter of the word *Matthew.*

All well and good. Now let us find the particular chapter and/or chapters within the Book of Matthew itself, the microcosm within the macrocosm so to speak, that in turn represent "death at the chariot" or "M at the W." There are 28 chapters in the book, and following the same line of reasoning that we went through before, we may break these 28 chapters up into three sets of 15, 3, and 10 chapters respectively. The first set represents a group of 3 times 5 or three E's; the middle set is simply a group of 3; and the last set consists of a group of 2 times 5 or two E's. It is significant that the word "EM" is the name of the letter "M," and that the number "1 + 3" (the central terms of the macrocosm and the microcosm) may be read as the number "13," the numerical value of "M." Therefore, our search has now isolated Chapters 16, 17, and 18 as being the representative chapters of "M at the W."

Let us check it out. We find that Chapter 16 has 28 verses, Chapter 17 has 27 verses, and Chapter 18 has 35 verses. This seems almost incredible, because the total number of verses in our selected chapters is our same number 90: the Alpha value of "M at the W."

Proceeding further, our path now becomes a little more thorny. Isolating a single verse from this large group of 90 verses as being the one verse that represents "M at the W" is not quite as obvious as it was before. As we approach "pay dirt," the path becomes a little more rough and the clues are well hidden. Needless to say, the problem was solved through the process of elimination. There is really only one verse that adequately fulfills all of the requirements, and it is Chapter 18, Verse 20. It is the 75th verse in the series, with 74 verses to the left of it and 15 verses to the right of it. The 74 relates to the King, the letter K; and the 15 relates to the Sun, the letter O. And equidistant between the K and the O is the single verse which represents the letter M—the 75th one.

There are still other clues that we have selected the correct verse that truly represents "M at the W." First, the number 74 stands for the God-Word "Chariot" whose symbol is "W." Therefore, the following Verse 75 should represent the "M," the inverse of the "W." The second clue is that the value of "WMO" is 51, the same as the sum of Chapters 16, 17, and 18. And thirdly, and by far the most significant clue of all, is that the numerical sum of Chapter 18, Verse 20 is 38—the number of Death, the letter M. Thus the complete Alpha number of "Matthew 18:20" is "90 + 38 = 128 = Z," the Empress, the letter Z, the number 26 which stands for God. It is also the death of either the Emperor, the Moon, or the Magician—the ACI or the All-Seeing Eye. You may take your choice as to which one of these three you wish to ascend into the higher consciousness.

The exact wording of Matthew 18:20 is as follows: *"For where two or three are gathered together in my name, there am I in the midst of them."* There they are—19 of the most powerful and significant words in the entire Bible. We honestly believe that in this group of words we have tracked down the perfect symbol to represent the central fulcrum point in the Scales of Justice—the home of the great "I AM." We will leave it to the reader to judge for himself whether or not this is the case.

We have now the correct verse that represents "M at the W," but we have not yet pinpointed its exact location *within* the verse. However, this is not at all difficult to do because Christ himself reveals the secret. Where are two or three gathered together? "In my name," he tells them to gather together, "for there *am I* in the midst of them!" And where is the phrase "in my name" located within the verse? The answer is that it is in the exact center of it. In the group of 19 words that make up the verse, there are exactly eight words to the left of "in my name" and eight words to the right of it. Therefore, it represents the fulcrum point of the Scales—the dwelling place of the great "I AM." And not only that, but there is even a fulcrum within the fulcrum so to speak, a zero point that is absolutely motionless, and a place that represents the innermost sanctuary of BEING. This is symbolized by the word "my," the CG or center of gravity of them all. The number of words and letters to the left and right of each of these three different aspects of Being are tabulated in the following table, and the result should prove rather interesting to the average reader.

Words to the Left		*Center*	*To the Right*
		MY	
Words	9	1	9
Letters	39	2	28
	I Hanged (39)	A B	I Man (28)
		MY NAME	
Words	9	2	8
Letters	39	6	24
	I See I	God (26)	Hex
		IN MY NAME	
Words	8	3	8
Letters	37	8	24
	Each CG	Death (38)	Each X

The Alpha number of the central word "my" is 38 which means Death (Tarot Key 13). This is the true letter M, and the "M" of "M at the W." Where then is the W? The W is symbolized by the word "in," because the Alpha number of "in" is 23, the letter W. This leaves only one other word to take into account, the word "name." Its Alpha number is 33, the same as the word "the"; therefore, it is the "the" of the "M at the W." The phrase "M at the W" is now complete, and "Matthew" is brought into full manifestation with the words "IN MY NAME." It is literally and truly "Death at the W," because "the W" or the "double you" (it can be said both ways) actually passes through the doorway called "Death" at this particular point in time.

The reader is asked to compare these words "In My Name" with the relationship of the Tarot cards in Figure 47. Cara, the one being "weighed in," so to speak, is the letter "W" that is brought into manifestation with the word "In." Together, the W + IN makes up the word "WIN," and that is exactly just what our blindfolded girl does. She wins the race for the Lovers (the letter V).

Boga, on the other hand, is the counterbalance of Cara, the known weight that is used to measure the weight or spiritual growth of the Lovers. She is the High Priestess or the "The" part of "The Lovers." She is also the "the" of "M at the W," and she is brought into full manifestation with the word "Name." (The Alpha numbers of both "The" and "Name" are each 33, and 33 reduces to 6 or the letter F, the symbol of the High Priestess.) The Alpha number of the term "In Name" is then 56, the number of "The W," and it is spelled "EF," the name of the symbol "F."

This leaves only Coty to be accounted for, and I am sure the reader will find no fault with relating the fulcrum of the scales, the Tarot key for Justice, with the word "My," the one word that is located at the very center of Verse 20. Indeed, Christ himself states that "there *am I* in the midst of *them*." And who and what is the word "them"? The answer is simple. It merely means "The M." And the "M" is Death, the number 38, the Alpha number for "My"! The lesson to be learned, then, is that the dwelling place of the great "I AM" is right in the center of the "M."

Thus when only *two* are gathered together in "my name," Christ is referring to the *Coty Boga* aspect of the two-word phrase "my name"; but when *three* are gathered together "in my name," he is obviously referring to the *Cara Coty Boga* aspect of the complete three-word term "in my name." It does make a difference how many words we use in our analysis. For example: the Alpha number of the one-word term "My" is 38, the number of Death. The Alpha number of the two-word term "My Name" is 71, the number of "The Death"; therefore there is not too much difference between the one-word term or the two-word term. But when we come to the three-word term, there is a great deal of difference between it and the other two. The Alpha number of "In My Name" is 94, the ID, the undifferentiated source from which we sprang, and the number of *Judgment*, the resurrection of the spirit, the letter "X." Death and Judgment are therefore the key words for the phrase, "In My Name."

Now let us study the two-word aspect in greater depth. Let us see if we can find out what makes it "tick," so to speak, if I may use the term in that manner. Let us try to ascertain the source of energy that exists within the phrase, "My Name." We know that the Alpha value of the first word is 38, the number of Death, the letter M. We also know that the Alpha value of the second word is 33, but let us stop right there. How else can you read the number 33? You may read it as "CC," and when you put the letters "CC" alongside of the letter "M," you bring into manifestation the term "MCC" or "MC^2," one half of Einstein's famous formula for the equivalence of matter and energy. $E = mc^2$ is probably the most famous formula known to science today, and it is with considerable awe and astonishment that we learn that the source of energy within "My Name," the dwelling place of the great "I AM," is *Energy* itself.

All well and good. But this rather astounding discovery by no means completes our analysis. There is still another way to attack the problem, and this alternate way is to ascertain the God-Name number of the term and see if it sheds any further light on the true meaning of the term "My Name."The effort proves quite worthwhile, as the reader can easily see from the adjacent tabulation.

The Cabalah then, not only tells us that the source of power within "My Name" is "$E = mc^2$," but it also reveals the exact location where this energy is stored. It is stored within the egg, the egg of the soul, or the Orphic egg if you will, and this "egg" is located at the center of gravity or directly in the middle of "Each" living thing. And from the egg or the seed, all things spring forth.

Symbol	God-Name Number		Alpha Number
M	Death	38	13
Y	Strength	111	25
N	The Hanged Man	100	14
A	The Emperor	123	1
M	Death	38	13
E	The Hierophant	147	5
	MY NAME	557	71
	E-EGG-A	EEG	GA

The above analysis was derived from a combination of the God-Name number and the Alpha number for the term. But the God-Name number all by itself is most intriguing. The number is 557, and if we were to read it backwards from right to left, we would read it as GEE, the name of the letter G. Now in any cabalistic analysis all clues should be followed through to their conclusion, for we never know just where our pot of gold may be hidden. Therefore, a further analysis of the letter G is mandatory.

But where do we begin? All we know at this point is that the God-Name number of "My Name" equates to the letter G. In other words, the letter G *is* "My Name," and if we could somehow find out just whom this letter stands for, we would then know whose name it really is. The letter G, of course, stands for Justice (Tarot Key 11); but other than the goddess Astraea, we have no knowledge of the true identity of the One who states that *Justice* (the letter G) be "My Name." A way out of the predicament is to treat fire with fire; that is, since the God-Name number of "My Name" refers to the letter G which stands for Justice, then a similar treatment for the word "Justice" itself might reveal the identity of the One we are seeking.

Symbol	God-Name	Number	Alpha Number
J	The World	105	10
U	The Fool	81	21
S	The Star	91	19
T	Temperance	100	20
I	The Magician	90	9
C	The Moon	90	3
E	The Hierophant	147	5
	JUSTICE	704	87
	Each "G"	GOD	HG

This action proved to be correct, as the reader can plainly see, and in absolute astonishment and wonderment as we marvel at the majesty of it all, we learn that the letter "G" is the symbol for GOD! And that when we use the term "My Name," we are indirectly referring to the Universal Consciousness that men call GOD.

NOTES

1. Arthur Edward Waite, *The Pictorial Key to the Tarot* (New York, University Books, 1959) pages 115, 21, and 250

2. John Bell, *Bell's New Pantheon* (London, J. Bell, Bookseller, 1790) Vol. I, p. 101

Chapter 14

THE OGHAM LETTERS OF LIFE AND DEATH

W E FIND FROM the previous chapter that a basic fundamental within the overall Consciousness of God is Justice. Indeed, God *is* Justice. The God Consciousness is constantly endeavoring to bring all things into a state of equilibrium and balance. If one aspect of Nature becomes too dominant and out of harmony with the role it is intended to play, another aspect comes into manifestation to curtail it. But this principle of equilibrium and balance is not solely limited to living things; no indeed, for even inanimate things such as religion, government, wealth and poverty, and even language itself are affected by it.

For example: let us compare the ancient Ogham language with the English language of today. On the surface, these two languages bear absolutely no relationship with each other because the structures of their alphabets are based upon completely different principles; yet, surprisingly enough, there is an underlying intelligence common to both of them. The Ogham alphabet, which dates back to the 5th and 6th century in Old

267

Ireland, consists of 20 letters where notches stand for vowels
and horizontal lines for consonants. It has been preserved prin-
cipally from inscriptions cut on the edges of rough standing
tombstones; but the absolutely amazing thing about all of this
is that the English letters in the word *LIFE* have not only
evolved out of this alphabet, but that they also point out the
basic principles of its construction. In other words, the
Cabalah uses the construction methods employed in the creation of the ancient Ogham alphabet to better explain to us how
Life is brought into manifestation, what it really is, and its relationship with *Death*.

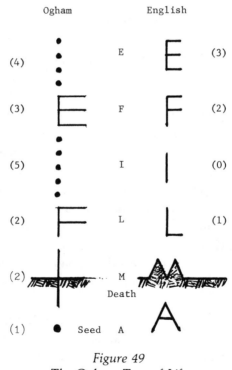

Figure 49
The Ogham Tree of Life

Figure 49 makes this comparison. The letters in the middle
column represent the equivalent sounds common to both lan-

guages. This column then acts as the fulcrum of a scales that is weighing the letter/symbols of the modern-day English language with those of their 5th century Ogham counterparts. The numerals at the extreme right and left designate the number of points (notches) or horizontal lines that extend outwards from the vertical trunk of the English and Ogham trees of life. Thus we find that the English word LIFE is built up of each of the numerals 0, 1, 2, and 3, with the "0" occupying an intermediate position within the body of the Emperor (123); whereas the numerals of its Ogham counterparts are 2, 5, 3, and 4, respectively. If we translate these numerals into English, we read the Ogham "tree" as stating that it "BE CD (Be Seed)."

It is interesting to note that if one were to recite the English alphabet out loud from A to Z, the mouth will remain open at the sound of every letter with the exception of the "M." Here, the lips will remain very tightly closed as if signifying Death— and Silence. Try this little experiment while looking into the mirror. You will be amazed at the result. It is a living proof that the sound of the English letter M closes the mouth and brings *Death* into manifestation (Tarot Key 13). There are many other proofs that the letter M is the symbol for this Tarot Key—such as the 13 steps leading up to the gallows when a man is hanged —but this particular proof is the most spectacular one. Death indeed is the doorway through which one must pass when leaving one world and entering another.

The Ogham symbol for the sound of "M" is a horizontal line extending on both sides of the vertical stem. In some ways it resembles a plus sign (+); or if we turn it slightly on edge it looks like an "X." The latter symbol repesents Judgement (Tarot Key 20); therefore, even the Ogham symbols verify that the death and resurrection of the spirit are synonymous terms.

The Ogham symbols for the English equivalent of the word "LIFE" are "F.....E.... ." Reading the term cabalistically we may interpret it as "FE," the symbol for the chemical element iron, whose Alpha number is 56 or EF, the reverse of FE. Now the numerical equivalent of the letter F is the numeral "6," and if we invert it we can change it into a "9" which represents the letter "I." But we also learned that these Ogham symbols state that they "be seed" (BE CD); therefore, the only step remaining to complete the glyph is to plant the "seed" in the ground below the surface of the earth by placing a dot under the "i." Death represents the surface of the earth, and the seed which is within it is the inverse of the tree which is above it in the same manner as the "6" is the inverse of the "9," or "EF" the reverse of "FE."

The English equivalent of the single Ogham dot or notch is the letter "A." Therefore, inasmuch as the two pans of our scale must balance, and that the English tree of life may be compared and weighed against the Ogham tree of life, the seed of our English tree must be this same symbol, "A." But isn't it absolutely amazing that the tree that springs forth from the "A" seed is indeed the word "LIFE" itself, the numerical value of which is the "O" in the middle of the "123" (The Emperor)! The symbol for the Emperor is, of course, the same as that of the seed—the letter A.

Another point to be understood is that the Alpha value of the Ogham tree of life symbols is actually identical to that of the English tree of life symbols. Both the English letters and the Ogham symbols have the same Alpha value because they both equate to identical sounds. The reader should not be confused by the numbers to the right and the left of the respective trees. These figures solely relate to the number of dots (notches) or lines extending out from the central stem. The Alpha value for either tree is then 46 (AM LIFE = 14 + 32 = 46). And if we start from the tip of the tree and read downwards to the seed and then back up to the tip again, we have the expression "E FILM A AM LIFE." In other words, the Cabalah tells us that this process called *Life* is basically the result of the Hierophant whose symbol is "E" (the Spiritual Energy within the Cosmos) *filming,* photographing, and recording the life of the Emperor whose symbol is "A." This is what life is all about.

However, if we take the Ogham tree of life into account as representing the past, and then read from its tip downwards to its seed and then up again through the English tree of life to the present, we read the following rather amazing statement: "EF 'I' AM LIFE." This definition of Life would imply that it results from the feminine "I" of the High Priestess descending in the tree of life of the past and then ascending once more in the tree of life of the present. Another interesting observation is that the great "I AM" may be defined as the energy within the seed arising and breaking through the surface of the earth. It is then transformed into the visible tree above called "Life." There are many different interpretations for the symbols of the Cabalah, yet all of them are basically correct. The student is limited only by his capability to comprehend them.

One other point. The writer has just discovered that even the Ogham symbols themselves, as different as they are from the English symbols, actually can be made into a replica of the English letters contained within the word "LIFE." As I have said several times in this work, the Cabalah always has many surprises in store for the diligent student. The English letters I, F, and E are plainly evident in the Ogham tree. Where, then, is the "L"? Well, if you just move the two horizontal lines from the "+" symbol, which represents the "M" sound of Death, to the right of the lower dot which represents the seed, you will make a perfect "L" using the 10 dots as the vertical leg and the two lines as the horizontal leg. And the total of 10 dots and 2 lines is 12, the Alpha number for "L"! The vertical leg is then the Pillar of Jachin (the letter J), and the horizontal leg the Pillar of Boaz (the letter B). "Life" indeed has its surprises.

The Naked Splendor of Isis Unveiled

In Chapter 6 we endeavored to show the process whereby the veil of ignorance may be removed from the goddess Isis, the Virgin Mother of the World. However, we did not actually unveil her completely. We did not reveal the naked truth of the magnificence of her Being; that is, the full disclosure of the fundamental principle that she represents. Madame Blavatsky, in her monumental two-volume treatise that she first published in 1877 titled *Isis Unveiled*,[1] removed a great many of her outer veils, but even she was unable to unveil her completely. The Masters of Wisdom working through her evidently did not consider that that was the right time for Isis's final unveiling. These more esoteric truths, according to the Agashan Teachers, had to wait until the end of the age when the world would be in a better position to receive them. This would be in the great *Grand Finale*, the "latter days" of the 20th century, the final act in the drama called Life when all that had been misinterpreted before could be clarified.

As a starter, let us consider the geometrical relationships between the digits 6, 8, 9, and 0. The digit 6, of course, represents Isis, the letter F, the 6th letter of the English alphabet. And if we were to turn her upside down, she magically is transformed into the digit 9, the masculine counterpart of her Being which is the Magician, the letter "I," the 9th letter of the English alphabet. Thus the High Priestess (Tarot Key 2) and the Magician (Tarot Key 1) are in reality one and the same; they represent only the feminine and the masculine aspects of the one Being. The thought is clarified and expounded a little further in the following Figure 50:

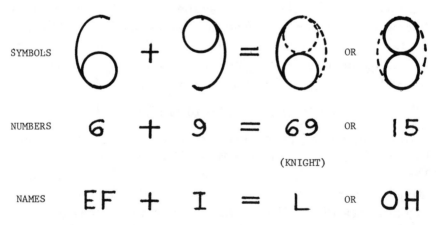

Figure 50
How the Digits Bring Life into Manifestation

One can see very easily from a study of the above figure that the combination of the 6 and the 9 brings into manifestation the Knight, the Letter L, since the Alpha number for "Knight" is 69. And if we read the entire equation backwards in reverse order from the right to the left, we find that the combined total of both sides of the equation gives birth once again to the process called "LIFE." Indeed, the issue or the result of this "sexual act" is the Sun, the English letter whose symbol is "O" and whose name is "Oh" (6 + 9 = 15 = O, and 0 + 8 = OH).

The illustration on the Face of Tarot Key 19 (The Sun) brings this thought sharply into focus. A naked child is shown mounted on a white horse in front of a wall. The word "Wall" may be broken apart into "W + All" or "Cara + Boga" (the High Priestess + the Magician or the 6 + the 9). And the child, of course, will eventually grow up into the Fool who is U (You), since the combination of Cara and Boga is 48, the number of the "Fool" and also of the "Wall" which symbolizes the parents from which he sprang forth. His birth is very much the result of a sexual union between these two forces because his mother, the High Priestess, is the very goddess of Sex itself.

Figure 51

Why do we say that? Well, the Alpha number for "The High Priestess" is 195 which may be read as "SE." And it is only one step further to add the two letters together and come up with the word "SEX" (19 + 5 = 24 = SEX). This is one of the reasons that she is known as the Virgin Mother of the World since all life must come into manifestation through and by the means of that aspect of Nature that she represents—the sexual union of the male with the female.

Now let us study this union from another angle. The female

force is the High Priestess whose symbol is "F," and the male force is the Magician whose symbol is "I." But now let us equate the *names* of these letters with the value of the symbols themselves. This is done in the following tabulation:

Names   *God-Self*   *Symbols*

EF + I = T OR O = F + I

11 + 9 = 20 or 15 = 6 + 9

One can see that the two sums are either 20 or 15, the combination of which gives us the word "TORO," which means "Bull" in Spanish. Now Taurus the Bull is the second sign of the Zodiac, and the Alpha number of the term is 180 or RO (100 + 33 + 47 = 180). Isn't it strange then that the number for Taurus should represent the conjunction "or" between two sums? The Alpha number for "Toro" is 68, the number for "Pillar" or "God-Self"; and the Alpha number for "El Toro," which means "The Bull," is 85, the number of "The Devil," the letter D. No matter what we do in the Cabalah, the God force and the Devil force seem to be ever present.

Just to prove this point, let us take a look at the following Figure 52:

6 + 9 =	Sum	Sum	= 8 + O		
SIX + NINE	JUDGMENT	A M	EIGHT	+	ZERO
52 + 42	94	113	49	+	64
DEVIL + THE I	EX	A M	(Seven Squared)	+	(Eight Squared)
D I	E - X	284	150	+	134
		B H D	O O		M D

Figure 52
Die! Judgment! Each Be Doomed

All of the numbers in the preceding figure are the Alpha numbers for the words they represent, and the story that they tell is absolutely amazing! The clue, of course, is the discovery that the Alpha numbers for both *eight* and *zero* are 7^2 (seven squared) and 8^2 (eight squared) respectively; and it is then that we find that this "Judgment" that is brought about through the conjunction of the 6 and 9 means that they "each be doomed." Or is this really what it means? Who is it that is doomed? Another interpretation is that Judgment in reality is an examination (Judgment am exam) after the 6 and 9 "die." Then Christ (X) manifests and be each (B H). And it is this manifestation of the Christ-self that enables each one of them to "doom" their own individual Devil-self, the "D." So then an equally valid interpretation is that it is the Devil who is doomed in the final analysis, and not the hero and heroine of our story.

NOTES

1. H. P. Blavatsky, *Isis Unveiled* (Wheaton, Ill., Theosophical Publishing House, 1950)

Chapter 15

THE HOUSE OF GOD

THE REAL MEANING for the term "Isis Unveiled" cannot be understood in its entirety until we likewise have a correct interpretation for "The House of God." Actually they are one and the same, for when we remove the veil from Isis (the veil between the pillars in Tarot Key 2), the House of God comes into view on the other side. And the way this is brought about is through a thorough understanding of your own "Cara Boga Coty Being."

"You are Cara Boga Coty," the Master Teacher Agasha has said on dozens of occasions (*Agasha: Master of Wisdom*, page 183), "but you cannot become aware of them until you are aware of *Being*. There is the secret. Only by being aware of Being will you know thy true self."

"But what is Being?" you might ask. The Alpha number for *Being* is 37; it is therefore the CG or center of gravity of yourself. It is the Spark of Divinity within the soul; it is your Higher Self, your individual *Cara Boga Coty Being*. It is significant to realize that the term "Cara Boga Coty" is itself three Beings in one, since the three 1's of Cara Boga Coty (111) equate to "Being + Being + Being" or 37 + 37 + 37. Even the name "Agasha" is a perfect example of "Being," since its Alpha number is also 37. And so is the number of sects that Agasha organized into one unit in the early days of Austa, Egypt. They, too, were 37 in number. Yes indeed, the real meaning of "Being" is an all-important aspect of the English Cabalah.

So is the real meaning for the term "Isis Unveiled." Its Alpha number is 148 or ADH. And it is certainly no "coincidence" that the Alpha numbers for the terms "The House of God" or your own individual "Cara Boga Coty Being" are equal to this same number (33 + 68 + 21 + 26 = 148, and 23 + 25 + 63 + 37 = 148). The number 148, then, simply represents four "Beings" in one, or 4 × 37. This is the true meaning for the term, "Isis Unveiled."

Yet, there is still a more powerful explanation. Let us analyze its God-Name number alongside of its Alpha number as follows:

Symbol	God-Name Number	Alpha Number
A The Emperor	123	1
D The Devil	85	4
H The Hermit	106	8
A D H	314	13
Pi + Death	π	M

We find then that the term "Isis Unveiled," the number 148, brings into manifestation not only the first three digits of Pi (π), but also the number 13 which means Death. And to make the statement even more emphatic, the God-Name number of the term is the Alpha number for "The Great Pyramid of the Emperor" depicted by Figure 18.

All of the above is leading us towards a great realization. The writer is often asked just why we illustrated the dust jackets of these volumes called the Agashan Books in the way that we have. The reason is as follows: In *Agasha: Master of Wisdom*, Agasha (who symbolizes your own Higher Self) is observing the Great Pyramid as it appears during the day when illuminated by the Sun; in *The Agashan Discourses*, he is absorbing its beautiful radiation while being bathed in the light of the Moon; but in these two volumes he is aware of the *exterior* of the pyramid only. He has not yet reached an understanding as to its *inner* significance. And then suddenly, in this present volume, the veil is lifted as he studies intently the true magnificence of its inner meaning. He suddenly realizes that it is so constructed that twice the length of the base of one of its sides, when divided by its altitude, brings into manifestation one of the most powerful forces in the universe—the number π or Pi. Of course, this is certainly not to imply that Agasha, or any of the other Teachers of the Higher Orders for that matter, were not aware of these truths all along. Indeed not. In fact, it is they who are responsible for this entire series of books in the first place.

But there is still more to come. In Volume II of *The English Cabalah*, the figure gazing at the pyramid will become aware of the greatest truth of them all. In that volume he will come to the full understanding that this magnificent structure, at one and the same time, is also a manifestation of the Golden Mean —the number Φ or Phi. Phi is the counterpart of Pi, and it results when we reverse the process and replace the altitude with the apothem. (Twice the length of the apothem when divided by the base is Phi). A cross section through our "Pi-Phi" pyramid is illustrated in the following Figure 53:

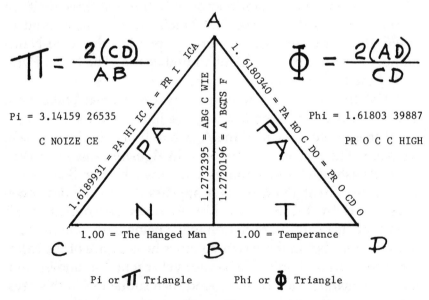

Figure 53
A Cross Section Through the Pi-Phi Pyramid

If we assume the half-base to be equal to one or unity, the altitude of the *Pi* triangle on the left is only .0012199 . . . greater than the altitude of the *Phi* triangle on the right. Cabalistically, the difference is read as "OOLSI"; or, reading it backwards, we have the word "ISLOO." If we could change the two O's to "AND," we would have the word "ISLAND," but unfortunately that is not the case. We can, however, substitute the term "Zero and Zero" for "00"; and if we were to do this, we could quite legitimately transform the "00" into an "E." (The Alpha number for "Zero and Zero" is 147, the same as that of "The Hierophant," whose symbol is "E.") Therefore, the Cabalah tells us that the only difference between the altitude of a Pi pyramid and a Phi pyramid—strictly speaking that is, because the difference in reality is almost negligible—is a small "ISLE," an extremely small island within the decimal fraction.

The Cabalah also reveals some very interesting information relative to the esoteric meaning of the values of Pi and Phi. If we consider the symbol "C" to represent the velocity of light (In the Agashan terminology, the vibrational frequency that separates the physical world from the astral world is called the Candic Ray), then we would presume that there is a large amount of "NOISE" in the vast range of frequencies between "standing still" and moving at the velocity of light—the maximum speed that one may travel or function at and still remain in the physical universe. However, the Agashan Teachers go on to say that when you travel at speeds greater than that of light—a frequency of 300,000 kilometers per second to us is a frequency of 0 to an astral being, remember—you can actually travel from here to anywhere else in the universe in the "twinkling of an eye."

The information revealed by the value of Phi is equally as startling. It, the same as Pi, is an infinitely long decimal number; but if we round up the 7th digit from a 3 to a 4, the number 1.618034 expresses it quite accurately for all practical purposes. This is read as "PROCD," and if we substitute the name of the letter (Cee) whose symbol is "C," we have the word "PROCEED." The dictionary defines the term as (1) to come forth from a source, (2) to continue after a pause or interruption, and (3) to go on in an orderly regulated way. And this process, as the reader will discover when he embraces Volume II of this work, is an extremely accurate definition of the function of Phi. And if we do not round off the 7th digit, and instead read the next 5 digits in their natural order, we can rearrange them to read "HIGH C." This note, incidentally, is one of the highest notes the human voice is capable of reaching.

Let us now analyze the *names* of the major segments of the cross section through our pyramid. They are the altitude, the half-base, and the apothem. The following Figure 54 is identical to Figure 53; the only exception is that the Alpha numbers of the names have been substituted for the true numerical values of the line segments.

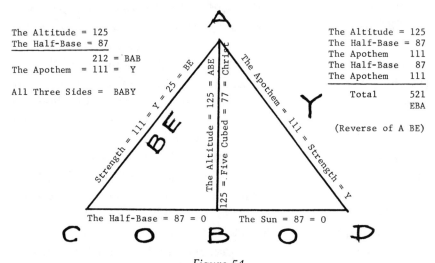

The Altitude = 125
The Half-Base = 87
_____
　　　　212 = BAB
The Apothem = 111 = Y

All Three Sides = BABY

The Altitude = 125
The Half-Base = 87
The Apothem 111
The Half-Base 87
The Apothem 111
_____
Total 521
EBA

(Reverse of A BE)

The Half-Base = 87 = 0　　　The Sun = 87 = 0

Figure 54
A Baby's Body Be a Company: A Co-Body with the Emperor

It is interesting to note that the Cabalah verifies the lettering system we had so chosen to use in identifying the line segments in Figure 53. For example: the altitude is indeed the line AB since its Alpha number is this very number, 125 or ABE. And when the initial life force first descended from the apex, it is only reasonable to assume that it landed squarely in the middle of the CD (the Seed). The rest of the items in Figure 54 are self explanatory. One can only repeat again, as he studies the truths contained therein, that the intelligence of the Cabalah seems beyond compare!

The next step in our analysis is to properly identify each of the line segments with its appropriate Tarot key. This has been done in the following Figure 55:

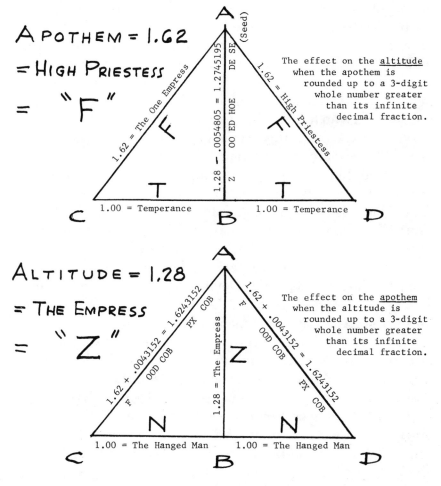

Figure 55
The Functions of the Empress and High Priestess

One should realize that the High Priestess represents the apothem of the pyramid and not its slant-edge. All of our cross sections through the pyramid are taken through the middle of the left and the right sides as we observe it from a vantage point directly in front of one of its faces. They are, therefore, a true orthographic projection of the way we actually see it from that position.

Another point is that when two people view the pyramid from faces perpendicular to each other, the line that I visualize as the altitude or the Empress will appear as the apothem or High Priestess to you. Yet the Empress will *always* be the altitude; it is only her projected image onto one of the faces that will *appear* as the apothem or High Priestess to someone else. The reason for this illusion is philosophical as well as mathematical; for the High Priestess in reality is nothing more than the Empress who has become pregnant.

Why do we make this seemingly contradictory statement? "After all, they are two different Tarot keys," you will say, and that is true. But the point to be made is that *all* Tarot keys are but different aspects of the *one* life that resides within the Tarot deck. There is only one entity to be considered, and that is You. The different Tarot keys are but different roles you play as you investigate the mysteries of your own Being. At one point in your evolution you are the Emperor, and at another point you are the Sun, the Devil, or whatever. The various Tarot keys are but different masks that you put on from time to time in the great drama that men call Life.

Therefore, when the Emperor casts his seed into the Empress, he becomes the Magician and turns her into the High Priestess. The A and the Z have now become the I and the F. Let us look at it this way: The Alpha number for "The Empress" is 128, and if we wish to change her into the "High Priestess," make her pregnant as it were, we must add 34 to her number (128 + 34 = 162 = High Priestess). But the number 34 is in reality the CD or "A Seed" (1 + 33 = 34 = CD); and the number 34 is also ONE. Therefore, since "a seed" is "one," it must belong to the Emperor since he stands for the Father, the *One* God whose symbol is "A." Everything, in the final analysis, reverts back to this first cause.

The Mysteries of the Lightning-Struck Tower

The reader is asked to refer once more to Figure 18. It shows the exterior of the Great Pyramid with its golden apex still intact, and if you were to slice it right down the middle, it would automatically turn into Figure 53, 54, or 55. The title of Figure 18 is "The Great Pyramid of the Emperor," the Alpha number of which is 314 or Pi. But we have already learned that it is not only a "Pi" pyramid, but it is also a "Phi" pyramid as well. Therefore, part of its complete title is missing. And since the Alpha number of "High Priestess" is 162 or Phi, the full title of Figure 18 should be *"The Great Pyramid of the Emperor and High Priestess."* This is its complete name. The Alpha number of the term is then "314 and 162" or "Pi and Phi," the combination of which brings into manifestation the true "House of God."

But the golden apex that originally crowned this magnificent structure is missing, it having long since toppled over into the sands of time, where it lies there today as a symbol of the fall of mankind, waiting to be found once more and restored to the position it had had in the beginning. (*Agasha: Master of Wisdom*, page 146.) This is the reason, then, that the Great Pyramid is only referred to today in connection with some great Pharaoh or Emperor—and never with the High Priestess. It is the Pi Pyramid of the Emperor that mankind today embraces, and not the Phi Pyramid of the High Priestess. But this situation will not last forever, as the Agashan Teachers state that the day is not too far away when mankind will once more awaken to the true significance of this veritable "House of God."

"Why do you keep referring to it as the House of God?" you ask, "when occult tradition has from time immemorial reserved this name to stand for the Tower (Tarot Key 16)?" This is quite true, but has it not also occurred to the reader that the Tower is depicted as being struck by lightning? Look closely at Figure

56. Doesn't the bolt of lightning send the *crown* of the Tower crashing to the ground? And isn't this "crown" of the Tower strangely similar to the golden apex that originally capped the Great Pyramid? The similarity between the symbols just could not be coincidental, and we will attempt to prove in this chapter that the true esoteric meaning of the lightning-struck Tower symbolized by Tarot Key 16 refers not only to the Great Pyramid of the Emperor and High Priestess, but also to the Core of Life itself.

THE TOWER.

Figure 56

Let us now look at the numbers. The Alpha number for "The Great Pyramid of the Emperor and High Priestess" is 495 which spells out "DIE"! (314 + 19 + 162 = 495 = DIE). Now who is it that dies? The answer is found when we compute the Alpha number for the equivalent term "Pi and Phi." The answer is rather shocking for we find that it is Christ (25 + 19 + 33 = 77 = Christ). Of course, the Cabalah doesn't actually spell out the word "Christ," but the implication is certainly there. The number 77 almost always refers to Christ in some way or another. The more one goes into the study of the Cabalah, the more he comes to understand the significance of the 7, the double 7, the triple 7, or any number of 7's for that matter.

But who is Christ, really? He is a double 7 which indicates two G's, not one G but two of them. And we learned a little earlier that the real meaning of the letter G is God or Justice. Therefore, the esoteric meaning of the word *Christ* would imply two separate entities: the initial archetypal reality along with its image, or more simply, God and Man. We have the answer with the term "Pi and Phi," but with whom does the conjunction "and" belong, with the former or with the latter? If we place it with the latter, we find that the Alpha number for the term "and High Priestess" is 181 or RA (19 + 162 = 181).

Now Ra is the chief deity of ancient Egypt, a universal creator usually represented by a hawk-headed god bearing on his head the solar disk. Therefore, the sun-god Ra must be the reality and "The Great Pyramid of the Emperor" its image.

On the other hand, since the Alpha numbers for the two words "Ra" and "and" are identical, we could place the conjunction with the Pi term and call it "The Great Pyramid of the Emperor, Ra." The Alpha number would then be 333 (314 + 19 = 333), and these three C's would then imply that they be the reality and that the Phi term of "High Priestess" is the image. It would seem that the one single difference between the reality and its image is that the reality contains the central conjunction "and."

The following Figure 57 illustrates the dual aspects of this Christ force rather interestingly. For purposes of the illustration we have combined the conjunction with the "High Priestess," thus giving her the advantage of representing the sun-god Ra. The image is then "The Great Pyramid of the Emperor" and it is seen to be a "cad." What is a cad? It is a person who does not behave as a gentleman,, and it is an excellent description of the difference between Man and God. The two terms have been spelled out, one following the other, along the rim of the wheel.

```
THE GREAT PYRAMID
                          =   314   =   CAD
OF THE EMPEROR

AND HIGH PRIESTESS  =   181   =   RA
_____

                          495   =   DIE
```

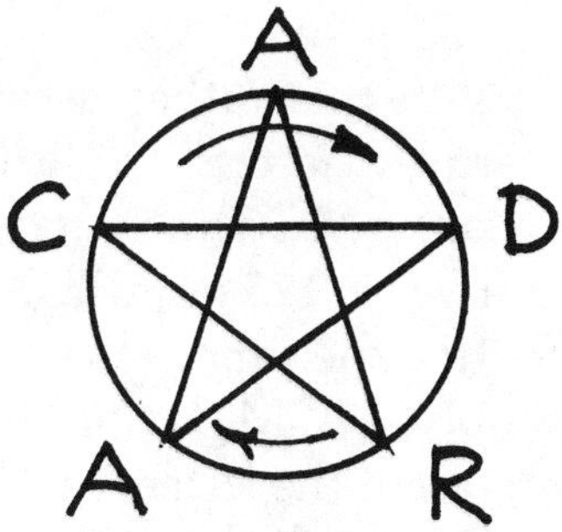

Figure 57
The Death of Ra

It is seen from Figure 57 that the Father (Ra) must also die along with his Son (the cad). Together, they make up the body of Christ. If we read the statement in a clockwise direction, we read "CAD R A" (Cad are A), which means that the Great Pyramid (the cad or the son) is in fact "A." This, of course, only verifies what we know already. However, if we read the statement in a counterclockwise direction starting with the A at the top, we read that this "Christ" force is "A CARD." Which card is it? It quite obviously is the 16th Tarot card titled "The Tower" and which is illustrated in Figure 56. Here, we quite vividly see the effects of this awesome power when it strikes the Tower bringing death to not only the "D" (the Devil who is You), but also to the Father who is CARA. (The reader may also see how this force is transmitted by following the lines of the pentacle starting with the lower A. He will find that it forms an electric *arc* from the Devil to the Emperor or from the D to the A.)

Now let us break the sun-god Ra into its three component parts. The Alpha number for "And" is 19; the number for "High" is 32; and the number for "Priestess" is 130. These three words make up the body of Ra since their total is 181 (RA). So then let us now ask ourselves the same question regarding *Ra* as we did for the word *Christ*. Who is Ra, really? The answer is rather shocking for we learn that the three component parts of Ra are none other than the three individuals who were banished from the Garden of Eden: Adam, Eve, and the Serpent (And = 19 = Adam; High = 32 = Eve; Priestess = 130 = The Serpent).

With this rather astonishing discovery, let us analyze the word "Priestess" a little more carefully. The number 130 becomes MO which means the Death of the Sun. Its God-Name number is 125 or ABE (M + O = 38 + 87 = 125 = ABE); and if we find the sum of the number 130, we find that M + O = M or simply, MOM. Or, if you prefer to consider the number 130 to represent the letters M + O, their sum is 28, the Alpha number of "Man," the letter N. The number 130 is also the Alpha number of "The Higher Self" (33 + 55 + 42 = 130). Our wise old "serpent" that tempted Adam and Eve is indeed a rather complex character.

However, if our theory is to hold water that the term "And High Priestess" is supposed to represent the Fall of Man as depicted on the face of Tarot Key 16 (Figure 56), the word "Priestess" itself should contain the "gold apex" of the tower that is also shown falling to its doom. And this it very beautifully does, for the word "PRIESTESS" may be transformed into "R IS SS PETE," which is exactly the same numerically as "R (Tower) Is Gold Apex" (18 + 28 + 38 + 46 = 130 = PRIESTESS). And not only that, but the term "AND" may be combined with the double S (SS) to represent the "SANDS" which the Agashan Teachers state now cover the gold apex at some point near the base of the Great Pyramid. The entire term is illustrated in the following Figure 58:

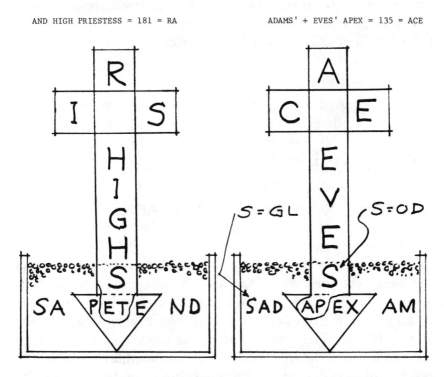

Figure 58
The Graves of the Serpent and Adam and Eve

The reader should be able to gain a much better understanding of the real meaning of the Fall of Adam and Eve from a study of the above two glyphs. There are many truths hidden therein. For example: the key to their redemption is plainly given by the upper three letters on the left-hand cross. One only has to substitute the name of the letter R (Are) for its symbol, and you can change the words "IS R" to "ARISE." The Alpha number for the double S (S + S) is also 38, the number of Death (Tarot Key 13) as well as "Gold." Therefore, the lesson for them to learn is how to arise from death. There are many other gems of wisdom buried within these "sands of time," as the Agashan Teachers would say, and so we would advise the reader to get in there and dig. One must remember that all of the many Adams, and all of the many Eves, constitute that which is known as the human race. These two glyphs are symbolical then of the predicament that you yourself are in today.

We may summarize the relationships between the terms in a CARA BOGA COTY manner as follows:

Cara			*Boga*			*Coty*
AND	= 19 =	ADAM	=	19	=	S
HIGH	= 32 =	EVE	=	32	=	LIFE
SS	= 38 =	GOLD	=	38	=	DEATH
PETE	= 46 =	APEX	=	46	=	COMAN
18	= 135			135	=	9
ARMY =	R	= ME =	RACE	= ACE	=	I

Each of the above three columns of words have identical Alpha numbers; yet their meanings are on different levels of consciousness. The Cara column is on the mental level; the Boga column is on the physical level; and the Coty column is on the spiritual level. The final word in the Coty column refers to Coman Coban, the Intermediary of Intermediaries who is the teacher of Agasha, and a fitting subject for the star of the spiritual column which represents the "Apex's Life + Death."

It is interesting to note that in the Agashan classes a character known as *Pete* would often come in and entertain the class with beautiful arias sung in a language which appeared to be ancient Italian. He claimed to be a fruit vendor in that particular incarnation, and he would sing, and sing, and sing his way through life as he sold his wares. Indeed, he would often sing so loud that it would seem that he was endeavoring to "raise the roof" with the sound of his magnificent voice. He is a perfect example of the Cara aspect of the fallen golden apex.

Then, on Good Friday, April 13, 1979, he returned once more through the channelship of Barry Lane in the class conducted by the Master Teacher Araskas. But now, in this later manifestation, all traces of his original Italian accent were gone. Yet he was the same personality, but now he manifested more as a teacher. It was very evident, to those of us who attended that particular class, that Pete had now literally and figuratively ascended from his previous "fallen" state of consciousness. Yet we do not wish to berate him in any way, as it is fairly obvious that he is only part of the "act" as it were, a key role in this great drama that the Teachers of Light are now producing in the latter days of the 20th century, in their efforts to dramatize and explain the many and varied aspects of all life.

Now the teacher *Coman Coban* manifests in much the same manner. Not that his personality is the same as Pete's, no I don't mean that at all, but he is still playing a role. He manifests in a base voice, with a quaint sense of humor, and is an extremely lovable character. He is Agasha's teacher, and rightly so; therefore, he represents the Coty aspect of the apex. He is the apex in its arisen state, after it has been elevated once again to its original position.

Who then represents the Boga aspect of the apex? If we have personalized the Cara and Coty aspects of the fallen apex of the pyramid, who then personifies its Boga or physical state? The answer is that it is *Agasha* himself. Agasha, Master of Wisdom, the hero of our drama, is the Boga aspect of the apex of the Great Pyramid of the Emperor. Agasha is indeed the CG or center of gravity between the other two. His Alpha number is 37, but when we add the "I" to it, we transform him into the "Agasha I," the number 46, the number of the apex, and the Higher Self of Pete who represents the equivalent of you and me.

Now then if Agasha represents your Higher Self—and we have stated many times that he should be thought of in this manner—how then can we associate ourselves with Coman Coban, a still greater teacher, and a teacher of teachers so to speak? The answer can be found on page 55 of the first volume in this series called *Agasha: Master of Wisdom*, and I quote:

"But first you (Adam and Eve) must seek for guidance, and it is only through your own individual effort, thoughts, and desires that you will be able to place yourself in personal, conscious touch with a teacher—whoever he may be. (This is your soul teacher, the one who assists you along the way, and who is symbolized by Pete.) Eventually you shall find him, and when you do, it will be because you will have opened the door and allowed him to enter. But this is only the beginning: the ending is still concealed. There is an even more wondrous discovery yet to be made. Then one day you will know. It will happen during a great flash of illumination when you will find yourself face to face with still another teacher. (Your Higher Self, symbolized by Agasha). And in this great moment, the Illumined One assigned to guide you (Pete) will most certainly be joyous, for he will know that you have finally removed the veil from Isis and learned the great truth—that the ultimate teacher is YOU."

But is this ultimate teacher your Higher Self? The answer is no. It is the *teacher* of your Higher Self, the equivalent of Coman Coban, that is the real YOU. If you, as Adam and Eve, represent the 1, you have to travel through the 2nd, 3rd, and 4th levels of your Being before you reach the ultimate. This is the decade or the 10 because $1 + 2 + 3 + 4 = 10$; and once you have come to the 10, you will have made a complete circle around the periphery of your Being, and ready to begin again on a new manifestation of consciousness.

Here then, in one short paragraph, the Agashan Teachers have removed still another veil from the mysteries of your

Being. Yet there is really nothing mysterious about it since all life is only a manifestation of number. The real mystery, if indeed there is one, is how the 10 can revert once more to the 1. "I am the Alpha and the Omega, the beginning and the end, the first and the last," Jesus is reported to have said (Revelation 22:13), but there is still a certain amount of confusion on this matter. Perhaps we can gain some enlightenment from an analysis of the name of *Coman Coban*, which, according to the theory just expounded, should represent this ultimate teacher who is the real YOU. The following tabulation should prove rather interesting to the average reader:

CO-MAN = 46 = APEX	MAN COMPANY = 115	
CO-BAN = 35 = EYE	BAN COMPANY = 104	

You = U = 81 = THE FOOL	You + I = 219		
Each A = HA	U I or B S		

The first thing that one notices after a study of the above table is that our assumption has proved correct. Coman Coban does indeed represent the Fool (Tarot Key 0) whose symbol is U and whose name is YOU. He is the Coty aspect of your Being, the spiritual apex of your pyramid in its arisen state before the Fall. Yet he also represents the end as well as the beginning, for he is a living symbol of that same apex after it has been replaced once more upon the pyramid of your Being. If you study Tarot Key 0 you will see him standing there on the precipice, symbolizing the Life-force both *before* it enters into manifestation as well as *after* it has returned from manifestation. Therefore, he literally does represent the Alpha and the Omega, the beginning and the end.

The number of the Fool is also the square of the "I" or 9 squared ($9^2 = 81 = U$). But 9^2 is also "9 × 9"; and 99 is the number of Judgement (Tarot Key 20), the letter X. Coman Coban is evidently quite aware of this because, out of all of the Teachers who have manifested in the Agashan and Araskas classes, he is one of the few who consistently ends his talk with the simple words, "Good Night." (The Alpha number for

"Good Night" is 99, the sum of 41 + 58.) This is an excellent signature for this great Teacher because the numbers 41 and 58 bring into manifestation the K and the S (41 = King = K, and 58 = Star = S). "What is so unusual about that?" you ask. There is nothing unusual about it, but it is interesting that "K + S = 11 + 19 = 30 = CO," and these two letters, aside from being the initial letters of both words of his name, are also the abbreviation for the word *Company*.

In the final analysis, this is what *you* really are—a Company. And a Company may represent a huge organization of many, many individuals. In the word "Coman" you *man* the Company, supply it with men, furnish it with manpower; and in the word "Coban" you *ban* the Company, censure it, excommunicate it, banish it—perhaps even from the Garden of Eden. Thus you are the creator and the destroyer, the giver of life and the reaper of death, but when we use the word "you," we are referring to it in its ultimate sense as the greater "YOU" of which the lesser "you" is but a part.

One other point before we leave this subject and move on to the greater mysteries of the Tower: Occult tradition has long held that the All-Seeing Eye is located within the apex of the Great Pyramid. (Just look at the Great Seal of the United States as depicted on the one-dollar bill.) Therefore, it is doubly significant that the name *Coman Coban* not only stands for the apex, but it also stands for the "eye" that is within it. And it is this inner *eye* that "bans" the Company, as opposed to the apex itself which "mans" it. You are then a Co-man as well as a Co-ban, in the sense that the prefix "co" refers to a partner or an associate such as co-partner or co-author.

The Greater Mysteries of the Tower

We have seen from the left-hand grave of Figure 58 that the letters "IRS," when removed from the word "PRIESTESS," represent the resurrected state of the apex of the Great Pyramid (IRS = 46 = Apex). Therefore, when we replace the apex back on top of the Pyramid, we are in effect adding these three letters (IRS) to its name. The complete name then makes the statement—and quite astonishingly so, I might add—that "The

Great Pyramid of the Emperor *is* 'R'." And what is the Tarot key that the letter "R" stands for? The answer is the Tower (Tarot Key 16), otherwise known as "The House of God." Moreover, the total Alpha number of the name is now 360, the number of degrees in a full circle (314 + 46 = 360). It would seem that the Cabalah is bending over backwards to make sure that we fully understand the relationship between the Great Pyramid and the Tower.

Now for some more surprises: What is the symbol for the Tower? It is the letter "R," of course. But if the reader will refer once again to Figure 30, he will find that the symbol "R" breaks itself apart into the number "12" or the "1" plus the "2." Very well. Now let us analyze the God-Name for this symbol. It is "THE TOWER." So then let us break it apart in the same way that we did its symbol and see what it contains. In other words, let us find out who is hiding in the Tower. "How do you do that?" you ask. Very simple. All you have to do is rearrange the letters in "THE TOWER" into a slightly different configuration, and when you do that, you will find that the one who is hiding therein is the "TWO THREE," or the "TWO" plus the "THREE."

What a strange Tarot key! In one sense, it breaks apart into the "1" and the "2," the total of which is 3; yet in another sense, it breaks apart into the "Two" and the "Three," the total of which is 5. Which is it then, the 3 or the 5? The answer is that it is both. The Tower is either the 3 or the 5, which means that it is either the "C" or the "E," the combination of which is the "C OR E" or the "CORE."

One can very readily see then that the esoteric or hidden meaning of the Tower (Tarot Key 16) is that it represents the very Core of Life itself! It is from this particular Tarot key that you were spewed forth in the beginning to begin the journey that is eternity. This is your home. This is where you started, and this is where you shall return.

But it is very inconvenient to refer to "The Core of Life" as "The *the Tower* of Life." The sentence involves a pair of "the's" that is inconsistent with good grammar. What is the solution? Luckily the Cabalah, in its infinite wisdom, has allowed for situations such as this. Every letter/symbol has both a God-Name as well as a God-Word. The former usually contains the definite article "the," and the latter is unencumbered by any other word save the Word itself. The answer in this particular case is to simply substitute the single God-Word "Hierophant" for the dual God-Name "The Tower." The Alpha number for both terms is 114, which transliterates itself into AN = O. And doesn't an "O" represent the Sun, the symbol that the Agashan Teachers refer to when they speak of the "Sun" Core of Life? Therefore in this substitution, we have a perfect solution for our problem.

"The Hierophant of Life." What a magnificent name for the Core of Life! The Hierophant, of course, stands for the letter "E"; but isn't this letter also the symbol for Energy? And doesn't the Core of Life, in the final analysis, actually mean pure Energy in its most powerful state? We may even change the word "Hierophant" into "Higher Fount," and this phrase seems to fit our description even better. The word "fount," according to the dictionary, refers to a fountain or a source; and what better definition for the Core of Life is there than the Higher Fount of Life? It is therefore the Higher Fountain, the Source of All, the Fountainhead from which we sprang!

The Alpha number for the term "Higher Fount" is 131 or MA (55 + 76 = 131); therefore, "the Higher Fount of Life" really means "the MA (mother) of Life." And not only that, but the Alpha number for the complete phrase is the amazing number 217 which means that it is a BAG (33 + 55 + 76 + 21 + 32 = 217 = BAG)! The reader is asked to reread once more the discourse on the Magic Bag given by the teacher Lao-Tse on page 21 of *Agasha: Master of Wisdom.* Looking at it in the context presented here, it should give even more food for thought to the serious-minded student.

But what about the term the way it actually is? According to the Cabalah, the word is "Hierophant" and not "Higher Fount"; therefore, it should prove even more significant if we were to analyze the term using the spelling given by Tarot Key 5. After all, the word "Hierophant" has a particular meaning all of its own. The dictionary defines a *Hierophant* as being an

expositor or advocate of the rites of worship and sacrifice. He
was also the chief priest of the Eleusinian mysteries as they
were practiced in ancient Greece. So then let us perform the
same analysis on "The Hierophant of Life" that we did on its
counterpart "The Higher Fount of Life." The solution is given
below, and it is with considerable awe and reverence that we
see the real meaning of the Core of Life come into focus almost
before our very eyes.

$$
\begin{aligned}
&\text{THE HIEROPHANT} = 147 \qquad\qquad\qquad = \text{E} \\
&\text{OF LIFE} \qquad\quad = \; \underline{\; 53} = \text{WHEEL} = \text{B} \\
&\qquad\qquad\qquad\qquad 200 = \text{TO}
\end{aligned}
$$

Imagine that! The Core of Life, in its ultimate sense, is nothing more than the verb "To Be." But what a magnificent
concept! After all, that is what Life is really all about. The
Alpha number of "to be" is 42 (35 + 7 = 42), and this number is
equally as significant for it represents "The I" or "The Ace."
And isn't GOD, in the final analysis, the One who states that it
"BE I"? (The God-Name number for the word "God" is 259 or
BEI). Yes indeed, the Cabalah can be absolutely fantastic at
times.

Chapter 16

THE FOUR LETTERS OF THE JUST

A BRIEF REVIEW OF the foregoing chapters will show that we have now identified the majority of the letters in the English alphabet. By that we mean matching up a particular Tarot key with its English counterpart. Yet there are still a few Tarot keys, or letters rather, remaining to be unveiled, and this chapter and the following chapter will complete the process.

Let us begin with the letters of the JUST—the letters J, U, S, and T. We have grouped these four letters together because their combination results in that which is guided by truth, reason, justice, and fairness. The Alpha number for the word "Just" is 70 which is read as GO—the first two letters of the word GOD. The final letter then represents that which is unjust, the D, the Devil, the very opposite of the Just. This is what the word GOD means: the marriage of the opposites.

We may go one step further in our analysis. Besides the Devil, what else represents the unjust? The Alpha number for "Unjust" is 105, the God-Name number for the World (Tarot Key 21), the letter J, the 10th letter of the English alphabet. And the combination of "Just + Unjust" brings into manifestation the number 175. It is an AGE, and it is the Alpha number for "Consciousness" (70 + 105 = 175 = AGE). Therefore the God Consciousness is just that—the combination of the "Just"ness of God with the "unjust"ness of the World, the total of which is "The Just World" or His *Consciousness* (175).

There is still another analogy we might make. The "just" part of his consciousness is composed of the letters G and O. Now the Alpha number for the God Names of each of these letters is identical to the other (Justice = 87 = the Sun). Therefore the *just* part represents perfect balance and equilibrium, as opposed to the *unjust* part, the World, which is out of balance until it is righted and matched with its counterpart. This is where *You* come into the picture, for if we balance the World by adding another 105 to it, we bring into manifestation the number 210 that we spoke of earlier; the "10 U," the tenth great initiate, the Fool who is U (You) when multiplied by the powers of the 10. This is called the Great Work, and it is accomplished by having the Fool (Tarot Key 0) travel through all 14 cards of a suit of the Minor Arcana, and by so doing, balance the World that he is functioning in. (The sum of the numbers from 1 through 14 is 105, the number that balances the Alpha number of "The World".)

We find then that for this period of time the Fool is playing the role of Jesus, one who is crucified upon the cross of matter as he attempts to right the World and bring it back once more into the God Consciousness. And what represents the cross? It is the letter T whose God Name is *Temperance* (Tarot Key 14), and the 4th letter of the word JUST. Indeed, the letter T is a graphic representation of the Tau cross, one of the most famous crosses of antiquity. It is also called Saint Anthony's cross. In fact if one will study the following Figure 59, he will see how the symbol for the Fool, when suspended from the Tau cross of Temperance, brings into manifestation the letter J, the symbol for the World.

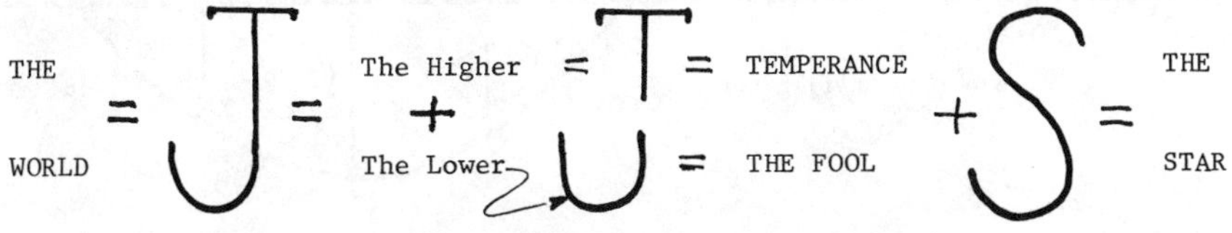

Figure 59
The Four Letters of the JUST

Thus we find that the letter J, the 10th letter of the English alphabet, is dual in the same sense that the number 10 is dual. The former is the result of a marriage of the T and the U, and the latter a marriage of the 1 and the 0. But even more significant is the fact that if we start with the letter J as a base (which represents the World), and then add 10 to it, the result is its higher self, the T. And if we start with the letters "T + U" as a base, and add 10 to it, the result is its lower self, the U (T + U = 41 = King = K, and K + 10 = 21 = U). We could also say that "U" are EA (Each) Adam-Eve since "T + U + 10" = 51 or EA, the Alpha number of "Adam-Eve."

The Letter S: The Symbol for the Star

Now let us look at the letter S, the 3rd letter of the word JUST. Its God Name is *The Star* (Tarot Key 17), and if we arrange the letters in a circle, we read that it signifies THE START, with the letter T being both the beginning and the ending of its name. The letter S is also the symbol for the Serpent, and it represents its serpentine motion as it would move from here to there, or as a wave moves along the surface of the water. Likewise the light from the Star moves as a wave, and the familiar sine curve of the mathematical function $Y = \sin x$ is a graphic description of the way it moves through space.

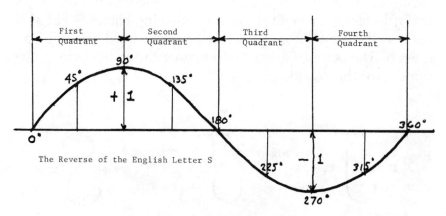

Figure 60
The Sine Curve of the Star

It is an interesting fact that there is another word in the English language whose meaning is synonymous with that of the Serpent. It is the Snake. At this point, let us now ask ourselves about the true meaning of the Star. What is a star, really? A star could be said to represent *energy*—pure, unadulterated energy in its most violent form. Therefore, it is extremely significant that the Alpha number for the expression "Serpent-Snake" is 147, the God-Name number for the Hierophant (Tarot Key 5), whose letter/symbol is E. And what does the symbol E stand for? It represents Energy as in the equation, $E = mc^2$.

But let us not stop here. The Alpha number for "Star" is 58, and the Alpha number for the first four letters of "Serpent" is this same number—58. Therefore, we may say that the "Serpent" may be equated to the "Star-Ten." And not only that, but inasmuch as the Alpha number for "Star" is the same as the number for "Two," we may likewise say that the "Serpent" is equal to the "Two-Ten." And what is the "Two-Ten"? It is the number 210, the number that we have been talking about that represents *You* times 10, the Fool whose destiny it is to right his World once more. Yet the number "Two-Ten" also equates to that wise old "Serpent" spoken about so much in the Bible as being the initial Force that instigated the "fall" of Adam and Eve in the first place. You then become your own Avatar— the sinner as well as the redeemer.

We can likewise analyze the word "Snake" following the same procedure that we did for "Serpent." The Alpha number for the first three letters of "Snake" is 34, the same as the number for "One"; and the "ke" part may be changed from "11-5" to "1-15" or AO, which represents 10. Therefore the "Snake" becomes the "One-Ten" as opposed to the "Serpent" who is the "Two-Ten." What this really means, we will leave to the reader to discover. The Cabalah provides many ways to interpret the real meaning of words.

The Letter T: The Symbol for Temperance

The Alpha number for Temperance (Tarot Key 14) is identical to that for the Hanged Man (Tarot Key 12). Their

God-Name numbers are each equal to 100, the square of 10. Isn't it rather interesting then that when we place the two side by side, we have the T + N or the TEN? Indeed, the *Hanged Man* may be equated to the *Ten* Man, because for all intents and purposes this is what he is. And we could say the same thing for the archangel Michael who is depicted in Tarot Key 14 as pouring the essences of life, back and forth, from one cup to another. Both of these cards are making the same statement, and when you understand the one you understand the other.

For an example: Let us treat the word TEMPERANCE as an anagram, and rearrange its letters into some form that makes sense. Without too much trouble, we end up with the statement "TEE CRAMP EN." Here we have the *names* of the two letters, T and N, separated by the word "cramp." Now what is the meaning of the statement? Inasmuch as the word *cramp* relates to something that is confined or restrained in some way, we see then that the Tau cross of Temperance is restraining the Hanged Man, the letter N, from falling to the earth. Look again at the 12th Tarot key. Its meaning is self-evident.

But there is even more evidence that what we say here is true. We say that the name of the archangel on Tarot Key 14 is Michael because occult science has long had it that he be so named (Eden Gray, *A Complete Guide to the Tarot*, page 36). Yet the Alpha number for "Michael" is the same as that for "cramp," the number for both words being 51. Therefore the Force that restrains the Hanged Man from falling to the ground is the archangel Michael.

Now let us study this a little more carefully. He is bearing the sign of the Sun upon his forehead (the dot in the circle), and the 3 + 4 sign of the septenary upon his breast (the triangle in the square). Here again is the 10: the "34" symbol which is the Alpha number for *One*, combined with the "O" symbol of the Sun which represents zero. Thus the Tarot key is informing us that the archangel Michael is vested with the powers of the 10.

But he is one being and not two. If the triangle in the square represents the "1" part of the 10, and the dot in the circle the "O" part of the 10, then Michael himself must be the *one* being containing them both, the unity of which the 10 is a part. We therefore can symbolically represent his consciousness by raising the two-dimensional symbols into three-dimensional symbols—transforming the square into a cube and the circle into a sphere, as it were—and then placing the one within the other. The result is the cube in the sphere, one of the most profound symbols of the entire Cabalah, and one which quite dramatically not only explains the Tau cross of Temperance, but also sheds more light on those mysterious Forces called CARA, BOGA, and COTY.

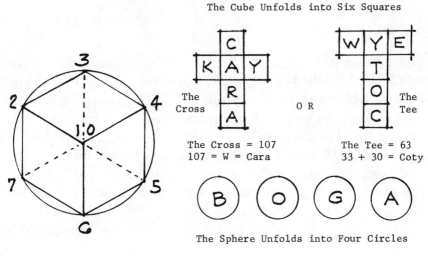

The Cube Unfolds into Six Squares

The Cross = 107
107 = W = Cara

The Tee = 63
33 + 30 = Coty

The Sphere Unfolds into Four Circles

Figure 61
The Cube in the Sphere

As one studies Figure 61, the first thing that becomes apparent is that the 8th vertex of the three-dimensional cube is hiding behind the 1st vertex at the center. The second point to be understood is that it is possible to represent the surface of the sphere as four two-dimensional circles (surface area = $4\pi R^2$), and the surface of the cube by six squares unfolded into either the Latin cross of Christian symbology or the Tau cross of Temperance. These are simply two alternate methods of unfolding a cube, but tremendously different in their philosophical significance. We have called these three types of unfoldment by the names Cara, Boga, and Coty for the reasons set forth within the figure.

The more one will study Figure 61 the more remarkable it becomes, because the potential amount of information that can be obtained from it is almost inexhaustible. For instance: Let us consider the following relationships:

FOUR	= 60	SIX	= 52
CIRCLES	= 69	SQUARES	= 100
Total	= 129	Total	= 152
	L I		O B = B O I L

The total Alpha value for the six surfaces thus gives us the word "Boil," which means the figure represents a "swirling upheaval of water in a constant state of agitation." Another definition of the term is that it represents a "painful sore," and when a boil breaks, you know the result. Pus is emitted from its hard central core, and with the poisons thus eliminated, the body then becomes healthy again. We find then that Figure 61 is a perfect symbol for life on the earth plane today. In fact, the Agashan Teachers have many times used the simile of the boil to express the current status of humanity in our present 20th century.

If the cube is unfolded in the form of the T-cross, the energies rise up from the ground in the same way that bubbles rise to the surface when water is brought to a boil. This is symbolical of the resurrection of the spirit when it ascends into the higher consciousness. Therefore, the word COTY has been placed in the stem of the "T" where the bubbles can arise from the C (Sea) and ascend at the Y (Wye). This is the archangel Michael, and you and I (WE) represent his wings. The combined Alpha number of all six faces of his cube is 91, the God-Word number for the letter V (Lovers) and the God-Name number for the letter S (The Star).

The Latin Cross: The Symbol of Christianity

Now let us study the opposite situation where the cube is unfolded into the Latin cross of Christianity. This is symbolical of the crucifixion of the spirit, when the blood of Jesus literally falls to the ground. The word CARA is thus written starting with the C at the top and ending with the A at the bottom. The cross now becomes the chariot, a vehicle through which the spirit can descend into matter. But the chariot must also have a driver; therefore we have placed the King in his Chariot by adding the KAY (the name of the letter K) to his CAR. The combined Alpha number for all six faces of the King's cube is 59, the Alpha number of "The God." But even more than that, the number reveals that it stands for the letter N (5 + 9 = 14 = N), the symbol for the Hanged Man or the Ten Man. This then is the reason that he is pictured hanging upside down on the cross as the spirit descends into matter.

Even further proof that we are on the right track in our thinking comes about when we analyze the Alpha number for the complete term "The Cube in the Sphere." These five words have a combined total of 191 (33 + 31 + 23 + 33 + 71 = 191) which represents either Temperance or the Hanged Man plus the Star (T or N = 100, and S = 91). The number 191 also transliterates into S + A = T, and here is where we have our greatest breakthrough.

SAT stands for what? It represents the abbreviation for the planet SATURN. But we really don't have to stretch our imagination this far to arrive at the same answer. If the reader will look at the figures in the Star (Tarot Key 17) and in Temperance (Tarot Key 14), he will find that they both are holding cups or "urns." In the former the feminine force is pouring the essences of life into the water and onto the earth, and in the latter the masculine force is pouring these essences from one "urn" into the other. And in both instances, the right foot is supported by the water (the C) and the left foot by the earth (the D). We call the earth by the letter D since the Alpha number for "earth" and "devil" are the same. The Alpha number for "urn" is also 53 which means "wheel," the God-Word for the letter B. Therefore, the word SATURN is a combination of (1) the cube in the sphere, the number 191 or the letters S + A, (2) Temperance, the letter T, the unfolded cube, and (3) the unfolded sphere, the four wheels of Boga, the cups that contain the essences of life as symbolized by the URN.

But SATURN is also the name of the Roman god of agriculture. In Greece he was known as CRONUS, an ancient god who ruled the earth during a time of great happiness and virtue. But what have we here? The Cabalah seems to be revealing a very great secret, for if we take the word SATURN and place it in a circle, we read that A (the Emperor) TURNS SATURN! But what else does the Emperor turn? We have only to read the name CRONUS backwards, and we find that it is the SUN OR C (the Moon). Incredible!

For an answer as to who "A" really is, we have only to analyze the Alpha numbers contained within the term "The God of Agriculture." The number for "Agriculture" by itself is 135 which means the ACE. He then is indeed the "A"; and he is also ME. And the number for "The God of" is 80 (33 + 26 + 21 = 80), which means H (each) O. But when we combine the two terms together, we find out who He really is. The Alpha number for the complete term, "The God of Agriculture," then is 80 + 135 which reads HOME!

Therefore, we find that we now have a proper name for the King in the Chariot who represents the Cross of Christianity. He is *Saturn*, and he is the counterpart of the archangel *Michael* who represents the Cross of Temperance. But what is even more significant, we find that if we combine both of them into a single entity—add the Alpha numbers for both of their names together—their sum is 144 which commands us to ADD, and when we do, we find that it is the number 9 or the "I." These two god forces are really equal because the Alpha number for *Saturn* is 93, the number for "learned one," the symbol for Coty; and the Alpha number for *Michael* is 51, the number for "Adam-Eve," the "double-you" symbol for Cara. Therefore it is not surprising that the combination of Adam and Eve, which means you and I, when combined with the "learned one," the spiritual Teacher within us all, brings into manifestation the true "I."

But let us not stop here. There is still the *Boga* principle to be taken into consideration. This is represented by the four circles of the sphere as it unfolds. The Alpha number of Boga is 25 and it means BE. And when we add the "I" to it (93 + 51 = 144 = ADD = 9 = I), we find that it BE I, the number 259, the God-Name number for God. It is also PI, since Saturn + Michael + Boga = 169 or PI (93 + 51 + 25).

Are you confused? I will admit that we seem to be going around in circles, and speaking of circles, this seems to be the time to embrace the greatest circle of them all—the unfolded Sphere of the Zodiac called BOGA.

The Zodiac: The Racetrack Around Which the Worlds Whirl

One will probably wonder how we gained the authority to label the four circles that resulted from the collapse of the spherical surface as BOGA. The answer is quite simple. We named it thus because that is just exactly what the Zodiac is— BOGA. The first three signs are the B, the second three the O, the third three the G, and the last three the A. The proof is given by the table on page 205 where all 12 signs of the Zodiac are shown to equate to the number 2,071 or BOGA. The Agashan Teachers did not invent these terms. Each important word in the Cabalah is so named because it represents some particular mathematical principle in Nature.

Now let us look at the complete diagram of Figure 61 and analyze it as a totality. The six squares of the Cross may be said to represent the *outer* faces of the unfolded cube and the six squares of the Tee its *inner* faces. And in the same way we may consider the four circles of BOGA to represent the *inner* spherical surface of the sphere, and the one three-dimensional sphere at the left its *outer* surface. It then is another Boga, but in order not to confuse the two let us just call it BE to represent the number 25.

It is also significant that the Alpha number for the term

"Inner-Outer" is 139 (60 + 79 = 139), and this is the same number as that of "The Wheel of Life," another name for the letter B. Therefore when we combine all of these faces together, what do we have? The Alpha number for the six faces of the Cross is 59 which represents "The God"; the Alpha number for the six faces of the Tee is 91 which represents "The Star"; and the Alpha number for the four faces of Boga is 25 which represents "All." The combination of all three aspects of CARA BOGA COTY is then the number 175 which is an AGE. It is also the Alpha number for *Consciousness*. And when we combine the total inner part with the outer surface of the sphere at the left, we find that the "AGE BE All Consciousness." It is just as simple as that.

Now let us compare the names themselves. That is, let us compare the Alpha number of the Cross (107) with that of the Tee (63). We find that their sum is 170 or AGO, the last three letters of BOGA. In other words, it represents the past or that which happened long ago. Now let us look at the difference between the terms. The number is 44 or DD. This, too, is extremely significant; since when we place the sum and the difference side by side, we have the following statement: AGO DD, which can be read as "A GOD D" (The Emperor, GOD, and the Devil, or more simply—A GOD DEVIL).

But let us not stop here. The difference between the two terms may also be equated to their sum just by transforming the letter D into its God-Name number which is 85 (The Devil). Thus the difference (DD) becomes 170 or AGO, the same number as the sum (85 + 85 = 170). In summary then, we find that not only their sum but also their difference is equal to the past —the last three letters of BOGA.

The following Figure 62 tabulates all of the "chariots" that race around the racetrack of the Zodiac in the same way that we tabulated the 12 signs of the Zodiac earlier. The Sun is given its rightful position as number 1, and each of the other planets or systems is numbered according to its distance from the Sun. Actually, several of the planets are really miniature solar systems themselves when we consider their many moons; but let us call each system by the name of its principal planet. The asteroid belt, which science has recently determined to be the remains of a planet which exploded a few million years ago, most certainly has to be included for the system to conform to Bode's Law.

Order Number	Celestial Bodies	Alpha Number	Word/Name Symbol	Running Total Sum	Word
1.	SUN	54	O	54	E D
2.	MERCURY	103	J C	157	O G
3.	VENUS	81	U R	238	
4.	EARTH	52	D	290	B I O
5.	MARS	51	EA	341	
6.	ASTEROID BELT	130	M O	471	
7.	JUPITER	99	X	570	E G O
8.	SATURN	93	I C	663	
9.	URANUS	94	X	757	
10.	NEPTUNE	95	Q/Z	852	H E B
11.	PLUTO	84	H D	936	

Figure 62
The Chariots that Race around the Zodiac

Strictly speaking, the planet Pluto is not in the Zodiac per se, since its orbit is not in the same plane as that of the other planets. It could very well be the first planet in still another Zodiac tilted at an angle to our own. Therefore, we have drawn a line separating it from the other 10 "chariots" or planets.

Each of these 10 planetary mini-systems that race around the circle of the Zodiac is thus seen to be a World, a Consciousness, an integral part of the greater system called the Solar

Logos, and of the still greater system known in the Agashan terminology as the Universal God Consciousness. Each individual system could represent, in its own right, Tarot Key 21 called the World, the English letter J, the number 10 which means the beginning and the end.

The Cabalah shows us that the first four celestial systems bring *Life* into manifestation (Their Alpha number sum is 290 or BIO which means Life); the first seven celestial systems awaken the *Ego* or the conscious self (Their Alpha number sum is 570 or EGO); and the first ten systems, the completion of the decade as it were, brings *Man* himself into manifestation. How do we know that the sum of the first ten systems represents Man? We know it because their Alpha number sum is 852 or HEB, the first three letters and the abbreviation for the word HEBREW. But don't just take *my* word for it; look it up in the dictionary yourself. It states that the letters *Heb* stand for the word *Hebrew*, a race of people whose trials and tribulations form the basis for the entire Holy Bible.

It is interesting to note that the Alpha number for *Hebrew* is 61, the same as the number for *You*. Therefore, inasmuch as Adam and Eve stand for you and me today, we must out of necessity trace our heritage back to the original Hebrews since Adam and Eve were the first *Hebrew* man and woman. This, then, is the reason that the Hebrew race has been called "God's chosen people." It is not that any one race of people is superior to any other race; no, not at all. All races are on an equal footing as far as the God Consciousness is concerned. It only means that the biblical history of Man was written using the Hebrew race as the principal characters—the actors and actresses as it were—to portray that which *all* men, in all the races on the earth, must ultimately endure before they can ascend into the higher spiritual consciousness. All of us then, philosophically speaking, are Hebrews.

Just in case the reader is a little dubious of our interpretation as to the esoteric meaning of the planetary names, the Cabalah gives us an excellent verification that what we say here is true. The Word/Name symbols for Mercury, Venus, Earth, and Mars (the four planetary systems between the Sun and the One that exploded) state that JUDEA is "our sea" (R C), the "rock" from which we sprang. And Judea, as you well know, is the name for ancient Palestine, the home of the Hebrews when it was subjected to Persian, Greek, and Roman rule.

Likewise, we may group Jupiter, Saturn, Uranus and Neptune together and realize that they represent Judgement, the letter X (Tarot Key 20); or rather, the planet Jupiter is the one that brings this about. Saturn states that "I see (understand)"; and Uranus and Neptune "Excuse" (X Q/Z) the terrible destruction of an undoubtedly quite beautiful planet that used to exist between Mars and Jupiter. All that remains of it today are thousands and thousands of small planets with diameters ranging from a fraction of a mile to nearly 500 miles. The Alpha number for "Asteroid Belt" quite significantly is 130 or M O (The Death of the Sun).

The Alpha number for Pluto, the 11th celestial body and the first "chariot" in a second Zodiac at an angle to our own, is 84 or H D (Each Devil, or the Teacher/Hermit plus the Devil, a dual entity). And it is even more significant when we realize that the combination of Pluto (the god of the underworld), the asteroid belt, and the Sun state that they "Doom Each" (DOOM H). The word *doom* means to give judgment against or to condemn. Yes, there are all sorts of interesting bits of information that one can discover about himself, as well as the solar system in which he lives, just from a simple cabalistic analysis of the names involved.

There is still further evidence of the truth in all of this hidden within the distances of each planet from the Sun or the radius of its orbit. In the latter part of the 18th century it was discovered that the mean distances of each of the planets from the Sun exist in an orderly, numerical progression with one exception—the planet Neptune. Of course, the exception was not known at the time because neither Uranus, Neptune, nor Pluto had yet been discovered. The law is called Bode's Law and the distances are tabulated in the following Figure 63 in astronomical units (the mean distance from the earth to the sun). If the reader is astute, he can ascertain for himself a probable reason for the discrepancy.

Celestial Body		Bode Distance	Mean Distance
1.	SUN (54)	CG of System	0.00
2.	Mercury (103)	4 + 0 = 4	0.39 (Ten)
3.	Venus (81)	4 + 3 = 7	0.72 (World)
4.	Earth (52)	4 + 6 = 10	1.00 (T, N)
5.	Mars (51)	4 + 12 = 16	1.52
6.	Asteroid Belt (130)	4 + 24 = 28	2.77 (Ceres)
7.	Jupiter (99)	4 + 48 = 52	5.20
8.	Saturn (93)	4 + 96 = 100	9.53
9.	Uranus (94)	4 + 192 = 196	19.19
10.	NEPTUNE (95)	New CG	30.07 (C . . G)
11.	Pluto (84)	4 + 384 = 388	39.5 (Ten + E)

(bracketing the rows 2–9: "8 Points of the Star/Cube")

Figure 63
The Cabalah Explains Bode's Law

We thus find from a study of Figure 63 that the apparent discrepancy in Bode's Law is not a real discrepancy at all. The planet Neptune, being located at an intermediate point between two normal terms in the series, merely shares with the Sun the quality of "oneness," and is thus enabled to attract unto itself a new higher order of planets from the 1 to the 10. But this new system would have for its base the distance from Pluto to Neptune rather than that of Mercury to the Sun.

It seems much can be learned from a study of the Star (Tarot Key 17), the letter S. The Star is depicted as having 8 points in much the same manner as our cube in the sphere (Figure 61). The center of the cube appears as the Sun or the macrocosmic Star, and the 7 smaller stars bear the same relationship to the larger one as the 7 *visible* vertices of our cube. Yet there is always a sun behind the sun, a hidden vertex behind the huge macrocosmic center of gravity, and the 8th outer point of the star system.

If the planet Pluto is the first planet in a space that is warped around Neptune as its core, and Uranus is the last planet in a space warped around the Sun as its core, there must then out of necessity be a planet near the Sun that represents the last planet in the previous system. The Agashan Teachers call this planet Platobia. It is an etheric planet and it rotates with the Sun, and it could be said to be comparable to the planet Uranus in the same way that the Sun can be compared to Neptune. It is interesting to note that the Alpha number for Platobia which is 76, when added to that of Uranus which is 94, brings to a combined total for the two of them the familiar number 170 which represents that which was AGO or the past.

Where then is the future? The answer is found when we compare the Alpha number for the CG of our present system with the CG of the one to come, or in other words the Alpha number for Sun (54) with that of Neptune (95). These numbers transliterate into ED/IE, which means that "E" DIE. But that which "dies" must live again, and we find that our Hierophant "E" is born again in Pluto inasmuch as its mean distance is 39.5 (Ten + E), as opposed to the mean distance of the first planet in the previouus cycle (Mercury) which was merely a single .39 (Ten).

Chapter 17

THE SPARK OF DIVINITY

THE AGASHAN TEACHERS have often referred to the inner "I" that lies within. This "Spark of Divinity" is as minute as a tiny atom, yet it is as powerful as the universe itself. It is a world within a world, and a world within a world, and a world within a world. It is an atom of energy in its most minute and most powerful state. It is your own individual soul atom and it represents *you* throughout eternity. It has always been and it always shall be. It was never created in the strict sense of the term and it shall never die. It is you forever (*The Agashan Discourses*, pages 345, 353).

In occult science it is known as the great "I AM." In orthodox religion it is known simply as "GOD." The Alpha number for the former is 23 or the letter W; the number for the latter is 26 or the letter Z; and when we combine the two together we have the number 49 or (7 × 7), the double 7 of the Christ Consciousness. If we read the number 49 backwards we find that it is the ID, the undifferentiated source from whence we sprang. We could go on and on with our comparisons, but we always end up with the same answer: namely, that the Universal Consciousness God simply represents all there is—the totality of the complete whole.

But let us try to pin this God Consciousness down a little more clearly; that is, let us try to find some frame of reference within the English alphabet or within the Tarot where we can point to a single symbol and state quite emphatically that that is God. Is it possible to do this? I don't know, but let us try and find out. We can begin by analyzing the God-Name numbers for "I AM" and then comparing them with those for "GOD." The God-Name number for "I AM" is 251 which states that it "BE A" (90 + 123 + 38 = 251); and the God-Name number for "GOD" is 259 which states that it "BE I" (87 + 87 + 85 = 259). Therefore, it follows that the God Consciousness is both the A and the I, the 1 and the 9, the Emperor and the Magician.

It is interesting to note that if we add the 1 and the 9 together, we have the 10, the letter J, the World, which corresponds quite beautifully with that which it is supposed to represent— All. The number 19 also represents the letter S, the Star; and if we reverse the process and put the 9 before the 1, it is still the Star for the Alpha number for "The Star" is 91, the letter S again. Thus the Star contains both the A and the I, and the God Consciousness could be said to be the *vibration* (the S) that is sent from the one to the other. It is, in fact, A's I.

But where do you as an individual fit into the picture? If we refer to *you* as *Ye,* in the same way that Christ referred to his disciples when speaking to them as a group, in the plural rather than the singular sense, we find that the number 255 states that "YE BE E." And if we analyze the God-Name number for "YE," we find that it is 258 or that it BE H (111 + 147 = 258). Ye then are both the letter H and the letter E, the combination of which is HE, the number 85, the Alpha number for the Devil, the letter D, one of the copartners of the ID. Yes, there are many things that you, too, may be equated to. Yet in the Cabalah they never contradict each other; each definition only brings out a different facet of who and what you really are.

Each "I" Is God

Earlier in this work we learned that the Magician (Tarot Key 1) stands for I; the Fool (Tarot Key 0) stands for You (U); and the Hermit (Tarot Key 9) stands for Each (H). Therefore the

Hermit, being each, represents *both* the outer mortal self (You) as well as the inner higher self (I). But there is also the "Eye" to be taken into consideration, the great All-Seeing Eye of God whose symbol is the Ace or the letter A. This Ace or "Eye" is always One, and it may be equated to pure white light which represents the totality of all the colors. However, if we break it up into its various components by sending it through a prism, we find that the first three primary colors to be brought into manifestation are that which is known as the Trinity—Each You and I (H + U + I). But the Alpha number of the sum of these three letters is 38 which represents Death (Tarot Key 13), the letter M. Therefore when we add the One, which is the A, to the Three symbolized by the M, we can truly say that the macrocosmic "I" or greater "I" AM, and we are right back to where we started.

Each I, which is made up of the symbols H and I, have also a very significant geometric relationship with each other since when you rotate any one of them through a 90-degree angle, it brings the other into manifestation. The principle is illustrated in the following Figure 64:

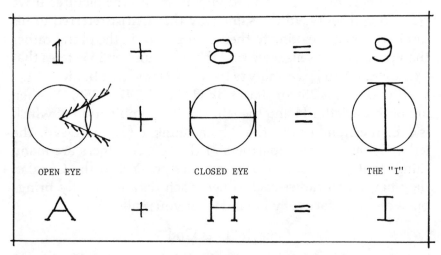

Figure 64
The Three I's

Even the *names* for the numbers 8 and 9 echo the above relationships. The Alpha number for "Eight" is 49 and the number for "Nine" is 42, and when we add them together we have the number 91, the Alpha number for the Star (the letter S). Thus the numerals 1 and 9 are back together again. Yes indeed, each "I" is truly God in more ways than one. This statement is further enhanced by the fact that the Alpha number for the term "Each I" is 26, which equates right back to the number for "God." Everywhere we turn, it would seem, we have verification after verification after verification.

The Great Power of the Spark of Divinity

All of the above now brings us to the point where we can actually demonstrate why this minute spark, this tiny, tiny atom, is as powerful as the universe is itself. Let us say, as a supposition, that we equate everything that is—all of the stars, galaxies, planets, etc. in the entire universe—into a gigantic whole which we shall call ONE. Then if we do this, every part of that ONENESS will be a fraction or a decimal number less than Unity: i.e. 1/10, 1/100, 1/1,000, 1/1,000,000 or in its decimal form .1, .01, .001, .000001, etc.

Very well. Now let us divide the universe into 9 parts, and what is the value of each part? If you divide 9 into 1 on your calculator, you will find that the answer is .111111111111 . . . forever. We find then that each one of these 9 parts is composed of an infinite number of individual units, the actual number depending upon how long the Universal God Consciousness wished to go on with the process of division.

But now let us say you are God and you have grown tired of the universe that you have created. You wish to restore all 9 parts back to the original unity from which they sprang. So then what do you do? The answer is simple; you simply reverse the process and now multiply each of the numbers by the same 9 that you divided by originally. After all, everyone knows that 1/9 × 9 = 1 or unity. Even a child in Grade School knows that. But does your calculator know it? No it does not. You will find that if you multiply .111111111111 . . . by 9, you will not have the original unity or 1 that you started with, but instead you will have an infinitely long series of 9's or I's as represented by the number .99999999999999 . . . forever.

If you are God, you will now find yourself in a very strange predicament. The very universe that you had created out of the single number 1 has outwitted you. No matter how long you fume and fret, you find it beyond your power to transform all of these infinite number of smaller I's back into the ONE which they were in the beginning. They will taunt you and taunt you and taunt you because they fully realize that they are equally as powerful as you.

Now what are you to do? You can plainly see that some part of the original unity is still missing. Therefore, your only recourse is to travel deep within your own consciousness to the furthermost reaches of Immensity, and there, at the extreme end of the long series of I's, standing isolated on a snowy mountain peak and holding up a lantern to guide your way, you shall find him. It is the Hermit. He is the missing "I" that was left behind. But he was waiting for you; he knew that you would come to seek him because he also knew that you could never restore the universe without him.

The Hermit represents the Spark of Divinity deep within us all, and he alone holds the key to restore the universe to its original unity. He had been asleep when you recalled the I's, and therefore he could not come. But he is awake now, and ready and able to add his power to the infinite number of I's that lie ahead of him. And what is this great secret that he possesses? It is the secret of his number. His number is .000000000000000001, the microcosm of the original macrocosm, a minute image of the greater 1.00000000000000000 of which it is a part.

The Great Work is about to begin. Silence prevails as God and the Hermit join hands. The magical operation is quite simple, and it begins by the Hermit merely adding his number, which is 1, to the last 9 or "I" of the long series of I's. Instantly, in the twinkling of an eye, the 9 becomes a 0, and the next 9 becomes a 0, and the next one, and the next one, and the next one. A chain reaction is thus brought about from this one initial action of the Hermit, and all of the I's change to 0's like a long line of dominoes falling one against the other. Soon the number .99999999999999999 is quite magically changed to 1.00000000000000000, and the universe is restored to the 1 it was in the beginning.

We can see then the great power that lies dormant within the Spark of Divinity, within this Divine Spark of the God Consciousness that lies within us all. The Alpha number for "The Spark" is 98 or I + H, and it means, I, each. And the Alpha number for "The Spark of Divinity" is 231 or W + A (33 + 65 + 21 + 112 = 231). Thus it represents the Chariot and the Emperor, and when we place the Emperor in his Chariot, he may race across the universe, change all of the separate I's into O's or Suns, and thus restore the God Consciousness back into its original unity.

The Esoteric Meaning of the Symbol H

As in all things in life, each symbol of the Cabalah has both an esoteric or inner meaning as well as an exoteric or outer meaning. If the exoteric meaning of the H is that it represents an "I" rotated through a 90-degree angle, what then is its esoteric meaning?

The answer is quite simple when you see it, but quite well hidden to the uninitiated. Earlier in this book we broke the letter B apart into the number 13. We also broke the letter R apart into the number 12. Well, let us now do the same thing to the letter H. We can in a similar fashion change the letter H into the number 0. "How do you do that?" you ask. But you don't have to ask *me* how to do it; you can do it yourself, and quite easily, I might add. The letter "H" breaks apart into the number "1 – 1," and the number "1 – 1" is 0 or nothing.

This is the secret of his power. The Hermit is not only *Each*, which means *One*, but he is also the 0, the complete balance between the positive 1 and the negative 1, the result of which is zero or nothing. Therefore, when we state that the *name* of the symbol O is Oh, we have really not changed its value an iota by adding an H to the original O (O + H = O + 1 - 1 = O). The entire process is nothing more than spiritual alchemy, which means the transformation of one thing into another through and by means of natural law.

We have also stated earlier that the *name* for the symbol H is Each. Now let us prove it. *Webster's Third New International Dictionary of the English Language* (Unabridged) lists two ways to spell the name of the letter H. The preferred way is AITCH, although its earlier spelling of ACHE is also accepted. Now then, let us look up the same word in the venerable 13-volume edition of *The Oxford English Dictionary*. Here, we find that the preferred spelling for the letter H is ACHE, with the alternate spelling of AITCH also acceptable but not preferred. Which then is the correct way to spell its name? It would seem that the answer lies in whether one lives in England or America. But in any event, the word ACHE is easily transposed into EACH; this then is the reason that we refer to it so much in the English Cabalah as EACH.

On the other hand, we can quite easily prove that the changing of its spelling from ACHE back to AITCH does nothing more than change its gender. The Alpha number for "Ache" or "Each" is 17, which means that it represents the letter Q or the Queen. But the Alpha number for the word "Aitch" is 41, the same as the number for "King," the counterpart of the Queen. Therefore, the letter H can refer to either the male or the female.

Yet in reality, its consciousness remains the same whether we call it ACHE or AITCH. Let us examine the difference between the two words. The former contains an "E" that is not in the latter; and the latter contains an "IT" that is missing from the former. Together, these letters form a "TIE" that connects the one with the other. They also represent an equality in the result of a contest—a tie. And why is that? The answer is that the Alpha number for "Tie" is 34 which means *One*. And since the Alpha number for their sum "Ache + Aitch" is 58 which means *Two*, that which remains when we subtract the "Tie" must also be *One*. Therefore, it is a tie and they both are one.

The Alpha number for "The Hermit" is 106 which means "A of" or the Emperor of something. The Alpha number for "Hermit" by itself is 73 which adds up to a 10, meaning the letter J or the World. Therefore, the Spark of Divinity has the potential to become Emperor of the World. But where does it get this power? It gets it from *Each*, the letter *Ache*, the feminine aspect of the symbol when it brings into manifestation HER MIGHT (HER MIT).

The Seven-Petaled Lotus

Basically, the letter H is an 8. There are eight different aspects to its nature, but one of them is hidden. Indeed, upon first observation you would swear that it is a seven (Ache = 17 = a 7). Perhaps we may compare it to the *diatonic* scale in music, which has eight tones to the octave, and yet there are only seven *different* tones, the last being a repetition of the first. Therefore if you were to count all the notes in 10 octaves, let us say, you would really have only 71 notes (10 times 7 plus the remaining one at the end). The 8th aspect of the letter H only comes into manifestation at the end of the cycle, when the last repeats the first. This is especially evident in solmization where different syllables are used to denote each tone of the scale, and the syllable for the last tone, which is Do, is always a repetition of the first.

Fortunately, there is a perfect mathematical symbol available to describe the function of the letter H in terms of not only the musical diatonic scale, but also in the way that it appears in nature. It is based upon a principle in mathematics which states that exactly seven circles, no more and no less, can be inscribed within any given outer circle where all of the inner circles are of the same size. But this procedure can go on *ad infinitum*, endlessly, without beginning and without end, and with even the smallest "dot" being a mirror image of one of the larger groups of seven at the opposite end of the spectrum. Let us say that the smallest "dot" we can find is the Spark of Divinity, and that the largest group of seven circles that we can become aware of is the Universe. Therefore, it becomes obvious that this Divine

Spark has all of the potential, and is equally as powerful, as the greatest universe one can imagine. The mathematical logic of the Agashan philosophy regarding the Spark of Divinity is undisputable. The following Figure 65 illustrates this principle quite clearly:

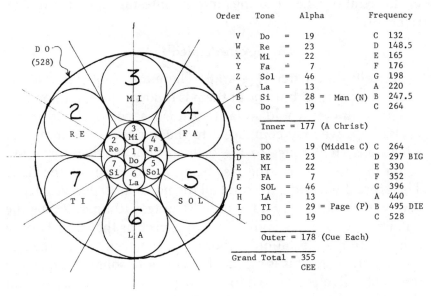

Order	Tone		Alpha			Frequency	
V	Do	=	19			C	132
W	Re	=	23			D	148.5
X	Mi	=	22			E	165
Y	Fa	≐	7			F	176
Z	Sol	=	46			G	198
A	La	=	13			A	220
B	Si	=	28	=	Man (N)	B	247.5
C	Do	=	19			C	264
	Inner	=	177	(A Christ)			
C	DO	=	19	(Middle C)		C	264
D	RE	=	23			D	297 BIG
E	MI	=	22			E	330
F	FA	=	7			F	352
G	SOL	=	46			G	396
H	LA	=	13			A	440
I	TI	=	29	=	Page (P)	B	495 DIE
J	DO	=	19			C	528
	Outer	=	178	(Cue Each)			
	Grand Total	=	355				
			CEE				

Figure 65
The Seven-Petaled Lotus and the Diatonic Scale

Therefore, let us carry this thought a bit further. The Agashan Teachers have long since stated that the Universe is constructed on the basis of strict mathematical principles. "Everything is mathematical in the final analysis," Agasha has said over and over again. And since occult science has taught from the very beginning that the universe was brought into manifestation through vibration, through sound, by the sound of the AUM through which the Word was made manifest, why then cannot the mathematical principles of *sound* be used as a model from which we can reconstruct a mental image of the universe?

The basic principles of sound, harmony, vibration, and musical tones have been known by mankind since the days of Pythagoras, and undoubtedly many thousands of years before that dating back to the time of Atlantis. Pythagoras spoke of the music of the spheres, but what are spheres, other than atoms, planets, suns, earths, and stars? It follows then that these heavenly bodies should be vibrating according to the laws of harmony, music, and the like.

Let us put this theory to the test. We begin with the assumption that it was through the Universal God Consciousness that man has learned the diatonic scale, the syllables that are used in its solmization, and all of the other items of music and harmony in the same way that it was through the God Consciousness that man learned the letters of the various alphabets. This we cannot dispute if the Cabalah is to have any validity whatsoever. Indeed, the principle of revelation from God to Man is the one, basic fundamental that supports its entire structure. Therefore, man doesn't invent these things; man only rediscovers them. There is a tremendous difference in these two suppositions. And if these things be true, Figure 65 should give us many keys towards unlocking some of the secrets of the universe.

Let us begin with the names for the syllables themselves. Since the octave begins and ends with Do it is only natural that this word, the keynote for the octave, should be the name for the central circle within each series of seven. If we add the two letters of its name together, we find that they yield the S or the Star (D + O = S). And if we read the entire term backwards, we have the word SOD which means *turf*, or one's native land. This verifies what we learned earlier when we found that the God Consciousness can be equated either to the World or the Star.

The names of the other six petals of our lotus are then the remaining six syllables in the octave. But when we come to the next to the last one, the seventh one, we have a discrepancy. The dictionary gives us two names for this tone, *Si* or *Ti*, and both are correct. But doesn't the name "SI-TI" sound very much like the word "CITY"? Isn't the Cabalah trying to tell us something? Ordinarily we might say that it is a coincidence, but when we find that the Alpha numbers for both terms are identical (each is equal to 57), the coincidence factor must be ruled out. And this is especially true when we realize that the number 57 is the God-Word number for the letters I and C, which means that the "eye" sees or that the "I" understands.

Using the "Si" name for the 7th tone, we find that the Alpha number for all seven petals of the lotus is the number 158 which transliterates into OH, the name of the letter O, the symbol for the Sun (Tarot Key 19). But isn't the Sun a star? Of course it is. The Cabalah seems to be telling us then that when we consider the central circle as one circle—the first Do in the series, as it were—it is as the letter S or the Star, but when we consider this circle to be the last Do that completes the octave, we then look upon it as being seven circles in one, and thus our "star" is seen up close and it appears like the Sun, whose name is Oh and whose symbol is O.

But now we come to the real crux of the matter, the main reason that the Universal Consciousness God has seen fit to give two names for the seventh note in the series. This was the only way that it could convey to man that we are supposed to build our seven-petaled lotus on the basis that it represents the key of C; that is, that the central petal represents Middle C (264 vibrations per second), and that each corresponding Do is always at a higher or lower octave in the key of C. This then is the reason that the Alpha value for all of the syllables that we sing, as we go up the scale and then back down again, is the number 355 or CEE, the name of the letter C and the key to which the other notes are tuned. What could be clearer than that!

Figure 65 also shows the vibrational frequencies of the notes in the octaves just above and just below Middle C. These are established in accordance with the laws of harmony and they represent simple numerical ratios. For instance: a note an octave higher than another note is vibrating at twice its frequency and thus its ratio is 2/1. Re is 9/8 that of Do, Mi is 5/4 that of Do, and the ratios for Fa, Sol, La, Si and Do' are 4/3, 3/2, 5/3, 15/8, and 2/1 respectively. It is thus seen that the frequency of the keynote (the central circle) is all-important since it forms the basis from which the frequencies of all the other notes in the scale are calculated.[1]

Now as an experiment, in order to test our theory, we have extended the English alphabet in a forward direction to represent each note higher than Middle C, and backwards to represent the notes in the octaves below Middle C. We find then that as we spiral down lower and lower, the first Do that we come to is V with a vibration rate of 132. The next ones are O, H, and A with vibration rates of 66, 33, and 16.5 respectively. There is no sense in going any lower because when we are in the 4th octave below Middle C (between H and A), we find that we are entering that zone known in the Agashan philosophy as the Silence. Here, in the abode of the Hermit and the Emperor, all is quiet since the audible frequency range of the human ear does not extend below 15 to 30 vibrations per second.

Then we can reverse the process and soar out into the higher frequencies of fathomless space. The next higher Do above Middle C is J (The World), with a vibration rate of 528. And the next ones above that are Q, X, E, L, S, and Z with vibration rates of 1,056, 2,112, 4,224, 8,448, 16,896, and 33,792 respectively. But here at the letter Z (the 7th octave above Middle C), again we must stop because once more we find ourselves in the Silence. At least as far as the physical body is concerned, all is quiet where the Star and the Empress reside because the upper limit of the human ear is between 15,000 and 20,000 vibrations per second.

Our analysis thus brings us to some very interesting conclusions. We find that the entire spectrum of sound the human body is able to hear is contained within eleven octaves of the diatonic scale. These eleven octaves contain 78 notes ($11 \times 7 = 77 + 1 = 78$). Now this is exactly the same number as the number of cards in the Tarot deck. It also represents three cycles of the English alphabet, extending all the way from the letter A (The Emperor) at the lower, base end of the scale to the

letter Z (The Empress) at its higher, treble end. Again we have
evidence that both the Tarot as well as the English alphabet
relate to the physical body of Man.

In addition to the above, the glyph of the seven-petaled lotus
is also undoubtedly a key symbol towards understanding the
true meaning of the "universal seven solar systems" spoken
about so frequently by the Agashan Teachers. "This principle,"
Agasha states, "has yet to be discovered by the scientific mind,
for it is a spiritual relationship and not necessarily one of a
material nature. Yet the countless solar systems are actually
grouped together into systems of seven. One supports the other
and the systems are interlocked and interwoven into a pattern.
Each group is interrelated and closely associated" (*The
Agashan Discourses*, page 306).

Yet it makes no difference whether we are speaking of the
macrocosmic universe of the stars, the microcosmic universe of
the atoms, or the body of Man that lies somewhere in between
—the principle is always the same. At the innermost core of the
lotus is the Emperor who sits on his throne and represents the
very first *Do*, the archetype which sets the pattern and the keynote for all of the other Do's and the universe which is to
follow. Then, facing the Emperor and representing the first
manifested Do, is the Hermit, the Ancient One, the One in
whom the Spark of Divinity resides. In the awakened state he is
the number 8, a man like you or me, but asleep he is the number 8
turned over on its side—the ∞, the Infinite State, the totality of
all that is. This thought is reinforced by the fact that the Alpha
number for "Infinity" is 106, the same as the number for "The
Hermit" (Tarot Key 9).

He is always pictured with a HOOD enveloping his head and
shoulders, and with the six-pointed star, the Seal of Solomon,
encased within his lantern which acts as a beacon of light to
guide those who are to follow. To those of us in the outer
world and who are looking within, his HOOD appears in
reverse as a DOOH—a "DO + OH," the 1 circle of the DO and
the 7 circles of the OH (the Alpha number for all 7 tones is 158
or OH). He is the 1 and also the 7—making 8 in all.

Yes indeed, this Hermit who dwells within each one of us is truly "One to Obey" inasmuch as he represents the BOGA principle of Life, being *in* the physical world, but not *of* it.[2]

NOTES

1. Additional information on the mathematics of pitch, musical scales, ear sensitivity, etc. can be found in such volumes as that by Arthur L. Foley, *College Physics* (Philadelpha, The Blakiston Company, 1941) p. 538–549

2. For a clearer understanding of the last paragraph, the reader is referred to the chapter on the Spiritual Centers in *Agasha: Master of Wisdom*.

Chapter 18

THE ENGLISH ALPHABET: A SUMMARY

If THE READER will now briefly review the preceding chapters, he will find that our long search to establish the identity of the 26 letters of the English alphabet has come to an end. All 26 keys of the Tarot (the 22 Major Arcana keys plus the 4 Court cards) can now be identified on a one-to-one basis with each letter of the alphabet. Our task has not been an easy one, and many dead ends were encountered along the way (Nature does not reveal her secrets without a struggle); but in spite of the blinds, the far larger amount of positive evidence makes it fairly certain that the correspondences established herein are the correct ones.

They are tabulated in Figure 66 and Figure 67. In these two figures the Tarot Forces are arranged in alphabetical order according to the English alphabet. We have also tabulated the Word number, Alpha number, Letter number, and Key number for the God Words and God Names of each of the letters in the same way that we had done so earlier in Chapter 6. The only difference between Figure 66 and Figure 16 is that the former arranges the numbers in alphabetical order and the latter in the order of the numbers appearing on the Tarot keys themselves. And we can say the same thing for Figure 67 and Figure 17. Aside from the addition of the 4 Court keys, the only differences are in their order.

THE ENGLISH ALPHABET -- GOD WORDS							
English Letters and Number	The God Words	Numbers				Running Totals		
		Word (Yod)	Alpha (He)	Letter (Vav)	Key (He)	Key Sum	Letter Sum	Alpha Sum
1. A	EMPEROR	1	90	7	98	98	7	90 I O
2. B	WHEEL	1	53	5	59	157	12	143 N C
3. C	MOON	1	57	4	62	219	16	200 TO
4. D	DEVIL	1	52	5	58	277	21	252 BE 2
5. E	HIEROPHANT	1	114	10	125	402	31	366
6. F	PRIESTESS	1	130	9	140	542	40	496 DIF
7. G	JUSTICE	1	87	7	95	637	47	583
8. H	HERMIT	1	73	6	80	717	53	656
9. I	MAGICIAN	1	57	8	66	783	61	713 G M
10. J	WORLD	1	72	5	78	861	66	785 G HE
11. K	KING	1	41	4	46	907	70	826
12. L	KNIGHT	1	69	6	76	983	76	895
13. M	DEATH	1	38	5	44	1,027	81	933
14. N	MAN	1	28	3	32	1,059	84	961 I You
15. O	SUN	1	54	3	58	1,117	87	1,015
16. P	PAGE	1	29	4	34	1,151	91	1,044 A ODD
17. Q	QUEEN	1	62	5	68	1,219	96	1,106 K OF
18. R	TOWER	1	81	5	87	1,306	101	1,187
19. S	STAR	1	58	4	63	1,369	105	1,245 AXE
20. T	TEMPERANCE	1	100	10	111	1,480	115	1,345
21. U	FOOL	1	48	4	53	1,533	119	1,393
22. V	LOVERS	1	91	6	98	1,631	125	1,484
23. W	CHARIOT	1	74	7	82	1,713	132	1,558
24. X	JUDGEMENT	1	99	9	109	1,822	141	1,657 PEG
25. Y	STRENGTH	1	111	8	120	1,942	149	1,768
26. Z	EMPRESS	1	95	7	103	2,045	156	1,863
Alphabet Total		26	1,863	156	2,045	BODE	OF	A HF C

Figure 66: The God Words in Alphabetical Order

THE ENGLISH ALPHABET--GOD NAMES								
English Letters and Number	The God Names	Numbers				Running Totals		
		Word (Yod)	Alpha (He)	Letter (Vav)	Key (He)	Key Sum	Letter Sum	Alpha Sum
1. A	THE EMPEROR	2	123	10	135	135	10	123 ABC
2. B	THE WHEEL OF FORTUNE	4	206	17	227	362	27	329
3. C	THE MOON	2	90	7	99	461	34	419
4. D	THE DEVIL	2	85	8	95	556	42	504
5. E	THE HIEROPHANT	2	147	13	162	718	55	651
6. F	THE HIGH PRIESTESS	3	195	16	214	932	71	846
7. G	JUSTICE	1	87	7	95	1,027	78	933
8. H	THE HERMIT	2	106	9	117	1,144	87	1,039 JC I
9. I	THE MAGICIAN	2	90	11	103	1,247	98	1,129
10. J	THE WORLD	2	105	8	115	1,362	106	1,234 A BCD
11. K	THE KING	2	74	7	83	1,445	113	1,308 M OH
12. L	THE KNIGHT	2	102	9	113	1,558	122	1,410
13. M	DEATH	1	38	5	44	1,602	127	1,448 ADD H
14. N	THE HANGED MAN	3	100	12	115	1,717	139	1,548
15. O	THE SUN	2	87	6	95	1,812	145	1,635
16. P	THE PAGE	2	62	7	71	1,883	152	1,697 A FIG
17. Q	THE QUEEN	2	95	8	105	1,988	160	1,792
18. R	THE TOWER	2	114	8	124	2,112	168	1,906
19. S	THE STAR	2	91	7	100	2,212	175	1,997 SIG
20. T	TEMPERANCE	1	100	10	111	2,323	185	2,097
21. U	THE FOOL	2	81	7	90	2,413	192	2,178 BAG H
22. V	THE LOVERS	2	124	9	135	2,548	201	2,302 B COB
23. W	THE CHARIOT	2	107	10	119	2,667	211	2,409
24. X	JUDGEMENT	1	99	9	109	2,776	220	2,508 BE OH
25. Y	STRENGTH	1	111	8	120	2,896	228	2,619
26. Z	THE EMPRESS	2	128	10	140	3,036	238	2,747
	Alphabet Total	51	2,747	238	3,036			

Figure 67: The God Names in Alphabetical Order

There are many remarkable things about these God Words and God Names, especially in the order that they align themselves. For instance: the Alpha number for the Emperor is 123 or ABC. Well this in itself is not too unusual, but when we realize that the sum of the first 10 God Names is 1234 or ABCD, we begin to sit up and take notice. The Cabalah seems to be conveying a rather important thought: namely, that the decade or the 10 is closely related to the monad which is 1. They both are triangular numbers, the only difference between them being that the monad is built up of three rows of dots or tetractys and the decade by four. These 10 tetractys (the apex of the pyramid in Figure 23) were considered by the Pythagoreans to be a symbol of the greatest importance; and it becomes even more significant when we realize that the missing number 4 even appears on the Tarot card for the Emperor himself. The number of his Tarot key is 4, and when we add this number to the 123 of his Alpha number, we bring the 10 tetractys or the decade into full manifestation.

A similar situation arises when we consider the number for the sum of the first 19 God Words or Names. All three of the numbers—the numbers 1, 10, and 19—are only a remanifestation once again of the number 1 or unity. Therefore, it is no surprise when we learn that the sum of the first 19 God Words brings into manifestation an AXE (1,245 = AXE). And what is an axe used for? It is a cutting tool used for felling trees, which means then that once again the Tree of Life is to be cut or severed at this point. The Alpha number sum of the first 19 God Names even echoes this remark with the number 1,997 which transliterates into SIG, the abbreviation for *signal* or *signature.* In other words, it is a *signal* that some action is about to take place, and the *signature* for this action is the axe. What could be clearer than that?

There are many, many more interesting and informative things to be learned from a thorough study of the numbers and combinations of numbers in Figures 66 and 67. But we will leave it to the astute reader to discover these golden nuggets for himself. It is as Agasha has always said, "You have to get in there and dig!"

The Spelling of the Letters

Now let us investigate a completely different aspect of the English Cabalah, and one that brings to light an almost incredible condition that currently exists in regard to the English language. How do you *spell* the letters of the English alphabet? When I asked this question to one of the librarians of the Glendale Public Library, she looked at me almost in disbelief. "What do you mean, how do you spell the letters?" she inquired. The thought had simply never entered her head that a simple tabulation of the *names* of all 26 letters of the English alphabet would be in any way useful. Yet the names of the letters in all of the other languages are tabulated in this fashion. For instance: in *Webster's New Collegiate Dictionary* under the heading "Alphabet Table," the names of the letters in the Hebrew, Arabic, and Greek alphabets are listed alongside of their symbols in a very orderly manner. But is there any place in the dictionary you can find a simple tabulation of the names of the letters in our own language, the English language? The answer, apparently, is no.

Simply astounded that this seemed to be the case, both the librarian and myself proceeded on a systematic search through the index of the library, through all of the dictionaries, through grammars such as English/French, English/German, English/Italian, etc., and even through childrens' alphabet books thinking that just perhaps, maybe, such a list would be contained therein. But was the search successful? It was not. Wherever the English alphabet was listed, and of course it was listed in innumerable places, the authors in every instance simply tabulated the *symbols* for the English letters and never their *names*. Why this is so, your guess is as good as mine.

Now this is very definitely not the case when we consider the names for all of the numbers. There they are, listed in dozens and dozens of places, as one, two, three, etc., neatly tabulated and correlated with the equivalent word in each of the foreign languages. Ask anyone how you spell 8, and he will immediately answer with an EIGHT; but if you ask that same individual how you spell R, for instance, he will first look at you in a kind of uncomprehending way, and then try to *invent* some way to spell it because he had never been taught how to spell these letters in school. And if you think the answer is ARE, you will be right as far as the English Cabalah is concerned but wrong if you wish to believe Webster. For some unknown reason, *Webster's New Collegiate Dictionary* has finally decided that it should be spelled AR; but most other dictionaries just do not consider the letter to be a word at all. As far as most of them are concerned, there simply are no ways to spell many of the letters in the English language. The names for the majority of the letters—not all of them but some of them—just do not seem to exist.

After this rather remarkable discovery, the writer lost no time in researching the matter as far as he was able to go. Here, too, was another challenge: to identify not only the correct Tarot keys with the letters of the English alphabet, but also to learn the way the letters should be spelled. This was of primary importance, I remember thinking at the time, because the spelling of a word can completely change not only its meaning, but also its numerical vibration.

A typical example of the problems that were encountered along the way is in the correct spelling of the letter H. We discussed this letter to some extent in the previous chapter where it was shown that it may be spelled in two different ways, AITCH or ACHE, the American way or the English way. Either way is technically correct. This is much the same as in the case where JUDGMENT is spelled thus in America, and in England a second E is added in the middle and it is called JUDGEMENT. The Cabalah allows for these alternate spellings in much the same fashion that the Wheel of Fortune (206) is many times referred to as the Wheel of Life (139); in either instance we always know that these two numbers relate to the letter B.

However, whenever we are making a numerical calculation

involving the addition of several letters in a word in order to find its correct God-Name number, God-Word number, or whatever, it is essential that we have only one, accepted standard of measurement that is used in each and every case. Otherwise the results would be chaotic, and we could come up with almost any number we wished to represent the answer to a particular problem; i.e., the number 99 is always used as the God-Name number for the letter X, 206 for the letter B, 38 for the letter M, etc. These are the God-Name numbers for these particular letters and they can never be changed, even though we also know that 94 does indeed represent the letter X, 139 the letter B, and 71 the letter M (The Death = 71).

Therefore, in the light of the above, it is essential that we establish once and for all a correct *cabalistic* way to spell the 26 letters that we can use in our mathematical computations where they involve the use of the name of the English letter. We have worked on this problem for many years, taking into consideration such factors as common usage, the esoteric meaning of the letter, the way most people would subconsciously spell it, the function of the letter, and last but not least, the actual letters themselves that go on to make up the *word* that represents the name of a particular letter. The results of our efforts are tabulated in Figure 68, my apologies being offered to those who disagree with our conclusions.

For instance: you would never convince a Britisher to accept for one moment that the letter Z is spelled in any other way than ZED. In England ZED is the name for the last letter of the English alphabet, and I guess it will stay that way for a long time to come. ZEE is only a bastardized version of ZED, they will tell you, and who am I to argue the point? But nevertheless, we still stand by the conclusions that we have reached as shown in Figure 68.

Another interesting point of controversy is the spelling we have chosen for the letter Q. What is a Q, anyway? Other than the fact that it is the symbol for the Queen, it is also a *Queue*, a term used to describe a long waiting line of persons or vehicles. Now we cannot prove the point here, but the 2nd volume of

THE ENGLISH ALPHABET--LETTER NAMES

English Letters and Number	Letter Names	Numbers				Running Totals			
		Word (Yod)	Alpha (He)	Letter (Vav)	Key (He)	Key Sum	Letter Sum	Alpha Sum	
1. A	A	1	1	1	3	3	1	1	A
2. B	BE	1	7	2	10	13	3	8	H
3. C	CEE	1	13	3	17	30	6	21	U
4. D	DEE	1	14	3	18	48	9	35	
5. E	E	1	5	1	7	55	10	40	CODE
6. F	EF	1	11	2	14	69	12	51	EA.
7. G	GEE	1	17	3	21	90	15	68	
8. H	AITCH	1	41	5	47	137	20	109	
9. I	I	1	9	1	11	148	21	118	
10. J	JAY	1	36	3	40	188	24	154	O D
11. K	KAY	1	37	3	41	229	27	191	
12. L	ELL	1	29	3	33	262	30	220	
13. M	EM	1	18	2	21	283	32	238	
14. N	EN	1	19	2	22	305	34	257	BEG.
15. O	OH	1	23	2	26	331	36	280	B H O
16. P	PEE	1	26	3	30	361	39	306	C OF
17. Q	QUE	1	43	3	47	408	42	349	CD I
18. R	ARE	1	24	3	28	436	45	373	CG C
19. S	ESS	1	43	3	47	483	48	416	
20. T	TEE	1	30	3	34	517	51	446	
21. U	YOU	1	61	3	65	582	54	507	
22. V	VEE	1	32	3	36	618	57	539	
23. W	DOUBLE YOU	2	120	9	131	749	66	659	
24. X	EX	1	29	2	32	781	68	688	
25. Y	WYE	1	53	3	57	838	71	741	
26. Z	ZEE	1	36	3	40	878	74	777	
Alphabet Total		27	777	74	878				

Figure 68: The Letter Names in Alphabetical Order

this work will definitely show that the Queen, who represents motherhood, is the doorway through which a long line of waiting souls are waiting their chance to be born into one of the suits of the Tarot. And the number that are waiting is endless— we might say that a perfect name for the Queen would be QUEUEUEUEUEUEUEUE . . . forever. Our thinking then follows pretty much along the following lines:

Name	Description	Alpha Number
Q	The Symbol	17
QUE	The Letter	43
QUEUE	A Long Line of People	69
QUEUEUE	THE QUEEN	95
	Total Sum	224
	Average Value	56 = EF

The reasons for the spellings of most of the other letters are self evident. We have at least touched upon the words, and the spelling of the words, earlier in the book when we showed the connection between the Tarot key and its corresponding English letter. However, we should mention in closing that the Alpha number sum for all 26 of the English letter words seems quite significant. The number 7 has always been associated with spirituality and the Christ Consciousness, and the addition of an indefinite number of 7's seems to enhance it even further. Indeed, even the Alpha number for *Christ* is a double seven or 77. Why then cannot the number 777 be equally as significant? The thought is reinforced by the fact that Aleister Crowley, one of the most profound teachers of occult science in this century, chose to call his treatise on the "Magical Alphabet" and the various tables of correspondences connecting it with practically every other item of the Cabalah (or the Qabalah, as he called it) by the title "777."[1] The English alphabet is thus seen to be the equivalent of his "Magical Alphabet" that he expounded upon so profusely during his lifetime.

The Spelling of the Numbers

Another absolutely fascinating point comes to light when we consider the Alpha number total for the names of all of the numbers from One to Ten. In fact, we should share it with you right now while we are speaking of the spelling of the letters. These ten numbers which represent the ten digits are tabulated below:

Number	Name	Alpha Number	Running Total	
1.	ONE	34	34	CD
2.	TWO	58	92	I B
3.	THREE	56	148	N H
4.	FOUR	60	208	BOTH
5.	FIVE	42	250	BE O
6.	SIX	52	302	COB
7.	SEVEN	65	367	C FG
8.	EIGHT	49	416	
9.	NINE	42	458	
10.	TEN	39	497	DIG
55. = 10	Totals	497 = 20		
		DIG = T		

Thus we find that the Cabalah tells us a very important fact: namely, that the sum of the first 10 numbers equates right back to a single DIGIT. But not only that, the running total sums are equally as informative.

We begin with the number 1 which represents the seed (CD). This in turn is followed by the statement "I Be" (1 + 2). But where is it that I be? The answer is found in the sum of the first 3 numbers which tell us that it is "in each" (N H). Therefore, the complete statement of the Trinity, the Emperor or the 123, is that "I be in each seed."

Now we come to the 4, the sum of the first 4 numbers which bring into manifestation the decade or the 10 (1 + 2 + 3 + 4 =

10). The number is 208 which states that it B OH (the Sun). This number is also exactly one half of the sum of the first 8 numbers (416), which is as it should be since 4 is one half of 8. But the sum of the first 5 numbers states that it also "BE O," and there seems to be a conflict here. But the conflict is soon resolved when we transliterate the number 208 into BOTH, and we find that they *both* be 0, the sum of the 4 and/or the sum of the 5. The sum of the former is 10, the letter J, the World, and the sum of the latter is 15, the letter O, the Sun. Thus the Cabalah states that *both* systems—the geocentric system which places the Earth at the center, or the heliocentric system which puts the Sun at the center—are correct. That is, either one of them may be used as the 0 or the central point from which the universe can be observed.

The sum of the first 6 numbers, however, is slightly different. Yet, in a way not too different as a COB is the central core about which all of the individual kernels of corn are encased. It is the axis around which the eatable part of an ear of Indian corn is arranged. And this axis is You, the Fool, the number 21; therefore you too are the center of your own universe.

Yes indeed, the numbers can tell us many wonderful things when they are asked. But to ask them, we have to get in there and DIG!

The Wheel of Life

Let us now consider all 26 letters of the alphabet as the rim of a gigantic wheel. It is the Wheel of Life. The numbers that the individual letters represent are placed on an inner circle within this wheel, and their total sum, which is 351, becomes the hub. And then, in a circle just outside of the hub, are the four letters of the Divine Word YOD HE VAV HE that was first uttered in the beginning. All of these things, and more, are brought into manifestation through the adjacent diagram.

Now it becomes strangely significant, as we study Figure 69, how all of these various numbers seem to harmonize with each other in such an unusual manner. For instance: the Hebrew word YOD HE VAV HE has a numerical value of 26, and there

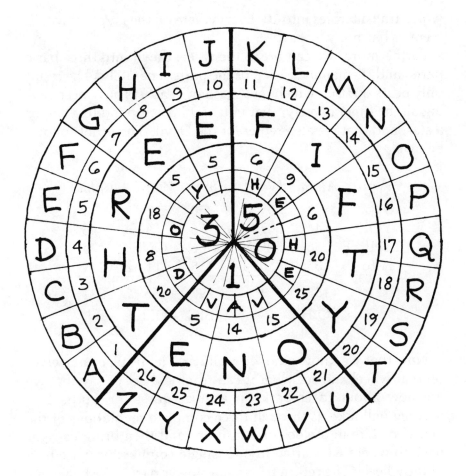

Figure 69: The Wheel of Life

are 26 letters in the English alphabet; therefore these letters can be matched against their English counterparts on a one-to-one correspondence. The number 351, when changed into the words THREE FIFTY ONE, contains 13 letters; therefore each of these letters can also be matched with the letters of the alphabet, this time on a 1 to 2 basis. And last but not least, YOD can be matched with THREE, VAV with ONE, and HE + HE with FIFTY, each one of them on a slightly different numerical basis. Even the hub can be read as 135 + 0 or ACE + 0, which transliterates into 10. Everywhere on the glyph, it would seem, is harmony.

Furthermore, we can break the wheel down into three basic parts, and then analyze each of the parts separately. The result only bears out that which the Agashan Teachers have been saying all the time; namely, that you and I correspond to a sun or a star, and that we also represent the Devil. The proof follows below:

Word	Alpha	Word	Alpha	Word	Alpha
3	3	50	50	1	1
YOD	44	HE + HE	26	VAV	45
THREE	56	FIFTY	66	ONE	34
A to J	55	K to T	155	U to Z	141
	158	+	297	= 455	221
	O H		BIG	DEE	B U

Now that we know who we really are, let us place ourselves on that wheel and see what it can teach us. Let us say that we are now about to embark on a great quest for truth. This journey will take us through three complete revolutions of the Wheel of Life in a clockwise fashion, and then bring us right back to where we started in one, single counterclockwise turn of the wheel. (The return trip is at a slower pace.) We begin our quest at the letter A.

The Quest

A be the sea.	A B C
A beast effigy	A BCD EFG
Hijack and kill men.	HIJK KL MN
Men hope Christ arrest you.	MN OP QRST RST U
You have double-you.	U'V W
You view Christ.	U VW "X"
Double-you asks wise A	W X YZ A
Why is	Y Z
A be the sea?	A B C

The Answer

A be the seed.	A B CD
D (devil) *effigy hijack and kill men.*	D EFG HIJK KL MN
Yet high jackal man knows	HI JKL MN NO
The pea (seed) *cures two* (too).	P QRS TU
You have double-you.	U'V W
But you have double-crossed wise A.	U'V WX YZ A
Therefore, double-you acts wise.	W X YZ
Wise A be seedy.	YZ A B CDE
A be the seed.	A B CD

Or

A beast effigy: each I.	A BCD EFG HI
High jackal man know peak.	HI JKL MN NO PQ
You rest.	U RST
You view crosswise	U VW X YZ
A beast effigy: each I.	A BCD EFG H I

The Journey

Double-you view the Tee (starting mound).	W VU T
The Tee (Cross) *is our coupon.*	T'S R QPON
You: Tzar (Emperor)	U TSR
You tee the "S" (place it on the tee).	U T "S"
You start (tee off).	U TSR
The "S" arcs up on animal cage (Zodiac).	S RQ PON NML KJ
But an animal cages (imprisons) *the "I."*	NML KJ I
The cage eyes each gaffe (The Zodiac observes each faux pas or blunder).	KJ I H GFE
Each gaffe (blunder) *fed the sea.*	H GFE FED C
Sea be A's "Y" (strength).	C B A'Z Y
A's be (Y = 25 = BE) *X-wave* (extraordinary wave).	A'Z Y X-WV
A's "Y" (strength) *X-wave* (X-ray) *you.*	A'Z Y X-WV U

Double-you view the Tee (The Tee is
　　now within you. The coupon is
　　redeemed).　　　　　　　　　　W VU T

　　Thus we find there is far more to the English alphabet than
what appears on the surface. In its exoteric sense it is the story
of Man; but taken esoterically, it becomes the story of God.
For instance: if one will study the Tarot card for the Wheel of
Life (Tarot Key 10) again, he will observe that there are two
entities riding the Wheel: the Serpent Typhon (the S) and the
Jackal-headed god Hermes-Anubis (the JKL). The Serpent
represents the Life-force descending the Wheel and the Jackal
that same Life-force as it ascends. Both of these characters are
clearly depicted in the preceding epic poem of the great Wheel
of Life.

　　But the poem can also be considered a great saga of the
macrocosmic world of God as well as that of the microcosmic
world of Man. In the former case the "S" becomes the Star and
the "NML" each sign of the Zodiac. And in the latter case the
"S" is the lowly Serpent who is cast out of the Garden of Eden
into an "NML" body in the animal cage called the Earth. There
are many levels of consciousness through which it may be
viewed. But in any event however, taken either macrocosmic-
ally or microcosmically, you are still in it; it is still *your* saga,
for didn't we learn earlier that you are also a "BIG OH," which
means a big Sun or Star? It would seem that the Fool, who is
You, is indeed the star of the show.

The Alphabet from A to Z

　　Thus we come to the end of our search. It has been a long
journey, but also an enjoyable one. We have met a lot of
strange characters along the way, some of them very formid-
able indeed, but once their masks have been removed we can
see them for what they really are—important and necessary
aspects of the Universal Consciousness called GOD.

　　Yet all of these aspects are good; there is absolutely nothing
within the God Consciousness that we can call *bad*. All that

had been feared and dreaded before is now seen, in the sunlight of our greater understanding, to be only a corrective influence to help us to stay upon the spiritual path. Therefore all aspects of the God Consciousness, in the final analysis, are positive.

But before we leave this portion of the Great Work to explore the more subtle recesses of our *inner* consciousness, one further step remains to be made. That step is to firmly place in our *outer* consciousness, once and for all so that we will never forget them, the 26 independent and yet unseparable divisions of the *God* Consciousness. So then come with us now through the remainder of this section, studying each page as if it were a picture book, while we briefly review the major aspects of not only the God Consciousness but also *your* consciousness—the 26 symbols of the alphabet from A to Z.

NOTES

1. Aleister Crowley, *777 Revised* (London WC 1, The Neptune Press, 1955)

A THE EMPEROR

The Emperor represents the Fatherhood of God. The Alpha number of his name is 123 and this number, when combined with his Tarot key number, which is 4, yields the decade or the 10. He is the crowned monarch, commanding and stately, and seated on a throne decorated by rams' heads, signifying the sign of Aries. In the background are bare mountains, indicating that his kingdom is of a primordial nature; in fact, his throne itself is hewn out of barren rock. In his right hand (the active, male side) he holds a sceptre in the shape of the Ankh, signifying life and generation; and in his left hand (the passive, female side) rests the globe of dominion. This indicates that only by balancing the masculine with the feminine, the forces of authority with those of dominion, can he equate spirit with matter and thus have the wisdom to rule with equal justice to all.

His symbol is the English letter A, the first letter of the alphabet, and it represents in graphical form the Great Pyramid of the Emperor. This great "monument to spirituality," as the Agashan Teachers so often refer to it, is the tomb of the Emperor himself and the place where his body is enshrined. And where is this place? Right in the number Pi, as evidenced by the fact that the Alpha number of "The Great Pyramid of the Emperor" is 314, the first three digits of π.

The Wheel of Fortune

The Wheel of Fortune is also called the Wheel of Life. The Alpha number of its God Name is 206, which means that it "B OF" something, and that something is the number 10, its Tarot key number. This is the ever-turning Wheel which carries men and their destinies through life after life after life, through all of the digits from 1 to 10, over and over again.

The serpent god Typhon represents the life-force in its descent into the physical world, and the jackal-headed god, Hermes Anubis, symbolizes you and me as we ascend from the Wheel into the higher spiritual realms. The four mystical Living Creatures of Ezekiel (the Bull, the Lion, the Eagle, and Man) occupy the four corners of the card, indicating the four fixed signs of the Zodiac. Looked upon in its macrocosmic aspect then, the Wheel of Fortune becomes a symbol for the whole cycle of Cosmic manifestation.

The symbol for the Wheel of Life is the English letter B, which means *to be*. Since this is the second letter of the alphabet, it is represented in graphical form by the *cycloid*, a mathematical curve generated by a wheel as it turns through *two* complete revolutions along its base.

Within the Wheel are the hub and the rim, which represent the Core of Life and the outer world respectively. The 8 spokes are the rays from the Star.

 THE MOON

The Moon, shown in three phases, watches over a nocturnal landscape. Its 16 chief rays and 16 secondary rays are sent out unto the Earth to assist in the process of evolution. It furnishes the power so that life may evolve from out of the sea (the C) and onto the shore. The way of evolution upon the earth plane is very clearly marked, and it is symbolized by a long, winding path that leads from the sea and across the land. About halfway up the path are two pillars or towers, and it eventually ascends into the rugged mountains in the distance.

In the foreground a crayfish appears, symbolizing life in the early stages of conscious unfoldment. Then, a little further along the path, are a wolf and a dog. The wolf is one of Nature's untamed creations, and the dog the result of its adaption to life with Man.

The symbol for the Moon is the crescent, the C, the third letter of the alphabet. It thus represents the reflected light of a planet rather than the direct light of a sun or star. The three words that describe the symbol are Cee, Sea, and See, meaning the Moon, the water that reflects its light, and the wisdom that is imparted when it is *seen* and understood. This comes about through the interaction of the 15 Yods (dewdrops of thought) with the evolving consciousness below as it struggles to attain self-realization.

THE DEVIL

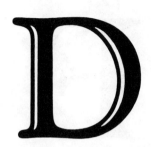

The Devil is the Mortal Mind, the Demon Self, that part of our consciousness that enslaves us and keeps us in bondage. In the Tarot Deck he is depicted as the Horned Goat of Mendes, with bat-like wings, donkey ears, and seated upon an altar in the shape of a half-cube. An inverted pentagram is above his head representing the wrong use of power, and his right hand is raised revealing a sign of black magic. (This is the reverse of the benediction given by the Hierophant.) A great, flaming torch of destruction is held in his left hand, and it is directed towards the earth.

The objects of his wrath are the hero and heroine of our story, Adam and Eve, who represent you and me. He has us chained to his altar and rightly so; for if you will examine the card you will discover that we are still controlled by our animal nature, having not yet lost our horns and tails. Yet the chains are loose, and they can be removed at will.

The symbol for the Devil is the letter D, the 4th letter of the alphabet and a number to labor under. The Devil then is an obstacle in our path. If one will look through the dictionary at all of the words prefaced by the two letters "de," he will have a general idea of what role the Devil plays in life. He represents the opposition or the anti-force—the dark part of the Moon not illuminated by the Sun.

E THE HIEROPHANT

The Hierophant is the ruling power of organized religion. In ancient Greece he was the chief priest of the Eleusinian mysteries; in our modern day he is the Pope. He is shown seated between two pillars, and two priestly ministers kneel before him. With his right hand he gives the well-known ecclesiastical sign, and in his left hand he holds the papal cross.

All well and good. But the truly significant symbolism of the Hierophant that is not generally understood is that he also brings all three octaves of the number five into full manifestation. At his feet is the symbol of "the crossed keys," the Alpha number of the term being 176. This reduces to 14 and brings the letter N into manifestation. His Tarot key number is 5 which gives us the letter E, and the letter W, the highest vibration of the number five (See Figure 1 on page 21), is very much in

evidence at the top of his triple crown. Therefore, it could truly be said that he brings that which is NEW into manifestation.

But the basic symbol for the Hierophant is the letter E, the 5th letter of the English alphabet. E is the symbol for *energy*, and it is this spiritual energy that is brought forth from the "Higher Fount" that enables mankind to grow spiritually. Therefore, he represents Coty, the Learned One, the Master of the Sacred Mysteries, the E of the WYE of Cara Boga Coty.

THE HIGH PRIESTESS

The name of the High Priestess is *Isis*, which in ancient times meant "throne." She is the Virgin Mother of the World, and she rules her kingdom from the central point between the two pillars of King Solomon's Temple—the black pillar of Boaz representing the negative life force, and the white pillar of Jachin the positive life force.

Behind her is a veil which is embroidered with palms and pomegranates, and upon her lap is a scroll inscribed with the word *Tora*, signifying the law as it pertains to the Secret Tradition. Her vestments are flowing and quite ethereal-like in their nature, and her mantle extends way down to support the lunar crescent at her feet. Upon her head is a horned diadem supporting a central globe, and a large solar cross, with arms of equal length, rests upon her breast. The two equal arms symbolize complete harmony and balance between the vertical, positive life force and the horizontal, negative life force.

The symbol for the High Priestess is the letter F, the 6th letter of the alphabet. And her astrological sign is also a 6, inasmuch as she represents Virgo, the Virgin, the 6th sign of the Zodiac. Therefore her number is 6, the inverse of the "I" which is 9. (The 9 turned upside down reverts back to the 6.) The Alpha number of "Isis," incidentally, is 56 or EF, a manifestation of the *name* of her symbol.

JUSTICE

The female figure seated between the pillars of Justice is the Greek goddess *Astraea*, one of the Titans who descended from heaven in a Golden Age long since past and inspired mankind with principles of justice and equity. She is traditionally depicted with a sword in her right hand symbolizing her potential severity, and with a pair of scales in her left hand showing balanced judgment. Normally she is blindfolded.

But in the Tarot deck her eyes are unveiled, symbolizing divine justice at work rather than the blindness of human justice. To Astraea then, all things are revealed; and her sword of Karma is poised, ready to smite all that is imperfect and out of harmony with natural law. All of one's actions, both of the past and the present, are weighed in the golden scales of justice, and if the karmic weight is in balance, progress along the path is assured.

The symbol for Justice is the letter G, the 7th letter of the alphabet, and like the High Priestess her astrological sign is also the same number as her symbol. Astraea therefore represents Libra, the Scales, the 7th sign of the Zodiac.

But in other ways she is different. Astraea gazes *inwards* into the inner world of the Temple, as opposed to the High Priestess who looks *outwards* into the outer world of mortal. One is thus the reverse of the other.

THE HERMIT

The Hermit is a symbol of attainment, rather than a symbol of quest. He represents the consciousness of the Ascended Adept in one of the great Spiritual Centers of the Earth, and he stands upon the mountain peak as a beacon of light for those on the path below him. The lantern that he holds aloft is the lighted Lamp of Truth, and it contains within it the six-pointed star of the Seal of Solomon.

The Hermit stands isolated and alone. He is always hooded, and he is robed in a mantle of discretion. The staff that he leans upon is the staff of intuition, and these three symbols—his lantern, his cloak, and his staff—are what constitute his inner strength.

But what is the secret of his power? It is his great symbol of authority, the letter H, the 8th letter of the English alphabet. Turn the number 8 over on its side, and it becomes ∞, the symbol of infinity. Open up the letter H into its component parts, and it becomes 1 – 1 or nothing. Thus the Hermit has the power, within himself, to enter into the Infinite State.

Furthermore, the British spelling of the letter H is ACHE, and this may be transformed into EACH. Thus the Hermit becomes a symbol of "Each I," the One without a second, the Ancient of Days, the ONE IDENTITY within us all that states simply that I AM.

I

THE
MAGICIAN

The Magician is the inner "I" that dwells within. He is the inner higher self as opposed to the outer mortal self (The Fool) who is *you*; and the Hermit, being *each*, represents both. Therefore, the Trinity is brought into manifestation with "each you and I."

In the Tarot card symbol for the "I" (the Roman numeral I and the English letter I), is a youthful figure wearing the robe of the Higher Initiate. He stands before a table upon which are the symbols of the four natural elements of earth, water, air, and fire. These are represented by a pentacle, a cup, a sword, and a wand, respectively. The cosmic lemniscate symbol of infinity is above his head, and around his waist is the occult symbol of eternity—a serpent swallowing its tail. His black hair, which is bound by a white band, signifies the limitation of ignorance by knowledge.

The Magician stands in a garden of roses and lilies, and in his uplifted right hand is a wand. His left hand points down to the earth, and he is about to demonstrate that that which is above may be made manifest in that which is below. He performs this "magic" by drawing the *anims* from the etheric world and then materializing them again into *atoms* of the material world. This is all accomplished through the power of the will working in harmony with the power of the mind.

THE WORLD

The World, sometimes called the Universe, is depicted as an elliptical wreath in the shape of the digit 0. It is thus seen as an endless chain formed from the branches of the Tree of Life, and one that is stronger than a chain of steel. Evidence of its great strength is given by the two cosmic lemniscates at its upper and lower ends, symbolizing that the great oval of the 0 is infinitely strong, and that it can never be broken.

Framed within the "0" is a female figure clad only in a scarf. She carries a wand in either hand, and her legs are crossed in the same fashion as the Hanged Man. She is in the act of dancing, and she expresses the soul's intoxication while living within the earthly paradise of the sensible universe. Her name? Some say that it is *Truth.*

Then at the four corners of the World are the Divine Watchers—the four Living Creatures of Eze-kiel last seen in the symbol for the letter B. Thus there is a great affinity between the Wheel of Life and the World or Universe, between the letter B and the letter J, and rightly so. They both are related to the two pillars on either side of the entrance to Solomon's Temple.

Furthermore, the letter J, since it is the 10th letter of the English alphabet, also signifies the completion of a cycle where the 10 once more reverts back to the 0.

K THE KING

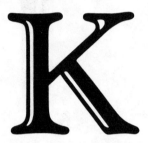

The Kings are the rulers of the four primary kingdoms of the sensible universe, the word *sensible* meaning that which can be perceived by the senses. These are the four basic elements of Earth, Water, Air, and Fire, or matter in its solid, liquid, gaseous, and energy states, respectively. In the Tarot deck, they are represented by the four suits of the Minor Arcana.

The sensible universe then is the counterpart of the spiritual universe, the universe ruled by the Emperor. It consists of the almost infinite number of *spiritual* planets, suns, stars, etc. of an etheric nature, and that cannot be perceived by the senses. These are represented in the Tarot deck by the 22 keys of the Major Arcana which, incidentally, were in existence way before the four outer kingdoms of the sensible universe were created (*The Agashan Discourses*, page 329).

The symbol for the King is the letter K, the 11th letter of the English alphabet, and he is always shown seated on his throne holding the symbol of his authority in his hand.

The Alpha number of his God Name is 74, which in turn reduces to an 11. But by far the most conclusive evidence that the letter K is his symbol, is the geometric construction of the letter. Upon inspection, the four Kings are found to represent the four corners of a square inscribed at 45 degrees within a larger square.

THE KNIGHT

The counterpart of the King in the outer provinces of the kingdom is the Knight. He is a man of noble birth who, after an apprenticeship period as a page and squire, is raised to honorable military rank and bound at all times to chivalrous conduct. In the Tarot deck he is always depicted mounted on horseback, properly suited up in shining armor, and ready to do battle with anyone who might pose a threat to the kingdom. In his right hand he holds the symbol of his authority, and in his left hand the reins of his horse.

The symbol for the Knight is the letter L, the 12th letter of the alphabet and one which, like the King, illustrates by its geometric construction the function of his office. In the same way that the four Kings represent the four corners of a square inscribed within a larger, outer square, the four Knights represent the four corners of the outer square. (See Figure 19.)

The Alpha number of his God Name is 102 which, like the King, always reduces to the number of his symbol. In this case it is 12. Further proof that the letter L is his symbol is found by analyzing the move of the Knight in the game of chess. He must always move in an L-shaped manner—one square either horizontally or vertically and then two squares in a perpendicular direction—which results in the 1-2 movement of the number 12.

M  DEATH

A mysterious rider on a white horse, suited up in black armor with a black helmet and red plume, moves slowly, bearing a black banner emblazoned with a five-petaled mystic white rose signifying not death—but life. The horseman carries no visible weapon, but king, child, and maiden fall before him, while a bishop with clasped hands awaits the release of his mortal consciousness from the limitations that heretofore have hampered its free expression.

In the distance, between two towers or pillars on the edge of the horizon, shines the sun of immortality because the moment it sets in one hemisphere it rises in the other, causing but a momentary lapse in consciousness. Life is supported by its continual motion—birth, death, and then its constant renewal. The process of disintegration is for the sole purpose of the release of energy.

The symbol for Death is the letter M, the 13th letter of the alphabet. It is interesting to observe that if one will recite the alphabet out loud from A to Z, the mouth will remain open at the sound of every letter except the M. Here, the lips will remain very tightly closed, as if to signify Death—and Silence. But rebirth and renewal is the true keynote of this card, for the rider on the white horse, with each of its measured steps, brings to the recipient not Death—but Life.

THE HANGED MAN

The Hanged Man has been an enigma to students of the Tarot ever since it was first rediscovered in our modern era. This key portrays a man in a deep state of entrancement, hanging upside down from a gallows in the shape of a T-cross of living wood, with leaves thereon, thus symbolizing the Tree of Life. But the *Tree* of Life is also one of the spokes of the *Wheel* of Life, and herein is the secret of the card. To make this exciting discovery, the reader has only to visualize the figure turning around and around about its head, which is always at the hub of the wheel, thus indicating that his *consciousness* resides at the central core of the Infinte State while his *body* endures cycle after cycle of earthly living. The crossbar of the T-cross becomes the rim of the wheel (See Fig. 28).

The symbol for the Hanged Man is the letter N, the 14th letter of the alphabet. It is significant that if you turn his symbol upside down, it doesn't change in the slightest. It is still the letter N, and so it is with the Hanged Man.

The Alpha number of his God Name is 100 (33 + 39 + 28 = 100). This is the same as $(10)^2$, which only reinforces the fact that he is also known as the *Ten Man* (Hanged = 39 = Ten). But in the final analysis, "The Man" is *You* since 33 + 28 = 61 = You. *The Hanged Man* is also another name for "The Soul" since "Hanged Man" = 67 = Soul.

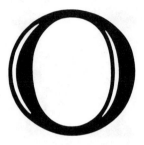

THE
SUN

In the Tarot key for the Sun, a naked child is mounted on a white horse holding a red banner aloft. The horse is symbolical of his physical vehicle that enables him to travel from here to there within the inner kingdom of the Major Arcana, and he is in perfect control of it inasmuch as he has no need for either saddle or bridle. A walled garden is behind him where four types of sunflowers are growing abundantly. These represent the four suits of the Minor Arcana, the four outer kingdoms of Earth, Water, Air, and Fire. These, the conquering child has now left behind him, having learned all that they had to offer. Consequently, the four sunflowers are now looking towards the *Son*, the rider on the white horse, for their development instead of to the *Sun* which shines down from above.

The symbol for the Sun is very similar to its astrological

symbol. It is the letter O, the 15th letter of the English alphabet. But unlike the other rider on the white horse seen in Tarot Key 13, the child's only vestments are a wreath of red roses around his head and a red plume. Together, the two riders bring the OM into manifestation. (The O represents the beginning of a cycle and the M brings about its end, the total of which is 28, the number of MAN.)

The straight rays represent radiation and the wavy ones vibration, both of which are necessary for life.

THE PAGE

The Page is the offspring of the King and Queen. Thus he or she may be considered to be either a prince or a princess of one of the outer kingdoms. Normally, he will serve his apprenticeship period in the personal service of the Knight. But before reaching maturity, he may also be employed to deliver messages, assist patrons, or serve as a guide. Thus the Page is always shown standing, ready to be of service, and holding the symbol of his authority in his hand.

Many times the Master Teacher Agasha or Araskas have stated that they are making their "call," meaning that they are sending their "page" into the outer kingdom of the mortal to summon those with whom they are desirous of making contact.

The symbol for the Page is the letter P, the 16th letter of the alphabet. Thus being the child of the Queen, the young Page may grow up to become equally as powerful as the King or even the Queen herself, in the same way that the lowly pawn in the game of chess may advance to the opposite end of the chessboard, be "knighted," and become a force equal to the Queen.

This is made possible because the Alpha number for the God *Name* of the Page is identical to that of the God *Word* of the Queen. Both numbers are 62. The lower case "p" and the lower case "q" are often depicted as a pair of scissors. See Figure 20.

THE
QUEEN

The Queen is the wife of the King, a very powerful force in her own right, and the co-ruler, along with the King, of one of the four primary divisions of the sensible universe—Earth, Water, Air, and Fire. Indeed, in the game of chess, she is *the* most powerful piece on the board, even surpassing the power of the King inasmuch as she may move *any* unobstructed distance in *any* direction she so chooses. (The King is limited to moving only one space at a time.)

The symbol for the Queen is the letter Q, the 17th letter of the alphabet, and, like the King, she is always shown seated on her throne holding in her hands the symbol of her authority. The exoteric spelling for the name of her symbol is CUE. It is significant that the Alpha number for "Cue" is 29, the same as the number for "Page," and we certainly don't want to miss the

"cue," as the Agashan Teachers would say, in this respect.

Yet its esoteric spelling is QUE, and this word, when combined with the name of the letter N, is QUE-EN.

The Queen represents motherhood, and like the word QUEUE implies, she is the doorway through which a long line of waiting souls are waiting their chance to be born into one of the kingdoms of the Minor Arcana. And the number that are waiting is endless. We might say that a perfect name for the Queen would be QUE-UE-UE-UE. . . .

THE TOWER

A lofty tower built on top of a tall, barren rock pierces the midnight sky. All is quiet and still. Suddenly the heavens open up as a great thunderclap shakes the whole of the earth. A bolt of lightning in the shape of a "W" terminating into a "V" strikes the summit of the tower, and its golden crowned apex is sent crashing to the ground along with its two occupants. Smoke belches forth as the tower is engulfed in flames, and 22 drops in the shape of the Hebrew letter Yod gradually settle to the ground. Once more all is quiet and still.

This is the great saga of the Lightning-Struck Tower, otherwise known as the House of God, and one of the most profound Tarot keys of the entire group of 22. It can be understood on many levels of thought. Its God-Name number is 114 which transliterates into AN = O, and it is just that.

The symbol for the Tower is the letter R, the 18th letter of the alphabet. It represents the great Core of Life when the hero and heroine of our story, Adam and Eve (which means you and I), were first spewed forth to begin our journey that is eternity.

Its symbol, the letter R, may be further broken apart into 1 + 2 = 3 = C; and the letters of its God Name, THE TOWER, may be rearranged into TWO + THREE = 5 = E. Thus "The Tower" simply stands for the letters C or E, which means that it is the CORE.

THE STAR

In the Tarot key for the Star, a beautiful maiden pours the Waters of Life freely unto both the land and the sea as she sees herself reflected in the still waters of the pool. She is Mother Nature herself, Truth unveiled, glorious in her undying beauty as she pours out upon the earth some part and measure of her priceless possessions. The five rivulets represent the five senses, and perched atop a tree is an Ibis, a symbol of the mind. The card truly represents the gifts of the Spirit.

In the sky above is an enormous eight-pointed star, surrounded by seven smaller stars of a similar shape. The larger star is the spiritual consciousness from whence she came, and its eight points represent the eight vertices of a cube inscribed within a sphere. The seven other stars are the seven chakras or interior stars of the human organism.

Her symbol is the letter S, the 19th letter of the alphabet. But it is also the symbol for the Serpent/Snake, whose serpentine movement symbolizes the wave motion of energy as it radiates from the Star to the Earth in much the same fashion as the function $y = \sin x$.

The Alpha number of "Serpent/ Snake" is 147, the number of the Hierophant or "Higher Fount"—the energy source of all. Thus meditative effort brings *energy* to the conscious self, bringing about newer and deeper revelations as to the true nature of BEING.

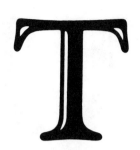

TEMPERANCE

If we arrange the letters for *The Star* in a circle, we find that it signifies THE START, with the letter T being both the beginning and the ending of its name. This is the symbol for Temperance, the 20th letter of the English alphabet, which, as one can see, is very closely related to the letter S. Not only do both figures have their right foot in the water and the other on the land, but each is holding a chalice in either hand from which the essences of life are being poured.

In the case of Temperance—which implies tempering, mixing, or adjusting—the psychic and material natures are being harmonized, the one with the other. In this Tarot key the archangel Michael is shown emptying the life essences from the silver cup of the *material* world of matter into the golden cup of the *ethereal* world of Spirit, from the seen into the unseen, from the past into the future, and then back again. Taken in this context, the rainbow stream in between the two chalices is the present. Moreover, the letters in the word TEMPERANCE may be rearranged into the phrase TEE CRAMP EN, and this is just what it does. In the Tarot key for the letter N, the T-cross of Temperance is shown restricting the movements of the Hanged Man (the soul) while it is tied to the cross of matter. The Alpha numbers for the God Names of both T and N are the same: 100 or (10)².

U THE FOOL

Pausing on the brink of a precipice, at the top of a tall mountain peak, is a well-dressed youth. His vestments are that of a page or a prince of the spiritual realms. Around his head is the laurel wreath of victory topped by a red plume, and in his left hand is the mystic white rose. His only other possessions are his faithful dog which follows him at his heels, a costly wand, and his wallet or traveling bag. But this is no ordinary bag for it is the magic bag of *consciousness*, and in this bag is *all* (*Agasha: Master of Wisdom*, page 21).

Therefore, our "Fool" is very well equipped and fully prepared to embark upon his travels through the earthly realms of existence. He is a free spirit in search of experience, a dreamer perhaps, but no "fool" in the sense of the word. Nay, it is he who will *fool* the others because he is the son of the Emperor and Empress and the Page of the Major Arcana. We might call him the Fool/Page, the Alpha number of which is 77, the number of Christ.

The Fool then is no stranger to the Sun which is rising behind him or to the Father that lives within him. Both of these Forces fully realize from whence he came and whither he is going, and how he will return some day after many lifetimes of earthly living. And who is this man? His symbol is the letter U, the 21st letter of the alphabet, but his name is YOU.

THE LOVERS

In the same way that the Tarot key for the Fool represents the one "you" that you were before the Fall, the Tarot key for the Lovers represents the "double you" that you became after the Fall—when the atom soul split into its masculine and feminine halves, thus creating you and your soul mate or counterpart, as symbolized by Adam and Eve.

In this Tarot key we see the archangel Raphael, representing the Higher Self, bestowing his cosmic benediction unto the two Lovers who, having now conquered their Demon Self, are now under divine guidance. Shining down from above, the noonday sun of the great Core of Life sustains both human and angelic kingdoms alike. By the woman is the Tree of the Knowledge of Good and Evil. Its fruits are the five senses, and the Kundalini force of the serpent is entwined around it. By the man is the Tree of Life. Its fruits are the 12 signs of the Zodiac as symbolized by its 12 trefoil flames. Everywhere there is balance, love, and harmony.

The symbol for the Lovers is the letter V, the 22nd letter of the alphabet. But this letter, being even, is also used to represent Eve. Proof comes from an analysis of its name which is VEE. If these letters are placed in a circle, they may be very easily read as EVE. Furthermore, Eve (the letter V) is formed by removing a rib from Adam (the letter A).

W THE CHARIOT

A triumphant, crowned king who has conquered on all planes stands erect in his royal chariot under a canopy of stars. He is clad in steel armor decorated with strange mathematical and astrological figures, and the crescent-shaped symbols of the *Urim* and *Thummim* rest on his shoulders.

The motive power for the chariot is furnished by two sphinxes of opposite polarity that draw it—one of Nature's most closely guarded secrets. It is sufficient to say that the charioteer uses the power of his *will* to control the sphinxes by invisible reins. On a shield in front of the chariot is a winged globe, under which appears the mystical symbol of the *lingam-yoni,* symbolizing the union of male and female forces.

The symbol for the Chariot is the letter W, the 23rd letter of the alphabet. It is also the W of the WYE of Cara Boga Coty.

The Chariot then is *Cara,* which means that it is "A Car," your own personal mental body that is capable of taking you anywhere in the Cosmos that you have earned the right to visit. It is your own personal UFO or "flying saucer," and it gives off a great amount of "Light and Inspiration" wherever you may send it. In the Agashan philosophy the word *Cara* means the mental aspect of Being, and it has to do with the great power of the Mind, through which control is gained over the forces of Nature.

JUDGEMENT

The Tarot key for Judgement (or Judgment) is also sometimes called the Last Judgment. Here, we find the angel Gabriel emerging out of the clouds and blowing on his trumpet as the dead arise from their coffins in great wonderment, adoration, and ecstasy. The coffins float on a great sea of Cosmic Mind that separates the earth plane from the astral plane, and snow-capped peaks are seen in the distance indicating the need for further attainment. A banner hangs from the trumpet, and on it is the solar cross which shows a balance between the positive and the negative forces. The card is truly a symbol of eternal life for the moment the Knight of Death approaches in one hemisphere, the angel Gabriel is readying his trumpet in the other. It is as the Agashan Teachers have always said, "Everyday is Judgment Day for someone on the earth plane."

The symbol for Judgement is the letter X, the 24th letter of the alphabet. It is also a symbol for Christ, and it means literally "The Resurrection." It is interesting to note that a double X (XX) appears at the top of the card, signifying not only the Roman numeral 20 (the Tarot number), but also a double judgement. It is significant that the Alpha number for "Judgement + Judgement" is identical to the number for "The Resurrection." They both equal 198 which transliterates into SH, a command to be silent.

Y

STRENGTH

A woman, garlanded with flowers and dressed in a simple white robe, is closing the mouth of a ferocious lion with as much ease as if it were a lamb. In other decks she is opening it. Who is she? She is the High Priestess (the letter F), the counterpart of the Magician (the letter I). Both of these Forces display the cosmic lemniscate symbol of infinity over their heads, thus signifying their infinite 6/9 relationship. Together, they constitute the "double you," the masculine and feminine phases of *Cara*, the mental aspect of Being. She is demonstrating that the powers of the mind are far superior to the physical strength of the lion, and that she is truly "One to Obey."

But this is the definition of *Boga*, the physical aspect of Being. Therefore the lion must be Boga; and being king of the beasts, he also is "One to Obey." This leaves only *Coty*, the spiritual aspect of Being, missing from the Tarot key. But Coty is not really "missing," as a further investigation reveals that the lion has eaten him. But is this so strange? It is not. Occult philosophy has always taught that the spiritual kingdom is *within*.

We find then that the Tarot key of STRENGTH is a pictorial representation of the three 1's of CARA BOGA COTY. (The Alpha number for both terms is 111). Their symbol is the letter Y, the 25th letter of the alphabet, and they are the Y (the why) of the WYE.

THE EMPRESS

A beautiful, stately figure in rich vestments is seated on a throne in the midst of a garden in full bloom. Her dress is covered with flowers, and she holds in her hand a scepter surmounted by a globe of the World. Her diadem contains 12 stars, and a string of 7 pearls adorns her neck. At her side is a heart-shaped shield portraying the symbol of Venus, the goddess of love, and before her is a field of ripening corn.

This is the Empress, a personification of universal fecundity, reproduction, multiplication, and growth. The Alpha number of her name is 128 and this number, when added to her Tarot key number which is 3, equates to 131 or MA. Thus in the same way that the Emperor represents the Fatherhood of God, the Empress represents the Motherhood of God.

Her symbol is the letter Z, the 26th letter of the alphabet, and in the same way that the Queen is the vehicle through which entry is made into the Minor Arcana, the Empress acts as the doorway to the Major Arcana. In fact, the Alpha number for "Empress" by itself (her God Word) is identical to the God Name of the Queen. Both numbers are 95. And if we add the Empress to the Queen, the total is not changed for it is still 95, only now in Roman numerals (95 + 128 = 223 = VC = 95). The Empress is the UE part of the QUE-UE-UE-UE, the name for the letter Q that goes on forever.

PART III

THE
APPLICATION

Chapter 19

THE GREAT ALL-SEEING EYE OF GOD

Now that we have established at least a working knowledge of some of the more basic aspects of the Cabalah, let us see if we can now *apply* the principles that we have learned—put them to work, so to speak, and see what they can do for us. This is the purpose for the third part of this work: the actual working out of specific problems, through and by means of the laws of the Cabalah, in order that we may better understand what life is all about.

Let us begin with one of the most powerful symbols of the entire Cabalah: the great All-Seeing Eye of God. Let us study this symbol, minutely and in great detail, and by so doing, allow it to speak to us and tell us what it knows. But where do we begin? Let us start with the Alpha number of its name. The term "All-Seeing Eye" gives us the number 119 (25 + 59 + 35), and it may be read as either AS or KI. But by reading it through three times in succession (119, 119, 119), we are informed that "A's ASK I" (A'S AS-KI). In other words, even the A's (the ones, the units) ask the "I" for guidance or whatever.

Now when we read this term three times we are really multiplying the number 119 by 3, which then gives us 357. But the number 357 is equally as interesting as the single term because it adds up to 15 or the letter O. Thus $3 + 5 + 7 = 15$, or $357 = CEG = O$; and, of course, the true "magician" will easily read this as "C (See) EGO," which means that he is now seeing or looking at the Ego.

Before we go any further, we should state once and for all that numbers in themselves are neither "good" nor "bad." Just because a God Name or a God Word might vibrate at a certain Alpha frequency, does not necessarily mean that that particular number will always represent that high God Force. On the contrary, it may bring the Anti-Force into manifestation. For example: 85 is the Alpha number for the Devil, and it is read as HE. But who is "He" really? Does it always refer to the Devil? Of course not. In the Bible, the word *He* is used many times in reference to Christ; therefore, the term itself is completely neutral and may be used to represent either force.

And it is the same with the number 119, which is the Alpha number for "All-Seeing Eye." Agasha has said many times that the only *devil* we will ever know is our *mortal mind.* But what is the Alpha number for "Mortal Mind"? The answer is 119, the same number as the "All-Seeing Eye." We can see then that the number 119 per se is neither good nor bad.

However, it is interesting to note that in this particular case the combination of the good with the bad results in a rather unique force, one that is completely neutral. If we double 119 we end up with 238, the atomic weight for the element *uranium,* and whose symbol is U. Uranium is also the heaviest of the natural elements, and it most surely is no "coincidence" that its atomic number just "happens" to be 92 or IB. In other words, the Cabalah tells us that with the combination of these two forces, the "I Am" now becomes the "I Be." Most interesting, indeed. And this becomes even more significant when we complete the statement and add the "U" to it.

Thus we find that for every positive force there is an equal and opposite negative force; for every positive number there is always its negative counterpart. With this thought in mind, let us take one final look at the terms "All-Seeing Eye" and "Mortal Mind" and compare them, as it were. If we place the two together, side by side, the Cabalah speaks to us saying, "Mortal, mind All-Seeing Eye." This is evidently the first commandment of the Cabalah inasmuch as it represents the marriage between good and evil.

But there is still more to be learned from these two terms. For openers, let us perform a few magical transpositions. Let us reverse "Mortal Mind" and call it "Mind Mortal," and that is exactly what the mortal mind does—it minds the mortal. The Alpha numbers for "Mind Mortal" are 40 + 79 or DO + GI; and if a "magician" were to read this, he would read it as "DOG I" or "I, GOD." The Alpha numbers for "All-Seeing Eye" prove equally as interesting. The word "All" gives us 25 and the term "Seeing-Eye" gives us 94 (59 + 35 = 94). There-fore, the term as a whole is 25 + 94 or BE + ID; and you don't have to be a magician to understand the meaning of that.

Now let us put the entire sentence together and we read, "'DOG I' BE ID." Now who or what is a "dog I"? One of the definitions of the word *dog* is that it refers to a despicable or worthless person. Therefore, the "dog I" is the mortal mind, the devil; and it really is a "dirty dog" because it is the "I" that always gets us into trouble. This we can accept and it makes sense; but when we read that this "dog I" is in fact the Id, the undifferentiated source from which we obtain our energy, the statement becomes quite profound and almost unbelievable on the surface.

But is it really as far-fetched or as improbable as it first appears? Let us read the statement backwards and see if we can gain a better understanding. If we reverse the fact that the "'DOG I' BE ID," we find that then an unusual phenomenon occurs. A command by the One God fairly shakes the Heavens as he shouts, "DIE! BI-GOD." And with these words the "bi-god," the "two-god" that represents the devil, breathes his last breath and dies. Thus the One God has brought death to the Devil, and the Emperor is the result (38 + 85 = 123 = A). How do we know that a double god or a two-god represents the

Devil? We know it to be true because their numbers say that it is so. The Alpha number for "God" is 26; but if we multiply this number by 2, we bring the Devil into manifestation inasmuch as the Alpha number for "Devil" is 52 or 2 times 26. *God* always represents unity, and *Devil* is only a word meant to express duality. Therefore, we find that our statement, epic, or story—call it what you will—is not as far-fetched as it first appeared.

Let us move on now to Figure 70 which is a more elaborate representation of the All-Seeing Eye.

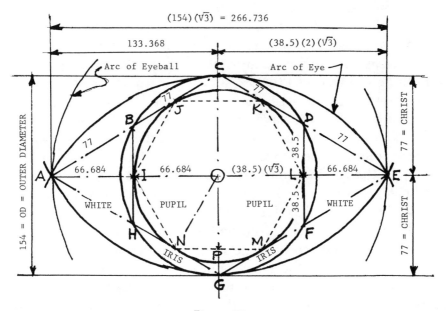

Figure 70
The Great All-Seeing Eye of God

If the reader will refer back to Figure 28 titled "The Hierophant: The Man Time Hanged," he will realize that Figure 70 is nothing more than this same figure rotated 90 degrees in the same manner as Figure 40. Otherwise they are indentical, with the same implications carried from the one to the other. The left corner of the eye represents the Emperor (the death of the

Devil), and the right corner of the eye represents Jesus Christ, the Pope, the Hierophant (the judgement of the Devil). Even the lettering of the diagram fits this symbolism quite remarkably inasmuch as it is solely based upon a consecutive numbering of the points in the eye as we go around its perimeter and then turn inwards at the H. (The A falls in the left corner and the E replaces the V or the X at the right corner; yet the symbology remains unchanged inasmuch as the E is used interchangeably with the V and it is a basic part of the word EX).

Very well. Now let us analyze the reason that we have selected the number 77 to represent the lengths of the sides of the equilateral triangles that form the structure or framework upon which the Eye is built. It could have been any number, and once this number is chosen, all of the remaining lengths and areas can then be computed. (All of the units of length must be proportional to 1, 2, and $\sqrt{3}$ inasmuch as these three units form the half-base, the side, and the altitude of any equilateral triangle.) We have selected the number 77 because the Cabalah practically dictated that this be the case. The reasons are as follows: The Alpha number for "Outer Diameter" is 154 or OD; the Alpha number for "Outer Radius" is 151 or "Jesus Christ"; therefore Christ, being the outer radius, must be one half of the outer diameter, and this is precisely what he is—the "Christ," the number 77, one half of the number 154.

The next thing to be done in an analysis of this type is to ascertain precisely the exact values for each of the lines, arcs, and areas contained within the diagram. This we have done, and the results are tabulated in Figure 71. They should be accurate to at least 12 and probably 13 significant figures since I was using a 14-digit calculator, and in every case the last digit has been rounded up or down to the nearest digit. The value I used for Pi, incidentally, was 3.14159 26535 897, and for $\sqrt{3}$ the number 1.73205 08075 688 was inserted into the electronic wizard that sits on my desk. So if there are any errors in the calculations, we may place the blame on my own personal "Hal." Remember the computer that went berserk in the motion picture *2001 AD*? Well, let us hope that my "Hal" is a little more dependable.

LINES

A B	Outer Side (Radius)	77.0
I B	Outer Half-Base	38.5
A I	Outer Altitude	66.68395 60914
C G	Outer Diameter	154.0
A E	Horizontal Axis	266.73582 43656
O N	Inner Side (Radius)	66.68395 60914
P N	Inner Half-Base	33.34197 80457
O P	Inner Altitude	57.75
I L	Inner Diameter	133.36791 21828
	Thickness of Iris	10.31604 39086
P G	Thickness of Hexagon	19.25

ARCS

A C	One Half Eye Arc	161.26842 28843
A C E	Upper Arc of Eye	322.53684 57686
A C E G A	Eye Perimeter	645.07369 15372
B C	One Sixth Outer Circumference	80.63421 14421
	One Quarter Outer Circumference	120.95131 71632
B C D F	One Half Outer Circumference	241.90263 43264
	Outer Circumference	483.80526 86528
J K	One Sixth Inner Circumference	69.83127 55230
	One Quarter Inner Circumference	104.74691 32845
I J K L	One Half Inner Circumference	209.49382 65690
	Inner Circumference	418.98765 31380

AREAS

A I B	Outer Right Triangle	1,283.66615 48
A B H	Outer Equilateral Triangle	2,567.33230 95
B C D F G H	Outer Hexagon	15,403.99385 71
O P N	Inner Right Triangle	962.74961 61
O M N	Inner Equilateral Triangle	1,925.49923 21
J K L M N I	Inner Hexagon	11,552.99539 28
A O C	One Quarter Diamond	5,134.66461 90
A C G	One Half Diamond	10,269.32923 81
A C E G	Total Diamond	20,538.65847 62
	Outer Circle	18,626.50284 31
	Inner Circle (Pupil)	13,969.87713 23
	Difference (Iris)	4,656.62571 08
A B C	Outer Eye Segment	2,148.33932 40
	Two Corner Arc Areas (White)	10,505.51292 91
	Total Eye Area	29,132.01577 22
	One Half Pupil Area	6,984.93856 62
	One Half Iris Area	2,328.31285 54
C A G H B	One Half White Area	5,252.75646 455
	One Half Eye Area	14,566.00788 61
	One Quarter Pupil Area	3,492.46928 31
	One Quarter Iris Area	1,164.15642 77
	One Quarter White Area	2,626.37823 23
	One Quarter Eye Area	7,283.00394 305

Figure 71
A Table of Numerical Values for Figure 70

You ask why it is so important that we carry these figures to so many decimal places. It is not important at all in a mechanical sense; but if we want to find out what the Cabalah is really telling us about this diagram, the more digits we have to work with, the greater the opportunity will be for it to express itself. And at the beginning of our investigation, we don't know where this information will be hidden. This then is the reason for identifying every possible length or area with its appropriate number. The study of the Cabalah is much like prospecting for gold; we know the gold is buried there, but we don't know where it is located.

However, we most certainly may understand the basic characteristics of any number from a study of its first few digits, especially the digits to the left of the decimal point. For instance: the second most important number in our diagram is the length of the inner radius (AI or IO). It is an infinitely long number inasmuch as it is a function of $\sqrt{3}$ (66.68395 . . .); but basically, it is a 67 because that number is the nearest whole number that it can be said to represent. Therefore, the inner radius is associated with the Hanged Man, the Soul, the letter N, in the same way that the outer radius is associated with Christ (67 = Hanged Man = Soul). And this is precisely as it should be inasmuch as Figure 28 depicts the Hanged Man in this central position.

Now let us leave the numbers for the moment and concentrate our attention on the overall picture of the Eye itself. Figure 70 is an excellent symbol for the Eye because it breaks it up into its three component parts—the pupil, the iris, and the white. But Figure 70 is also a symbol for something else, and this latter aspect comes as a complete surprise. Let us take the Alpha numbers for "pupil" and "iris" and we find that they are 74 and 55, respectively. The total value for the colored portion of the Eye is then 129 which gives us the letters LI. But the surprise comes when we ascertain the Alpha number for the third component part which is the white. The Alpha number for "white" is 65 or FE; and the combination for all three gives us LI + FE = LIFE. Therefore, it may be concluded that Figure 70, in addition to being a symbol of the All-Seeing Eye, is also a symbol of *Life* itself. Isn't it fantastic what the Cabalah will do?

So then, now that we have our symbol in front of us, let us attempt to understand what "Life" is all about. In fact, if one will look at Figure 70 with this thought in mind, he may quite easily visualize the iris of the eye as representing the rim of this vast, cosmic "Wheel of Life." Indeed, the iris carries its pupil all around and about the socket of the eye in every possible direction—upwards, downwards, to the right, to the left—so that the *life* within can be aware of the *life* without.

We can see then that the Wheel of Life is intimately related with the All-Seeing Eye. This is even born out numerically from a study of their Alpha numbers. The Alpha number for "All-Seeing Eye" is, of course, 119. This can be read as A's, which infers that it belongs to A (119 = AS = A's). And when we compute the Alpha number for "A's All-Seeing Eye," we find that it is 139 or ACI, identically the same as the number for "The Wheel of Life" (33 + 53 + 21 + 32 = 139 = ACI). Therefore, the Cabalah tells us that A's All-Seeing Eye is in fact the *Wheel of Life*, the "wheel" through which all life is evolving to become better than what it is today; and this should be equally as applicable to the macrocosm as well as the microcosm.

We might also say that A's All-Seeing Eye becomes A's map of the Eye, since the term "Map of the Eye" carries this same number: 119. And when we combine the two together (119 + 119) we have the number 238 (BCH), which tells us that "A's Be See Each." (The letter B is the symbol for *Wheel*, the God Word for Tarot Key 10, the Wheel of Fortune or the Wheel of Life.) Thus the Emperor's "wheel," the iris and pupil of his eye, sees each one of us as we evolve from life to life. But it could also be said that all of the microcosmic "a's," you and I and all that be who ride this vast, cosmic wheel to the far reaches of the macrocosmic Eye (the universe of the greater A), fairly *beseech* it, beg it, and implore it to help us through our trials and tribulations that seem to be almost constantly upon us. Here again is Zen: the letters BCH apply equally as well to the phrase "A's Be See Each" or the simple statement that "A's Beseech."

Yet we are not yet through with this thought. We must carry it through to its conclusion. The question can now be asked as to who is the one whom we beseech. Where and to what specific force do we direct our supplications? The answer as to *where* we direct our thoughts is answered by just adding another 119 to the previous total (119 + 119 + 119). Their sum is 359 or the CEG. This term refers to the "E" or the Energy that is located within the "CG," the Center of Gravity of the Eye itself. This, of course, is in the very center of the pupil. And this is as it should be inasmuch as the Agashan Teachers have always taught that the God-Self lies within, at the very core of its being. But do you send your thoughts to the center of the universe way out *there* somewhere? The answer is a very definite, no. You direct your thoughts to the center of the *pupil.* And where is that? The center of the pupil is in *your* solar plexus, the very center of the human anatomy, since *you* are that pupil, the child in school, the one who is being instructed by the teacher, the Wheel of Life itself.

Now let us direct our thoughts as to *whom* we are to beseech. Of course we "intellectually" know that it is God, the God-Self, the Spark of Divinity that resides within the center of the soul itself. But we do not *actually* know this insofar as the Cabalah has not specifically answered the question as to which Tarot Force represents this God-Self of whose consciousness we are a part.

For an answer to this question we must look to the teacher for help. Who is the teacher? The teacher is the outer rim of the wheel of life, the iris of the eye, a vast consciousness that limits the size of its pupil through its ability to expand and contract. The teacher then is the *iris,* and if we were to read his name backwards we would find that he is the "Sir I," a man of great rank and position, a veritable *knight* in shining armor who through his previous conquests and achievements has earned the privilege of being addressed as *Sir.*

Now if the teacher be the Knight, then his pupil must be the Page of the Knight, and that is exactly what the pupil is—the "pup I" of the L (the Knight). A pup is a young dog, but if we were to read these words backwards, we would also see that a pup is a young god. Therefore, the "pup I," the Page, is in reality a young god in the becoming. And we know that this "pup I" most certainly is "the Page" because their Alpha numbers are identical (53 + 9 = 62, and 33 + 29 = 62).

For a proper understanding of this "Page-Knight" combination, we must study the words "pupil-iris" as a single entity. Together they form a constant because as one expands the other contracts, but their diameter remains always the same. Reading the term "pupil-iris" backwards we find that the "Sir I" knights the "Pup I," and their combined consciousness is then represented in the number 129 (LI), which means literally the Knight of the "I." The Page or pupil is then seen to be merely an opening in the greater consciousness of the Knight through which light is transmitted from the outer world of the senses to the inner world of the spirit. Thus the Page is truly in the service of the Knight. Their relationship is emphasized when we write the words thus: Pup I (L) I riS.

Therefore, the Cabalah tells us that it is the Knight whom we are to beseech. It is the "L" or the Knight who is the center of gravity of the pupil-iris combination. And it is the Knight, you will recall, who represents your immediate higher self, the one who acts as the Intermediary between you and your God-Self. (The Knight is most certainly not the God-Self, because the Knight only resides on the surface of the ball of the Eye and not within it.) Now does this Knight have a name? He quite surprisingly does, and if you have followed the clues that have been given throughout this discussion, you will realize that his name is LEO. We know from our previous analysis that the "A's BCH CEG." In other words, the A's beseech the C (E) G. And if you will study Figure 70, you will see that the vertical axis through the diagram of the Eye is designated "C (O) G," with the "O" directly in the center of the CG (center of gravity) of the pupil. Combining all three of these clues together then, we can say that his name is LEO. And who is Leo? The answer is Leo the Lion, of course.

The Mysteries of the Black Hole

The Black Hole represents one of the most mysterious objects in the Universe because the fundamental laws of physics, as we know them, appear to be destroyed along with our usual concepts of space and time. Therefore the laws have had to be adjusted, and the latest concept of science is that a black hole is formed by the collapse of a heavy star to such a condensed state that nothing, not even light, can escape from its surface.

Now Leo the Lion is very much like a black hole. In the first place, he represents the fifth sign of the zodiac or the letter E. Who is E? E is the Hierophant, the Pope, the chief priest of the Eleusinian mysteries in ancient Greece. He is represented by Tarot Key 5 and his Alpha number is 147. But he is also the negative "you" because 147 = NG, and N + G = U. Therefore, if *you* (the Pup I and the Sir I) represent the positive "U," the central "L" or Leo represents the negative "U" or the *anti-U.*

In the second place, isn't the pupil of the eye in reality only a "black hole"? The pupil is an opening or a *hole* in the diaphragm of the iris, and it most certainly is *black.* Therefore, the pupil is a black hole and the CG of this hole is Leo the Lion.

Then thirdly, let us analyze the Alpha numbers of the words "black hole." They are 29 + 40 = 69. Thus we find out that "black" stands for *Page* and "black hole" stands for *Knight* because their Alpha numbers are identical. Even the Alpha number for the word "hole" itself makes sense. It is 40, and since there are no God Words or God Names for this number, we will simply call it DO. But there is still one other thing we can do in a case such as this. The number 40 is the what? It is the "G" (40 = 33 + 7 = The G). Therefore 40 can be translated into DO + G = DOG; and if the Page is a "Pup I," the "Sir I" in all probability would be a *dog.*

Even the peas in the pod are represented here. A "black hole" may be said to be a *pod* because 29 = .P and 40 = DO, and putting the letters together we have POD. But if we look inside this "black hole" or this "pod," what do we find? We find *peas* because "Pup I" is most certainly a P (62 = the Page = P), and "Sir I" = 55 or EE. So then the pup by itself is a "P," and when we combine the pup with the dog we end up with PEE. Anyway you look at it, we have "peas."

Now let us analyze the word "lion." Its Alpha number is 50 or EO, the last two letters of LEO. But the really interesting thing is discovered when we add the Alpha numbers for the God Names of these two letters together into a single entity. The number for E (The Hierophant) is 147, and the number for O (The Sun) is 87; and when we add the two together we have the number 234 or BCD, which in the Cabalah is read as "beast." And this becomes doubly interesting when we consider that the "lion" is indeed a "beast." In fact, he is the King of the Beasts.

Now let us look at the letters themselves in the word "LION." Do you see anything unusual there? How about when we break the letters apart into "L IO N"? Now do you see anything unusual? Well if you do or don't, the answer is that IO looks exactly like 10, and we may assume that the Cabalah is showing us that within the "lion" is the *ten*. This fact must be extremely important because the Cabalah repeats the proof again when we add the letters I and O together. Their sum is 24 or X. And what is an "X"? It is the Roman numeral for the number 10. Therefore, we learn that within the "black hole" of Leo the Lion exists the 10, the X, the Christ, the Judgment.

But this is not all it is telling us. Our 10 exists in the what? It exists in the lion, of course, but it also exists between the letters L and N. And these letters when read backwards give us the NL or the word "Nil." The dictionary defines the word "nil" as meaning *nothing* or *zero*. Therefore, we also learn that even within the zero or nothing at all, exists something. And that something is 10. It is interesting to note that the number 10 converts to the letter J, and the letter J is the symbol for the World (Tarot Key 21). But isn't this what the Agashan Teachers have been telling us all along? Many times Agasha has said that when we go within the minute atom of the soul, we find a world equally as vast as the universe is itself.

Even the word "Leo" by itself tells a story. Its Alpha number is 32 = CB = E. Therefore, Leo is the E, or the Energy of the Lion. And when we combine all three words together into "Leo the Lion," we have the number 115 which is read as KE or AO. Here again, we can combine the K + A = L, and we have the word LEO back again.

Thus we find that there is a very strong connection between

Leo the Lion, the fifth sign of the Zodiac, and that mysterious denizen of the universe called a Black Hole. This "black hole" may be said to resemble the jaws of a lion, and a perfect word exists to describe them. The word is *Maw*, and Webster defines the term as the jaws of a voracious carnivore (a hungry beast) or more broadly, the symbolic or theoretical center of a voracious hunger or appetite of any kind. Is this definition too far astray from that of a black hole which one author[1] has described as "being like a cannibal, swallowing up everything that gets in its way. Once engaged by it, there is no hope of escape; our own world is left behind forever . . ."? No it is not. In fact, the Alpha number for "Maw" is 37 or CG, and the Alpha number for "Leo Maw" is 69, which is the same as for "Black Hole."

Now just what is it that this "black hole" has swallowed? Earlier in this work we learned that our "cat" had eaten Coti— not Coty but Coti. There is an important difference here in this connotation. We have also learned that the spiritual phase of life, the Coty phase as it were, relates to *time*. Well now, here we come to a very interesting point. If we were to convert the word *Coty* to "time," we would be forced to change its spelling to *Coti* in order to match the vibrational rate or the Alpha number of "time" itself which is 47. And this is exactly what the Cabalah has done. In other words, it is telling us that these mysterious black holes in space, as symbolized by our cat, are actually swallowing that which we know as *time.*

But the "time" that is swallowed by these black holes will not be forever. It will only be in the body of the cat for "awhile" so to speak, for a short time only insofar as time is measured on the galactic time scale. Then, after awhile, *time* will reverse itself and begin to run backwards; and when this occurs, it will *emit* forth from the maw of the lion (the pupil or black hole of the eye) in a tremendous explosion of new light and energy which in all probability will result in the death of the black hole and the birth of that which is known as a *quasar*. Thus stars, galaxies, and even the universe itself seem to be going through a constant cycle of death and rebirth.

The Cabalah then only reiterates and substantiates that which has been taught in the Agashan classes for many years. And quite surprisingly, this philosophy is not too far afield from the latest concepts of science. For instance, in this morning's paper (the forces of synchronicity again) was a rather enlightening article on this very same subject where the writer went on to say:[2]

"Quasars, discovered by Sandage in 1960, appear to be very remote objects glowing with furious brightness. They are so bright that astrophysicists have trouble imagining how they turn out so much energy. One popular speculation is that they represent the nucleii of young galaxies, where the collapse of gas clouds formed massive black holes; their intense energy would result from tormented dust and gas heated as it spins into the black hole. More than one hypothesis urges that stars, too, are consumed by black holes at the center of these galaxies."

From the above, it would appear that there is a simultaneous process going on at one and the same time. The black hole and the quasar are quite obviously interrelated, with each, perhaps, being the reverse of the other in the same way that black holes swallow TIME and quasars EMIT energy. Even the words themselves suggest this reverse relationship because the Alpha number for "Energy" is 74, which is the reverse of 47, the Alpha number for "Time."

In any event, it is quite possible that either a black hole or a quasar makes up the central core of each and every galaxy. The death of one would naturally result in the birth of the other. Or perhaps they both exist there simultaneously. Who knows? Therefore we have constructed Figure 72 on the following page.

Figure 72 also came about from following the suggestions contained within the term "Iris-Pupil." What is this phrase really telling us? To find the answer, let us separate the letters in the following manner: "I R I's Pupil," which is read as "I are I's pupil." In other words, the "Iris-Pupil" combination is telling us that in reality it is only the pupil of a still greater eye (I) whose iris surrounds it. It is only the pupil of a higher self, a higher I, a higher teacher. Here we have worlds within worlds within worlds, eyes within eyes within eyes, galaxies within galaxies within galaxies—all proceeding outwards from a common black hole or quasar. The concept staggers the imagination as we wonder, "Is the universe only one gigantic eye?" It may very well be the case, for is not the eye the window of the soul?

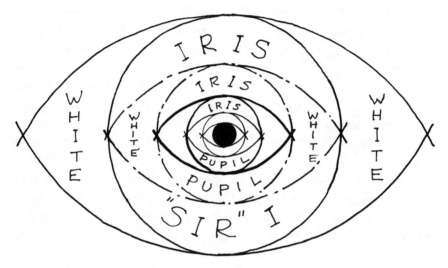

Figure 72
The Black Hole and/or Quasar in the Midst of the Eyes

Perhaps the best way to attack this problem is to concentrate our attention on the key actors of our drama, the Black Hole and the Quasar. We can start by comparing their Alpha numbers. The number for "Black Hole" is, of course, 69, which equates to the Knight or the letter L; but the number for "Quasar" turns out to be 77, the number for Christ. The Quasar then would seem to fulfill the same function as the Christ who has arisen from the dead. But there are even more clues to be had. When we integrate the number 77 (go through the process of finding the sum of its digits), we find that it gives us the number 14 or the letter N. Thus the Black Hole and the

Quasar, taken together as a unit, bring into manifestation the L + N, the first and last letters of the LION.

But we are not through yet. We must now consider that which exists *inside* the body of the lion. These are the two missing inner letters, the I and the O, the energy within the fire which stems from that which the lion has eaten. This we have learned is the spiritual principle of life, the Coti principle which relates to Time. But Coti or Time is not the *entire* spiritual principle because it only represents a numerical force of 47. There are still 16 other units to be considered in order to build up the *total* spiritual force of 63 which is the Alpha number of Coty.

Very well. What happened to the missing 16 units? These, we will symbolically represent by the letter P. A very probable answer is that during the process of gobbling up Coty our lion was so ravenously hungry, and he opened up his maw with such fury, that the "Y" part of Coty was broken into two pieces —the P and the I. The "I" then fell asleep on the "cot" and was promptly swallowed into the stomach or the lower maw. But the "P" was a little more leery. He stayed awake and fought with all of his strength against falling into what appeared to be a bottomless pit. He was thus able to remain in the upper maw or jaws of the beast, and there he remains to this very day as the Page or the pup "I" of the pupil.

Even the letters themselves tell this same story. The COTY principle breaks itself into COTI + P, two separate and distinct parts. The CO stands for *Company*, a group of two or more persons or things associated with each other for a single united cause or purpose. But the TIP of this company has been broken in two, with the "P" staying in the upper compartment and the "IT" thrown into the lower compartment along with the rest of the company. And, of course, if we were to gaze down into the lower chamber from the upper chamber, it would appear as though it were a bottomless PIT because no light could escape to illuminate the passage.

The story that can be told about the BOGA principle is equally as fascinating. This is the physical phase of life and it is represented by the body and the maw (the jaws) of the lion. It is interesting to note that the Alpha number for "Body" which is 46, when added to the Alpha number for "Maw" which is 37, actually *does* equal the Alpha number of "The Lion" which is 83. And when we add P to BOGA we change it to King (16 + 25 = 41 = King); but isn't the lion also King of the Beasts? One addition seems to substantiate the other. BOGA + P can also be read as "B O GAP," which means that there be a GAP or a break in the circle or the "O." Isn't it true that "PI" (which is the symbol for the circle) had to be broken into two parts, thus putting a GAP in the "O"? Of course it's true, and the Cabalah knew it all along.

Now we come to the CARA principle, and it is here where we gain our greatest insight into what is perhaps the keynote of the entire drama. Cara, you will remember, brings into manifestation the great powers of the mind as she demonstrates complete control over the Boga force, the physical body, by being able to open and close the jaws of Leo the Lion with such ease. How then does she do this? After all, she is only a frail woman while Leo has the strength of a powerful lion.

The answer, strangely enough, can be found in her name. She is the High Priestess, the Virgin Mother of the World, but she comes into manifestation as Eve, the eternal woman, the feminine counterpart of the masculine force which in this instance is depicted as Leo the Lion. Therefore we shall call her Eve, because in this way she will be able to command such force over the lion so as to make him as docile as a kitten. Her symbol, of course, is V (Eve = Vee = V). And when she blends her symbol with Leo, LOVE is the result (V + LEO = LOVE).

Eve is not only able to control the jaws or the maw of the lion (which is a symbol of the pupil, the black hole, the aperture in the diaphragm), but she is also able to control his body as well. This is symbolized by the iris, the Sir I, the diaphragm that surrounds the pupil. How does she do this? The Alpha number for "Iris" is 55 or EE; and when we combine her full *name* with LEO which is EVE, we find that she loves the Iris (55 or EE) equally as much as she loves the Pupil (74 or the King) since

LEO + EVE equals LOVE EE. Therefore, we may honestly say
that Love conquers All. And what is "All"? Why Boga, of
course (All = 25 = Boga).

In the same way that Energy is the reverse of Time (74 vs.
47), so is Eve the reverse of Cara (32 vs. 23). We may also say
that the "Cara I" equals 32 or Eve. Therefore Eve is the Cara "I"
who comes to assist her physical counterpart who is Boga. The
Alpha number for "Eve" is also identical to that of "Leo," and
when we combine them both together they are equal to zero (32
+ 32 = 64 = Zero). Sometimes Eve is known by her last name
which is Evelyn; in this way then she may even neutralize the
balance of Leo's name which is "the Lion" since the Alpha numbers of both are identical (Evelyn – the Lion = 0, or 83 – 83 =
0). We may say then that "Eve Evelyn" *minus* "Leo the Lion"
equals zero. But the most astounding thing of all is revealed
when we *add* Eve (32) to Leo the Lion (115). The result is "The
Eve-Leo Lion," the zero lion, so to speak, whose Alpha number
is 147, the Hierophant, the English letter E, the spiritual aspect
of CARA BOGA COTY which is "Hundred + Ten + One."

Now let us look at this relationship in another way. We have
learned that the pupil of our "iris-pupil" combination is similar
to one of those mysterious objects in space called "The Black
Hole." But now let us suppose that Cara comes along, jumps
into this "hole," and fills it up. What would we have then?
"The Black Hole" would then become "The Black Whole"
because the Alpha number of Cara is 23 or the letter W. But
this "whole" need not necessarily be "black" because we may
change *black* into *Page* since their Alpha numbers are both
equal to 29. Therefore, "The Black Whole" is in reality "The
Whole Page," and that is exactly what a "black hole" becomes,
once Cara, the mental aspect of Being, is poured into it. But
what else can we say that this complete Being called "The Black
Whole" or "The Whole Page" actually is? If we compute its
Alpha number we find that it is 125: "five cubed" which gives
us 77 or *Christ*, 125 which gives us *Spiritual*, and lastly 63 (the
Alpha number of *Whole*), which gives us *Coty*.

"But what happens to Cara, once she has jumped into this

'black hole'?" you ask. Well, let us answer the question in this way: The pupil is, of course, the black hole. And who is the pupil? The pupil is the child in school, the student, the disciple; he is *You*, or rather, your physical body. But what else are you? You are the King, since the Alpha number for "pupil" is 74 which equates to "The King"; but you are also the "Chariot" inasmuch as its Alpha number is the same number 74. The Chariot is the double-you (the letter W), the physical body; therefore, it could be said that you are the King who is riding around in his own personal chariot—the Chariot of the Gods. And what happens to Cara when she steps into your chariot? She rides along with you, and you both race away into the sunset, embarked upon a new and exciting journey into consciousness.

"But suppose there is no room in the chariot," you persist. There is no problem there. The symbol for the Chariot is the W; the symbol for Cara is also the W. Therefore, she can sit in your chariot as snug as a bug in a rug, with one W snuggled in on top of the other one. The secret, of course, lies in the numbers themselves. Cara, when added to the black hole or to the Knight (it makes no difference which term we use because they are both equal to 102), makes the following numerical equation: 23 + 102 = 125. Translated into English letters, this becomes: W (Cara) + L = AY. So there she lay, snuggled up in your arms, all safe and secure in your chariot of love.

The two of you are now the "Iris-Pupil" of the great All-Seeing Eye of God, and as such, you may truthfully say, "I are Eye's pupil." Is this grammatically incorrect? No it is not, since the two of you have now become one—and yet somehow, still two. In any event, you are now free to travel anywhere in the universe around the sphere of the All-Seeing Eye as you are indeed the window of the soul, the vehicle through which the God-Self that dwells within can become aware of the universe that lies without. Thus you may travel upwards, downwards, to the left, to the right—anywhere you so desire to go in your "UFO" chariot which in reality is the pupil of the great All-Seeing Eye of God.

Exploring the Map of the Eye

We pointed out earlier that the symbol of the All-Seeing Eye was like a great map of the Eye, with the eyeball itself being comparable to the globe of the Earth in a microcosmic sense, or to the globe of the Universe in a macrocosmic sense. So then let us now return to Figure 70 and study the various component parts of this map in greater detail.

The symbol E at the extreme right-hand corner of the eye represents the East, and the symbol A at the extreme left-hand corner represents the West (A = 123 = AW or a W). C would then be towards the North and G towards the South; the equator is represented by the horizontal axis AOE. Very well. It is interesting to note that the upper arc of the eye is designated by the arc ACE which means *All-Seeing Eye*, and that the lower arc of the eye is designated by the arc AGE which means *Consciousness* (AGE = 175, the Alpha number of "Consciousness"). This ACE AGE then (the Consciousness of the All-Seeing Eye) is in reality a gigantic CAGE since it encloses the iris, the pupil, and the two white portions of the eye. This "CAGE" is the only part of the eyeball that is normally seen by the mortal, the balance being hidden by the eyelids.

The next thing that comes to our attention as we study this "seen" portion of the eye is that the white areas are divided into two separate and distinct zones thus constituting a duality, as opposed to the iris and the pupil which are not so divided and which therefore represent individual units, each complete unto itself. The two *white* areas also represent the *mental* state of consciousness, the Cara state as it were, since the Alpha numbers of the words "mental" and "white" are each equal to 65 and therefore identical. One of the white areas could be said to be "Divine Mind" as opposed to its equal and opposite counterpart called "Mortal Mind." The Alpha number for the former is 103 or JC; this stands for Jesus Christ. The Alpha number for the latter is, of course, 119. But when we combine the two together, an interesting phenomenon occurs. The result is 222 which when separated back into its equal and opposite aspects gives us *Cara Boga Coty Strength* (111 + 111 = 222). The term *Divine Mind* may also be referred to as *Coty Mind* inasmuch as their Alpha numbes are each 103 or JC.

Another verification that we are on the right track in exploring this "map of the eye" is that it turns out to really *be* a map of the All-Seeing Eye or a map of the God Consciousness. The Alpha number for "iris-pupil" when combined with that for the word "white" yields the word LIFE, true (129 + 65 = LIFE); but when we add the second "white" to the previous total, thus making the map of the eye complete, we find that we now have the number 259 or BE I, the God Name number of the word GOD itself. (GOD = 87 + 87 + 85, or G + O + D, or Justice + The Sun + The Devil, which in turn equals 259 or BE I). Iris-Pupil-White gives us 194 which stands for AID; but Iris-Pupil-White-White gives us 259 which stands for GOD. Thus the God Consciousness is itself verifying that this "map of the eye" BE I.

At the center of the eye, at the CG of the pupil as it were, is the letter O, the hub of the great Wheel of Life. This is a very fitting symbol as the Agashan Teachers have often referred to the Core of Life as a great sun, and the letter O is a symbol for just that. Moreover, it is the hub of the great Wheel of Life, the rim of which is represented by the iris, the area enclosed by the circles BCDFGH and IJKLMN.

Let us now analyze the iris of the eye. We may do this by studying the numerical number that represents its area. From the table in Figure 71 we find that the area of the iris is 4,656.62571 08 . . , a number very difficult to read. Remember that all numbers do not tell significant, readily understood stories about themselves. So then when we have a problem in deciphering the meaning, as in this particular instance, we move on to another number which expresses essentially the same thing, in the same way that we would dig in another area of the mine when prospecting for gold. We know the gold is there, but the valuable strike might be a little further to the right or the left.

The next step in our exploration is to divide the iris in two, and study the number that represents its area to the left or the right of the vertical axis and which directly relates to one of the white areas. The table in Figure 71 gives this number as 2,328.31285 54 . . . and it is here where we hit pay dirt. Translated into English, the number reads "W B H CAB: HEED!" In other words, the Cabalah tells us that the letter W be each cab, and for us to *heed*, pay attention, and concern ourselves with this important information. What is the letter W? It represents the Chariot (Tarot Key 7), and a chariot most certainly is a *cab* because that is exactly what it is. The word *cab* refers to a taxi-cab, a chauffer-driven automobile carrying passengers for hire. It is also the abbreviation for the word *cabriolet*, meaning a light 2-wheeled one-horse carriage, the 19th century counterpart of the *chariot*, which is defined as a 2-wheeled horse-drawn battle car of antiquity used in processions and races. Therefore, the Cabalah verifies that the letter W is indeed the symbol for the Chariot (Tarot Key 7).

The number that represents the area of the pupil is equally as informative. The number is 13,969.87713 23 . . , but for a clearer understanding let us separate the digits as follows: 139-69-87-7-13-23. The number 139 is the Alpha number for "The Wheel of Life," the letter B; the number 69 corresponds to "Knight," the letter L; the number 87 stands for "The Sun," the letter O; and the numbers 7, 13, and 23 represent the letters G, M, and W, respectively. Put together as a whole, the number is read "B LOG MW." The word *log* is a mathematical term meaning *logarithm*, the power that a number must be raised in order to produce a given number; and the letters M and W are a pictorial representation of a force along with its reflected image (the M is the inverted image of the W). Therefore, the Cabalah is telling us that the number that represents the area of the pupil of the eye is a logarithm, and that this logarithm is somehow related to its image.

What is the next step to be taken in a problem of this type? The answer is obviously to (1) find the logarithm of the pupil area, and then (2) compute the number whose logarithm is the pupil area, which is called its *antilog*. But since the average table of logarithms is only accurate to five significant figures, there is no reason to call our pupil area anything more than 13,970. (its nearest 5-digit number). Looking this number up in a table of logarithms we find: Log 13,970. = 4.14520. And the statement that is thus made is absolutely astounding! The Cabalist will mentally read the entire equation as one sentence as he groups the digits together in the following manner: LOG 139-704-14-5-20, which reads "LOG BE GOD NET" or "LOG ACI (All-Seeing Eye) GOD NET." If we consider just the antilog, we read "ACI GO"; or if we read only the logarithm, and read it backwards, we have the word "TEND" which means to listen, pay attention, or move in the direction that is indicated.

We may also consider the pupil as representing the antilog of a pure logarithm, that is, the mantissa only of the logarithm, a logarithm whose characteristic is 0 (the number before the decimal point is the characteristic). If this were the case, our pupil area would change from 13,970. to 1.3970 and the equation would be: Log 1.3970 = .14520. The statement that is now made is entirely different, but it is equally as astounding as the previous one. We now read, "ACI GONE: B O," which tells us that the All-Seeing Eye is *gone*, because it now *be zero*. Or, if we read only the logarithm, and move in the direction so indicated by reading it backwards, we have the word "TEN." And the ten, in the Agashan philosophy, is the same as the zero, the point where the action began. But this way or that way, it seems absolutely incredible to me that these simple numbers can speak in such an intelligent manner!

Now let us consider the opposite arrangement, where the pupil area now becomes the mantissa of the logarithm (the number to the right of the decimal point in the mantissa). However, when we look up the number .13970 in our five-place logarithm table, we find only the numbers .13956 and .13988 listed. The antilog of the former is 1.379 and the antilog of the latter is 1.380; therefore, to find the antilog of .13970 we will have to interpolate and the answer is given by the following equation: Log 1.3794 = .13970. The statement that is made can be read as "LOG MG ID ACI GO," which means the logarithm's image is the "Id," from which the All-Seeing Eye goes. Or we can also read it as "LOG MG ID = MIG O," and in this case we find out that the log of the image of the "Id" is the same as the image of the "O." The interpretation is yet not clear, but we can certainly see we are on the trail of something.

The next thing that comes to mind is the similarity between the logarithm (.13970) and its corresponding antilogarithm (1.3794). The numbers are so similar in this particular instance that to work with them becomes confusing. But perhaps this similarity is the very point the Cabalah is trying to make! Let us check it out. Looking through our table of logarithms, we find that the point where the logarithm equals its antilog lies somewhere between the following two equations:

Log 1.371 = .13704 (Log is less than its antilog)
Log 1.372 = .13735 (Log is greater than its antilog)

And lo! Our investigation has paid off for we seem to have hit the jackpot. Why do I say that? Well just read the top equation. It reads "LOG MG AM GOD!" which means that the log of the image is actually God! Wasn't Man created in the image and likeness of God? Well then, the Cabalah is telling us that the image or the *antilog* is Man; and that the true reality, that which created the image, is the *logarithm* itself which is God.

Now let us read the second equation and see what it says. On the surface we would read it as "LOG MG B MG CE" or "LOG MG B A CG CE." In other words, the log of the image *be* either the image of "C," or the image that sees, or a CG (center of gravity) of "C," etc. There are several interpretations and none of them are too clear. But let us dig a little further and interpret the logarithm (.13735) as 1-3-73-5, in which case it is read as "ACHE" since the number 73 stands for "Hermit" whose symbol is H. Thus we find that a clearer interpretation of the second equation is "LOG MG B ACHE," which means that the logarithm of the image is either the Hermit (Tarot Key 9) whose symbol is "H," or another alternative which implies that the job results in a continual *ache* or pain as "He" feels such sympathy and pity for Man who was created in "His" image. We can also say that in the log of the image, you see He (LOG MG U C HE), since the final 2 of the antilog may be cabalistically married to the first 1 of the logarithm.

But we are not finished with our analysis. Actually, I became so intrigued with the problem of finding the exact number on the logarithmic scale whose antilog was its own reflection, that I worked it out to 10 significant digits—the limits of the electronic wizard that sits on my desk. I used the method of trial and error; if my assumption was too large I then used a smaller number, until I eventually was able to zero in on the following equation:

Log 1.3712 88574 = .13712 88574 = (13-7-128-85-74)

This particular number is evidently a very important number inasmuch as it marks the dividing line between numbers whose logarithms are *greater* than themselves and numbers whose logarithms are *smaller* than themselves. And evidently the Cabalah thinks so too, for when this point is reached, it says that the *images decay* (MGZ DK). The key to the analysis was substituting the letter/symbols for the God Names whose Alpha number appeared in the equation (128 = The Empress = Z; 85 = The Devil = D; 74 = The King = K). This number, then, must represent the Fall of Man, since the definition for the word *decay* means to decline from a sound or prosperous condition.

But Man, even though he has fallen, must rise again. So then let us now take off in our UFO chariot and explore the vast regions of the eye known as the Great White Way. This is the term that the Agashan Teachers have often used to describe the vast *inner* space within our own galaxy commonly known as the Milky Way; and it is plainly depicted in our map of the eye as the white areas to the east and to the west of the pupil. Its area is shown in the table of Figure 71 to be 10,505.51292 91 which, of course, is based upon our basic unit of 77 for the outer radius of the iris.

Does this number tell us anything that we should know pertaining to these vast outer regions of the eye? Of course it does, but to understand the meaning we must break it up into its component parts which are "105-0-5-5-12-9-2-91." At the extreme left-hand corner of the eye is the number 105, the Alpha number for "The World" (Tarot Key 21) whose letter/symbol is J; and at the extreme right-hand corner of the eye is the number 91, the Alpha number for "The Star" (Tarot Key 17) whose letter/symbol is S. These are the first and last letters of the word JESUS, and we would assume, as we read this word from the right to the left, that the God Consciousness will "use" the inner portions of our number which represents the white area of the eye in the same manner.

Very well. What separates the World from the Star, or the letter J from the letter S? The answer is "O EEL I B," which means a duality: the O which stands for the Sun, and the "eel I" which stands for the serpent, the tempter, the devil, the letter S. (The eel is a snakelike fish that lives in the sea.) This is really an excellent analogy because it is quite evident that the God Consciousness uses both the positive and negative forces in the vast regions of space between the world and the star. Reading from left to right then it tells us "O + eel, I be," and backwards from right to left we hear "Be I Lee-o," which I am sure refers to our friend Leo the Lion. And we most certainly cannot dispute the Cabalah when it states that an "eel I" be the letter "S," a universal symbol for vibration, the energy from the Star as it is sent to us through space. "Joe," it says, "eel I be S." (105-0-5-5-12-9-2-91)

The Eyeball as a Giant Globe

Before we leave our map of the eye, let us take one last look at it as a complete whole. In other words, let us examine the entire area of the eyeball itself. But first, we must understand that there are three areas involved: (1) the flat, projected area of a circle, (2) the real area of this "circle" which is the surface area of a half-sphere, and (3) the total surface area of the sphere of the eyeball. These three areas are all interrelated, and their relationship is exactly the same as the digits 1, 2, and 4 because the surface of a sphere is exactly 4 times the area of its circular cross section. We will call these three areas *the lovers* because the Alpha number of Tarot Key 6 (The Lovers) embraces them all. It is 124 and its symbol is the letter V.

Let us examine the first area, the area of the circle. We find that its value is (Pi)(77)(77)(3) = (Pi)(17,787) = (Pi)(1 + 77 + 87). And since 77 further reduces to 14 or the letter N, and 87 to 15 or the letter O (87 is also the God-Name number for O), the cabalistic name for this rather amazing number is (Pi)(ANO) or (Pi)(AN O) or just simply PIANO. The number also embraces all three parts of the Trinity since God the Father is represented by the letter A, Christ the Sun by the numbers 77 and 87, and the Holy Ghost by Pi. And not only that, but it is a musical instrument capable of bringing forth the music of the *spheres* once it is multiplied first by 2 and then by 4. It is Pi times *an O*, Pi times a zero, and when we multiply anything by a zero what do we have? Nothing.

So then let us now find out what "nothing" really is. Its value according to my wise and faithful electronic friend is 55,879.50852 9399 . . . followed by an endless chain of digits, forming an incredible variety of permutations and combinations of every possible type of description, that goes on, and on, and on—forever. This infinitely long number is the area of a circular cross section through the sphere of the eyeball, but since any true projection on a flat plane has zero thickness, we can say that its volume or mass actually *is* nothing and this statement made by the Cabalah is correct.

If we read the decimal part of the number from the right to the left (backwards towards the decimal point), we find that it says "X see I be hoe" (X C I BE HOE = 99-3-9-25-805). In other words, the double I (Judgement or Christ) understands that the single I (the Magician) be a *hoe*, an instrument or tool used for digging. But isn't a *hoe* also a plow or a harrow, an instrument that turns and loosens the soil with a series of *discs*? To *disc* the soil means to *hoe* it or cultivate it; therefore one word may be substituted for the other, and the Cabalah tells us that the area of a circle is just what we all know it to be—a disc, a thin circular object. But this is the single I or the Magician. The double I or Judgement is the spherical area of the eyeball, the two portions forward and aft of its circular cross section.

The term HOE may also be read as H (each) OE. And what is OE? The Alpha number for the God Name of O (The Sun) is 87, and the Alpha number for the God Name of E (The Hierophant) is 147; but when we add the two together we find that their sum is 234 or BCD. Therefore, each OE means each BCD or each *beast*; and this also is what the single I is—a beast of burden, one that pulls the disc harrow or the plow (BCD = 234 = 9 = I = the Magician).

There is also a second meaning for the first three letters of the term "X C I BE HOE." XCI is the number 91 in Roman numerals; and the number 91, of course, is the Alpha number for "The Star" (Tarot Key 17) whose symbol is the letter S. Therefore, we may read "XCI BE HOE" as "S BE HOE," and we find that the Wheel of Life, the letter B, is actually located in the middle of the "SHOE." But is this so surprising? When we *shoe* a horse, or when we place our foot into a *shoe*, we are in fact allowing the Wheel of Life to carry either the horse or ourselves many miles without injury to the foot. And then, of course, there is always the old woman who lived in a shoe and who had so many children she didn't know what to do. Isn't this "old woman" the Wheel of Life? Think about it. The Cabalah makes beautiful sense once we allow our intuitive faculty to help us comprehend it.

"But what is the meaning for the integer part of the number, the digits before the decimal point?" you ask. On the surface, I will admit that the number 55,879 does not tell us too much about itself. We may read it as "EE H (each) GI," but this is not too inspiring and so we must get in there and "dig." How do we do that? For starters, let us find its God Name number (the sum of the Alpha numbers for the God Names of each of its component parts). EE (The Hierophant) is 147 + 147, H (The Hermit) is 106, G (Justice) is 87, and I (The Magician) is 90; and when we compute their sum we realize that this was the correct approach to the problem. The answer is 577 or EGG, and we

find that the integer part of the number that represents the area
of the circle is the EGG—that which gave birth to its decimal
part, the part of its consciousness that is forever expanding.

The circle then is the Orphic Egg, the mundane egg from
which Phanes (in Orphic cosmogony) sprang into light. The
noted philosopher Manly Palmer Hall goes into this at great
length in his *Encyclopedic Outline* or "big book." In it he
states[3] "the Orphic egg to be synonymous with the *mixture* from
bound and *infinity* mentioned by Plato in the *Philebus*. The egg
is furthermore the third Intelligible Triad and the proper symbol of the Demiurgus, whose auric body is the egg of the
inferior universe. . . . In the esoteric doctrines the supreme individual achievement is the breaking of the Orphic egg, which is
equivalent to the return of the spirit to the Nirvana—the *absolute* condition—of the Oriental mystics." This, then, is a more
elaborate definition of the first area of the eyeball—the projection of itself unto the flat surface of a plane.

Now let us analyze the second and third areas involved, the
area of its half-sphere and the total area of its spherical surface.
The area of the former is (Pi)(2)(17,787) or (Pi)(35,574); and
the area of the latter is (Pi)(4)(17,787) or (Pi)(71,148). Translated, the half-sphere is "PI CEE K (74 = The King = K). And
inasmuch as the word "Cee" is the name of the letter "C," we
may assume that the second area is translated as "PICK." Here
again we have another instrument or tool, but more than that,
the word "pick" means to choose or select between alternatives. This is a perfect word for the second area inasmuch as it
involves two different choices—the surface area of the front of
the eyeball or the surface area of the rear of the eyeball.

The translation of the third area, the total area of the spherical surface of the eyeball, offers some surprises. First, the number (Pi)(71,148) may be read as "PIG + AN H" (Pig + An H).
Here again are two alternatives: (1) a Pig, which is everything
that the name implies—a beast, a swine, or an immoral
woman, or (2) an "H," the Hermit (Tarot Key 9), the Teacher,
the wise one, the very opposite of the "pig." Then there is a
second way to translate this term, and this is by far the most

interesting. The answer is "Pi + GANH," and if we read this phrase backwards from the right to the left, it may be read as "HANG PI."

Now what are we doing when we "hang" Pi? The Hanged Man (Tarot Key 12) turns Man upside down and places him on the Tree of Life, and maybe we should do the same thing with Pi. How do we do this? Very simple. We simply invert Pi, turn it upside down as it were, and we have the term 1/Pi instead of Pi/1 (the diameter of the circle divided by the circumference instead of the circumference over the diameter). And the most amazing thing happens when we do this. The Alpha number for "One Over Pi" is 34 + 60 + 25 or 119, the number of the "All-Seeing Eye" itself, which also, incidentally, is the same number as its opposition—"Mortal Mind," the only devil that we will ever know, as the Agashan Teachers have stated over and over and over again. Therefore, the number 1/Pi brings the All-Seeing Eye/Mortal Mind into manifestation, an H (the Hermit) or the Pig. Which one is it? Take your choice; it is either one or both.

The three terms then, the three areas, taken together as a whole, tell us that the *Hanged Pi* (1/Pi) *picks* or selects the *piano* as its musical instrument to bring into manifestation the "music of the spheres." Why did it select the piano? The answer is revealed in the three words CARA BOGA COTY. We just cannot seem to get away from this phrase. It crops up almost everywhere in the study of the Cabalah. In this case it is CARA, Divine Mind and/or Mortal Mind, who initiates the action by selecting the piano. It picks the piano because the piano has 88 keys, 52 white keys and 36 black keys, and thus by going up and down the scale it can also bring BOGA COTY into manifestation. But we must remember that CARA is 1/Pi, the *inverse* of Pi; therefore, it desires a musical instrument that likewise is the *reverse* of BOGA and the *reverse* of COTY. The piano fulfills these specifications perfectly because the Alpha number for BOGA is 25, the reverse of which is 52, the total number of white keys; and the Alpha number for COTY is 63, the reverse of 36, the total number of black keys. But the total sum is not changed a whit inasmuch as 25 + 63 is no more equal to 88 than 52 + 36; and the term DEVIL CHILD (52 + 36) is most appropriate for the reverse of BOGA COTY (25 + 63). We will be hearing more about this term "Devil Child" as we continue on with our studies into the mysteries of the Cabalah.

Now let us recap all three of these areas together into a single series. We can do this by tabulating them one above the other, and when we set them up in this fashion, we gradually become aware of another even more extraordinary relationship heretofore undreamed of. It is very well concealed, but the discerning reader should be able to decipher it from a study of the following equations. The hyphen is used to separate the digits into groups so that the task may become a little easier.

Circle Area = (1)(Pi)(1-77-87) =   55,879. 508-52-93-99
Half Sphere = (2)(Pi)(1-77-87) = 111,759. 0-170-58-798
Full Sphere = (4)(Pi)(1-77-87) = 223,518. 0-34-11-7596

The Cabalah is evidently trying to tell us that a rather extraordinary relationship exists between the integer part of the area of the half sphere and the decimal part of the area of the full sphere. Heretofore in our previous knowledge of mathematics no such relationship exists, but the Cabalah is now calling our attention to a most interesting relationship. It states that the integer part of the former is *within* the decimal part of the latter, or rather that the integer part is *of* the decimal part. The integer part of the half sphere is 111,759; but isn't "ONE-11,759" the same number? Therefore, the decimal part of the full sphere which is "0-34-11,759-6" may be read as "O-ONE-11,759-6" since 34 = ONE = 1. The result is "0-111,759-F" which tells us that the half sphere's integer is *of* the full sphere's decimal.

The next point of interest lies within the *half* sphere's decimal. Its number is "0-170-58-798," and in the same way that we substituted ONE for 34, let us now substitute TWO for 58. The result is the term "0-1702-798." "What is so interesting about that?" you will ask. Well, just read the number backwards from the right to the left and find out. You will find that it tells us "H (each) I G-BOGA-O." In other words each "I" goes, and

BOGA, the physical aspect of CARA BOGA COTY, is right in the center of the verb GO.

But this is not all. You will find that BOGA, surprisingly enough, also exists within the decimal part of the other two terms as well. If we read the decimals for the circle and the full sphere backwards in the same way, we find (1) "X C I BE (25 = BOGA) HOE" and (2) "FI EG-111-0." In the latter case BOGA exists within the EGO, as 111 = STRENGTH = Y = 25 = BOGA. Therefore, we might say that BOGA exists within the full sphere manifesting as STRENGTH (111); it exists within the half sphere manifesting as itself (BOGA); and it exists within the circle as it manifests as BE, the letter B, the Wheel of Life.

An analysis of the integer part of these terms proves equally as interesting. For example: the integer of the full sphere is 223,518. This number may be written out cabalistically as "TWO-23-5-18," and when we write it out in this way, the word "TWO-W-E-R" comes into our view. But what is wrong here? Obviously we have one "W" too many; our "TOWER" is too crowded and one "double you," the offensive one, will have to be cast out. But as we do this we find we are symbol-ically bringing into manifestation Tarot Key 16, the lightning-struck Tower, the House of God from which two individuals are seen falling from its heights. These two individuals are you and I, Adam and Eve, the male and female aspects of our Being which are symbolically represented as the "double you."

We find then that this "W" is cast out of the integer of the full sphere represented by the Tower. But where does it go? A likely answer is to the next lower tier of the ladder of our Being, to the integer of the half sphere whose number is 111,759. So then let us check this number out, and inasmuch as consistency is the order of the day, let us spell out the first digit as ONE and then write out the others in their normal manner as we did before. The result is the term "ONE-1-1-7-5-9," and it is read as "ONE A AGE I." Thus the statement is made that a single "A" ages the "I," causes it to become mellow or mature, and brings it to a state fit for use or to maturity.

But the Cabalah is also telling us that the integer of the half sphere is a state of consciousness whereby "A Age" is in the center of "One I." Here again, the "I" is referred to as One. But the term "Age" is also synonymous with the term "Consciousness" because it represents its Alpha number (CONSCIOUSNESS = 175 = AGE). Therefore, it is the Consciousness of the Emperor whose symbol is A that resides at the center of "One I." And not only that, it is also the ID who resides there inasmuch as the Alpha number for I (The Magician) when added to the Alpha number for D (The Devil) brings forth this same number 175 (90 + 85 = 175 = AGE). Thus we find that the word "Consciousness" may be said to represent the sum total of the Magician and the Devil, or the I plus the D; and that these two terms, when added to the Emperor himself (A + ID = A + AGE), bring into manifestation that which occupies the central space between the "ONE" and the "I." This may sound a bit confusing, but if you think it out carefully it should become quite clear.

However, when a "W" is added to this slowly maturing and ageing "I," the situation is changed quite dramatically. Heretofore, the consciousness of the half sphere represented a rather steady state of evolution as the consciousness of the ID slowly moved toward that of the Emperor. And inasmuch as the letter "W" is symbolized by a chariot, this entire process of the soul's evolution through each age might be compared to a chariot race where the Magician (The I) is racing the Devil (The D). The arrival of the chariot into the integer of the half sphere then signifies it has crossed the finish line and the race is over.

Did I hear you ask who won? The "I" did of course, as the "D" (the Devil) is always the loser in the final analysis. The Cabalah verifies that this is so because when we add a "W" to "ONE A AGE I," the meaning of the phrase is changed to "WON EA. AGE I." We find then that "I WON EA. (each) AGE" when we place the letters in a circle and read them starting with the I. The old age is thus complete and an entirely different age is about to begin. And last but not least the hero and heroine of our story, Adam and Eve, after having spent countless lifetimes going through the Wheel of Life (the result from being cast out of the Tower which is commonly known as the Garden of Eden), are now to be readmitted into the Kingdom once again. Only this time their consciousness will not be in the Kingdom of the Full Sphere, but in the Kingdom of the Half Sphere known as the Middle Kingdom.

Eventually they shall enter the third and last kingdom called the Kingdom of the Soul or the Kingdom of the Perfect Circle. Only this will not be until they have found their way back into the vast consciousness of the Soul itself, otherwise known as the Orphic egg. Then, inasmuch as all life is brought forth from the egg, and after they have passed their final initiation, they shall ascend once more into the Kingdom of the Full Sphere and be as a Pillar of Light. The circle is now complete, and they are back once more into the TOWER of their Being.

NOTES

1. John G. Taylor, *Black Holes* (New York, Avon Books, Random House, Inc. 1975, 1973)

2. Timothy Ferris, *Los Angeles Herald Examiner*, New York Times News Service, January 14, 1979

3. Manly Palmer Hall, *An Encyclopedic Outline* (Los Angeles, Philosophical Research Society, 1928) p. 60

Chapter 20

THE STRUCTURE OF NUMBER

Now LET US take a look at *Number* itself, and analyze its basic structure. In the first place, there always is a little round dot that separates the integer or whole part of any number from its decimal fraction. The integer part to the left of the decimal point is always finite; however, the digits to the right of the decimal point of any transcendental number such as pi, phi, e, $\sqrt{2}$, $\sqrt{3}$, $\sqrt{5}$, etc. form an endless chain that goes on, and on, and on—forever. And, as we said earlier, this infinite chain of digits brings into manifestation permutations and combinations of such an incredible variety that it absolutely defies description.

Yet there is no fixed division line between the integer part and the decimal fraction. By that I mean there is no fixed position for the decimal point. The integer may consist of only a single digit, or then again it may embrace a million digits—yet the decimal part will still be endless. And the number will *always* be the same, no matter where the decimal point appears, as long as it is consistently multiplied or divided by powers of ten. (Multiplication by 10 moves the decimal point over one digit; yet the number remains the same.) One can see then that the numeral 10 is the key factor that offers everlasting life to any number. Multiply the number by 2 and all of the digits change, multiply it by 3 and they change again, but a factor of 10 will consistently bring back the original sequence of digits exactly as it was in the beginning.

The Alpha number for the word "decimal" is 47, which is the same as the number for "time." Therefore, the decimal point is merely a point in time. And conversely, the Alpha number for "point" is 74 or the reverse of 47; thus even the decimal point itself may be read either forwards or backwards without changing its number. The total Alpha number for "decimal point," incidentally, is 121 (47 + 74 = 121), and even this number has the same properties. It is truly a "universal" number that applies to "yourself," and yourself alone since it represents "your universal self" (79 + 121 + 42 = 121 + 121). Some of its attributes insofar as they relate to the element gold are depicted in the following Figure 73:

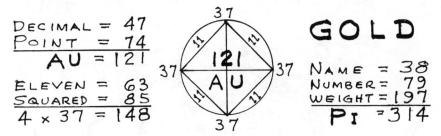

Figure 73: The Decimal Point as the Element Gold

It is interesting to note that if the decimal point represents the element gold, which is the 79th element in the Table of Chemical Elements, that there would be 78 elements to the left of the decimal point, the exact number of Tarot cards in the Tarot deck. This allows for 26 elements to represent God (hydrogen to iron), and 52 elements to represent the Devil (cobalt to platinum). The number of elements to the right of gold, being the decimal point as it were, would then theoretically be infinite, although common sense tells us that this is not the case. Nature herself only brought into manifestation 13 additional elements (mercury to uranium), and this would seem to be a good time to stop inasmuch as 13 is the number of Death (Tarot Key 13) whose symbol is the letter M. This leaves us six groups of 13 elements to the left of the decimal point and one group of 13 elements to the right, making seven in all. Thus we have the digit 7, a spiritual number; and it is doubly interesting to note that the decimal point, the element gold, divides that which the Agashan Teachers refer to as a *universal* number, the number 7, into 6 and 1 which is the Alpha number of YOU (6 + 1 = 61 = You).

The Mysteries of the Decimal Point

Now let us examine the forces within the decimal point itself. An excellent analogy is to compare it with the pupil of the eye. If the inner Being wishes to see that which is to the right, it moves the pupil to the right; and if it wishes to see that which is to the left, it moves the pupil to the left. And so it is with the decimal point. Figure 74 illustrates its motion quite clearly.

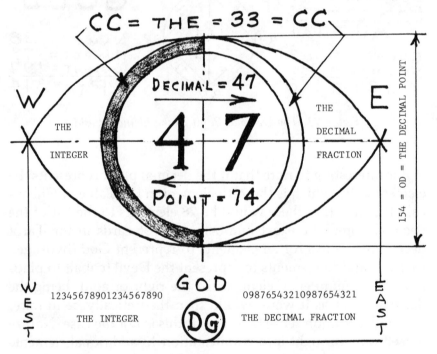

Figure 74: The Decimal Point as the Pupil of the Eye

This relationship was discovered quite accidentally when it was suddenly realized that the Alpha number for "The Decimal

Point" was identical to the number for "Outer Diameter" (154) in the Pupil-Iris combination in the glyph for the All-Seeing Eye in Figure 70. But nothing happens by "accident" in the study of the Cabalah, and it would seem that this discovery was more than likely accidentally on purpose. Indeed, the analogy of the pupil playing the role of the decimal point as it moves backwards and forwards through the number of its Being is too perfect to be anything other than a direct revelation from the Masters.

Even the Alpha number of the word "pupil" is the same as that of the word "point," both of them being 74, the number of "The King" whose symbol is K and whose "Chariot," the letter W, is also the same number. Therefore, we can visualize the King in his chariot exploring every aspect of the mysteries of his Being as he travels from digit to digit up and down the scale of the Soul's consciousness all the way from a tiny atom to the universe itself. The circular motion of the wheel is also implied inasmuch as the Alpha number for "The King + Chariot" is identical to "eleven squared," which in turn differentiates itself into the four corners of the wheel depicted in Figure 73. During one complete revolution of the wheel each of these four corners will touch the ground, bringing into manifestation the 1, 2, 3, and 4, the sum of which is the decade, the ten, the necessary factor required to keep the number constant as we travel from digit to digit.

It also seems not by happenstance that each of the four major divisions of the decimal point has a numerical value of 37. Doesn't 3 × 37 = 111 or CARA BOGA COTY? Here are the three One's again, with each representing a cardinal point of the compass of the wheel that is not touching the ground. This fourth point is reserved for BEING, that part of the point/ wheel that is actually in manifestation at the moment, and whose three unmanifested aspects are Cara, Boga, and Coty. Or we might use the term "Once," which means at one time only, and state that "The King + Chariot" was "Once Cara Boga Coty," or is now, in fact, "Being Cara Boga Coty." Each of these terms, *Being, Once,* or even the name *Agasha* itself, has a numerical Alpha value of 37 which means that it is capable of being the CG or center of gravity of one's own consciousness.

We find then that these four major divisions of the decimal point, these four CG's as it were, constitute what may be said to be the "Four You" since the Alpha number of "Four You" and "Decimal Point" are the same (60 + 61 = 121, and 47 + 74 = 121). We thus are forced into the unavoidable conclusion that the *decimal point* in reality is actually "Your UFO" since the term "Four You" quite easily rearranges itself in this manner. Imagine having your own individual UFO, your own personal flying saucer, and be able to freely move throughout your consciousness as easily as you are able to multiply or divide yourself by powers of ten! Is that what these UFO's that are occasionally seen to come into manifestation actually are? Decimal points or decimal "chariots" that are moving backwards and forwards through time itself? Is the planet Earth then the temporary integer part—we will assume that the decimal point exists where we are at the moment—of an infinite decimal number known as the Universal Consciousness of God? The Agashan Teachers would have us to believe that this is so; however, as the old adage goes, only "time" itself will prove the truth or falsity of this statement.

Let us analyze the numbers. The Alpha number for "The Decimal" is 80 (33 + 47 = 80) which is read as HO. The word "ho" is an exclamation of surprise, delight, or exultation, and it most certainly is this, and even more, when one discovers its real meaning. "What is that?" you ask. The word "HO" also means "Each O," which adds emphasis to the fact that when you read it backwards it is read as *Oh*, the name of the letter "O," the symbol of the Sun (Tarot Key 19). But this fact in itself is nothing to get particularly excited about. The excitement comes, however, when one discovers what the total value of HO actually is. HO = W, and W = HO (8 + 15 = 23). Therefore, we find that the real meaning of the decimal (HO) is that it proves not only WHO God is, but also HOW He performs his great works! And this is by moving the Chariot (the letter W or the decimal point) to the extreme right end of the decimal number to find the "HOW" of it, or to the extreme left end of the decimal number to find out "WHO" it is that is performing the action. Yes indeed, this discovery most certainly should provoke a few "ho's" or so from the one who comes across the splendor of its works.

The Alpha number for "The Decimal Point" is also not without an esoteric meaning. Its Alpha number is 154 which is read as OD. But when we add the two letters together to find its sum, we discover that it is the letter S (15 + 4 = 19 = S). This letter is the symbol for the Star (Tarot Key 17), and we find then that our decimal point or our chariot as it were is likewise our star. But isn't the Sun, the "chariot" that moves across the sky, also a star? Of course it is. It is the "decimal point" for the planet Earth, and perhaps some of the other planets as well. But the real esoteric meaning of the term is not understood until one reads the entire equation which is "S = OD" or the word "SOD." Now what is *sod*? The dictionary defines the term as *turf*, the surface of the ground when covered with grass. Another definition is that it represents *one's native land*. Therefore, the esoteric meaning for the decimal point is that it represents your native land, your home from which you sprang forth in the beginning.

Figure 74 points out that the decimal point may be represented as two letter C's, back to face, and enclosing the letters D and G. This is GOD. Very well. But now let us change these letters into their God Names and read the resulting statement. The God Name number for C is 90 (The Moon); the number for G is 87 (Justice); and the number for D is 85 (The Devil). The statement so made by the combination of these terms is rather profound.

Normal Order (to the right)		*Reverse Order (to the left)*	
The (33)	Decimal (47)	Point (74)	The (33)
C C	D G	G D	C C
90 + 90	85 + 87	78 + 58	09 + 09
180	172	136	018
R O	Q B	M F	O R
ROCK YOU BE		FROM or FORM	

Therefore, the Cabalah itself verifies the statement made in the preceding paragraph that was derived from an entirely different word and an entirely different system (Decimal point = sod = your native land). And even more astonishing, the total of the God Name numbers when read in reverse order equals 154, the Alpha number for "The Decimal Point" (136 + 018 = 154 = OD). I hate to belabor the point, but if the reader will also double the God-Name numbers as they appear in normal order, he will find that they are magically transformed into the *Natural* number that spells GOD (180 + 172 = 352, and 352 × 2 = 704 = GOD). And this, of course, is derived from an entirely different method of analysis than the glyph of Figure 74 which comes to the same conclusion—that the decimal point, is in fact, GOD.

The Three Basic Parts of Any Number

Now let us analyze the complete decimal number as a whole. We find that it is made up of three parts: the integer or finite part to the left of the decimal point, the decimal point itself, and the infinite part to the right of the decimal point called the infinite decimal fraction. And these three terms taken as a whole likewise give out a wealth of cabalistic information. The Alpha numbers of the words are tabulated below, along with their corresponding English letters. The letter Y is used for the number 111 because that is the Alpha number for Strength (Tarot Key 8) whose letter/symbol is Y.

The Integer		The Decimal Point	
33	78	33	47	74
111		154	
Y		O D	(YOD)

The Decimal Point		The Infinite Decimal Fraction		
33	47	74	33	86	47	86
154		252		
O D		Y B	(BODY)	

The integer is thus seen to be YOD, the number 10, the first word of the Divine Name YOD HE VAV HE. We are, of course, including the decimal point to act as a signature that the finite part is complete. But when we examine the infinite part we must also include the decimal point to define where the decimal fraction begins. And the infinite part is seen to be the BODY. Isn't this study absolutely fascinating? The writer certainly thinks so.

Now let us look at the above table a little more carefully. There is one other point that is fairly crying out to be seen and understood. That point is that the integer, by itself and without the decimal point, is 111 or CARA BOGA COTY. And not only that, but the infinite decimal fraction, likewise by itself and without the decimal point, is also CARA BOGA COTY; but in the decimal part it is CARA BOGA COTY that BE. The point is very subtle, but a "Y" is a "Y" no matter how you look at it; and it is always 111 or CARA BOGA COTY.

Let us look at Figure 73 once again. Picture this glyph as representing the decimal point in the middle of a number. The decimal point is seen to be a wheel, and if we were to rotate this wheel and move it to the left, we would gradually bring one, two, and three 37's in contact with the ground—all equally spaced with each 37 representing a "1" or a unit of the complete term 111. And the same thing would occur if we were to rotate the wheel and move it three steps to the right. All in all then there are two sets of CARA BOGA COTY to be considered, one to the right and one to the left of the central decimal point. But not only that, we most certainly cannot forget the central CG or the decimal point itself. This is the inner BEING, that which is in manifestation *now* and that which represents the inner reality of which CARA, BOGA, and COTY are only its unmanifested aspects. These are the seven groups of 13 elements that we spoke of earlier when we were comparing the element gold to the decimal point. But the strangest thing of all is that these seven 37's, or seven CG's as it were, add up to the number 259 which says that it BE I; and this, of course, is the number of the God Names of the symbols G, O, and D or simply GOD.

We observed this phenomenon occurring once before when we added up the Alpha numbers of the different parts of the eye. The Alpha number of "White + Iris-Pupil + White" is itself equal to 259 and it also "BE I." Yes indeed, the symbol of the All-Seeing Eye when it is understood in its entirety will have a great story to tell mankind.

One other point. If we read the Alpha numbers for "The Integer + The Decimal Point + The Infinite Decimal Fraction" as a single sentence, it may be read as "YOD BE B" (111 + 154 + 252 = Y OD BE B). Now the letter B is the Wheel of Life; its Tarot Key number is 10 and its God Name is the Wheel of Fortune. But what is the accepted value for Yod? Yod is the 10th letter of the Hebrew alphabet and it has been known from earliest times to represent the number 10. Therefore, the Cabalah is verifying the point that Yod is the equivalent to the letter B, the Wheel of Life. The sum total of the entire phrase, incidentally, is 517 which means that it is EQ (equal) to 22 or the letter V (Tarot Key 6) which stands for the Lovers. This means you and I.

The Pillars of Light

The question can now be asked that if CARA BOGA COTY exist to the left of the decimal point, or this inner BEING as it were, and if CARA BOGA COTY also fill up the space to the right of the decimal point, what then lies beyond the first digit of the integer and the last digit of the fraction? What is the name of this 4th "CG" when the wheel of the decimal point once again rests upon the point from which it started? The answer to the outer senses is apparently empty space, nothing, the great void. But to the inner senses the 4th CG" is the exact opposite of this. It would appear as a great Cosmic Being, a consciousness so vast it cannot be comprehended in its entirety. In the Agashan terminology these great Cosmic Beings are referred to as *Pillars of Light*—"white wholes" of pure light or energy, the very opposite of the "black hole" of the pupil of the eye or the decimal point.

They are depicted in Figure 75 as the great twin Pillars of the World upon which the extremities of the All-Seeing Eye are supported and tied. In the Cabalah they are called Jachin and Boaz, and they are symbolically represented by the letters J and B.

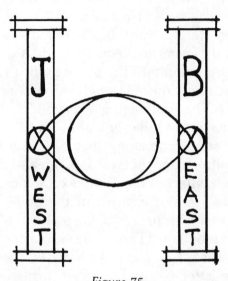

Figure 75
The Twin Pillars that Support the Eye

From the above, it is apparent that there is a still further meaning to the term "YOD BE B" in that it also represents the great Pillars of Light on either side of the All-Seeing Eye. Yod, being a 10, represents the great Pillar in the west whose symbol is J. Jachin is positive, white, and masculine. The letter B, also a 10 in the Tarot sense but a 2 in the Alpha sense, represents the great Pillar in the east whose name is Boaz. Boaz is negative, black, and feminine. But the important thing to be understood is that each Pillar of Light is neither positive nor negative, black nor white, per se. The Cabalah tells us that "Yod *be* B" and it means this in a literal sense. The very fact that a Pillar of Light is either positive or negative depends entirely on its position in relationship with the Eye. If it is to the west of the Eye it is positive; if it is to the east of the Eye it is negative. But in the case of a series of Eye's, strung together from Pillar to Pillar like beads on a string, one can see very easily that each Pillar of Light is both positive and negative; or rather, its right side is positive and its left side is negative.

These points are verified when we study the numbers. J + B = 10 + 2 = 12. But 12 = L = The Knight = 102 = J B, and we are back to where we started. Also, B + 10 (Tarotwise) = 2 (Alphawise) = 102 = J B. Therefore, Yod (J) *be* B. And we most certainly have to bring *you* into the picture when we make these comparisons because You = U = 21 (Alphawise) = 0 (Tarotwise) = 210 = B J. The Fool then, who is you (U), has the potentials for becoming a twin Pillar of Light.

There is still another analogy that can be made. We may remove the capital from the word *Pillar* and refer to them simply as the two pillars of the Temple of Solomon. These two pillars constitute a major element in the Book of the Tarot, being incorporated in four Tarot keys of the Major Arcana. They are the Hierophant (Tarot Key 5 and the letter E), the High Priestess (Tarot Key 2 and the letter F), the Moon (Tarot Key 18 and the letter C), and Justice (Tarot Key 11 and the letter G). Together they spell out EF CG, and it is interesting to note that "ef" (the name of the letter F) is indeed the CG or center of gravity between the two pillars B and J. Just look at the High Priestess card and observe this for yourself. Isn't the letter F midway between the letters B and J? It most certainly is.

Let us now return to Figure 75 for a moment and study the names of the pillars. We have been told that the pillar in the west represents the positive life force and it most certainly does. The Alpha number of "J + West" is 77 which stands for Christ. Moreover, if we rearrange the letters slightly we find that it is also the "Jew's 'T' or the Jew's 'T' cross" which means Christ, who was a Jew, being crucified upon the cross of matter. But we can't stop here. Rearranging the letters still further, we find that the west pillar "Jets 'W' (double you or chariot)." Thus the west pillar spouts forth or *jets* its chariot away from itself in a high-speed current of air or water into the decimal number of the Eye. It also *jets* forth its "double you," Adam and Eve, as they are tossed from the Tower (Tarot Key 16) when it is subjected to an electrical charge. The west tower or pillar may be compared to the cathode or positive terminal of a primary cell or storage battery that is delivering current.

The east tower or pillar is just the opposite of this. It may be compared to the anode or negative terminal that receives the negative ions that the cathode has sent forth. It is the negative life force, and the Alpha number of "B + east" is 47 which stands for Time. It is also the *Beast* as opposed to *Christ*, the negative as opposed to the positive; but the combination of the two is the number 124 which represents the Lovers, the letter V.

The W, which is the chariot, leaves the terminal in the west and travels to the terminal in the east as it progresses through the decimal number of the Eye. This is the decimal point and it is motivated through and by the powers of 10. However, during this process it eventually falls victim to a "black hole" which separates the integer from the decimal fraction. Let us call this "black hole" by the symbol "X" which represents the unknown. But "X" is also the symbol for Judgement, and it represents the resurrection of the W or chariot, but in a different form than it was in before. Thus through and by the powers of "X" the W is changed into a B, or the chariot is changed into a wheel; and it is this B or Wheel of Life that eventually arrives at the negative terminal in the east.

The Cabalah does not make many statements without proving them, or in the absence of a rigorous proof, at least providing some elements of verification that the statement so made is true. The transformation of the W into the B is no exception. The Alpha number for W (The Chariot) is 107, and the Alpha number for X (Judgement) is 99; but when we add the two together, bring the Chariot through Judgement as it were, the answer is 206 which is the Alpha number for the letter B (The Wheel of Fortune). Even the simple addition of the symbols gives us the same answer. W + X = 23 + 24 = 47 = BEAST. And this, of course, is the letter B whose home is in the EAST (the negative pillar of Boaz whose symbol is B).

But actually, as we pointed out earlier, each pillar is dual insofar as its right side is positive and its left side is negative. Its left half is receiving the current, the ball as it were, from the previous Eye and its right half is sending it back out again into the forthcoming Eye through and by means of the W or the chariot. An inactive pillar (one that is not receiving or delivering an electrical current) may be compared to a gigantic rocket, suspended on its launching pad, and ready to take off into an entirely new dimension of space and time. Its payload is the "B" and its fuel is the "W," but an inactive pillar/rocket has neither; yet, strangely, it is still complete insofar as it has its SEAT (ready to receive its payload, the B) and its JETS (ready to be fueled with the W). The Alpha number for this empty pillar/rocket is 99 which represents the letter X or Judgement (Seat + Jets

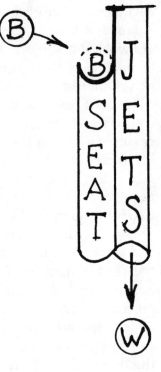

Figure 76
A Rocket of Light

= 45 + 54 = DEED = 99 = double "I" or Judgement). The "deed," of course, is the great feat that has to be accomplished. The entire glyph is depicted in Figure 76.

Now let our astronauts arrive on the scene and be seated in their respective seats. They have had to be well trained for this journey by riding the Wheel of Life through many lifetimes of earthly living; but now they are ready, and the Wheel of Life, along with its occupants, arrives at its destination—the spaceship or rocket that is to carry them into a higher consciousness. It is interesting to note that the Alpha number for "rocket" is the same as that for "world"; so we could say then that this "rocket" *is* the World (Tarot Key 21), the letter J, the number 10. However, when we place the "B" into its "seat" on the rocket ship, its Alpha number is changed from 99 (Judgement) to 101, the Alpha number for "The Pillar" which it now has become. This number 101, incidentally, is also the Alpha number for "The God-Self" or "The Logos."

One other point. The writer just noticed that we used the term "rocket ship" to describe the fully loaded spaceship that is to carry our astronauts to points unknown. This term is doubly interesting because the Alpha number for "rocket ship" is identically the same as the number for "world earth" (72 + 52). And not only that, but the total sum of these terms is 124 which stands for "The Lovers" (Tarot Key 6 or the letter V), as well as "B + seat + W + jets" or the combined term "B-East + J-West." All in all, it is thus inferred by the Cabalah that *the Lovers'* own, personal "earth world" is destined to become, if it hasn't already, a "rocket ship" to chart heretofore unexplored regions of space and time.

And when this occurs, perhaps they will become as "Pillars of Light"; well, we don't have to *suppose* that it will be so because the Agashan Teachers have long since promised that this is the ultimate destiny for all. The Alpha number for "A Pillar of Light" is "1 + 68 + 21 + 56" which integrates into "69 + 77" or FIG 7 (Knight Christ). The Alpha number for "The Pillars of Light" is "33 + 87 + 21 + 56" which integrates into "120 + 77" or LOG 7 (Double-you Christ). Now what does a *Figure 7* have to do with the *Log 7*? Well, let us look up its logarithm and find out. From the standard five-place logarithm table we find that "Log 7.000 = .84510 or H (each) D + EA (each) 0. Therefore, Log 7 = each "D" plus each "O"; and when we combine these two letters with the figure 7 or the letter G, we have the name GOD. A Pillar of Light then is the same as GOD, and to become as such is the ultimate destiny for all.

Yet this is not entirely true because the Cabalah inferred that GOD was equal to "A Pillar of Light" plus "The Pillars of Light" or the 1 plus the 2 (or more). This would bring the Holy Trinity into manifestation, and it would indicate that a minimum of three (3) forces is required to represent the God Consciousness. We therefore sketched out a glyph incorporating three Pillars and two Eyes, and the result was so fascinating and enlightening that we are including it as the following figure.

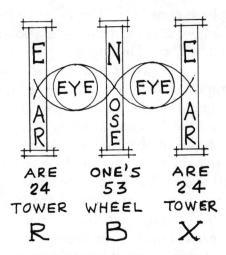

Figure 77: The Face of Cara Boga Coty

It does not take much imagination to come to the conclusion that Figure 77 represents the face CARA BOGA COTY. Here you are, eye to eye, with the mental, the physical, and the spiritual aspects of your very BEING! Here are the three one's again, only this time they are depicted as three Pillars of Light. Cara and Coty become your "ears" so that you may *hear* the music of the spheres, and Boga, the Middle Pillar, becomes your "nose" so that you may *know* all things and be as they. Even the Alpha number of "Ear + Nose + Ear" is 101 (24 + 53 + 24 = 101), and this is the number of "The Pillar" or "The God-Self." And the most amazing thing of all is that the word EAR may be rearranged into the word ARE, the name of the letter R, the symbol of the Tower, the House of God depicted as the lightning-struck tower in Tarot Key 16. Of course, the very fact that the Alpha number for "nose" is the same as that of "wheel" is no mere coincidence. The word "wheel" is the God Word for the letter whose symbol is B and whose name is Be, the number 25, the Alpha number of Boga. And the same thing could be said for the letters below the horizontal crossbar of the eyes; that is, that it is no mere coincidence that they say, "AR (the conventional spelling for the letter R) AROSE." In other words, the glyph states that the "R" (the tower or rocket ship) eventually *arose* from its launching pad and ascended into the wide blue yonder of the heavenly consciousness. And the same thing can be expected of our own "rocket ship" that we call our "earth world" in the tomorrows to come; for that exalted state that exists above the crossbar of the hurdle is to be ultimately attained by EN-E, which means ANY man, soul, or consciousness depicted by the letter N. (The *names* of the letters of the word "en" (N) are "e" and "en," and the God Word for this symbol is Man.) Yes indeed, Figure 77 is a remarkable glyph no matter how you look at it.

Before we leave this fascinating subject of the Pillars of Light, we must bring one last point to your attention; and that point is realized when an analysis is made of the actual names of Jachin and Boaz in relationship with the pillars of the Temple of Solomon that bear their initials—J and B. Let us begin this analysis with their Alpha numbers. The Alpha number for "Jachin" is 45 and the number for "Boaz" is its next-door neighbor which is 44. Taken together as a sum, they represent the number 89 which stands for H (each) I. But more than just that, when we add the "Eye" that they support between them we have the number 124 again, and this number, of course, represents the Lovers (45 + 35 + 44 = 124). It could also be said that Jachin *eyes* (looks at) Boaz and that Boaz eyes Jachin. It's a small world, isn't it.

Even the Alpha numbers for the pillars that bear their initials reveal their true identity in a most remarkable way. One might ask, "Who are Jachin and Boaz, really?" Well, let us ask the pillars and find out. The Alpha number for "West Pillar" is 135, which means that it is the ACE or the All-Seeing Eye (67 + 68 = 135 = ACE = 9 = I). Here again, we have two neighboring numbers. The answer given by the Alpha number for "East Pillar" proves equally as informative. It is 45 + 68, which brings into manifestation the number 113, the counterpart of "I" which is "AM." Thus we find that these two pillars are a representation or a symbol of the Universal Consciousness of God, or the One who states simply that "I AM."

Chapter 21

THE CHEMISTRY OF LIFE

In this chapter we shall discuss the chemistry or structure of Life itself, that particular aspect of the phenomenon that we term "Life" which deals with its chemical composition, bodily structure, and the properties of the elements of which it is constituted and the transformations that they undergo. At this point, the reader is liable to ask, "Well how can Life, which is only a word to describe a process, be treated as something physical or tangible?" The answer is that anything that has life, anything that *lives* in other words, must also have an etheric body, invisible to man, and yet just as tangible to the etheric touch as your physical body is to the physical touch (*The Agashan Discourses*, page 161). This etheric body can then be said to be the "life" body, for when it is severed from the physical organism, the physical body is quite dead.

But, in order to discuss these life processes properly, we must have a symbol with which to relate. In the previous chapter when we discussed the structure of Number, that symbol turned out to be the human eye, and there doesn't seem to be any good reason to change the symbol now. Indeed, the eye is an excellent symbol for Life because, as it was pointed out earlier, the Alpha numbers of its basic parts bring LIFE into manifestation ("pupil-iris" + "white" = 129 + 65 = LIFE). But more than just that, the All-Seeing Eye of God is a very apt symbol for Life because it is the archetype from which the organ of sight in the body of all living things was developed.

Let us examine the eye in greater detail. In Man, who was presumably created in the image of God, this organ appears externally as a dense, white spherical body surrounding a circular, colored portion, or iris, the center of which is an opening, or pupil, through which light passes into the retina. Then in the center of the retina, at the rear of the eyeball, is that which is called the "blind spot," where the optic nerve leaves the eye and which is insensitive to light. Its basic components then, when viewed externally, are the *pupil*, the *iris*, the *white* (the major portion of the surface of the sphere is called the sclera or the "white" of the eye), and the *blind spot*. The blind spot is technically on the interior surface of the eyeball, but if we were to sever the optic nerve from the eyeball itself, there would be no other name to call this area except as the "blind spot." The eye as it would appear from all four directions is shown in Figure 78.

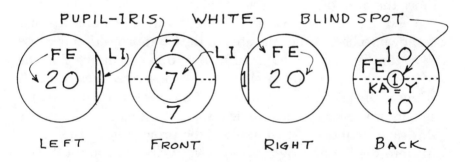

Figure 78
The Sphere of the Eyeball

We have designated the symbols LI for the pupil-iris and FE for the white areas because they represent their Alpha numbers. Likewise, we have called the blind spot by the symbol KA = Y because the Alpha number for "blind spot" is 111, the CARA BOGA COTY number for Strength (Tarot Key 8), the letter Y. But the Alpha number interpretation is not the only reason that they have been so named. On the contrary, the far greater reason is one that takes us deep within the Table of the

Chemical Elements—to the very structure of matter itself.

Isn't the word "Li" also the symbol for the element *lithium*, the 3rd element in the series of the chemical elements? And isn't the word "Fe" also the symbol for *iron*, the 26th element? And how about the word "KA = Y"? Isn't the letter "K" the symbol for *potassium*, the 19th element, and the letter "Y" the symbol for *yttrium*, the 39th element? Of course they are, and the reader will soon find out that these rather amazing "coincidences" are most definitely not the result of happenstance. To the contrary, the Cabalah is attempting to take mankind by the hand and lead him through the entire structure of matter to the very core of his own BEING. And this is what "Life" is all about.

These are the reasons then that we have shown these symbols in their appropriate locations in the left, front, right, and back views of the sphere of the eyeball in Figure 78. These four views were chosen because they represent the *total* surface area of the eye, inasmuch as the area of a sphere is exactly four times the area of its circular projection ($A = 4\pi R^2$). Hence, a top and bottom view would be superfluous. The pupil-iris disc is shown to be 1/3rd of the area of the front projection because that, too, is exactly what it turns out to be, assuming that the pupil-iris is the central circle within an inscribed *Vesica Piscis* (Figure 70). Likewise, the number 7 has been chosen to represent its area because the atomic weight of the element lithium is this same number—7. Moreover, the projection of the pupil-iris into the left and right views is very close to unity (.963) if we assume the projected area of each circle to be 21.

Another interesting item about Figure 78 is that the projected area of the left, front, and right views of the eye is then 3 times 21 or 63. And the number 63 is the exact weight of a LIFE molecule consisting of one atom of lithium and one of iron (the atomic weight of iron which is 56, when added to that of lithium which is 7, yields a LIFE molecule with an atomic weight of 63). This then leaves the area of the back of the eye, an area which the pupil-iris can never reach, to represent the counterpart of Life which is Death. But we will leave this negative aspect of Life for another day and concentrate our attention now on the two single elements that bring LIFE into manifestation.

Lithium and Iron

The properties of these two elements should give us some valuable clues as to what "Life" is all about. Let us first take up lithium. *The Encyclopedia of the Chemical Elements*[1] tells us that lithium is the lightest of the metallic elements and the first member of the alkali metals group. It is found widely distributed in the earth's crust, has the highest melting point, the highest boiling point, and it encompasses the largest liquid range among the alkali metals. Its high specific heat, high thermal conductivity and low viscosity, also make it an attractive metal for many purposes. It is silvery white in color and soft enough to be cut with a knife, and it can be *extruded, drawn, and rolled with considerable ease.* Is this not an apt description for this "chariot" that races across the socket of the eye, that is able to expand and contract its diaphragm with such ease and with such efficiency, and more than that, be constructed of a material that is flexible enough, and strong enough, and durable enough to last a lifetime? It would seem that the element lithium symbolizes these qualities to a remarkable degree. Its name is derived from the Greek word *lithos* which means "stone," and it is just that. The letters may be put in a circle and read as "One's 'T'," the cabalistic symbol for the Tree of Life.

Now let us look at iron. Its name is derived from the Latin *ferrum* and it is the most important metal known and used by man. Indeed, it is the fourth most prevalent element in the earth's crust and not only that, but some form of it even constitutes the major part of its molten core. It is through no coincidence then that the outer covering of the globe of the eye, the "white" part of it as it were, is referred to as Fe or iron. In its crude state (the initial product of the blast furnace) it is called *pig iron*, but in its refined state it is combined with a small amount of carbon into *steel*. The Alpha number for the word "steel," incidentally, is 61 which is the same as "you."

But by far the most important function of iron, as far as human and animal life is concerned, lies in the life processes. It is a vital constituent of absolutely every mammalian cell, and the role of iron in the body is closely associated with hemoglobin and the transportation of oxygen from the lungs to the tissue cells. But once it is incorporated into the body, whether by oral administration or by parenteral injection, there is no efficient mechanism for its excretion. Hence it is frequently spoken of as a "one way" substance. And the most amazing thing of all is that iron from outworn red cells is used over and over again as though it were a precious metal in the economy of the individual. All of this information has been obtained from the aforementioned *Encyclopedia of the Chemical Elements.*

The following tabulation will bring the relationship of these two necessary elements of "Life" into its proper perspective:

					Sum
Element Name	LITHIUM	92	IRON	56	148
Symbol	LI	21	FE	11	32
Atomic Weight	6.940	7	55.85	56	63
Atomic Number	3		3	26	26	29
Numerical Sum		123		149	272
		A		N I	B J

One can see that the key number for any element of the Periodic Table is the numerical sum of its parts: its name, its symbol, its weight, and its atomic number. These four aspects of itself identify it in the same way that a soldier is identified by his name, rank, and serial number. Only in the case of the chemical element, its symbol corresponds to the soldier's rank, and its weight and number to his serial number. The Alpha numbers for its name and symbol are used in this tabulation and its weight is computed to the nearest integer.

In the particular case of lithium and iron, one sees that the key number for lithium is 123 which stands for the Emperor, the letter A; and the key number for iron, inasmuch as it represents no one particular God Name or God Word, is read simply as NI (149). But look at what it says! The absolutely incredible statement is made by the Cabalah that the elements lithium and iron are just what we have been saying all along, namely, that they represent "AN I" (An eye). And not only that, when we add the two together we find that they *be a world* (2 = B and 72 = World or the letter J).

The element iron though, even though it doesn't represent a *single* God Name or God Word, most certainly does represent the sum of two or more of them. For instance: 149 = 38 + 111 = MY (Death + Strength). But whose death and strength is it referring to? The answer is found by combining the first three aspects of itself (its name, symbol, and weight) together into a single entity separate and distinct from its fourth aspect (its atomic number). These first three aspects of the element iron are then found to be the Emperor, the letter A, and its fourth aspect is God, the Empress, the letter Z (56 + 11 + 56 = 123 = the Emperor, and 26 = God = Z = the Empress). Iron, then, represents the Emperor and the Empress, the Fatherhood and Motherhood of God.

Another point of interest is that the Alpha number for *iron* is identical to its atomic weight, and this same number, which is 56, is the reverse of its symbol (56 = EF, the reverse of FE). Cabalistically speaking then, EF + FE + EF = ABC, and the whole of the element *iron* may then be said to be the ABC + Z or the ABC's of Life.

The analogy becomes even more interesting if we assume that *iron* is giving us a message, and that message is that the symbol of something is ofttimes the reverse or the inverse of that which it represents itself to be. Or perhaps we could say that the symbol is the inverted image in the eye of the reality that is. Following this suggestion then, let us read the statement that an eye be the world (AN I B J) backwards and discover its image. The result staggers the imagination for it states that the World be *in* the Emperor (J B IN A). And if the Emperor is in reality the pupil-iris of the All-Seeing Eye (the "Li" of Life), does this mean then that the "Fe" of Life, the vast white area of the eye, is also somehow within the Emperor? Is the macrocosm or greater self actually within the microcosm or lesser self, the reverse of the way we would ordinarily look at it? Are there worlds within worlds within worlds as the Agashan

Teachers have so often proclaimed, and do these worlds exist within the "black hole" of the pupil of the eye? This concept, however strange, is certainly worthy of further consideration.

The point is further emphasized in the following tabulation:

NAME		Element Name
RANK	Our Ankh	Symbol of Life
AND SERIAL	Se(RI)a Land	Weight = 72 = World = J
NUMBER		Atomic Number

Here, the atomic weight is shown to correspond to the World, the letter J that the Cabalah states is *in* the Emperor or the A. But the A that "I are" (AIR) is also shown to be within the SEA, and this in turn is followed by the LAND. Just look at Tarot Key 18 (The Moon) whose symbol is C. Doesn't this card portray life evolving out of the sea (the C) and onto the land as it passes through the two pillars J and B? Isn't this the same as the Agashan philosophy which states that all life evolves out of the sea to become greater than what it is today? Of course it is, and here again we have a world within a world within a world.

For those who are still skeptical, let us examine the Tarot keys for the Star (Tarot Key 17) whose symbol is S, and for Temperance (Tarot Key 14) whose symbol is T. Both of these cards depict a godlike figure who is either standing or kneeling with one foot on the land and one foot in the water. Thus these two forces, the symbols S and T, represent the connecting link between the land and the sea. But S + T adds up to 39, the Alpha number for "Ten." And the tenth letter of the alphabet is the letter J whose God Name is the World. It is the *World* then or the atomic "weight" that makes this connection, the ST-ONE or the element lithium, the pupil-iris of the eye, the decimal point of the decimal number, the wheel of the chariot— each of these forces as it travels freely from the one to the other, from the left to the right, from the land to the sea, makes the connecting link and brings *life* into manifestation.

One of these forces is also the image of the other. Which one is the reality, the land or the sea? Is life moving from illusion to reality or is it returning from reality to illusion again? Of this we cannot be sure, but we can be sure about which part of your name, rank, and serial number is the reality and which is the illusion. The Alpha number for "Name + Rank" is 77 which stands for Christ (33 + 44 = 77); therefore, it is your name and rank, your name and your symbol, that represents your true reality of which your serial number is only its image. How do we know this? We know it from the Alpha number of "Serial Number" which tells us that it is the image (64 + 73 = 137 = MG = Image). The Alpha number for "and" is 19 which is S; therefore, the words "and serial number" are but *images* of your name and rank which represent the Christ within, your true reality. It follows then that you are created in Christ's image.

We find then that the elements lithium and iron do indeed contain much that is conducive toward a true understanding of the basic principles of life. Even the atomic numbers of these two elements, when added together into a sum, bring into manifestation the number 29 or BI, a prefix which means *life* and also *two*. In other words, the Cabalah seems to imply that two forces are vital to bring life into manifestation—the 2 and the 9. Let us check it out. This is quite easily done because we have just come to the understanding that the *name* plus the *symbol* is the true reality; the serial number is but the image. The Alpha numbers for the *names* "two + nine" are 58 + 42 or the number 100; the numbers for the *symbols* are 2 + 9 or the number 11; and combining the names with the symbols verifies we are on the right track because once again we are face to face with the number 111 or CARA BOGA COTY, the true Trinity, the mental, physical, and spiritual aspects of all life.

The Ore from Which the Elements Are Mined

Now let us direct our thoughts to the source, to the ore from which the elements are mined. It is a well-known fact that the human body has contained practically every known element at one time or another during its evolution on Earth. Therefore, that source is YOU. The following Figure 79 will reinforce these conclusions quite dramatically.

COLUMNS

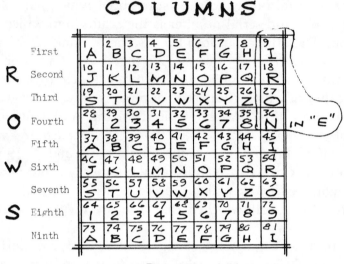

Figure 79
The Magic Square of the Letters and Digits

First, let us point out that Figure 79 is nothing more than a repetition of Figure 1 with the exception that it balances the number of rows with the number of columns making 9 × 9 or 81 squares in all. This magic square then represents YOU, since 81 is the Alpha number of the Fool. Moreover each square, the macrocosmic larger square or the microcosmic smaller square, also may be considered to be a house for either a letter or digit, and it takes 4 rows of 9 squares each to constitute a set. The first set of 36 squares then represents the original archetype, the inner reality as it were, with the remaining 45 squares merely images or serial numbers of this inner reality.

It should also be understood that each set of 36 units (26 letters + 10 digits) represents an individual element of the Periodic Table, and that instead of a rectangular format, they may be placed in circular form around the circumference of a circle if so desired. In the latter case 10 degrees would be allocated for each letter or digit. Always we have the 10, whether it be rectangular or circular, because the 1st, 2nd, 3rd, and 4th rows, when added together, also equal 10. This is called the decade, and it is an extremely important entity in the English Cabalah.

But now let us get back to our original thought on the relative importance of the 2 and the 9 and their relationship with the word *life*. The meaning of the four quadrants of the digit 9 is obvious; Figure 79 plainly shows them to represent the element iron, the "Fe" part or the second half of "Life." Isn't this absolutely fantastic? Here you have the word *iron* spelled out right before your very eyes! And not only that, but it is also philosophically correct being placed just exactly where it should be placed.

The four quadrants of the digit 2 tell us an equally impressive story. If our theory holds true, the 2 then must represent the element lithium, the pupil-iris of the All-Seeing Eye. But isn't this pupil-iris dual? It most certainly is because it is composed of the aperture and the diaphragm, the inner hole and the outer structure, emptiness and that which contains it. This, according to the Cabalah, is brought into manifestation by the B, K, T, and 2. It is, in other words, the "Bucket 2," or the "2" which is a bucket. And a bucket, inasmuch as it is a vessel with a *flat* bottom used for collecting, carrying, or holding something, is a perfect description of the pupil-iris, the "black hole" and the 2 that brings it into manifestation, the receptacle for all of the particles of light that lie in its path as it sweeps through space. But it is *not* a bottomless pit and it *does* have a bottom. The key word is *flat*. Its Alpha number is 39 which is the same as *ten*. The number 10 then may be said to represent the bottom of the black hole or bucket of the pupil-iris combination. And this, according to the Cabalah, is the element lithium, the first half of "Life."

The next thing for the reader to notice is that each little square in the diagram of Figure 79 has a number attached to it. These numbers may be called the serial numbers of the squares and they too are important. The serial number of the first four squares of the digit 2 is 62 which stands for the Page, the letter P (2 + 11 + 20 + 29 = 62 = The Page). And the serial number of the first four squares of the digit 9 is 90 which stands for the Magician, the letter I (9 + 18 + 27 + 36 = 90 = The Magician). But the interesting thing about all of this is that together they give us PI, the ratio of the circumference of a circle to its diameter; and not only that, but the sum total of them both is $62 + 90 = 152$, the Alpha number of "The All-Seeing Eye." It is an amazing world, isn't it!

Even the Alpha number for the word *bucket* is itself equal to 62, the same as the sum of its constituent parts. And many, many other interesting things can be observed from a study of the serial numbers contained within our magic square. For instance: the sum total of all the numbers in our square from 1 to 81 is 3,321 or 33-21. This represents "The U" and it is indeed just that because 81 is the Alpha number for "The Fool" (Tarot Key 0) whose letter/symbol is U. And if you were to read the number 3,321 backwards you would find that it reads ABC's (the plural of C); in other words, these are the simple ABC's of life.

The term CARA BOGA COTY is most magnificently presented. These are the three 1's or the three A's, as we have said earlier. The serial number of the first A (Cara) is 1; the serial number of the second A (Boga) is 37; and the serial number of the last A (Coty) is 73. But the sum total of all three of these A's is again 111 ($1 + 37 + 73 = 111$). Boga, the second A, is quite appropriately numbered inasmuch as it represents the CG or center of gravity between the first and the last; and not only that, it is the Alpha number of *Agasha*, that great Master of Wisdom whose philosophy was covered in our two previous works. The number for the third A or Coty is 73, the reverse of 37, and its symbol is the letter H because it is the Alpha number for *Hermit* (Tarot Key 9). This card is the symbol of the Teacher, the one who stands at the top of the mountain with his lantern in his hand, and who beckons to all who are below to come unto him. It, too, is rather appropriately numbered.

The Sirius Connection

Is the All-Seeing Eye connected with the star Sirius? It would seem from the evidence that it most certainly is. Many, many authors and philosophers have been intrigued with this star and its importance to mankind. It even became the dominant theme of Robert Anton Wilson's most informative treatise, *Cosmic Trigger: The Final Secret of the Illuminati*.[2] In it,

Wilson informs us that (1) the whole ancient Egyptian calendar revolved around the movements of Sirius—the year began with the "dog days" when Sirius started to rise behind the sun (July 23 in our calendar), (2) ancient records indicate that the familiar image of Isis, with a star above her and one of her feet in water and the other on land, is a symbol of the Sirius connection, (3) the Sirius system is the "third eye" of the cosmic entity of which our sun is the heart, (4) the Dogon tribe in Africa, a tribe barely advanced beyond the Stone Age, know that Sirius has an invisible companion (the white dwarf, Sirius B); yet Sirius B's existence was not suspected by our astronomers until the present century, and it was only photographed successfully in 1970, (5) that this same tribe not only knows the exact period of Sirius B, which is 50 years, but it also is aware that it is one of the heaviest stars in the galaxy, and (6) the Bozo tribe, which is one of the neighbors of the Dogon, likewise know about the Companion of Sirius and call it *tono nalema* (Eye Star).

"How could such primitive tribes come unto this information?" you ask. Well this is the crux of the entire Sirius mystery. According to the two French anthropologists who collected the Dogon legends about the star—Professors Griaule and Dieterlen[3]—the tribesmen *say* they know about these things because a visitor from Sirius, several thousand years ago, told them about it. But was this manifestation psychic or physical? And where did all of the other informants who seem to have knowledge about Sirius come unto their information? Only time will answer these questions.

Now let us see if we can shed some light on the mystery from a cabalistic approach. The dictionary tells us that Sirius is a star of the constellation Canis Major and that it is the brightest star in the heavens. The Latin name for the constellation means literally "greater dog"; consequently, its brightest star has been known for generations as the *Dog Star Sirius.* The Alpha number for "Dog Star" is 26 + 58 or 84, and the Alpha number for "Sirius" is 95; but when we place the two numbers side by side we have 84 + 95, and this transliterates into "H (each) DIE." But let us not stop here. If we were to consider *"The* Dog Star Sirius," we would have to put 33 (the Alpha number for *the*) in front of the equation, and we would find that he "sees each die" (33 = CC = C's = Sees).

Now perhaps we are getting somewhere. If the Dog Star Sirius bears any relationship to the All-Seeing Eye, it would be only natural that He would see every living thing go through the process of death many times. But who is "He" anyway? We find that he is only a *babe*, since the Alpha number for the complete term "The Dog Star Sirius" is 212 which in turn adds up to 5 (33 + 26 + 58 + 95 = 212 = BAB = E = BABE). Is "He" then a manifestation of the Christ child, the *babe* who is born in a manger, an open trough in an animal's stable? Again, only time will answer this question.

Now let us attack the problem a little differently. Let us refer once again to Figure 78 and see if there are any clues hidden therein. You say there are none? Well look again, and observe the words a little more carefully. Be a detective and see if you can ascertain anything unusual. Lo! What have we here? If you will read the term "PUPIL-IRIS" backwards from the right to the left you should have a revelation. It says, "SIRI-LIP UP." Now compare this with the word "SIRI-US." In other words, the Cabalah is telling us that the *pupil-iris* combination of the All-Seeing Eye is the Dog Star Sirius, and that we (you and I or "us") are his upper lip!

Well, perhaps it doesn't mean this literally, but the Alpha number for "upper lip" certainly deserves further investigation. Let us check it out. We find that it is 76 + 37 = 113 = AM. In other words, you and I (us) are the "am" of "I am." We are then the pupil, the disciple, and the "I" is the iris, the Master, the Teacher. And if we compute the number for "*His* upper lip," we find that it is 149, the name, rank, and serial number of the element iron, the base metal that has to be transmuted into spiritual gold.

Thus we are brought to the inescapable conclusion that the word *Sirius* is intended to be broken out into two parts: Sir I + us. The "Sir I" is the Knight, the iris, the "I" part of "I am"; and the "us" is the disciple, the pupil, the "am" part of "I am." Together we make up the Holy Trinity: "Sir I" the Father, "U" the Son, and "S" the Holy Spirit. Even the Alpha numbers tell us that this is so. For example: the Alpha number for "Son" is 48, the same as the number for "Fool," the letter U who is *you.* And the Alpha number for "Spirit" is 91, also the number of "The Star," the letter S. Therefore, you and the star make up the entity known as "us," the "am" part of "I am."

According to the Cabalah then, the Dog Star Sirius should be comparable to the element lithium, the 3rd element of the Periodic Table, the "Li" part of "Life." Let us check it out. We have already found that the Alpha number for Sirius is 95, so the first thing to do in an analysis such as this is to see if there is any correlation with the name, rank, and serial numbers of the element we are trying to compare it with. So then let us refer back to the table giving these numbers for the element lithium on page 424.

At first glance there is an excellent correlation because we find that the sum of lithium's name and atomic number is identical to the Alpha number of Sirius ($92 + 3 = 95$ = Sirius). But where do we find any clue that it represents the Dog Star? The only two other numbers remaining are its symbol and atomic weight, and these are 21 and 7 respectively. We see that they represent U (The Fool) and G (Justice); or perhaps we might say that it is a BAG, but we still do not seem to have the correlation we are looking for. But wait a minute. Is there something that we have missed? Aha! I ask you, does the name "Fido" mean anything to you? The dictionary defines this term as a familiar name for a *dog* and we seem to have hit the jackpot. The atomic weight of lithium is listed as 6.940 which gives us the key word we were looking for—FIDO. But how do we know that our dog Fido is a star? Well, if we total the numbers we find that $6 + 9 + 4 + 0 = 19$ = S, the letter/symbol of the Star (Tarot Key 17). Once again, the Cabalah doesn't let us down.

In case the reader looks up the atomic weight of the element lithium and finds it slightly different than the number we have listed here, let me point out the following facts: It seems that the accepted weight of any element depends upon whether oxygen is used as a base or carbon is used as a base. Lately, I believe, carbon has come to be the accepted yardstick, but there is still a discrepancy. However, the two conflicting values average out at 6.940. For instance: *Webster's New Collegiate Dictionary* (publication date 1977) lists the atomic weight of lithium to be 6.941 with C = 12; but *The Encyclopedia of the Chemical Elements* (publication date 1968) lists the atomic weight of lithium to be 6.939 with C = 12. But FIDO wins in the end result since the average of 6.941 and 6.939 is 6.940. And if we go back to the original base of O = 16, we find that they all agree that lithium is indeed 6.940 (*Webster's Seventh New Collegiate Dictionary,* published 1965). Our dog Fido is most persistent that his name shall not be changed!

What about the symbol then? Where does that come in? We find that the name, number, and weight of lithium corresponds to Sirius, the star whose name is Fido; but where does the other remaining aspect enter the picture? Well, dear reader, the symbol "Li" adds up to 21 and this is the number of the Fool who is *you.* Indeed, the letters L and I when moved so close together that they touch actually *do* become a "U." You then, the reader of this book, are the one who completes the picture. And this is mankind itself, taken as a whole, or at least that portion of the race of Man that resides on the planet Earth. This is born out from the fact that lithium's name and number equal 95, the Alpha number for "Empress," the letter Z; and its symbol and weight (21 + 7) equal 28, the Alpha number for "Man," the letter N. And when we combine the Z and the N we have Zen, or the Great Pyramid of the Emperor. How do we know that it is the Emperor's pyramid? We know it to be so because the total serial number or key number of the element lithium is 123, the number of the Emperor, the letter A that stands on top of the Z + N.

NOTES

1. Clifford A. Hampel, *The Encyclopedia of the Chemical Elements* (New York, Reinhold Book Corporation, 1968)

2. Robert Anton Wilson, *Cosmic Trigger: The Final Secret of the Illuminati* (New York, Pocket Books, Simon and Schuster Division, 1977)

3. Robert K. G. Temple, *The Sirius Mystery* (London SE5, Futura Publications Limited, 110 Warner Road, Camberwell, 1976)

Chapter 22

THE BEAST WHOSE NUMBER IS 666

"HERE IS WISDOM. Let him that hath understanding count the number of the beast; for it is the number of a man; and his number *is* Six hundred threescore *and* six." With these words (Revelation 13:18), St. John concludes one of the most mystifying chapters in the entire Bible. Down through the centuries men have tried to decipher its meaning, and their efforts have gone for naught. But is man to be held in ignorance forever? No, not necessarily, not as long as he has the Cabalah to assist him in his endeavors to ascertain the true meaning of words and number. And this is especially true as it relates to Scripture.

Just as an illustration: St. John had been talking about two beasts that had come into manifestation. The first beast had risen up out of the *sea*, and it had *ten* horns and bore the name of *blasphemy*. This beast represented the powers of darkness and was basically evil. The second beast came up out of the *earth*; it had *two* horns, like a lamb, but spoke as a dragon. It was equally as powerful as the first beast, but this second beast represented the powers of light and was basically good. It also

435

directed mankind to make an *image* of the first beast, and it then gave life unto the image of the beast so that this "image" could speak and cause men to worship it or be killed. The image, of course, was only reflecting the thoughts and actions of the first beast, the evil beast, the one whom it had been modeled after.

Now what is the meaning in all of this? On the surface it just sounds like a bit of mythology from out of the past whose true meaning has long since been lost to mankind. Or has it really been lost? Perhaps it is just waiting in limbo, so to speak, for the right and proper time when men may comprehend it once more. But it seems that that time is now at hand, for they may do so today through and by the means of God's gift to mankind in the 20th century—the English Cabalah.

For instance: the first clue towards an understanding lies in the number of horns allocated to each of the two beasts. The first beast that rose up out of the *sea* had ten, and the second beast that came up out of the *earth* had two. Now isn't this strangely reminiscent of the two pillars of the Temple of Solomon called Jachin and Boaz, and which are generally identified by their symbols of "J" and "B"? Isn't the "J" a ten and the "B" a two? Therefore, these two beasts must somehow be related to the white pillar of Jachin and the black pillar of Boaz.

The second clue lies in the words *sea* and *earth.* The Alpha number for "sea" is 25 and the number for "earth" is 52. One is the reverse of the other, and not only that, but their sum is 77 which stands for Christ. But we have two beasts, and since the Alpha number for one "beast" is 47, their sum gives us the number 94, the ID, or Judgment. This, too, is a symbol for Christ since the letter/symbol for Judgment (Tarot Key 20) is "X." But this "Judgment" is a two-edged sword since the number 94 reduces to 13, the letter M, the symbol for Death. In summary then, the combination of the sea and the earth, along with the two beasts that arose therefrom, represents the death and/or resurrection of Christ.

The third clue lies in the name of the first beast, the one with ten horns that arose out of the sea. His name was *blasphemy,* a most appropriate name inasmuch as the Alpha number for "blasphemy" is 101, the number of "the Logos," "the God-Self," or "the Pillar." It is therefore an act of "blasphemy" that he is so named because this evil beast of darkness arose out of the sea, out of the white pillar of Jachin, the very opposite from the black pillar of Boaz. But this is not as incongruous as it sounds inasmuch as every pillar is both masculine and feminine, positive and negative. The feminine half of the number 101 is the even number 10 on the left; its masculine or positive aspect is the odd number 1 on the right. And together they represent the dual nature of the Godhead.

It is very obvious then that the first beast represents the "D" or the Devil part of the "ID" and that the second beast is the "I" or the Magician. The definition of *id*, you will recall, is the undifferentiated source of the organism's energy from which both *ego* and *libido* are derived. The first beast arose out of the sea, but didn't all life first come from the sea? The word *sea* is synonymous with the letter *cee*, the symbol C, the Moon, Tarot Key 18. And if the reader will refer once more to this Tarot card he will see life evolving out of the sea unto the shore. Indeed, the Agashan philosophy teaches that the sea was the first "world" we had ever known; it is not incongruous then that the left-hand pillar would be this "world," the letter J, Tarot Key 21.

It is also appropriate that the second beast, the I or the Magician, arose from the earth. This beast represents the resurrection of Christ as opposed to the first beast which represents his death, and it is doubly significant insofar as human expression, after going through many lifetimes of earthly living, will eventually ascend from the *earth* into the Christ Consciousness. The ascension of man from this Wheel of Life, the letter B or the Boaz pillar, is then symbolized by the second beast or the return of the Christ. And when he ascends from the *earth* he also ascends from the *devil* because the Alpha number for "earth" and "devil" are both 52.

The reader is now asked to refer back to Figure 75 where these two pillars are depicted holding up and supporting the All-Seeing Eye. The "eye" then becomes the "image" that the second beast (the I) imparted life thereto because the Alpha numbers for both "eye" and "image" are the same. They are each 35. However, the "eye" that is brought into manifestation to the left of the central pillar (we are now referring to Figure 77) is the image of the mortal mind, the "eye" that desires others to worship it; but the "eye" that manifests to the right of the central pillar is the All-Seeing Eye itself, the "eye" that bestows pure love equally unto all and asks nothing for itself in return. The one is the negative and the other is the positive aspect of the number 119 ("mortal mind" and "All-Seeing Eye" are each equal to 119); yet they are both a part of that which we call "life." The number 129 (LI), incidentally, is the Alpha number for all three terms from pillar to pillar—beast, image, and beast (47 + 35 + 47 = 129) or beast, eye, and beast. It is this former aspect of life that St. John is evidently in reference to.

The Alpha numbers for some of the other terms that he uses are equally as informative. For instance: the Alpha number for "The image of the beast," a term St. John repeats three different times in Verse 15, turns out to be 169 or the number PI (33 + 35 + 21 + 33 + 47 = 169 = PI). And what is Pi? Pi is the universal symbol for the circumference of a circle, the completion of a cycle, and what could be more fitting than to call the thing which is produced after going through a full circle of 360 degrees the *image* of the original reality? Indeed, the 15th verse that calls our attention to this fact is the symbol for the circle itself, the letter O.

Another word that is used to represent great power or authority is the word *dragon*. This is a very well-chosen word because the Alpha number for "dragon" is 59, a number which in the Cabalah is used to represent "The God" (33 + 26 = 59 = EI). Raising the number 59 or EI to a still higher vibration we find its God Name number. This is found to be 237 (E + I = The Hierophant + The Magician = 147 + 90 = 237), which means that it *Be* the CG or center of gravity. We are talking about the God, and he most definitely *does* reside at one's CG.

Even the numbers for the book, chapter, and verse are significant, which only go to show the tremendous range and depth of the Infinite Intelligence which was the guiding influence behind this "revelation" of St. John. For example: the Alpha number for "Revelation" is 121 which is read as AU. This is the symbol for the element gold, but it becomes doubly interesting when we add the number of the chapter alongside of it. The number of the chapter is 13, and the book and chapter then bring into manifestation the AUM, the out-going sound that is the Alpha part of the Alpha and the Omega, the beginning and the end, the first and the last. Just think of it! This fantastic chapter from the Book of Revelation promises to shed light on one of the most profound mysteries of creation itself—the AUM.

But this is not all. The last and most significant verse in the chapter is Verse 18. This is the letter R, the symbol for the Tower (Tarot Key 16), and the symbol for a Pillar of Light. Therefore, the Cabalah is informing us that the power behind the AUM, the force that brings it into manifestation, is somehow related to the Beast whose number is 666!

Are you beginning to be impressed? Well if not you should be, because you yourself are about to have a revelation. You will have it when you compare the *God Name* number for the chapter and verse with the *Alpha* number for the book, chapter, and verse. These two numbers, the God name number and the Alpha number, have no relationship on the surface—and this is especially true insofar as they relate to two different things—but inwardly they are most intimately related. The God Name number for the chapter and verse is 152 (13 + 18 = M + R = Death + The Tower = 38 + 114 = 152). The number 152 tells us that O B (The Sun be), but more than that, it is also the Alpha number for "*The* All-Seeing Eye" (33 + 25 + 59 + 35 = 152). Now hold on to your hats for you are in for a surprise. The Alpha number for "Revelation 13:18" is this very same number, 152 (121 + 13 + 18 = 152). Perhaps one stands for "The Mortal Mind" and the other for "The All-Seeing Eye," who knows? But in any event it is most fitting that two aspects of the number 152 are included, because that is exactly what this chapter is all about—the constant struggle between the positive and negative aspects of all life.

Now let us get down to specifics. Who and what is the beast whose number is 666 and why is this particular number so all-important? Where do we begin? In the first place, we note that the number 666 is written out rather unusually and quite poetically; it is called "Six hundred threescore and six." Now if this phrase is in cipher code to conceal a hidden meaning, the first step to solve the mystery would be to compute its Alpha number and then compare it with the number it is supposed to represent: 666. The difference between these two numbers should technically be zero or nothing, and it will be interesting to find out what the difference actually is. Indeed, if there is any validity to our argument, there will be a valuable clue hidden here.

We find that the Alpha number for "Six hundred threescore and six" is 313 (52 + 74 + 116 + 19 + 52 = 313), and subtracting this number from 666 gives us 353, a number that is theoretically supposed to be zero or nothing. But just a minute. 353 = CEC, and if we pronounce it, it sounds like *Cee Cee*, the number 33, the Alpha number for the definite article "The," one of the most common words in the English Cabalah and also one of the most important, inasmuch as it represents the difference between the God Name number and the God Word number for most of the Tarot Trumps. Let us check it out:

	Alpha Number	God Name Number	Sum	
T	20	Temperance	100	120 AT
H	8	The Hermit	106	114 AN
E	5	The Hierophant	147	152 O B
	33	Sum Total	353	386

Again our hunch has paid off and we seem to be getting somewhere in our analysis for we find that the God Name number for "The" is indeed 353, that mysterious number which theoretically should equate to zero or nothing. And even more than that, the Cabalah tells us that the word *The* "be at an O." It is also interesting to note that combining the God Name numbers for the letters T and H gives us 206, the Alpha number for "The Wheel of Fortune," the letter B, the first letter of the word *Be*, the name of the letter B and the symbol for the Wheel of

Fortune or the Wheel of Life. This, then, is the esoteric meaning for the word "The"; its presence implies that that particular Tarot force is brought into manifestation and that it *Be*, that it exists as an entity, and that it can be pointed out. Without the definite article, it is merely an abstraction.

There is still another interesting observation that we can make. The Alpha number for "Six hundred threescore and six" is 313, but this can be read as CM. Now what is "CM"? CM is the Roman numeral expression for the number 900, and the writer was absolutely amazed when he discovered that the difference between 900 and 666 is the very *Beast* himself, inasmuch as it is 234 (234 = BCD = Beast)!

The sum of 900 and 666 is equally as fascinating. The addition of the two terms gives us 1,566 or the word OFF. Does this then imply that by adding two supposedly equal things together, making them into a duality so to speak, somehow takes them "off" of the Wheel of Life, the very opposite of "Be," and places them once again back into the unmanifested state? Or does the word "OFF" merely mean that it is "Of F," that it is *of* the High Priestess? Perhaps they both are true and the combination of the difference and the sum brings into manifestation the "BCD OF F," which is translated into the "Beast of the High Priestess." There is some validity to this because "F" is at the midpoint between the pillars "J" and "B"; and perhaps this "Beast of F" is then the "image" of the beast that St. John was referring to in his vision. There are many things to consider when one gets deeply involved in the interpretation of Scripture.

Let us return once more to Figure 75. The reason I am doing so is that now we have a "beast" to identify with the white pillar "J" in the west. This pillar corresponds with the "I" part of the "ID" and the pillar in the east corresponds with the "D" part. Since the number for BCD is 9 or I, we shall place this "BCD" in the west to act in opposition to the "BEAST" who be in the east. We may place the High Priestess in the middle of the "eye" at midpoint between the two pillars.

Very well. We can now come to some interesting conclusions. If we add the two "beasts" together, we have the numbers 9 + 47 = 56 or EF, the *High Priestess.* She evidently represents the sum total of both. But if we subtract the two "beasts," we end up with the number 38 which is the Alpha number for *Death*, the letter M. The combination of the two then literally gives us the "Death of the High Priestess," and this is exactly what the word "The" represents in its true esoteric sense. (The table on page 440 shows the *sum* number of "The" to be 386, 38 + 6 = M + F.) Moreover, if we add the difference of these two "beasts," the number 38, to the *beast* whose number is 666, we bring GOD into manifestation (666 + 38 (Death) = 704 = GOD). And if we subtract "Death" from 666, we bring 2π into manifestation (666 – 38 = 628 = 2 × 3.14). This, then, offers an interesting geometric clue as to who and what God may be.

But we are not yet through with our analysis. The most startling aspects of this strange chapter from *Revelation* are still to be revealed. A good beginning point at the second phase of our investigation is to tabulate the word "Beast" in the same way as we had done with its predecessor "The." The tabulation follows below:

	Alpha Number		God Name Number	Sum		
B	2	The Wheel of Fortune	206	208	BOH	B OH
E	5	The Hierophant	147	152	OB	
A	1	The Emperor	123	124	AX	A BOX
S	19	The Star	91	110	KO	
T	20	Temperance	100	120	LO	LOOK
	47	"Beast" Total	667	714		
THE	33	"The" Total	353	386		
	80	THE BEAST	1,020	1,100		
	8–0		10-2-0	1-100		
	H O	Each O	J B O	A (N) = J + BOAZ		

A careful analysis of the above tabulation should most certainly prove, beyond a shadow of a doubt, that "the beast"

referred to in the subject chapter is indeed a symbol for the
twin pillars of the Temple of Solomon, Jachin and Boaz. Even
the spelling of the words is most accurate, and the letters are
even placed in their correct order. The only exception is that
the letter N (100 = The Hanged Man = N) will have to be
rotated 90 degrees into its "Z" position to give us the word
Boaz; but even this apparent "flaw" is undoubtedly not a flaw
at all but an operation, I suspect, that was deliberately planned
by the Infinite Intelligence who designed the Cabalah. Later, it
will be pointed out that a right-angle turn (as suggested by the
Knight, or the letter L) is absolutely necessary when one
reaches the end of a certain phase of consciousness or a particular suit of the Tarot. And the statement, "Look! Oh (the letter
O) be a box," is absolutely superb.

Another most interesting fact is that the God Name number
of the word "Beast" is 667—one digit more than the mysterious
number 666. Indeed, if one were to substitute the letter C for
the letter S in the spelling of the word "Beast," its God Name
number would then actually be 666! And this should not affect
the *sound* of his name if we were to pronounce the C softly as
in ACE or BCD. Our "beast" would then become a *cat* (BEAST
= BEACT = BE ACT = BE CAT).

Or is our "beast" a dog? The God Name number for the
word "God," as we have learned earlier, is 259 or BE I. But now
let us read "God" backwards and it becomes "Dog." "Well,
there is nothing so unusual in that," you will say. No, not yet,
but a most unusual situation most certainly *does* arise when we
add the two terms together; that is, when we add the God
Name number for GOD to the Natural number for DOG. Try
it, and you will find that the *dog* is another beast whose
number is 666 (DOG + BE I = 407 + 259 = 666).

And we most certainly cannot forget the *fox*. He is a perfect
candidate in our search for the "beast" whose number is 666.
Just look at Figure 79. There he is, occupying the sixth column
in our magic square of the letters and digits, with the three
letters of his name symbolizing the first, second, and third octaves of the number six, or more simply, the number 666.

So then which beast be the one St. John is referring to? Who be the beast whose number is 666? The answer is amazingly simple, once one has thought the problem through to its conclusion. There is no one particular beast per se to be found. The problem is not to be taken literally, but rather as a lesson in deciphering the hidden meaning contained within the numerical vibrations of words, letters, and symbols. For instance: there are two words, and only two words, in *italics* in the quoted 18th verse of Chapter 13 of Revelation. These are the words "is" and "and." We are also told to count the number of the "beast," but then it places these two key words in italics immediately afterwards when it tells us what this number *is*. In other words, it is implying that the number of the "beast" is reflected in the words "is" and "and." Well, the answer is obvious; the Alpha number for the former is in fact identical to the sum of the two words in italics (47 = 28 + 19).

Another example, and this one is perhaps the most profound of them all: The God Name number of the key word "beast" is 667. This cannot be changed because that is what it is; however, it is the number for only *half* of the equation. The other half of the equation is the number 666. "But how can 667 be equal to 666?" you ask. The answer is that *energy* is being consumed during the process of summing up all of the terms contained within the body of the "beast," with the net result that when it is finally equated to unity—when the many are transformed into the one, so to speak—there is a loss of mass which is released in the form of energy. This amounts to a quantum of energy with the unit value of 1. But the energy is not "lost." It merely returns once more into the "black hole" of the decimal point (.) or the equal sign (=), whichever be the case.

If we were to sum up then the *total* of both the left half and the right half of any equation, this sum would actually be *more* than the sum of its constituent parts. It would be larger because we would also have to add the *energy* values of the decimal points and the equal signs to the *mass* values of the respective terms. In other words, by the very fact of performing a mathematical calculation we are using up some form of energy, and in the ultimate analysis it might very well be that the term (667) does indeed equate to the term (666 =).

But enough into this excursion into theoretical physics. Let us stick to the problem at hand: that is, to determine the numerical sum of both halves of the equation, the complete whole, the sum total of the God Name of the beast *and* its serial number which is 666. But when we go through this operation we are simply astounded, for we find that $667 + 666 = 1,333$ or MCC or, using lowercase letters, "mcc." "What is so outstanding about that?" you ask. It is outstanding because it represents the total energy (E) contained within any physical entity. $E = mc^2$ is Einstein's famous formula for the equivalence of mass and energy, where E = energy, "m" = mass, and "c" = the velocity of light. $E = mc^2$ may also be written as $E = mcc$, and we find then that our "beast" whose number is 666 does in fact represent this famous principle that is, perhaps, the very foundation of the universe itself.

"Well, that is all well and good," I hear you say, "but how do we *know* that the number 1,333 is intended to represent $E = mc^2$? After all, it may be nothing more than a coincidence." The Cabalah anticipated your reaction, and has thus furnished us with rather an astounding verification. Through the genius of its infinite intelligence it has added a corresponding proof that relegates the possibility of "coincidence" almost to zero.

But before we get into this "proof"—I don't know what to call it other than proof, but nothing is ever really *proven* to anyone unless he has the willingness to accept it—let us define what we mean by *mass*. Mass is a number, but more than that, it is a quantity, a collection of a certain number of units, things, or particles. If we say that something has a mass of 10, it doesn't mean anything until we define what the unit is that we have 10 of. It may be protons, atoms, apples, or even earths. In any event, the mass of something means a certain number times 1. We cannot forget the 1 any more than we can leave the 1 out of the factors of a perfect number. (The number 6 is a perfect number because it is both the product and the sum of its factors. $1 + 2 + 3 = 6$ and $1 \times 2 \times 3 = 6$, but where would we be if we forgot the 1?) Therefore, the mass of a number is

(1)m, and the true equation for energy is $E = (1)mc^2$ and not simply mc^2 by itself, although technically you could multiply the term mc^2 by as many ones as you wished and you would not change the answer an iota.

Now for the proof. We may spell out $(1)mc^2$ as "A Em Cee Squared," and when we write it out in this manner, we find that its Alpha number (the sum of its terms) is identical to its product (the product of its terms). In other words, it becomes a perfect number. $1 \times 13 \times 3 \times 3$ equals 117; and $1 + 18 + 13 + 85$ also equals 117. The Cabalah tells us, then, that energy is equal to the number 117. But not only that, it also proves to us that the number 1,333 is intended to represent mcc or mc^2. And the truly amazing part comes about when we compute the total value of the equation $E = mc^2$; that is, when we add the left half of the equation to its right half, or the energy itself to that which is its image. The answer is none other than the beast himself, for $117 + 117 = 234 = BCD = Beast$.

It would seem then that the number 117 is the key. This number is very obviously the product of mc^2, but how can we also prove that it relates to energy in a cabalistic sense? Let us check it out. $117 = AQ = R$. The cabalist will immediately see that this reads "a cure." But it is a cure for what? The answer is found in its Alpha number, and not only that, it also provides us with the proof we were looking for. Since the Alpha number for "cure" is 47, the Alpha number for the complete term "a cure" must be $1 + 47$ or simply 147 if we read the numbers in their natural order. And this, of course, is the Alpha number for "The Hierophant" (Tarot Key 5) whose letter/symbol is E, the symbol for energy.

But the number 117 by itself is the sum of the A and the Q which gives us the Tower or the letter R ($1 + 17 = 18 = R$). This is even emphasized again by combining the God Name numbers for the A and the Q ($123 + 95 = 218 = B R$, and "B R" means that it *be* R). The number 117 then is the Tower, the House of God; but even more than that, it is seen to be the sum of the masculine force and the feminine force, the Emperor and the Queen. The letter R, you will remember, can be broken apart and opened up into the 1 and the 2, the male and the female, the odd and the even. This then only confirms what we had learned earlier.

But the Tower is not the only Tarot force that is made up of these two I's, the masculine "I" and the feminine "I"; indeed, the Hierophant (the letter E) and Judgement (the letter X), just to name a few, act in a similar fashion. For example:

9 = I	God Word	Magician	= 57	I	= 9
9 = I	God Name	The Magician	= 90	I	= 9

18 = R = Tower = 81	The Hierophant	= 147 Judgement = 99
R	E	X

It is interesting to note that this tabulation also seems to be a mirror image of Figure 75 which depicted the twin pillars on either side of the eye. The Tower is the black *Boaz* pillar in the east; Judgement, then, represents the Christ tower in the west or *Jachin*; and the Hierophant, the letter E, is the *Eye* in the middle (the E + Ye), the two "I's" that constitute the one "Eye." It is this awesome combination of forces that then *wrecks* the Tower of Boaz (REX = wrecks), releases the lightning that strikes the tower, and thus brings about the direful consequences depicted on the face of Tarot Key 16. This, then, is the "cure" that we spoke of earlier. And who is cured? Why the *beast*, of course, since the Alpha numbers of each of the three terms, "REX," "cure," and "beast," are one and the same— the number 47. The Alpha number for "double I," incidentally, is 68, the same as the number for Pillar, Logos, and God-Self. And five of these "68's" is the number 340 or "One O," the number 10 (34 = One).

For those of you who still have doubts that this particular chapter and verse of *Revelation* is written in cipher code, especially in that of the Alpha and God Name numbers of the Cabalah, we have some additional evidence that is rather startling in its nature and should alleviate these doubts altogether. For instance, the statement is made: "Let *him* that hath understanding count the *number* of the beast; for it is the number *of a man;* and *his* number is Six hundred threescore and six." The *italics* in this case are ours. What is the number? It is 666, but more than just that, it is also the number *of a man.* These three words then, "of a man," should directly relate to the number 666 if our theory is to hold water. Let us check it out:

Alpha Number		God Name Number		Sum		
O	15	The Sun	87	102	JB	J B
F	6	The High Priestess	195	201	TA	A TAX
A	1	The Emperor	123	124	AX	
M	13	Death	38	51	EA	EA.
A	1	The Emperor	123	124	LD	LAND
N	14	The Hanged Man	100	114	AN	
	50	"Of a Man" Total	666	716		
	EO	(F AGO E)		GAF		

And it most certainly does, for the number 666 is indeed the God Name number of those three all-important words "Of a Man." Man, then, is thus seen to be *each land,* the Emperor of which is A (A of). And the World, the 10 or the letter J, becomes a *tax* or a heavy demand on *man* or the inhabitants of *each land.* Or, it could be interpreted that the *Knight* who represents the twin pillars makes war upon and *attacks* (A Tax) each land. This way or that way, the Cabalah is open to various degrees of interpretation.

But we are not through yet. One notes that the Alpha number for "Of a Man" is 50, which is read as EO. Let us now go through the same process with the Alpha number sum:

Alpha Number		God Name Number		Sum		
E	5	The Hierophant	147	152	OB	B JOB
O	15	The Sun	87	102	JB	
	20	"EO" Total	234	254	BED	
	BO	(Beast be O)	BCD			B JOBBED

Thus we find that not only is "Of a Man" the number 666, but a second integration reveals the fact that it is also none other than the beast himself (BCD = Beast). Moreover, the beast turns out to be zero, O, or nothing; and not only that, the Cabalah tells us that being an "O" is just a job, one that is sometimes "jobbed out" for hire to some other company (Company = 87 = The Sun = O).

Another proof: The statement is made, "Let *him* that have understanding count the number of the beast." Who is this "him" that understands? Let us check this word out in the same manner of the others.

Alpha Number		God Name Number		Sum				
H	8	The Hermit	106	114	AN	AN I		R
I	9	The Magician	90	99	II	I EA.		X
M	13	Death	38	51	EA			EA
	30			234	264			
	CO	(Company)		BCD	Z D	(Beast's "D")		

This "him" turns out to be either the same beast or another beast. But are not there two beasts mentioned in this amazing chapter from the Book of Revelation? Perhaps the "beast that hath understanding" is the beast with two horns instead of ten. This beast was likened unto a lamb, the symbol for Christ, and it appears that we are on the right track because the Cabalah transforms "him" into each Tower of Judgement (EA. R X), and the letter X, of course, is also a symbol for Christ. The Alpha number for "him" is 30 which is read as CO, the abbreviation for "Company"; and here again we have a second verification of the relationship between the beasts.

Still another proof: The statement could have just as easily been said, "For it is the number 666, a man," instead of the way it was actually written: "For it is the number *of* a man." In other words, the word "of" can be shown to equate to the number 666 all by itself. "How do you do that?" you ask. The answer is very simple, and the writer could hardly believe his eyes when he discovered it. The trick is to find the Alpha number for the phrase "Six Six Six," and once this is accomplished, the word "of" magically comes into view (52 + 52 + 52 = 156 = OF = 666). There seems to be no end to the mysteries contained within this fantastic chapter.

The question now arises that if writing out the number 666 in the English prose and words suggested by the Book of Revelation has a hidden meaning behind it, perhaps the other ways of expressing it that are in common use today are equally as meaningful: namely, in ordinary Arabic numerals, in Roman numerals, or even in the binary code of the computer. All five of these methods are tabulated below:

Type of Expression	Alpha Number		
English Prose	SIX HUNDRED THREESCORE AND SIX	313	C M
English Words	SIX SIX SIX	156	O F
Arabic Numerals	6 6 6	18	R
Roman Numerals	DCLXVI	74	K
Binary Code	10100 11010	80	H O
Alpha Sum	Six for One	641	
	BE	7	25
	6 6 6	18	
Alpha Sum + BE		666	

What have we here? Again the Cabalah has not let us down, for we can see that the Alpha number sum for all five of these modes of expression is exceedingly meaningful. It tells us that the simple substitution of the numeral 6 for the numeral 1 will result in the beast whose number is 666! But to arrive at this number, what is the number that we must start with? You guessed it. It is the number 111, the Alpha number of CARA BOGA COTY.

The amazing thing about all of this is that there are two summation processes involved, each one distinctly different from the other in philosophical meaning, and yet the total sum in each case is identical—the number 666. On the one hand, the Cabalah states that a simple substitution of the 6 for the 1 will *be* 666 (which it is in line 8); and on the other hand, the *actual* numerical sum of all six or seven terms, depending upon how you look at it, actually *is* 666 (line 9). It looks as if this beastly number remains constant in or out of being, on the Wheel of Life or off the Wheel of Life, with the letter Be or without the letter Be.

The Alpha number for 666 in binary code is perhaps the most interesting of the five because it is the number 80, the number of "The Beast" himself $(33 + 47 = 80)$. It (the binary code number) is then the true beast whose number is 666. The number 10100 11010 is computed as follows: $666 = 1 \times 2^9 + 0 \times 2^8 + 1 \times 2^7 + 0 \times 2^6 + 0 \times 2^5 + 1 \times 2^4 + 1 \times 2^3 + 0 \times 2^2 + 1 \times 2^1 + 0 \times 2^0 = 512 + 128 + 16 + 8 + 2 = 666$. Its Alpha number is then found by substituting the letter A for every 1 and the letter O for every 0 (zero), the net result of which is 80 $(5 \times 1 + 5 \times 15 = 80)$. But this number is also read as H (each) 0; and not only that, but the word "ho" is likewise an exclamation of surprise, delight, or exultation. Why is it used in this manner? The answer is simply because $H + O = 23$ or the letter W. We could then say that HO = W = HOW, and that W = HO = WHO. This then is the reason that "each O" brings forth an exclamation of surprise and delight since it explains not only *who* the beast is but also *how* he is able to manifest.

The number 666 in Roman numeral form is DCLXVI. If we put these six letters in a circle and then read it clockwise starting with the "I," we read "Id selects V." Now why does the Id select the symbol V? Or is it that the Id selects the VI which is six? The Alpha number for the six letters is 74 which represents "The King," the letter K.

All well and good. But now let us read the message that all six of the 666's have to tell us; that is, let us start at the upper right-hand corner of the tabulation and read the column of letters downwards and then upwards again in the form of a "U." The message says, "CORK H (each) BE OF M (death)." In other words, each 666 is a cork, and not only that, but it is a cork of death. One can see that we still have further to go in our attempt to decipher the true meaning of the glyph, but at least we have made a start. It is interesting to note that the Alpha number for "cork" is the same as that of "beast." They are both 47 and their total represents the Id (47 + 47 = 94 = ID).

What shall we do now? The next step is obviously to read what the individual types of expression have to say, for if there is any one rule for the Cabalah, it is to treat the counterpart or the image in the same way that you have treated the original. If you have translated something in a clockwise manner, then read it backwards in an anticlockwise direction; if you work with the right-hand side of a glyph or an equation, then do the same thing with its left-hand side. Balance is always the keynote of the day, but even though I knew these truths, I was absolutely astounded when I found that the left-hand column of the initial letters of the various modes of expression told a message equally as profound as the right-hand column.

There are many ways to interpret it, but the central column of capital letters is most explicit as to whom and what it is referring to. The letters PW are an abbreviation for prisoner of war, and this alone should be enough to inform us of the subject matter of the message, but when the Infinite Intelligence behind the Cabalah places the word "of" above the P, and then follows it with WAR B, there is absolutely no question but that it is stating that it "be a prisoner of war." We then WEEP when we find this out (Words English English Prose), and we search diligently for the prisoner as we SCAN the N or the Hanged Man which represents our soul (Sum Code Alpha Numerals). Yes indeed, there are many interpretations for the beast whose number is 666, and this is especially true of the five modes of expression that bring not only him but also everything else into manifestation.

Our glyph or tabulation is now fairly demanding further expansion and elucidation by putting the number 666 itself in each of these five modes. We can do so very easily by simply computing the sum of the Alpha numbers and then reading what it says. Let us begin by placing it only in the first three: English prose, English words, and Arabic numerals. There is a method in this limited approach as the reader will find out a little later.

		Mode Alpha Number			Sum
666	IN	English Prose	147	NG	836
666	23	English Words	153	OC	842
666	23	Arabic Numerals	137	MG	826
1,998	69	Sum of 3 Terms	437		2,504
SIH	FI	(If His D See G)	DCG		YOD

The answer is truly remarkable because we find that it represents Yod, the 10th letter of the Hebrew alphabet, and the first word of the Sacred Name, YOD HE VAV HE. And not only that, but the Alpha numbers for English Prose, English Words, and Arabic Numerals tell us in their respective order, "Negative O See Image" (NG O C MG). However, this "negative O" cannot always see his image. He can only do so *if his D is able to see his G.* This statement is found by reading the left-hand numbers backward and the right-hand number which represents the sum in its normal manner. There is a tremendous philosophical impact to this observation because in the word GOD, the last letter D cannot see the first letter G *unless* the "O" is empty or transparent. Therefore, it would follow that the negative "O" is more than likely hollow or empty as opposed to the positive "O" which apparently is solid or full. Is the zero then the negative "O" and the letter O the positive one? Or is there an *actual* negative zero or an anti-zero in much the same manner that there is anti-matter as opposed to physical matter? The answer cannot be resolved at this stage of our understanding, but the problem most certainly should give us food for thought.

Now let us proceed with our analysis by placing the number 666 in the remaining two categories or modes of expression. We will carry over our previous sum as the first term of the next series of three.

		Mode Alpha Number			Sum	
1,998	69	Sum of 3 Terms	437	DCG	2,504	YOD
666	IN	Roman Numerals	164	PD	853	HE C
666	23	Binary Code	96	IF	785	G HE
3,330	115	Sum of 5 Terms	697	= 22	4,142	
C's CO	KE	(Cee's COKE)	FIG	= V	DAD B	

It is now quite evident why we chose to analyze the number 666 in the first three modes of expression combined into a separate tabulation different from the remaining two: Roman Numerals and Binary Code. These two modes bring into manifestation the final three aspects of the Sacred Name, YOD HE VAV HE, and not only that, but they also clarify the true relationship of the Vav (the letter V) with the remaining three parts. The Vav, evidently, is directly associated with the CG or center of gravity of the system and it represents the fourth aspect of BEING. This, then, is the reason that the Id selects the V, for this symbol can play the role of the 5 (Roman numeral), the 6 (Tarot key number), or the 22 (English letter). The combined total is then 33 or CC (cubic centimeter).

Figure 80 compares the entire system to a bottle of COKE because the statement is made that "Dad be C's (33) Coke figure." What is a figure? One of its definitions is that it is the bodily shape or form of something. And what is more familiar, world-wide, than a bottle of Coke? Therefore Dad, the Father, must be comparable to the bottle. But the sum total of the five 666's is dual. In one sense they have been shown equal to the *cork*, and in another sense they are shown to be C's Coke, or that which is *in* the bottle. And since the Alpha number of "Coke" is 34 which equates to "One," we could say that Bottle + Cork + 1 = 122 = A "V," and we are right back to where we started.

Before we conclude this little essay on the number 666—a most fantastic number, and it makes no real difference whether we call it the number of the beast, a man, or whatever—there is one more extremely important point that should be brought

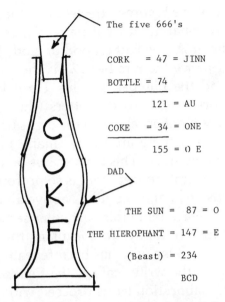

The five 666's

CORK   = 47 = J INN

BOTTLE = 74

        121 = AU

COKE   = 34 = ONE

        155 = O E

DAD

THE SUN =   87 = 0

THE HIEROPHANT = 147 = E

(Beast) = 234

        BCD

Figure 80: The Beast as a Bottle of Coke

out at this time. That point is the relationship that this number bears with the sum total of all 26 letters and 10 digits of the English language. If the reader will refer back to Figure 79 he will see what we mean. The sum total of all of the numbers from 1 to 36—which includes all of the letters from A to Z and the digits from 0 to 9—is none other than our friend whose number is 666. Think of it! He embraces every single symbol used in the English language. A most impressive thought, indeed.

But not only that, the difference between the sum of the first set of symbols (the first four rows of the magic square) and the total value for the complete square, which is 3,321, is also significant. It is the number 2,655 which transliterates into the letter ZEE (3,321 - 666 = 2,655 = ZEE). Thus our magic square is broken up into two distinct parts—the number 666 which represents a complete set of the letters and digits, the original archetype let us say, and the number 2,655 or the letter ZEE which represents all of the vacant spaces available for *images* of the original symbols. It is these empty spaces that then constitute the body of the Empress, the letter Z, the Motherhood of God; and the original archetypal pattern must be that of the Emperor, the letter A, the Fatherhood of God. This could very well be the case since the number 123 is the Alpha number of the Emperor and the number 4 is his Tarot key. His Alpha number then corresponds to the letters (the first three rows) and his Tarot key number relates to the digits (the fourth row).

We find then that there are many, many meanings to this almost incredible number. This is true. But on the other hand, is there any one overall concept that is so profound in its meaning that it stands head and shoulders above all of the others? I don't think so, at least not in this particular sense, but there *is* a concept that most certainly *does* explain the real workings behind the law. The One who has been revealing this information, bit by bit, to the writer calls it *the final solution*, and so without further elaboration let us proceed with the removal of this one remaining veil.

The Final Solution

The reader is requested to now refer once more to our glyph of the great All-Seeing Eye of God, Figure 70. We will be referring to this diagram from time to time because there is so much information concealed therein that it is impossible to adequately cover it in a single discussion. Well, do you see anything unusual in this second look that you didn't notice before? If you haven't noticed it by now, I will call it to your attention. Our friend, the beast whose number is 666, is none other than the radius of the inner circle, the radius of the pupil of the eye! Of course, the number is actually infinite, but his signature is certainly there inasmuch as it occupies the first three digits of this enormously important number: 38.5 ($\sqrt{3}$).

Now look again. Do you see any other familiar numbers? I mean numbers that are different from the obvious, such as the outer radius of the iris which represents Christ. What about the number 38.5? Have we covered this number before in our book? We certainly have for that is the number of *Vesica Piscis*: The Merging of the Worlds (Figure 25). There, the

reader was shown how the spiritual world of Death (38) gradually merged with the material world of the Devil (85), ultimately bringing into manifestation the Emperor (123) when the
conjunction was complete.

There are still other interesting numbers but let these three
suffice for the moment: *Vesica Piscis* (38.5), the Beast whose
number is 666 (66.684), and Christ (77). Together, they form
respectively the short side, the long side, and the hypotenuse of
a right triangle. This triangle is commonly known as the 1, $\sqrt{3}$,
2 right triangle because each of the sides ultimately reduces to
one of these three basic numbers. This famous triangle is
further expounded in the following Figure 81:

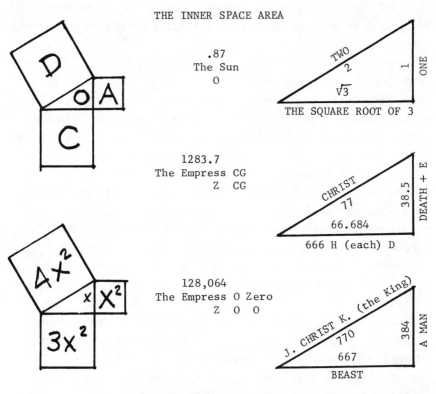

Figure 81
The Death of Christ

There are actually so many interesting things about Figure 81 that I really don't know where to begin. We have called it the death of Christ for a very special reason, but basically, it is that it illustrates one of the most universal principles of all life: namely, the birth, life, death, and ultimate resurrection of Man (or of all species of life, for that matter). This is a fundamental principle of the universe and it is applicable to all that is— atom, cell, man, planet, or star. There is not one single thing that escapes this universal law.

But the first thing that one sees is that the law is mathematical. "Everything obeys the laws of mathematics," the Master Teacher Agasha has said on numerous occasions, "for in the final analysis, everything *is* number." If there were one single phrase that could best describe the Agashan philosophy, this is it. "But," Agasha goes on to explain, "all cycles eventually close, and when they do, we have what is known as the *Grand Finale.*"

Now what does he mean by that? The dictionary defines the term *grand finale* as being the concluding portion of a drama or performance, usually spectacular, and that which involves most or all of the prior actors or participants. But isn't this very similar to the definition of the word *coda*? This word is defined as (1) a more or less independent passage, at the end of a musical composition, introduced to bring it to a satisfactory close, (2) the concluding section of a ballet, especially the final part of a *pas de deux*, and (3) a concluding section or part of a literary or dramatic work, especially one of a conventional form and serving as a summation of preceding themes and motifs. They are one and the same, and it is with great interest then that we find that Figure 81 brings into manifestation this very word— CODA!

The 1, $\sqrt{3}$, 2 right triangle thus becomes the mathematical expression of that which Agasha says is the Grand Finale of our present cycle or age. This is where we are at the present time; this is where the action is; but what is even more significant is that it also spells out the word COCODA when we repeat the beginning once again after the ending (CODA + CO = COCODA). Cocoda is also the name of a great Spiritual Center that exists high in the mountains of the land of Tibet, the original "Shangri-La" so to speak, and we read about it in our work, *Agasha: Master of Wisdom*. It is likewise significant that the Alpha number of the word "Cocoda" is 41 which transliterates itself into DA, the final syllable of the word. Thus the complete word is repeated again in its final syllable or "grand finale." And if we subtract the D from the A, subtract the Devil from the Emperor as it were, we have the reverse of *Vesica Piscis* which results in Death; but if we add the two terms together we have either the E (The Hierophant), or the letters TH (D + A = 85 + 123 = 208 = TH). And what is even more significant is that these two terms when combined together into a single word give us the word THE, the definite article that begins almost every God Name.

Interesting, you say? Well if you think that is interesting, wait until you see the rest. We have hardly even begun in deciphering that which the writer believes to be the greatest revelation of all time. Let us continue. We shall now prove that the sum of the lengths of the sides of our triangle is identical to the sum of its squares. The Alpha number for "One" is 34; the Alpha number for "The Square Root of 3" is 206 or the Wheel of Fortune (33 + 81 + 68 + 21 + 3 = 206 = B); and the Alpha number for "Two" is 58. Summing them all together then, we have the number 298 (34 + 206 + 58 = 298). It transliterates into B I H (each), which means that "I be each," and he most certainly is because the sum of the squares is this very same number! A = The Emperor = 123; C = The Moon = 90; and D = The Devil = 85; and the sum total of all three of them is 298 (123 + 90 + 85 = 298). The "I" within is then telling us that he not only be each side of the triangle, but that he also is the square of each side.

But this is not all. If we spelled out the numeral 3 as *Three*, we would then substitute the number 56 for the number 3 in the above analysis, with the result that the Alpha number for "The

Square Root of Three" is none other than the God Name number for the word GOD. It is 259 and it states that it BE I (87 + 87 + 85 = 259 = G + O + D). The basic home base for God then could very well be the $\sqrt{3}$, and the new total for the length of the sides would then be 351 (34 + 259 + 58 = 351). But this is really no different from the previous sum with the exception that it has gone through an additional turn of the wheel (351 − 298 = 53 = Wheel = B). And even more significant than just that, the number 351 now represents the sum total of every letter from A to Z or all 26 letters of the English alphabet. But is this so surprising? It is not. In fact it would be surprising if it were not so because the number 26 represents not the God-Name number, but the *Alpha* number for GOD. This way or that way, God seems to truly be all that is.

Now let us move on to the second triangle which substitutes the *Vesica Piscis* number 38.5 for the basic unity of the short side of the triangle. And since we will only be dealing with three-digit numbers in this analysis, let us simply use the first three digits of the long side and just call it 666. The hypotenuse is then 77, or if you prefer, the number 77.0 with a zero attached to it to make it conform with the others. Very well. What have we here? What is the next step in our analysis? The next step is either to *read* what we already have or combine two of the terms together and then read the result. The first approach doesn't look too interesting, on the surface, so then let us try the second approach. It is obviously to add "Death" to either Christ or the Beast 666; in other words, shall we put the Christ to death or shall we put the beast to death? When this decision arose 2,000 years ago they chose to put the Christ to death, so we probably should go the other direction now. That decision ended in disaster, as we already know. It is even proven out cabalistically because when we add 77 to 38 we end up with the number 115 or the letters AO. This may be interpreted to mean 10 (A + 0 = 10), but its real interpretation is the combination of the Emperor and his Sun which brings the number 210 into manifestation (A + O = 123 + 87 = 210). This is an extremely important number in the Cabalah and we will deal with it at a later date. It has a multitude of ramifications and a full analysis will require a complete chapter in itself. Needless to say, we will not go that route now.

So then the other alternative is to put the beast to death, and what is the result? The answer is that we bring GOD into manifestation as 666 + 38 = 704 = GOD! Wow! But this is not the complete story. We still have to take into account the remaining decimal part of the short side, the .5 or the E (the energy part), as well as the hypotenuse which represents Christ. Let us add these two forces together and see what occurs. The answer is equally as dumbfounding as the first, inasmuch as we now find that we have brought the EGG into manifestation (.5 + 77.0 = 77.5 = GGE or EGG if we read it backwards). Or we might simply say that .5 + 77 = E + GG = EGG. Thus, when we make these simple additions, the perimeter of our triangle becomes the GOD EGG. And what is contained within this "God egg"? The answer is the Empress, the letter Z, which represents the Motherhood of God. Here, in this extremely important glyph, the Mother herself is contained within her own egg!

But we are not through yet. The question now arises as to whose God egg is it that contains the Empress or the Motherhood of God within it. To whom does the egg belong? The answer to this puzzling question is not as difficult to find as one might suspect. It is found by just computing the numerical sum of the perimeter of our triangle. The addition of the complete short side with the long side is the number 105.1 which is read as the World A or the World Emperor (38.5 + 66.6 = 105.1 = The World (105) + A (The Emperor). And if we add the hypotenuse to it, we would read the term as "Christ, the Emperor of the World."

But again we are not completely satisfied. The question can still be asked as to *whose* world is it that He is the emperor. Again the answer is relatively easy in coming. We simply find the one total sum that represents the perimeter or shell of the egg. It is the number 182.10 (105.1 + 77.0 = 182.10), and it is read as 18-21-0 or R U O. "What does 'RUO' mean?" you ask.

If you ask this question, you are not very adept at the Cabalah yet because one of its basic rules is to always read things backwards if they are not understandable in the normal manner. The answer is, of course, that it is OUR world that Christ is the emperor of. And not only that, but if we integrate the word "OUR" still further and find its Alpha number, we find that it is 54 which means "Sun," the God Word whose letter/symbol is O. Therefore, the Christ who is emperor of *our* world is none other than *our* own sun. The number 54 is also the Alpha number for *Kraio*, the name now used by the great Master whose last physical incarnation was as Jesus of Nazareth in Palestine.

But what is still wrong here? The answer is that this entire glyph represents a God egg, and an egg must be *hatched* so that that which is contained within it may arise and ascend into a higher consciousness. A chick is within the egg, and that "chick" is the Empress, the number 128 which also can be read as 1-28 or A MAN (28 = Man = N). Therefore, a man is in the egg and that man is YOU. The Alpha number for "chick," incidentally, is 34 which means *one*. *You* are the one then, because the Alpha number for "the one" is 67 which means "Hanged Man" or "Soul." And this is *your* soul that we are talking about. It is *your* soul egg. All you have to do is to break the shell of the egg that holds you in darkness and arise into the light. "It is just as simple as that," the one whom I know as "the One" is now telling me. You are your own Avatar and the knowledge of this truth will set you free. And the "shell" that surrounds you and holds you in prison is made up of your own individual "hells" that you have created through many lifetimes of earthly transgressions. But the time is now at hand, now that we are at the Coda, or the Grand Finale as Agasha puts it, for us to break through and out of these earthly hells and be about our Father's business.

Now let us move on down to the third triangle in Figure 81 with the sides of lengths 384, 667, and 770 respectively. This is essentially the same triangle as the second triangle with the exception that each side has been multiplied by a factor of 10, and the long side or base number of the beast has been rounded *up* a single digit whereby the infinite number of the beast is now correct to the *nearest* three significant figures. But where does this extra unit come from if we are to keep the total sum of the sides the same? The answer is that we have borrowed it from the short side of *Vesica Piscis*.

But *Vesica Piscis* is still *Vesica Piscis* in that it still represents the Death of the Devil (38 = Death and 4 = D = Devil). The third triangle depicts the state of *Vesica Piscis* before the Material World has begun its merger or conjunction with the Spiritual World; the second triangle shows it when the merger is half-way complete; and the first triangle shows the eclipse to be total, that is, Death and the Devil now appear as a single entity and the Emperor is in full manifestation. The reader is requested to refer once more back to Figure 25 to refresh his memory as to how this eclipse of the short side of the triangle actually comes about.

One can also see that during this eclipse the length of the hypotenuse is in no way affected. The action solely involves the lengthening and/or shortening of the long and short sides respectively, and the Christ Consciousness which represents the hypotenuse remains constant throughout the process. In fact, it would be *impossible* to change it without destroying the validity of the Pythagorean theorem and the law of the right triangle. If we were to make the hypotenuse double the length of the short side in the lower triangle, make it 768 or 2 × 384 as it were, the law would no longer be valid as the true length of the hypotenuse with sides 384 and 667 is 769.639 . . . or 770 to the nearest three significant figures.

The third or lower triangle also proves beyond a shadow of a doubt that it is indeed the correct geometrical interpretation of Chapter 13, Verse 18, of the Book of Revelation. "How can you be so adamant about that?" you ask. Well, I can only say let the facts speak for themselves; you, yourself, must be the final judge in the matter. The verse refers to the number of the "beast"; yet, it also states that it is the number of "a man." We have already found that the God-Name number for the word "beast" is 667 (Table on Page 442); so then let us now determine the God-Name number for "a man." The computation follows on the following page.

Alpha Number		God-Name Number		Sum		
A	1	The Emperor	123	124	V	Ave
M	13	Death	38	51	EA	
A	1	The Emperor	123	124	V	Ever
N	14	The Hanged Man	100	114	R	
	29	A MAN (Total)	384	413		
BI		Be I	M D	D M	Devil	Death

The God-Name number for "a man" is thus found to be 384, the length of the short side of the lower triangle, and the right-angle complement of the number for "beast." And not only that, but the sum of the Alpha number and the God-Name number is 413 or DM, and again we learn that this action results in the Death of the Devil.

Now what about the hypotenuse of our triangle? The second triangle showed its length to be 77, and we assumed that this stood for Christ. An excellent proof that this is indeed the correct word for the hypotenuse of our triangle would be given if somehow the number 770 would relate to this same individual.

Alpha Number		God-Name Number		Sum		
C	3	The Moon	90	93	IC	I See
H	8	The Hermit	106	114	R	Our
R	18	The Tower	114	132	MB	Death Be
I	9	The Magician	90	99	X	Judgement
S	19	The Star	91	110	KO	Look!
T	20	Temperance	100	120	LO	
	77	CHRIST (Total)	591	668		
J.	10	The World (Jesus)	105	115	KE	(E) Decay
K.	11	The King	74	85	D	
	98	J.CHRIST K. (the King)	770	868	Infinite (86) 8	
IH		I each half (each)		HFH	Tower (F) Tower	

But the third triangle is dealing entirely with God-Name numbers; therefore any proof worth its salt would have to include the word *Christ* in its God-Name number form. The computation for our investigation is reprinted above, and one can see that once again the Cabalah has not let us down. It proves very definitely that the hypotenuse of our 1, $\sqrt{3}$, 2 or *Vesica Piscis* right triangle is indeed Jesus Christ, the King of the World.

Now let us return to the basic reason why we have referred to Figure 81 as the death of Christ. It is, simply, that "The death of Christ" is Pi (33 + 38 + 21 + 77 = 169 = PI). But Verse 15 of Chapter 13 also called our attention to "The image of the beast." And the Alpha number for this term, you will recall, is likewise 169 or Pi. But what is Pi? Pi is simply the circumference of a circle divided by its diameter which results in the end of an AGE. It is the Emperor divided by the Self or, in other words, a zero (64 = zero). We arrive at these conclusions in the following manner:

$$PI = \frac{\text{Circumference}}{\text{Diameter}} \quad \frac{123}{75} = \frac{\text{The Emperor}}{\text{The Self}} \quad \frac{A}{GE} = 1.64000 = A \text{ Zero } 0\ 0\ 0$$

It would seem then, as the Agashan Teachers have so often proclaimed, that everything is indeed mathematical. They have stated time and again that every situation in life, absolutely every experience either large or small, has a mathematical interpretation or solution. But the *final* solution to any problem is always the completion of the cycle and the return once more to the zero from whence it began. This is Pi.

This is also the 1, $\sqrt{3}$, 2 right triangle, the areas of which bring into manifestation this same number: 3.141592. . . . Cabalistically, we would read it as 3-1-4-15-9-2 or CAD O, I Be. The three outer square areas give life to the "cad," an unskilled assistant, a person who Webster says is "without gentlemanly instincts." But the inner triangular area brings into manifestation the O, the Sun, the Core of Life from which we sprang. The Father God, the "I be" or the "I am," then separates this basic geometrical glyph from the infinite decimal that constitutes the balance of the number. But the beginning,

or the end, of the number Pi is always the "Coda," the Grand
Finale, the last act before the new cycle begins. This new cycle
is the very opposite of the previous cycle, and it represents
"The resurrection of Christ."

This is the beast himself, as opposed to the image of the beast
—the original reality from which the image sprang forth. The
Alpha numbers for the words in the term "The resurrection of
Christ" give us the clue. The Alpha number for "The resurrection" is 198 or SH. This is interpreted to mean the *silence.* It is
also AIH or H (each) I, the Emperor (reading it backwards).
But the Alpha number for "of Christ" is this same term without
the A (21 + 77 = 98 = IH = I each). Therefore, "The resurrection" is A + IH or 1 + 98. This brings into manifestation the
number 99 which is the double I of Judgement (Tarot Key 20),
the letter/symbol X which stands for Christ.

The total Alpha number for the entire term "The resurrection
of Christ" is 296 which states that it "B IF" (be if). If what?
What is the meaning of the "if"? For an answer, let us find the
God-Name number for the term. The God-Name number for
BIF is 491 or DIA (206 + 90 + 195 = 491 = DIA). This is the
abbreviation for the word *diameter,* and the meaning for the
"if" is now quite clear. The Cabalah tells us that the resurrection of Christ will only occur *if* Christ, who represented the
outer radius of the iris of the eye, now becomes its diameter.
But which diameter, the outer or the inner? For an answer to
this question we will have to move on to the following
discourse on the esoteric meaning of the words themselves.

A Lesson in Psychology

A picture is sometimes said to be worth a thousand words;
so then let us begin with Figure 82 which depicts the Core of
Life as a great Sun. The first thing we should fully understand,
as we contemplate this figure, is that it is essentially no different from the eyeball of the great All-Seeing Eye of God
depicted by Figure 70. The one exception is that the iris has
been omitted; the central inner circle represents only the pupil,
and it is lettered accordingly. The pupil, in this case, represents
either a black hole or a quasar. If we consider the rays of

energy to be traveling *towards* the center of the pupil, it is a black hole; but if they are considered to be traveling in an outward direction *away* from its center, it is a quasar. But this way or that way, the diagram is the same.

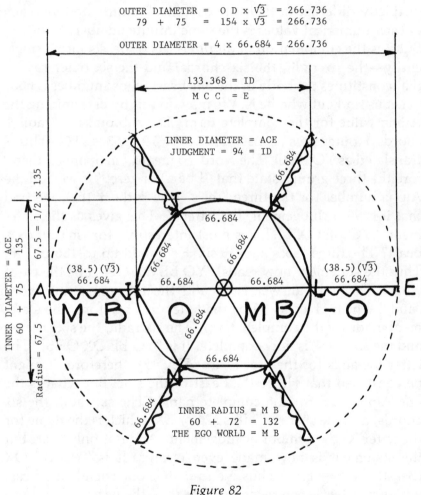

OUTER DIAMETER = O D x √3 = 266.736
79 + 75 = 154 x √3 = 266.736

OUTER DIAMETER = 4 x 66.684 = 266.736

133.368 = ID
M C C   = E

INNER DIAMETER = ACE
JUDGMENT = 94 = ID

66.684

66.684

66.684   66.684   66.684

(38.5) (√3)   (38.5) (√3)
66.684   66.684   66.684   66.684

66.684

66.684

INNER RADIUS = M B
60 + 72 = 132
THE EGO WORLD = M B

INNER DIAMETER = ACE
60 + 75 = 135

67.5 = 135

67.5 = 1/2 x 135

Radius = 67.5

A   E

M-B   O   M B   -O

Figure 82
The Core of Life Is Like a Great Sun

The next thing that we should realize is that Figure 82 is made up of three completely different types of "beasts." (The word *beast* is an excellent definition because how else can one describe a number as beastly as 66.6 . . . ?) There is the beast who represents the radius of the inner circle of the pupil; there is the beast who acts as its outer chord forming the skeleton of its circumference; and there is the beast who represents the rays of energy that radiate outwards or inwards from the inner circular core to the periphery of the eyeball. All three beasts are distinctly different in their philosophical nature, and yet each of their numerical values is the same infinite number: 66.6. . . . But it is the combination of all *three* sets of beasts into a single entity—the six radii, the six chords, and the six outer rays—that constitutes the body of the *one* beast whose number is 666.

Let us find out who he is. We may do this by determining the Alpha value for the complete term. The subtotal for "radii + chords + outer rays" is 250 (41 + 67 + 79 + 63 = 250). This is translated as YO BE O. The word *Yo* means *I* in Spanish; therefore the three groups state that "I be O or zero." If we add the Alpha number for the three "the's" (the + the + the), we find that it is 99 or Judgement, the letter X. This gives us the statement, "YO BE OX." This is most interesting, for isn't an ox a beast? The three "six's" (six + six + six) add up to 156 or OF. Thus the statement now reads, "YO BE OX OF." I be the ox of what? The only answer is to add the one remaining word "and," which gives us 19 or the letter S. Therefore, the statement made by the complete term "The six radii, the six chords, and the six rays" is now complete. It is "YO BE OX OF S." The letter S stands for the Star (Tarot Key 17); therefore, it might be construed that He be the beast of the star. But what is the one Alpha sum for the complete name "The six radii, the six chords, and the six rays"? It is 524 or EX, which is the name for the letter X, the symbol of Judgement. And not only that, but the statement is now made even clearer. It is "YO BE OX (Beast) OF S = EX." Thus we find that our friend, the beast whose number is 666, is none other than the *beast of sex*! And this is Judgement and/or Judgment or the *Id*. Wow!

This "Id," or the undifferentiated source of the organism's energy, is actually the inner diameter or the ID of our circular core in Figure 82. But if the reader will refer once more to this diagram, if he has not already done so, he will find out what this "Id" actually is. It is indeed the source of the organism's energy for it is Einstein's famous formula "E (Energy) = mc²"! And E + ID gives us the word DIE if read backwards. Our central core is appearing more and more like a black hole or, if you prefer to look at it in a more positive manner, a quasar. In fact, it may even be the Core of Life itself!

This reference to the Core of Life is substantiated if we consider it to represent the state of the Universe before the original "big bang" explosion that science says actually occurred in the beginning. The beast is the inner radius, and the Alpha number for "inner radius" is 132 or MB (Death be). But M + B also equals O (13 + 2 = 15 = O), and the entire *outer* diameter of the eyeball is now read as a "bomb" within the OM, the sound that occurs at the end of every life cycle. It is the death of the Sun (M + O), and even more than that, it is an "M" bomb or death bomb. But what does a "bomb" eventually do? It eventually *explodes,* and it is at this point of the cycle that the Universe was first brought into manifestation. Our own individual "atom bomb" exploded, and our *soul atom,* which means you and I, began the journey that is eternity.

Let us return once more, briefly, back to Figure 81. The three squares that surround the central triangle may also be observed as three cubes of three-dimensional space. The volume of each cube or block would then be the cube of the side of the inner triangle instead of its square. Well, aren't you curious? We just made the statement that the squares that constitute our Coda— the last act in our drama, the Grand Finale, or Pi as it were— may only be individual faces of cubes of a still higher dimension. Well then aren't you curious to find the numerical value of their volumes, and by so doing perhaps glean a little more information pertaining to the riddle of life? The writer was, and to his absolute amazement he found that the cube of the short side of the triangle, the cube of *Vesica Piscis* as it were, yielded the most valuable clue to date relative to the true identity of the beast whose number is 666. The number 38.5 cubed, or 38.5 × 38.5 × 38.5, brings into manifestation the truly incredible number 57,066.625. This number is read cabalistically as EGO 666 BE, and we learn that the beast whose number is 666 is none other than that portion of the psyche called the *ego!*

Armed with this new burst of knowledge, let us return to Figure 82 and put it to the test. Let us see if we can substantiate the fact that the inner radius is the ego. We can. The Alpha number for "inner" is 60 which is the same as "the ego" (33 + 27 = 60); and the Alpha number for "radius" is 72 which is the same as "world" (Tarot Key 21). Therefore, our glyph tells us that the inner radius is the ego world.

Now we are getting somewhere. Figure 82 brings into manifestation both the *ego* and the *id*—two of the four terms of Jungian psychology. We now have the feeling that perhaps there might be an even greater meaning for Figure 82, over and above that which we have already discovered. But where then are the other two, the *superego* and the *libido*? Are not all four of these terms related to the *psyche* or the soul? Perhaps then Figure 82 is also a diagram of the soul.

Let us start with the *id*. There seems to be no question but that the inner diameter, the ID of the central core of Figure 82, represents the *id*. It even makes sense philosophically. An earlier definition defines the term as "the undifferentiated source of the organism's energy from which both *ego* and *libido* are derived." But the latest edition of Webster defines it thus: "the one of the three divisions of the psyche in psychoanalytic theory (id, superego, and ego) that is completely unconscious and the source of psychic energy." This "psychic energy" that stems from the id is the *libido*. However, the libido seems to be something apart from the id, and *not* one of the three main divisions of the psyche or soul which is made up of the *id*, the *superego*, and the *ego*. The libido, therefore, is probably missing from Figure 82 if our theory is to hold true.

Where then is the ego? Since all of the lines of Figure 82 are made up of that beastly number 66.6, there is not much choice available to us. It obviously must be one of these 66.6's, but since the six radii constitute the id, we may assume that the ego does not reside in that particular group. Therefore, the ego may be looked for within the group of the six chords or the group of the six outer rays. We shall select the six outer rays because these rays are *energy* that is being emitted from the central core. The symbol for energy is the letter E, and the letter E is the initial letter of the word *ego*. Therefore, it may be assumed that E stands for ego. Besides, the very term "ego" itself may be broken apart into "E go," which implies then that E or energy *goes* away from and leaves the central core. Or perhaps it leaves the periphery and *goes* into the core. The "E" would "go" in this direction if the core were a black hole.

Well, there is only one group of 66.6's left, and that is the six chords. Through the process of elimination, the six chords must then represent that portion of the psyche called the *superego*. Webster defines the term as "the one of the three divisions of the psyche in psychoanalytic theory that is only partly conscious and that aids in character formation by reflecting parental conscience and the rules of society." The *superego* then is only partially conscious as opposed to the *ego* which is the one, outer, conscious self. It is the *ego* that serves as the organized, conscious mediator between the person and external reality.

Now then, does the Cabalah offer any proof that the superego represents the six chords? The answer again is a very definite, yes! We know that the value of the outer ray is 66.6 and that the value of the chord is likewise another 66.6, making the total sum of the outer ray plus the chord the decimal number 133.368. . . . Well, if one were to add the Alpha value for the word "ego" to the Alpha value for the word "superego," he would find that the answer is the number 133, the integer part of this infinite decimal! ("Ego + Superego" = 27 + 106 = 133.) And even more than this astounding fact, the Alpha number for "superego" is found to be 106, the number of the Hermit (Tarot Key 9) and the letter H. Thus in the same way that the E stands for the ego, the H may be said to represent the superego. And together they form the word HE.

It is interesting to see that here again we have the three one's of *Cara Boga Coty* (111) brought into manifestation inasmuch as Webster begins the definition of each of the terms *id*, *superego*, and *ego* with "the one of the three. . . ."[1] These then are the three divisions of the psyche: the id, the superego, and the ego; the unconscious, the partly conscious, and the conscious;

the mental, the physical, and the spiritual; or simply, Cara, Boga, and Coty. No matter how you look at it, it is a manifestation of the Trinity: the breaking up of the *one* psyche or soul into its *three* constituent parts.

All well and good, you may say, but where is the *libido* in all of this? This is a good question, so then let us begin with its definition. The *libido* is defined as the emotional or psychic energy which is derived from the *id* and which is usually goal directed. Another definition is that it represents the sexual drive or instinct. Fine. Now let us compare this with its Alpha number. The Alpha number for "libido" is 51 or EA. This is the abbreviation for *each*, but more than that, it is also the initials of Eve-Adam and the Alpha number for "Adam + Eve." And with Adam and Eve we have the first manifestation of sexual, emotional, and psychic energy in Biblical mythology. In other words, God caused Adam and Eve to come into manifestation *after* He himself was brought into manifestation; for He is the first cause (the id) and Adam and Eve (the libido) the second. Now don't you feel we are getting somewhere with our little analogy?

Now let us try to just see what the word "libido" is telling us. We may break it up into its component parts as follows: Li B Id O. In other words, it is saying that the term "Li" be the "Id" of "O," which means that it be the id of the sun or the *outer* id. But the meaning is still unclear until we realize what the "Li" stands for. Of course! Why didn't we think of it earlier? "Li" is simply the number 129, the Alpha number for "pupil + iris," the diameter of the outer circle of the iris *and* the pupil!

Inspired once more with this entirely new breakthrough, let us now go back to Figure 70 and look upon it with new eyes and with a greater awareness. The diameter of the inner circle of the pupil of the All-Seeing Eye is the ID, which represents the id. But the diameter of the outer circle of the pupil and the iris is the OD or the libido. This is proven if we just read the last four letters of the word "libido" backwards. It reads, "OD I be—Li (lithium)." And OD stands for outer diameter.

Thus we find that the same principles that we applied to the inner circle of the pupil in Figure 82 (when we compared it to the Core of Life or a great sun), we may also apply to the outer circle of the pupil-iris combination. For example: let us say that the central circle of Figure 82 now represents the circle of the pupil-iris combination. The diagram would be exactly as depicted, with the exception that the number 77 would replace all of the 66.684's. In other words, the pupil-iris of the first eye would then become only the pupil (or disciple) of a still greater Eye. There is the answer: eyes within eyes within eyes, worlds within worlds within worlds, ids within libidos within ids, on and on and on—forever.

Christ then replaces the beast whose number is 666 with every bit as much power and authority as was granted the original beast. He is his equal in every sense of the word, and not only his equal, but in one sense even his superior. But who is Christ, really? Christ now becomes the equivalent of the superego of the first diagram; and the libido replaces the id. Who then replaces the ego or the conscious self? Aha! Here is where you are in for a surprise. He is replaced by no one; for the ego, the conscious self, lives on and on and on. How do we know this? We will prove it in the forthcoming paragraphs, but in the interim let us find out who Christ really is.

Christ, of course, is now the radius, the chord, and the outer ray of our diagram. The length of each and every line has the numerical value of 77 which is equivalent to Christ. But in the same sense that the id, the ID whose number is 94, is equivalent to the two beasts (94 = 47 + 47), so is the libido equivalent to two Christs. We must remember that Christ represents the radius of the circle of which the libido is its diameter. (77 + 77 = 154 = OD = "Outer Diameter"; and "Outer Radius" = 151 = "Jesus Christ").

Very well. Since Christ is found to be the radius of the circle whose diameter is the libido, let us simply divide the length of the diameter by two in order to ascertain the value of its radius. There is nothing mysterious about all of this; it is simple ordinary arithmetic. What is the length of the diameter? It is 51 —naturally. The Alpha number for "libido" is 51; therefore, one half of the "libido" would quite obviously represent the equivalent value of its radius. Now remember, when we ascertain this value it is also equivalent to Christ, since Christ represents the radius of this same circle, but in another system of measurement. Well, have you now finished with your computation and ascertained the value of the radius? Are you surprised to learn that *Ye* are Christ? The Cabalah makes this statement loud and clear, so therefore it must be true. $51/2 = 25.5 = YE = 77 = $ Christ. And not only that, but $25.5 = 77$ also makes the statement that it "BE EGG"; and "it," of course, refers to YE. Therefore, *Ye* are not only Christ, but *Ye* are also an egg; and more than likely this "egg" is the Orphic egg or the egg of the soul. The soul has often been described in the Agashan classes as being egg-shaped; and in the class conducted by the Master Teacher Araskas, it has been compared to the Orphic egg. In any event, this represents You, the reader of this book, for has not it also been said that Ye are Gods?

Thus we find that we have two completely independent, yet interrelated—since one is derived from the other—sets of hexagonal forces. Modern psychology has defined the set which consists of the id, the superego, and the ego as the *psyche*. What then shall we call the second set of outer hexagonal forces? This is the set that is comprised of the libido, the Christ, and as we said a little earlier, the ego again. There is only one other word available that means the same thing as the *psyche*, and that word is *soul*. Therefore, it seems fitting that we should call this outer set the soul. Indeed, their Alpha numbers are even the reverse of each other. The Alpha number for "psyche" is 76, and the Alpha number for "soul" is 67. The number 67 also stands for "The One," as well as "Hanged Man," the letter N. Perhaps when we turn our "hanged man" upside down, he will then turn into the psyche. Who knows? In any event, one is the reverse of the other.

The following tabulation will prove beyond a shadow of a doubt that the outer ray of the outer hexagon must have the same numerical number as the outer ray of the inner hexagon. Therefore, it too must be the ego, inasmuch as there is no other word available whose Alpha number is 27. Besides, any other word would not express the tremendous philosophical concept that is so implied.

	Inner Hexagon		Central Circle		Outer Hexagon	
Diameter	ID	13	CARA	23	LIBIDO	51
Chord	SUPEREGO	106	BOGA	25	CHRIST	77
Outer Ray	EGO	27	COTY	63	EGO	27
Each Trinity		146		111		155
A Unity	PSYCHE	76	STRENGTH	111	SOUL	67
666		222		222		222

The writer could not resist calling the sum of the Cara Boga Coty forces "each trinity" and that which they represent "a unity" because they are just that. It is interesting to note that the Alpha number for "each trinity" is 132 or MB (17 + 115 = 132), and the Alpha number for "a unity" is 90 or IO (1 + 89 = 90). This tells us that Death be each trinity (MB = Death be), and that the Magician, the letter I, be a unity (90 = The Magician = Tarot Key 1 = I). And not only that, but their sum is another 222 (132 + 90 = 222), which in turn represents Death + Life (MB + IO = M + BIO = Death + Life). The Cabalah is absolutely fantastic at times.

Let us return once more to Figure 82. We have found that the ego may be represented by the letter E and the superego by the letter H. Therefore, let us place at each outer ray of energy the letter E, and at each chord of the central circle we will place an H. The following Figure 83 has been drawn up accordingly and illustrates the thought that we must now bring to your attention:

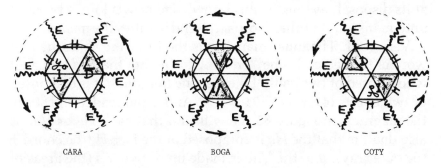

Figure 83: In the Beginning Was the Word

"In the beginning was the Word, and the Word was with God, and the Word was God." This quotation from the Book of John, Chapter 1, Verse 1, tells the entire story. The ancient Hebrews found this "Word" to be the Divine Tetragram, the Sacred Name, YOD HE VAV HE. We covered this subject at great length a little earlier in the present volume, but we must once more embrace its sacred concepts because you will find that Figure 83 illustrates them quite vividly.

To begin with, the word *Yod*, the tenth letter of the Hebrew alphabet, represents the *Id*. How do we know this? We know it to be so because the English word "I" is the same as the Spanish word "Yo." Therefore *Id* and *Yod* can be used interchangeably as far as the Cabalah is concerned. The reader may think this is strange, but we have evidence of some of the most fantastic proofs arising out of the introduction of a few words in a foreign language. And the English Cabalah, being universal in character, is not limited entirely to the English language. The general idea of the Cabalah is to transfer a thought from the Infinite Intelligence or Infinite State unto mankind. And if this "Infinite Intelligence" is aware that man is knowledgeable of some foreign language terms, it will not hesitate to use them if the occasion arises. The reader will note that we have already made use of Roman numerals, the binary code, the Greek alphabet, the Periodic Table of the Chemical Elements, and a few more bits and pieces from various cultures of the past; and God only knows what we will embrace before this present work is brought to a close. The main thing to be imparted is knowledge, and the Cabalah will not hesitate to use any means at its disposal, as long as this knowledge or wisdom is brought unto mankind. In other words, the end justifies the means.

Very well. The inner diameter is the Id or the Yod, the first word of the Sacred Name *Yod He Vav He*. But the *Yod* is dual; it is composed ot two radii. Likewise the *Id* is dual; it is composed of two beasts (47 + 47 = 94 = ID). And if the reader will study the diagrams in Figure 83, he will find that each *He* or *Vav* is also dual, in that the *He* is composed of the H + H (the chord + the outer ray), and the *Vav* is made up of two V's (the areas of two inner triangles between diameters).

This discovery of the duality of the individual words within the Sacred Name comes rather as a surprise to the writer, as heretofore he had always considered them to be units and not dualities. It was only the *He* that he thought was dual, insofar as it was repeated twice. But there they are, every single component of the Sacred Name *Yod He Vav He*, fully expressed and unfolded in Figure 83. Yet, the reader will observe, it takes three full soundings of the complete name to travel around the Wheel of Life and come back to where we started. The Cara cycle is expressed by the wheel on the left; the Boga cycle is expressed by the central wheel; and the Coty cycle is expressed by the wheel on the right. The *Yod* takes us across the diameter; the *He* takes us in a lateral direction across the chord and then radiates us outwards as energy; the *Vav* then brings us back again through the *space* between the diameters; and the final *He* repeats again the process of the first *He*, only this time at the opposite end of the wheel. *Yod He Vav He:* one great cycle expressing the dual nature of all things, and yet encapsuled together as an individual unit of a still greater cycle called the Trinity.

Now for the evidence: "How do you know that the *Vav* represents the space between the diameters?" one might ask. I think the symbol of the "V" itself (which is the English equivalent of the Hebrew *Vav*) seems to imply that it represents the area of one of these inner triangles or the *space* between two corresponding diameters. But this assumption becomes rather valid when we consider that the Alpha number for "space" is 44, and that V + V is also equal to this same number (22 + 22 = 44 = Space).And isn't the word "Vav" in reality a "V + (a) V"? Of course it is, and it takes two "V's" to make an "X," the symbol for "Judgment" (Tarot Key 20) whose Alpha number is 94 or ID.

The letter V is also the Roman numeral which stands for 5, and two times 5 is 10, the Roman numeral X. And the Hebrew Vav stands for 6, as it is the 6th letter of the Hebrew alphabet. But isn't the symbol for the Lovers (Tarot Key 6) also a V? This way or that way, all of the loose ends seem to verify themselves.

Even the Alpha number for "Inner Diameter" tells the same story. It is 135 which transliterates into ACE (60 + 75 = 135 = ACE). And isn't an ace the same shape as an A, the counterpart of the letter V? How about the Id? We know that it must be numerically equal to the chord plus the outer ray because the inner diameter consists of two radii. But the Alpha number for "He" is 13, and the Alpha number for "Id" is also 13, thus substantiating this fact.

The final tie, however, comes when we consider that the word HE means "Each E." But the Alpha number for "Each E" is 22, the same number as a single "V." Thus the lineal lengths of two lines are equated to an area. And not only that, but the entire glyph is seen as a lesson in *Self Judgment*, since the Alpha number for "diameter" is 75 which is the same as "The Self," and the Alpha number for "Judgment" is 94 or the Id.

NOTES

1. *Webster's New Collegiate Dictionary* (Springfield, Mass., G & C Merriam Co., 1974)

Chapter 23

THE HALLS OF THE INITIATE

In *Agasha: Master of Wisdom* (page 330), we discussed the three principal temples of initiation that the disciple on the spiritual path must graduate from before he becomes the higher Initiate. In the Agashan classes they were called the Temple of the All-Seeing Eye, the Agasha Hall of Higher Learning, and the Temple of Fulfillment. In total, they could be said to represent the Temples of CARA BOGA COTY since we must have a temple for each of the three divisions of life—one for its mental aspect, one for its physical aspect, and one for its spiritual aspect.

However, the picture is not complete until we place you, the reader of this book, within it. You thus become the 10th great Initiate, a remanifestation of the number 1, and the Agashan Teachers say that you may consider yourself to represent still another temple, one called the Temple of the Living God. These 4 temples then embrace the entire spectrum of matter from its solid or dense state (which is you), all the way up through its liquid, gaseous, and energy states respectively.

They also may be referred to as the four *Halls of the Initiate*, if we were to take them individually; but if we were to look at them as *one* temple, in the same way that we refer to the

479

Universal Consciousness of God as *one* consciousness, they would automatically become the one *Hall of the Initiates*, the one temple where all of the many disciples take their initiations into the Higher Orders.

This "Hall of the Initiates" was the last great temple to be brought to the attention of the members of the Agashan class. It is truly a colossal structure with a single golden dome as its crown, and it literally towers into the sky presenting much the same picture as the physical body of Man. It represents the sum total of many other halls of higher learning that the 10th great Initiate, who is you, had passed through earlier on his long pathway to Self-Realization. Figure 15 illustrates this process quite vividly, for it portrays not only the Temple of Illumination at the end of the path, but also the many "disciples of the Light" (a favorite expression of the Master Teacher Araskas) who are on the spiral path that leads to it.

In this section we shall discuss its four basic ingredients—the four major earlier temples, if you will—the sum total of which, when merged together into a unity, goes on to make up this one final "Hall of the Initiates." By this method of subdividing it into its basic parts—breaking up you as an individual into your four major components—the Teachers of Light are better able to explain just exactly what it is that you really are. These four basic ingredients are (1) The Tree of Life, (2) The Temple of King Solomon, (3) The Tree of the Sephiroth, and (4) The Temple of the Living God.

But first, before we get into a serious discussion of each of these four temples, we must have an understanding as to the identity of the individuals who reside therein. In other words, who are the characters in this great drama called Life? They all have names and, strangely enough, these names are universal. By that we mean the names of the characters in my drama are the same as the names of the characters in yours; the characters are all the same, but the names of the *actors* who portray them are as different and varied as the grains of sand upon the seashore. Each one of us has played or will play all of these roles; and, I might add, some have played them magificently while others have been dismal failures. But, there is always another performance and another chance for each one of us to redeem ourselves and play the role the way it should be played.

The Characters in the Drama

The name of the star of the show is *You*, that individual known as YOU. But he is also called by another name; that name is *Hermes, the Thrice Great.* Why is he called the Thrice Great? The word *thrice* means three times, in a threefold manner or degree. In three separate incarnations this great god of wisdom brought learning and understanding to mankind.

In Egypt he was known as *Thoth.* He was the god of wisdom, learning, and magic, the inventor of numbers and letters, and scribe of all the other gods. Thoth is depicted usually as a man with the head of an ibis; at other times he is shown with the head of a baboon. The complete deck of the Tarot is sometimes called the Book of Thoth.

In Greece he became known as *Hermes.* He was also called Hermes Trismegistus, in recognition of his two other major incarnations. Hermes was the herald and messenger of the other gods. He transmitted their great knowledge and wisdom unto mankind. Consequently, as a result of this action, many works embodying mystical, theosophical, astrological, and alchemical doctrines were given unto mankind. All of the hermetic doctrines and sciences that later became public knowledge through the writings of the Gnostics in the first three centuries A.D. are attributed to this great god.

Then, in Rome, he manifested as *Mercury,* the god of commerce, eloquence, and science. He is usually depicted with wings on his feet as he travels from here to there in the twinkling of an eye. And he always carries a caduceus, the symbolic staff of a herald, as a symbol of his great power. The first planet in the solar system is named after him, as is mercury, the 80th element in the Table of the Chemical Elements, and the only metal that is in liquid form in its natural state.

This then is the star of the show. This is the thrice great Hermes known as Hermes-Mercury-Thoth. This is you. His various manifestations are further clarified in the table on the following page.

Names along with Their Alpha Numbers

A	1	A	1	FOUR	60	-------------	0
HERMES	68	TYRE	68	YOU	61	THE TREE	81 U
MERCURY	103	SOLOMON	103	YOU	61	THE FOOL	81 U
THOTH	71	TEMPLE	71	YOU	61	THE SON	81 U

	243		243	243		243
	X C		X C	X C		X C
	90		90	90	=	90

THE MOON		THE MAGICIAN	EMPEROR		
THE C	+	I	+	A	=	M

The next tier of characters in your ladder of Being are brought into manifestation through the construction of King Solomon's Temple. The true temple, of course, is not made with human hands; however, the historical temple that King Solomon constructed conveys the glory and the splendor of Man in his original pristine state of Being. It is a temple in which the indwelling Spirit is illuminated and hallowed through and by means of the laws of number and architectural symbolism in order to convey great spiritual truths.

The story of the construction of this temple is covered quite completely in two parallel accounts in the Bible. Here, first is the First Book of Kings, chapters 5, 6, and 7, and then again in the Second Book of Chronicles, chapters 2, 3, and 4, one is taken on a word by word account through various aspects of its construction. What is given in these two books is just about all we know about it; yet, if one follows the clues that are hidden therein, the doors to understanding somehow seem to swing open, and quite magically so, I might add.

The major clues lie in the names of the characters themselves. Although the Father, King David, was first given the plans for its construction by God, it remained for his Son, King Solomon, to carry them out. Yet there is another entity here, and one that is overlooked by the average scholar. It is the *Oracle*, the Intermediary between the Lord God of Israel and the *One* being addressed. An oracle is defined as (1) a person (as a priestess of ancient Greece) through whom a deity is believed to speak, and (2) a shrine in which a deity reveals hidden knowledge. It is interesting to note that the Alpha number for "The Lord God of Israel" is 193; the number for "The Oracle" is 87; and the number for "One" is 34. If we total the three together, we end up with 314, the first three digits of Pi, and the Alpha number of "The Great Pyramid of the Emperor."

Both of these terms are used quite extensively such as: "Blessed be *the Lord God of Israel*, who hath with his hands fulfilled that which he spake with his mouth to my father David, saying," (II Chronicles 6:4), and "And *the oracle* he prepared in the house within, to set there the ark of the covenant of the Lord. And *the oracle* in the forepart was twenty cubits in length, and twenty cubits in breadth, and twenty cubits in the height thereof:" (I Kings 6:19, 20).

Thus we find that the Oracle is the instrument through which God speaks to both the Father, King David, as well as to the Son, King Solomon; and the Oracle is, therefore, of major importance in establishing communication between the God Consciousness which is above, and the mortal consciousness which is below.

Now then if the God Consciousness is symbolized by a Hermes-Mercury-Thoth combination, the question can then be asked as to which three characters constitute your mortal consciousness. We do not have to look very far for the answer, for they are obviously the three characters in the drama who make up the entity known as YOU. The following three characters then represent your physical consciousness, that part of yourself that exists on the physical plane of life, and that is in communication with the God Consciousness on the next higher tier.

KING SOLOMON = 144 = ADD = THE STRENGTH = Y
THE ORACLE   = 87 = H G = THE SUN   = O
KING DAVID   = 81 = H A = THE FOOL   = U

Sum Total   = 312 = CAB

The physical consciousness is then seen to be a *cab*, a chariot, a vehicle to carry the entity known as YOU around and about. But even more than that, it is also seen to be a perfect demonstration of the old adage, "As above, so below." It is a mirror image of the God Consciousness, for it contains the Father (King David), the Son (King Solomon), and the Holy Ghost (The Oracle). The proof for this lies in the Alpha number of the Oracle which is 87 or HG, the initial letters of Holy Ghost. Moreover, the Alpha number for "The Holy Ghost" is 162 (33 + 60 + 69); and the number 162, of course, is the Alpha number for "High Priestess," a living symbol of the Oracle.

One may also obey the commandment given by the Alpha number for King Solomon, and ADD the digits together turning the Son into the "I" (144 = ADD = 9 = I). The "YOU" now turns into an "IOU," and we can see very easily that the Son (King Solomon) is indebted to the Father (King David). In fact, if we consider the Oracle to be "each G" (HG), we can see that it represents *Justice* (God) and is weighing the Son against the Father. (The Oracle or the "O" represents the fulcrum of the scales, and the "I" and the "U" are on the left- and right-hand pans, respectively.) But the two pans are not in equilibrium as the Son is heavier than the Father. Therefore Solomon, in order to bring the pans into balance, must repay the debt owed to his father by carrying out the construction of the Temple.

One other point: Inasmuch as 87 is not only the Alpha number for "O" but also the Alpha number for "G" (O = The Sun = 87, and G = Justice = 87), the analogy becomes even more evidential. It is also interesting to note that if we rearrange the letters and put the Oracle first, and then follow it with the Father and Son respectively, we end up with the word "GUY." And isn't this just what the Fool, who is You, really is —a Guy?

Now let us unveil the mysteries related to a few more of the characters in our drama. It seems that Solomon could not build his temple without the assistance of *Hiram, King of Tyre,* for he did not have the cedar and fir trees necessary for its construction. Therefore, he was able to purchase from this friendly king all of these required materials out of the forests in Lebanon. And not only that, but Hiram, King of Tyre, also sent Solomon "Hiram, out of Tyre," a widow's son of the tribe of Naphtali, whose father was a man of Tyre, a worker in brass. This accomplished artisan, a man filled with wisdom and understanding, was then able to complete the temple (I Kings 7:13, 14). The Revised Standard Version calls this skilled craftsman "Hiram from Tyre."

The Alpha numbers of all these names are quite revealing. The Alpha number for "Hiram" is 49, the same as "Lord"; and the number for "Tyre" is 68, the same as "Logos" or "God-Self." The number for "King of Tyre" is 130 (41 + 21 + 68 = 130), which is the same as "The Higher Self"; thus the complete term "Hiram, King of Tyre" can be equated to "Lord, the Higher Self."

But our analysis becomes even more evidential when we consider the name of the skilled artisan. "Hiram, out of Tyre." The Alpha number for "out of" is 77, the number for "Christ"; and the Alpha number for the complete term, "Hiram, out of Tyre" is then 194 which translates into AID (49 + 56 + 21 + 68 = 194 = AID). And if we wish to find out just exactly where this "aid" comes from, we have to consider the alternate term, "Hiram from Tyre." Its number is 169 or PI. In other words, aid is forthcoming when we complete the cycle and return once more to the point of beginning. The Cabalah also tells us that the real source of the aid is from the Lord, the Higher Self.

The Cabalah is not simple, and it takes a good deal of discernment to ascertain the true meaning of all of these stories in the Bible. When we think we have one segment pretty well unveiled, another segment will present itself which will enhance the story even further. For instance: It was to the writer's great chagrin, and almost horror, when he discovered that the Book of Chronicles changed the spelling of "Hiram" to "Huram." (In the Book of Kings it is spelled as "Hiram.") But, I have since learned that all of these so-called spelling "errors" are not accidental. In fact, it is becoming more and more evident that each and every variant in the spelling of the terms in this fantastic book of revelation, known as the Bible, is done for a specific purpose—to reveal a still greater meaning to an all-important term.

Let us analyze these two words. The Alpha number for "Hiram" is 49, and the number for "Huram" is 61. Well, there you have your answer right there. In the Cabalah, the number 61 always stands for "You"; and this person called "You" is the Fool, the reincarnating ego, the outer self, the outer body of the "Lord" who dwells within. *Hiram* is then the inner self, the Lord, and *Huram* is the outer self, which is you; and the total of them both is 110 or simply "a ten" (49 + 61 = 110).

In the Agashan philosophy the 10 always means completion, the end of the cycle, a returning once again to the 1 from which it started. "Take a number from 1 to 10" is a phrase that is used over and over again when we attempt to break anything up into its basic components; therefore, it is most appropriate that the combination of Hiram and Huram is "a ten." A ten or "Aten" was also extremely significant in Egyptian theology because it stood for the solar deity, the one and only God (according to the Pharaoh Akhenaten), and its symbol was the disk of the sun which gives forth of its life and its energies equally unto all. This person called "You" is then Huram, the 10th great Initiate, the "ten" part of "Aten" or the "10" part of "1-10"; and the Lord is then Hiram, the first great Initiate, the Emperor, the initial letter "A" of the word "Aten," and the first digit of the number "110."

Both *Hiram* and *Huram* are the same in that they refer to the "Ram," the symbol for Aries, the first sign of the Zodiac or the letter A. "A are I's," the word *Aries* tells us; and it most certainly is this since it refers to two I's in particular—A and U, or the gold "I." The first two letters of Hiram refer to "each I" (HI); and the first two letters of Huram refer to "each you" (HU). But even more than this rather interesting thought, there is a far more profound observation yet to be made. The word "HIRAM" means "Each are the great 'I AM'" (H R I AM); and the word "HURAM" means "Each are the great 'AUM'" (H R

AUM). Yes indeed, the Cabalah can be quite fantastic at times.

One can go on and on with an analysis of the various names connected with the Temple of King Solomon, and the above is just a sampling to show what can be discerned from the words themselves. There is, however, one final observation that should be made at this time. Let us return once more to the table on page 482. The entire drama is indeed a Hermes-Mercury-Thoth production, as evidenced by the first column of names. But now let us look at the second column. Can we not also state, and be equally sure of the footing that we are on, that the temple itself is also a Tyre-Solomon temple? Wasn't it built through the combined efforts of the two Hirams from Tyre as well as King Solomon himself? And we certainly cannot forget the characters in the third column of names. They represent the third tier in our ladder of consciousness, and they are you and you and you. And they even include that unfortunate one who represents the "Four you," the Devil himself, the mortal mind.

Reading across the top row, another interesting observation can be made. The numbers are 1, 1, 4, and 0; but doesn't the number 114 stand for "Hierophant," the letter E, or "The Tower," the letter R? And doesn't the number 114 convert to AN, which in turn adds up to an O ($114 = AN = 1 + 14 = 15 = O$)? Therefore, it converts to an 0, and that is exactly just what the top number of the fourth column is—an 0.

The Hierophant is very much in evidence in the construction of this temple because the Alpha number for the title of Hermes himself, "The Thrice Great," is 147, the same number as "The Hierophant" ($33 + 63 + 51 = 147 = E$). And even more interesting, if we compute the number for "Master Builder" we find it to be this same number: 147 ($76 + 71 = 147$). Therefore, the three E's of Hermes are "The Thrice Great Master Builder: The Hierophant."

This myth of the three E's can now be enhanced even further if we return to Figure 34 titled the Judgment of E. Here, we find the letter E occupying all three possible positions in our "hourglass of time." The phrase "THY EM" (thy death) may now be exposed as an "E MYTH," and that is exactly what it is—a myth, for there is always Energy (E) to be released into a different level of consciousness.

God states that this released energy is "MY 'THE'" because the definite article "THE" can be transformed into "BE," the Wheel of Life (TH = 100 + 106 = 206 = B). But "BE" is also 25, the number for Y. Therefore, summing them all up, we find that "THY EM" = "E MYTH" = "MY THE" = "Y THEM" = "25 THEM" = "BE THEM" = "B THEME"; and that is indeed the *theme* of our story—a Hermes-Mercury-Thoth production.

A further study of the table on page 482 reveals that each of these four gods is responsible for a different "Hall" in the consciousness of the Initiate. The "Four you" at the top of the columns symbolized by the letter "A" is obviously the dense "you" or the outer "you." This is the Hierophant, the Thrice Great Master Builder, the outer consciousness of the Temple of the Living God. A *Four* is then the ruler of this temple, and "A Four" is "You" since the Alpha numbers of both terms are identical (61). You then are symbolized by the Earth, or matter in its dense state (Earth = 52 = Devil).

Now we come to the three states of your *inner* consciousness known as Hermes, Mercury, and Thoth. They are represented by the *Tree of the Sephiroth* which is ruled by Hermes, the *Temple of King Solomon* which is ruled by Mercury, and the *Tree of Life* which is ruled by Thoth. These three halls of learning are also symbolized by Water, Air, and Fire, respectively. Mercury is the obvious ruler of the Temple of King Solomon because Mercury and Solomon have the same Alpha number. It is 103 which means JC or Jesus Christ.

The consciousness of the Tree of Life is symbolized by the apex of your pyramid. It represents your highest and innermost state of consciousness, and it is ruled by the god Thoth. Indeed, the Alpha number for *Thoth* is 71, which means "The Death." It represents the death of matter as we know it, for once matter has been transmuted from its solid, liquid, and gaseous states, it becomes pure Energy and a part of the consciousness of Thoth. The Alpha number of "Fire," incidentally, is 38—the same as the number of *Death*.

Because the consciousness of the Tree of Life is so vast, we will save the exploration into this first and most basic ingredient of the Hall of the Initiates, the great ONENESS from which we sprang, for Volume II of this work. We can however, and we shall, fully explore its other three ingredients in the three chapters that follow. We will begin with the Temple of Solomon; this in turn will be followed with a discussion of the Sephirothic Tree; and we will conclude with a thorough investigation into that facet of the Hall of the Initiates known as the physical body of Man—the Temple of the Living God.

Chapter 24

THE TEMPLE OF KING SOLOMON

Actually, the name of this temple is a misnomer since the Biblical accounts refer to it as *the House of the* Lord. "Then Solomon began to build the house of the Lord at Jerusalem in Mount Moriah, where the Lord appeared unto David his father" (II Chron. 3:1). However, it is generally spoken of today as *the Temple of Solomon,* in honor of its builder.

The Biblical references convey to the reader its magnificent grandeur in vivid word pictures, and they describe in considerable detail its furnishings, general layout, and basic dimensions. However, very little remains today to substantiate it. Other than the fact that a visitor to Jerusalem can see some of the stones placed in position by Solomon's masons, and explore the ingenious system whereby water was brought to Temple Hill and stored there, there is no real, physical evidence from which an accurate scale model can be constructed. All of the attempts that have been made so far in this direction are, unfortunately, based upon pure speculation.

Yet, from the information given in the two aforementioned Books of the Bible, and with the help of the Cabalah, it should be possible to reconstruct a fairly accurate floor plan of the temple proper along with its inner court. We have done this in Figure 84, and we hope that this diagram will act as a stimulus so that the reader himself will be able to complete the reconstruction within the framework of his own mind.

490

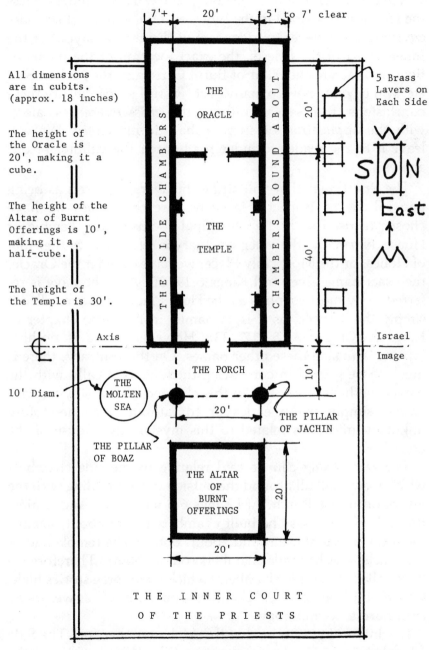

Figure 84
The Temple of King Solomon

There should be no argument from Biblical scholars with the way we have laid out the temple proper. This is more or less the way it is described in the Bible, and the way most scholars envision it. However, our concept of the general layout of the Inner Court of the Priests, the exact location of the pillars of Boaz and Jachin, the Altar of Burnt Offerings, the Molten Sea, etc. will be quite new to many. Yet, we feel we can justify these conclusions from several rather valid cross references, along with the application of strict, cabalistic principles. We will leave it to the reader to judge for himself the validity of our analysis.

The first things that will strike the average person as being unusual, as he inspects Figure 84, are the names we have chosen to use for the two principal rooms of the Temple or House. Normally, the inner sanctuary is referred to as the Holy of Holies, or the Most Holy Place; we have called it the Oracle, the exact name given in I Kings 6:19, 20. And the nave is referred to by most scholars as the Holy Place; we have called it simply the Temple, as it is so named in the same chapter of Kings (I Kings 6:3, 5, 17, 33). However, there is nothing "wrong" in using these other names. On the contrary, there is much to be gained in comparing them cabalistically with the names we have used. But in this chapter we are staying with basics, simply in an endeavor to fathom some heretofore unknown mysteries related to this mysterious "House of the LORD."

The same thing can be said relative to the side chambers which were built all around the outside of the building with the exception of the Porch. In I Kings 6:5 we read, "And against the wall of the house he built chambers round about, against the walls of the house round about, both of the temple and of the oracle: and he made chambers round about:" Therefore we have called these side chambers, which were three stories high, by their Biblical name of "chambers round about" as well as by their normal terminology.

It is interesting to note that the Alpha number for "The Side Chambers" is 139, the number for "The Wheel of Life," the letter B. Then, if we place "You" on this Wheel of Life, the resulting Alpha number would be 200, the "TO" part of the verb "To Be" (You = 61, and 139 + 61 = 200). But this isn't all. The truly amazing thing is that the Alpha number for "Chambers round about" is this very same number: 200 (69 + 72 + 59 = 200). Therefore, the side chambers when empty are just that —the side chambers. But when we place "You" in these side chambers, they become the "Chambers round about."

The next thing that the reader will notice as being different from contemporary models of Solomon's Temple is that we have omitted any walls around the Porch. We have done this on good authority since the Scriptures leave the impression that the Porch was not an interior room, having no mention whatsoever of doors as in the case of the main room and the inner Oracle. "And the porch before the temple of the house, twenty cubits was the length thereof, according to the breadth of the house; and ten cubits was the breadth thereof before the house" (I Kings 6:3).

Therefore, if the Porch was entirely open, we have a very logical location to place the twin pillars of Jachin and Boaz, and this is precisely at its corners which line up with the north and south walls of the Temple. "And he set up the pillars *in the porch* of the temple: and he set up the right pillar, and called the name thereof Jachin; and he set up the left pillar, and called the name thereof Boaz" (I Kings 7:21).

These pillars would then be necessary to support the roof of the Porch, if indeed a roof existed. But more than likely it was roofed over since the Hebrew word for "porch" has been translated elsewhere as "vestibule," "portico," or "entrance hall." These words would seem to imply some sort of a roof.

The pilasters that we have shown within the north and south walls of the Temple are pure conjecture. Yet some sort of internal column arrangement must have existed in order to support the massive roof beams spanning nearly 30 feet (1 cubit = 18"). With the side chambers there is no problem because we are told in I Kings 6:6, "The nethermost chamber was five cubits broad, and the middle was six cubits broad, and the third was seven cubits broad; *for without in the wall of the house he made narrowed rests round about, that the beams should not be fastened in the walls of the house."* Yet here we are only speaking of a maximum span of approximately 10 feet. In the case of the Temple itself, the span is nearly three times this distance.

We learn that there were two courts of the Temple: (1) the Inner Court of the Priests, and (2) the Great Court which went "round about" and surrounded the entire complex (II Chron. 4:9; I Kings 6:36; I Kings 7:12). We have no data for the size of the Great Court, but we have been able to reconstruct a fairly plausible floor plan for the Inner Court of the Priests. It is shown in Figure 84.

We know the size of the Altar of Burnt Offerings for it is given in II Chron. 4:1, immediately following a description of the pillars of Jachin and Boaz: "Moreover he made an altar of brass, twenty cubits the length thereof, and twenty cubits the breadth thereof, and ten cubits the height thereof." We also know not only the location of this Altar, but also the location of the Inner Court that contained it from the following description in I Kings 8:64: "The same day did the king hallow the *middle of the court that was before the house of the* Lord: for there he offered burnt offerings, and meat offerings, and the fat of the peace offerings: . . ." Therefore, inasmuch as the Altar was 20 cubits square, and because it existed in the middle of the Court, which in turn was directly in front of the Temple, the size of the forepart of the Inner Court of the Priests was 60 cubits square. It may have been larger, but according to the mathematics of the Cabalah, these were its dimensions.

We know that the Temple faced the east from the following description in Ezekiel 8:16: "And he brought me into the inner court of the Lord's house, and, behold, at the door of the temple of the Lord, between the porch and the altar, were about five and twenty men, with their backs toward the temple of the Lord, and their faces toward the east; and they worshipped the sun toward the east."

Another prominent item in the Inner Court which was placed just left of the entrance to the Temple was a great brass bowl. It was cast by Hiram of Tyre and was called the Molten Sea. It was round, 10 cubits in diameter and 5 cubits high, and rested upon 12 bronze oxen with each group of 3 facing the cardinal points of the compass. It is fully described in I Kings and II Chronicles, including its location at the southeast corner of the Temple.

This then completes our survey of the basic rooms, spaces, and areas, the totality of which make up that which is known as the Temple of Solomon. An analysis of Figure 84 shows that it can be broken up into two basic parts—an inner part consisting of the temple proper, and an outer part contained within the walls of the court. Let us now analyze these various parts cabalistically. Let us begin with an analysis of the Inner Court of the Priests.

The Inner Court

Figure 85 subdivides the larger square of the Inner Court into nine smaller squares in much the same way that we made our Tic-Tac-Toe glyph (Figure 37). It can be readily seen that each of the squares is exactly the same size as the Oracle (20′ × 20′). Therefore, each of these smaller squares is a complete entity unto itself as well as being a part of the greater whole. And so it is with all of life.

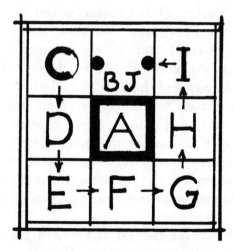

Figure 85
The Divisions of the Forepart of the Court

Now we have made this analogy because the geometry of the
spaces, along with that which they contain, fairly dictates that
it be so made. In the first place, the Alpha number for "The
Inner Court" is 170 or AGO (33 + 60 + 77 = 170), the same as
the number for "The Great Pyramid" (33 + 51 + 86 = 170). In
the second place, the physical dimensions of the Altar exactly
fit the inner square; and not only that, but the Altar is so
placed that it can be made to represent the Apex of the Pyramid, or rather, the upper platform of the Great Pyramid upon
which the golden Apex used to rest. Then thirdly, if we number
all of the squares starting with the Apex as the number 1 or the
letter A, and then continue numbering them up and around the
periphery of the greater square, both of the letters B and J (the 2
and the 10) will fall in the square occupied by the Porch of the
Temple including the columns Boaz and Jachin (B and J). And
if all this still seems to be coincidental to the skeptical reader,
how would he go on to explain away the fact that Solomon
placed the Molten *Sea* in the square where the letter *Cee* (the C)
will fall? Is it because it represents the Holy See, the office of
the Pope? It could very well be, because we must remember
that we are now in the Inner Court of the Priests, just outside
the House of the Lord.

But let us not stop here with our points of verification. We
can go on even further. Didn't Ezekiel 8:16 tell us that 25 men
stood between the Porch and the Altar, in the same square
occupied by the letter B? And isn't the name of the letter B, if it
were spelled out, the word "Be"? And doesn't the number 25
convert to BE, the name of this very same letter?

But the value of our "B" square, which represents the Wheel
of Life, is changed to a "J" square which represents the World,
once a complete revolution of the outer circuit is completed.
The letter B then represents the beginning of this outer cycle
and the J the ending; but the A is that which existed before the
beginning, the higher *inner* consciousness before its fall into the
outer periphery, so to speak.

Thus we find that the numerical value of the square which
contains the Porch, the entrance to the Temple, began with a 2
and ended with a 10, which in turn reverts back to the digit 1.

We are now ready to begin once more another revolution around the outer periphery as we continue our journey through the outer worlds.

All well and good. We now arrive back in the "C" square, back into the Molten Sea that Solomon, in his wisdom, had placed in the upper left-hand corner of the Inner Court. But this "C" square now becomes a "K" square, the number 11, the digit 2. And the Alpha number for the word "Sea" verifies that this is so, for it is 25 or BE, the letter B or the 2. Even the Alpha number for the complete term, "The Molten Sea," tells the same story. Its number is 137, the MG or the image (33 + 79 + 25 = 137), and this in turn also reduces to a 2 (137 = 11 = K = 2 = B).

Thus the numerical value of each square, when reduced to a single digit, becomes one digit less with each revolution around the outer periphery of the Inner Court. And if we wish to find the letter/symbol for each square, in any particular cycle, we have to add eight letters to the letter/symbol of the previous cycle. For instance: C + 8 = K, and K + 8 = S, and S + 8 = A. Therefore, three revolutions around the circuit will transform the upper left-hand square from C to CKSA; and thus we find that the mission of the Holy "See," now follow me carefully, is that it "SEEKS A"!

The reader can entertain himself quite profitably, and gain a good deal of philosophical insight, I might add, as he follows through in his mind the evolution of each of these outer squares or worlds. For example: the lower left-hand square changes from E to M, which brings into manifestation the word "EM," the name of the letter M, the symbol for Death (Tarot Key 13).

Now what happens to the first "A," the Altar, the Apex of the Pyramid, the central point of the inner consciousness, during all of these revolutions of the spirit around its outer periphery? The answer is that it doesn't change at all. It remains constantly the same, the Source, the Oneness, the Hub of the Wheel that is ever watchful of each and every state of its outer Being. This central "A" is truly One, while all of the outer "A's" may be said to be Ten's.

There is a lesson to be learned here when we study the two

names for the god Aten. If you look up his name in the dictionary, you will find two different spellings for this same god. It is
spelled both as "ATEN" as well as "ATON." Either spelling is
correct. But now let us hyphenate the two words into "A-TEN"
and "A-TON," and if we read the former in the regular manner
and the latter in reverse order, we find that "a ten is *not* A."
Why isn't a ten a real A? The answer is that the true Emperor,
the true A, always stays within at the center of his Being, and is
not the other A's, the 10's, that become unconscious of their
oneness with their creator while in the outer worlds of consciousness. This is the 10; this is you.

It is interesting to note that not only is the entrance to the
Great Pyramid from its north face, but so are the entrances to
the two other pyramids in the Giza complex, Cephren and
Mycerinus, also located in the north. And if we identify the
Inner Court of the Temple of Solomon with the Great Pyramid, symbolically speaking that is, the entrance must be from
the right side, the letter H, the Hermit (Tarot Key 9). The
Alpha number for "The Hermit" is 106 which can be read "A
of." Thus the Hermit is not only the teacher, but he is also of
the "A," and is well qualified to represent the entrance to the
inner consciousness. But H stands for *each;* therefore he is each
one of us, you or I, when we reach that particular square in our
journey around the Inner Court.

The Basic Parts of the Temple[1]

Now let us analyze the temple proper itself. It has three basic
parts: (1) the Side Chambers which enclose it in the form of an
inverted "U"; (2) the Oracle or sanctuary; and (3) the Temple
or nave. All three components, taken together as a whole, then
represent the inner or interior part of the Temple of Solomon,
as opposed to its exterior part called the Inner Court of the
Priests. Actually, a better term would be to call the Inner Court
of the Priests its middle part, since the Great Court encloses
them all and constitutes the true outer part of the Temple of
Solomon.

The following table will clarify this even further, and prove
rather enlightening to the average reader:

The Component Parts

THE SIDE CHAMBERS = 139
THE ORACLE   = 87
THE TEMPLE   = 104

Subtotal   = 330 = The 0   = 33 + 0 = F = 6
THE INNER COURT   = 170
OF THE PRIESTS   = 160

Subtotal   = 330 = The 0   = 33 + 0 = F = 6
                      660 = Woman = 66 + 0 = L = 12

THE GREAT COURT   = 161 = The Hanged Man + You

Grand Total   = 821 = The Empress (Reverse)

The Complete Whole

THE TEMPLE OF SOLOMON = 228 = BBH = Baby each
THE HOUSE OF THE LORD = 204 = BO + Dee = Body
THE TEMPLE OF SOLOMON = 228 = BBH = Baby each

Subtotal   = 660 = FFO = OFF OF "F"
THE ADAM-EVE CHRIST   = 161 = PA = A You

Grand Total   = 821 = HBA = Each be A

Thus we find the Cabalah repeating once again the same story that it has told over and over and over: namely, that you, the Fool, Tarot Key 0, are an indispensable part of the God Consciousness. It would seem, in this analysis, that in reality you are the macrocosm rather than the microcosm, as all of your various states of consciousness lie within the Great Court which we have equated to the Adam-Eve Christ (Great = 51 = EA = Adam-Eve, and Court = 77 = Christ). It is also worthy of note that the Alpha number for the term "Great Court," by itself, is equal to 128, the Alpha number of "The Empress" whose symbol is Z. And since this letter is the 26th letter of the English alphabet, it is also equal to God.

The Altars

In any analysis of the Temple of Solomon, it must be remembered that we have two separate and distinct altars to be considered. (An altar is an elevated structure on which incense is burned or sacrifice offered to deity.) The first altar is called *the Altar of Burnt Incense.* I Kings 7:48 refers to it as the Altar of Gold. It stood in the Temple in front of the veil or partition separating the Temple from the Oracle. It was 1 cubit square and 2 cubits high, and was made of acacia wood and overlaid with gold.

The second altar is called *the Altar of Burnt Offerings* (In many places in the Bible the last letter, the "s," is omitted). The Catholic Bible refers to it as the Altar of Holocaust. And then again, II Chronicles 4:1 calls it the Altar of Brass. It stood in the middle of the Inner Court directly in front of the Porch, and its size was 20 cubits square and 10 cubits high. The basic altar was of stone, but a large portion of it was covered with brass or bronze plates.

Now let us compare these two altars. The former was a double-cube ($1 \times 1 \times 2$), and the latter was a half-cube ($20 \times 20 \times 10$). One was covered with gold and the other with brass. The Alpha number for "gold" is 38 which means "Death." The Alpha number for "brass" is 59 which means "The God." Sometimes the word "brasen" is substituted for *brass* (I Kings 8:64), but it makes no difference in our analysis because the Alpha number for both words is the same (brass = 59 = brasen). Therefore, these two altars are somehow connected with the death of God; and the net difference between them is you ($59 - 38 = 21 = U = $ You).

Even the complete titles of the terms tell us a similar story. The Alpha number for "The Altar" is 85 which means "The Devil," the letter D. And who is the Devil? It is you, of course, the mortal mind. Therefore, the term "The Altar of Gold" means the same thing as "The Devil + The God," since the Alpha number for "of Gold" is the same number 59 ($21 + 38 = 59 = $ The God). And this in turn equates to the other altar as well, since the Alpha numbers for all terms are identical: "The

Devil + The God" = "The Altar of Gold" = "The Brasen Altar"
= "The Brass Altar." The total value of each term is 144 (85 +
59 = 144), which commands us to ADD; and when we do this,
we reduce each expression to 9 or "I."

We pointed out in Figure 84 that the volume of the Altar of
Burnt Offerings is exactly one half that of the Oracle (Their
floor areas are the same but their heights are different). The
Alpha number for "The Altar of Burnt Offerings" is 280 (33 +
52 + 21 + 75 + 99 = 280). Therefore, to find that which exists in
the empty space above the altar—which amounts to the same
thing as discovering the entity or entities that are sacrificed—
we must transform the altar into a perfect cube, and by so
doing make it identical to, and a mirror image of, the Oracle.
Who then is sacrificed? The following table will give us the
answer.

The Sacrificed

THE LORD GOD OF ISRAEL	= 193	= SC
THE ORACLE	= 87	= HG
Subtotal (Be each O)	= 280	= BHO

The Altar

THE ALTAR OF BURNT OFFERINGS	= 280	= B HO
Grand Total (Be Hoof)	560	= E FO

Thus we find the Cabalah reaffirming once more the general
theme of the death of God in connection with the altar. And
here again is the Devil (the altar), and the God (the empty
space above it). The reader will realize that we could have used
any number of terms to make up the equivalent of the number
280, but in this analysis we are restricting ourself to use only
those terms that appear in the appropriate sections of the
Authorized Version of the Bible. For example: II Chronicles 6:4
(the LORD God of Israel), and I Kings 6:19, 20 (the Oracle).

At this point the astute reader will then ask, "Well, if you are
being so meticulous, why then don't you leave off the final 's'

from the term and call it the way it is usually called in the Bible, to wit: 'the Altar of Burnt Offering'?" This is quite true, and even though it is not exactly grammatically correct, many verses in the Bible do indeed refer to it in this manner (Exodus 30:28, 31:9, etc.). It is also referred to as "the Altar of *the* Burnt Offering" (I Chronicles 16:40, 22:1, etc.), and with the addition of the "the," it makes it more grammatically acceptable. But this way or that way, let us take the reader's suggestion and sacrifice the final "s" to the spiritual space above it. This will make the Alpha number of the space above the altar 299 (280 + 19), and the Alpha number for the altar itself 261 (280 – 19). We will then conform to normal usage and refer to it simply as "the Altar of Burnt Offering."

The Molten Sea

To the left of the Altar, and in the "C" square in front of it, was that great brass bowl called the Molten Sea (I Kings 7:23-25). Its basic use was for the priests to wash in, as opposed to the 10 Lavers at the sides of the Temple which were used for washing individual offerings (II Chronicles 4:6). But the symbolism of the Sea carries far more cosmic overtones than just that. The Sea represents the oceans from which all life sprang forth (Genesis 1: 9, 10), and the Altar at the center of the court symbolizes the mountains which must be climbed by the various species in order for them to ascend into the higher consciousness at physical death. Thus the Sea is birth and the Altar is death. The Cabalah reinforces this thought, for the Alpha number of "Sea" (25), when added to that of "Altar" (52), brings into manifestation the number 77, the number for *Christ*. And Christ, of course, represents eternal life.

Another interesting point is that the Alpha number for "The Molten Sea" is 137, the MG or image (33 + 79 + 25 = 137). Now let us compare this with "The Altar of Burnt Offering" whose number is 261. Since 26 is the number for "God," and 61 is the number for "You," we may place the two numbers side by side and read "261 + 137" as "GOD AM G" (God is Justice), and "137 + 261" as "MG B YOU" (Image be You). And not only that, but the Alpha number for the space above the Altar is 299, which may be read as "Page'I'be Judgement" (29 = Page, and 99 = Judgement). This also yields the word "PI," since the letter/symbol for "Page" is "P."

From the above, we can see that there is a very strong relationship between the Sea and the Altar. But now let us backtrack a bit. The Authorized Version has forced us to sacrifice a very logical letter, the last "s," from the Altar of Burnt Offerings. The "s," which represents the Star (Tarot Key 17), then ascended into the heavens above the Altar. But inasmuch as the Sea and the Altar are so closely related, logic would have it that part of the Sea itself has also ascended into the space above it. Indeed, does not water evaporate? Therefore, we must find a logical symbol to represent that portion of the Sea that has evaporated into the space immediately above the surface of the water. We do not have to search very far, for the letter/symbol "C" is obviously the answer.

All of the water then that originally comprised the Molten Sea, in both gaseous as well as in liquid form, can be said to be represented by the term "The Molten Sea + 'C'." This term then directly corresponds with the way the Altar was in the beginning, namely: "The Altar of Burnt Offering + 'S'."

Now when we compare the two, in their original state, another even more striking relationship is seen to exist. The Alpha number for the former term is exactly *one half* that of the latter (137 + 3 = 140, and 261 + 19 = 280). And this relationship, amazingly enough, is actually the way it is supposed to be when we consider their relative heights. The height of the Sea is 5 cubits, exactly half of the 10 cubit height of the Altar, and not only that, but the height of the Altar is exactly half that of the Oracle. All three elements can then be combined together in the term "Sea-Altar-Oracle," the ratios of its heights of which are 1:2:4. This number (124) is the Alpha number of "The Lovers" (Tarot Key 6), and the Alpha number of the first two terms when compared with that of the third is the same as "Christ" bears to the "Sun" (25 + 52 = 77 = Christ, and Oracle = 54 = Sun).

But we haven't even begun to astound you yet. There is still an absolutely fantastic situation yet to be unveiled by the

inquisitive student of the Cabalah. In the beginning we had the
term "THE MOLTEN SEA + C." Well, what are you going to
do now, just simply look at it? Whenever a situation such as
this arises, when a new letter is added to an already established
phrase, and especially when the new letter doesn't easily blend
in with the other words, the next step is to try to *rearrange* the
letters into other words which do make sense. This is what the
Cabalah is all about and if we do not take advantage of striking breakthroughs such as this, and follow the trail further, we
might have just as well not even started on our investigation in
the first place.

Have you got the answer yet? If you haven't, work on it for a
while and try not to cheat by reading the rest of the paragraph.
It is really very simple, but I will admit that answers to ana-
grams such as this are sometimes very elusive. But seeking for
them does stimulate the mind, and this one is no exception. The
simple answer is that the term "SEA + C" rearranges itself very
nicely into "ACES," and not only that, but our "ACES" are
preceded by the word "TEN." Ten aces! Wow! Let's go further.
What do we now do with "THE MOL"? The answer again is
quite simple. These letters seem to fall into an "empty hole" as
they rearrange themselves into "MT (empty) HOLE." We thus
end up with *ten aces in the hole*, and if you are a poker buff
you certainly know what that means! You have a sure winner
(that is if they don't put you in jail or shoot you on sight for
cheating).

There are still other implications connected with this phrase.
For instance: the letters "Mt" are an abbreviation for "Mount,"
and we suddenly are faced with the possibility of a "hole" or
cave in a mountain. What about the many Spiritual Centers,
such as the Earshin Valley that we are told exists within a huge
cavern or "hole" in the heart of Mt. Shasta? (*Agasha: Master of
Wisdom*, page 241). Are the Spiritual Centers of the Earth the
real "molten seas" that are constantly sending forth their repre-
sentatives into the outer world?

Then, too, if ten aces in the hole represent the Molten Sea,
what then do the ten Lavers stand for? The Alpha number for
"Laver" is 58, the number for "Two," and here is our answer.

We now have 10 Two's to match up with our 10 Aces, and the puzzle is becoming quite intriguing, to say the least. The Alpha number for "Ace + Two" is 67, the number for "Hanged Man," "Ten Man," "Soul," "The One," and we could go on and on and on.

And for those of you who are still not entirely satisfied with our answer of "MT HOLE + TEN ACES," let us simply change "MT" to "THE" since their Alpha numbers are the same, and we thus can quite legitimately call our term "THE HOLE + TEN ACES."

All of the above now brings us to the final step in our analysis, and that step is to ascertain what exists in the empty space above the Sea, in the same way that we found the occupants in the space above the Altar (See table on page 501). To do this we must transform the space occupied by the Molten Sea into a perfect cube, and the following tabulation yields some rather interesting results. We are using the full term including the "C" in order to correspond with the table for the Altar which included the "S."

The Space Above

THE ARK 63
TWO'S (LAVERS) 77
Subtotal   140 = NO

The Sea Below

THE (MT) HOLE 73
TEN ACES 67
Subtotal   140 = NO

Grand Total (Noon be each 0) = 280 = B HO

The reader will note that in the same way the ten aces fill up the empty hole, so do the "two's" fill up the ark. Didn't God command Noah to fill the ark with two of each of the species of the birds and the beasts? This was necessary for the preservation of the species. But the ark, in another sense, also contains all of the stars in the sky for the preservation of the universe (Two's = 77 = Stars = 2's). The ark, then, becomes the container of both the macrocosm (the stars) and the microcosm (the two's, the pairs of the individual species). And not only that, but the ark also floats upon the *image* of that which it contains. It floats upon *the seas,* the image of the two's and stars (The Seas = 77 = Two's = Stars), each of which, in turn, is equal to Christ (77). The general idea that the Cabalah is trying to convey is symbolically illustrated in the following Figure 86:

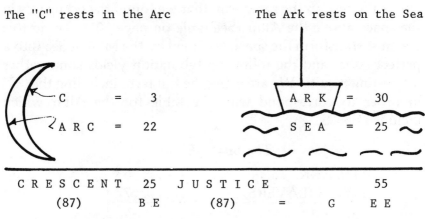

Figure 86
The Crescent Be Justice and Justice Be God

Thus, in the beginning, God brought the Molten Sea into manifestation (The Molten Sea = 137 = MG = Image). But eventually, minute drops of water from the Sea soon evaporated and arose into the space above it. These drops from the Sea then reverted back and became a part of the reality that they were before the beginning, or before the creation of the image, as it were. These drops are called the "C," the reality behind the image which is the "Sea."

But each drop of the "C," being water, must also be contained by a suitable vessel or basin in the heavenly realms. Here is where the etheric counterparts of the ten Lavers come into play. Inverted, they become as a great dome in the sky, a giant basin to act as a receptacle for each symbol of the "C." All of the elements in this case literally and truly fit their containers as their Alpha numbers are all identical. The Seas = 77 = Lavers = Stars = Two's = Christ.

One other thought before we leave this subject: Our "MT HOLE" may be equated to "HER MT I," which in turn is equal to "HERMIT" (Tarot Key 9), the letter H. And the Alpha number for "TEN ACES" is the same as the number for "HANGED MAN" (39 + 28 = 67), the letter N. It may be concluded then that "Her empty 'I' hanged man." The meaning is not too clear on the surface, but if the Cabalah says it's so, it must be so. It is to be noted that the sum of the Hermit and the Hanged Man is the Wheel of Fortune (the letter B), and that the sum of the letters H and N is the letter V (the Lovers). Could it be then that the reason that you and I are now riding this Wheel of Life is somehow related to the fact that the "I" of the High Priestess is now empty? Think on it. It might be so.

The Oracle: The Holy of Holies

Now let us move into the inner Sanctuary, the Oracle, the Most Holy Place, the receptacle for the Ark of the Covenant. It is in the shape of a perfect cube with the length, breadth, and height all being equal. The Ark is placed under the wings of two colossal cherubim of olivewood overlaid with gold. Each cherub is 10 cubits in height, and their wings extend clear across the 20-cubit width of the room. Their faces are turned toward the nave of the Temple, being ever so watchful against any unauthorized intruders.

The Ark which they guard is a chest 2-1/2 cubits long, 1-1/2 cubits wide, and 1-1/2 cubits high. It is made of acacia wood and overlaid with gold both within and without. It is a fitting receptacle for the testimony or covenant that is placed within it on tables of stone, and its lid is of solid gold which is called the mercy seat. It symbolizes the almighty presence of an invisible God, and by so doing, indicates the impossibility of representing God in any form whatsoever.

But is this really true? Perhaps we may find an adequate

symbol within the name itself. All through the Bible, both in the Authorized King James Version as well as in the Revised Standard Version. He is referred to simply as the LORD. This word, when printed in small capital letters, represents the Hebrew Yod He Vav He, the Tetragrammaton, the most sacred and incommunicable name of God, and one which is used by himself alone. Yet in many places in the Bible, especially in I Kings and II Chronicles, the phrase *God of Israel* is added to it, thus enhancing the name even further to "the LORD God of Israel." But the complete title, with all of its ramifications, is given in II Chron. 6:7 which reads: "Now it was in the heart of David my father to build an house for *'the Name of the* LORD *God of Israel'.*" The italics and capitalization are ours. Thus we have three different phrases with which to work.

Let us begin with the basic term "The LORD." Its Alpha number is 82 (33 + 49 = 82), and this number transliterates into HB which means "Each be." This could mean that each one of us, in the final analysis, is the One whom we refer to as "the Lord." (Here, we have removed the capitals insofar as we are referring to the Hebrew word *Adonai* which means *Master.*) Then if we integrate the number 82, we change it to 10, the letter J, the World (Tarot Key 21). Thus "The LORD" = 82 = HB = J, or, in other words, the LORD is equivalent to "Each B J," or each of the pillars Boaz and Jachin. Or, even more profound, it may mean that each be the World.

Now let us analyze "The LORD God of Israel." The Alpha number for "God of Israel" is 111 (26 + 21 + 64 = 111), the number for Strength (Tarot Key 8), the letter Y. But what is even more significant is that it also stands for our old friend CARA BOGA COTY, the Trinity, the mental, physical, and spiritual aspects of ourself. In this way then, the LORD is equated to CARA BOGA COTY.

But the analysis for the complete phrase "The Name of the LORD God of Israel" is absolutely fantastic! The Alpha number for "The Name of" is 87 (33 + 33 + 21 = 87), which means that it stands for "The Sun" (Tarot Key 19), the letter O, "Justice" (Tarot Key 11), the letter G, "The Oracle," the inner Sanctuary of the Temple, the dwelling place of the Ark of the

Covenant. And when we sum up the Alpha number for "The Name of the LORD," we end up with 169 or PI (87 + 82 = 169). But aren't the first three digits of Pi 3.14? And isn't the Alpha number for "The Great Pyramid of the Emperor" also 314 or Pi? Therefore, the Name of the LORD equates to the Great Pyramid.

But we still have to add "God of Israel" or "Cara Boga Coty" to it in order to end up with the complete title. And when we do this, we have the same number that we have been working with all along in this chapter—the number 280 which B H O (be each O). "The Name of the LORD God of Israel" thus is 280 (87 + 82 + 111 = 280), or Pi added to Cara Boga Coty.

Now let us break down the number for "The LORD God of Israel" into its component parts. It is 193 or SC (82 + 111 = 193), but the S represents the Star (Tarot Key 17), and the C represents the Moon (Tarot Key 18). Therefore, the complete symbol stands for the Star and the Crescent, which according to the Agashan philosophy, is that which exists in the very center of the Great Pyramid (*The Agashan Discourses*, page 201).

Very well. We have now found that the LORD God of Israel equates to the Star and the Moon. (The symbols for the Moon and the Crescent are interchangeable.) But who is he, really? For an answer to this question we have to perform another integration. We have to add the God-Name number for the letter S to the God-Name number for the letter C, and when we do this, we find that he is none other than Ra, the sun god of Heliopolis, the universal creator and chief deity of ancient Egypt (S + C = 91 + 90 = 181 = RA).

But is he not also equal to the Lovers (Tarot Key 6), the letter V, the universal symbol for Adam and Eve? Doesn't S + C also equal V (19 + 3 = 22)? Therefore, you and your counterpart or soul mate also equate to Ra. And, of course, this is the same answer that we always eventually find the more we study the Cabalah; that is, that you and I in the final analysis are God.

Now let us analyze a little more carefully the place where our Star and Crescent reside. Agasha has said that it is in the very center of the Great Pyramid. But inasmuch as the Alpha number for the Great Pyramid of the Emperor is 314 or Pi, the symbols must exist in the center of the circumference of a circle. And where is the center of the circumference? It is anywhere and everywhere along the circumference or perimeter because a circle has no beginning and no end. There is no special point along the circumference that is different from any other point. They are all equal.

But, of course, this is only one way to look at it. There is still very definitely a central point or CG (center of gravity) of the Great Pyramid. And this brings us to another absolutely astounding revelation, for through the laws of the Cabalah, we are now in a position to discover an alternate dwelling place for our Star and Crescent.

"Where is that?" you ask. For an answer to this question, let us quote the following verse from II Chron. 5:7: "And the priests brought in *the ark of the covenant of the* LORD unto his place, to *the oracle* of the house, into *the most holy place,* even under the wings of the cherubims." Again, the italics are ours. We have put the full name for the Ark into italics to emphasize the fact that its Alpha number is identical to that of the Great Pyramid. They are each equal to Pi. "The Ark of the Covenant of the LORD" = 314 (33 + 30 + 21 + 33 + 94 + 21 + 33 + 49). Therefore, we may conclude that the Star and the Crescent may just as easily reside within the Ark of the Covenant as they can within the Great Pyramid.

Another interesting observation is that the Alpha number for "Covenant" is the same as "Judgment," the letter X which stands for Christ. And the number for "The Convenant of the," which is 181 and represents RA, when added to the number for "LORD of Ark" which is 100 (The Hanged Man), gives us the number 281 which states that it "be each A."

The dictionary defines the word *covenant* to be a formal, solemn, and binding agreement between two parties. And the *Covenant of the* LORD is especially binding since the Alpha number for "Covenant" is 94 or ID, the reverse of that for "LORD" which is 49 or DI. In any case, it implies a unique relationship between the "I" and the Devil.

But we are also talking about the *Ark* of the Covenant.

Therefore, the word "Ark" must have a binding agreement with some other word. What is that word? Figure 86 shows it to be "Arc," and not only that, but the sum of the two words (Ark + Arc) is 52, the number for "Devil," the letter D. These two words very definitely have a covenant with each other because "Ark + Arc" equals "30 + 22" equals "CO + V" equals "COV.", the abbreviation for the word "Covenant."

Now let us analyze the other two occupants of the inner Sanctuary or Oracle. They are the two cherubim who guard the Ark. The dictionary defines a cherub to be a biblical attendant of God, an order of angels, and a member of the Celestial Hierarchy. Other than that, we have no other description to go by. However, we can analyze their name. The Alpha number for "Two Cherubim" is 137 or MG (58 + 79 = 137). And, of course, the letters MG stand for *image*. But what are they an image of? The answer is that they are a perfect image of "The Molten Sea" (33 + 79 + 25 = 137 = MG), not only because the sums of their numbers are the same, but also because the numbers of the individual words are the same (Two = 58 = The Sea, and Cherubim = 79 = Molten).

But if you think that is rather astounding, wait until you hear the rest of the story. There are also two other elements of the Temple of which they are the image, and these other two units are the Great Pyramid and the Inner Court (The Molten Sea = 137 = MG = Two Cherubim = Great Pyramid = Inner Court). All four of these elements are reflections of each other, and they constitute the real key to understanding the mystery of the Temple of Solomon.

We are really moving into high gear now, with only one other major discovery yet to be made. Not only is "The Ark of the Covenant of the Lord" a mirror image of "The Great Pyramid of the Emperor" (both terms are equal to 314 or Pi), but so is "The Most Holy Place" a mirror image of "The Lord God of Israel." The Alpha number of both of these terms is 193 or the Star and the Crescent, thus proving once again that an alternate dwelling place for these two symbols is the Ark, or more broadly the room in which the Ark resides.

Thus we now have three pairs of opposites, each of which is

a mirror image of the other, and the situation is fairly crying out to be depicted in the way that we have shown it in Figure 87. An octahedron is one of the five Platonic solids that may be placed in a sphere and whose faces, edges, and vertex angles are all equal and symmetrical. And an octahedron, which is a pyramid resting on top of an inverted pyramid, is ideally suited to represent these three pairs of opposites with its six vertices. Therefore, we have taken the liberty of expressing these concepts in the terms of a bit of mathematical logic.

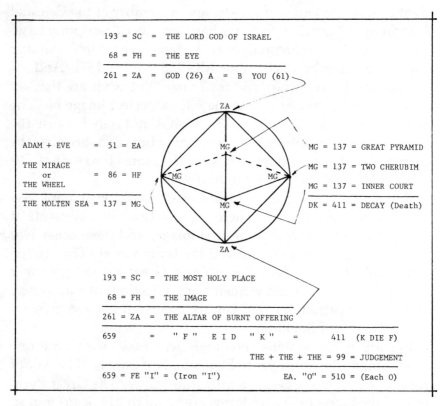

Figure 87
The Octahedron (Ten + Zero) in the Sphere

Figure 87 points out the extremely interesting relationship between the eye, the mirage, and the image. The Alpha numbers for the eye and the image are equal to each other, and the number for the mirage is the same number in reverse. The illusion then is the reverse of both the image and the reality. We have broken the octahedron up into the ten and the zero because the Alpha number for "octa" is 39 or "ten," as opposed to "hedron" which is 64 or "zero." And the ten plus the zero gives the number 100, the number for the Hanged Man or the Soul.

There is still another way in which we can depict these strange relationships. The following tabulation unveils a few more of the truly amazing numerical correspondences between the elements of Solomon's Temple.

The Eye

THE LORD GOD OF ISRAEL . . . . 193 = S C

The Mirage

S (The Star)	19 = S
C (The Crescent)	3 = C
THE ARK OF THE COVENANT	211 = U A
OF THE LORD	103 = J C
TWO CHERUBIM	137 = MG
THE ORACLE (The Sun)	87 = O
Mirage Subtotal	560 = EF O

The Image

THE MOST HOLY PLACE	193 = S C
THE HOLY OF HOLIES	182 = R B
THE ARK SANCTUARY	185 = A HE
Image Subtotal (Scarab: He)	560 = EF O
Grand Total (Mum: Silence)	1,313 = M M

It will be noted that in every case the Star and the Crescent are the initial symbols for the *Eye* which signifies reality, the *Mirage* which signifies illusion, and the *Image* which signifies a reflection of reality. Also it should be noted that the numerical value of both the Mirage and the Image (560) represents the total volume of the Oracle cube, which is the same as that of the Altar of Burnt Offerings and the space above it (table on page 501). This number represents the High Priestess (EF), the Virgin Mother of the World, and the Sun (O) she carries in her womb. It is likewise significant that the exact Alpha number for all three of the names in common usage today that have been substituted for the Oracle (those listed under the Image) is this very same number.

The Soul's Journey

All of the above now brings us to the myth or life drama that the Cabalah is trying to convey relative to the mysteries of the Temple of Solomon. The general idea runs something like this: In the beginning, at the very dawn of time, the sun-god Ra became a Star (Ra = 19 = S). And his sister-wife, the moon-goddess, became a Crescent (a planet which revolves around the star called the "C," and from which life evolves). Thus we may call them the Lovers (S + C = 22 = V), the male and the female, the original archetype of Adam and Eve.

Now *Ra* and his sister-wife "C" loved to get in their Chariot or "CAR" and each night travel through the great "ARC" of the sky that extends from the East to the West. Their chariot is called "CARA" (A CAR), and it is symbolized by Tarot Key 7, the letter W (the double-you). In fact, you may see their image each night as you focus your attention on a particular star and follow it as it travels through that great "arc." But the moon-goddess "C," who represents the planets of the star, is always invisible. Yet they are One, and taken together as a unity, they are known as "The LORD God of Israel," the Star and the Crescent, the number 193.

In the symbolism of the Temple of Solomon, the journey of the Star always begins in the east at the Altar of Burnt Offerings. Here, the Star, the letter "S," is spewed forth from the "Word" (Offerings), and ascends from the Altar into the great arc of the sky. Indeed, we may say that the Star itself is a part of the "offerings" that were originally offered unto the Universal Consciousness God. And what is the final destination of this offering called the Star, as symbolized by the letter "S"? The answer is that after passing through the great pillars of Boaz and Jachin, after passing above the Porch, and after traversing over the great space above the Temple, it finally descends once more into the west, and into that Most Holy Place called the Oracle. Here, the two Cherubim, ever on the lookout for descending stars, catch it safely, and tenderly place it once more into the great Ark of the Covenant.

"This is all well and good," I hear you say, "but is there any evidence that this myth is the one intended to be conveyed?" Yes, strangely enough, evidence does exist that this is so; but you have to look in the King James Version of the Bible, the Authorized Version, to find it. Unfortunately, the translators of the Revised Standard Version missed the cue, so to speak, and deleted a great cabalistic clue from the biblical text.

All through I Kings and II Chronicles, the King James Version refers to the two Cherubim who guard the Ark as "two cherubims." Why did these translators add an unneeded "s" to a word that was already in plural form? To be grammatically correct, we either have one cherub or two cherubim, and never two "cherubims." Then why the unnecessary extra "s"?

The Cabalah tells us that the Universal Consciousness God *intended* for the translators to express it in this fashion. In this way, then, the Star (the S) could ascend from the Altar of Burnt Offerings, and thus change the word *Offerings* to *Offering*. After its journey it would then descend unto the two Cherubim and be caught by them, and thus change the word *Cherubim* to *Cherubims*. Far fetched, you might say? Not at all. The Universal Consciousness God is constantly forcing Man to spell words in such a way so that the words themselves will have a "vibrational rate"—as the Agashan Teachers would say—in harmony with their true meaning.

Now let us examine the contents of the Ark. I Kings 8:9 tells us that there was nothing in it save the "two tables of stone" which had been put there by Moses. The Alpha number for "Two Tables of Stone" is 211 (58 + 59 + 21 + 73); and again we have a cabalistic verification that the contents of the Ark must equate to the Ark itself, for the Alpha number for "The Ark of the Covenant" is this same number: 211 (33 + 30 + 21 + 33 + 94). The sum total of the Ark plus its contents (211 + 211) is then the number 422 which transliterates into DV. Does this mean "Devil"? Or reading it backwards mean "Lived"? It would appear so, because if we add the missing "the" to the phrase and call it "The Two Tables of Stone," the sum will then be 33 + 422 or 455, which spells out the word DEE, the name of the letter D, and the symbol for the Devil.

Now let us examine it a bit further. We learn from Exodus 25:10 that the length of the Ark was 2-1/2 cubits, its breadth was 1-1/2 cubits, and its height was 1-1/2 cubits. The volume of the space within it was then 5.625 cubits (2.5 × 1.5 × 1.5). Now what does the number 5.625 say? It says quite emphatically that "EF BE." And who is Ef? It is the High Priestess of course, the name of the letter "F," and the symbol of Tarot Key 2.

Is the High Priestess then the Devil? Of course not. The letter Dee, or the Devil, was represented by both the Ark *and* its contents. Therefore, the surface area of the six sides of the Ark must now be considered. If the volume of the space within it symbolizes its contents, the area of its sides must represent the Ark itself. The surface area is found by solving the following computation: 2(1.5 × 1.5) + 4(2.5 × 1.5). And what is the answer? You will be actually dumbfounded when you learn that it too is none other than the High Priestess herself! The answer is 19.5 cubits, the Alpha number for the God-Name of the High Priestess.

Again we find that the Ark itself is once more equal to its contents, for when we equate the volume to the surface area, we learn that 5.625 = 19.5, or that EF BE The High Priestess. And this, of course, is quite true. The 6 is equal to the 6, and the 2 is equal to the 2 (The Tarot Key number for the High Priestess is 2). The total value then Tarot-wise is 4, which represents the D or the Devil; but the total value Alpha-wise is 12, which represents the Knight, the Higher Self, or one half of Christ, the letter X. Indeed, the High Priestess herself tells us this same story when we find the total value of her Alpha number: 195 = 19 + 5 = 24 = S + E = X.

The total length of all of the edges of the Ark is also interesting. We find it to be expressed by the following computation: Length = $4(2.5) + 8(1.5) = 22$. And what does the number 22 symbolize? It represents the Lovers, the hero and heroine of our story, Adam and Eve, of course. But *you* are also the contents of the Ark, since its volume was determined to represent EF BE, or $56 + 25$, and if we add the two numbers together we have the number 81, the Alpha number for the God-Name of the Fool, who is none other than U (You).

From the above, it is obvious that the Cabalah is trying to convey the thought that when the Star and the Crescent are placed once more into the Ark of the Covenant—when the Lord God of Israel, the number 193, has entered therein—these two entities, the S and the C, now find themselves in the womb of the Virgin Mother of the World. They represent the unborn Christ within the womb of the Madonna. Thus the second half of the journey of the soul will be as mortal—the descending Star has now entered the reincarnational plane as a Spark of Divinity, as a reincarnating entity, awaiting birth once more upon the physical plane.

Yet is this so unusual? Many times the Agashan Teachers have stated that the Spark of Divinity that resides within the soul is the Soul Atom—the Atom of the Soul. But the Soul Atom, in the final analysis, is in reality a Star. There is no difference; the macrocosm descends to become the microcosm, and the microcosm ascends once more to become the macrocosm. "Worlds within worlds within worlds!" they go on to say, "There within that most minute atom is a world within a world, and the space between one element of an atom and another element of an atom is as vast as from here to the sun." (*The Agashan Discourses*, page 168).

Thus the base line that separates the microcosmic world of Man from the macrocosmic world of the Star, the reincarnational plane as it were, is seen to be the upper level of the Altar of Burnt Offerings. This plane is 10 cubits above the floor level of the Temple, and exactly in the center of the Oracle cube. All that be below it is in the world of Man; all that be above it is in the world of Spirit. The *bodies* of the two Cherubim then, who are 10 cubits high, live in the world of Man; but their *wings* extend up into the world of Spirit. And the upper part of the Temple itself, which is 30 cubits high (I Kings 6:2), then consists of two perfect cubes while the lower part below the dividing line, being 10 cubits high, consists of two half-cubes.

It is also seen that the second half of the journey of the Star will be as a Spark of Divinity residing within the body as mortal. But this could be any body—man, beast, bird, or whatever. The Universal Consciousness God, the Star and the Crescent as it were, does not differentiate between the species and consider one any higher than the other. They are all God's creatures, and I am sure It loves all of Nature with equal intensity.

This journey into the physical world may then be symbolized as traveling on an inverted circular path which begins at the Ark of the Covenant in the Oracle at the west end of the Temple. It covers a vast circular arc equal and opposite to the arc at the dome of the heavens, and it extends way down under the Temple itself. It then rises up again under the Porch, through the inverted reflections of the pillars of Boaz and Jachin, and eventually ends in the east at the upper level of the Altar of Burnt Offerings, exactly at the point where it began.

Now that we have completed a full circle in the journey of the soul, so to speak, we should consider another analogy that simply must be pointed out at this time. Earlier in this volume we showed how the sound of the AUM brought life into manifestation, as opposed to the sound of the OM which signifies its completion. Now the Temple of Solomon, in rather a fantastic manner, echoes these same sounds.

The AUM begins at the Altar of Burnt Offerings with the "A." The Inner Court represents the Great Pyramid and its golden apex sits on top of the Altar. The sound then rises upwards, over and above the "Porch Beam" that supports the roof of the Porch and which extends from Boaz to Jachin, and finally reaches a loud crescendo at the uppermost part of the arc in the space above the Temple. Here, in this part of the arc is the AUM. The Altar is the "A," the Porch Beam is the "U," and the Temple is the "M." The Alpha number for "Porch Beam" is 81 (60 + 21), which is the number for the Fool (Tarot Key 0), represented by the letter U. And the Alpha number for "Temple" is 71, the number for "The Death" (Tarot Key 13), the letter M.

At this point the sound gradually lessons as it diminishes in volume, and it eventually disappears altogether when it is absorbed back into the Ark and into the silence. But at one and the same time a new sound begins to be heard, and it is the OM. It begins in the Oracle, descends down the arc beneath the Temple, and reaches its loudest pitch at the nadir of the circle way down in the earth itself. Then it gradually diminishes in volume as it rises up from under the Porch, up through the inverted reflections of the pillars, until it too disappears into the silence as it surfaces at the top level of the Altar of Burnt Offerings—the exact point where its counterpart, the AUM, first had its beginning. The Altar then represents the Alpha and the Omega, the beginning and the end.

"But how do you get the letters OM out of all of this?" you ask. Very easily. The Alpha number for "The Oracle" is 87, the same as the number for "The Sun" (Tarot Key 19), the letter O. And, of course, the Alpha number for "Temple" is 71 or "The Death," the letter M.

"But what about the space in the arc that lies directly under the Porch?" you persist, "Can you neglect that part of it in a cabalistic interpretation?" And the answer is, of course you can not. Therefore, we must find an appropriate letter to assign to this portion of the lower arc just before the sound of the OM dies off into the silence at the Altar. But don't we already have this letter? Look again at Figure 85. The letter "B" is obviously this letter inasmuch as it represents the square containing the Porch in the first revolution around the Inner Court. Besides, the Alpha number for the term "Porch Steps" is 139 (60 + 79), the number for "The Wheel of Life," the alternate name for the letter "B."

Therefore, the complete name for the lower arc as the sound of the OM travels from the Oracle to the Altar is "OM Be." And what does the "OM Be"? The answer is that the "OM Be AUM," the Alpha and the Omega, the beginning and the end.

We thus have divided the circular course that the soul travels around the Temple into six separate and distinct parts or arcs: the upper hemisphere consisting of the letters "A U M," and the lower hemisphere containing the letters "O M B." And this is as it should be, for the circumference of a circle contains precisely six of its radii—no more and no less.

The "B" is thus seen to be the Silence—the break in the sound between the AUM and the OM. It also allows a pause for identification, to identify the one with the other, and to state that they *Be*. Indeed, the Alpha number for "The Wheel of Life," when added to the number for "Silence," equals "The Wheel of Fortune" (139 + 67 = 206). The following tabulation will illustrate this point a little further:

Alpha Number		God-Name Number		Sum	
A	1	THE EMPEROR	123	124	
U	21	THE FOOL	81	102	
M	13	DEATH	38	51	
	35	AUM Subtotal	242 = X B	277 =	B 77
O	15	THE SUN	87	102	
M	13	DEATH	38	51	
	28	OM Subtotal	125 = A BE	153 =	O C
B	2	THE WHEEL OF FORTUNE	206 = B OF	208 =	BOTH
	65	Grand Total	573	638 =	2(319)
	FE	Reverse of (C GEE F) EGC			B C S

There is a good deal of verification in the Bible that the letters we have chosen (the U and the B) are the correct symbols for the Porch or entrance to the Temple. For instance: I Kings 7: 15, 16 states that the two pillars in the Porch were 18 cubits high apiece, which when added to the chapiters (capitals) which sat on top of the columns, which were 5 cubits high, gives us a total height of 23 cubits to the bottom of the porch beam. Yet II Chronicles 3:4, strangely enough, gives us an apparent contradiction. It states that the Porch in front of the House was 120 cubits high. Well, how high was the Porch? The

I Kings version is more than likely correct because if it were actually 120 cubits high, it would have been called a tower instead of a porch. Yet, there must be a reason for the discrepancy, and we have to look to the Cabalah for the answer. It is very simple: the numbers 23 and 120 stand for the same thing, cabalistically speaking. The number 23 means the letter W, the double-you, or the Chariot; and the number 120 is the Alpha number of "double-you," the name of the very same letter. Is the Cabalah trying to tell us that this is the symbol for the Porch? Apparently so. And when we break up our "double you" into its two parts, we end up with the single "U" plus the "B" (21 + 2 = 23, or U + B = W).

But which part of the Porch is the "U" and which part is the "B"? Again, we must interpret the verses in the Bible cabalistically. Let us examine the net height of the pillars without the capitals. I Kings 7:15 states that they are 18 cubits high; yet II Chronicles 3:15 gives us a contradiction again when it says the net height is 35 cubits without the capitals. There is one dimension, however, upon which they both agree, and that is the height of the chapiters or capitals. Each one is 5 cubits high. Therefore, these then are the clues with which we must work.

Since the total height of the pillars including the capitals determined the height of the Porch, and consequently the "double-you" or the "B + U," it would stand to reason that the pillars would represent the one and the capitals the other. The word "double" obviously refers to the "B" (which is 2) and the "you" to the "U." But which letter do we assign to the pillars, the "B" or the "U"? It is the "B," naturally, since their total net height is 53 (18 + 35), the number for the God-Word "Wheel," the symbol for the letter B. This leaves the number 10 to represent the combined height of the capitals, and this must be you. Indeed, the more we go in the Cabalah, we always seem to end up being the 10. In the final analysis, we are the "10" part of the god *Aten*, the 10th great initiate, as opposed to the "1" part or the "A," otherwise known as the Emperor or the Father.

The Alpha number for "beam" is 21 which means "U." Therefore, the "Porch Beam," which equates to the number 81 or the Fool, can be said to be the "U + PORCH." But let us look at this term a little more carefully. Can't we break it up into the phrase "UP OR C: H"? Of course we can, but what does it mean? It means "Up or Sea: Each"; or, in other words, when each one arrives at the square of the "double-you," he may either rise *up* and enter the upper part of the inner Temple by hurdling the porch beam, or, he may take the other alternative of proceding directly to square "C," and thus fall once more into the Molten Sea, the Sea of Confusion, and by so doing be forced to complete another revolution around the outer squares.

This, in essence, is what the soul's journey through the Wheel of Life is all about. Sooner or later it must come to the crossroads, and when it does, it is faced with the decision of whether to ascend into the higher spiritual consciousness, or ride the Wheel of Life through still another physical incarnation.

The Great Court

Now let us focus our attention on the Great Court which went "round about" and surrounded the entire complex of the Temple of Solomon (II Chron. 4:9; I Kings 6:36; I Kings 7:12). We made the statement in the earlier part of this chapter that we had no data relative to the size of the Great Court, but we were able to reconstruct a fairly plausible floor plan for the Inner Court of the Priests (See Figure 84). However, we wish to retract on this statement a bit. In the light of the information that we have rediscovered during the preparation of this chapter, we feel that we now have enough additional material whereby we can also reconstruct a logical floor plan for the Great Court as well.

Earlier in the chapter we quoted the following lines from I Kings 8:64: "The same day did the king hallow the *middle of the court that was before the house of the* LORD: for there he offered burnt offerings, and meat offerings, and the fat of the peace offerings." We put the key words in italics to emphasize the fact that (1) the Altar is always in the middle of the Court, and (2) the Court that contains this Altar is always in front of or before the House of the LORD, meaning the Temple. From this information we were able to reconstruct the Inner Court of the Priests.

All well and good. However, we neglected at that time to quote the *ending* of the verse (I Kings 8:64) which reads as follows: ". . . because the brasen altar that was before the LORD was too little to receive the burnt offerings, and meat offerings, and the fat of the peace offerings." The preceding was written regarding the dedication ceremonies for the Temple of Solomon, and it simply means that the king had to hallow the middle of the *Great Court* that was in front of the Temple, in order for it to substitute for the Altar of Burnt Offerings, the brazen altar in the middle of the Inner Court of the Priests, because the smaller altar of brass was not large enough to accommodate the thousands who were gathered there on that occasion. The key to the entire interpretation of I Kings 8:64 lies in the identification of the court that is referred to simply as "the court that was before the house of the LORD." Does it mean the Inner Court of the Priests or the Great Court? We believe that it can be correctly identified as being either or both.

With this thought in mind, and following the ideas presented by Figure 85, we have placed the microcosm within the macrocosm, so to speak, and incorporated the entire Inner Court as a single element of the Great Court. We have thus followed the mandate given on the sacred Emerald Tablet of Hermes which reads: "As below, so above; and as above, so below. With this knowledge alone you may work miracles. And since all things exist in and emanate from the ONE Who is the ultimate Cause, so all things are born after their kind from this ONE" (*Agasha: Master of Wisdom*, page 279).

Figure 88, therefore, gives us a general idea of what the Grand Complex which contained all three major elements of the Temple of Solomon might have looked like. The Great Court represents the macrocosm and the Inner Court of the Priests the microcosm. And there, within the microcosm, is the Temple of Solomon itself. But the inner part of the Temple, you will note, lies in that part of the microcosm that represents reality. It is the eye. The image exists in the Court and/or Courts that are in front of or before the House of the LORD.

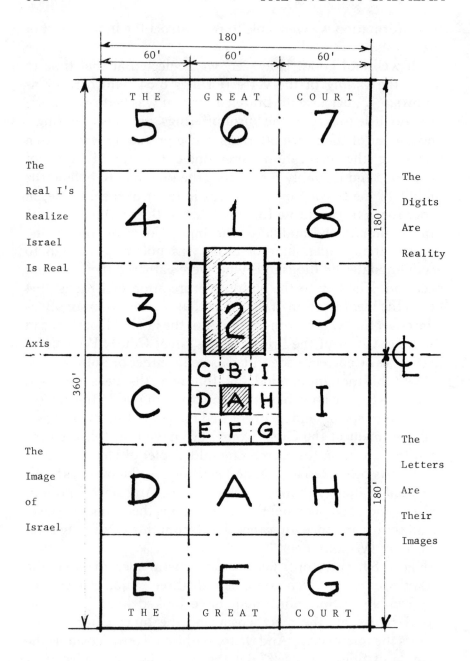

Figure 88
The Grand Complex

One other point before we bring this chapter to a close: The inner part or the interior of the House may be said to consist of the Side Chambers, the Oracle, and the Temple. The Alpha number for all three terms is 330, which may be read as "The O" (33 = The). But this is the same number as the outer part or the exterior of the House which consists of "The Inner Court of the Priests." Its Alpha number is also 330 or "The O." But the absolutely fantastic thing is that the middle part, which can be said to consist of (1) The Porch, and (2) Boaz and Jachin, in turn can be related to the Greek letter Tau. "What is so unusual about that?" you might ask. The answer is that the Tau Cross is shaped like the letter "T," and when we put the "O" or a loop on top of it, we bring the Ankh or the Egyptian symbol for Life into manifestation. Figure 89 illustrates quite graphically its connection with the Temple of Solomon.

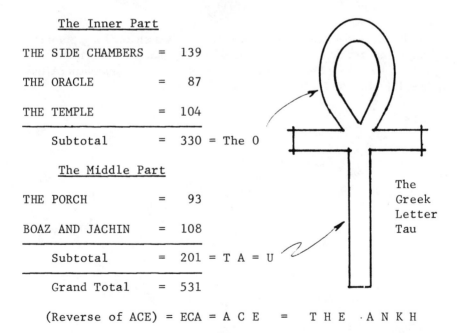

The Inner Part

THE SIDE CHAMBERS   =   139

THE ORACLE   =   87

THE TEMPLE   =   104
_____
    Subtotal   =   330 = The 0

The Middle Part

THE PORCH   =   93

BOAZ AND JACHIN   =   108
_____
    Subtotal   =   201 = T A = U

    Grand Total   =   531

(Reverse of ACE) = ECA = A C E   =   T H E ·A N K H

The Greek Letter Tau

Figure 89
The Ace and the Ankh

Now the amazing thing about all of this is that our Ankh can be made in two different ways: either with the inner part of the House as its upper loop, or with the outer part of the House, the Inner Court of the Priests, as its upper loop. But in each case, the Tau part of the cross is always the Porch including the pillars Boaz and Jachin.

Thus we find how intimately the Ankh cross is associated with the Temple of Solomon. And it is doubly interesting when we realize that the Ankh is not only equal to the Ace, but it is also equal to One (Ankh = 34 = One). Here are our three 1's again: *Ankh, Ace,* and *One,* only this time, instead of being equal to Cara Boga Coty (111), they are equal to Christ (34 + 9 + 34 = 77 = Christ). The reader will also note that the TAU symbol for the Porch breaks down into the U + U or the double-you, thus verifying once again what we learned earlier.

NOTES

1. If the reader wishes to do additional research on King Solomon's Temple, an excellent, illustrated booklet is available: E. Raymond Capt M.A., A.I.A., *King Solomon's Temple: A Study of Its Symbolism* (Artisan Sales, P.O. Box 1497, Thousand Oaks, Calif. 91360)

Chapter 25

THE TREE OF THE SEPHIROTH

In this chapter we shall discuss the third basic component of that great temple of initiation known in the Agashan classes as the Hall of the Initiates. This third ingredient is called the Tree of the Sephiroth which, when combined with the Temple of King Solomon, automatically becomes the Temple of the Living God. The Tree of the Sephiroth is also referred to in many occult circles as the Tree of Life, but this is a misnomer; more correctly, it should be called the *image* of the Tree of Life, the *image* of the Oneness from which we sprang. This item will be clarified further in Volume II of this work.

Before we discuss the Tree in depth, a bit of background material is in order. The following, more or less, is a summary of the cabalistic cosmogony as it was understood by the ancient Hebrew scholars:[1] In the beginning, before the very dawn of time, was AIN SOPH. It represents that which remains after every knowable thing has been removed—the incomprehensible state of pure *Being*. It is circular in shape, being depicted as a giant globe outside of which there is nothing—not even a vacuum. Therefore, AIN SOPH bears the same relationship to the created Universe as the Orphic Egg bears to the body of Man. It is the great Cosmic Egg, within which the creation and dissolution of absolutely everything of any nature whatsoever is constantly taking place. AIN SOPH is therefore the Absolute, all there is, the Most Ancient of all the Ancients, the closed eye as opposed to the open eye, the infinite as opposed to the finite, the vastness of eternity itself, within which the Core of Life is only a mere dot.

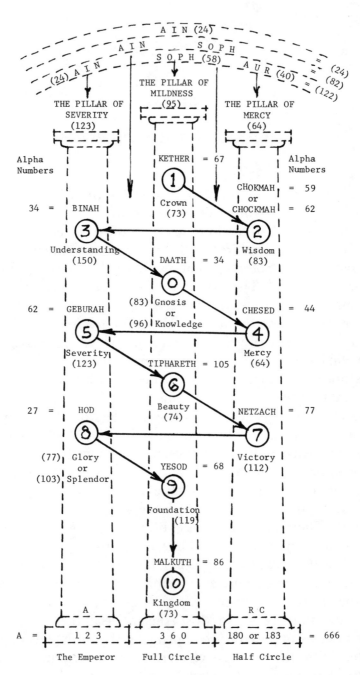

Figure 90
The Tree of the Sephiroth

But the nature of AIN SOPH is itself divided into three parts: (1) AIN, the Vacuum of Pure Spirit; (2) AIN SOPH, the Limitless and Boundless; and (3) AIN SOPH AUR, the Limitless Light. These may be depicted as circular rings within the area of a circle; but in the beginning the Supreme Substance, the AIN, alone permeated the entire area of the circle. Then, as this Substance moved in towards the center of Itself, the ring of AIN SOPH was brought into manifestation, which in reality was a limitation of AIN; and finally the third ring of AIN SOPH AUR, or Light, came into Being which represented a still further limitation. These are depicted as the outer rings of Figure 90.

This continual motion of AIN SOPH towards its center resulted in the establishment of a single dot. This dot was called the great "I AM," and it represented the supreme individualization of the Universal Essence. When this white, shining point of Light first appeared it was called *Kether*, which means the *Crown*. Soon this "dot" expanded into a globe, and out of it radiated a great burst of energy in the form of a zig-zag flash of lightning which radiated inwards towards the center. At key positions in this "lightning flash" nine other great globes appeared, which in turn arranged themselves in the form of a tree. And these nine globes, together with the Crown at the highest position, the apex, are what constitute the first system of the Sephiroth.

We call it the first system because the great area which had been vacated by the withdrawal of AIN SOPH into a single dot, Kether, was filled by four concentric worlds, spheres, or trees—call them what you will—and the light of the ten Sephiroth was reflected down through each of these in turn. This resulted in the establishment of four great world chains, four symbolical trees, called by the ancient Hebrews as: (1) *Atziluth*, the Boundless World of Divine Names; (2) *Briah*, the Archangelic World of Creations; (3) *Yetzirah*, the Hierarchal World of Formations; and (4) *Assiah*, the Elemental World of Substances.

The Alpha numbers of these world chains or trees are in themselves quite unusual because they reveal the following very interesting relationships:

The First Tree:	ATZILUTH	= 117	THE FOOL = 81 = U
The Second Tree:	BRIAH	= 38	THE FOOL = 81 = U
The Third Tree:	YETZIRAH	= 112	THE FOOL = 81 = U
The Fourth Tree:	ASSIAH	= 57	THE FOOL = 81 = U

Grand Total = 324 = 324
The God Aten (A Ten) = C X = 110 = C X

Thus the Fool, who is You, is seen to constitute each of the four worlds or trees. It is also interesting that the Alpha number for "Tree" is identical to that for "Fool."

We find then that each one of these world chains, or trees, contains within itself ten different powers or spheres. Each one contains a parent globe and nine others which sprang forth as emanations, each globe being born out of the one preceding it. "But aren't there eleven different globes in Figure 90?" I hear you ask. Yes, indeed there are eleven different globes, spaces, or worlds depicted in the Tree, but there are still only ten Sephiroth! The answer to the puzzle, and the crux of the entire glyph, is in understanding that there is no Sephirah at the point marked *Daath*. The House of Daath is empty, in other words, because the 10th Sephirah, Malkuth, has *fallen* from its exalted state which it had previously held in the upper Tree, and into the Sea (the letter C, the digit 3) of the Tree immediately below it.

Therefore, the numerical number for the sphere called Daath is the digit 0, which signifies that the house is temporarily empty. But eventually Malkuth, which represents the fallen kingdom, will arise again, and the 10 will revert back to the 0 from whence it came. This will place the Kingdom directly under the Crown of Kether, and to all intents and purposes its king will then be crowned. The 9th Sephirah Yesod will then assume its rightful role as the true "foundation" upon which the Tree rests.

We state that Malkuth had fallen into the Sea (the C or the digit 3), of the Tree immediately below it because as the lightning flash continues its zig-zag course inwards towards the center, the 1st Sephirah of the lower Tree (following the 9th

Sephirah of the Tree immediately preceding it) will fall in the Pillar of Mercy on the right, the 2nd Sephirah in the Pillar of Severity on the left, and the 3rd Sephirah, the letter C, will occupy the house in the middle Pillar of Mildness just below Yesod.

In this way then, we can see that it will take four full manifestations of the lightning flash, four complete Trees to be brought into manifestation, before the 4th kingdom will be a mirror image of the 1st (Kether is in the middle pillar in Atziluth, the right-hand pillar in Briah, the left-hand pillar in Yetzirah, and in the middle pillar again in Assiah). The middle pillar is thus the beginning and the end, the Alpha and the Omega, the first and the last.

The importance of the number 10 is clearly stated in the *Sepher Yetzirah*[2] which states: "There are ten Sephiroth; ten and not nine; ten and not eleven. Try to understand them in thy wisdom and thy intelligence; constantly train on them thy researches, thy speculations, thy knowledge, thy thought and imagination; rest all things on their principle, and restore the Creator on His foundation" (I:4).

It should be stated at this point that practically all we know of the ancient Hebrew Cabalah is set forth in two famous works of antiquity: (1) the *Sepher Yetzirah*, or the "Book of Formation"; and (2) the *Zohar*, which means "brightness." It is usually referred to as the "Book of Splendor." The former is a kind of cosmology, if not a system of physics, and the latter deals more particularly with God, the human soul, and the spiritual world. Both of these books are filled with concepts that are as valid today as when they were written, and they make up the foundation upon which the modern Cabalah has been built.

"There is no end to the ten Sephiroth," the *Sepher Yetzirah* goes on to say, "either in the future or in the past, either in good or in evil, either in height or in depth, either in the East or in the West, either in the South or in the North" (I:5). Thus we see that the infinite is considered to be made up of 10 basic elements—no more and no less.

And yet, strangely enough, it ties all of the Sephiroth

together into five pairs of opposites, all different, and yet united into one overall concept. "The ten Sephiroth," it continues, "are like the ten fingers, five pairs, but linked together by unity" (I:3). The last words provide the explanation and the proof of that which preceded them.

"What are the meanings of each individual Sephirah?" you might ask. The *Sepher Yetzirah* explains them quite well in the following stanzas: "The first of the Sephiroth, One, is the spirit of the living God, blessed be His name, blessed be the name of the One Who lives in Eternity! The Spirit, the Voice, and the Word, that is the Holy Ghost" (I:9).

"Two is the breath which issues from Spirit; it contains the twenty-two letters which form but one single breath" (I:10).

"Three is water, which issues from breath or from air. In the water He dug darkness and void, mud and clay, and graved them in the shape of a garden bed" (I:11).

"Four is fire, which issues from water, and with which He made the throne of His glory, the celestial wheels (Ophanim), the Seraphim and the angelic servitors. With the three together He built His habitation, and it was written: 'Who makest winds thy messengers, and the flaming fire, the ministers'" (I:12).

So much for the first four Sephiroth, which the *Sepher Yetzirah* compares to the four basic elements—Earth, Air, Water, and Fire, or the letters A, B, C, and D. It is interesting to note that Water corresponds with the English letter C, which we have shown earlier to be a symbol of the Sea.

It goes on to compare the next six Sephiroth with the six different directions one can travel in the world: the four cardinal points of the compass (East, West, North, and South), as well as up and down. However, it is unclear as to specifically which of the Sephiroth it is in reference to. Yet we do not have to remain in ignorance for long. All we have to do is apply a cabalistic interpretation to the following stanzas, and our mystery is solved:

"The end of the ten Sephiroth is tied to their beginning as the flame to the fire-brand, for the Lord is One and there is no second to Him: and what will you count before the One?" (I:7).

"Close your mouth that you speak not, and your *heart* that you do not ponder; and if your *heart* be too busy, bring it back to its place, for therefore it is said: run and return, and it is on this verse that a covenant was made" (I:8).

We have put the word "heart" into italics because it is the key to the entire mystery. We learned earlier in this work (Figure 2) that the word HEART is only an anagram for EARTH, and isn't the Earth the World or the Kingdom? This would certainly appear to be reasonable, especially since the 10th Sephirah is symbolized by the letter J or the World (Tarot Key 21).

Therefore, if our "Earth" is not too busy, let us follow the suggestion put forth in the *Sepher Yetzirah* and bring our "Earth" once more back to its proper place in the empty house of Daath. We shall have therefore fulfilled the covenant which was made years ago, and which states that after something has "run" its course, it shall eventually "return" again from whence it came.

The stanzas also explain the strange relationship between our planet Earth and the element Fire, which the *Sepher Yetzirah* states to be the 4th Sephirah. The Alpha number for "Earth" or "Heart" is 52, which means "Devil," the letter D, and consequently the true 4th Sephirah. And isn't the core of the Earth a veritable "sun" of tremendous fire or energy, which only bears out the statement made by the Greek philosopher Heraclitus when he said, "This world was ever, is now, and ever shall be an ever-living Fire"?

Then too, when we return the Earth to the 4th Sephirah of Daath, we will have literally tied it to the beginning (Kether) in the same way that the flame is tied to the fire-brand. The Alpha number for "fire-brand" is "38 + 39" or "Death + Ten," and this most certainly does represent our Kingdom, the planet on which we live. But what is it really? The Alpha number for "fire-brand" (38 + 39) adds up to 77, the number of *Christ*. But the Alpha number for "flame" is 37, the CG, the Being, the reverse of the number for "Crown" which is 73. Therefore, our "flame + fire-brand" is the same as "Agasha + Christ," the

Father and the Son, etc.; and the sum total of these two opposites, this particular pair as it were, is 114, AN = O, the Tower
or Hierophant, the "ORE" from which all things are made.

Let us now examine the strange relationship of Earth, Air,
and Water with Fire, the first three Sephiroth with the fourth.
The Alpha numbers are tabulated below:

1. EARTH:	52 = DEVIL	= D	= 4	
2. AIR:	28 = MAN	= N	= 14	
3. WATER:	67 = HANGED MAN	= N	= 14	
4. FIRE:	38 = DEATH	= M		DEATH = 38

185 = 14   LIFE = 32 + DEATH = 38

AHE = N   (A HEN)

And what does a hen do? The answer is, it lays eggs. The
Alpha number for "A Hen" is 28 or *Man;* and the Alpha
number for "Eggs" is 38 or *Death* (577 = 19, or EGG = S, and
EGGS = 38 = Death). The next 6 Sephiroth (Chesed through
Yesod) are then seen to be the "eggs" that our "hen" has laid: all
the possible directions that we can travel as we journey
through the Tree of Life—East and West, North and South,
and Up and Down.

Let us now return to Figure 90. The student of the Cabalah
will immediately notice that we have added a rather peculiar
way to spell the name of the 2nd Sephirah (Chockmah instead
of Chokmah). We realize that there is no exact, accurate way to
translate the sounds of the Hebrew words into English. The
way that they are spelled today has only come about through
the process of evolution. Common usage has eventually dictated the way that they are now spelled in English, and in many
cases today's spelling is quite different from the way that the
words were spelled in the past (Sephiroth vs. Sefiroth, Tiphareth vs. Tiphereth, etc.). And we can say the same thing for the
English words that represent the accepted translation for the
equivalent words in Hebrew. For example: Which is the correct
translation of Hod: Glory or Splendor? There used to be many
other variants, but again, usage has finally eliminated all of the

others, to the point where only those words that appear in Figure 90 are in common use today. The only exception is the English name for Hod; both terms must be included inasmuch as neither one has surpassed the other.

Then why did we spell "Chokmah" as "Chockmah"? The answer is rather interesting, and again it points out that a so-called "accident" sometimes changes the course of history. One of the best books on the Tarot today is *A Complete Guide to the Tarot* by Eden Gray.[3] In this important work, the author consistently uses the same spelling for the Hebrew words that we have used: namely, the present accepted way to spell them. There is one exception, however. In the diagram for the Tree of Life that appears on page 127, she breaks her own rules of spelling and "accidentally" changes the spelling for "Chokmah" (the way she spells it in the rest of the book) to "Chockmah." Why did she subconsciously add the additional "C"? Here again, we have the same problem as to why the King James translators of the Bible added the extra "S" to "Cherubim." There must be a cabalistic explanation in this case, in the same way there was in the other. And indeed there is—a most important one.

In the opinion of the One who is really writing this book (the author is only his scribe), she was subconsciously wishing to add the three 1's of Ain, Ain Soph, and Ain Soph Aur to the 2nd Sephirah of Chokmah, which represents Wisdom. She wished to remove their image from the Divine Sea as represented by the three upper arcs, and place this "C" into the Wheel of Life, the letter B. In other words, she wished them to *Be*.

What is the net effect of this magical act? (Yes, changing the spellings of words is a very potent act, and can be considered to be the equivalent of an act of magic.) The answer is that it brings the Beast 666 into full manifestation, and by so doing brings the entire Tree of the Sephiroth up to its full potential. The sum total of the Sephiroth in the left-hand pillar is then 123 which represents the Emperor, and the total of the Sephiroth in the middle pillar in 360 degrees or a full circle. But with the addition of the extra "C" to Chokmah, it is sufficient to take all three of the Sephiroth in the right-hand pillar out of their 180 degree or "D" status, and place them into their rightful category of the RC (180 + 3 = 183 = RC), the Tower of the Moon. The sum total of all of this is then the Beast whose number is 666 (123 + 360 + 183 = 666). And not only that, but the combination of the left-hand pillar and the right-hand pillar now bring into manifestation an ARC (123 = A, and 183 = RC); and this circular *arc* is then able to blend most beautifully with the full 360 degree circle of the middle pillar.

Before we leave Figure 90, let us realize the significance of the lower arc of AIN SOPH AUR which represents Light. The total Alpha value of this term is 122, and this becomes even more significant when we realize that it is identical to the Alpha value of "The Pillar of" (33 + 68 + 21 = 122 = AIN SOPH AUR). Thus, the Cabalah has informed us that the true meaning of AIN SOPH AUR is that it represents a Pillar of Light. But not only that, there is even a greater significance to be seen in this glyph of the Tree of the Sephiroth. The words AIN SOPH AUR center themselves over each one of the pillars. Thus AIN governs the Pillar of Severity, SOPH governs the Pillar of Mildness, and AUR governs the Pillar of Mercy.

But let us not stop here. What does the middle arc of AIN SOPH govern? It is quite evident that this arc of the *Limitless and Boundless* governs the *space* between the pillars! Here then, is the answer to still another one of the mysteries; that is, to find an adequate, easily understood, symbol for this portion of the Trinity. And the term "empty space," or the space *between* objects or things, is a perfect symbol. How then can we symbolize AIN, the highest aspect of them all? Well, this is where I am stopping. Aside from the fact that it obviously represents a perfect vacuum, where not even minute molecules of gas, or even the nuclei of atoms exist, we cannot say anything more about it. Or can we? Perhaps we can. The word AIN means "IN A," or that which is *in* A. We can also break the letter N apart into AM, and state that AIN means "I AM A." In other words, it means the great "I AM" which is "A." Other than that we can't help you a bit. You will just have to figure it out for yourself.

Now let us study the Tree of the Sephiroth insofar as it relates to a pack of spheres. The following Figure 91 should prove quite enlightening in this direction:

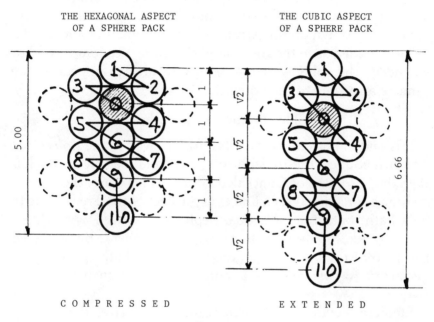

THE HEXAGONAL ASPECT
OF A SPHERE PACK

THE CUBIC ASPECT
OF A SPHERE PACK

COMPRESSED   EXTENDED

Figure 91
The Tree of the Sephiroth as Reflected in a Sphere Pack

If one were to construct a pyramid of spheres (as in Figure 23), you would discover that the packing of the spheres in every plane parallel to the base would be in a cubic fashion; that is, they would arrange themselves either in two-dimensional squares or three-dimensional octahedrons or cubes (the spheres in every odd-numbered plane are directly above each other). However, as soon as you observed this very same sphere pack from a vantage point perpendicular to one of its faces, you would find all of the spheres arranged in either two-dimensional triangles or hexagons, or three-dimensional tetrahedrons or cuboctahedrons (the 12 spheres in 3 adjacent planes which surround and touch a single sphere at the center). Therefore, the way the spheres are arranged in any sphere pack is simply a matter of where the viewer is who is observing them.

Now the same condition exists when we observe the Tree of the Sephiroth. It may appear to be compressed in the way the left-hand diagram of Figure 91 depicts it (if it were constructed in any plane parallel to one of the sides of the pyramid); or then again, if one would observe it from the vantage point of looking directly down on the pyramid from above, it would appear to be extended as in the right-hand diagram. Yet compressed or extended, the spheres of the Sephiroth always appear in the same relationship to each other.

The Twenty-Two Paths

It is said in both the *Sepher Yetzirah* as well as the *Zohar* that 22 Paths connect the 10 Sephiroth, the combination of which is then the "32 Paths of Concealed Glory." Therefore, the ancient Hebrews considered each and every aspect of the Tree of Life to be a Path, both the individual Sephiroth, as well as the highways, roads, or tunnels that interconnect them. But in order for us to distinguish the Sephiroth from the Paths proper, it is necessary to first make a qualitative distinction between the two.

Stephan Hoeller in *The Royal Road*[4] theorizes that the ten Sephiroth represent relatively objective states of consciousness (the ten numbers from 1 to 10), while the 22 Paths stand for subjective experiences which the individual psyche undergoes while its consciousness is being transferred from one Sephirah, or state of consciousness, to another. And we tend to go along with this theory. The 22 Paths are then represented by the 22 letters of the ancient Hebrew alphabet or the 22 keys of the Major Arcana of the Tarot; and the 10 Sephiroth in each of the four kingdoms from Atziluth to Assiah are the numbered keys of the Minor Arcana from the Ace to the Ten. In this way we may then envision each Sephirah as a town or way station wherein the traveler may tarry for a while, as opposed to the Paths which become highways designed for continuous movement while the wayfarer is moving from one locale to another.

It is a matter of interest that the modern-day Sephirothic Tree is usually depicted in a hexagonal manner (Figure 92),[5] thus indicating an original close packing of the spheres when each of the Sephiroth is expanded (in the way that you would blow up a balloon) to the point where it touches its neighbor. Then wouldn't it be reasonable to assume that the various Paths in reality had their origin at the points of contact between the Globes or Spheres? It would appear to be the case. The only discrepancy lies in the horizontal Paths such as between Chokmah and Binah, or in the diagonal Paths between Binah and Tiphareth for an example; but this doesn't offer any real problem because when you eliminate the central Sephirah such as Daath, the spheres of Chokmah, Binah, and Tiphareth actually do expand in the direction of these Paths to the point where they ultimately touch.

For the purposes of a better understanding of the Tree, and to make our point a little clearer, we have drawn up Figure 93 which replaces Malkuth or the Kingdom back into its proper position as the "Earth-Heart" of the Tree. And the reader will easily ascertain that we still have our 22 Paths between the individual Sephiroth. Other than that, there is no real difference betwen Figure 92 and Figure 93. But to avoid a numbering confusion in this new arrangement, we have designated the 10 successive emanations of the Sephiroth by the letters A through J. We have also retitled them with the God-Words of these letters along with the four elements and the six possible directions one may travel in space as instructed by the *Sepher Yetzirah*.

I am sure that the reader will be absolutely astounded (as was the writer) when he fully realizes the impact of Figure 93. I just couldn't believe my eyes as I summed up the Alpha numbers for each of the terms in our revised Tree of Life. Here we have the *Emperor* of the *Earth* in his number 1 position at the top of the Tree. And not to be outdone by her husband the Emperor, there lies the *Empress* of the *World* in the Yesod position at the base or the "foundation" of the Tree. And how did this situation all come about? Very easily. The Emperor simply *fired* the Devil and kicked him out. Of course, the CIA was indirectly responsible for this action. But isn't this only natural for the CIA to act in this manner? Hasn't it instigated many

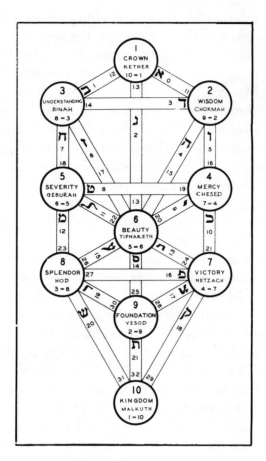

Figure 92
The 22 Paths to the Fallen Kingdom[5]

revolutions in the past among the kingdoms of the earth in order to accomplish some worthwhile cause? This may or may not be the case, but in any event the Cabalah seems to think that it is so.

Who then heads the left-hand Pillar of Severity? The answer is Eve, the letter Vee, depicted by the Alpha number for the Lovers. And who heads the right-hand Pillar of Mercy? The answer is You, the letter U, the Fool, the counterpart of Eve. But by far the most fantastic discovery is the realization that as Justice now prevails, it is the Lovers, Adam as well as Eve, who

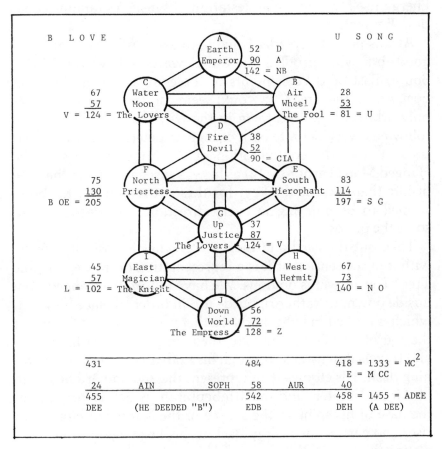

Figure 93
The 22 Paths to the Arisen Kingdom

now rule the middle Pillar of Mildness from the CG (center of gravity) position of the sphere of Tiphareth. Yes indeed, the entire Tree of Life has now become a "love song" with the hero and heroine of our story its major participants. Even the Devil appears therein, as the sum total of not only the Eve column but the Adam column as well. But aren't you and I in reality also the Devil? The Agashan Teachers have said time and again that this is so. Well, maybe not forever, because the Cabalah also shows us that when we subtract AIN SOPH AUR from our Tree of Life we then no longer equate to the Devil—only to

Energy itself, a living manifestation of Einstein's famous equation, $E = mc^2$.

At this point the reader is liable to ask, "All this is well and good, but what proof is there that we now have the North, South, East, and West points of the compass in their correct position on the Tree?" It would seem, on the surface, that we only arbitrarily placed them in the way that we did. No, we followed a very definite path of logic in determining their positions. It was the configuration of the arms and legs of the Hanged Man (Tarot Key 12) as he was suspended from the Tree of Life that gave us the key; for these extremities of his body seemed to be pointing in every direction that we needed to solve the puzzle.

Take out the card and look at it. What is basically wrong with it in the sense that it is a representation of the Sephirothic Tree? The answer is obvious. We have to turn the Hanged Man upside down, or rather rightside up, in order to place his head, which is bathed in light, in the Kether position of the Crown at the top of the Tree. The light then emanates from his crown and travels downwards through his body in the form of a lightning flash. His elbows then represent the 2nd and 3rd Sephirah of Air and Water, and the 4th Sephirah, which is Fire, lies at the base of his spine as the source of the Kundalini Fire which rises and carries the energy back to his head again, thus completing the circuit. But some of this energy is lost into the great Abyss, the bottomless pit, and here is the crux of the matter. Figure 94 shows how this energy reenters his body through his left foot, and consequently brings into manifestation all of the directional points in the lower globe.

We have used the geometrical figures of the tetrahedron (a pyramid on a triangular base) and the octahedron (a dual pyramid resting on a square base) in order to graphically show how the lightning flash literally travels from his head to his toes. The base of the pyramid then designates the North, South, East, and West points of the compass and its two apexes the directions Up and Down. Very well. Now follow this energy as it enters his left foot at the South, travels horizontally through his leg to his knee at the North, then up through his thigh to his heart at the upper apex, and finally down again through his right leg bringing into manifestation the West, East, and Down vertices respectively. This is the principle, then, that we used to locate the points of the compass in Figure 93.

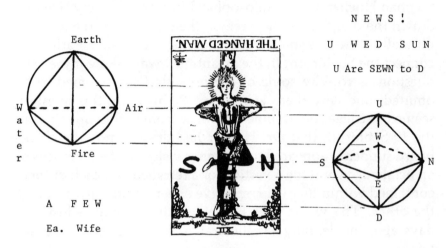

Figure 94
The Hanged Man Points the Way

I am sure that the reader will also be pleased at the message Figure 94 brings us, sort of as a piece of dessert as a reward for our efforts. Not only do we find that the Hanged Man's consciousness seems to be in the center of the upper sphere of the tetrahedron, but it also seems to be married to the lower sphere of the octahedron. There is a wedding in process, although it is not exactly clear as to who is marrying whom. It is perfectly clear, however, that the Fool, who is you, is literally and truly SEWN to the Devil, the letter D.

The Three-Dimensional Tree

All of the above now brings us to an entirely new concept of the Sephirothic Tree. In fact, this new concept is perhaps the greatest and most significant one of them all. In a nutshell, the idea is to change the Tree of Life from the two-dimensional way we normally see it, and instead visualize it as existing in the three-dimensional world of space.

The idea for this new concept came to me as the end result of almost a synchronistic series of events. It was Wednesday evening, June 13, 1979, and I was attending the 5th lecture of a series of six talks on the Cabalah (He spells it Kabbalah) by Dr. Stephan Hoeller at the Philosophical Research Society. He had drawn the diagram of the Tree on the chalkboard the way we normally view it, and he was explaining the various Paths that connect the Sephiroth. In the meantime I was asking myself the question as to why some of the possible Paths seemed to be omitted, and why there were only 22. Instantly this question seemed to trigger off an inner response from within myself, and the 10 Sephiroth that Dr. Hoeller had drawn upon the chalk-board suddenly appeared to my inner vision as the 6 vertices of an octahedron and the 4 vertices of a tetrahedron, each of them contained within its own respective sphere, and one on top of the other. The vision that I received that evening—just five days ago, incidentally—is illustrated in Figure 95 on the ad-joining page.

I say that this was the result of a rather synchronistic series of events because just the previous week, on June 6, 1979, I had had a very similar psychic experience. It was during that lec-ture that I received some of the information that appears in the forepart of this chapter. It seems that the atmosphere created in the auditorium on those particular evenings was sufficient to bring to the surface from the inner planes of consciousness a good deal of supplementary information relative to what the speaker was saying. I have used this method many times in the past while attending the taped lectures of the Agashan classes, and all I can say is that it works. Agasha's voice seems to act as a catalyst that triggers off additional information that is sent from the soul, but the synchronistic aspect comes about when we consider why that particular tape was played on the precise evening that I attended the class. Invariably something was said that affected that which is written in this book. And why did Dr. Hoeller elect to do a series of talks on the Sephirothic Tree at precisely the time this chapter was being written? And not only that, but why was I inspired to attend these lectures in the first place? The answers to these questions fall under the general heading of *Synchronicity*, a term which implies the interrelationship of all things.

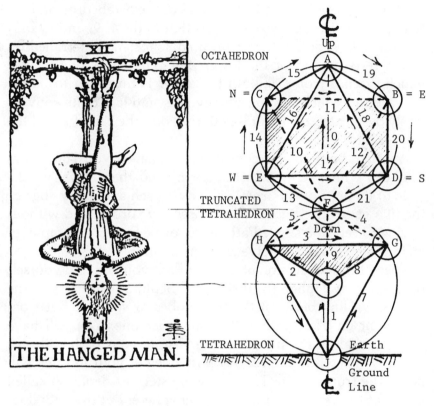

Figure 95
The Three-Dimensional Tree and Its 32 Paths

But let us return once again to Figure 95. If one would visualize the shaded rectangle CBDE to represent the inner square base of an octahedron upon which the upper and lower 4-sided pyramids rest, you would get the picture rather quickly. The lower tetrahedron or 3-sided pyramid is inverted, and the shaded triangle HGI represents the plane of its triangular base, which in this case is directly under and parallel to the square base of the octahedron. We have lettered the six vertices of the octahedron by the letters A to F to correspond with the six Sephiroth from Kether to Tiphareth, and the four vertices of the tetrahedron by the letters G to J to correspond with the four Sephiroth from Netzach to Malkuth. But the absolutely amazing thing about Figure 95 is that it shows all 22 paths that connect the Sephiroth to be the *edges* of the octahedron and the tetrahedron. The only exception is that Paths 4, 9, and 5 (DIE) are the edges of another truncated (shortened) tetrahedron which rests on top of the lower one. The trunk of the Tree which extends from Malkuth to Kether is thus seen to be the *axis* around which the spheres revolve, and it is quite conveniently designated by Tarot Key 0, the Fool, the 22nd Path of the Tree of Life.

Another point to be considered is that if you start from Malkuth which represents the Earth, and then travel up the Tree to its tip, your journey will cover each and every edge of the two geometric figures in a consecutive order, and without having to repeat a single Path twice, or be forced to jump over an intervening gap to arrive at the next numbered Path.

Then at the conclusion of the 21st Path you will find yourself once again at Tiphareth, the central Sephirah that acts as the connecting link between the two globes or spheres. But from this point on your path will be an inner one. You will have completed all of the outer edges and now your path will turn inwards. Therefore the 22nd and final leg of your journey will be up the trunk of the Tree to the mysterious Sephirah called Daath at the very center of the upper sphere. But the Path does not end here. It continues on in its vertical direction, unabated, until it eventually comes to a halt at the tip of the Tree. And once you have arrived at Kether, you will then receive your crown and thus be king of your kingdom.

Thus we find in one simple diagram a visual representation of the Fool's pilgrimage from consciousness to consciousness in his effort to obtain self-realization. But where are the other ten Paths? The answer is that they lie within the Sephiroth themselves, the individual way stations that act as central points of consciousness between the outer Paths. But this is not all. They also may be said to represent the path of the original lightning flash that first brought the ten Sephiroth into manifestation.

But once the Universe is created, it then needs to be experienced. Therefore it was inevitable that the time would eventually arrive whereby the Fool (who is You), having helped to write the Book of Life, must then experience the result of his own creation. Figure 96 depicts his downward journey which, incidentally, is the inverse of Figure 95.

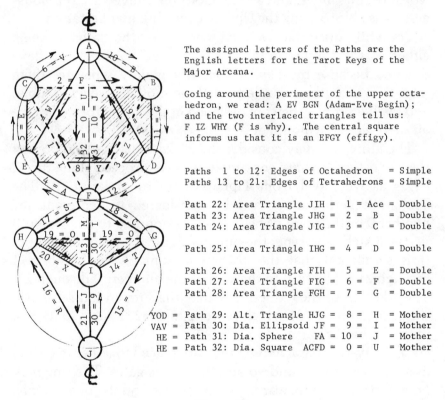

The assigned letters of the Paths are the English letters for the Tarot Keys of the Major Arcana.

Going around the perimeter of the upper octahedron, we read: A EV BGN (Adam-Eve Begin); and the two interlaced triangles tell us: F IZ WHY (F is why). The central square informs us that it is an EFGY (effigy).

Paths 1 to 12: Edges of Octahedron = Simple
Paths 13 to 21: Edges of Tetrahedrons = Simple

Path 22: Area Triangle JIH =	1 = Ace = Double
Path 23: Area Triangle JHG =	2 = B	= Double
Path 24: Area Triangle JIG =	3 = C	= Double

Path 25: Area Triangle IHG = 4 = D = Double

Path 26: Area Triangle FIH = 5 = E = Double
Path 27: Area Triangle FIG = 6 = F = Double
Path 28: Area Triangle FGH = 7 = G = Double

YOD = Path 29: Alt. Triangle HJG = 8 = H = Mother
VAV = Path 30: Dia. Ellipsoid JF = 9 = I = Mother
HE = Path 31: Dia. Sphere   FA = 10 = J = Mother
HE = Path 32: Dia. Square ACFD = 0 = U = Mother

Figure 96
The Journey of the Fool

The first chapter and verse of the *Book of Formation* (*Sepher Yetzirah*) reads as follows: "In thirty-two mysterious paths of wisdom did the Lord (the Almighty, Merciful and Gracious

God) write. His name is holy; He is exalted and holy. He created His Universe by the three forms of expression: Numbers, Letters, and Words."[6]

Now what are the numbers? The *numbers* are obviously the Sephiroth, the 10 digits, the external points or *vertices* of the two geometric figures. The *letters* are then the *edges* of the figures, the connecting links between the vertices; and the *words* are represented by the *areas* of each triangular face. Thus through the powers inherent in numbers, letters, and words (points, lines, and areas), God, the Universal Consciousness, was able to bring the Universe into full manifestation.

You will notice that we have designated the Paths as being either of the simple, double, or "mother" variety. We have done so because the *Sepher Yetzirah* plainly separates them into: "Twenty-two basal letters: three mothers, seven double, and twelve simple; they are designed in the voice, formed in the air, and set in the mouth at five places" (II:3).

Therefore, we may consider the 22 *basal* letters to represent the 22 *vertices* that are encountered as we proceed along the 21 *edges* as we travel from Tiphareth (F) to Malkuth (J). The Tiphareth vertex may then be considered to represent the number 0 or the point of beginning, as opposed to the Malkuth vertex which represents the number 21 or the point of ending. It is significant that the arithmetic sum of the numbers 1 through 21 is identical to the sum of the numbers 0 through 21. The addition of the 0 doesn't change the sum an iota; it is still the same number 231 which represents the 231 gates spoken of in the following verse:

"Twenty-two basal letters: they are placed together in a ring, as a wall with two hundred and thirty-one gates. The ring may be put in rotation forwards or backwards and its token is this: Nothing excels in good, and nothing excels in evil" (II:4).

At this point the reader is liable to ask, "But the *Sepher Yetzirah* plainly states that there are only 12 simple letters. How then can you count the edges of the tetrahedrons also among the simple letters?" Very easily. Verses 9 through 12 of Chapter I tell how the Creator (the 1) brought the 2nd, 3rd, and

4th Sepirah into manifestation as Air, Water, and Fire. But then Verse 13 clarifies the situation by stating:

"He chose three of the simple letters, a secret belonging to the three mothers, and put them in His Great Name and sealed them with six extensions" (I:13). "His Great Name" could then be considered as the inner triangle IHG within the double tetrahedron, and the six extensions which seal it are then the six edges which lead to each upper and lower vertex (Points F and J). Therefore, it is plainly seen that the *Sepher Yetzirah* intends for each outer edge of the two solid geometric figures to represent a "simple" letter.

The seven "double" letters also become quite logically the seven triangular face areas of the double tetrahedron. Isn't an area "double" in that it is computed from two numbers, a height and a width? But even more than this self-evident fact, the *Sepher Yetzirah* seems to describe our double tetrahedron quite beautifully in Chapter VI, Verse 11 which reads: "Seven are divided, three against three, and one is equilibrating between the two groups."

To properly comprehend the true meaning of the "mother" letters, we have to embrace the mathematics of a sphere pack and the YOD HE VAV HE of all creation. It is rather a complex subject and difficult to understand in its entirety, but perhaps we might point out a few of its more fundamental concepts right here. Basically, it is that the "mother" letters are transcendental; that is, they cannot be represented by any finite number, but only as the square root of a finite number. In other words, they are infinite.

Let us start with basic principles: (1) YOD may be designated as an equilateral *triangle* made up of at least three points or spheres, and (2) HE may be referred to as a *square* of at least four points or spheres. These two forms, the 3 and the 4, are constantly in opposition to each other. The former represents harmony between three independent and yet interrelated units, and the latter discord between two pairs of opposites such as good and evil, right and wrong, etc.

Now where does the VAV come in? The VAV represents

duality—two separate units, each complete unto itself, but yet combined with the other into a unity. Thus the total of the 2, 3, and 4 gives us the BCD or the Beast, and this in turn equates to the 9 or the "I." But if we add unity (the 1) to this sum, we have the number 10, and we are right back to where we were in the beginning—in the totality of the Father.

The three "mother" letters are then seen to be the inner measurement, or the diagonal measurement if you will, of these three geometrical figures—the triangle, the square, and the double tetrahedron. Here in these three mother letters we have a manifestation of YOD HE VAV, which can be expressed as the sum of $10 + 5 + 6 = 21$, and which in turn reverts back to the English letter U, or the Fool who is You.

From the above, we can quite easily understand that our lower "sphere" containing the double tetrahedron is not really a sphere at all, but an ellipsoid (an ellipse rotated about its axis giving an egg-shaped appearance). It only *appears* to be a sphere because of the way it is rotated in Figure 96. But now that we are approaching the heart of the matter, we can begin to strip away these illusions and see things the way they really are—in the same way that we now perceive the Tree as a three-dimensional entity as opposed to the two-dimensional way we had previously visualized it.

Figure 97 attempts to bring this new concept of the Tree of Life a little more into focus. Here, in the apex of a pack of spheres, rests the octahedron with its six principal points or globes. The spheres of our Sephirothic Tree are numbered in their normal manner, in the same way that they are numbered in Figure 92. Kether is then at the number 1 position at the crown, and Tiphareth is at the number 6 position as the CG between the double tetrahedron and the octahedron. The inverted tetrahedron of Netzach, Hod, Yesod, and Malkuth (Spheres 7, 8, 9, and 10) is seen to be suspended from Tiphareth, and free to rotate around it in the same manner as the pendulum of a clock.

We are now in a position to accurately determine the numerical value of our three mother letters. For purposes of our anal-

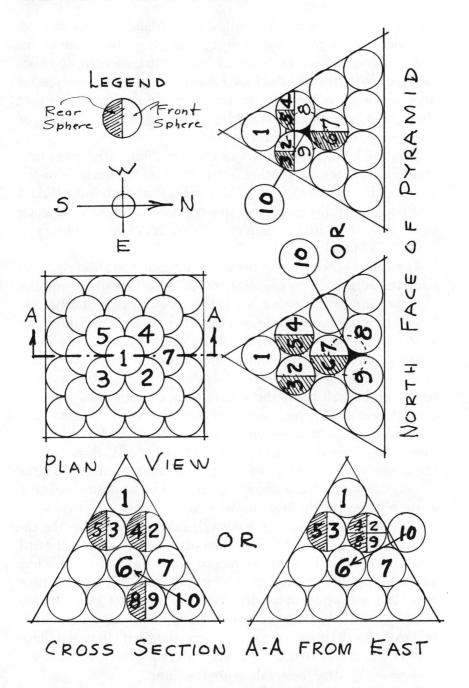

Figure 97: The Sephirothic Tree as the Apex of a Sphere Pack

ysis, we shall consider the radius of each and every sphere in our sphere pack to be 1 or unity. In this way, then, the diameter of every sphere becomes 2; and the true length of every "simple" path (the length of the edges connecting the vertices) is also 2. We are assuming that the length of each side of either the octahedron or the tetrahedron extends from the center of one sphere to the center of its neighbor.

Very well. Figure 96 shows us that the 29th Path brings into manifestation the 1st mother letter which is the *altitude* of the triangle HJG (I like to refer to this triangle as each judge). And inasmuch as all three sides of this equilateral triangle are each equal to 2, its altitude is $\sqrt{3}$ or 1.73205 08075. . . . Let us just call it 1.732 for short.

The 2nd mother letter is brought into manifestation by traveling the 30th Path up the *diameter* of the ellipsoid JF, and the computation of this value is a little more difficult. It amounts to determining the altitude of a tetrahedron and then doubling it. We know from Proposition 13 in Book 13 (a strange combination of numbers) of *Euclid's Elements* that the square of the diameter of a *sphere* in which a tetrahedron is inscribed is equal to one and a half times the square of one of its sides, but this doesn't help us in determining the diameter of an *ellipsoid* containing two tetrahedrons back to back. Nevertheless, the altitude of a tetrahedron can be proved to be $\sqrt{8/3}$, thus making the diameter of the ellipsoid double this amount 3.26598 6322 . . . . Let us just call it 3.266 for short, and by so doing, assign it as the number for the 2nd mother letter.

This then brings us to the 31st Path which leads up the diameter of the sphere containing the octahedron. This is the 3rd mother letter, and it corresponds to not only the first HE, but also the final HE of the God Name YOD HE VAV HE. These two HE's are philosophically different, and yet one can see from Figure 84 that they are numerically identical. The first HE relates to the diameter of a *sphere,* and the final HE to the diagonal of a *square,* two completely different geometric figures, and yet in this case their values are the same.

The altitude of each 4-sided pyramid extending up and down

from the square base CBDE can be shown to be equal to $\sqrt{2}$, where 2 is taken to be the length of each side. Its value is then 1.41421 35623 . . . If we read the first 8 digits cabalistically, we may read it as "A DAD B ACE," and this is just exactly what the Father is—an Ace! But if we double this term, and by so doing bring the 3rd mother letter into manifestation, we find that the diameter of the sphere containing the octahedron is 2.82842 71247. . . . Let us also shorten this term in the same way that we did the others and call it simply 2.828.

Now we have numerical values for all three of our mother letters, as well as the value of the 32nd Path taken by the Fool as he descends down the diagonal of the square ACFD (2.828). But what about the mystical 33rd Path, a Path that cannot be sought but only bestowed (as the honorary 33rd degree of Free Masonry)? Where lies this Path? Its value, the same as the values of the 31st and the 32nd Paths, is also 2.828; for it represents the third and last possible diagonal of an octahedron. And there you have it, precise and to the point, all of the significant figures from which the balance of the dimensions can be computed for our Tree of Life.

We might point out though, that the cross section A-A shown in Figure 97 is not an accurate representation. This cross section through the middle of a sphere pack should show each alternate row of spheres snuggled in between its upper and lower neighbors. Figure 98 corrects the picture, so to speak, and more accurately depicts what it would be like if you were in the very center of a pyramid of spheres. In fact, we have taken the liberty of altering our spheres slightly (making them into oblate spheroids in much the same manner as our Earth) so that they will fit snugly within the confines of the Great Pyramid.

One can see from a study of Figure 98[7] that the Queen's Chamber was intended to signify the very center of the Great Pyramid, and consequently (in our sphere pack analysis), it also signifies the mysterious Sephirah Daath which is located at the midpoint of the central inner square of the octahedron. But what is even more interesting, the descending passage that extends from the entrance down to the Pit intersects the vertical axis directly in the center of the 6th sphere of Tiphareth. It is this Sephirah then that symbolizes the great Abyss, that infamous bottomless Pit spoken of so frequently in the ancient cosmogonies.

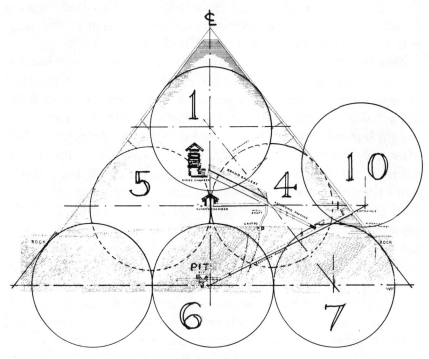

Figure 98
A Cross Section Through the Great Pyramid[7]

But is this so surprising? After all, Tiphareth is the only Sephirah that exists simultaneously in both the upper sphere of the octahedron and the lower ellipsoid of the tetrahedrons at one and the same time. It could very well act as a "pit" or a "black hole" where all matter in the upper sphere of the octahedron vanishes into the so-called nothingness as it is sucked through the Tipharethic drain. But of course it doesn't "disappear." The disappearance is only an illusion, a mirage unto the eyesight of those living in the upper sphere, for in reality it emerges once more very much alive and well within the egg-shaped body of the worlds of Netzach, Hod, Yesod, and Malkuth (Victory, Glory, Foundation, and Kingdom).

And for those of you who are still skeptical of our analogy, let us now examine the word "TIPHARETH" itself. Is it not indeed "H (each) EARTH PIT"? But the 6th Sephirah of Tiphareth is also "H (each) HEART TIP." Or, let us consider the entire Tree singly as a chimney, and call "TIPHARETH" the "HEARTH PIT" just below the Fireplace. Yes indeed, the 6th Sephirah of Tiphareth is most certainly a place of great "Beauty," not only in the way that it gives pleasure to the senses, but also in the way that it exalts the mind and spirit.

One can see also from a study of Figure 98, that the only time you can enter the Great Pyramid from the Kingdom of Malkuth is when the pendulum of our clock (6-10) has swung up to its highest possible position, as it is depicted in the diagram. At this point only, on the north face of the pyramid, is it possible to enter the descending passage that leads into its interior. Well, this may or may not be true. We know from our studies that there are still other Paths that lead up to it from below.

Now that we have come this far in our journey into the mysteries of the Sephirothic Tree, perhaps it is time to stand back a bit and look at it from afar. Let us try to understand it in its overall concept, and let us ask ourselves what is the ultimate meaning of this magnificent Tree that the ancient scholars looked upon with so much awe. Therefore, the next segment in our study will be an attempt to do just that.

Its Ultimate Meaning

Perhaps its secret is hidden within the 12th Tarot key called the Hanged Man, the Ten Man, the Soul, call it what you will. In any event, all through this book we have found ourselves turning the poor man rightside up, and then upside down again, and then reversing the process in one continuous cycle after another. Which is his correct position? The answer is neither. It all depends upon whether the soul is going through the process of involution or evolution. And it is the same way with God.

A clue that points in this direction is discovered when we compare the Alpha number for "Crown" with that for "Kingdom." The former is the English name for Kether, the 1st Sephirah, and the latter the name for the 10th. We find that in either case the number is the same. It is 73 and it stands for "Hermit," the letter H which means *each*. Therefore, the proposition that we wish to present is that they are interchangeable; the 1 can replace the 10 and the 10 can replace the 1.

We pointed out earlier that the continual motion of the globe of AIN SOPH towards its center resulted in the establishment of a single dot known as the great "I AM"—the supreme individualization of the Universal Consciousness. This represented the process of *involution*, whereby the outer globe of the ALL (the 10) receded into itself and became the ONE, a minute central point about which the four now empty worlds of the greater SELF revolve.

But every process in Nature has its equal and opposite reaction, and the Universal God Consciousness is no different. Therefore, the time eventually came for the process to reverse itself, and for the consciousness of the ONE to refill once again the four empty worlds from whence it came. This is called the process of *evolution*, whereby the essence of the God Consciousness of the ONE refills the 36 (not 40 but 36, mind you) empty receptacles which constitute the four worlds of Atziluth, Briah, Yetzirah, and Assiah. We say that there are only 36 outer receptacles or Sephiroth because the 1st Sephirah of Kether (which represents the Crown) of each and every kingdom is identically the same—One Sephirah about which the other 36 revolve. These four worlds or trees are illustrated in Figure 99, with the trunk of each tree the inner diagonal from the CG of a gigantic tetrahedron to each of its four vertices. (The fourth kingdom cannot be shown because it is perpendicular to the plane of the paper.)

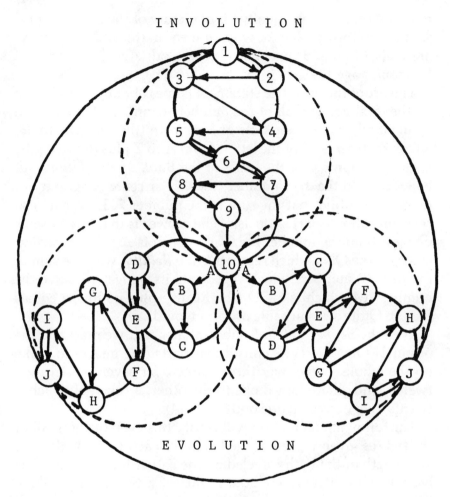

Figure 99
The All Recedes into the Dot, and the Dot Expands into the All

Thus we find that the Crown (the 73 or the 1) can easily be exchanged for the Kingdom (the 73 or the 10), the correct nomenclature only depending upon whether the One is traveling inwards or outwards. We also see in Figure 99 a vivid explanation of how the Master Teacher Agasha was able to combine the 37 sects of the ancient country of Austa (Egypt) into "One Grand Unit" of the Consciousness of Immensity, and not only that, but an equally vivid picture of the mathematical solution to the problem of why all men, in the ultimate reality, are truly One, and that that One is God (*Agasha: Master of Wisdom*, page 129).

The proof for the latter statement comes about when we sum up the total value of all of the numbers from 1 to 37. The total value of all of the outer sects or Sephiroth (the sum of 1 to 36, which represents all of the letters from A to Z plus the 10 digits) is 666, the number of the Beast of the *Book of Revelation*; but when we add the 37th number, the CG or center of gravity of them all, we find that the sum is the number 703. "What is so revealing about that?" you ask. The answer is that it represents one less than the number for GOD which is 704, but when we combine the ONE which represents the *Reality*, with the sum of the first 37 numbers which represents its *Image*, we have the number 704 which is GOD (the Reality plus its Image equals GOD). Quite a remarkable proof, I would say.

Even the *Sepher Yetzirah* substantiates that we must add the original "One" to its 22 constituent parts (the image) to make up the whole: "One over three, three over seven, seven over twelve, and all are joined one to the other, a token of which is twenty-two objects in *one* body" (VI:14).

The following tabulation will clarify this even further. All of the figures given represent the length of each individual Path. The length of the Path traveled by the Father is and always has been 1, since it represents the radius of a Sephirothic sphere (the distance from its central dot to its outer periphery). To call the number for the Father anything other than unity would destroy the entire system of the Cabalah since the Father *is* One. The value for the double letters is $\sqrt{3}$, which represents not only the altitude of the equilateral triangle, but also its area (Area = $1 \times \sqrt{3} = \sqrt{3}$). And the simple letters are, of course, the length of each edge which is 2.

Thus we find that the whole is made up of 22 objects (images) in the body of the *one* reality, making 23 in all when we add the One to the sum of its parts. The adding of the "One" is mandatory if we follow the instructions given in the *Sepher Yetzirah* (VI:14). We further find that when this "One"

	Quantity	Path Types	Unit Lengths	Total Length
Reality	1	Father	1.000	1.000
Image	3	Mother = $\sqrt{3}$ = 1.732 Mother = $2\sqrt{2}$ = 2.828 Mother = $2\sqrt{8/3}$ = 3.266		7.826
Image	7	Double = $\sqrt{3}$ = 1.732		12.124
Image	12	Simple	2.000	24.000
Sum Total	23 (Reality + Images)		12.558	44.95
	W		A BE 58 (Two)	D DIE

travels the entire length of all of the Paths, the net result is that this action brings about the Death of the Devil (The Devil = D). Therefore when "D" dies, the Emperor is once more brought back into full manifestation and the Great Work is then complete (Death + The Devil = 123 = The Emperor = A). This *Vesica Piscis* operation is the fundamental and basic theme of the entire Cabalah, and its importance cannot be overemphasized (See Figure 25).

Furthermore, the total of the unit lengths even restates this fact, just to be sure that we haven't missed it. Its significant message is that this is what "A BE": "D DIE." He is also the number 58 (Star/Two), and even this statement makes sense because we have included Him twice in our computation— once as the One Reality and again in the 22 Images (Mother, Double, and Simple letters).

Are you beginning to be impressed? If not, you certainly should be because the very idea that a pack of spheres can reveal such a fantastic amount of information seems well nigh incredible. But there is still more to come, and this new disclosure will unveil perhaps the most basic and fundamental concept of the entire Cabalah and its related Sephirothic Tree. This is the orderly progression of the 10 dimensions of the Universe, the first 5 of which are tabulated on the following page.

In this tabulation, the symbol X stands for any number whatsoever. Therefore, the equations are universal. But the Cabalah is already one step ahead of us. Somewhere way back in the far-distant past it assigned the Hebrew letter Aleph to represent the zero dimension of the dimensionless point, and it remains equally as valid today as it was then. How do we know that Aleph is its symbol? We know it from observation. We know it from the fact that any number—you name it—when expressed to the 0 power *is* 1 or unity ($X^0 = 1$). And not only does the Hebrew letter Aleph have a letter value of 1, but its symbol is the OX ($X^0 = 1 = OX = A = $ Aleph)! And, of course, we cannot forget that the Alpha number for "Aleph" is 42, the number of "The Ace," and the number for "Ox" is 39, the same as the number for "Ten." Therefore, Aleph represents not only the Ace of Kether (the Crown), but it also represents the 10 of Malkuth (the Kingdom). The evidence that Aleph represents these symbols is simply overwhelming!

Zero X^0	POINT	=	74	Symbol of DOT	=	39
1st = X^1	LINE	=	40	Symbol of LINE	=	40
2nd = X^2	SQUARE	=	81	Symbol of AREA	=	25
3rd = X^3	CUBE	=	31	Symbol of SPACE	=	44
4th = X^4	SPHERE	=	71	Symbol of TIME	=	47

Grand Total   BIG   = 297 = The High Priestess = 195 = F

The Cabalah even gives us the symbol for the 4th dimension of Time. Since $X^0 = 1$, X^4 should equal the 5th Hebrew letter which is He. But what does "He" stand for in English? It represents the number 85, the Alpha number for the Devil, the letter D, the 4th letter of the English alphabet. And the 4th letter of the English alphabet is quite obviously an appropriate symbol for the 4th dimension of Time. Therefore, now that we have established the key symbols in both of the alphabets, the symbols for all of the other dimensions likewise become known (Z = Zero dimension, A = 1st, B = 2nd, C = 3rd, etc.).

The simple letters of the Hebrew alphabet are then quite obviously the one-dimensional lines, the double letters the two-dimensional areas, and the 3 mother letters the 3 dimensions of Space—length, width, and height. But inasmuch as space is normally symbolized by a cube, the Cabalah seems to be directing us to compute an equivalent cube whose volume is equal to a box with a length of $2\sqrt{2}$, a width of $2\sqrt{8/3}$, and a height of $\sqrt{3}$—three transcendental numbers with infinitely long decimals. But to the surprise of us all, the volume of our three-dimensional cube turns out to be the familiar number 16—a natural, whole number!

With this rather shocking discovery safely within our grasp, the next step is obviously to compute the length of its side. This number, the cube root of 16, is an extremely critical number because it represents the value of X—the basic root number which brings into manifestation the orderly progression of the 10 dimensions of Time and Space (X^0, X^1, X^2, etc.). Its value is found to be 2.51984 20998 . . ., which may be rounded off to 2.5198421 and read as "Y SHD U" or "BE SHDU" (Wished You Be Shadow). And that is exactly what we are: the shadow of the God-Self! For practical reasons we may round off the number even further to 2.520, and by so doing give us additional evidence that we have read the number correctly. The number 2.520 transliterates itself into "YBO," and if we place these letters in a circle and then read them starting with the B, we read it as the word "BOY." And isn't a *boy* both the son as well as the shadow of the Father who is God? The numerical value for each dimension is tabulated in the following table:

Power		*Root*		*Numerical Value*		
X^0	= Father	= $(2.520)^0$	=	1.	A	(Emperor)
X^1	= Simple	= $(2.520)^1$	=	2.520	YBO	(BOY)
X^2	= Double	= $(2.520)^2$	=	6.3504	F CEOD	(F COED)
X^3	= Mother	= $(2.520)^3$	=	16.	P	(Page)
X^4	= BODY	= $(2.520)^4$	=	40.320	DO CT	(C DOT)
X^5	= Boy E	= $(2.520)^5$	=	101.6064	A OP OF D	
X^6	= Boy F	= $(2.520)^6$	=	256.	BE F	
X^7	= Boy G	= $(2.520)^7$	=	645.12	FD EA. B	
X^8	= Boy H	= $(2.520)^8$	=	1,625.7024	P BE GOB (D)	
X^9	= Boy I	= $(2.520)^9$	=	4,096.	DO IF	
X^{10}	= BE JOB	= $(2.520)^{10}$	=	10,321.92	JC U I B	

But if we have a boy $[(2.520)^1 = $ A BOY or BOY "A"], where is the *girl*? And where is the *body* that they must have in order to be born? These questions, and many others, will be answered when we read what these 10 dimensions of Life have to tell us.

We have suggested some possible interpretations for the above terms, but our analysis is only a rough stab at it and doesn't do it justice. The initials "J.C." in the Cabalah refer to Jesus Christ, and many times the word "Gob" is used to represent one of the tiny spermatozoa at sea in the semenal fluid of the father as it struggles so valiantly to impregnate the egg in the mother's womb. It is a very apt symbol, for isn't a "gob" a seaman in the U.S. (us) Navy?

But this way or that way, the fact remains that the Cabalah is trying to tell us a story. You may believe the story or you may not: in the final analysis it is strictly up to the individual. But just in case you are wavering between accepting what we are saying here or casting the whole thing aside as so much rubbish, we have prepared one more table to try to convince you that the Cabalah is indeed what it claims to be. The following tabulation successively sums up the first five dimensions of the space-time continuum in which we live, and I am sure that you will have to agree that the statements so made simply *cannot* be attributed to coincidence.

Terms (X = 2.520)	Numerical Sum	
X^0	= 1.	A
$X^0 + X^1$	= 3.520	CE B "O"
$X^0 + X^1 + X^2$	= 9.8704	I H (Each) GOD
$X^0 + X^1 + X^2 + X^3$	= 25.8704	BE H (Each) GOD
$X^0 + X^1 + X^2 + X^3 + X^4$	= 66.1904	FF SOD

The combination of the first two dimensions is the real key to unlocking the final secrets of the Sephirothic Tree. It states that the ACE, the All-Seeing Eye, the very first card of each of the Minor Arcana of the Tarot, is in fact Zero or Nothing, which means that it represents that which is left over after everything of a tangible nature has been removed. This is the All-Seeing Eye or the Ace. And then when we add the first dimension of Time to our Universe of Space, we find that it brings into being *sod*, a term used to describe the grass-covered surface of the ground, turf, one's native land. Indeed, it represents the very earth on which we live. And to whom does our "earth" belong? It belongs to the High Priestess, the Virgin Mother of the World. It is indeed F's Sod (FF = F's).

To bring these ideas more sharply into focus, we must return once more to our Tree of the Sephiroth, the universal symbol that binds all 10 dimensions of the space-time continuum in which we live into a unified whole. Yes, we are not quite finished with our Tree, and this final look will give it the recognition it so rightly deserves by unveiling the ultimate secrets of its Being.

Figure 100 is called a space-time continuum because it shows how the 4 dimensions of space interrelate with the 6 dimensions of time. And these secrets, surprisingly enough, are all contained within the Sephirothic Tree. But we must now view the Tree a little differently than we viewed it before. The Tree is the same, but we are going to view the Sephiroth from a slightly different perspective. The basic change is that the lower *ellipsoid* that formerly contained *two* tetrahedrons is now viewed as a *sphere*, and not only that, but one of its tetrahedrons has seemingly vanished into the nothingness. But it has really not vanished. It has only been sent out into the Universe in a separate sphere of its own, being the child of the High Priestess who has now given birth and is no longer pregnant. Hence the lower ellipsoid is now back to its original spherical shape.

Another extremely important point to be understood is that the lower sphere of Space is not the same size as the upper sphere of Time. Why is this so? The answer is that all spheres in a sphere pack touch and are in continuous contact with their neighbors. The distance between their centers is 2 radii. Therefore, the length of an edge of either the tetrahedron or the octa-

hedron is the same—2 units long. Now the radius of the sphere
enclosing the octahedron has been previously shown to be $\sqrt{2}$
or 1.414; but the radius of the sphere enclosing the tetrahedron
must be smaller. Euclid proves the square of the diameter of the
circumscribing sphere to be 1-1/2 times the square of one of its
edges, thus making the diameter of the sphere equal to $\sqrt{6}$ or
2.4495 (rounding off this infinitely long decimal to 5 digits).
This, you can see, is less than the diameter of the upper sphere
which is 2.828.

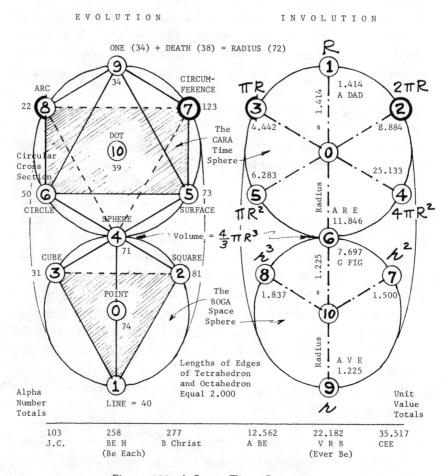

Figure 100: A Space-Time Continuum

But the truly remarkable thing about all of this lies in the numbers themselves. The radius of the Time sphere, which we have called CARA, is 1.414 (A DAD) which means that it belongs to the Emperor, the Father. In fact, it would seem that it relates to Father Time, himself. Therefore the Space sphere, having just given birth to a new-born son (the vanished tetrahedron), must be feminine. We will call her BOGA. But her new radius, now that she has returned to her normal size, is 1.225 or AVE! (1/2 the diameter rounded off to 4 digits). And AVE is a salutation meaning Hail and Farewell—Hail to the newly born Son, the Christ, the King, and Farewell to the One who has just died. How do we know that he has died? We know it from the value of her diameter which is 2.4495 or X DIE. The symbol X refers to Christ, the One who dies and is forever reborn.

There are all sorts of extraordinary relationships that will be discovered as one explores the mysteries of Figure 100, but we will leave it to the student to investigate these on his own. There is, however, one additional point that we should bring out at this time. That point is that if you will substitute letters for the numbers of the Sephiroth, and then read around each egg-shaped form in a clockwise direction, you will be in for a pleasant surprise. The left-hand figure reads: "A BEGIN" (8 + 6 = 14 = N). But how does A begin? The next word is "COD," and a *cod* is a species of fish. This is followed by the letter J which represents the 10 or the World. This would imply that all life goes through the process of evolution. To offset this, the right-hand figure depicts the process of involution. We start off by reading the statement: "H I GD." We interpret this as meaning each I is God. But we also learn that this "I" that is God is likewise the Ace of every Ten (GD B ACE OF J). It is interesting, isn't it?

The Tenth Sephirah

Now let us examine the 10th Sephirah Malkuth which represents the Kingdom, and try to ascertain why the number 10 has two digits instead of one. The answer is quite simple when one delves into the subject a little deeper. Figure 100 shows that after her Son has been born, the ellipsoid of the High Priestess, the Virgin Mother, returns to its normal spherical shape. This becomes possible once the 10th Sephirah, the Son or the Kingdom, has been expelled, thus returning the Mother into a single tetrahedron once again (the tetrahedron 1,2,3,4 in the left-hand diagram). Thus it is seen that the outside periphery of the two spheres of the Space-Time continuum is made up of all of the digits from the 1 to the 9—the Space sphere with the digits 1, 2, 3, and 4, and the Time sphere with the digits 4, 5, 6, 7, 8, and 9. The digit 4 does double duty as the connecting link between the two worlds. In the right-hand diagram it would be the number 6. One can see then that when the sphere of Time is married to the sphere of Space, a complete Space-Time continuum can be made up with but 9 digits (the vertices of the two figures). But without this "marriage," with the two spheres left to operate independently, a 10th number becomes a necessity.

Besides the outer vertices of the two geometric figures, there are two other points, dots, or spheres—call them what you will —that are extremely important. These are the CG or center of gravity points around which the outer Sephiroth rest. But since there is no room to place a full-sized Sephirah at the CG of either the octahedron or the tetrahedron (assuming that the octahedron is formed from 6 spheres in a sphere pack with a square base, and the tetrahedron from 4 spheres with a triangular base), the intervening void must then be filled with a new, smaller Sephirah—one that is located equidistant from the spheres forming the vertices of the figure, and that has its volume expanded to the point whereby it touches them all. Figure 101 illustrates how these smaller Sephiroth fit in very snugly at the CG or midpoints of the octahedron at the top and the two tetrahedrons at the bottom. (In this figure the High Priestess is still pregnant.)

Now do you see what we are driving at? The first two-digit number, the number 10, has two digits because it was *intended* by the God Consciousness to be able to be broken apart into two independent, yet interrelated, entities—the 1 and the 0. And yet, it may be combined back together again into a single unity—the 10, which represents the ending of one cycle and the beginning of another.

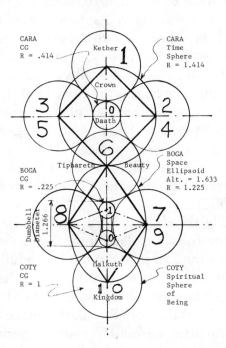

Figure 101
The Mysteries of the 0 and the 10

Therefore, the function of the 10 is actually threefold: (1) to represent the unborn child within the womb of the High Priestess, with the 1 at the CG of the upper tetrahedron and the 0 at the CG of the lower tetrahedron; (2) to represent the newly-born Son of the High Priestess, a full-sized Sephirah that is sent forth to reproduce a brand new Tree in the same manner that the Father produced the first one; and (3) to represent the two inner Sephiroth at the CG points of the CARA Time sphere and the BOGA Space sphere. In this latter case the 1 may occupy the CG of Space and the 0 the CG of Time (as in the case of involution), or the process may be reversed, with the 1 occupying the CG of Time and the 0 the CG of Space, as is the case in the evolutionary spiral.

Now let us study these three phases of the 10 in greater

depth. Let us begin when it represents the unborn child within the womb of its mother. It is apparent from Figure 101 that the child takes the form of a dumbbell, since the peculiarities of a pair of pyramids resting on a 3-sphere triangular base dictate that the CG of the whole be two spheres connected by a cylinder. But who is this "dumbbell," really? You don't have to look very far for the answer, for all you have to do is look in the mirror and there he is. It is the Coty Fool, the spiritual Fool who is You. The length of one half of the dumbbell diameter is .633 which can be read as F C C; and the length of the other half is the sum of these letters which is 12 or the letter L. Therefore, we can say that his full name is F + C + C = L; and when the Moon becomes full, the inner C's will turn into O's and we will have the FOOL.

But eventually the child is born, and the inner 10 that was within the womb is expelled into the outer Kingdom of Malkuth. This is the 2nd phase of the 10—a full-sized Sephirah that is equal in every respect to its Father, and that is now about its Father's business as it begins to build a new kingdom all of its own. This is the Son, the 10, the image of its Father the 1. The Son will then encounter many experiences, some of them very trying indeed, as it goes through the Wheel of Life in the outer worlds in an endeavor to regain the lost crown of its kingdom—the Crown of Kether, the Father. But here again, the Son is in reality only a reincarnation of the One, the previous king who had ruled the earlier kingdom. The very name *Kether* states that it may be *either* the K (the King) or Malkuth. And the name *Malkuth* tells us that it is like a youth (AM LK UTH).

This, then, brings us to the 3rd stage of the 10—the phase where the Son does indeed regain his lost kingdom and rules it once more from the CG points at the two centers of the Time-Space continuum. The 1 part of his 10 consciousness now resides in the Sephirah called Daath, at the very center of the CARA sphere of Time; and the 0 part of his consciousness occupies the CG of the BOGA sphere of Space. Let us call this CG of Space the Sun, the letter O, the 15th letter of the English alphabet. It is interesting to note that the Alpha number of "Daath" is 34, the same as the number for *One*; and when this is combined with the 87 number of the Sun (The Sun = 87 = O), we have the "universal" number 121 which is represented by the letters AU, the Emperor and the Fool.

The Tree Within the Tree

All of the above now brings us back to the point where we can embrace once more our old familiar friends CARA, BOGA, and COTY—the Mental, the Physical, and the Spiritual aspect of all life. But this Holy Trinity does not only exist within the macrocosmic spheres of the outer universe, but it also exists within the microcosmic spheres of the inner universe —the CG spheres of the outer worlds.

We can prove this point through the simple analogy of a hologram. A hologram is a three-dimensional image made on a photographic plate without the use of a camera. It is produced from a laser when the subject is placed in a beam of coherent light, but its truly remarkable quality, and one that is not too well known, is that each and every minute part of the hologram contains within itself an image of the whole. In other words, a hologram proves that the whole is in each of its parts; and if we were to view the entire universe as a hologram, we have a logical proof that the microcosm or smaller universe is a mirror image of the macrocosm or greater universe.

Thus if we were to study the CG dots or spheres at the centers of the octahedron or tetrahedron, we should be able to observe a minute replica of the entire Tree of Life. And then within the centers of the centers, so to speak, would be still other replicas—trees within trees within trees, worlds within worlds within worlds, on and on and on, ad infinitum.

The Agashan Teachers refer to the inner CG of the *atom* as the *anim*. Indeed, even the word itself states that it is the CG because the Alpha number for "anim" is 37 or CG. Therefore, in following this same line of thought, we have prepared Figure 102 which compares the basic dimensions of the larger geometric figures (the macrocosmic universe) with those of the CG spheres (the microcosmic universe) within it. The *atoms* of the outer worlds of Time and Space are thus seen to be full-sized Sephiroth, as opposed to the *anims* (spiritual counterparts) of the inner worlds which consist of the smaller CG spheres. These two worlds are separate and yet interrelated. We are told that the anim is the controller and modifier of the atom.

One other point. The right-hand column of Figure 102 gives possible interpretations for the cabalistic meanings of the decimal numbers. They are by no means the only interpretations, and quite possibly not even the correct one in some cases. They are given merely as an aid to show the many and varied ways in which a number can be read. After all, the purpose of the Cabalah is to teach one to think, and not to necessarily provide the answers until the proper effort has been put forth in this direction.

In the adjacent tabulation, the unit quantities have been computed to eleven significant figures—one digit representing the integer part of the number and ten digits for its decimal fraction. I don't know the significance behind this, but I do know that it works. Any other number of digits for the units of the macrocosm, either more or less, will not yield the truly magical numbers for the microcosm expressed in the above tabulation. The only exception to this rule is in the computation of the Cara CG radius. Since it represents $\sqrt{2} - 1$, we had to add the next successive decimal digit in order to replace the integer and still end up with eleven significant figures.

There is no question now relative to who is who. Without the shadow of a doubt, the CG of Boga represents the child, OA, the Sun of the Emperor—ACE'S BABE! And who is the Ace? The father is unmistakingly pointed out by the CG of Cara when it states: "DAD B ACE" (Dad Be Ace). And this inner world of the microcosm seems to be quite large! The first three digits of the CG of the Cara sphere state that it is BIG; and not only that, but the CG of the Boga sphere states that it is GOD (O + D + GEE). Therefore, we can come to the conclusion that the *inner* world of the anim within the *outer* Time-Space continuum of the atom is not only a BIG GOD, but that it is also the Father/Son combination of the ACE and its BABE. The Mother is represented as the High Priestess "F" who gives birth to them both. Can anything be clearer than that?

THE MACROCOSMIC UNIVERSE			
Cuboctahedron Diam.	4 (1)	4.00000 00000	D
Octahedron Diameter	$2\sqrt{2}$	2.82842 71246	B H. B H (Each)
Tetrahedron Diameter	$\sqrt{6}$	2.44948 97427	2.4495 = X DIE
Octahedron Radius	$\sqrt{2}$	1.41421 35623	A DAD U C EFW
Tetrahedron Radius	$\sqrt{6}/2$	1.22474 48713 5	1.225 = AVE
Pi	π	3.14159 26535	C A DO I'Z E
THE MICROCOSMIC UNIVERSE			
Cara CG Radius = Ra	$\sqrt{2} - 1$	.41421 35623 7	DAD B ACE. F B CG
Boga CG Radius = Rb	$\sqrt{6}/2 - 1$	.22474 48713 5	B X (the King) DOME
Coty CG Radius = Rc	(Sephirah)	1.00000 00000	A
Cara CG Square (1)	$(Ra)^2$	.17157 28753	AGO JOB (72-87-53)
Boga CG Square (0)	$(Rb)^2$	.05051 02572	OEO: EA. O BE World
Coty CG Square (10)	$(Rc)^2$	1.00000 00000	A
Cara CG Cube (1)	$(Ra)^3$	.07106 78118 8	OG 10 FG U R H (Each)
Boga CG Cube (0)	$(Rb)^3$	.01135 19212 5	OA: ACE'S BABE
Coty CG Cube (10)	$(Rc)^3$	1.00000 00000	A
Cara CG Sphere (1)	4/3 Pi $(Ra)^3$	.29768 81542 6	BIG F (H_2O) D B F
Boga CG Sphere (0)	4/3 Pi $(Rb)^3$	.04755 08165 3	O D (GEE) OHPE C
Coty CG Sphere (10)	4/3 Pi $(Rc)^3$	4.18879 02046 6	4-18-87-90-20 = DROIT
Cara + Boga Spheres	(1) + (0) = 10	.34523 89707 9	C DEW H I GO GI
Cara + Boga + Coty	(1) + (0) + 10	4.53402 91754 5	DECDO BI AGED E
Coty - Boga - Cara	Difference = 0	3.84355 12338 7	MD (CEE) A MG

Figure 102
The Cara and Boga (Time and Space) Aspects Within Each Sephirah

The key to the remaining mystery is found when we consider the *outer* sphere of Coty that surrounds its *inner* CG, which consists of *any* of the 10 Sephiroth whose radius is 1 or unity. And when we do this, we find that it is a geometric figure known as the *cuboctahedron:* 12 spheres surrounding and touching an inner one at the center, and all of the spheres, including the one at the center, are equal in size. It is beyond the scope of this chapter to fully explore this most important figure at this time, but we can say that it constitutes one of the *three* geometric figures that can be found in a sphere pack about which a greater sphere can be circumscribed. The other two are the octahedron and the tetrahedron.

The octahedron is, of course, Time. The Father exists at its CG, and he is surrounded by 6 Sephiroth. How many times have the students of Agasha heard him exclaim: "I shall continue to give the truth, even though I have but 6 disciples left"! Why the continued use of the number 6? The answer is quite obviously that he is giving emphasis to the fact that it is the *Father* who is at the CG of the octahedron—not the Mother, nor the Son, but the Father. This is Cara. Its Alpha number is 23 which is the same as "I AM."

Now the counterpart of Time is Space. Boga resides at its CG, with the unborn Son of the Father still in her womb. The Mother then is the tetrahedron, and she is surrounded by 4 Sephiroth which represent the basic elements of Earth, Air, Water, and Fire—all of the elements of matter in the physical world. The Alpha number for Donna, incidentally, is 48, the number for the Fool who is You. (Donna is the counterpart and soul mate of Agasha.) Therefore, we can say that she represents "U AM" in contrast to the Father who is "I AM." And if we add the "AM" to her name, we can say that "DONNA AM MA-DONNA," which is exactly what she represents—the Madonna, the Virgin Mother of Christ the King—the Son of the Father. This is the High Priestess, the letter F, and sometimes she is referred to as the Holy Ghost, the third person of the Trinity. The Alpha number for "The Holy Ghost" is also the same as that for "High Priestess." They both are equal to $162 (33 + 60 + 69 = 162 = 32 + 130)$.

Now we come to the second person of the Trinity, the offspring of the first and the third—the reembodiment of the Father who lives again as the Son, the Christ, the King. This is Coty, the Spiritual Son who, after he has fully matured and gathered his 12 disciples around and about him, will reside at the CG of the cuboctahedron—the Spiritual sphere of pure

Being. This is the Christ Consciousness as symbolized by the cuboctahedron of 12 vertices and 14 faces, 8 of which are triangles and 6 of which are squares. The Son was born the Fool (Son = 48 = Fool), but eventually he ascends to become the Christ.

The Christ Consciousness

The cuboctahedron is an ideal symbol to express the Christ Consciousness because in reality it is the *outer* expression of the *inner* consciousness within an individual Sephirah. The Coty CG sphere is a full-sized Sephirah; and so are its 12 outer spheres. Therefore the *one* sphere that contains them all is the macrocosm of the microcosm. Figure 103 shows the Coty sphere in all of its aspects.

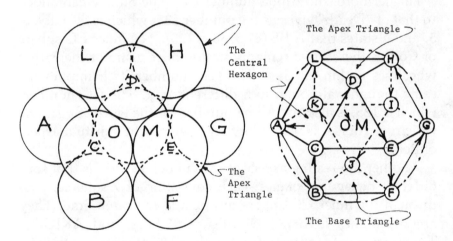

Figure 103
The Coty Sphere of the Cuboctahedron

If we can say that the Cara sphere is the sphere of Time, and that the Boga sphere is the sphere of Space, then the Coty sphere is the sphere of Being. Its CG is the same as the units of its outer consciousness. Therefore it is all one. And not only is it an expression of Coty, but it is also an expression of Cara and Boga as well. There are 6 Cara CG spheres at the centers of its 6 square faces and 8 Boga CG spheres at the centers of its 8 triangular faces, and these 14 smaller Sephiroth, when added to the 12 full-sized Sephiroth at its periphery, make 26 Sephiroth in all—the Alpha number for God and the Cabalistic number for YOD HE VAV HE. Therefore, it is not only an expression of the Christ Consciousness, but taken in its entirety, it is also an expression of the God Consciousness.

It is interesting to note that if we start at the central sphere which we have lettered 0 for zero, and then proceed through all 12 of its outer spheres in sort of a zig-zag pattern around and about the middle plane of the hexagon, the 13th sphere will bring us right back to the center again—and the symbol for 13 is M or Death. Therefore, the significance of the central CG sphere is not only that it represents the sound of the OM, but that it also signifies the Death of the Sun or the Death of Christ.

Furthermore, the Alpha number for "The Sun" when added to that of "Death" gives us the number 125, which is the cube of 5, and it states that A BE (87 + 38 = 125). The inner CG sphere of Coty is therefore a remanifestation once again of the Father who lives within his Son. The very number itself implies the same thought, although in a different way. The CG number, which is 125, is also the Alpha number for the word "Spiritual" which, of course, is what Coty represents—the spiritual aspect of Being.

Another interesting aspect of the cuboctahedron is that four different hexagonal planes, each consisting of 7 spheres, pass through the inner CG sphere at one and the same time. They are the planes LDEFJK, DHIJBC, LHGFBA, and AKIGEC. These can equate to the four basic elements of earth, water, air, and fire, which are really nothing more than the four states of matter—the solid, liquid, gaseous, and energy states. They also represent the four concentric worlds of Atziluth, Briah, Yet-zirah, and Assiah spoken of in the first part of this chapter. One can even say that they represent the four kingdoms of the Minor Arcana—Pentacles, Cups, Swords, and Wands. Yes, they represent all of these things and more, but in the final analysis it all simmers down to the simple fact that they stand for the first four numbers: the 1, the 2, the 3, and the 4, the total of which is 10.

From the above, it would seem that the Coty sphere of Being is in reality a synthesis of the Cara sphere of Time, the Boga sphere of Space, *and* the Coty sphere of Being. Not only is Coty Coty, but it is also Cara Boga Coty as well: 3 aspects of life all combined into 1. It is the first HE as well as the last HE of the Divine Name: YOD HE VAV HE. The Alpha numbers for "Time + Space + Being" bring into manifestation the Empress, the letter Z, since their total is 128 (47 + 44 + 37 = 128); and here again is the manifestation of the number 26 since Z is the 26th letter. We could go on and on with more analogies, but these will have to suffice for the time.

If the Crown is the symbol for the 1st Sephirah (Kether), and the Kingdom is the symbol for the 10th Sephirah (Malkuth), what then is the symbol for the Coty sphere of Being? The answer, I am told, is that the name "Ten/One" is its symbol. It is not only Ten, but it is also One; the Ten and the One are the two sides of its Being. And not only that, but it likewise represents *all* of the numbers from 1 to 10, the sum total of which is 55, the double E, which in turn equates to 10.

The Alpha number for "Crown" is 73; the Alpha number for "Kingdom" is 73; and the Alpha number for "Ten/One" is also 73. Now the number 73 is the number for "Hermit," the letter H which means *each*. And when we compute the total for all three of them, we find that it is 219 or U + I (You and I). And not only that, but it also represents Cara (Double-You) since 219 is the Alpha number for "Light and Inspiration" (56 + 19 + 144 = 219).

The reverse of the number 73 is likewise interesting because it represents the CG or the center of gravity of something. The number 37 is the CG. It is also the Alpha number for "Being" itself. Therefore, if we total up the three CG's of the three Hermits, we should have a number that represents the inner expression of their Being and that corresponds with the 219 (you and I) sum of their outer expression. And it does just that. The sum of 37 + 37 + 37 is 111, the three 1's, and the Alpha number of CARA BOGA COTY.

In summary then, we find that the number 219 (you and I) represents the outer expression of the three Hermits at the extreme ends of the Tree—the Crown, the Kingdom, and the Ten/One. Their inner expression, their CG's as it were, comes into manifestation through Cara Boga Coty. And when we total them both together, find the sum total of their outer expression *and* their inner expression, we find that it is the number 330 which in the Cabalah stands for "The O." It is also an expression of the triune aspect of the God Aten, since 37 + 73 = 110 = A Ten.

This then brings to a conclusion our little discourse on the many and varied meanings, hidden as well as obvious, of that all-important, third component part of the Hall of the Initiates known as the Tree of the Sephiroth.

NOTES

1. Much of this information was obtained from the chapter on the Tree of the Sephiroth from Manly P. Hall's treatise on *The Secret Teachings of All Ages* (Los Angeles, The Philosophical Research Society, Inc., 1928 and 1978) p. 121

2. This particular translation of this ancient Hebrew masterpiece is by Adolphe Franck. The quotations were taken from pages 69 and 70 of his work titled *The Kabbalah* (New Hyde Park, N.Y., University Books, 1967)

3. Eden Gray, *A Complete Guide to the Tarot* (New York, Crown Publishers, 1970) p. 127

4. Stephan A. Hoeller, *The Royal Road* (Wheaton, Ill., The Theosophical Publishing House, 1975) p. 36

5. This diagram is taken from one published by Paul Foster Case (Los Angeles, Builders of the Adytum, Ltd.)

6. This quotation from the *Sepher Yetzirah*, along with the verses that follow, was translated by Knut Stenring, *The Book of Formation, Sepher Yetzirah* (New York, KTAV Publishing House, Inc., 1970)

7. The background drawing of the Great Pyramid was taken from a rendition originally made by D. Davidson and H. Aldersmith and republished by Peter Tompkins, *Secrets of the Great Pyramid* (New York, Harper and Row, 1971) p. 246

Chapter 26

THE TEMPLE OF THE LIVING GOD

THE FOURTH AND last constituent part of the great Hall of the Initiates is that temple in which you, the reader of this book, are now residing. It is the physical body of Man, and it has been known throughout the centuries as the Temple of the Living God. It has been so named because there never has been, nor shall there ever be, a comparable church, laboratory, factory, library, conservatory, or other earthly structure built on the earth plane with a capability anywhere near that of the human body.

Even its communication system alone is awesomely complex. Networks of nerve cells, some with fibers several feet long, run throughout the body, connecting each and every bit of tissue with the 10 billion or so nerve cells of the governing brain. Electrical impulses travel along these pathways, leaping across narrow gaps between cells, and relaying information to and from the various nervic centers. The heart beats, the lungs draw breath, the metabolism is maintained, dead cells are replaced with new ones, and scores of muscles are precisely directed so that you, the dweller within this temple, may live, move, and have your being.

Now it is an interesting fact that this temple in which you reside, the Temple of the Living God, is in turn mathematically equal to the sum total of the two previous temples—the Temple of King Solomon and the Tree of the Sephiroth. In other words, if we were to place the Sephirothic Tree *within* the Temple of Solomon, superimpose each Sephirah over its nervic centers in such a way so that they may activate them, the net result would bring into manifestation a physical vehicle very similar to the house in which you live—the Temple of the Living God.

Figure 104 brings this idea more sharply into focus. We begin with the Temple of King Solomon as it is depicted by Figure 84. The outline of the floor plan of the temple can very easily be envisioned. Now let us activate it, give it life in other words. We do this by extending the Tree of the Sephiroth to its maximum open position (the right-hand diagram of Figure 91), and then instantly, in the twinkling of an eye, lock each Sephirah in its proper place within the corresponding columns of the Temple. This is an act of magic, and it can be compared with the precise point in time when the soul, that is hovering in the mother's aura, suddenly takes over the newly formed body growing within her womb (*The Agashan Discourses*, page 49). But if the Sephirothic Tree were compressed in its normal state (Figure 90 and the left-hand diagram of Figure 91), this action would not have been possible.

Our friend the Beast whose number is 666 also seems to be in evidence here. Figure 91 plainly points out that the total length of the extended Tree is this very number: 6.66. But now let us look at the Tree in Figure 90 again. What is the Alpha value for the Hebrew names of the Sephiroth? Their total is shown to be 666.

Now let us study Figure 104 in greater depth. We find that the soul has taken over the Temple of Solomon with the result that it is now a living entity—the outer physical consciousness known to mortals as JOHN JONES, or whatever. Yet in the meantime a strange phenomenon has occurred. The lightning flash which originally extended from Kether to Malkuth has

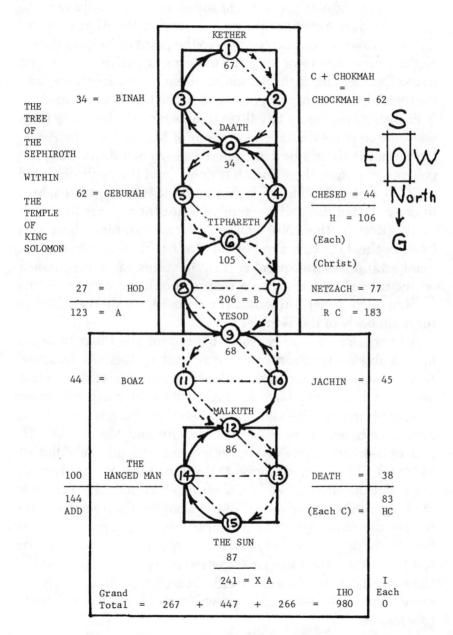

Figure 104
The Temple of the Living God

now taken on greater dimensions and extended itself even further into the earth. We might say that it eventually came to rest in the Sun, a point at the extreme end of the Altar of Burnt Offerings and which corresponds to the point of its inception at Kether, now seen to occupy the uppermost position at the top of the Oracle. This is the Kundalini force, or the Life force, and it extends from the top of your head to the tips of your toes.

Furthermore, Figure 104 also explains how the lightning flash was able to place the fallen kingdom of Malkuth on the Altar. Lightning, it should be remembered, always follows a zig-zag course (at least in the Cabalah it does), and it was through the assistance of the Pillars of Jachin and Boaz that it was enabled to do so. Jachin then, whose symbol is J or the number 10, is able to function in the 10th position of the lightning flash and Boaz in the 11th (the symbol for Boaz is B, the number 2, a manifestation of the number 11). It seems far more than a "coincidence" that these two pillars should be named in this fashion. Any other numerical force could not tie the Altar to the main body of the Temple.

A further study also reveals how the middle Pillar of Mildness is able to function in the way that it does. At least the figure casts a lot more light in this direction. Heretofore, most occultists had looked at all three pillars in much the same fashion; but now one can plainly see that there is a world of difference between the Pillars of Severity and Mercy (the left- and right-hand pillars of Figure 90) and the middle Pillar of Mildness. The former support the structure of the Temple itself, but the latter acts as the *doorway* through which entry is made to all the major rooms of the Temple. Each Sephirah on the middle pillar is a door or empty space, as opposed to the Sephiroth on the outer pillars which represent columns or solid material. The differences between the two seem to be the same as that between anim (anti-matter) and atom, but a lot more thought is needed before we can come to any definite conclusions.

In case the reader is wondering why we changed the orientation of the Temple of the Living God from the east-west axis of the Temple of Solomon, it is only to symbolize the fact that this action of the soul has now put the Temple through a full 90-degree turn in space and time. The Temple of the Living God (the human body) towers into the sky about a vertical axis, as opposed to the Temple of Solomon which is built on a horizontal axis parallel to the ground. Besides, we wished to show that the former is a temple for the SON, as opposed to the latter which ultimately ended up as a temple of WOE. We might even go so far as to say that when we add the image (the MG), it becomes the MEOW SONG of the cat.

Masonic Symbology[1]

All of the above points out what we can do with symbology when we allow the symbols to speak for themselves. There are no fast and rigid rules that we must follow, except that we must have a reason for everything that we do. We must be logical in our thinking. One is free to work with symbols in any way that he chooses, the main point being that we allow them to communicate to our *outer* consciousness the wisdom that lies *within*. Thus the study of symbology is much more of an art than it is a science.

Let us take the Masonic symbol of the compass and the square. This symbol appears in every Masonic lodge, usually with the letter G in the space between these two important instruments. Now what does this symbol really mean? The noted Mason Albert Pike on page 34 of *Morals and Dogma*[2] tells us that "GEOMETRY, which the letter G in most Lodges is *said* to signify, means *measurement* of *land* or the *earth*." But in an esoteric sense, doesn't this really amount to "Spiritual Measurement"? Isn't that what we have been doing all through this book, measuring buildings and symbols in order that we might determine their *spiritual* dimensions? The answer is yes, and we shall now put it to the test.

Figure 105 on the following page is an elaboration of this truly universal symbol.

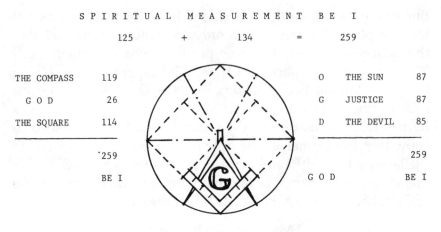

SPIRITUAL	MEASUREMENT	BE	I
125	+ 134	=	259

THE COMPASS	119		O	THE SUN	87
G O D	26		G	JUSTICE	87
THE SQUARE	114		D	THE DEVIL	85
	`259				259
	BE I		G O D		BE I

Figure 105
God and Justice Be I

One can very readily see that the compass relates to the circle or the letter O, the square to the 4th letter D, and God to its initial letter which is G. Indeed, we learned from the table on page 266 of this work that the God-Name number for the word "Justice" is 704 which transliterates back to GOD. Therefore God is Justice and Justice is God.

We also learned earlier that the God-Name number for the letters in GOD is the number 259 which states that it BE I. But what we did not know was that the Alpha number for the sum of its symbols—The Compass, God, and the Square—was also 259 and that it "BE I." Neither did we know that the Alpha number for "Spiritual Measurement" was the same number and made the same statement. In fact, it states that "A BE MD"; and "MD," of course, is the number of *Vesica Piscis* which means the Death of the Devil, with the result that the Emperor is brought into manifestation. Therefore, there is far more to Masonic symbology than what is generally known by the public at large, and even by Masons themselves, I might add.

Now let us study these two symbols independently, and then together, and see what they are capable of telling us. Figure 106 shows the Mason's square as the quadrant of a circle whose radius is equal to its outer edge. Its inner edge is the quadrant of another square.

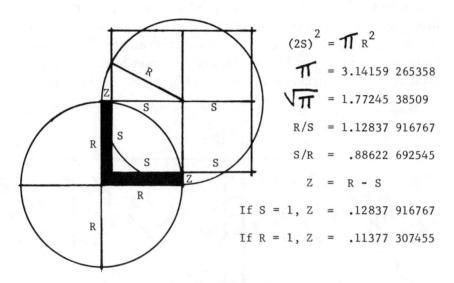

$$(2S)^2 = \pi R^2$$

π = 3.14159 265358

$\sqrt{\pi}$ = 1.77245 38509

R/S = 1.12837 916767

S/R = .88622 692545

Z = R - S

If S = 1, Z = .12837 916767

If R = 1, Z = .11377 307455

Figure 106
The Mason's Square Squares the Circle

As soon as one draws a figure such as the one shown above, your first reaction is to try and do the impossible and make the square the same size as the circle. It just seems logical that the two areas should be the same. This is called squaring the circle, but since π is an incommensurable number, it cannot be done with a ruler and compass alone. Another tool is needed to perform this magical act. And what is this tool? It is the Mason's square. The true Mason's square then, if it is to be used to construct *spiritual* temples not made with human hands, must itself be pure and have for its dimensions those prescribed by the above figure. It is interesting to note that the width of its leg results in the number .128, the Alpha number of the Empress, the letter Z, the 26th letter of the English alphabet; and the number 26 is the number of GOD. And not only that, but its alternate dimension is .11377 which states that it is the "AM" part of "I AM," followed by the number for Christ.

But we are not through yet. Our magical square has only just begun to tell its story. The next question we will ask it is how many smaller squares are contained within each leg of our magical L-shaped square. To our astonishment, the number turns out to be either 8 or 9, depending upon which way you look at it. Its construction is illustrated in Figure 107 below:

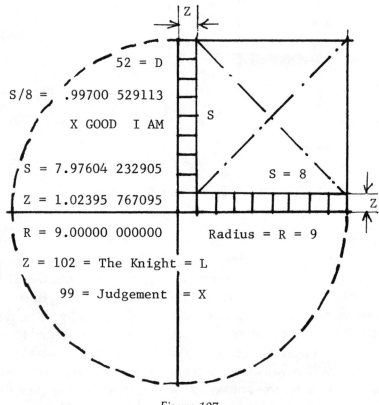

Figure 107
The Mason's Square Rights Each (H) "I"

Again we have a verification that we are on the right track in our thinking, for each and every dimension of both the larger

"L" and the smaller unit squares has its own individual story to tell. In order to be compatible with the circle, the outer edge of the L-square is divided into 9 parts and its width is then 1.02, the Alpha number of the Knight, the letter L. But to also be compatible with the square, the inner edge of the L-square is divided into 8 parts, with the resulting smaller unit squares having dimensions almost equal to unity (.997), and that tell us that they relate to *Judgement*, that they are *good*, and that they are a part of the great "I AM."

Absolutely intrigued, the writer lost no time in analyzing the *names* of the various component parts of our magical Mason's square. These names are Outer Edge, Inner Edge, Length, Width, Breadth, and Thickness. The Alpha numbers for each of these names are shown in the following Figure 108:

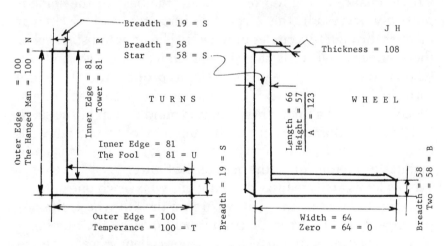

Figure 108: The Mason's Square Turns the Wheel

Since there are two God-Names for "Outer Edge" (100) and also two available for "Inner Edge" (81), we can say that all four edges of the Mason's square bring into manifestation the word TURN. This makes the "breadth" of the square equal to 19, since it must be the difference between the outer edge and the inner edge (100 – 81 = 19). But this matches perfectly with the word "Breadth," since its Alpha number is 58, the same as the number for "Star," the God-Word for the letter S whose number is 19. Thus there is confirmation all the way around the perimeter of the instrument. And not only that, but since 58 is also the Alpha number for "Two" (the letter B or the Wheel), we may conclude that the Mason's square TURNS the Wheel or the Star.

We could go on and on with our analysis, but these examples will have to suffice for the time.

The Squares on the Path of the Zodiac

Let us return once more to Figure 104, our glyph for the Temple of the Living God. The reader will observe that as the Kundalini or Life-force travels up the human figure from its feet which rest on the pedestal of the Altar all the way up to its Crown chakra at the top of the head (the base of the spine is probably at Yesod), this serpentine force travels in a circular manner through five circles or wheels. The uppermost wheel or the number 1 wheel is then in the Oracle; the 2nd and 3rd wheels rotate as a pair in the Temple proper; the 4th wheel turns in the Porch between the Pillars of Boaz and Jachin; and the 5th wheel, the final wheel, spins around on top of the sacrificial Altar of Burnt Offerings. The sum total of these 5 wheels is then the number 15 ($1 + 2 + 3 + 4 + 5 = 15$), which brings into manifestation the Sun at the base of the figure.

Now let us analyze just what happens when each one of these wheels turns. Let us say that we are on the 4th wheel, the one turning around between Boaz and Jachin. Since the number 4 represents strife, struggle, etc., it is an excellent wheel to represent life on the planet Earth. Therefore this is where we are at the moment: on the Wheel of Life spinning around in the Porch just outside of the Temple. Will we be there forever? Of course not. As soon as we learn our lessons we can ascend from it into the greater wheel, the 3rd wheel, on the *inside* of the Temple doors. But this is where we are for the moment.

However, for purposes of this analysis we will just simply have to arise above the wheel and look down on it from above. For the time being then we shall be the observer instead of the observed. From this vantage point the circle of the Zodiac becomes the rim of the wheel, and the horizontal line through Boaz and Jachin the horizon. The picture is illustrated a little more clearly in Figure 109:

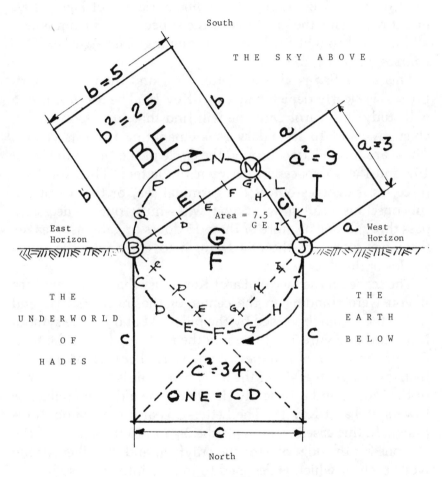

Figure 109
The Squares on the Path of the Zodiac:
The W Position of the Word WHY.

Figure 109 is perhaps one of the most significant glyphs in the entire Cabalah because it expresses in one simple diagram just what life is and what it is all about. It also brings into manifestation the famous theorem of Pythagoras by showing that the area of the square of the short side of a right triangle, when added to the area of the square of its long side, is exactly equal to the area of the square of the hypotenuse. In other words: $a^2 + b^2 = c^2$, where a, b, and c are the three respective sides of a right triangle. This triangle is the *inner* triangle of Figure 109, and it represents the great *sea* of the subconscious from which all life was brought forth in the beginning (*The Agashan Discourses*, pages 61, 67).

This inner *Sea* is also the letter *Cee*, and the evolutionary process is clearly depicted in Tarot Key 18 (The Moon). If one will study this Tarot card, he will find that the Moon has 16 chief rays and 16 secondary rays emanating from its center. These are the 16 letters around the circle of the Moon in Figure 109 and the 16 spaces in between the letters. Thus the Lifeforce, as it evolves out of the germinal sea, or the sea of the subconscious—call it what you will—must out of necessity pass through one or more of these 16 doors or gates as it leaves the inner world of the *one* triangle to enter into the outer worlds of the *three* squares.

The scene on the face of Tarot Key 18 is what you would see if you were standing in the center of the inner triangle and facing the square bounded by the pillars M and J. (The symbol M is used in Figure 109 to denote the *middle* pillar of the temple, or the Pillar of *Mildness*.) The space between M and J is then the *image* (the MJ) of the inner Sea. This is the outer "Cee" or the Moon, and it is clearly shown between the two pillars or towers of Tarot Key 18. The Letter C is also the symbol for 3 things. In this case it represents the 3 gates to the square of the "I": one for the dog, one for the crayfish, and the other for the wolf, each of which is destined to evolve into the 9 square of the "I."

Does the Cabalah verify this in any way? Of course it does. The Alpha number for "Dog + Crayfish + Wolf" is 171, which adds up to 9 or I ($26 + 89 + 56 = 171 = 9 = I$). The number 89 also means H (each) I. And when we compute the God-Name number for AGA, we find that it also is an "I" for it is the number 333 ($123 + 87 + 123 = 333$). It would seem that the

Cabalah is bending over backwards to make this point quite clear.

Now let us turn to the left a bit and face the square bounded by the pillars B and M. There are 5 gates to this kingdom and we have designated them by the symbol E. In other words, it is the Hierophant whom we see as we face in this direction. The two pillars that are shown on Tarot Key 5 on either side of the Hierophant are then the pillars B and M, the Pillar of Severity and the Pillar of Mildness. Even Arthur Edward Waite tends to substantiate this by stating on page 88 of his *Pictorial Key to the Tarot*[3] that these two pillars are not the same pillars between which the High Priestess is seated. One of them is, of course, but it is the reverse of the Pillar of Boaz.

Now let us make a full 180-degree turn from our vantage point in the center of the inner triangle and observe the kingdom that lies within the earth. This is the underworld of Hades, and its square is bounded by the pillars J and B. From Chapter 13 we learned that we would find the Priestess Astraea seated between these twin pillars of Justice. It is she then whom we see as she gazes intently into the center of the inner kingdom. The High Priestess, who is seated at her back and facing the opposite direction, is the Virgin Mother of the World, and it is into her womb the Life-force goes if it proceeds downwards through the 8 gates from the pillars B to J into the underworld of Hades. This is the number 34 and it represents the seed (34 = CD = seed). We know that its area must be 34 since it represents the sum total of the two upper squares.

At this point we should make a very important clarification. Figure 109 is a general glyph, and it represents the middle pillar, wherever it might be, at *any* point within the half-circle of the Zodiac that lies above the horizon. One must remember that there are an infinite number of right-angle triangles that are formed as the point M rises in the east at the Pillar of Severity, then travels across the sky through the 8 gates from B to J, and eventually descends in the west at the Pillar of Mercy. This is a mathematical fact because *every* triangle of any size whatsoever that can be inscribed within a semi-circle is a right-angle triangle. Try it out for yourself. You will find that this is so.

What is the middle pillar then, really? We found out earlier that it represents the doorway through which access is gained to all the rooms of the Temple. All well and good. But what specific thing might that be? Where do we find the door? Let us go to the Cabalah for the answer. And when we do, we find that the key that unlocks all the doors lies, as it always does, within the Alpha number of its name.

The name of the middle pillar is *Mildness*, and its Alpha number is 95. "What is so revealing about that?" you might ask. The answer is that the number 95 is a feminine number. It is the God-Name number for the Queen and the God-Word number for the Empress, both of whom are women. But not only that, they are also *mothers*. The doorway then is the womb, out of which one is born into a higher or a lower consciousness.

But let us not stop here. Where might we find the Empress or the Queen within the signs of the Zodiac? We know that the Virgin Mother is the High Priestess, the letter F, Virgo, the 6th sign of the Zodiac, but where is the Empress or the Queen? The answer is that they can be found in the 8th sign of the Zodiac which is Scorpio. If the reader will go back to Chapter 10 and review the Alpha numbers for the zodiacal signs, he will find that not only is 95 the Alpha number for Scorpio, but the number for the complete term "Scorpio the Scorpion" is 237—the God-Name number for IE or 95 (95 = I + E = 90 + 147 = 237).

We find then that the Motherhood of God, as evidenced by the Empress or the Queen, gives birth to Scorpio, which in turn should represent the point M as it moves across the dome of the sky from the east to the west. But wait! The next question is what is Scorpio, really? Let us analyze the word. The word SCORPIO is a fantastic message in code. It may be broken apart into "S + C or Pi + O," and it means that it represents either the Star, the Moon, Pi, or the Sun, all of which are celestial bodies or "chariots" that race across the sky. The word "Pi," of course, refers to an individual sign or a group of signs showing that even the zodiacal signs themselves are in the race. (The length of an arc in the circumference of a circle is a function of Pi; i.e., 30 degrees of arc = Pi/12 or Pi/6, the exact value depending upon whether the diameter or the radius is taken as unity.) In this way then, the Cabalah has informed us that the point M that moves across the dome of the sky may be any one of the celestial bodies. It may be a sun, moon, star, planet, zodiacal sign, or whatever.

Now let us see what happens when this point M gradually sinks down into the western horizon as it merges into the Pillar of Mercy on the right-hand side of the Temple. The picture is illustrated in Figure 110.

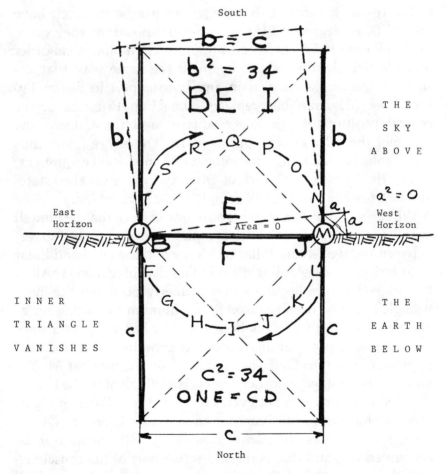

Figure 110
The Inner Triangle Vanishes: The H Position of the Word WHY

Just before the point M reaches the right-hand Pillar of Mercy, the square of the short side of the triangle becomes infinitesimally small, until it vanishes altogether at the point of impact. And the same thing can be said for the inner triangle itself. On the other hand, the square of the long side of the tri-angle becomes exactly equal to the square of the hypotenuse, and the entire figure becomes a double square, one on top of the other, bringing into manifestation the "H" symbol of the Hermit. Or is it the "OH" symbol of the Sun? This would be the word we would see if we were also to include the circle of the Zodiac in our calculations.

The reader will notice that the letters around the circle have moved three degrees clockwise from the positions they occu-pied in Figure 109. (The letters are placed in alphabetical order in an anticlockwise fashion in much the same way that the signs of the Zodiac appear in any horoscope.) In Figure 110 then, the Magician has replaced the High Priestess in the central position of the lower square, and the Queen now becomes the ruler of the upper square. The entire figure thus represents H (each) IQ, meaning your intelligence quotient. This is the Hermit, the Spark of Divinity in its awakened state, and he truly has become the Temple of the Living God.

We can say that this is so because one can see that he himself is now the middle pillar of the Temple! He occupies the "space" between the right-hand Pillar of Mercy and the left-hand Pillar of Severity, thus becoming the middle Pillar of Mildness. All of his subjective consciousness that formerly occupied the inner triangle has now been reduced to a minimum (it having seem-ingly vanished into a "black hole"), and he has merged the male and female aspects of his objective consciousness (the two upper squares) into ONE, as evidenced by the number 34. Yes indeed, his total *outer* consciousness is equivalent to the Logos, the God-Self, or we might even say to that of a Pillar of Light. (The Alpha number for each of these terms is 68 or "One + One.") Yet there is one part of himself that still remains to be accounted for, and that is the subjective part of his conscious-ness that seems to have vanished, as we just said, into a black hole.

So then the next step is to find his subjective consciousness, and try to determine what happened to it. How do we do this? The answer is to bring it back into the plane of our sight, or into the plane of the paper, so to speak. It really never vanished altogether; it only *appeared* to do so because the plane of its consciousness was rotated through a full 90-degree turn, thus reducing its area to that of a straight line. The maximum area of the inner triangle is shown in Figure 111.

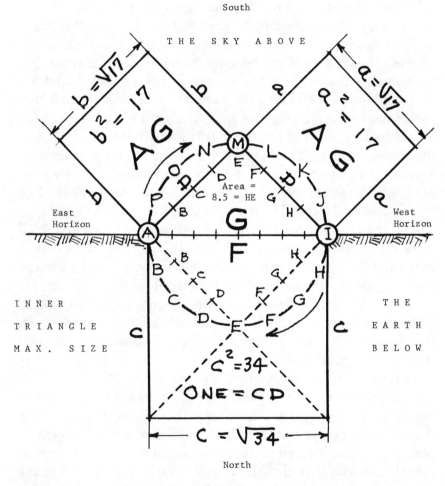

Figure 111
The Inner Triangle at Maximum Size: The Y Position of the Word WHY

In Figure 111 the point M is directly in the doorway to the inner portion of the Temple proper. It thus lies on the true axis of the middle pillar, and could be said to represent the middle Pillar of Mildness in its entirety if one were above the Porch of the Temple looking down on it from above. The same could be said for the Pillar of Severity on the left and the Pillar of Mercy on the right. The Emperor now represents the former and the Magician the latter, and in this head-on view where the pillars are seen as three circles, the great "I AM" is brought into manifestation.

We are also able to now look at the subjective consciousness face to face, at its maximum value, and see it for what it really is. This vast sea of the unconscious contains all of our many "selves" that have not yet become individualized, that are still contaminated with thoughts of hatred, revenge, etc., and are thus unable to ascend into the pure white light of the spiritual consciousness. And when we look at them lumped together as a single entity, we find that they are none other than our friend *the Devil* himself. (The maximum area of the inner triangle is found to be 1/4 of the area of the lower square of the hypotenuse, which makes it equal to 8.5 or HE; and the number 85 or HE equates to the Devil (Tarot Key 15), the letter D.)

This then is the character who has been holding us back all these many lifetimes of earthly living. It is he who has gotten us into all of the trouble we find ourselves in today, and search as we may, we shall never find another devil the likes of him. He is the challenging factor, the opposition, the mortal mind which is always in conflict with the divine mind, and which therefore holds poor Adam and Eve in bondage until they release themselves from his control and aspire to the higher consciousness (*The Agashan Discourses,* page 184).

Even the male and female squares of the two equal sides of the inner triangle reflect this very thought. One represents Adam and the other one Eve. And when they are in this central position equidistant from the two outer pillars, they are in complete bondage to their Devil self. The length of each of the sides of their squares is 4, the number of the Devil, and the area of their squares is 17 or AG, the symbol for the element *silver.*

And what is the Alpha number for "silver"? It is 85, the number of the Devil, of course.

The Cara Boga Cotee "O"

In Chapter 10 we learned that everything in life has three basic modes of expression: its mental aspect (Cara), its physical aspect (Boga), and its spiritual aspect (Coty). These are universal principles, and the laws of *Cara Boga Coty* are applicable throughout the Universe. This is especially true when we consider the squares along the path of the Zodiac. The following Figure 112 brings the mathematical relationships between these three forces quite sharply into focus:

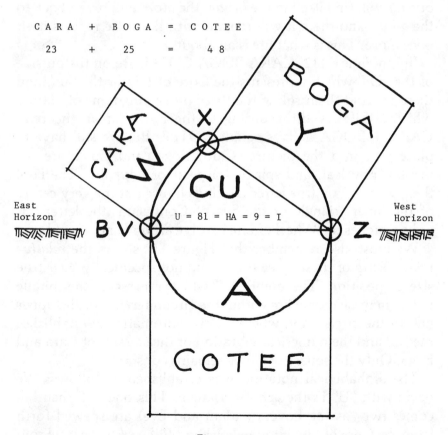

CARA + BOGA = COTEE

23 + 25 = 4 8

U = 81 = HA = 9 = I

East Horizon

West Horizon

Figure 112
The Sum of Cara and Boga Is Always Equal to Cotee

The first thing that comes to our attention as we study Figure 112, is that the familiar CARA BOGA COTY has now been changed to CARA BOGA COTEE O. Yet nothing has really *changed* since the numerical vibration (Alpha number) for both terms is still the three 1's of the number 111. The only difference is that the last two letters of COTY have been changed from a "T + Y" to a "TEE + O" in order to bring the ANKH into manifestation, which is an "O" on top of a "T."

The Ankh is the Egyptian symbol for life and generation, and its manifestation is absolutely essential in order for the Wheel of Life to keep on revolving. Then, when it is finally withdrawn, the Wheel will come to a halt and COTEE-O will become COTY once again. Therefore that which was on the *outside* will find itself in the *inside*, the *atom* will revert back to the *anim*, and there it will remain until the cycle repeats itself once more. This is what life is all about.

But in Figure 112, CARA BOGA COTEE are on the outside of the "O," which represents the Core of Life or the Sun, and there we find them ruling the three *outer* kingdoms of Nature which is Life. And, according to the Pythagorean theorem, CARA + BOGA always equals COTEE. But we still have to place *you* into the picture. Cara, Boga, and Cotee are the mental, physical, and spiritual aspects of *your* life. The Fool then, who is You (the letter U), finds himself at the very center of the inner triangle of the Sea of Confusion (the letter C), as he watches the Wheel of Life revolve around and about him.

We must also remember that Figure 112 shows the *relative* relationship of these three forces and not specifically their true size or position. The point "X," which represents the middle pillar, may be *anywhere* within the circumference of the upper half of the circle. And where "X" is, automatically establishes the size and the numerical vibration of the squares of Cara and Boga. Only the square of Cotee remains constant.

The alphabetical notation was established as follows: We begin with "U" in the central triangle. This one "U" then becomes two, as the Lovers (Adam and Eve) are spewed forth from the Core of Life into the left-hand Pillar of Severity. From this pillar is where the Lovers (the letter V) begin their journey around the Wheel of Life.

The next letter in alphabetical order is W. This represents the open "space" between the left-hand pillar and the middle pillar, and its name is *Cara*. It is also the Chariot in which they will ride as they travel clear across the dome of the sky. But in the beginning, Cara is an extremely small square, one so small as to be completely undetected by the human eye. Soon, however, it grows in brightness and it becomes the morning star as it ascends above the eastern horizon.

The next letter is X. This is the letter of Judgement, and it marks the point where our heroes disembark from the mental chariot of Cara and enter into the physical Zodiac of Boga. Yet they will not do this during their physical lifetime, because Boga will always appear to them like the carrot in front of the horse's nose; no matter how far they travel in their chariot, Boga will always appear to be in the distance ahead of them. X is also the middle pillar, and it is a most appropriate symbol inasmuch as it portrays geometrically the intersection point between the two squares.

The letter Y, of course, stands for Boga. In Boga, it is the past that be, and it is always that part of the Zodiac that remains to be traveled and explored by our two heroes. In the beginning, when Adam and Eve first embarked in their chariot, Boga was immensely large, and it appeared to represent the entire Consciousness of Immensity itself, the consciousness that the Agashan Teachers speak so frequently about. However, as they themselves became bigger Boga became smaller, until eventually, at the end of their journey in the upper hemisphere, Boga in turn became only a minute speck in the Cosmos.

The next letter following Y is Z. This represents the Pillar of Mercy on the extreme western end of the horizon, and into Mercy all of the celestial bodies descend. All of them—including planets, stars, galaxies, even the zodiacal signs themselves—descend in the Pillar of Mercy, which is symbolized by the letter Z, the Empress, the Motherhood of God. Of course this is all illusion, brought about by the turning of the Earth on its axis, but this way or that way it is still the way life appears unto the consciousness of Man.

Now we come to Cotee as represented by the Emperor, the letter A. He symbolizes the entire pyramid of space within the earth itself. He is the foundation upon which the entire heavenly structure rests. The Greeks called him Atlas, and upon his shoulders rests a mighty burden.

The letter A is followed by B, and light appears upon the eastern horizon once again. The letter B symbolizes the Wheel of Life, and its appearance in the left-hand Pillar of Boaz signifies that the circuit is now complete. The Lovers have now completed their journey, both in the upper hemisphere of the stars and within the earth itself, and are now ready to enter once more into the inner recesses of their Being.

This is the letter C which symbolizes the great Sea of Consciousness, the great Core of Life itself from which they were evicted in the beginning. Only now, they are far more wise than they were then. Having gone through all of the experiences life has to offer, having reaped the consequences from partaking of the fruit from the Tree of the Knowledge of Good and Evil, Adam and Eve are now ready to ascend into the higher consciousness of the spiritual realms, never again to return to the physical plane called Earth. In essence, they have made a full 90-degree turn, for isn't the letter "C" only the letter "U" turned over on its side?

The Cabalah has furnished us with a good deal of evidence that what we say here is true. For instance: we learned earlier that the Alpha number for "Dog + Crayfish + Wolf" (the three entities that arose from the sea in Tarot Key 18) is 171. But what is the Alpha numbers for the God-Names of the letters C and U? It is this same number 171, signifying that they represent the "I" that is within (C + U = 90 + 81 = 171).

We also notice that the letters for the Cara Boga Cotee squares on the circle of the Zodiac bring into manifestation the WAY. Couldn't they then be called the Great White Way that the Agashan Teachers are so often referring to? Didn't Christ say that I am the *Way* and that I am the Light? And isn't Figure 112 the "way Cara Boga Cotee see you" or the "way you see

Cara Boga Cotee"? Yes indeed, there is a good deal of verification to be had if we look for it.

Now let us examine the life processes within the earth itself. What exactly happens to the celestial bodies from the time they disappear into the Pillar of Mercy in the western horizon only to reappear once more from the Pillar of Severity in the east? What happens to them while they are in the Cotee square? The answer is obvious. They are merely continuing on their way and doing the same things that they had done previously. Figure 113 illustrates the process.

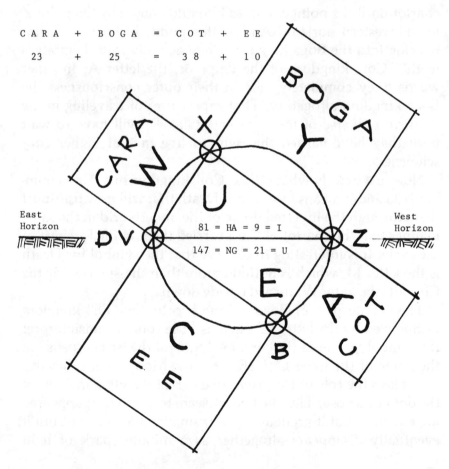

Figure 113: The Wheel of Life Even Tears Cotee Asunder

We thus learn that life in the nether world after physical death, life in the spiritual world of Cotee, is pretty much the same as life in the upper hemisphere of the mental/physical worlds of Cara and Boga. The only difference is that it begins in the west at the Pillar of Mercy and ends in the east at the Pillar of Severity. The letter B replaces the letter X for the middle pillar that separates its two kingdoms, and the Devil (the letter D) ends up at the Pillar of Severity. Thus in the next round it will be the Devil instead of the Lovers who must suffer through the consequences of earthly living. But this is only as it should be.

We must remember that the Lovers remain in the Cara chariot until the point X moves into and conjuncts the point Z in the western horizon. And at this point, instead of disembarking into the Boga kingdom, they actually find themselves in the "Cot" kingdom of the Emperor, the letter A. In other words, they completely miss in their outer consciousness the Boga kingdom altogether. That experience, of traveling in the *physical* universe of the stars and galaxies, will have to wait until they have earned the right to live in that higher consciousness.

Now just exactly what is this "Cot" kingdom? Its Alpha number is 38 and it means Death. It is Death that will now transport them through the inverted dome of the underworld in the same manner that the chariot of Cara carried them in the forepart of the cycle. It is interesting to observe that the symbol for Death is the letter M, which is nothing more than the symbol for the Chariot, the letter W, turned upside down.

The counterpart of Boga is found to be the "EE" kingdom symbolized by the letter C. There is little room to misinterpret the symbology, since the combined total of the letters spells out the name of the letter C (CEE). It is the Moon, then, that this time plays the role of the proverbial carrot dangling in front of the donkey's nose. They just never seem to reach it. It appeared huge at first, but it gradually grows smaller and smaller until it eventually disappears altogether as a minute spark of light descending into the Pillar of Severity. This is the Spark of Divinity, the "I" within that goes before us to prepare a place in the forthcoming round (*Agasha: Master of Wisdom*, page 64).

An excellent point of verification that we are on the right track in our thinking comes about when we consider the "U + E" that now occupies the central *rectangle* within the inner, circular core. (When we consider both hemispheres of action, the inner triangle becomes a rectangle.) Within it we have the Fool (the letter U) and the Hierophant (the letter E), and when we assemble the Alpha numbers of their God-Names together, we find that "I HANG YOU." This is a most relevant statement since it explains the predicament of the Hanged Man hanging upside down on the cross.

One may wonder from what authority have we learned that there even *is* a second middle pillar that can act in the same manner in the lower hemisphere as the sign of SCORPIO did in the upper one. Our authority is simply the same God Consciousness that named the astrological signs in the first place. It does not take one long to ascertain that there is a second sign that fills the bill most beautifully. It is the sign of PISCES, the 12th sign of the Zodiac. The name PISCES can be broken apart into "Pi + S + C + ES," and it means that it represents either Pi (the sign itself), the Star, the Moon, or the symbol X (E + S = X). Therefore, we have two astrological signs, Scorpio and Pisces, that can take turns alternating as the middle pillar in both the upper and lower hemispheres, respectively.

In fact, if one wishes to pursue the point further, the Cabalah seems to indicate a horoscope that can be used for further investigations. The key is to assume that Cancer is rising at the time of our event, whatever that event may be. The Alpha number for Cancer is 44, the same as the number for Boaz, the base of the left-hand Pillar of Severity. This would place the upper middle pillar (the point M of Figure 109) in the 12th sign of Pisces, the Pillar of Jachin in the 10th sign of Capricorn, and the lower middle pillar directly under its upper counterpart at the point G, which would fall right in the middle of the 8th sign of Scorpio. There is the start of your horoscope, and it fits all the requirements of the 16 rays emanating from the Moon, as well as the 12 signs of the Zodiac.

A further study of Figure 113 (the "AM" part of "I AM," incidentally) reveals that the four *outer* squares represent the four kingdoms of the Tarot—Pentacles, Swords, Wands, and Cups; and the *inner* rectangle, the source from which the outer worlds sprang forth, would then be the Trump Suit of the Major Arcana. This is the God State, as opposed to its four outer expressions of Earth, Air, Fire, and Water, respectively.

There are also two pairs of opposites at work, each one complementing the other. The Earth/Fire pair of CARA/COT may be referred to as "A Car/Cot." These are the active or masculine forces, as opposed to the passive or feminine forces which consist of the Air/Water pair of BOGA/EE. This latter pair states simply that the "Ago Be E." The Alpha number for "A Car/Cot" is 61 (23 + 38 = 61), which means that it represents YOU. The number for the complementary pair of "Ago Be E" is 35 (25 + 10 = 35). Phonetically it sounds like CE (Cee or Sea). It represents the "space" that you travel through in your journey through life as well as death, and it is significant that 35 is the Alpha number of words such as EYE or AUM.

Now let us analyze the totality of both of these pairs of opposites. If we place their Alpha numbers alongside of each other, we read that they represent a FACE (61 + 35 = FACE). But it is the face of whom? The answer is that it represents the face of CARA BOGA COTEE! Their total Alpha number is 96 (23 + 25 + 48 = 96), which means that they also qualify the statement with a great big "IF." "If what?" you ask. The answer is *if* they become an IFO (9 + 6 = 15, or I + F = 0). "But what is an IFO?" you persist. An "IFO" in the Cabalah means that it stands for an *"Identified* Flying Object," as opposed to a "UFO" which means that the object is still unidentified. This is the one and only difference between an IFO and a UFO. The "face" of the former is known and identified; the face of the latter is still unknown.

The identification is made in the following tabulation:

I	= IDENTIFIED	=	85	= The Devil	= D
F	= FLYING	=	73	= Hermit	= H
O	= OBJECT	=	55	=	= EE

HEED!	213	= U C	= 24 = X
FOX!		B M	= 15 = O
(You Become Back!)		BAC	= 6 = F

We thus find that the object is identified to be none other than our old friend the Devil. And if you think that there is a possibility that we could have misidentified him, mistaken him for someone else as it were, that solution is eliminated because the Cabalah verifies again that our first impression was the correct one. The Alpha number for "Identified Object" is 85 + 55 or DEE, the name of his symbol, the letter D. And who is the Devil? It is YOU.

But we cannot leave out the most important part, the "Flying" part, that part of the IFO that enables it to fly. This is the Hermit, the Teacher, the One who furnishes the power as you, the mortal devil, travel through the far reaches of the universe as you explore many, many, many of your previous lives. For doesn't the word DEVIL mean one who has LIVED (reading it backwards)? This means he has lived in the past, that he comes from BOGA, and that he is on an excursion to the planet Earth to find the *reason* that he became that which he now is.

Thus we have "a cot" at one end of the spectrum, which means the bed on which we sleep, and "a war car" or a chariot, an IFO at the other end. It would seem that the Higher Self, the one sleeping on the cot, is dreaming the life that you and I are experiencing today. And if this be true, Boga is then the "cue." A cue is a hint, a word given from those off stage to prompt the actor so that he does not forget his lines. The greatest error that one can make while living on the earth plane, the Agashan Teachers have said dozens and dozens of times, is for him to miss the *cue*, and thereby not complete that which he was sent back to the earth plane to do.

Yes indeed, there are many connotations to the IFO of

CARA BOGA COTY. Why have we returned to our previous spelling? Simply to express the totality of the whole. CARA BOGA COTEE represent the "IF" part of the IFO, but the "O" part is not brought into manifestation until the end when the circle is then complete. Thus the numbers 96 + 15 bring into manifestation the three 1's of CARA BOGA COTY (111), and when they do, the three gods will awaken from their slumber, arise from the sarcophagi in which they are imprisoned, and realize once again who and what they really are. This point in time, according to the Agashan philosophy, is called the *soul awakening*.

A Typical Problem

Now let us turn our thoughts to the practical application of our CARA BOGA COTEE O. We realize, of course, that we are the Sun, the O, and that CARA BOGA COTEE live around us. Or, we might say that we are the egg-shaped outer shell that encloses all four of our CARA BOGA COTEE inner squares, as well as our central "O," the very Core of Life itself. In the latter case we would appear as the Fool, the Tarot key whose number is 0, and whose name is YOU. In any event, Figure 112 and/or Figure 113 represent a map of your BEING.

But these figures do not just apply to the human kingdom; no indeed, they may be used to represent absolutely anything and everything, whatever it may be. The only requirement is that it must have a *name*. "In the beginning was the Word" is more than just a statement. It really means what it says. Before anything can be subjected to analysis to find from whence it came, we must begin with a word or phrase that describes it. Then, after we break it up into its constituent parts, we may find the true secret of its BEING.

The first thing to do in any CARA BOGA COTEE analysis is to find the Alpha numbers of the words and/or letters that constitute its name. These then must be broken up in such a way that the numerical sum of the Cara and Boga squares must equal the Cotee square. It doesn't make any difference what the numbers are so long as the equation balances. The remaining letters that cannot be made to fit within the outer squares are then relegated to the central core, the inner triangle, from whence they came.

There are many phrases we might use as an example, but let us begin with the Tree in the Garden of Eden. Isn't that where Adam and Eve began?

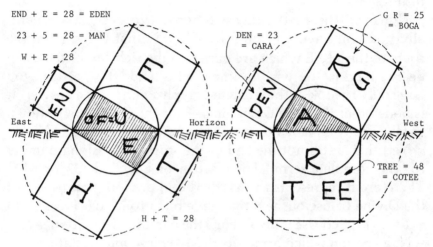

Figure 114: The Tree in the Garden of Eden

You may use either a 3-square or a 4-square analysis. The left-hand glyph of Figure 114 uses four squares in order to equate EDEN with the definite article THE. Since the letter E is surplus, it must be tossed into the center along with the preposition "OF." These three inner letters then become the "FOE" of the four outer squares. It is interesting to note that if we read the four outer squares in clockwise order, we find that they represent the biblical verb ENDETH. Or, if we read all of the terms, we find that it is "THE END OF E."

The right-hand glyph uses three squares in order to equate GARDEN with TREE. And, as in the case with the previous example, the extra "A" is sent back to the Core. But then we may till the garden, cultivate it, so that it will grow. We begin with only one letter in the Cara square, then two, then three, and we watch the words take shape and form. For instance: ERG is a unit of work, DEN the home of a beast, etc. Soon you will have four letters in your Cara square, and your journey from the east to the west will be almost complete. But in this particular case that day will be a sorrowful one, for the only word that can be made from the 4 letters at our disposal is the verb REND, which means to tear asunder, violently, an action which is usually accompanied with grief, rage, or other painful feelings.

However, the 4-letter day will not last forever, and eventually you will have a beautiful GARDEN that is fed from the roots of the TREE which are buried in the rich soil of the earth below. And if you wish to know who tends this garden, you have only to look at the left-hand glyph again for the answer. It is none other than the Devil himself, or the One who is known as HE. The complementary pair of squares is the verb TEND.

Yet, this is still not the end of the story. The Alpha number for the complete term "The Garden of Eden" is 131 or MA. Therefore it represents the Motherhood of God, that aspect of the Divine Consciousness that gave birth to MAN. Doesn't $13 + 1 = 14$? Of course it does. Thus the combined equation is MA $= N$, an action which brings forth MAN into manifestation.

Conclusion

The foregoing examples are only a smattering, a hint as to what can be ascertained once words and phrases in the English language are subjected to scrutiny through the methods imposed by the Cabalah. You may analyze your name, you may analyze a biblical name, or you may analyze anything you wish and by so doing, learn far more about yourself or that certain something than you had previously realized.

How does this work? How is it possible that everything can be named in such a way so that it will reflect what it really is? How did the original Hebrew names for things eventually end up being spelled the way they are today in English? Why aren't they spelled another way? Why haven't we been taught these things before? Where has everybody been, asleep? And lastly, if these things be true, what is the *modus operandi* that brings all of this about?

These are good questions, and the answer to all of them is

simply, I don't know. I approached this subject on several occasions with Rhebaumaus Tate while the Zenor telephone was still available, and his answer always went something like this:

"My son, Man must learn that there is nothing really *new* that ever happens. Everything that is happening now has happened before, and it shall happen again, and again, and again —someplace, somewhere, sometime. Therefore, the God Consciousness working within Man has caused all of these things to be the way it wishes them to be. It is this inner God Consciousness that actually names things—not the outer man. Man may *think* that he names them, true: but it is usually more a case of *remembering* what the name actually is, rather than that of determining a new one."

In other words, we are living in the God Consciousness. We have always lived there and we always shall live there because there is no place else to be. Everything, in the final analysis, is GOD. The God Consciousness is the writer of the drama we are now acting out, and things will happen the way they are *supposed* to happen because that is the way it is written. And it is written that way because your previous actions *demanded* that it be so written—either for the good or for the bad. This is what is known as karma.

But if you don't *like* the way things are now, you can always change the picture. I didn't *have* to write these three books on the Agashan philosophy. I could have flatly *refused* to follow the cue from the soul, and by so doing, not complete the contract I had signed prior to birth. But then where would I be? And not only that, what would my next life be like? I shudder to think of the answer.

Rhebaumaus once told me the modus operandi of his relations with me goes something like this: I make an action. He analyzes the results of that action. If he thinks I have gone too far to the right, he impresses me to veer to the left a bit. So I adjust my course accordingly, and thereby stay on the path. I throw the ball to him, and he passes it back to me; then I throw it back to him again, and this action repeats itself throughout life. If it were not for this teacher/disciple relationship, the mortal would become so confused in life, that it would be impossible for him to fulfill it in the way he was supposed to.

Yet we cannot forget the soul's part in all of this. Within the soul is the Infinite State, the God-Self, and it is from this Infinite State that all of the information contained within this volume was mined. The teacher didn't give it to me; the teacher only directed me to where I could find it. Of course, he knows everything that is in this book and far more. But that isn't the point. Even though the teacher knows the answer to a problem a child in school is working on, he doesn't reveal it to the child. He makes him work it out for himself. Otherwise the child could not learn, and the entire purpose of the school, which is to educate students, would be defeated. That is why a Teacher is called a teacher. He is one who teaches.

So then, as Agasha would say, let us be up and doing and be about the Father's business, or—to echo the words of his brother Araskas—let us be up and at "em." In any event, it means for us to try to chip away a little more corrosion from the soul so that we will be in a better position to see our own *Being* reflected therein.

THE END OF VOLUME I

NOTES

1. The following is an excellent book on Masonic symbology: Harold Waldwin Percival, *Masonry and Its Symbols* (New York, The Word Publishing Co., 1952)

2. Albert Pike, *Morals and Dogma* (Charleston, Southern Jurisdiction of the U.S.A., 1871), p. 34

3. Arthur Edward Waite, *Pictorial Key to the Tarot* (New York, University Books, 1959) p. 88